COURT QUEENS

COURT QUEENS

CELEBRATE THE PLAYERS, TEAMS, AND HISTORY OF WOMEN'S BASKETBALL

Emma Baccellieri and Jordan Robinson

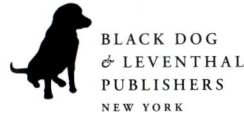

BLACK DOG
& LEVENTHAL
PUBLISHERS
NEW YORK

Black Dog & Leventhal Publishers
Hachette Book Group
1290 Avenue of the Americas, New York, NY 10104
www.blackdogandleventhal.com
BlackDogandLeventhal   @BDLev

First Edition: March 2026

Published by Black Dog & Leventhal Publishers, an imprint of Hachette Book Group, Inc.
The Black Dog & Leventhal Publishers name and logo are trademarks of Hachette Book Group, Inc.

Black Dog & Leventhal books may be purchased in bulk for business, educational, or promotional use. For more information, please contact your local bookseller or the Hachette Book Group Special Markets Department at Special.Markets@hbgusa.com.

The publisher is not responsible for websites (or their content) that are not owned by the publisher.

Additional copyright and photo credits may be found on page 241.

Photography research and direction by Carolyn E. Davis
Print book jacket and interior design by Katie Benezra

Library of Congress Control Number: 2025020963

ISBNs: 979-8-8941-4134-3 (hardcover); 979-8-8941-4135-0 (ebook)

Printed in Dongguan, China

TLF

10   9   8   7   6   5   4   3   2   1

CONTENTS

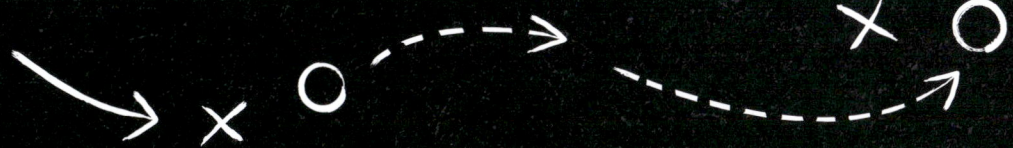

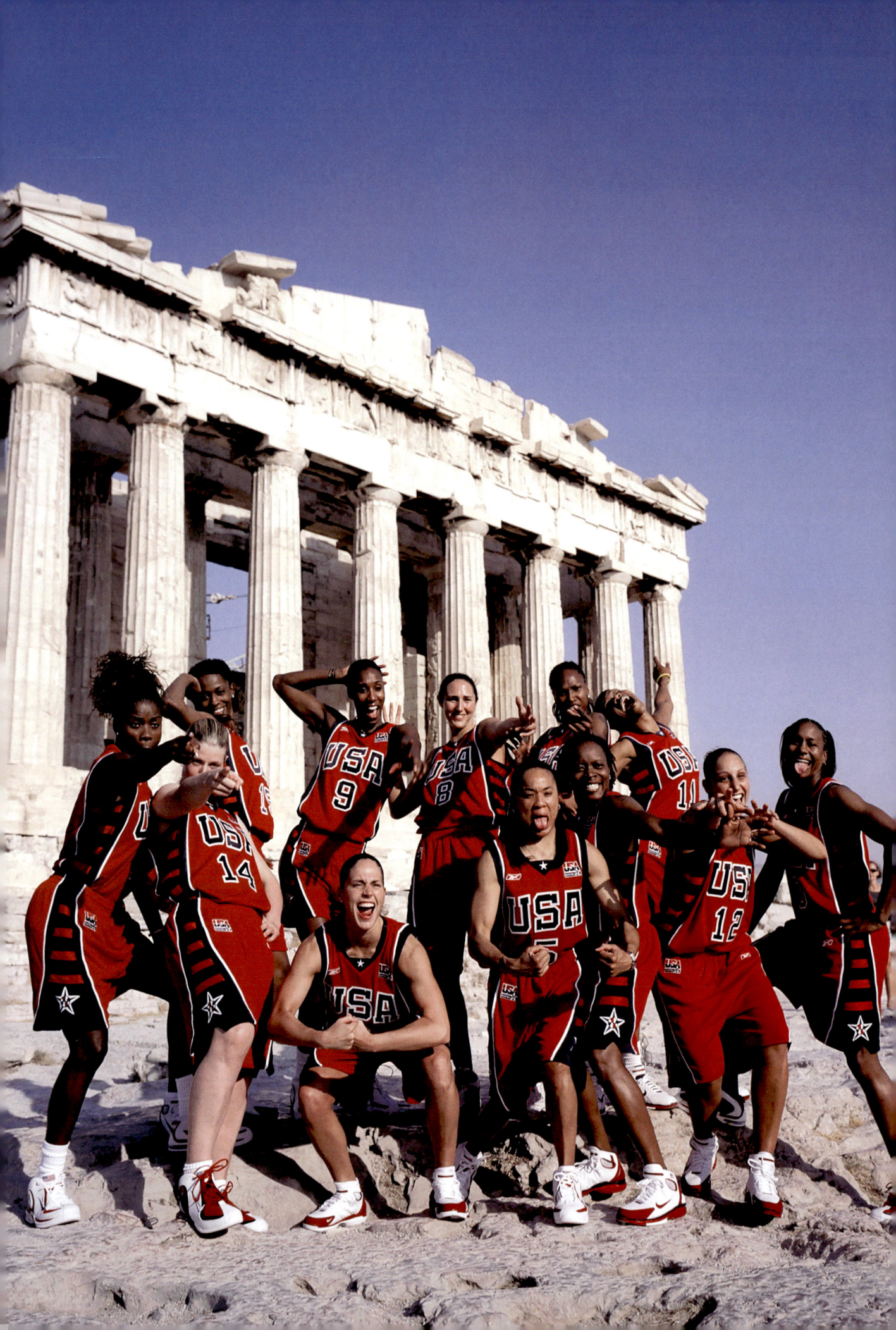

PREFACE

Welcome to our love letter to women's basketball. That was how we described this book from the very beginning: The two of us wanted to write something that felt like a celebration of our favorite game and the many incredible people behind it. What we did not realize was just how many new stories there would be for us to fall in love with along the way.

Every woman in our research led us to discover five more. For every name we knew, there were rivals and teammates we did not, and every single one had an engaging story all her own. It made for a process that was both inspiring and maddening. There have been strong, brilliant women on the hardwood for nearly a century and a half, and so many of them never got the shine they deserved.

So we'd like to think of this book as just a starting point. Every woman mentioned in these few hundred pages could fill an entire volume of her own. This history is so much bigger than anything that could fit in one book. But that's a blessing. The process of writing this made us fall even more deeply in love with the game that we had already loved for our entire lives, and we hope that reading it does the same for you, too.

The two of us wrote this from opposite ends of the country. We talked to women young and old, of various backgrounds, with very different playing experiences. Yet it was striking just how much there was tying all of us together.

All of the stories in here build on each other. Cheryl Miller walked so JuJu Watkins could run. Ora Washington jumped so A'ja Wilson could fly. Nancy Lieberman dished out the assist that Caitlin Clark would catch decades later. The game evolved from nine-on-nine to six-on-six to five-on-five. Uniforms went from bloomers to tunics to shorts. Opportunities went from AAU to the AIAW to the NCAA to the WBL to the ABL to the WNBA. But the passion stayed the same. The women in the first chapter did whatever they could for a chance to play—even if it meant dying their heads bright red like the barnstorming ladies of the All-American

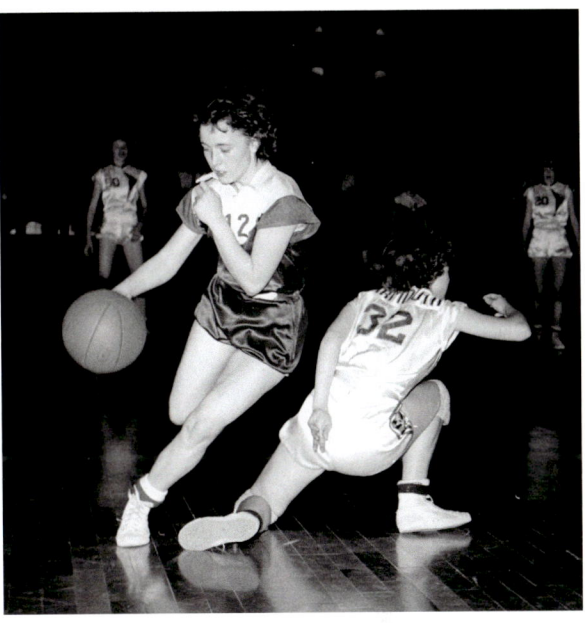

Red Heads. Their journeys made it possible for the women in the last chapter to build serious careers as modern professionals.

And that progress keeps on building. While we were writing this book, more records were broken, new superstars were born, and fresh champions were crowned. The game continues to sprout new fans and water longtime followers. Hopefully, this book will be part of that experience, too.

Thank you to everyone who opened their personal collections and scrapbooks to us. Thank you to organizations like Legends of the Ball that work so hard to preserve the history of the game. Thank you to the public libraries and newspaper archives that made our research possible. And thank you to every woman who has ever laced up her sneakers and hit the court. You all made this possible.

OPPOSITE: The 2004 US Olympic team plays around in front of the Parthenon en route to a third consecutive gold medal.

ABOVE: An Iowa high school player shows off her crossover in a game of six-on-six.

CHAPTER 1

1890s–1960s

THE PIONEERS

WOMEN HAVE BEEN HOOPIN' SINCE THE GAME OF BASKETBALL WAS INVENTED. EVEN WHEN IT REQUIRED CREATIVITY—OR FIGHTING JUST TO BE ON THE COURT IN THE FIRST PLACE—THEY CARVED OUT SPACE FOR THEMSELVES AGAIN AND AGAIN IN THE EARLY DECADES OF THE GAME.

RIGHT: Ladies line up for a free throw, 1899.

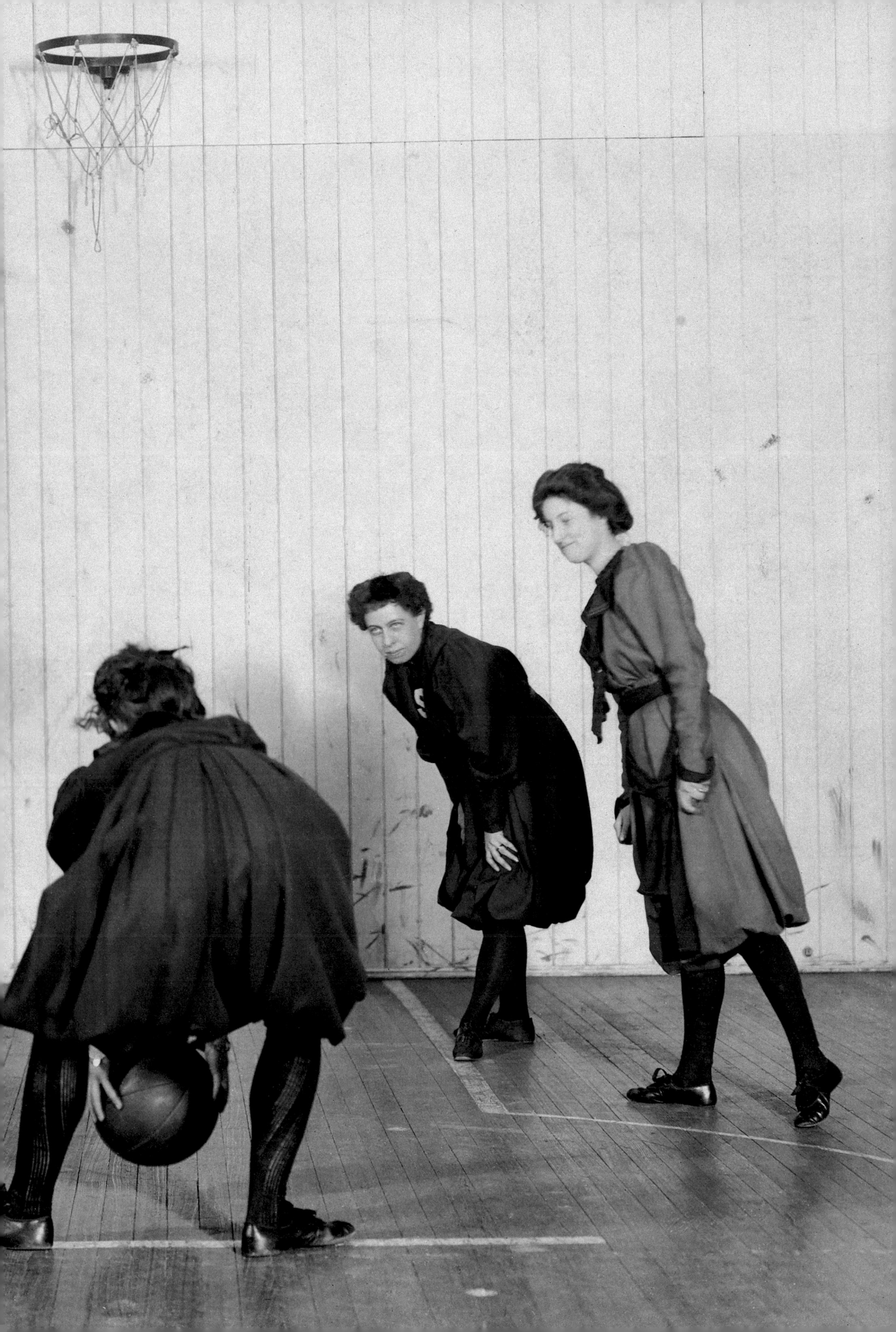

THE MOTHER OF THE GAME

SENDA BERENSON

THE FIRST TO BRING THE GAME OF BASKETBALL—AND ITS OPPORTUNITIES FOR TEAMWORK AND FREEDOM—TO WOMEN

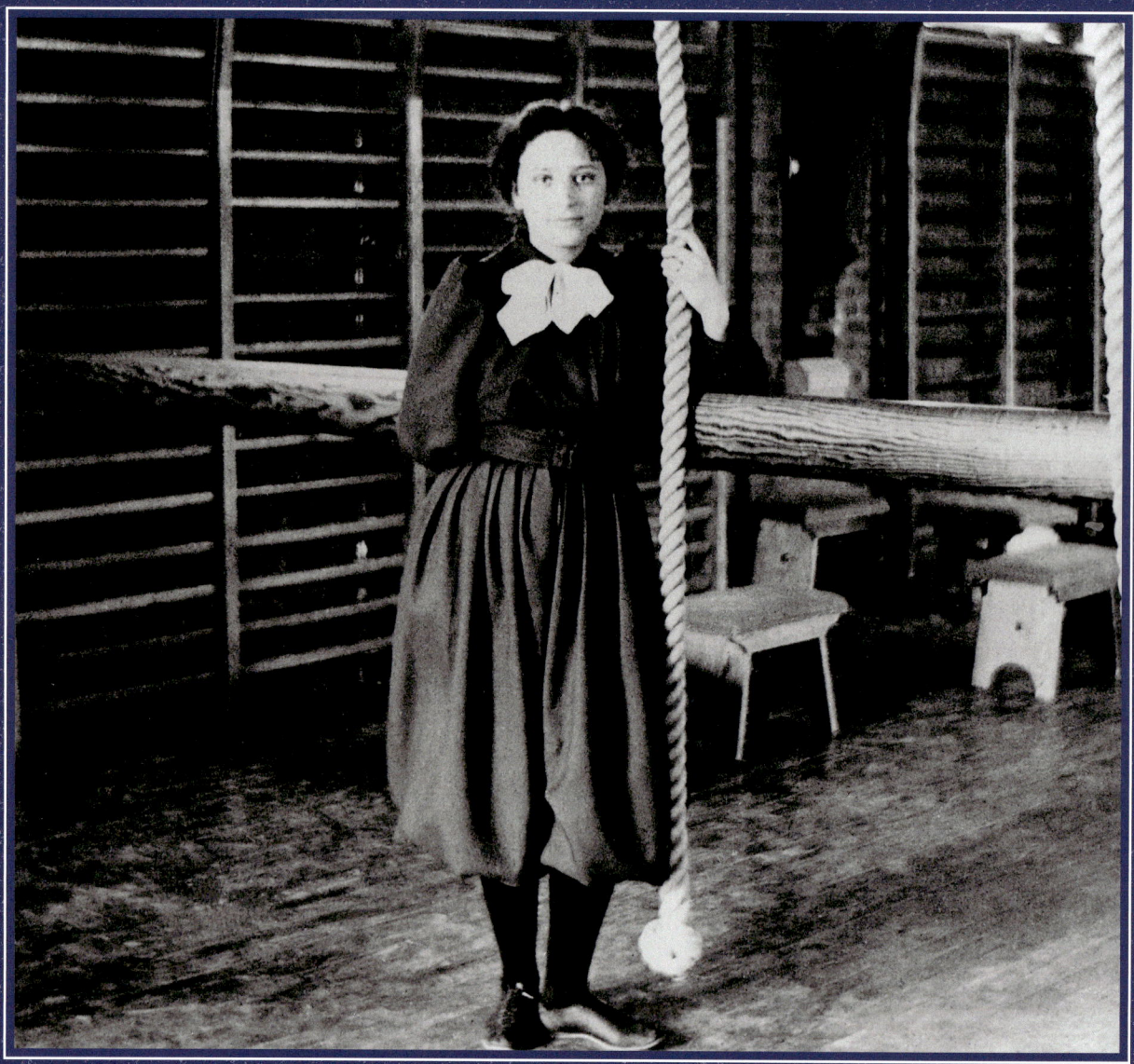

ABOVE: Senda Berenson at Smith College, where she taught for nearly two decades and built the foundation of women's basketball.

By the spring of 1890, Senda Berenson was desperate.

It felt like she was losing whatever grip she once held on her future. The twenty-two-year-old had always been physically delicate but had recently been growing even more so. She had been forced to leave her classes at the Boston Conservatory of Music: Her back was so weak that she could not sit up straight enough to play her beloved piano. Berenson once fostered dreams of becoming a concert musician. Now she was as physically frail as she had ever been, and she found herself slipping into depression.

She had turned down a marriage proposal not long ago in hopes that she could build a grander life for herself. But that meant she was still at home with her overbearing father. Their close-knit Jewish immigrant family left Eastern Europe for the United States when Berenson was a child and ultimately settled in Boston. Her father had very high standards for his children—and was not pleased with supporting a grown daughter who had declined marriage for reasons he did not understand. Berenson's home life grew increasingly miserable. She was too sick to escape into her usual loves of art or music. Her favorite brother had gone abroad, writing about how she might love what he saw in France and Italy, wishing that she had the same opportunities he did. She felt completely trapped.

Then came a suggestion from a friend that changed not just the course of her life but the future of women in sports.

Berenson would visit the Boston Normal School of Gymnastics.

It was not a natural fit. The school had recently opened to educate teachers in the growing field of physical education. Berenson fit none of the admission criteria: She had not finished high school because she had sometimes been too weak to attend class, and she clearly did not meet the standards for physical health. But the founder of the school decided to admit her. What better way to prove their curriculum than by showing it could work even on the frailest of young women? Berenson did not suffer from any specific illness. Like many Victorian women, she had been considered weak from youth, and her condition had seemingly become self-reinforcing. The founder of the school believed that basic exercise could make her stronger, and her example might be one for many, many other young women.

Berenson enrolled as soon as she could.

She immediately discovered it would be more difficult than she had expected. "How I hated that school for the first few months!" she later wrote. She had never tried much exercise before. Even going on walks had been rare for her. She could not complete the regular exercises with the other students: Instead, she would spend five minutes at a time standing up straight before lying down across three stools, a move designed to strengthen her back. It was painful. But it worked. After three months, she felt a little better, and by the end of the school year, she could participate in the standard exercises. Berenson was finally strong enough to play the piano again, but she had also found a new passion in exercise.

"It is impossible to tell how my life had altered," she wrote. "I had changed an aching body to a free and strong mechanism, ready and eager for whatever might come."

It felt as if an entire world opened up to her. After enrolling at the Normal School for one more year, Berenson was approached about a different opportunity. There was an opening for a physical education teacher at Smith College, a women's school a few hours away in Northampton, Massachusetts. She wasn't sure if she was ready, but her teachers persuaded her. Who better to connect with girls who believed exercising had no purpose? Berenson left for Smith in January 1892.

The experience was overwhelming. Many of her new colleagues looked down on her department: Smith had offered physical education for years, but there were still plenty of people who found it unnecessary, or even unladylike. Some students simply would not show up to classes. Berenson found herself frequently defending the purpose of her work.

One day, she found a description of a new game called basket ball, published in the January 1892 monthly newsletter from the YMCA International

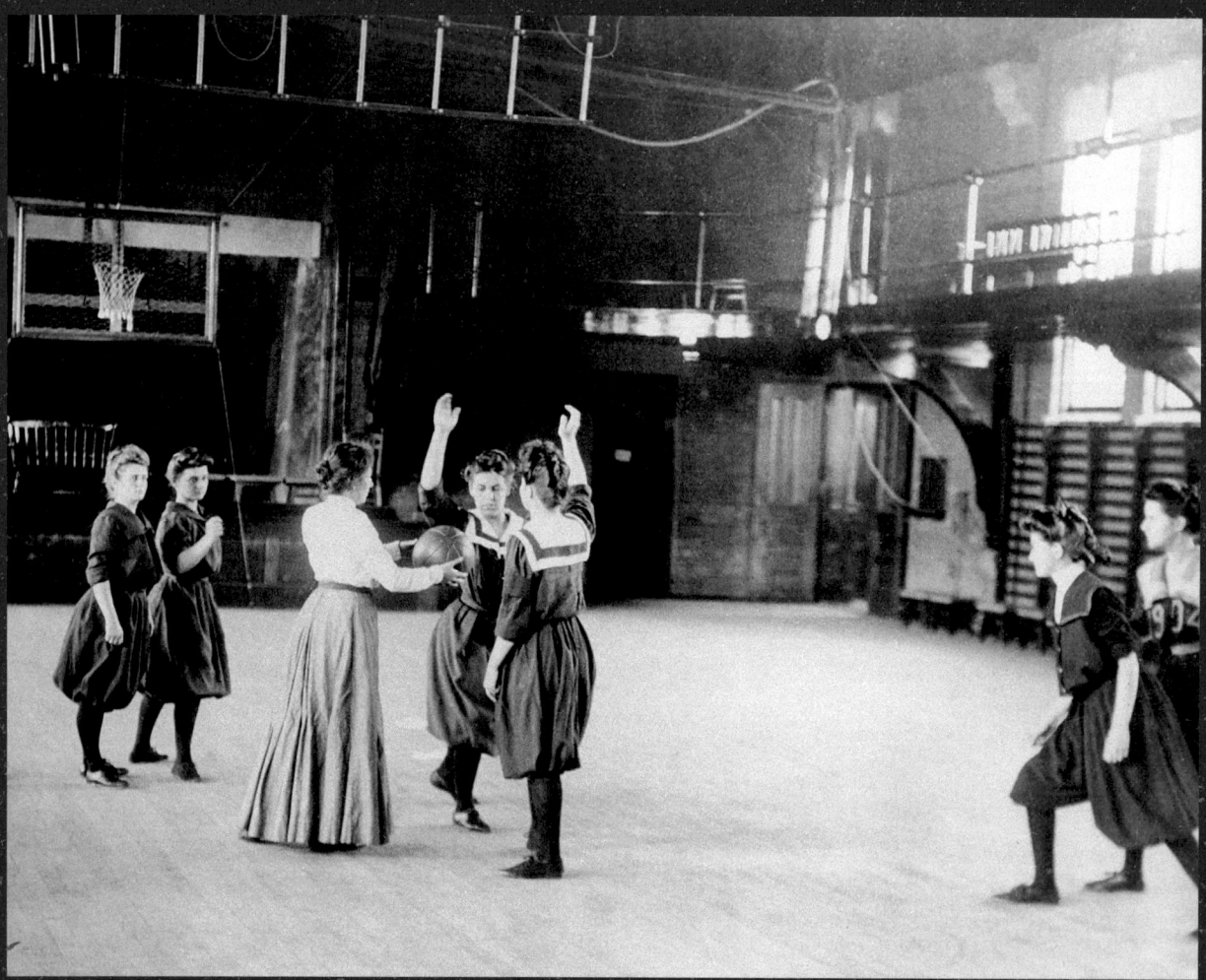

Training School in nearby Springfield. She was immediately curious.

The game had been invented by a fellow physical education teacher. Dr. James Naismith had been looking for something to play indoors with his classes in December 1891: He sketched out thirteen simple rules that laid the foundation for modern basketball. For those first games, Naismith hung peach baskets on the wall of his gym, dividing students into teams and directing them to throw the ball into the opposing basket. He considered it enough of a success that he published the rules a few weeks later. It was a game designed for and created by men. However, there was nothing saying it could not also be for women.

In those early rules, Berenson saw an opportunity, and she went about finding some baskets. She hung them from the balcony of the gym with no great hopes for what might follow. Berenson saw those first days of women's basketball "as a dubious experiment, it must be confessed," she later admitted. Yet even in those early, fumbling attempts, many of her students knew they loved the game. So did Berenson, and she quickly found something powerful that she had not expected. Her students generally did not work in groups: They did gymnastics, walking, and swimming, and some girls had experience with golf, tennis, fencing, or horseback riding. There was steadily increasing cultural support around physical activity for women, but that centered almost entirely on individual

---

ABOVE: Berenson prepares a jump ball for a game in one of her classes.

pursuits. Many of her girls had never been on any kind of team before—academically, socially, or athletically.

A sport like basketball was a revelation. "Above all does the teamwork develop that in woman which both training and tradition have kept dormant in her," Berenson later wrote. "Willingness to surrender the individual to the common good—all this unconsciously to the girl basket ball will bring out in her if she gives her best to it."

She continued using basketball as a class exercise, but some of her students wanted even more. Eventually Berenson decided to do something new: She would organize an official game. A team of freshmen would play a team of sophomores—nine versus nine—and they would invite the rest of campus to watch. The college had never hosted anything like this before. On March 22, 1893, hundreds came, packing both levels of the gym, their feet dangling from the balcony. Students brought banners and dressed in class colors. Not all of them knew the rules. But they cheered loudly all the same.

This was a setting consisting entirely of women. Berenson had fixed a sign to the door earlier that morning: "Gentlemen are not allowed in the gymnasium during basket ball games." This would be just for her girls.

It was the first game in the history of women's college basketball. (It was not without drama: One player dislocated her shoulder. "We took the girl into the office and pulled the joint into place, another center took her place and the game went on," Berenson recalled.) The freshmen-versus-sophomores game became a yearly tradition at Smith. "The scene in the gymnasium at 3:30 was most inspiring," *The Boston Globe* wrote of the game in 1894. "Not a man was to be seen. The thousand girls kept up a continual hum." Women's basketball started catching on all over the country in the

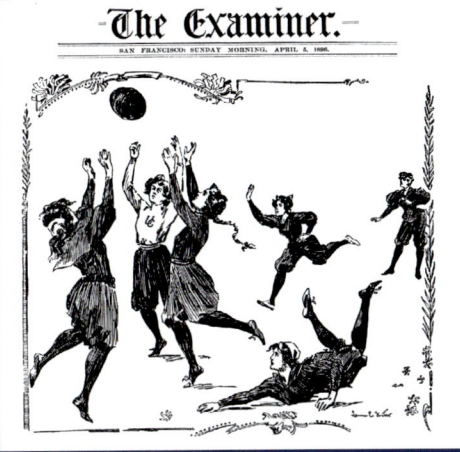

COLLEGE BALL TIPS OFF

The first intercollegiate game was played on April 4, 1896, when Stanford and the University of California, Berkeley, met in downtown San Francisco. The game had been discussed in the local papers for weeks. (All of the 700 tickets were for women: No men were allowed in the gym, but some listened to the action from the corridors outside, and a few even climbed up to look in the windows.) Those early games on divided courts featured very little scoring: Stanford won, 2–1, and the players were greeted by cheering students and serenaded by the school band when they returned. But the squad did not last. In 1899 Stanford banned female students from intercollegiate sports, citing health concerns for women. That kind of backlash was common in the decades to come: As the game spread, it often met concerns about women exerting themselves, sometimes resulting in outright bans like this one. More than half a century would pass before Stanford had an official team again.

ABOVE: No photographs of the 1896 game were taken, but the action was illustrated in newspapers like the *San Francisco Examiner.*

years that followed. As it grew, Berenson refined her vision for the game, and she opted for some changes. She wanted new rules.

She felt basketball had to be safer for women. Berenson was concerned about players getting hurt—especially those who did not have much experience with sports—and she did not want them to tire out too quickly. Most important, she wanted the driving principle of the game to be teamwork, and she felt that was being threatened by rough play. She called for a ban on grabbing the ball from opponents' hands. But her biggest change was dividing the court into three sections. The players would be separated into forwards, centers, and guards, and each group would have to stay in their designated sections, rather than running the length of the floor. Berenson recommended that women play six-on-six or nine-on-nine: This would give an equal number of players in each section. (Naismith's original rules did not mention the number of players on each team, but already men were settling into playing five-on-five.) It was a decision that shaped the game for women for decades.

Berenson's rules became the most popular version of women's basketball. The sporting-goods company Spalding asked her to edit a rule book that was published annually, starting in 1901: Copies were advertised in newspapers all over the United States and Canada and sold for ten cents each. (Spalding published dozens of sports guides, from boxing to football to archery, but this was the first specifically for women.) The divided court made a clear break with men's basketball. That was critical not just for safety but also for strategy, Berenson argued.

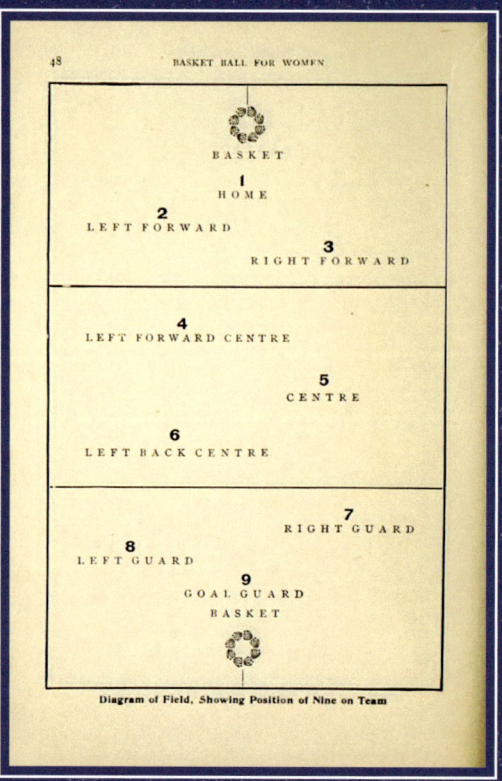

Diagram of Field, Showing Position of Nine on Team

"It does away almost entirely with 'star' playing, hence equalizes the importance of the players, and so encourages team work," she wrote in the rulebook. "This also encourages combination plays, for when a girl knows she cannot go over the division line to follow the ball, she is more careful to play as well as possible with the girls near her when the ball comes to her territory."

It would be decades before the women's rules aligned more closely with the men's. (Some would later argue that this delay was essential: Without rules like Berenson's, the sport might have been deemed too rough for women altogether in the early 1900s, and it may not have caught on as it did.) Among those who defended Berenson's rules were her players from Smith. They insisted they never felt slighted by her vision of the game as she had presented it.

"She never lowered any standard because some people thought that 'girls couldn't take it!'" said one of her players. "She knew better and made us know it, too."

Berenson recognized early on that basketball might be transformative for women. "Certain elements of false education for centuries have made woman self-conscious," she wrote. She felt that sports could be a remedy. In golf and tennis, she often saw that same kind of self-consciousness, with young women playing as if they were posing. They

ABOVE: Berenson divided the court into thirds, like this, for nine players. She had guards playing defense near the opposing basket, centers staying in the middle of the floor, and forwards playing offense.

could not seem to shake the instinct to perform for whoever might be watching. Basketball was different. Here, they performed only for themselves and their teammates, moving so fast as to lose themselves in the game entirely. Berenson saw great freedom in that.

"It is impossible to pose in basket ball," she wrote. "The game is too quick, too vigorous, the action too continuous to allow any element to enter which is foreign to it. It develops quick perception and judgment—in one moment a person must judge space and time in order to run and catch the ball at the right place, must decide to whom it may best be thrown, and at the same time must remember not to 'foul.' It develops physical and moral courage, self-reliance and self-control, the ability to meet success and defeat with dignity."

There may not have been a more unlikely candidate to introduce the sport to women. Berenson's early life was ruled almost entirely by her fragility. Yet sports would ultimately give her not just strength but purpose. She left her job at Smith in 1911—she had received a marriage proposal that she finally wanted to accept—but she continued to edit the official rule book and serve on the United States Basket Ball Committee. More than anyone else, Berenson shaped the early decades of the game, opening it up to women and determining how it should be played. And if aspects of her approach would eventually come to feel dated, her passionate, protective spirit around the game was timeless: "A bit temperamental, of course, but we adored her," said one of her players.

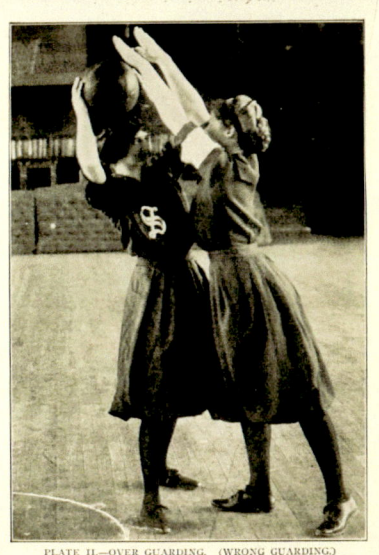

PLATE II.—OVER GUARDING. (WRONG GUARDING.)

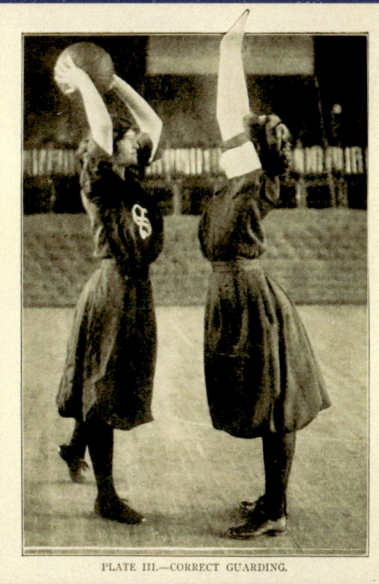

PLATE III.—CORRECT GUARDING.

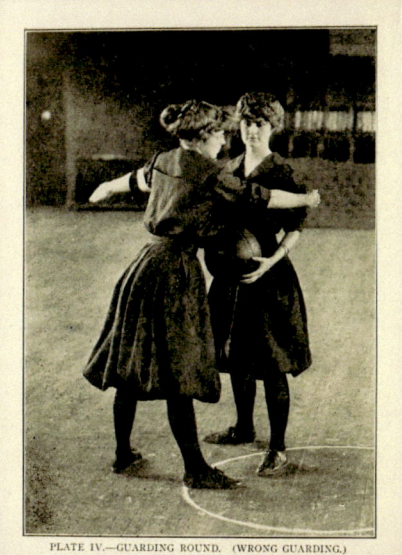

PLATE IV.—GUARDING ROUND. (WRONG GUARDING.)

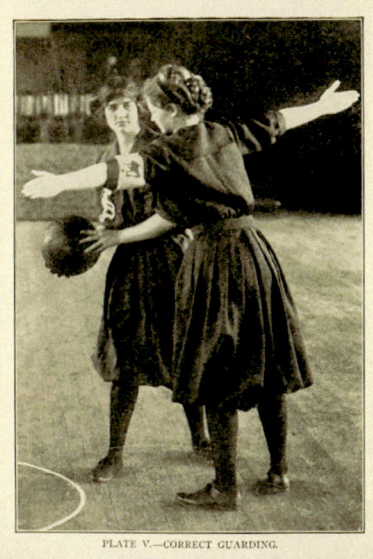

PLATE V.—CORRECT GUARDING.

ABOVE: By 1913, Senda Berenson's guides for Spalding included photographic demonstrations, like these on how to play defense.

THE GAME SPREADS

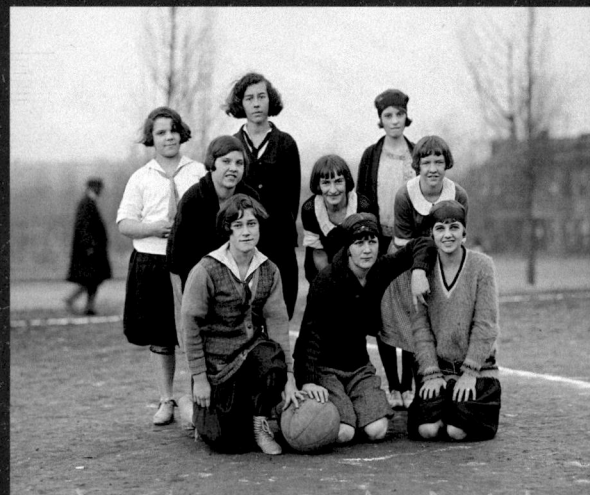

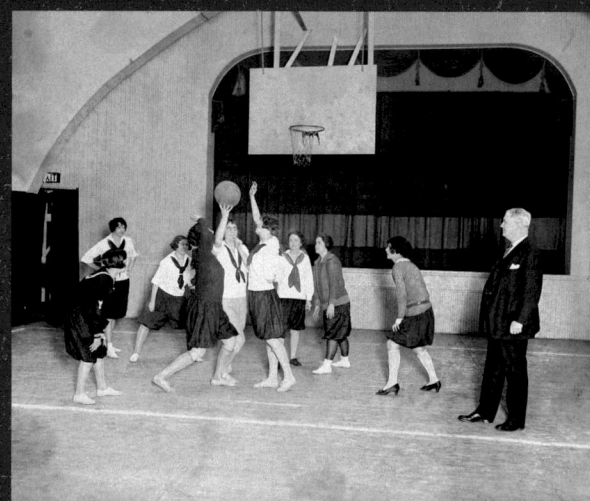

In the years after Senda Berenson tossed up that first ball at Smith, the game began catching on with women around the country, establishing itself on blacktops and in gyms all over.

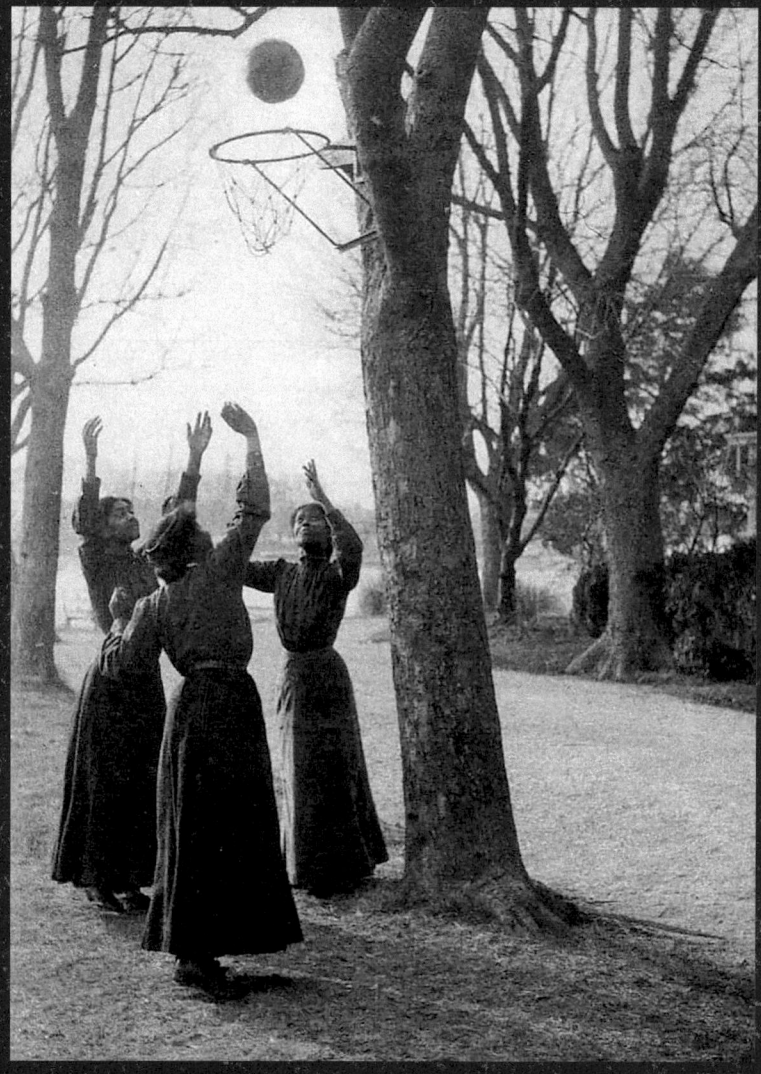

ABOVE LEFT: Even though basketball had been created as a game to play indoors during cold winters, it soon found a place outside, where it thrived on playgrounds. This is the Rosedale Playground Girls' Team in Washington, DC, in 1924.

ABOVE RIGHT: Basketball also established itself as a workplace pastime. Here, US postmaster general Harry New watches a 1926 game among female employees of the Post Office Department, which hired unmarried women as clerks and secretaries.

RIGHT: The sport quickly found a place at Black colleges and universities, including what is now Hampton University in Virginia, where these three young women were photographed playing outside in 1907.

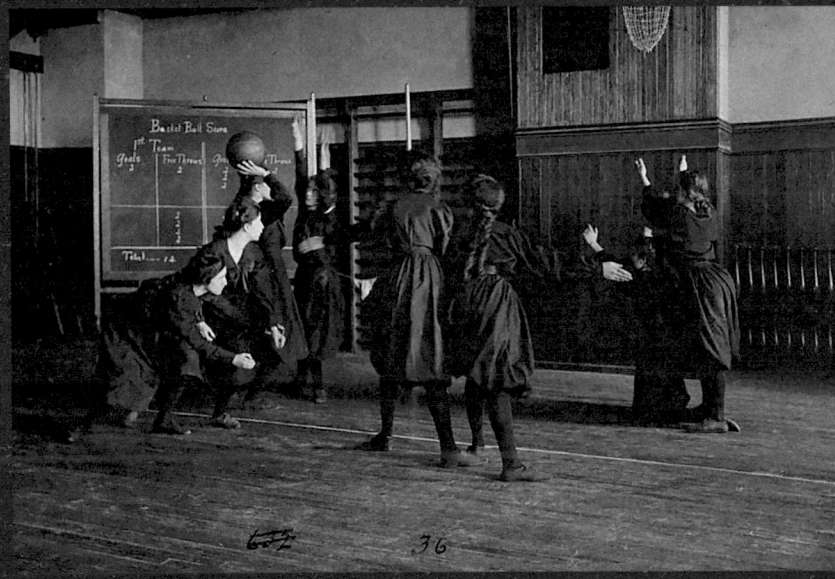

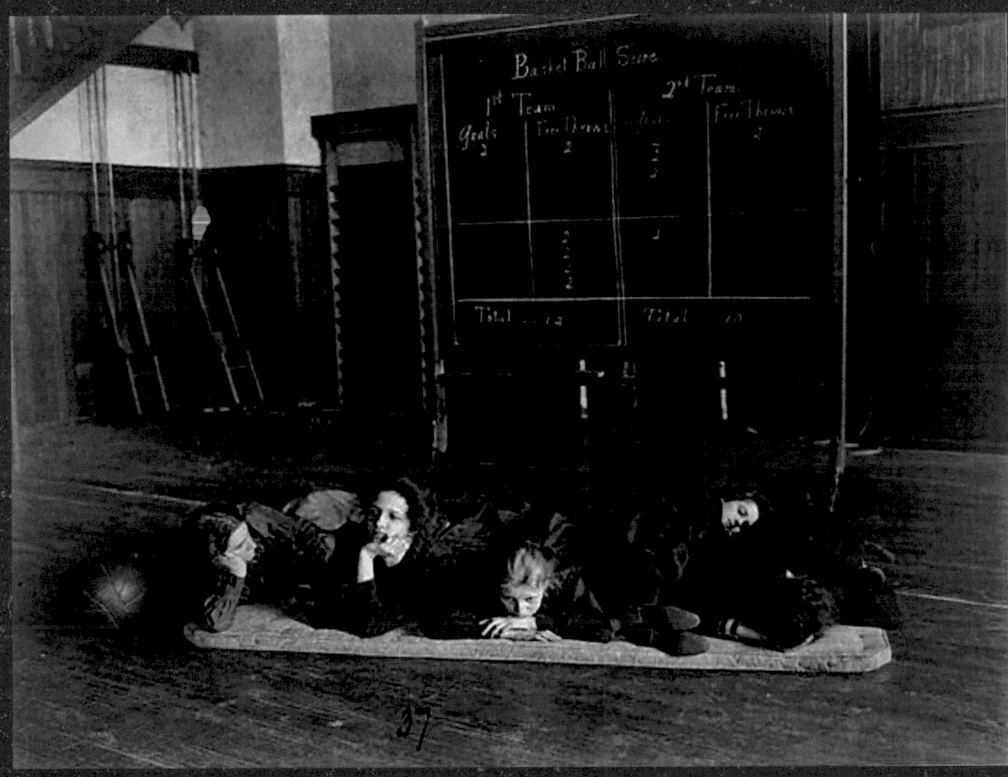

ABOVE: While the game first spread to colleges, it quickly took root in high schools, too. In physical education classes like these at Western High School in Washington, DC, in 1914, girls kept score on a chalkboard, and they relaxed in front of it afterward.

ORA WASHINGTON

The Early Days of Black Women in Hoops

Sometime in 1910, Ora Washington traveled to nearby Milford, Virginia, and boarded a northbound train. She'd leave her father and eight siblings behind as a preteen seeking more freedom. Hours later, she hopped off a train car in bustling Philadelphia to kick-start her new life. Like many African Americans at the turn of the century, she migrated north to escape the harsh, racist realities of the Jim Crow South. Her Aunt Mattie had moved to Philadelphia a few years prior, and now Washington would follow. Soon after, one of America's best sports stars would be discovered.

Pennsylvania wasn't exactly a utopia. Race tensions were still high there as well, and opportunities for young Black women were dwindling. Washington next appears in the 1920 census, working as a live-in housemaid in her early twenties—a typical job for women then. Four years later, Washington joined the Germantown Black Young Women's Christian Association (YWCA), where they encouraged physical activities to the recent migrants. Attending college wouldn't have been an option for someone like Ora, but the YWCA offered Black women a sense of community and an opportunity to participate in organized sports.

The freshly laid tennis courts first caught Washington's eye, and a YWCA instructor approached her about joining the sport. She'd never played before, but she picked it up *fast*. She was a natural and developed a killer serve. Those weekly lessons would lead Washington to enter her name into local all-Black tournaments and dominate. Starting in 1925, she'd win almost every tennis trophy available to a Black woman in prewar America, including the American Tennis Association, a Black national tennis organization. She'd win twelve straight women's doubles titles and seven straight single titles by 1936.

"She was probably the best women's tennis player

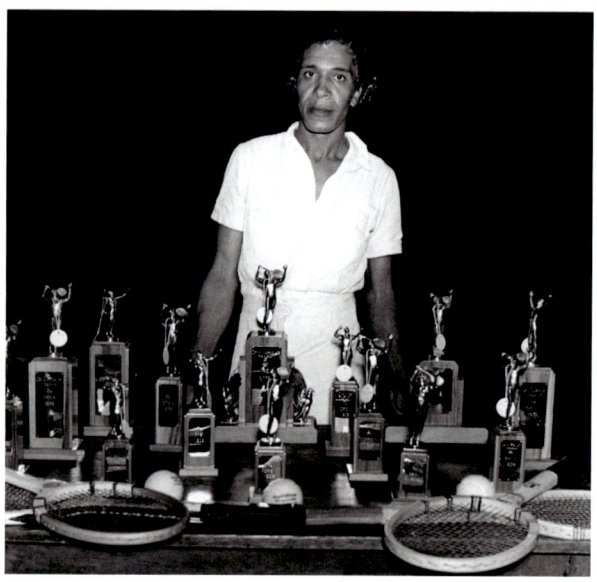

in the country for over a decade and had to struggle in anonymity because of the color of her skin," NBA legend Kareem Abdul-Jabbar said of Washington. "People like Ora Washington labored in obscurity but it made it possible for what we have now."

Standing five feet, seven inches tall, Washington had big hands and a square jaw. Her short, curly bob was often slicked back out of her face. Her baritone voice boomed no matter the arena she played in. In *Shattering the Glass: A Remarkable History of Women's Basketball*, she is described as "powerfully built, with broad shoulders and sharply defined muscles as well as lightning speed." She was fierce, and her athleticism and competitive edge stood out despite her taking to sports later in life.

By the late 1920s and early 1930s, Washington found a winter sport to keep her in shape for

ABOVE: Ora Washington, aka the Queen of Two Courts, posing with her tennis hardware. She was the reigning champion of the all-Black American Tennis Association (ATA) from 1929 to 1935.

her spring and summer tennis tournaments—basketball. She joined the Germantown YWCA Hornets all-Black basketball team. Basketball was beginning to grow in popularity for women in Philadelphia. It was often referred to as "Fives" shortly after the sport was discovered in 1891 or "Quints," with all-Black teams becoming known as "Colored Fives" or "Black Fives." (For women, the number of players on the court was still evolving.) Washington became the star due to her height, natural agility, and quickness. Washington's teammates included her tennis doubles partner, Lula Ballard. The Hornets started winning, with Washington being a force at the rim.

On April 9, 1931, her Hornets faced the Rankin Femmes, a team from near Pittsburgh, for the National Girls Basketball Title. A reporter from *The Pittsburgh Courier* was there, courtside: "The game was a thriller from start to finish with the teams putting in a fine exhibition of basketball as girls should play it," they wrote. "The Rankin community Quint featuring a smooth working five-cylinder attack, making the game harder for the visitors." It was tied 10–10 at halftime, but Washington—the Hornets' team captain—started to take over. She'd score twice in the final three minutes, helping the Hornets take the title, 22–19. "The tribe for the Hornets, however, can almost be completely summed up by two words: Ora Washington," the article continued. "This flashy, aggressive girl center was all over the floor, making the tail-tail field goals which decided the contest."

It became clear that the Black press loved documenting Washington's climb as the premier dual athlete in the state. They often called her Queen Ora or the Queen of Two Courts. *The Pittsburgh Courier* provided her basketball scoring statistics during the 1931 season. *The Chicago Defender* snapped a photo of Washington surrounded by all her trophies, awards, and medals. *The Philadelphia Tribune*, the city's top Black newspaper, selected her as an all-star pick in March 1932, with sports editor Randy Dixon saying she was "the greatest girl player of the age . . . Ora can do everything required of a basketball player."

Washington caught the eye of another women's hoop star, the manager and coach of the Philadelphia Quick Steppers, West Philly's own Inez Patterson.

"Pat," as her friends called her, dedicated her life to "breaking down barriers set up against Negro women in sports" as the exhibit *Pool: A Social History in Segregation* described. She was a bona fide athlete herself. She was her high school's only Black field hockey player, and by the time she enrolled in nearby Temple University, she was an elite competitor in javelin, hurdles, tennis, volleyball, dance, and basketball. Patterson was also known as the Mermaid of Philadelphia because she was a record-breaking swimmer, too. She spent most of her time in the 1920s teaching lessons to Black boys and girls about water safety at various neighboring YWCAs.

Patterson wrote a weekly column, "Girls in Sport," for the *Tribune*. In the early 1930s, she shamelessly recruited for her own all-Black semipro basketball team, with Ora Washington at the top of the scout list.

With Washington on her roster, Patterson pitched a team sponsorship opportunity to the newspaper. They already had a men's team, so why not a women's counterpart? she thought. Her basketball team would get a sponsor to travel and buy uniforms, and the *Tribune* could sell more papers—it was a win-win. It was green-lit, and throughout the 1930s, the Tribune Girls sprouted as a vital part of the Philadelphia sports scene. The eight players donned high-waisted belted shorts and cap-sleeve tops with an all-caps TRIBUNE across the chest.

> "She passes and shoots with either hand. She is a ball hawk. She has stamina and speed that make many male players blush with envy."
>
> —RANDY DIXON, SPORTS COLUMNIST, *THE PITTSBURGH COURIER*, 1939

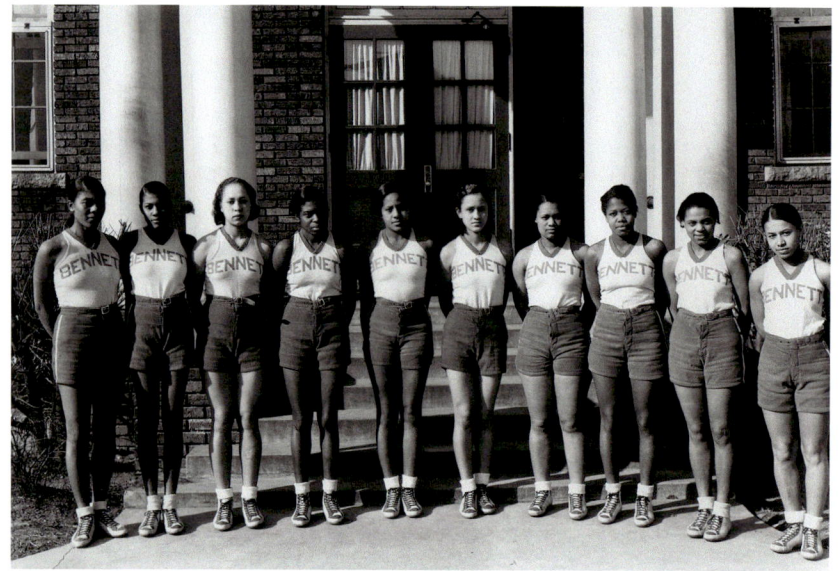

halftime shows or rising stars standing center court singing the national anthem. Your ballgame ticket served a dual purpose: a game *and* a show.

This type of dynamic advertising and charging for admission for the Tribune Girls allowed players like Washington to get paid. It wasn't much, but until then, she was only an amateur.

Briggs became confident in the team's crowd appeal, and in 1934, they headed on a South and Midwest tour, scheduling games against the top college and semipro teams in the area. One of those opponents would be Bennett College for Women, one of the most dominant Black Fives teams ever. While most programs during the Great Depression were scaling back their athletics, Bennett went all in on their basketball. Bennett player Ruth Glover, who enrolled in fall of 1933, would lose only one college game in her four-year varsity career.

The Tribune Girls scheduled a weeklong three-game series against Bennett College in Greensboro, North Carolina, to decide the National Black Women's Championship. The series drew thousands of fans to the spacious city arena to watch what a local newspaper called "the fastest girls' team in the world" led by "the indomitable, internationally famed and stellar performer, Ora Washington." In one game, the Trib Girls defeated Glover's Bennett Belles 31–22, with Washington scoring 13 points in the win.

"She was one of those strong players," Ruth Glover explained to author Rita Liberti in the

Patterson tapped Otto Briggs to run the promotions for the Tribs. Briggs, a former Negro League baseball player, was the newspaper's circulation manager and was married to the *Tribune*'s president. He framed them as entertainment rather than a competitive sporting spectacle. "Girls! Beautiful Girls! And How They Play!" a 1933 advertisement promised.

The Tribune Girls were a hot ticket. "Don't miss seeing Ora Washington and Inez Patterson in action. They are two of the greatest girl players in the world," a 1932 promo read. "They make you forget the Depression." For twenty-five cents, you'd get to see the National Colored Champions square off on the court, followed by a dance featuring live music by Jenning's Orchestra ("They are considered the peppiest orchestra this side of Hades," the poster wittingly touts.) Basketball became a hub for Black entertainment, especially during a country-wide economic crash when everyone—Black and white people alike—was experiencing financial troubles. The sport became a welcome distraction for people concerned about their pocketbooks. It wasn't out of the norm to have the women's games be doubleheaders with the most prominent jazz superstars of the day, such as Ella Fitzgerald or Duke Ellington. These spectacles were precursors to the current arena basketball-game experience, with A-list hip-hop artists performing electric

---

ABOVE: Between 1933 and 1937, the Bennett College Belles of Greensboro, NC, only lost one game. The all-Black, all-women teacher college was hailed as "the nation's best female cage team" of the decade. Their star forward, Ruth Glover, is third from left.

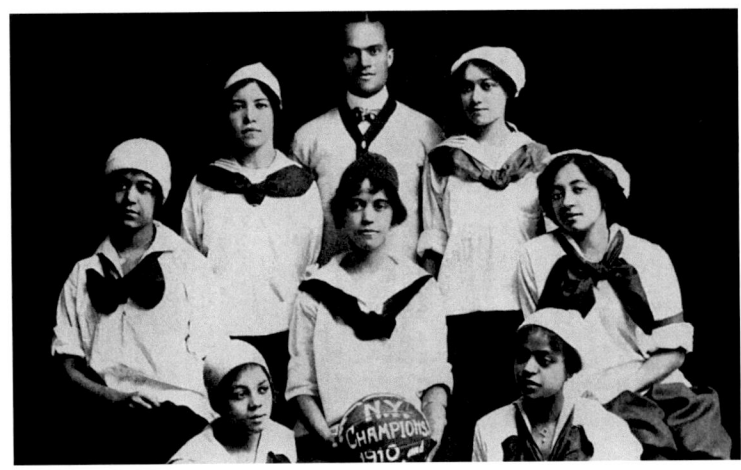

article "We Were Ladies, We Just Played Basketball Like Boys." "She wasn't a huge person or very tall. But she was so fast. And see, they fed her the ball. . . . The team was built up around her."

Unlike Washington, who didn't learn basketball until her twenties, young skilled players like Glover resulted from a boom of playground basketball courts popping up around the country in the 1910s and 1920s. The easily accessible sport gave Black boys and girls an outlet. Coinciding with the number of historically Black colleges and universities (HBCUs) rising in the 1920s, the sport's growth—especially for Black women—was unprecedented. Conferences like the Southern Intercollegiate Athletic Conference gave out men's and women's basketball championship trophies, and the Tuskegee University of Alabama women's team was often a title holder throughout the thirties and forties. Varsity players like Alice Coachman were a part of both basketball and track teams, which made their team's speed nearly impossible to keep up with. In addition to a successful hoop career at Tuskegee, Coachman competed in track-and-field at the London Olympics in 1948 (due to World War II, there were no Olympic Games in 1940 or 1944). She was the sole American woman to win gold that year and the first woman of African descent to win a gold medal.

Players like Coachman, Glover, and even Washington are the offspring of their women's basketball founding Black mothers. The original all-Black Fives team was the New York Girls in 1910, the sister team to the Alpha Physical Culture Club men's basketball squad. Their crosstown rivals were the Spartan Girls Club from Brooklyn and the Jersey Girls out of Orange, New Jersey. The first recorded game of all-Black women's teams was the New York Girls versus the Jersey Girls in March of 1910, with the New Yorkers winning 12–3. As *The New York Age* described it in an article titled "Young Women Play Basketball": "The players, winsome and charming in their dainty white blouses, showed up well in practice, but it was when the referee's whistle started the game that the real surprise came," it read. "These lassies demonstrated that they could play! The audience, eager and expectant, had been attracted by the novelty of the affair. They expected to be amused. However, they were agreeably surprised when the young women put up a clever and even scientific game, playing fast and vigorously, as several hard falls on the floor attested."

From then on, women's basketball among Black women was here to stay. By the time Ora Washington stepped away from sports in her mid-forties after eighteen years of play, she had only lost a total of six basketball games, all to men's teams. She was one of the most decorated female athletes of all time, but with little to show for it. Despite her countless trophies and championship titles, she made little money playing tennis and basketball. Not enough to ever quit her day job as a housemaid. She laid the groundwork for Black tennis star Althea Gibson, the first Black woman to win the US Open and the first to integrate the sport in the 1950s. Washington was a trailblazer for what is now a women's professional league made up of almost 80 percent Black players.

ABOVE: On March 3, 1910, *The New York Age* declared: "These lassies demonstrated that they could play!" while recapping the first recorded basketball game between two independently organized all-Black women's teams. The New York Girls defeated the Jersey Girls 12 to 3.

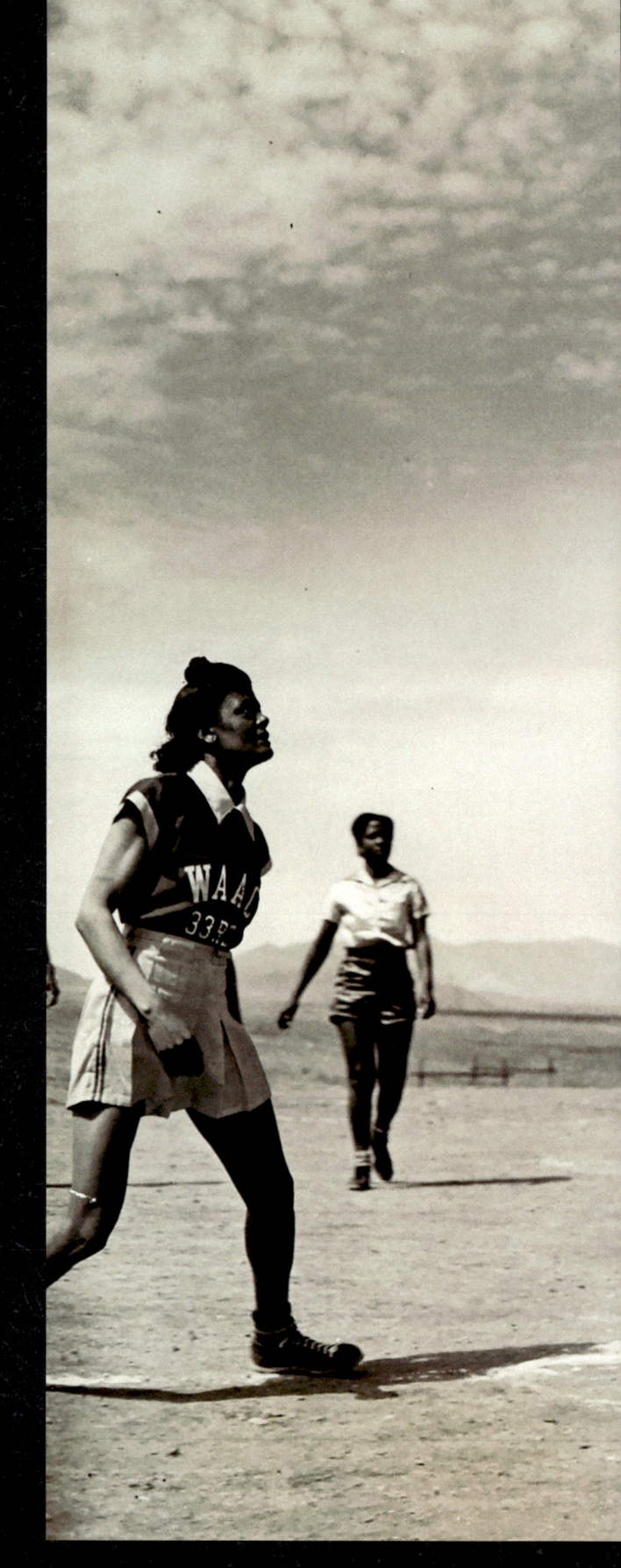

RIGHT: Members of the all-Black 32nd and 33rd Company's Women's Army Auxiliary Corps (WAAC) basketball team, playing at Fort Huachuca in Arizona, 1941–43. World War II was the first time women could officially serve in the military besides nursing and clerical work. Sports, like basketball, served as bonding time for the soldiers and boosted morale.

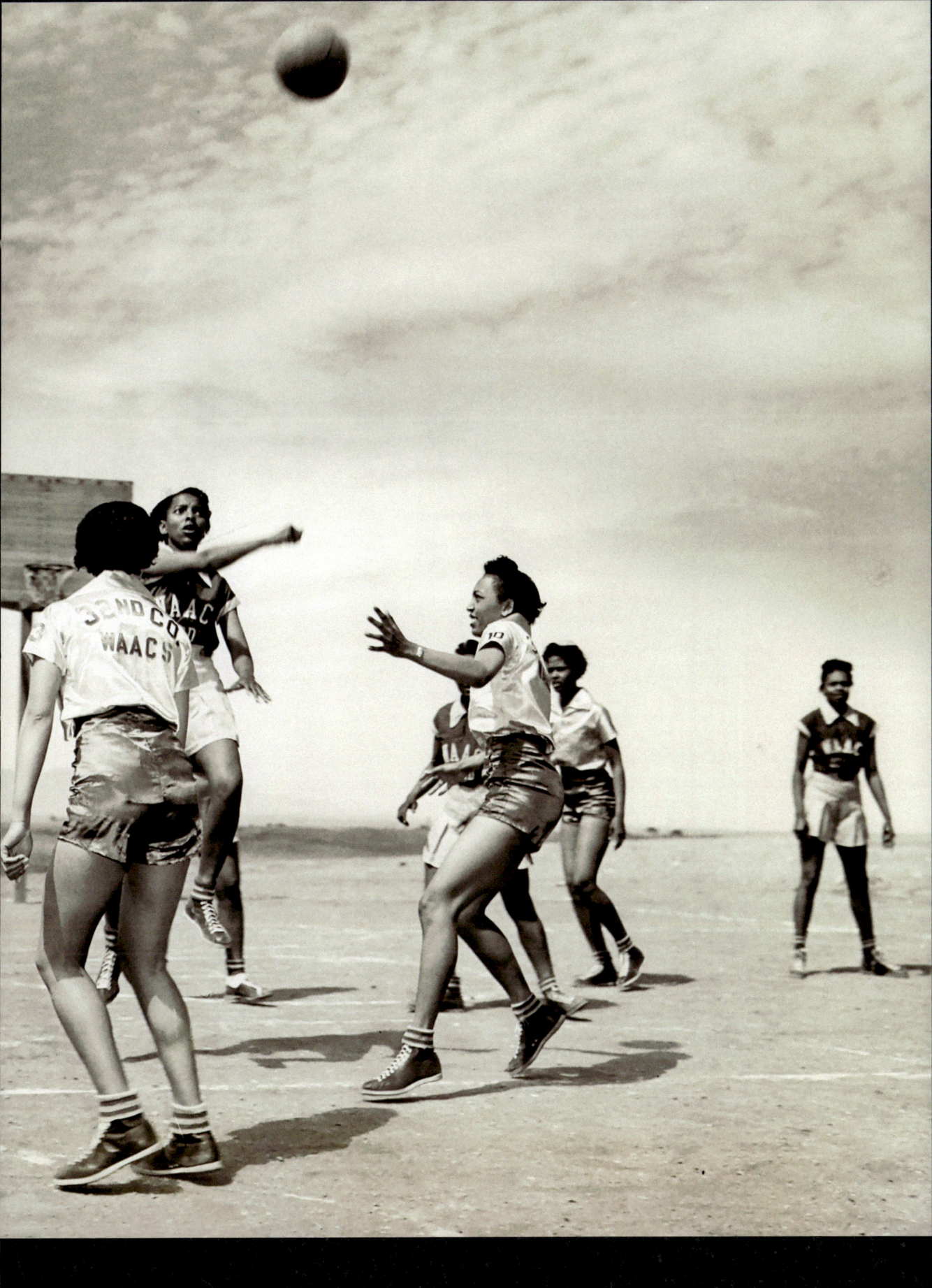

SIX-ON-SIX

A Game of Their Own

There were only a few years between the invention of the game and the publication of the very first rule book. But it would be decades before standardized rules were adopted for women across the country. In some areas, girls were invited to play five-on-five, just like the boys. In others, they played nine-on-nine, using a court divided in three sections. A different model was growing popular by the 1920s—one that represented a compromise between those systems. This was six-on-six. It would rule the game for women for the next four decades, and in some communities, its influence would last even longer.

In six-on-six basketball, the court was divided in half, with three players from each team on each side. Each was assigned to play either offense or defense: There was no crossing half-court. (Some variations designated one or two "rovers" who could run the length of the floor.) Players had to either pass or shoot after just two dribbles. It offered more hustle and physicality than in the nine-player version, but not as much as in five-on-five. There were still pockets of women around the country who played with the same rules as the men. But the version of the game that spread the most widely, gaining a foothold with high schools, factory teams, and small colleges, was six-on-six.

It especially thrived on farmland and in rural areas. The cultural pushback that kept girls from playing basketball in wealthier communities was largely absent: Many of these girls did plenty of strenuous physical activity in their daily lives. If they were already working on the farm like their brothers, why not play sports, too? And no sport captured them quite like six-on-six. It gained steam in these communities throughout the 1930s and 1940s. Many small-town high schools eventually built just as much support for their girls playing six-on-six as for their boys playing five-on-five.

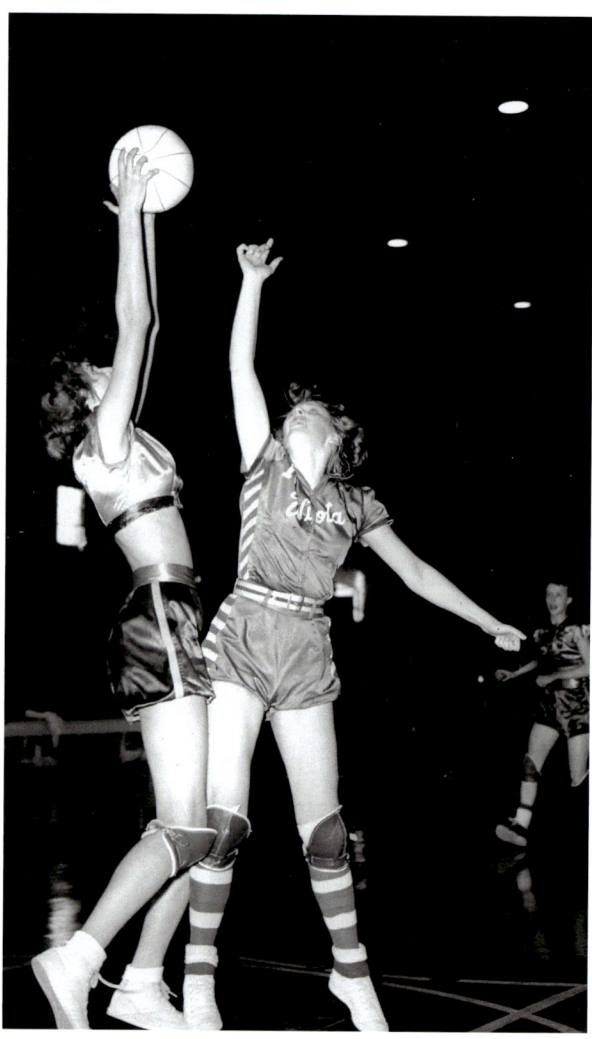

In 1950, for instance, North Carolina hosted a girls' basketball exhibition with four of the best high school teams in the state. All were from small towns. The Raleigh *News & Observer* published an explainer: "Girls' basketball long ago was dropped

ABOVE: Six-on-six basketball thrived even in the tiniest Iowa towns. Wiota, IA, had a population of just 246 in 1940. But it still had a competitive girls' basketball team, seen here.

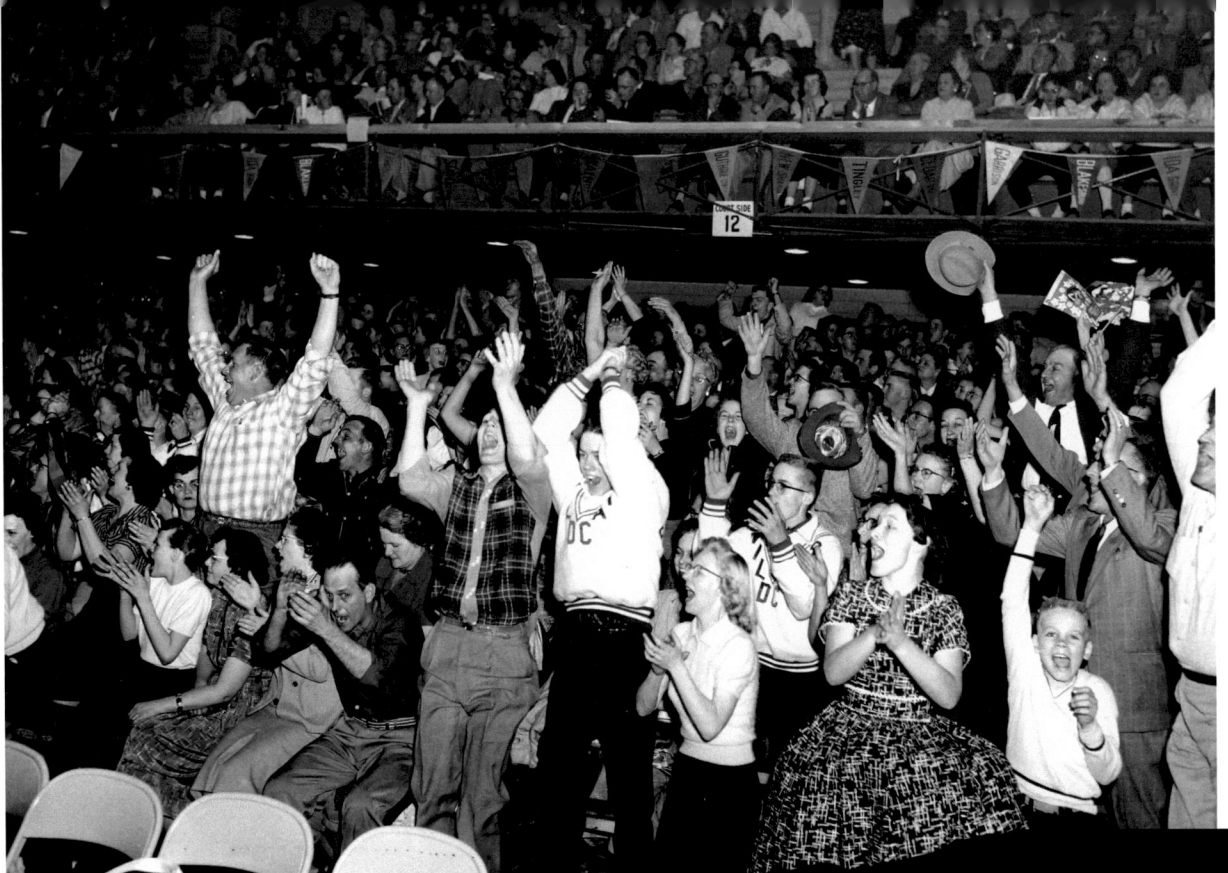

from high schools the size of Raleigh," wrote the newspaper. "But in smaller towns, the girls' basketball teams usually draw more spectators than the boys and therefore are directly responsible for the success of the drawing power." The paper guaranteed a show for anyone who might be skeptical: "There are as many thrills and spills as in the men's game." The exhibition drew 6,000 people, thought at the time to be the largest crowd for girls' basketball anywhere in the South.

But there was nowhere that loved six-on-six basketball as much as Iowa. The state high school tournament was a huge annual fixture. Iowa had organized its first girls' state tournament in 1920—some states would not have an equivalent for decades—and it had become a massive draw by the 1950s, televised throughout the Midwest. It was a high-scoring, fast-moving style of play unlike anything else in basketball. (This meant the biggest stars could average more than 50 points.) The game became part of the fabric of the state.

There were other parts of the country where girls and women ended up discouraged or even

> "Gentlemen, if you attempt to do away with girls' basketball in Iowa, you'll be standing at the center of the track when the train runs over you!"
>
> —JOHN W. AGANS, SCHOOL SUPERINTENDENT, IN A DEBATE ABOUT THE SPORT AT THE IOWA STATE TEACHERS' CONVENTION, 1925

banned from playing basketball. Concerns about overexertion and unladylike behavior made it very difficult for girls to play in some areas. That was not the case in Iowa where the team was deeply embedded in the local culture. It was so beloved that even when the rest of the country eventually moved on to five-on-five, Iowa clung to its history of six-on-six, not holding its final state tournament until 1993.

ABOVE: The girls' high school championship was serious business for Iowans. The crowd seen here took in a tournament game in 1957.

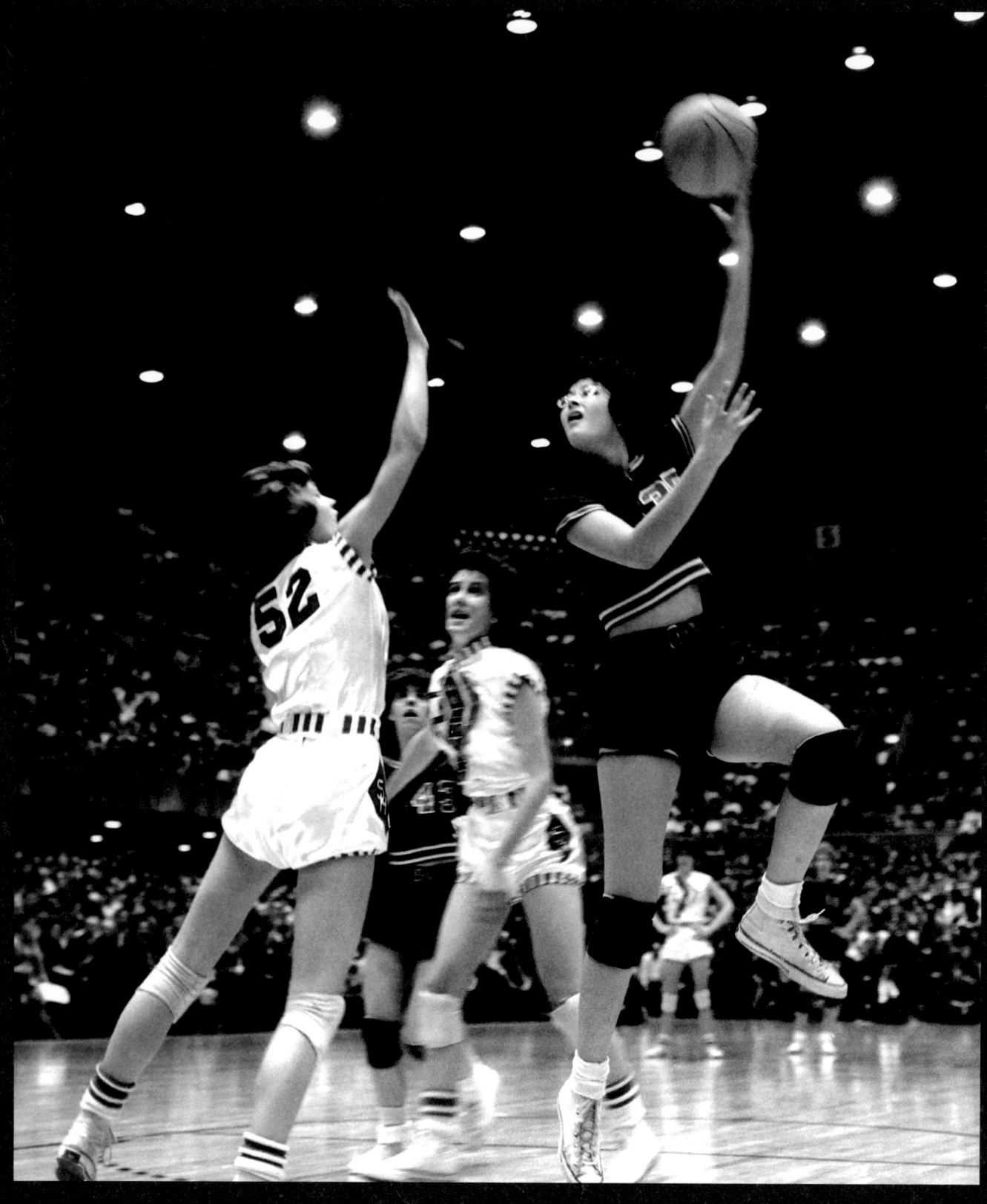

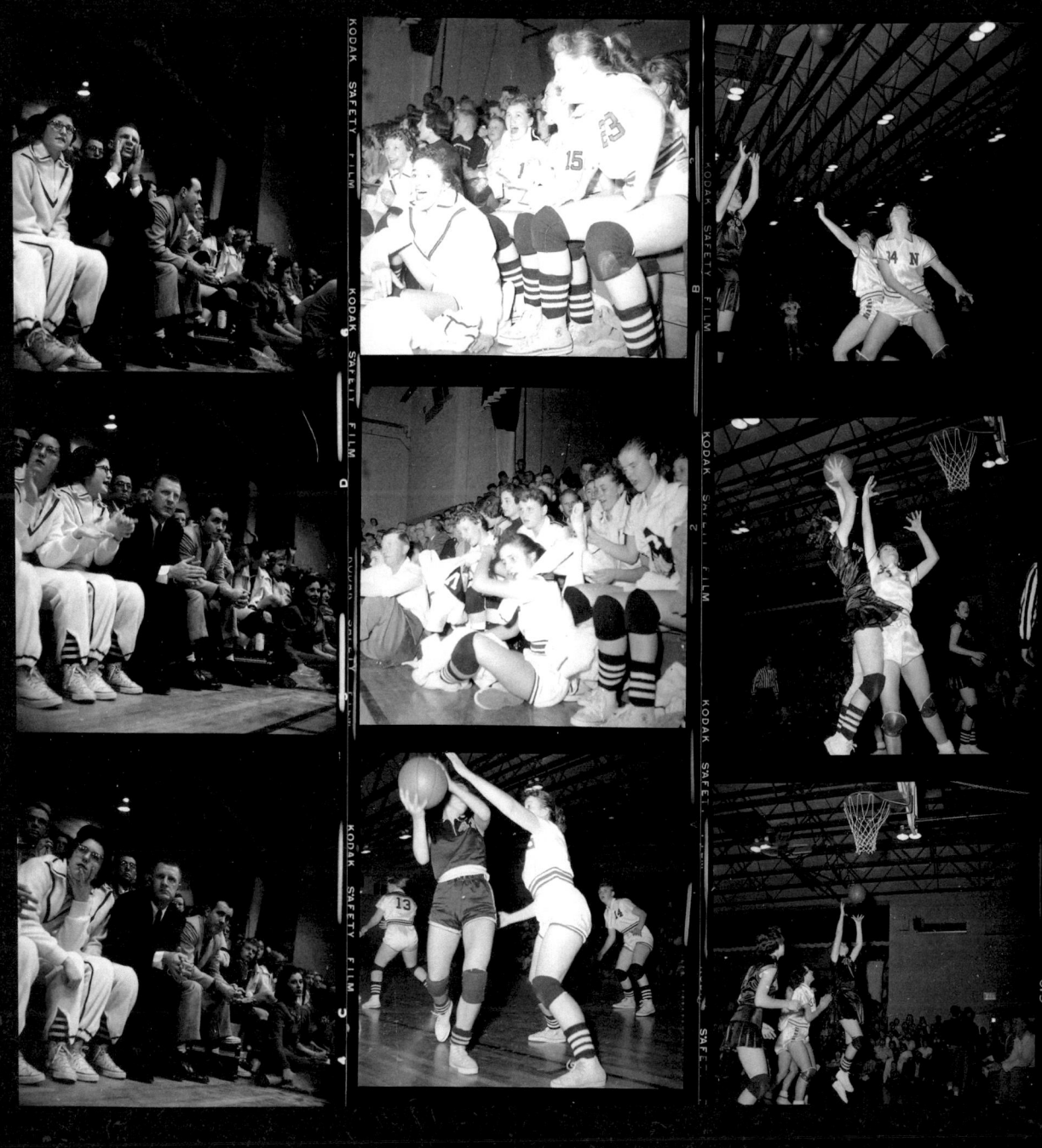

OPPOSITE: An Iowa high school player shows off a sky hook. The fact that six-on-six was so different from five-on-five would be described by some players as an asset: It meant they were rarely compared to the boys or made to feel lesser. They were simply playing their own game.

ABOVE: A sheet of negatives from an Iowa state tournament shows the excited crowd, the action on the court, and the aftermath.

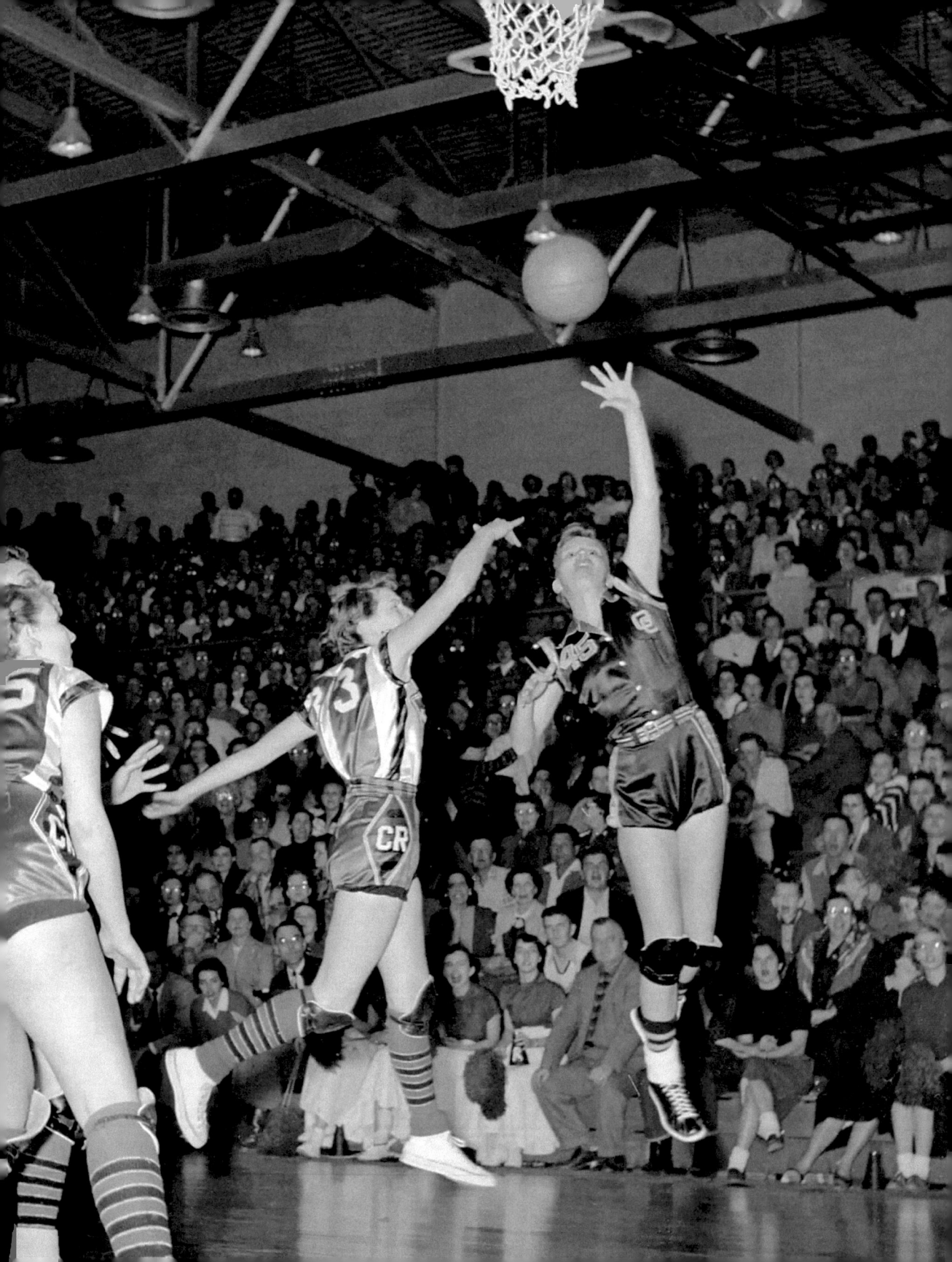

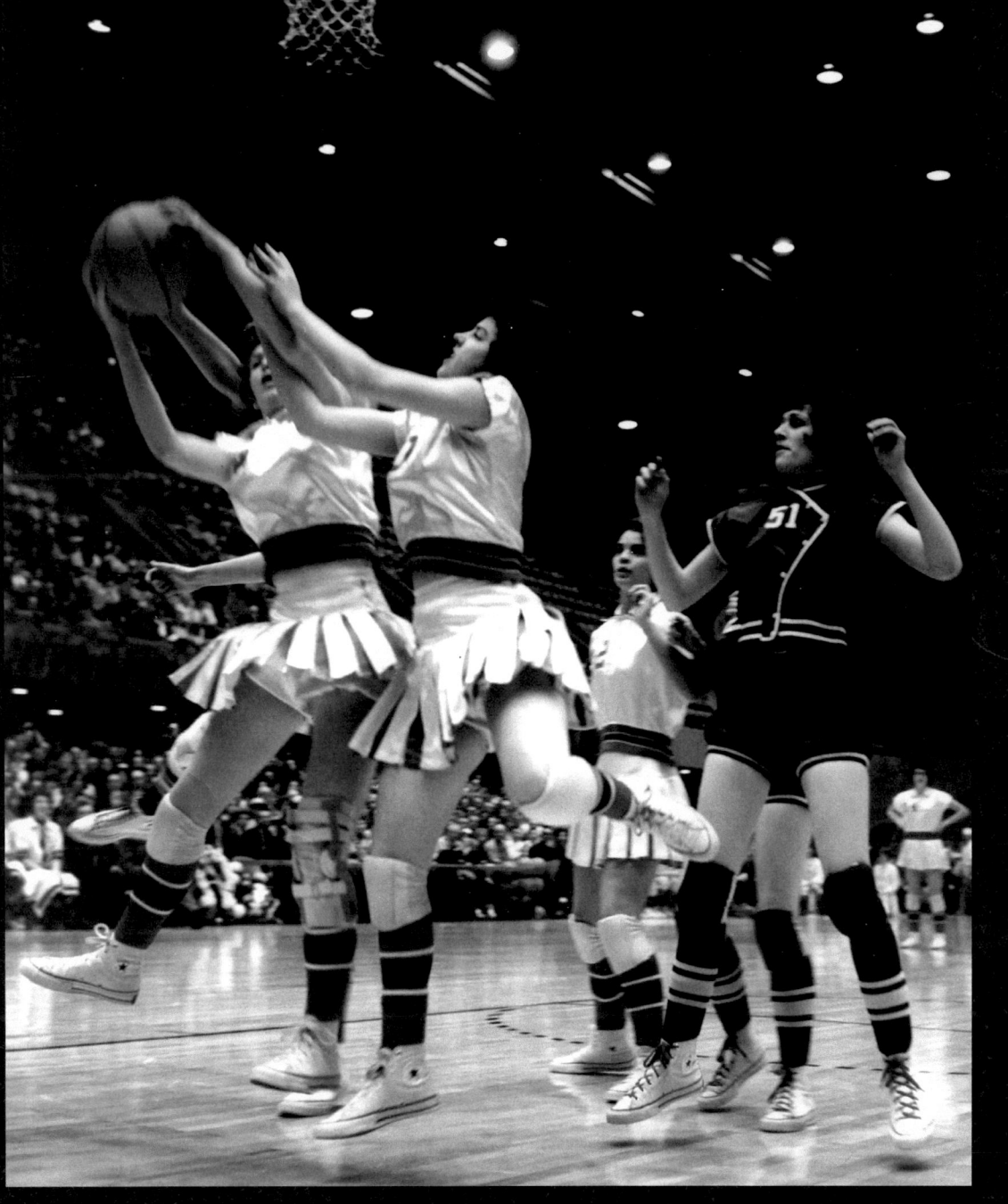

OPPOSITE: Guthrie Center and Coon Rapids are two small towns in Iowa: Neither has ever had a recorded population above 2,100. But their six-on-six teams could still pack a gym.

ABOVE: The six-on-six uniforms could vary widely by school in the 1950s and '60s. Some players wore one-pieces or shorts. Others wore pleated skirts, like these, seen in a 1964 game between Everly and Oxford Junction. But the footwear was nearly always the same: Chuck Taylor Converse.

DENISE LONG

From Iowa to the NBA

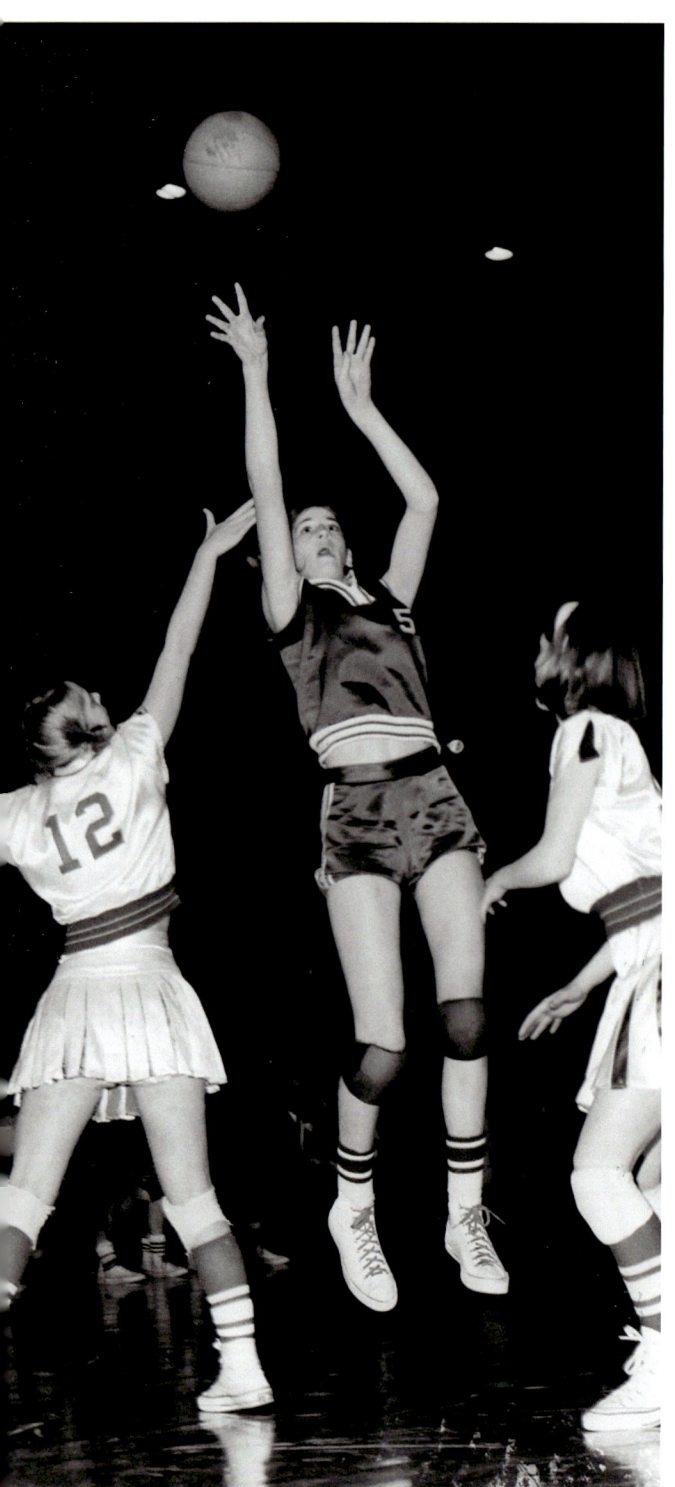

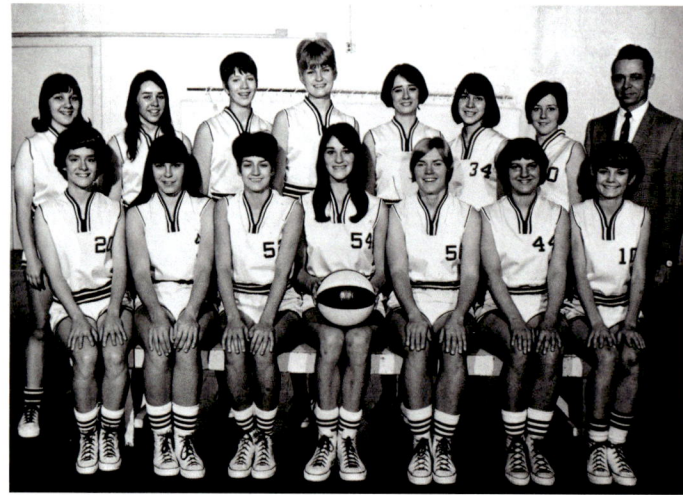

I f all the great Iowa six-on-six players, there was none quite like Denise Long. From the small town of Whitten, she captivated the state with her scoring in the 1960s. She gained notice the first time she dropped more than 100 points. And the second time. And then the third. (Her record was 111.) She took her tiny high school team to the state championship, where Long scored 64 points in an overtime victory, securing a title before 15,000 fans in Des Moines.

That brought her stardom outside Iowa. In May 1969, the spring of her senior year, Long showed up to school and was greeted with a message: *Congratulations, you've been drafted.* "Into the army?"

LEFT: In high school, Denise Long was all but unstoppable, leading her tiny school to a state championship and breaking 100 points on three separate occasions.

ABOVE: Denise, center, holding ball.

OPPOSITE: Denise Long goes up for a shot against a San Francisco Warriors player.

she blurted out. Not quite. She'd been picked the night before in the thirteenth round by the San Francisco Warriors—the men's professional team. Long had just become the first woman selected in the NBA Draft. (The pick was nullified—the fact that she was in high school alone was an automatic disqualification.) It seemed at first like just a publicity stunt, but there was a real plan from Warriors owner Franklin Mieuli. He wanted to have women play on the court before home games and during halftime.

Mieuli ultimately recruited four teams of women, and the star was Long. (While the women did not get paid, Mieuli covered Long's tuition at the University of San Francisco for the year, and he leased her a spectacular car to get around town in—a purple Jaguar.) It lasted just one season, but it provided an opportunity for her to keep playing and to brush shoulders with the biggest stars in the NBA.

They included Lakers' center Wilt Chamberlain, best known for scoring 100 points in a game in 1962, who *knew* that he recognized the name "Denise Long."

"Aren't you the young lady who broke my record?" he asked.

"Yes," she said, though ever polite, quintessentially Midwestern, she quickly added a qualifier: "But I didn't mean to."

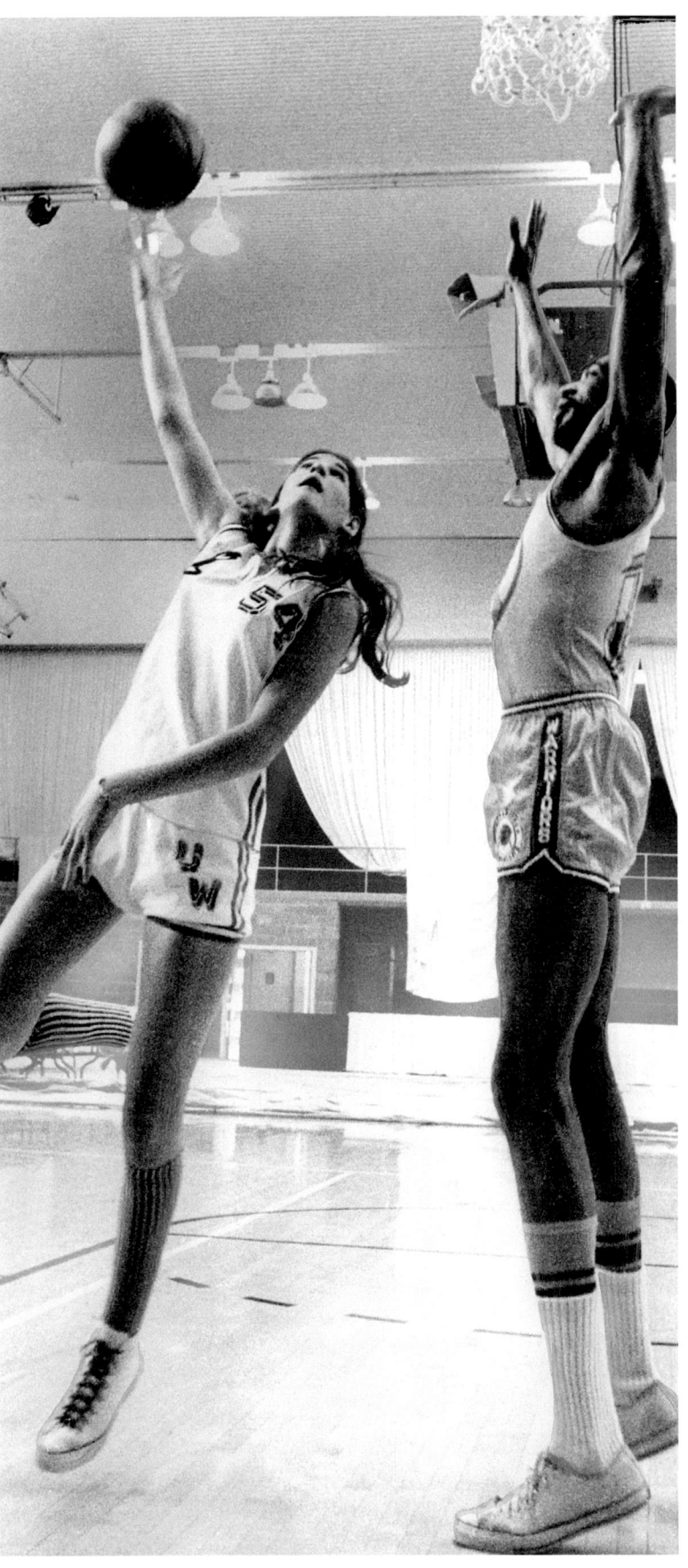

THE ALL-AMERICAN RED HEADS

These Women Took Barnstorming to a New Level

In the pretelevision era, the leading women's pro team was the All-American Red Heads. The players dyed their hair red as a gimmick, and they'd crisscross the country in makeshift station wagons and limos, playing hoops against men's "barnstorming teams" with men's basketball rules. The team of seven would thrill audiences with their tricky handles, clever moves, and rousing misdirection plays that were guaranteed to get you off your seat. Think Harlem Globetrotters but with *way* cooler hair.

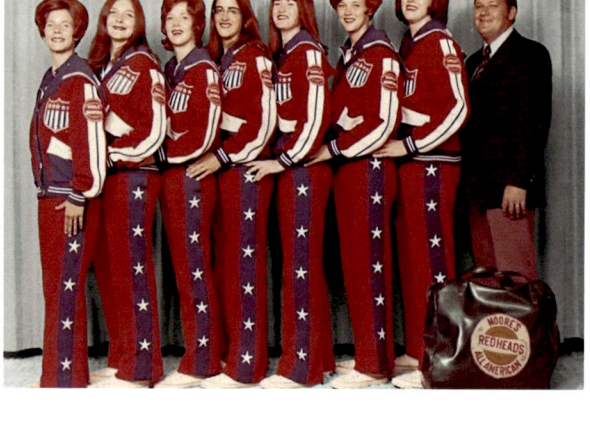

C. M. "Ole" Olson of Cassville, Missouri, had the bright idea of a traveling barnstorm women's hoops team in 1936, but they had to be unique. Ole was always gimmicky: He was said to be the first person to throw a behind-the-back. His wife, Doyle, was a hairdresser and owned five local beauty shops. She originally joked about the players having fiery red tresses, but Ole ran with it. He taught the ladies creative tricks on the court, dressed them in shiny red, white, and blue uniforms, and had them all dye their hair—Miss Clairol 33, to be exact.

"I called it Bozo red," Lynn Thomas, who played from 1971 to 1973, said to the Missouri Sports Hall of Fame. "If you didn't rinse it out and then played and sweated, that red dye would run down your face."

Orwell Moore and his wife, Lorene "Butch" Moore, purchased the team in 1954 and moved them to Caraway, Arkansas, where they ran and operated the Red Heads for over thirty years. Orwell was the coach, and Lorene was their star player; she finished the all-time Red Heads' leading scorer with 35,426 points in eleven seasons.

The Red Heads could ball. They won ninety-six consecutive games and played upward of 200 games per season. The demand got so high during 1964–71 that three teams traveled at a time across all fifty states, even making stops in Mexico, Canada, and the Philippines.

They had special plays like the dipsy-doodle, where a player would dribble toward the basket, between her legs, lean forward, and shoot over her own back. And the piggyback: hopping on a teammate's back and dunking the ball.

The Red Heads were enshrined in the Naismith Basketball Hall of Fame in 2012, the first women's team to receive the honor. With their last game in 1986, their fifty-year stint makes for the longest-running women's professional franchise in the history of women's hoops.

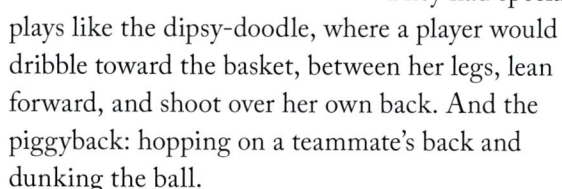

ABOVE: The Red Heads traveled over 60,000 miles by car every 200-game season, always in style.

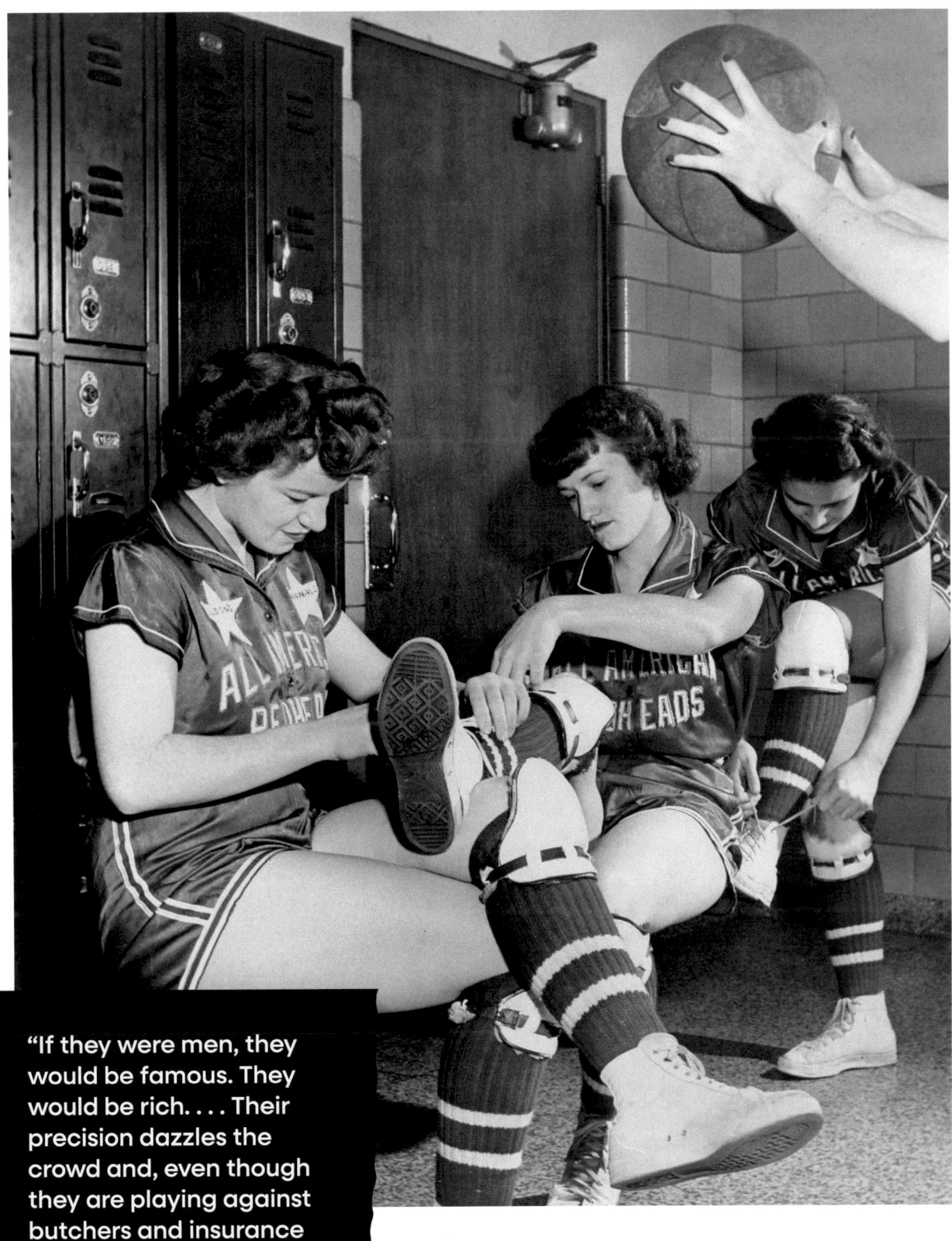

"If they were men, they would be famous. They would be rich. . . . Their precision dazzles the crowd and, even though they are playing against butchers and insurance men and car salesmen, the All-American Red Heads are plainly a splendid basketball machine."

—*SPORTS ILLUSTRATED*, 1974

ABOVE: Pre-game, star player Red Mason (left) laces the sneaker of teammate Myrtle Wallace in a locker room circa 1950.

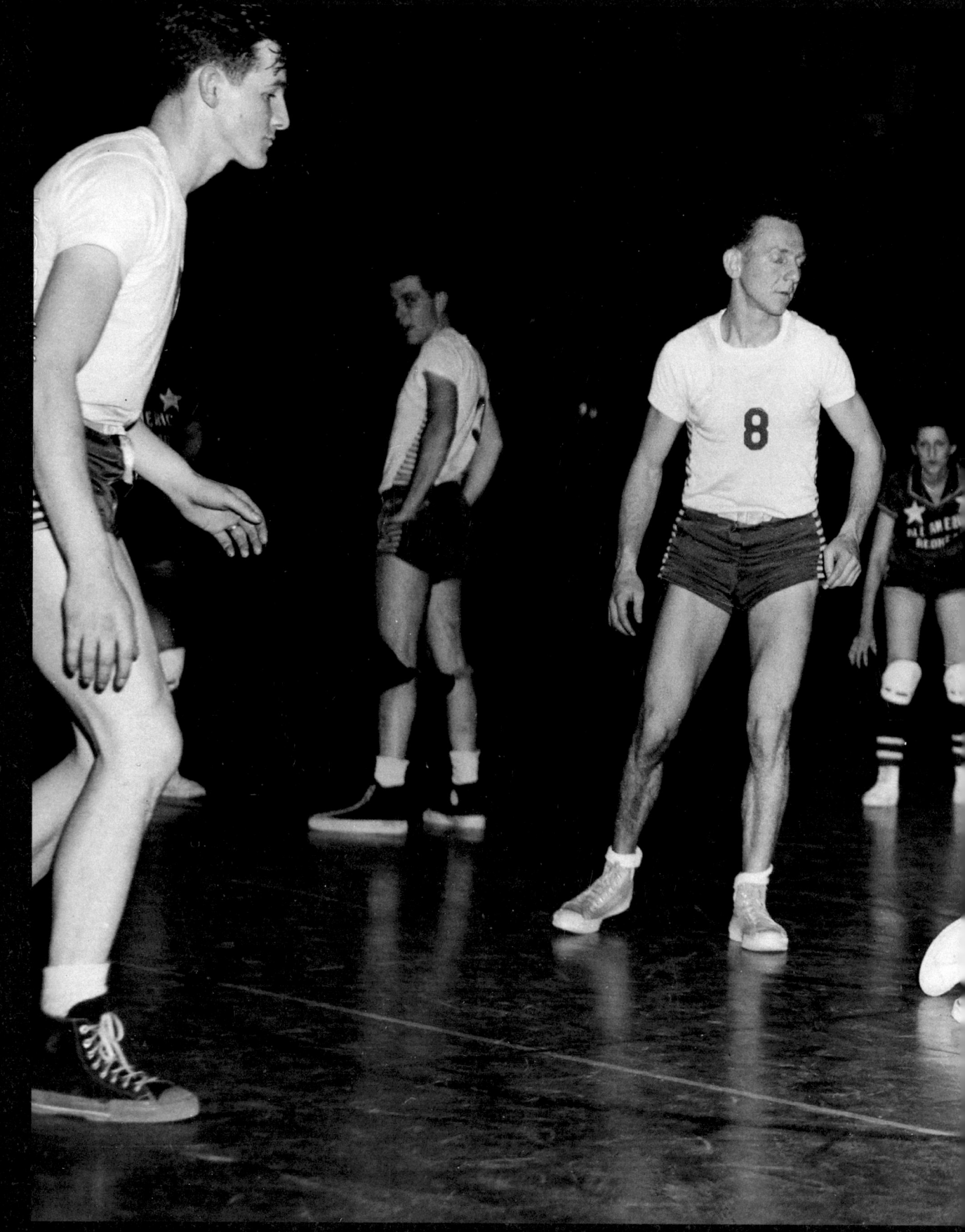

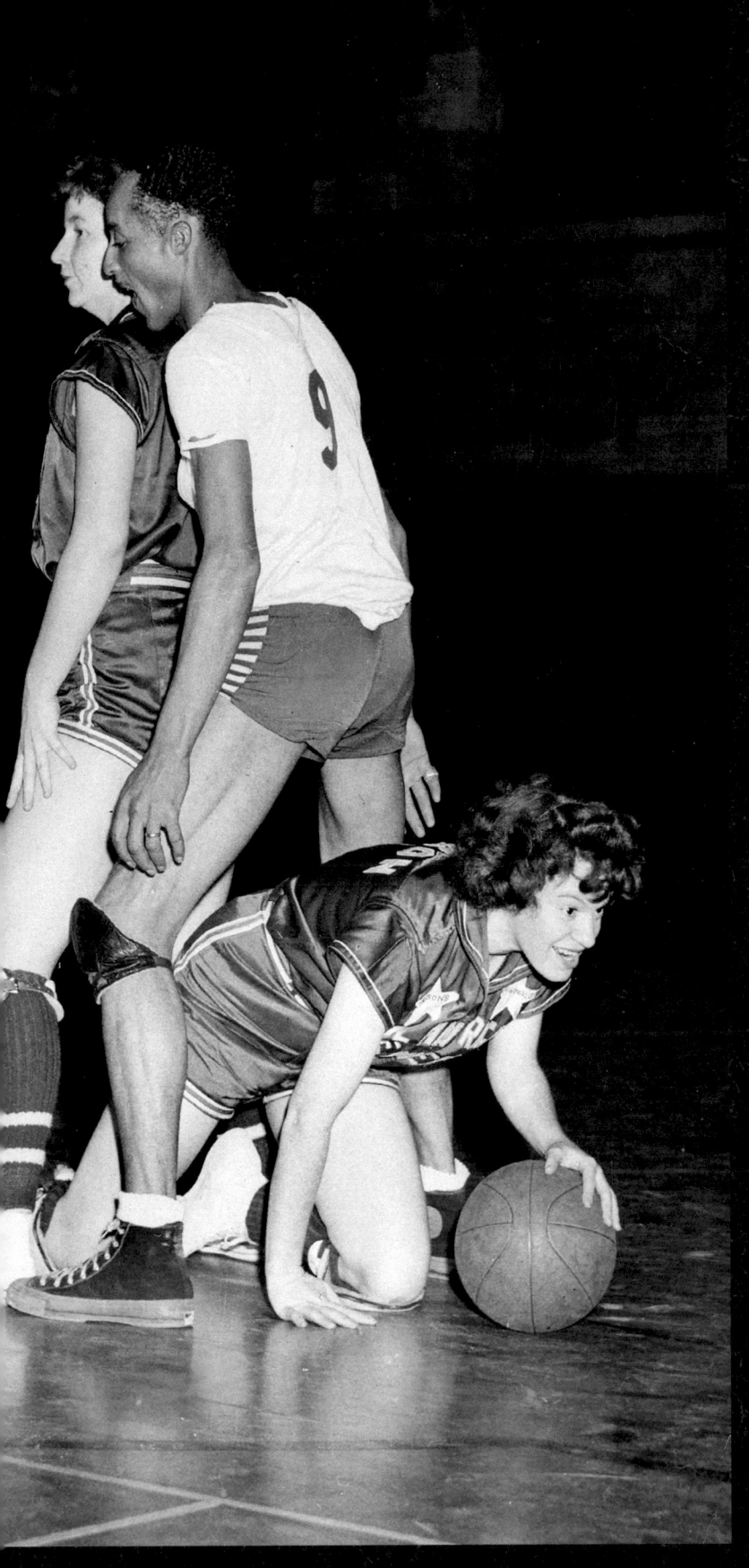

LEFT: The All-American Red Heads had their fundamentals down pat, but were firstly entertainers. Like this tricky move, for instance, when a player dribbled through her teammate's (and the male defender's) legs for an easy layup.

WAYLAND BAPTIST FLYING QUEENS

A Winning Streak Like No Other

There may not have been a more curious setting for the first women's college basketball dynasty than Wayland Baptist College in the 1950s. A tiny religious school in a small West Texas town, its female students were not allowed to dance, play dominoes, or wear pants around campus. But they could play basketball. And did they ever.

There was no formal governing structure yet for women's college basketball. (It would be decades before the NCAA included women.) A number of schools had teams—but their best option for competition was the Amateur Athletic Union, or AAU, which oversaw a national championship tournament and offered the biggest stage for women playing basketball after high school. This was long before the AAU became known for its focus on youth sports: These were generally adult women, and most played on *industrial teams*, teams sponsored by the companies they worked for. Those boomed as women took jobs in factories during World War II, with teams like the Hanes Hosiery Girls, Pine-Sol Queens, and Martin Aircraft Bomberettes. The companies paid all their expenses and used basketball as an advertising opportunity. (The experience was more semipro than amateur.) But that made it difficult for any college squad to seriously compete. That changed with Wayland Baptist.

The school's president began supporting women's basketball in hopes of drawing more female students to the tiny campus. The program quickly ran up against a logistical problem. Not all of the most talented players could afford to attend Wayland. (Tuition and fees totaled roughly $800 a year then.) If they wanted to compete with industrial teams in the AAU and gain any kind of serious recognition, they would have to draw better

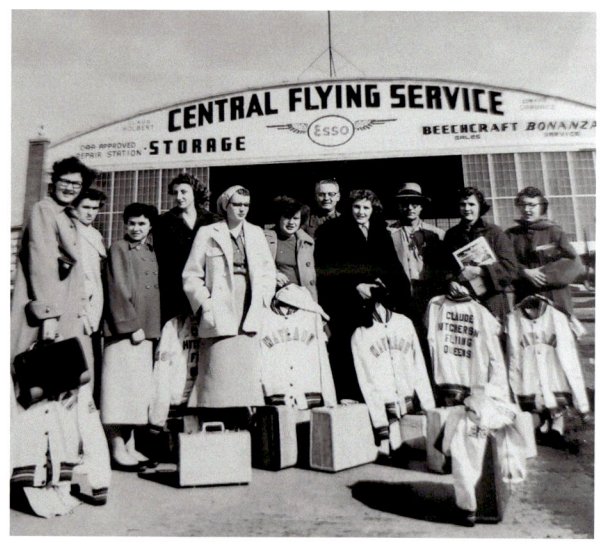

players to Plainview, Texas. So why not arrange to cover tuition and room and board for every player?

They had just created the first women's college basketball team where every player would be on scholarship.

That alone would have been enough to set them apart. But they got another major boost from a local alumnus named Claude Hutcherson, who owned a "flying service," or air travel company. He and his wife, Wilda, loved the idea of sponsoring the team and signed on in 1951. They agreed to fly the players to games all over the country, and the team became the Wayland Baptist Flying Queens.

They quickly became one of the most successful teams of their day. (It helped that coach Harley Redin was an early proponent of the full-court press: They played six-on-six, with two players

ABOVE: The Flying Queens traveled in style like no other team.

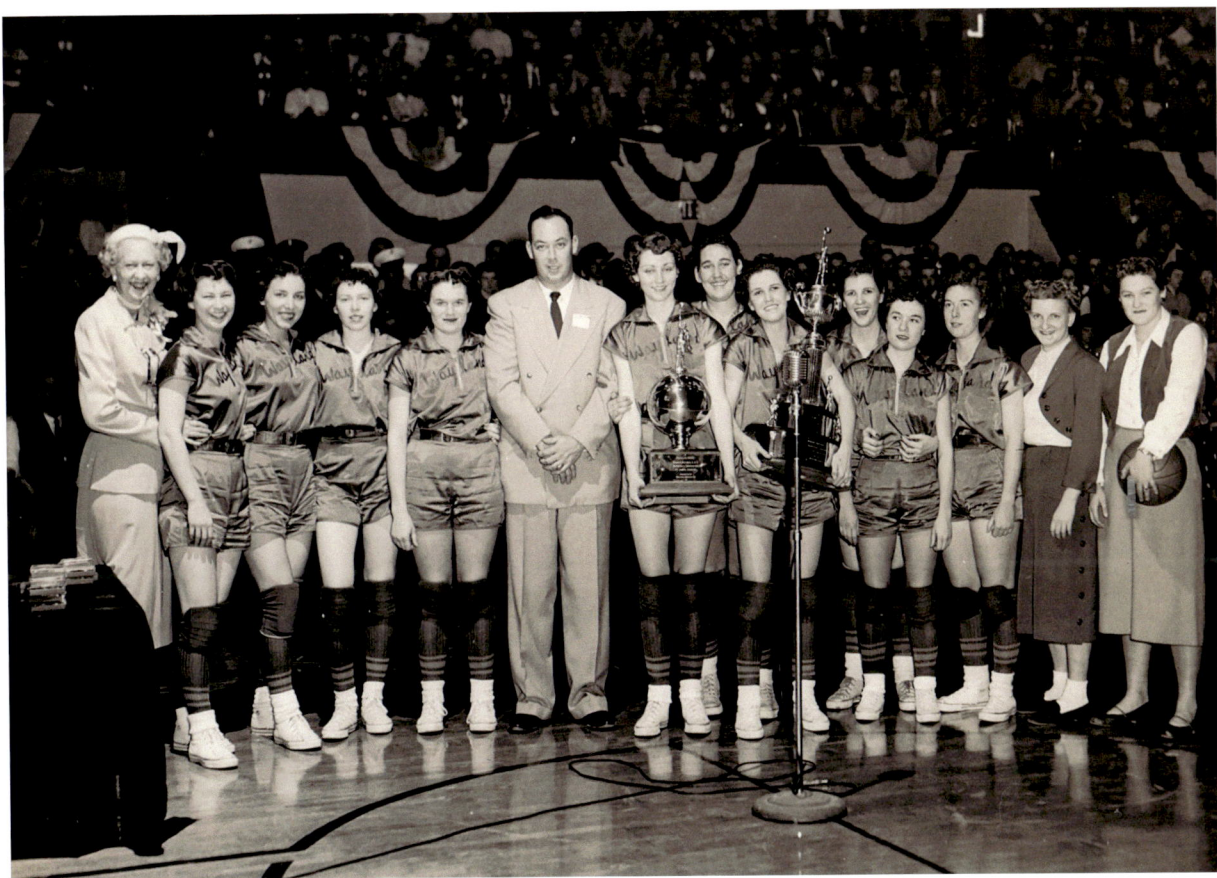

designated as offense, two as defense, and two as "rovers," able to cover the length of the court. Redin was one of the first to actually *use* those rovers to run the floor.) They had fancy uniforms and stayed in the nicest hotels. (That came with surprising perks: They once found themselves staying in the same place as the Harlem Globetrotters. Redin convinced them to use an empty hotel ballroom to teach his team a few tricks.)

Once the team started winning, it took a very, very long time for them to stop. Wayland Baptist won 131 consecutive games from 1953 to 1958. That is not an official college record (it was, after all, technically the AAU), but it remains the longest win streak recorded by a college team, men's or women's, for any level of competition. College basketball had never seen anything like the Wayland Baptist Flying Queens. And no one has matched them since.

AAU SQUADS

Some were sponsored by colleges, some were organized by workplaces, and some were just local. Teams included:

- Atlanta Peaches
- Jacksonville Pepsi-Cola Six
- Amarillo Dolls
- Snow White Launderettes
- Milwaukee Real Refrigeration Girls

ABOVE: The 1954 AAU Championship came right in the middle of the Flying Queens' record winning streak.

MATTER OF FACT
1890s–1960s

Numbers, People, and Moments That Defined the Era

NUMBERS

2 In 1962, a rule change allowed each team permission for two players to rove the entire court, no longer needing to stay in their section.

30 The thirty-second shot clock was made optional in 1966. Also, continuous, unlimited dribble becomes the official rule, making the game much faster.

'68-69 Coaching from the sideline is no longer a foul. The previous rule only allowed coaches to talk to their players during time-outs and intermissions.

156 Points scored by Maryland high school player Marie Boyd Eichler on February 25, 1924, still the all-time record for points in a high school game.

PEOPLE

Arguably the best player of the AAU era, **NERA WHITE** stood six foot one and could do just about everything on the court. The native Tennessean played for a team sponsored by Nashville Business College and helped them win ten national championships in fifteen years. She was tournament MVP in all ten.

The first women's college basketball national championship was held on March 23, 1969. The invitational tournament included sixteen teams who played six-on-six and was set up by West Chester State coach **CAROL ECKMAN**. Her players tore through the bracket to win it all.

MISSOURI ARLEDGE starred in the 1950s for Philander Smith College, which was a historically Black school in Arkansas. Every other college roster and company team in the AAU national championship bracket was entirely white. "Big Mo" Arledge led the team to the quarterfinals, and she became the first Black player named an All-American.

1896

Bloomers were introduced as a playing uniform at New Orleans' Sophie Newcomb College by **CLARA GREGORY BAER**. She wore them while playing "Newcomb Ball," an early form of volleyball.

1913

New York Girls center **DORA COLE** was the director of dancing of the world-renowned historical pageant *The Star of Ethiopia*, written by famed playwright W.E.B. Dubois.

1904

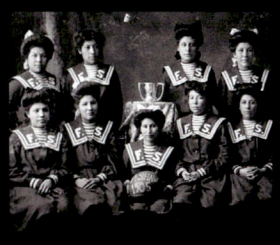

A team of Native American girls from the **FORT SHAW INDIAN BOARDING SCHOOL** gained notice playing all over Montana—which they parlayed into a trip to the St. Louis World's Fair in 1904. They handily beat the competition there and were crowned world champions. A centennial memorial was dedicated to them in Fort Shaw in 2004.

SEPT. 1924

Debut of *THE SPORTSWOMAN*, a periodical about women's sports. Their motto: "Every girl and every woman to play something, whether she may excel at it or not."

BERENSON TROPHY

The Berenson Trophy, named for Senda Berenson, is given to inductees each year at the Women's Basketball Hall of Fame.

RIGHT PLACE, RIGHT TIME

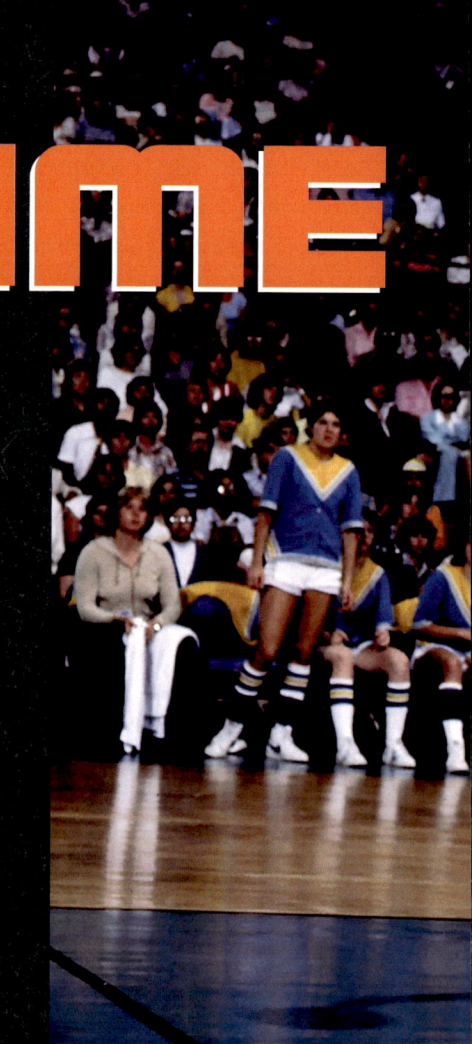

THE WOMEN'S GAME
EXPLODED IN THE 1970s.
LADIES STARTED TAKING OVER
COLLEGE COURTS, GOING PRO,
AND WINNING MEDALS IN THE
OLYMPICS. THE LANDSCAPE
WAS FOREVER CHANGED.

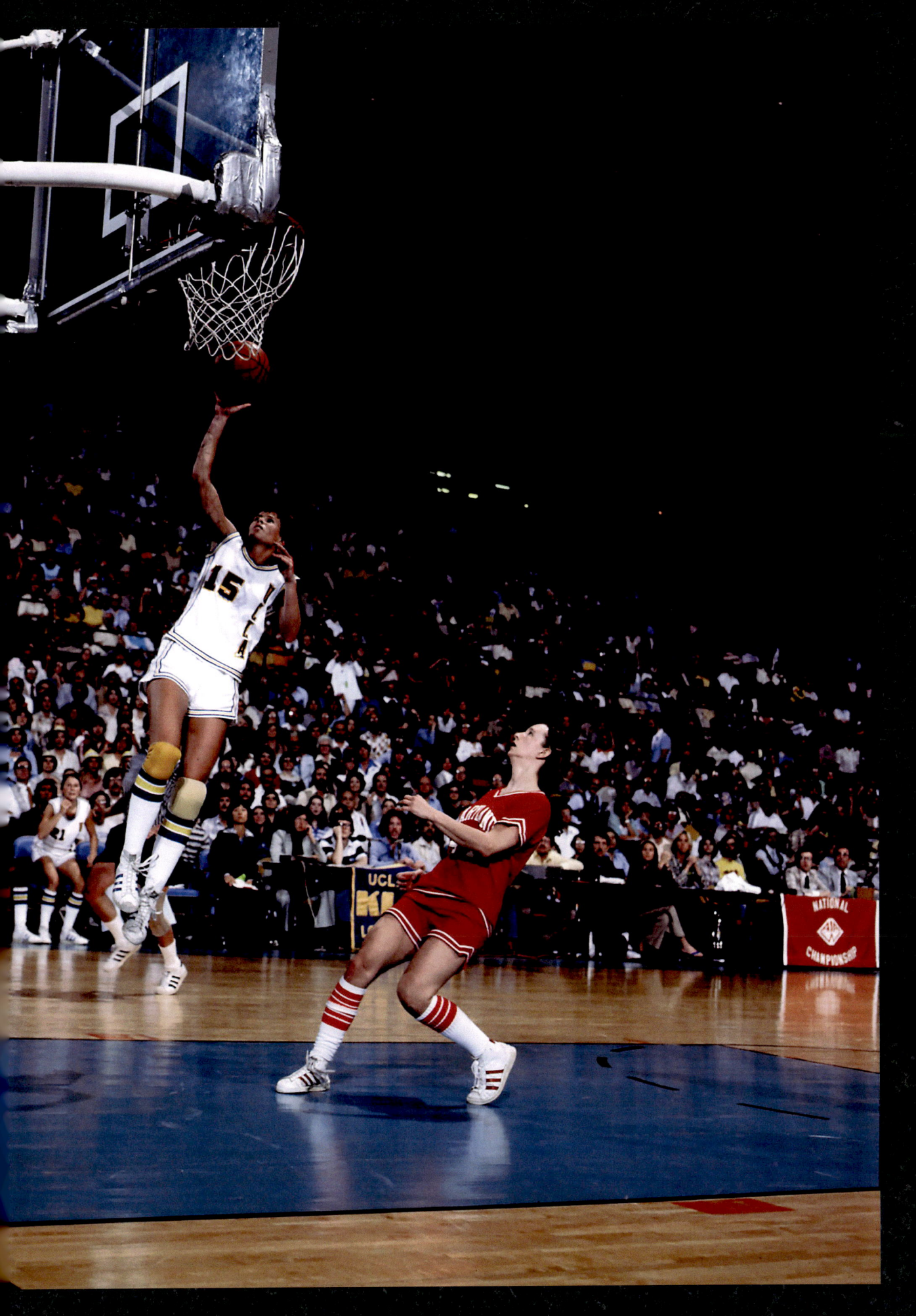

THE BIRTH OF THE AIAW

Women's College Basketball Gets Organized

"Must women follow that which is laid down for men by men?"

This was the question that drove the first delegate assembly of the Association for Intercollegiate Athletics for Women (AIAW). Their attempt to answer it would shape college sports for women through the 1970s and 1980s.

Before the AIAW, women's college sports were fragmented, often more like intramurals than serious competition. But there was appetite for change in the 1960s, which led to the creation of the AIAW in 1971. It was the first major governing body of intercollegiate sports for women—and it was very different from any of the structures that preceded it. When the women of the AIAW looked at the men of the NCAA, they saw a system rife with greed, commercial influence, and predatory behavior. They wanted something new.

The AIAW's founders agreed to a set of core principles. They wanted athletes to choose their schools for reasons beyond sports. That meant no restrictions on transfers and no aggressive recruiting. (In fact, athletes were encouraged to reach out to coaches, not vice versa.) At first, there would be no athletic scholarships, either: This quickly changed. It was a significantly different model for college sports, but it was one in which its leaders believed deeply.

The organization grew quickly. It set rules and ran national championships for women in eight sports in 1972. And none was bigger than basketball. The next few years would see hundreds of additional schools, a dozen new sports, and much more money.

All of that growth was partially a product of good timing. Title IX had become law in 1972. It

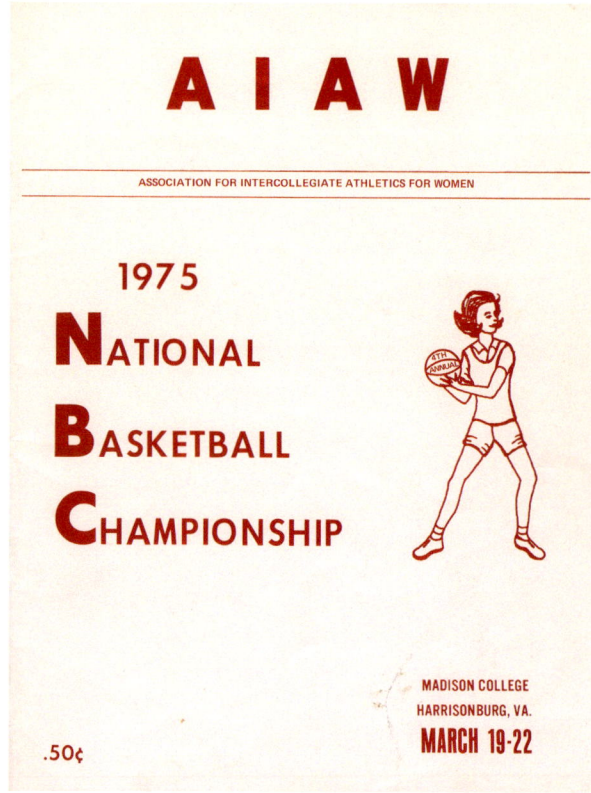

did not mean instant change for women's athletics: In fact, it took almost two years for the first draft of federal regulations on what it would entail for college sports, and it would be still longer before those regulations were enforced. But the law opened the door to seismic change and that change initially ran through the AIAW, with its vision that women's college sports might be run for women, by women.

ABOVE: The AIAW's national basketball championship was one of the biggest events for women's college sports by the mid-1970s.

"No person in the United States shall, on the **basis of sex**, be excluded from participation in, be denied the benefits of, or be subjected to discrimination under any **educational program or activity** receiving federal financial assistance."

TITLE IX

These thirty-seven words changed everything for women and girls on June 23, 1972. This one sentence was snuck into a larger section of the Education Amendments, which President Richard Nixon signed into law. By 1975 President Gerald Ford had made it clear that Title IX includes athletics, and gave athletic departments up to three years to fully comply.

THE MIGHTY MACS

THE FIRST AIAW NATIONAL CHAMPIONSHIP

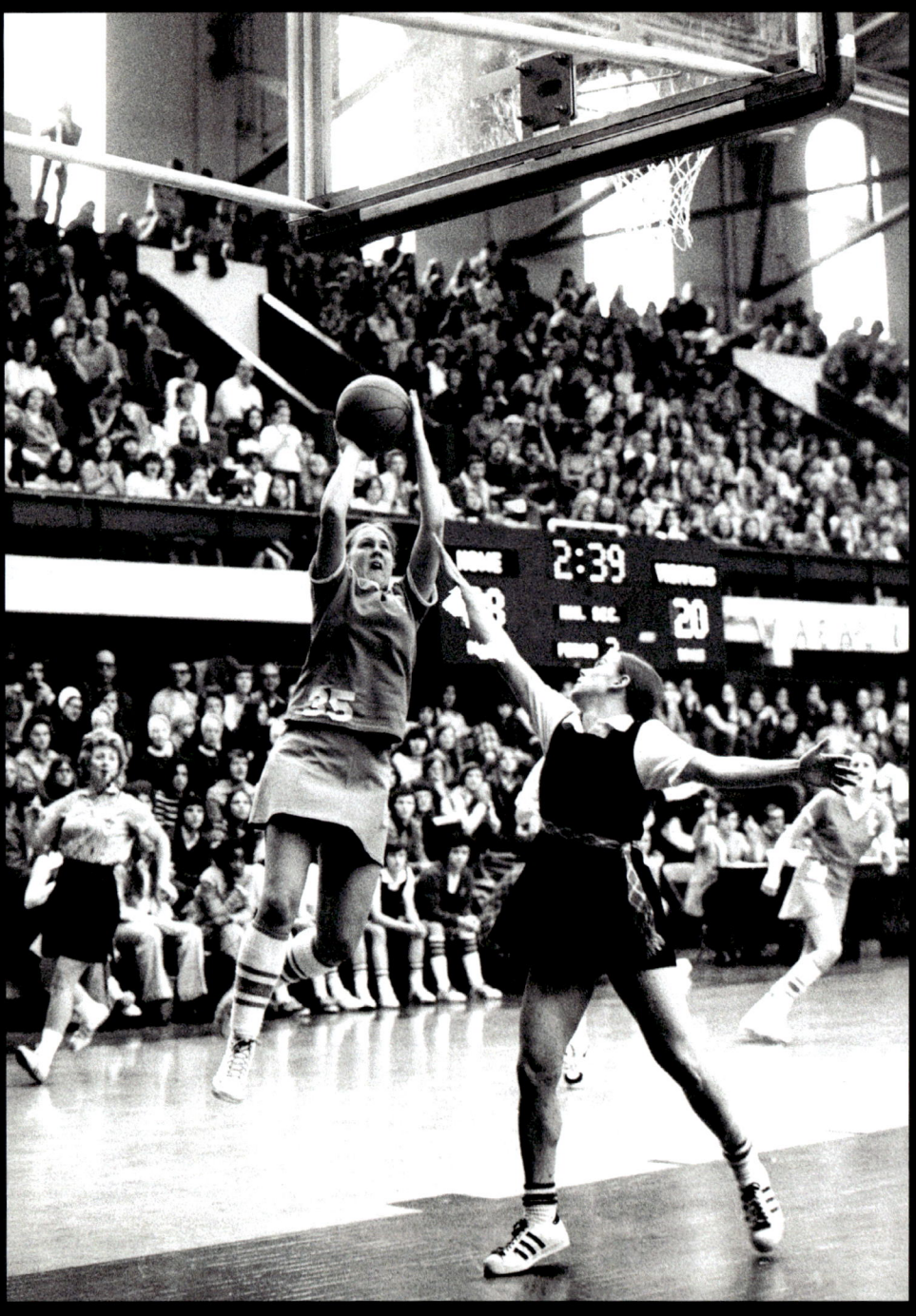

ABOVE: Don't let the tunics fool you. The Mighty Macs could hoop—and pack a gym.

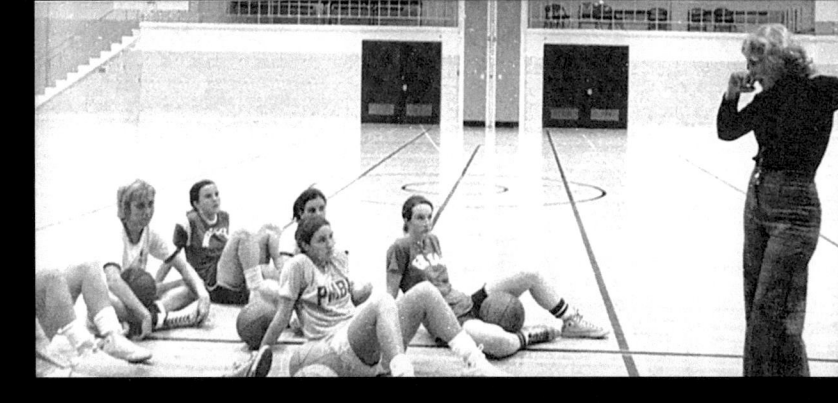

Cathy Rush had no expectations when she became the basketball coach at Immaculata College in 1970. The job was only part-time, and the annual salary was negligible, just $450. The gym had burned down and not been rebuilt. The small Catholic women's school enrolled only a few hundred students on its campus outside Philadelphia. The job still appealed to twenty-two-year-old Rush. She loved basketball. Plus, she had married an NBA referee, so while he was on the road during the season, she needed something to do.

"I really didn't think I could make anything out of it," Rush says. "It was a nothing job."

Her players felt similarly. They never guessed that basketball might define their experience at Immaculata. When they enrolled, serious college basketball for women simply was not something that existed in the popular imagination.

"There was no anticipation of some great athletic career," says Theresa Shank Grentz, who played at Immaculata under Rush from 1970 to 1974. "That was not anywhere near the picture."

Yet they became some of the first women to shape that ideal for the generations who followed. They arrived on campus right before the formation of the Association for Intercollegiate Athletics for Women, with Title IX around the corner in 1972, and they dominated those early years of the college game. None of them had known exactly what they were getting into when they came to Immaculata. They made basketball history there all the same.

Immaculata won the first modern college national championship in 1972. Nicknamed the Mighty Macs, they ultimately won back to back to back, repeating as champions in 1973 and again in 1974. They were also responsible for a slew of other milestones. Immaculata recorded the first official undefeated season. They were the first team invited to play outside the United States. (The Mighty Macs did a monthlong tour of Australia.) They were part of the first nationally televised game and the first game at Madison Square Garden. (They won both.) And it all started with an incredibly unlikely win in that first national title game in 1972.

The tiny school had limited resources. (Immaculata's basketball uniforms were also the field hockey uniforms: The players simply passed along their blue tunics at the end of the season.) Since there was no gym, they used a nearby basement facility that offered them access for two hours every weekday. But for everything the school lacked, Immaculata still had some major talent on campus. How? Some of the most competitive girls' high school basketball in the country was then being played in the Philadelphia Catholic League. (Many of those schools were single-sex: As a result, girls traditionally had not been forced to compete with boys for resources, which had stymied the growth of the game elsewhere.) When many of these girls finished high school, they went to Catholic women's colleges in or around Philadelphia, such as Immaculata. This was before the days of recruiting or athletic scholarships for women. But faith, geography, and fate combined to bring many strong players to campus.

This all meant there had been a basketball team at Immaculata since the 1930s. Traditionally more like an intramural squad, it had begun to evolve

---

ABOVE: Immaculata head coach Cathy Rush was young, but she had a mind for strategy and was obsessed with learning the intricacies of five-on-five.

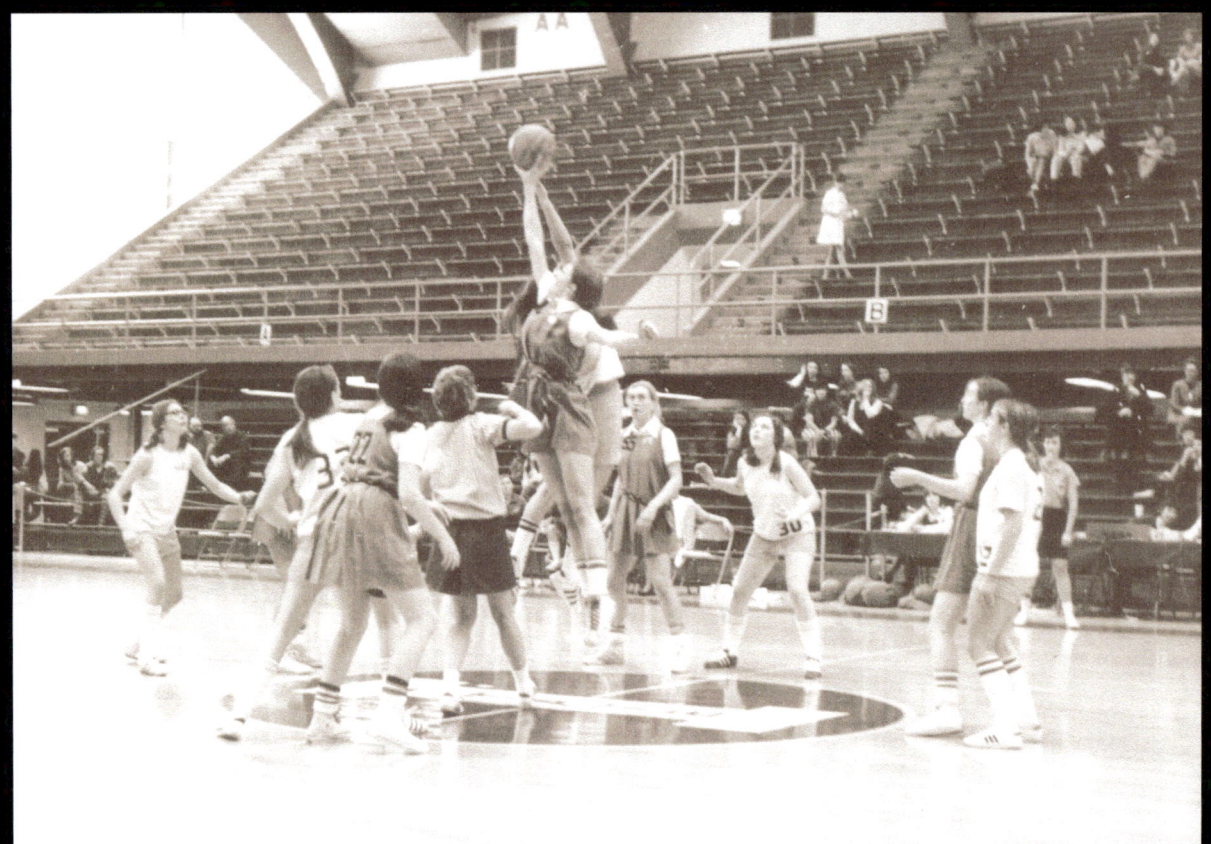

by the late 1960s, as organized intercollegiate play was growing for women. This was the environment Rush stepped into when she was hired in 1970.

When her first practice was over, Rush called her husband in the NBA, bursting to share what she had seen.

"Oh, my God," she remembers telling him. "I have Jerry West in a girl's body!"

That was Theresa Shank Grentz. The freshman center was six feet tall, the most physically dominant player on the floor, an excellent ball handler with a gorgeous fadeaway jumper. She had won three championships in the Philadelphia Catholic League. She was joined by several girls she had played with or against in high school. The group was unpolished, but still, Rush was thrilled.

It was going to be a season of change. Everyone here was used to playing six-on-six. That included Rush, who had played that style in high school and in college at nearby West Chester State, which was known for its physical education program and had a

strong basketball tradition. This would be the first season that Immaculata and other nearby colleges would switch to five-on-five. (Some colleges had begun adopting full-court, five-on-five rules for women's basketball in 1969, and it would become the national standard in the college game in 1971.) It would be a major adjustment.

Even though Rush had never played five-on-five, she'd watched plenty, including sitting in the stands at "dozens and dozens and dozens" of NBA games. She threw herself into reading about strategy, and she came away with a fast-paced, up-tempo style that she believed she could implement with her team.

They played well in Rush's first season at Immaculata, but it was the next year that would

---

ABOVE: There was hardly anyone in the stands for the 1972 AIAW national championship in Normal, IL, but the game sparked a dynasty all the same.

change everything for them. The newly established AIAW would begin overseeing women's college sports in 1971. That meant standardized rules (including that national switch to five-on-five) and more robust schedules. It also meant a full national championship tournament with regional qualifiers. (The event had grown out of an invitational national championship that had been held in each of the past few seasons and was originally played six-on-six.) Immaculata had no designs on seriously contending for that first title. They did not even know there would be a tournament until after the season had started. But they quickly put themselves in contention.

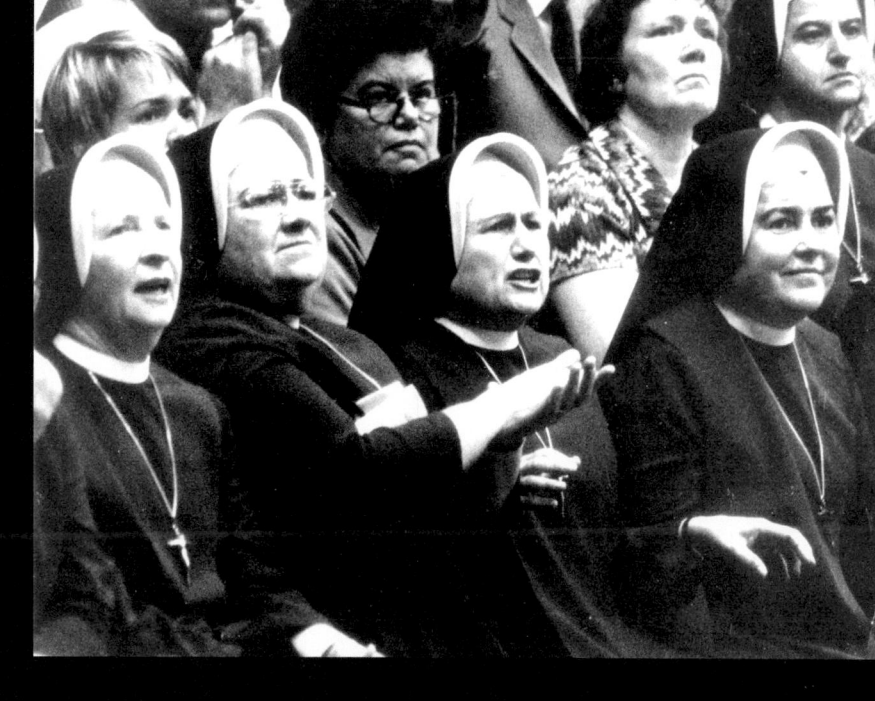

Immaculata dominated their competition and cruised through much of the regular season, but that ended at the regional qualifier for the national championship. After easily handling their early opponents, Immaculata had to face West Chester State, which had been declared the best team in the area. It took only a few minutes to learn just how richly deserved that label was.

This was the worst loss that most of the players would ever see. West Chester beat Immaculata 70–38. In the closing minutes, Rush looked up at the clock, desperate for it to hit zero. She felt like there was nothing else she could say or do.

"I remember that so vividly," Rush says. "Just hoping that the clock kept going."

Yet their season was not over. Their region would be sending two teams to the national championship: That meant West Chester *and* Immaculata. There was just one problem. The sixteen-school, four-day tournament was hosted by Illinois State, and there was no budget for postseason travel at Immaculata. (After all, the concept of a national tournament had barely existed a year ago, and it certainly was not a priority for the nuns who ran the college.) The team wasn't sure it could afford to play.

"All the nuns in there are thinking, 'There's no money,'" Grentz says. "Why would we send these eleven girls on this team to Illinois to play basketball?"

But they had one powerful advocate. The president of the college was a nun named Sister Mary of Lourdes. Many decades before she had gone into the convent, she had played high school basketball in the Philadelphia Catholic League, too. She won over the other nuns.

They quickly planned a pep rally and a series of fundraisers. It (mostly) worked. They'd scraped together enough money for nine plane tickets—which meant three players would have to stay behind. And just one of those tickets was guaranteed. (That one went to Rush.) The other

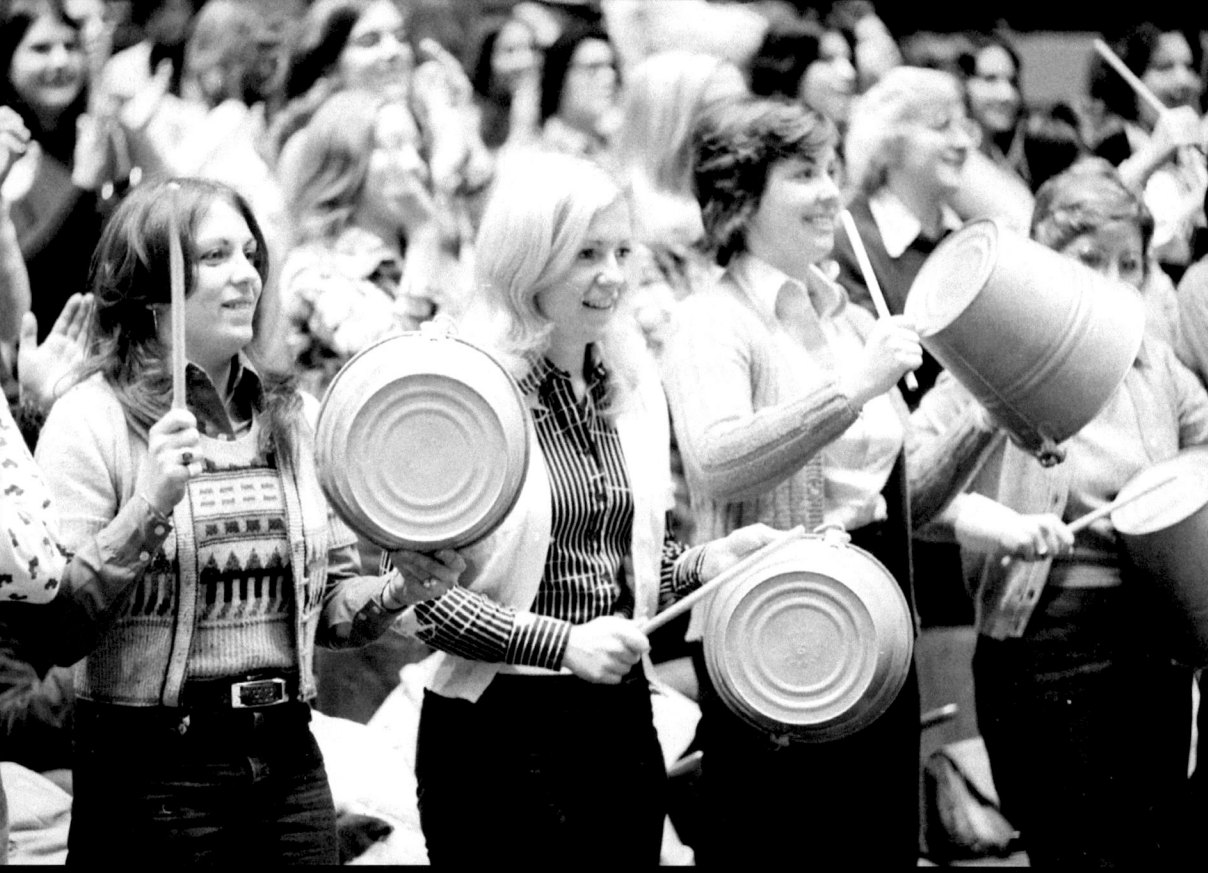

eight would all be flying standby. They worked up a contingency plan: *Here's who boards the plane first, second, third . . .* "For us to get there in itself was a miracle," says Grentz. When they landed, they piled into a pair of rental cars, with Rush driving one and her most responsible senior driving another, and they were off. They'd made it to the national championship.

"Mary of Lourdes, she's back on campus, and she has them all praying," Grentz says. "'Dear God, let them win one game and keep their self-esteem.' Because they all think we're going to get killed."

They had good reason. Most of the other schools had not left players from their bench at home, and they had not flown standby, and they were not sleeping four to a hotel room. "Everybody had the new polyester warm-up suits," Grentz says. "Not us." (She and her teammates noticed right away that if they made the second round, their likely opponent would be Indiana, a state flagship with an enrollment of 35,000. Immaculata's student body

numbered less than 500.) There were no divisions yet between small colleges and large universities: Any school in the country that sponsored women's sports was in the same pool. It meant that Immaculata was an obvious underdog.

But they could make that work. They handily beat South Dakota State. They escaped by 3 points over Indiana. They pulled off a remarkable comeback win over Mississippi College for Women. That left just one last matchup. The national championship game against highly favored West Chester State.

It was a possibility that had been circled on the bracket for them from the start. West Chester

---

ABOVE: The father of one of the players, Rene Muth Portland, owned a hardware store, and he started a tradition of filling the cheering section with buckets and sticks. He brought the buckets to every home game and passed them out to all the fans.

had been joking the whole time about wanting a rematch against Immaculata. Nothing sounded better to them than another easy out. But it had seemed impossible that it might actually happen: They had trounced Immaculata scarcely two weeks ago, yet the little school had now somehow knocked off a series of much bigger, stronger opponents. Now two schools that were located only a few miles apart would play for a title halfway across the country.

It became Immaculata women's college basketball's first Cinderella story.

"At that point, if we had played West Chester ten times, we would have lost nine of them," Rush says.

Their coach felt like they had virtually no chance. (Remember: Immaculata's score against West Chester in regionals had been 70–38.) Rush decided to go big: She dug into her limited bench to put her tallest possible lineup on the floor. That meant starting five-ten freshman Rene Muth Portland. When the game tipped off, Rush discovered something that gave her a bit of hope. West Chester was playing a full-court press, hoping to shut down this smooth, fast-moving offense, but what they had not accounted for was that no one could break a press like Grentz. "She was so dominant," Rush says. "I mean, just unstoppable." The sophomore center saw an opportunity to play the game of her life.

This matchup looked completely different from the one in regionals. Grentz made her presence known early. After relatively modest bench contributions in the early rounds, Portland scored 10 points, more than in the quarterfinals and semifinals combined. West Chester was clearly thrown by the bigger, more physical lineup from Immaculata and began fouling indiscriminately. (Three of their starters ultimately fouled out.) The

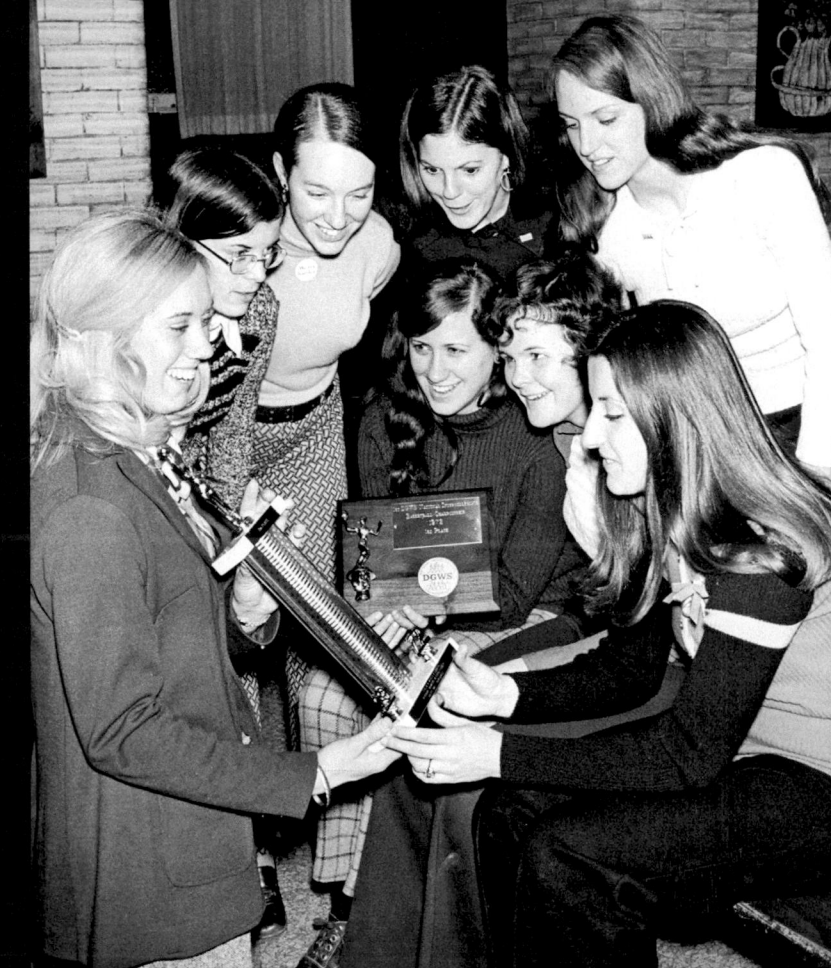

game was still close: With just under three minutes to play, Immaculata was clinging to a two-point lead, 44–42. But then came Grentz. She took over entirely in those closing minutes.

The final score was Immaculata 52, West Chester 48, with 26 points for Grentz.

"We didn't have a manager, so I couldn't even tell you how many points Theresa had, how many shots she took, how many she made," Rush says. "I didn't know any of that information. But I knew it was a miracle."

This was something none of them had imagined. (It had never been presented to any of them as being

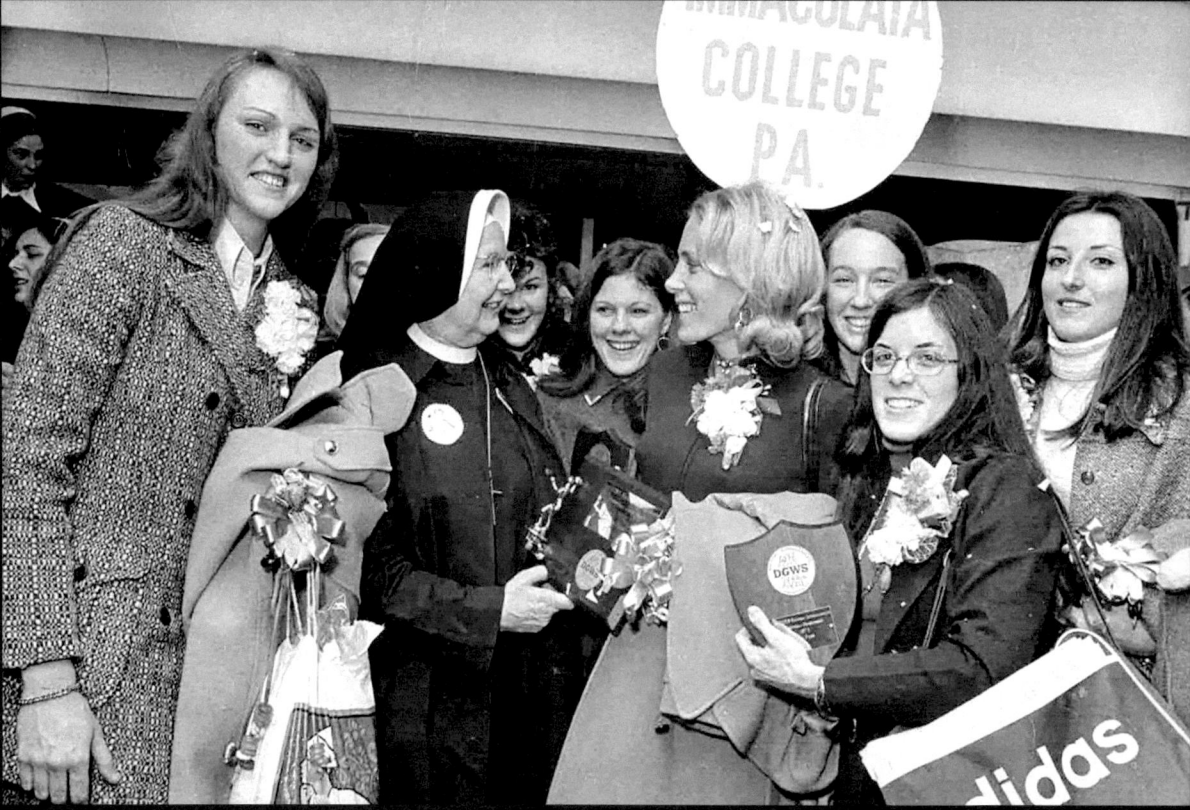

omething of which they could dream.) They were national champions. They didn't know what to do when they won: It didn't occur to anyone to cut down the nets. There were no family or friends to celebrate with, and there was no trophy, either. The team was instead handed little ceremonial plaques. And then came a question.

How were they going to get home?

Rush called Sister Mary of Lourdes. They had o return the cars, had no hotels booked that night, nd had no plane tickets, either. Mary of Lourdes called a local Catholic philanthropist who gave an even better answer than she'd hoped: *Tell them o buy first-class tickets on the next flight out.* Even petter, Immaculata was delighted to realize West Chester was on that flight to Philadelphia, too, only way back in economy.

Immaculata was greeted at the airport by the cheering section they had missed on the road: Here were their families and most of the student body nd, of course, dozens and dozens of ecstatic nuns. Airport passersby saw the celebration and joined in.

It was a reception that gave context that had been missing when they accepted their little ceremonial plaque on the court back in Illinois. This meant something.

"Once I got off that plane, my life changed for the rest of my days," Grentz says. "Because now I was the national champion, and nobody could ever take that away, whether we should have won, shoul not have won, whatever the case—didn't matter. It was so improbable."

That game swung everything. Rush discovered that her low-key, part-time coaching job was now far more intense. (Her life was changing in other ways, too: She had found out the week before the championship that she was pregnant with her first child.) Immaculata had finally rebuilt its gym on campus, but now, they could fill bigger facilities.

ABOVE: Sister Mary of Lourdes greets Cathy Rush at Philadelphia International Airport after the championship victory.

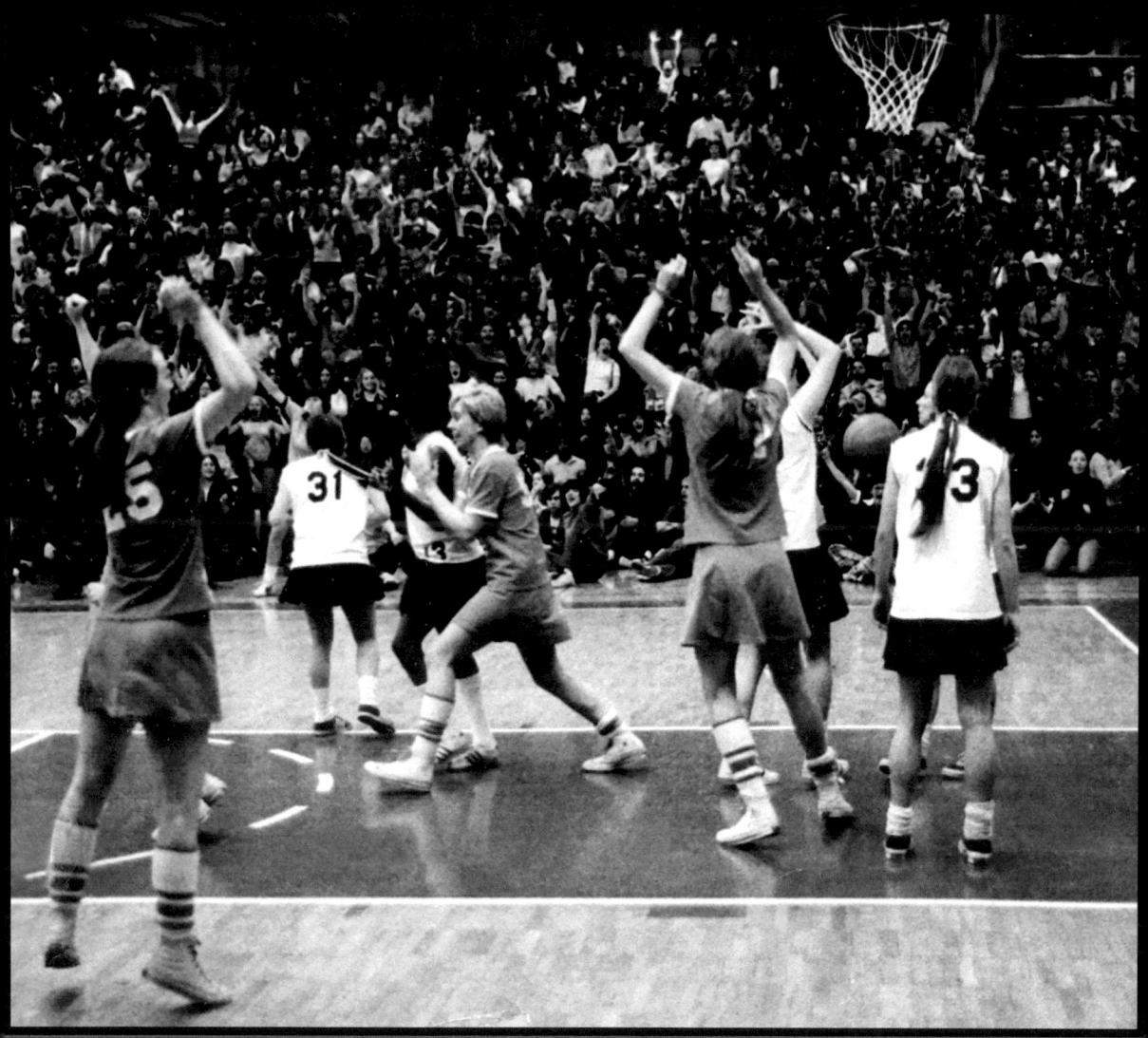

They went undefeated the next season and defended their championship. (Rush gave birth during the season and put her new baby in a portable crib on the sideline during practices.) Grentz became the first women's college player to get a full individual feature in *Sports Illustrated*. They won it all again a year later, and then came the parade of milestones, with the international tour and national television spotlight.

The magic lasted only a few years. As the landscape shifted in the late 1970s—when larger schools began meaningfully supporting athletic programs for women to comply with Title IX— winning became harder for a tiny women's college like Immaculata. Rush left coaching in 1977, and

the program would never quite regain its luster. But they'd won championships in a way that few schools would ever match. And they'd built another legacy, too, in the gyms they filled and jaws they dropped.

"We could bring the crowd to its feet," Grentz says. "It might have been fifty years ago, but the place was packed, every place. . . . People will come to be entertained, and when they watched us play, we entertained."

ABOVE: The Mighty Macs celebrate a close tournament win over Indiana in 1974.

ANN MEYERS

A Q&A with the First College Star

She was the first women's basketball player to receive a full athletic scholarship, thanks to Title IX. She had lightning speed and could score from anywhere on the court. She could defend all positions. Ann Meyers was ahead of her time and would become a pillar of women's hoops. In her own words, read about her Hall of Fame career from UCLA to the Olympics to the pros.

The best game you ever played in? Brag on yourself a little.

Certainly the AIAW national championship versus Maryland and winning [in 1978]. I had 20 points, ten rebounds, nine assists, and eight steals. I had 19 points—fourteen rebounds in the semifinal game versus Montclair State. We held Carol "the Blaze" Blazejowski to 40 points—her average. (No three-point line and regular size ball.) I also had a quadruple double versus Stephen F. Austin earlier in the year—the first one by a college player, male or female.

Favorite shoes you ever played in?

Ha! There was only one in the sixties: Converse! I switched from Converse to

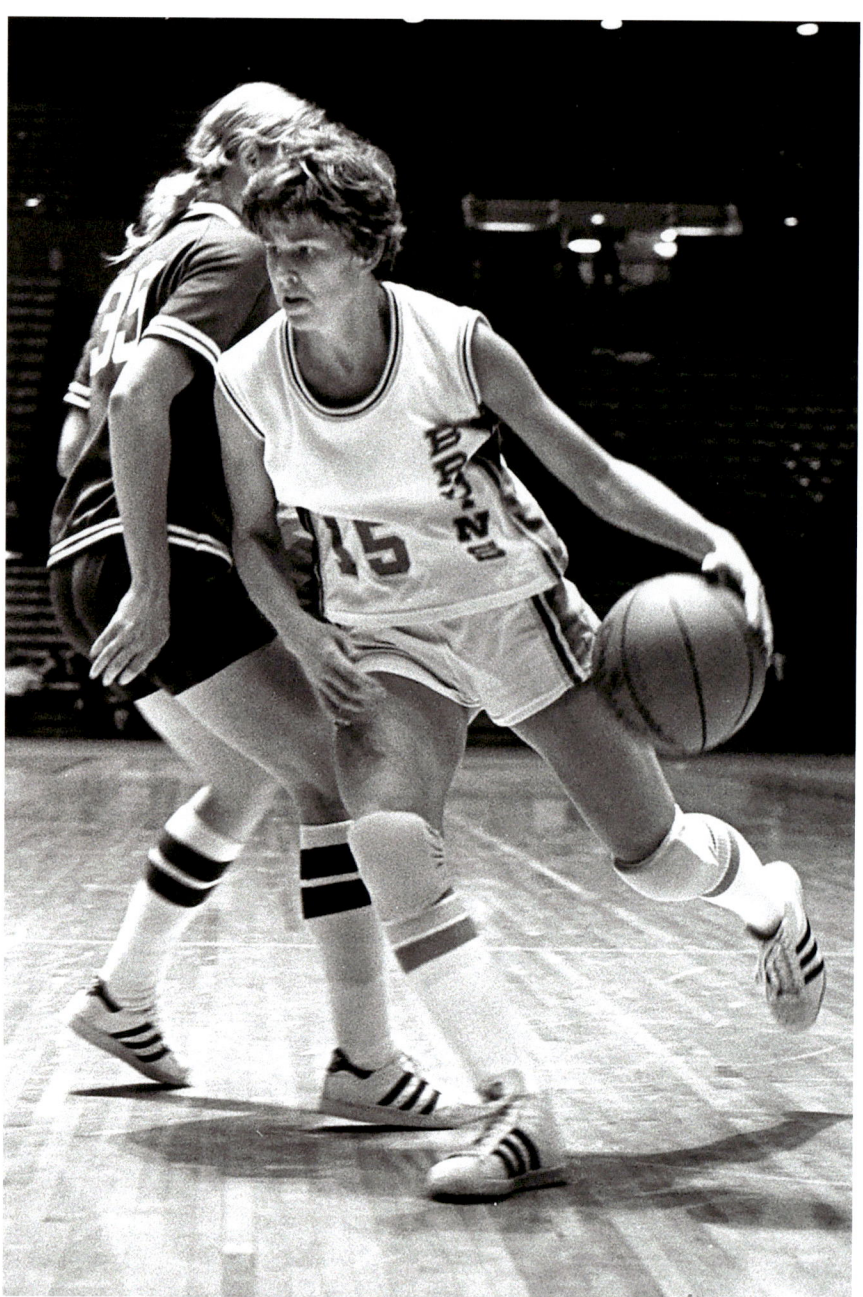

ABOVE: At five foot nine, Meyers was an All-American at UCLA, playing near all five positions.

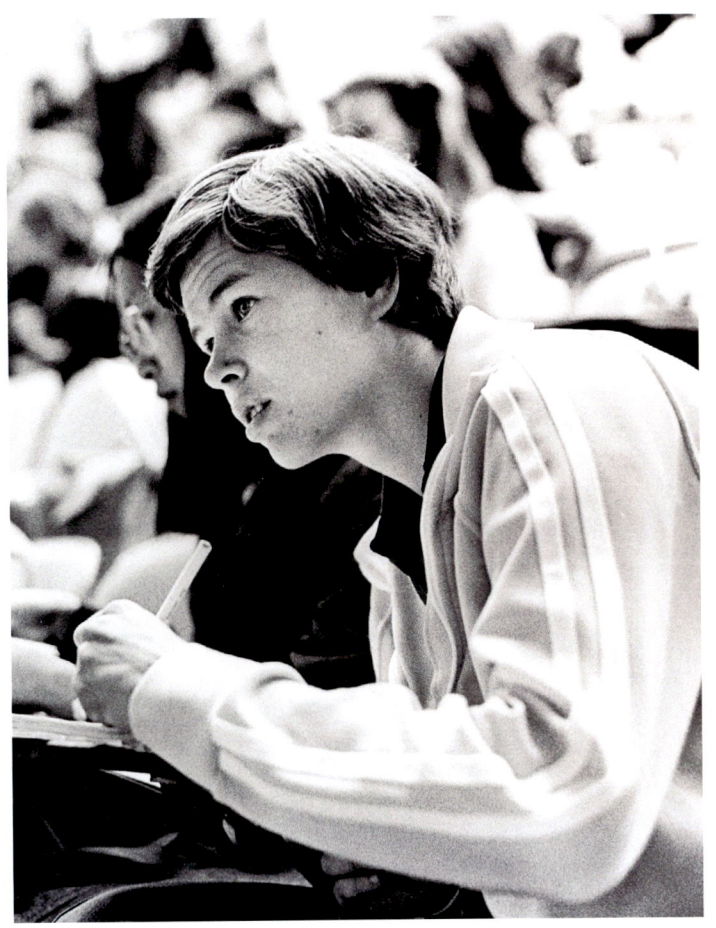

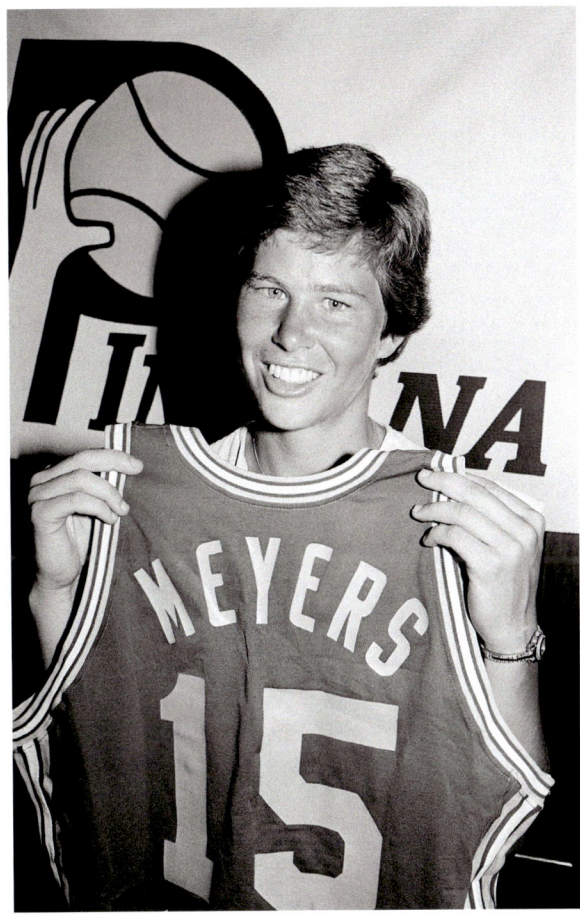

Adidas when I got to UCLA. We only got one pair each season. I played in those on the Olympic team and in the WBL (Women's Basketball League, see page 50).

If you could add something from someone's skill set to your game, what would you choose?

The game certainly has changed from my playing days. The three-point shot and small ball came in to the women's game when the WBL was created. Actually, I am very happy with what my skills were: balance, rebounding, defense, speed, physicality, setting picks, midrange, a willing passer, got to the basket, and got to the free-throw line. Because that was our game. Not many players played with my intensity on both ends. I just wanted to win!

What coaches had the biggest impact on your career?

Start with my dad. He coached all of us at home and on the playground. But Kenny Washington, Billie Moore, Sue Gunter, John Wooden. I played with Pat Head in the Olympic team in 1976 and she would coach me in 1979 for USA Basketball.

ABOVE LEFT: Meyers was the first woman to receive an athletic college scholarship. She studied sociology at UCLA.

ABOVE RIGHT: In 1979 Ann Meyers became the first woman to sign an NBA contract with the Indiana Pacers, for $50,000. She made it to the second round of cuts in spring tryouts.

LUSIA "LUCY" HARRIS

From Mississippi to the Hall of Fame

Growing up in rural Minter City, Mississippi, Lusia "Lucy" Harris's family had the only makeshift basketball hoop in the neighborhood. Her yard was the hot spot for the local boys and girls—and her ten siblings—to play ball. Lucy was tall. Her six-foot, three-inch stature unfortunately made her a target for school bullies, but it gave her an advantage on the court. She fell in love with basketball. "It just came natural," Lucy said.

She studied the game, too. Late at night as a kid, she'd put a blanket over her head and the TV, allowing herself to be as close as possible to the high-flying NBA action. Ethel and Willie, her mom and dad, would call for her to go to bed. She'd reluctantly agree but stay a few extra minutes anyway. Lucy would try to memorize the mechanics of Kareem Abdul-Jabbar's skyhook, Bill Russell's rebounding prowess, and (her favorite) Oscar Robertson's feathery jump shot.

Lucy became the top girls' high school basketball player in Mississippi after scoring 46 points in one game. She led her school to the state tournament. After graduation, she had originally planned to attend the historically Black Alcorn State University, about three hours south of her hometown. But they didn't have a women's basketball team yet, and she wasn't ready to stop playing. Enter coaches Margaret Wade and Melvin Hemphill. They were relaunching the women's team at Delta State University in Cleveland, Mississippi, about thirty minutes from Lucy's Minter City. Lucy agreed to suit up for the Lady Statesmen in 1973. She donned the number 45 proudly. Her tube socks went so high they brushed the bottoms of her kneecaps. She was the only Black woman on the team.

Immaculata College had been the crown jewel of women's hoops, winning the AIAW championship in the national tournaments' first three years, from

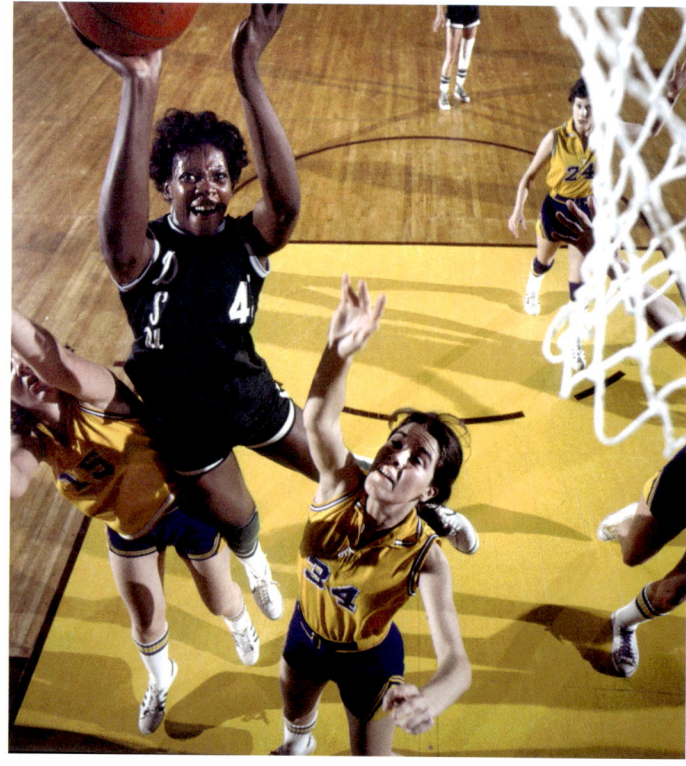

1972–74. That was until Lucy, Delta State's "Fab Five" starters, and Coach Margaret Wade's GIVE THEM HELL pin showed up the following year to ruin the party. DSU would go on to three-peat, in 1976 and 1977, led by Lucy's dominant postplay. During her four-year career there, she averaged 25.9 points and 14.4 rebounds per game, finishing with a total win record of 109–6. She is still the school's all-time leading scorer (2,981 points) and rebounder (1,662) and holds the single-game high of 58 points. Lucy was also named Homecoming Queen in 1976 and was a charter member of Delta Sigma Theta, a Black sorority.

ABOVE: Lusia Harris dominated the boards against LSU in the 1977 AIAW championship. Delta State University won the tournament, and Harris was the MVP.

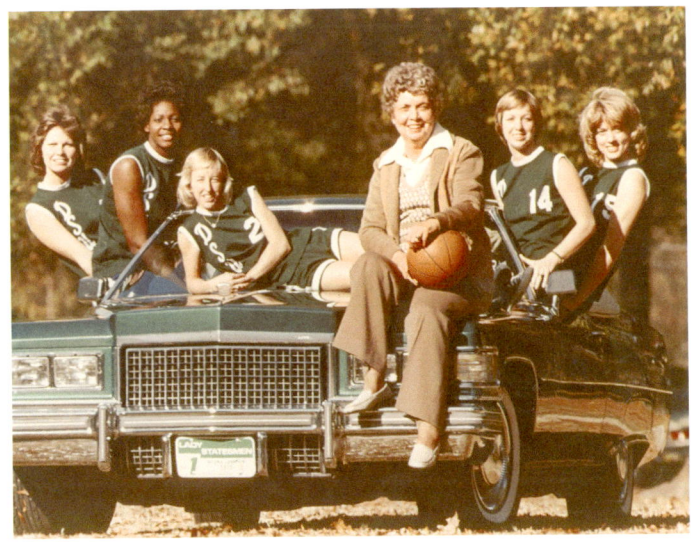

Her career is dotted with additional milestones that cement her place in women's basketball history. She scored the first basket in the 1976 Montreal Olympics, the first time women's hoops were in the Summer Games. She was the first woman to be drafted to the NBA in 1977, as the 137th overall pick in the seventh round by the New Orleans Jazz. (Denise Long was the first woman selected in the draft in 1969, but that pick was nullified.) Lucy thought it was a fluke, a publicity stunt. She never attended the offered tryout and ultimately believed she wasn't good enough.

"I had to be realistic," she said in an interview in 1999. "I really didn't think I could compete on that level. Not with guys. But it was a big honor."

She played in the Women's Professional Basketball League (WBL) for the Houston Angels from 1979–80. She also had a successful career as a teacher-coach in her hometown and raised four children. In 1992, she became the first female player to be enshrined in the Naismith Hall of Fame. After being introduced, the audience gave Lucy a much-deserved standing ovation, bursting with applause. As she walked to the podium, she was escorted by Oscar Roberston, her favorite player.

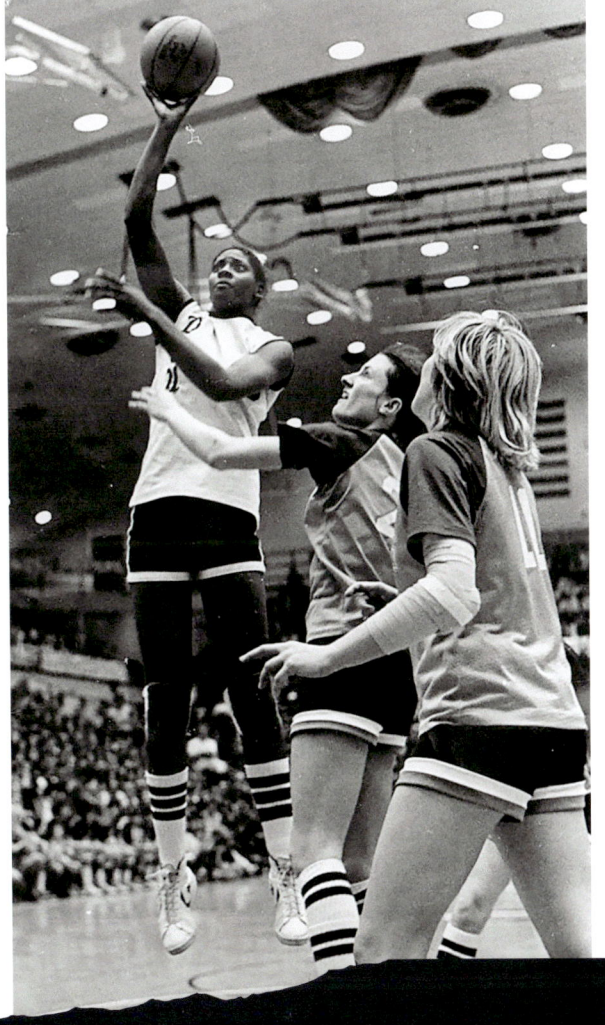

"She had such good moves inside. She was unstoppable. . . . They were an excellent team, and she was just the best."

— CATHY RUSH, IMMACULATA HEAD COACH

ABOVE LEFT: DSU's "Fab Five" starting lineup remained the same for all three championship runs. From left to right: Wanda Hairston, Lusia Harris, Debbie Brock, Coach Margaret Wade, Cornelia Ward, and Ramona Von Boeckman.

ABOVE RIGHT: Harris finished her college career atop the Delta State leader boards in points (2,981) and rebounds (1,662).

ALLEZ! TEAM USA IN MONTREAL

The First Olympic Games, 1976

The United States was not expected to medal at the first Olympic Games that featured women's basketball. There were real questions about whether Team USA would even *qualify* for the 1976 Summer Games in Montreal: The US women had just finished eighth in the 1975 World Championships. (Other countries had begun investing far more in their women's teams, especially the Soviet Union, Czechoslovakia, and Bulgaria.) But after retooling the roster—hundreds of women came to open tryouts across the country—they made a splash at the final qualifying tournament. Team USA won a surprising 5–0 to earn a spot in the Olympics. And they would soon earn even more.

Their roster was young and had very little experience playing together. The oldest player was twenty-four-year-old Pat Head, just a few years out of college, but already the head coach at the University of Tennessee. (She would soon become much better known by her married name: Pat Summitt.) She was joined by a collection of college players, including Lusia Harris from Delta State, Ann Meyers from UCLA, and Gail Marquis from Queens College, and even one high schooler: eighteen-year-old Nancy Lieberman. They had never been able to dream of the Olympics. While men's basketball had been part of the program since 1936, there hadn't been serious discussion of adding

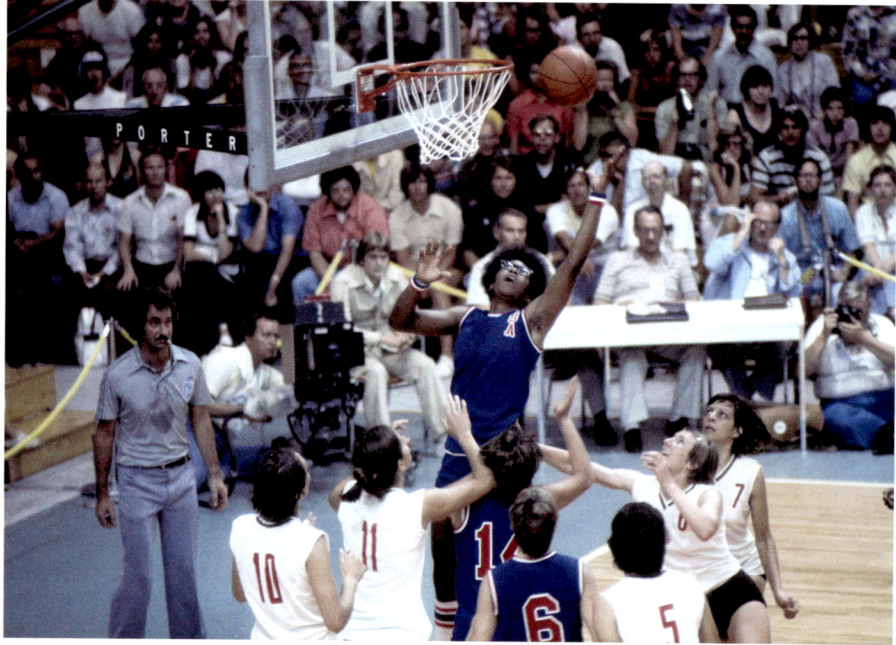

the sport for women until very recently, and some members of the national team had not known until that spring that it would be part of the Games. The opportunity felt almost too good to be true.

Team USA's first Olympic game tipped off at 9 a.m. against Japan. That meant getting up before dawn to prepare. But they had extra motivation. This was the opening game of the opening day—meaning they would be the first women ever to play

ABOVE: Charlotte Lewis (center) had never played organized basketball until she enrolled at Illinois State: There had not been a girls' team at her high school. But she was six foot two, with an incredible knack for rebounding, and she quickly stood out in the college game. That helped earn Lewis a spot on the 1976 Olympic team—where she got a specially made pair of athletic glasses (seen here) from sponsor Kodak.

basketball at the Olympics. Team USA was desperate to be the first to score and they were: Harris would be credited with the first basket in Olympic history. But they went on to lose the game, and in a six-team, round-robin competition, they knew that one loss might ultimately make all the difference.

However, they responded with a pair of dominating wins over Bulgaria and Canada. They knew they had virtually no chance against the historically dominant Soviets. (They lost 112–77.) It meant their chances at a medal would come down to their final game against Czechoslovakia. Head coach Billie Moore laid out the stakes for Team USA in her pregame locker room speech. She wanted her young women to know just what they were playing for.

"She looked at all of us and she said, 'Ladies, whatever you do today will change and support the course of women's basketball history for the next twenty-five years,'" Lieberman would later tell the Naismith Basketball Hall of Fame. "To have that type of understanding and vision about the historical element of what we are doing, when we're just thinking about getting loose in layup line, has never left me."

Moore called for them to play a 1-3-1 press. That stifling defense led to a final score of USA 83, Czechoslovakia 67, earning them an unlikely silver medal. It started a streak that still lives today: The US hasn't left the Olympics without a medal in women's basketball since.

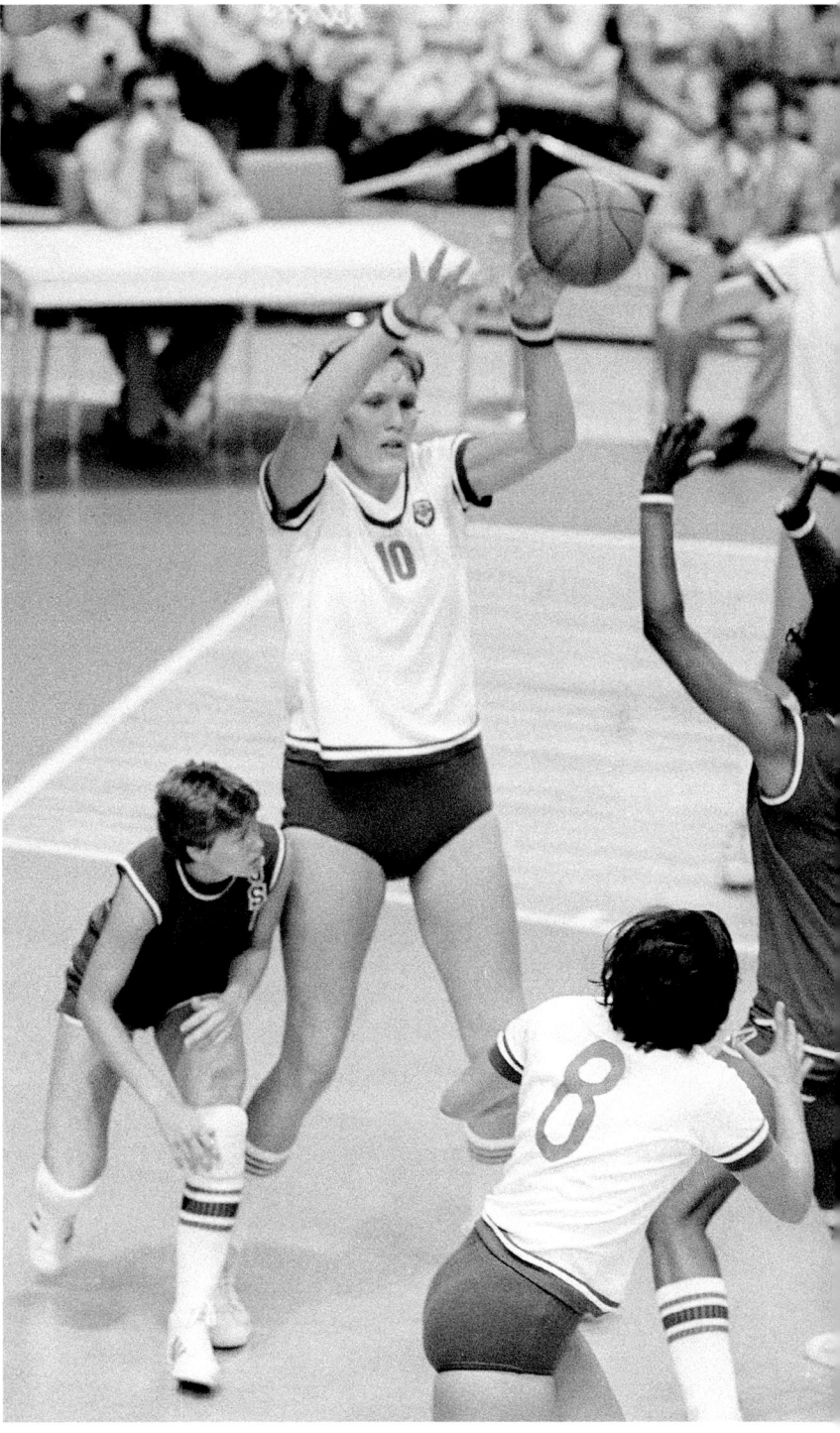

ABOVE: The toughest competition in the Olympics, by far, were the Soviets. Their best player was Uljana Semjonova (pictured here), who was seven feet tall and would eventually become the first foreign woman inducted into the Naismith Basketball Hall of Fame.

THE WBL
"UNASSUMING TRAILBLAZERS"

THESE LEGENDS SET THE STANDARD
FOR PRO HOOPS IN AMERICA

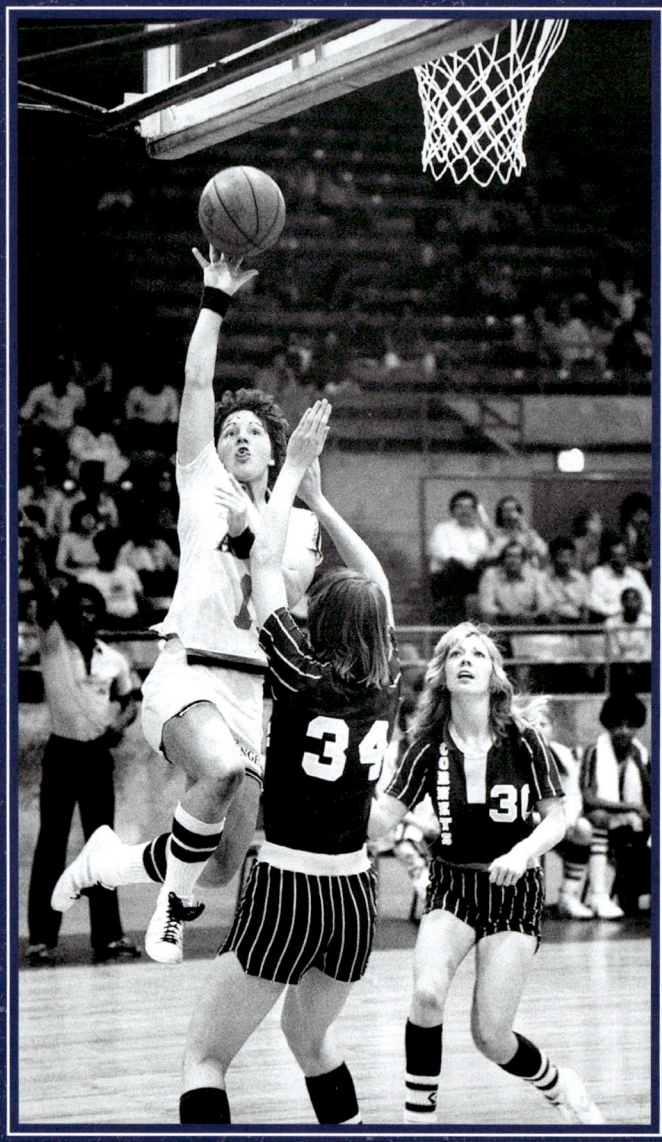

ABOVE: Houston Angels Karen Aulenbacher soars in for a layup versus the Iowa Cornets' defense in April 1979. The Angels won twenty-six of their thirty-four games in the opening WBL season and captured the league championship. Because of their aggressive and over-physical style of play, they earned the nickname "Houston Muggers."

t was April 10, 1979, the first round of playoffs in the first year of the first women's professional basketball league, the WBL. The Midwest Division crown was at stake, and the Chicago Hustle and Iowa Cornets had identical regular-season records of 21–13. The winner goes to the Finals. The Chicago Hustle had home-court advantage, and an advantage it was. A roaring, rambunctious crowd filled DePaul University's Alumni Hall. It wouldn't have been unusual to see Chicago celebrities dot the front row. NFL star Walter Payton from the Bears, or Ernie Banks from the Cubs, or Coach Jerry Sloane from the Bulls. Billie Jean King threw up a ceremonial jump ball one time. The Hustle was the lone winning pro sports team in the pre–Michael Jordan Chi, and the city immediately immersed them into their pro sports culture.

The Hustle-Cornets rivalry brewed deep, with most of their meetings going into overtime. This matchup was no different. Iowa came into town with their star guard "Machine Gun" Molly Bolin, armed and ready to shoot the long ball as she had all season long. Hustle's defensive specialist, forward Elizabeth "the Bandit" Galloway, had one job: to try to slow her down. Their coach, Doug Bruno, ran a fast break, run-and-gun style, similar to Galloway's University of Nevada, Las Vegas, college hoop days. She led the league in steals for a reason. Chicago's offensive juggernaut was league MVP and All-Star MVP Rita Easterling. At barely five foot six, Rita E would speed dribble through opponents and dish out dimes like candy. The local Channel 9 WGN TV station's camera continuously panned to keep up with the game's quick pace, a tricky feat.

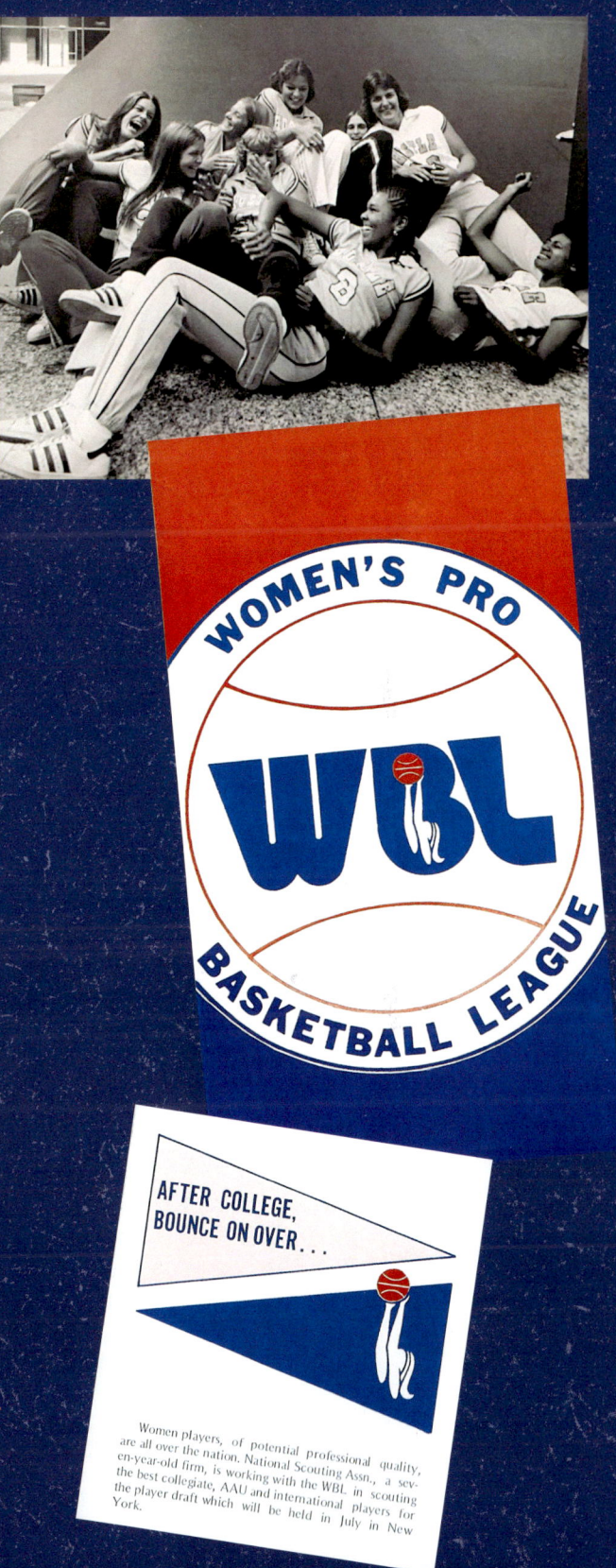

TOP RIGHT: Rookies from the WBL's Chicago Hustle squad smile and laugh together.

ABOVE RIGHT: "After college, bounce on over . . ." The WBL marketed to women's basketball players who weren't finished competing after their college glory days.

AFTER COLLEGE, BOUNCE ON OVER . . .

Women players, of potential professional quality, are all over the nation. National Scouting Assn., a seven-year-old firm, is working with the WBL in scouting the best collegiate, AAU and international players for the player draft which will be held in July in New York.

The Hustle stole the first game over Iowa in overtime, 112–107. Four Hustle players scored over 20 points and Bolin dropped 30 in the loss. (By the way, this was before the three-point line was installed in the 1979–80 season. These ballers were putting up some points!) Post-game, the Chicago players (and their opponent) would head down the hall to the Blue Demon Room, where fans would be waiting to celebrate, drinks in hand. Two days later, the Hustle traveled to Des Moines and lost 114–101, and then again two days after that by 1 point, 118–117. Iowa won the series 2–1. They headed to the Finals only to fall short against the red-hot Houston Angels, the league's first champion. Eight teams would finish the league's inaugural season still intact. But little did they know that only two more seasons would follow before the WBL shuttered for good.

"Of course, we feel like our decade, there's not one more important. And that's not because we were in it. That's because of what occurred during it, starting with Title IX, the AIAW taking over and creating a championship for women. The AAU was still around. And then the first women's professional basketball league," Elizabeth Galloway reminisced. "We're multiple trailblazers, and we just happen to be at the right place in time, born in the right decade."

The players of the WBL were achieving dreams they didn't know were possible. Before the league's inaugural game between the Chicago Hustle and the Milwaukee Does on December 9, 1978, Galloway says her college career at the University of Nevada, Las Vegas, abruptly stopped. She was heartbroken after the highs of being a part of the first team to receive a women's college basketball scholarship, upsetting cross-country powerhouses like Immaculata College and Delta State. She wasn't ready to hang up her sneakers *just* yet. What was she

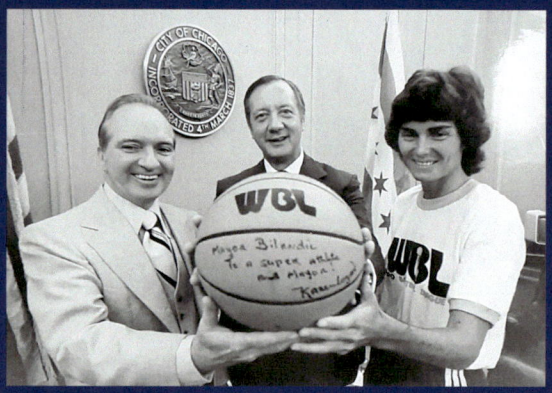

1978: THE 28.5-INCH WOMEN'S BALL IS BORN

Karen Logan had an idea. She'd been barnstorming for the All-American Red Heads for years and played with a men's ball and by the men's rules. There needed to be some changes. Her pitch was to create a smaller basketball specially made for women. It should be 28.5 inches in circumference and 20 ounces—a downsize of one inch and two ounces from the men's. Volleyball had lower nets, golf had different-sized clubs, and tennis had smaller racquets, all for women, and women's basketball deserved the same unique customization. Logan thought that because women's hands were generally smaller than men's, a smaller ball would improve ball handling, increase shooting percentages from long range, and allow passes to zip across the court. Wilson was the first to adapt the size-6 ball, premiering in the WBL in 1978. The NCAA later adopted the women's ball in 1984.

ABOVE: Karen Logan (right) and Chicago Hustle general manager John Geraty (left) present a signed commemorative WBL ball to Chicago mayor Michael A. Bilandic (center).

going to do? The Texas native could play overseas, thousands of miles away from familiar faces, or she could continue her education and attend graduate school. Into the UNLV gym walks Karen Logan, barnstorming women's basketball legend with the All-American Red Heads, with a sales pitch players couldn't refuse: She's helping to start up a women's basketball professional team in Chicago and wanted Galloway and a few of her teammates to try out. Logan excitedly explained that the women's pro league was founded by sports entrepreneur Bill Byrne. The goal was to piggyback off the success of the women's college game and the women's Olympic silver medal in 1976.

"It was so on," Galloway said fiercely. They didn't even know how many teams, how much they'd be paid—anything, really. They just knew they could still ball. "It was just pure joy that we not only get to continue to play basketball but women's *professional* basketball. We were going. We had a pioneering spirit, going into the unknown."

Nearly 1,500 miles away in Iowa, Molly Bolin received the same pitch. A small-town firecracker, Bolin could shoot the leather off the ball, and the WBL needed her star power to join their league. Her basketball love affair started in 1968 when her baton-twirling group performed during a high school girls' basketball game. She became infatuated with the atmosphere—the pep band, the cheerleaders, the sold-out crowd—and knew she wanted to join. Iowa was a hub for women's athletics dating back to 1925 when the Iowa Girls High School Athletic Union was formed, setting the precedent of organized girls' athletics. Bolin became obsessed with the sport, and the state wanted her to be its first star.

"The pitch I got was off the charts," Bolin said. She had wrapped two nonconsecutive junior college seasons, averaging 24.6 points per game, and was searching for her next school, but a new offer materialized. "They said they were forming a

pro team in Iowa, and they were also going to film a movie that summer, and they were guaranteeing me a spot in the movie and guarantee me a spot on the team. They staged my whole signing at the governor's desk at the state capitol."

Bolin was the first player to officially sign a one-year contract with the WBL, for $6,000. "Even

---

TOP: "Machine Gun" Molly Bolin had an epic nickname and an even better jump shot.

ABOVE: The WBL never sacrificed on style. Bolin's Iowa Cornets bomber jacket was almost as iconic as her game.

FOLLOWING: Despite the league lasting only a limited time, the game programs and media guides did not hold back on creativity.

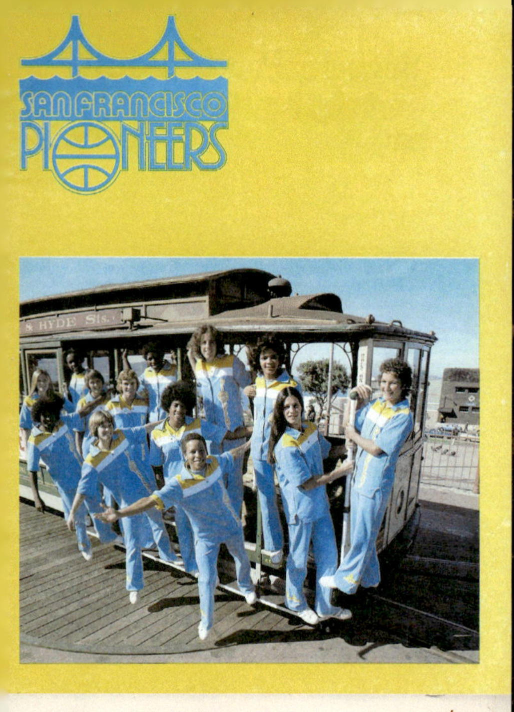

SAN FRANCISCO PIONEERS

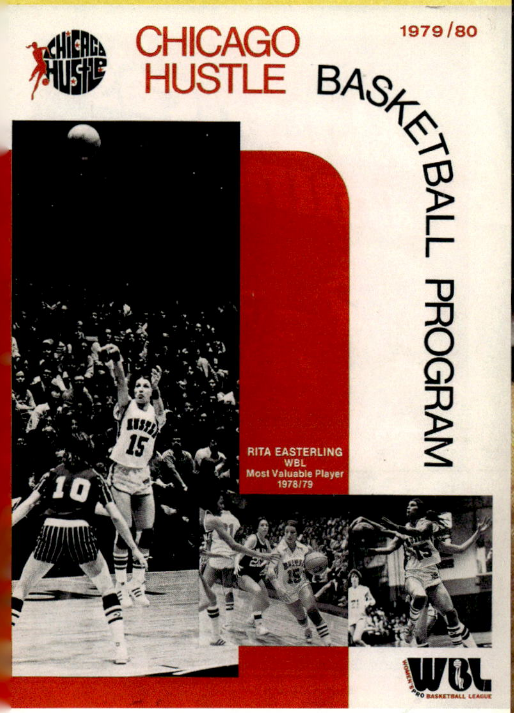

$2.00

WOMEN'S WBL PRO BASKETBALL LEAGUE

5 EAST

CHICAGO HUSTLE

1979/80

CHICAGO HUSTLE BASKETBALL PROGRAM

RITA EASTERLING
WBL
Most Valuable Player
1978/79

WBL

Official Guide
AND FACTBOOK/1979-80

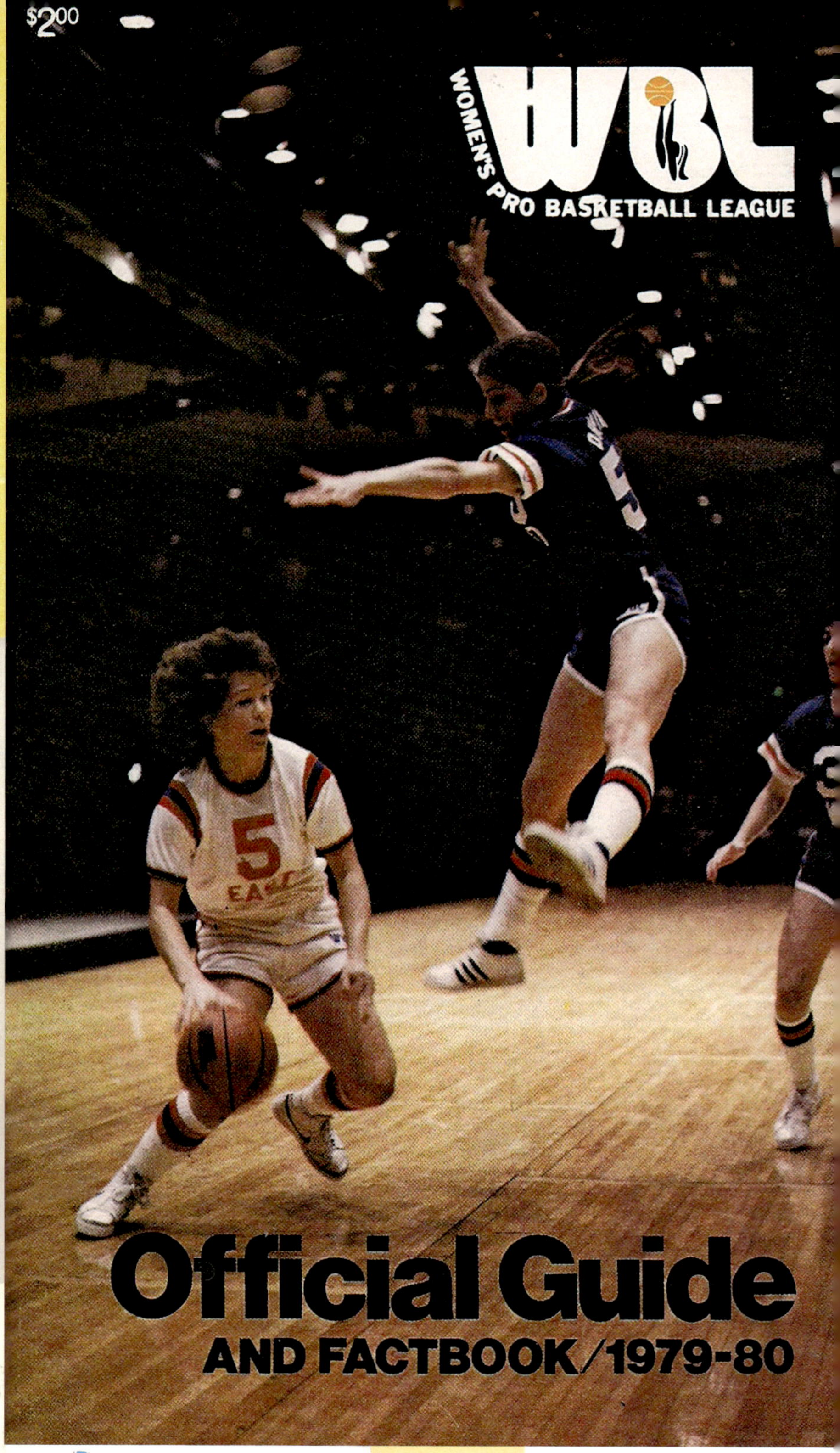

WOMEN'S WBL PRO BASKETBALL LEAGUE

24

10

15

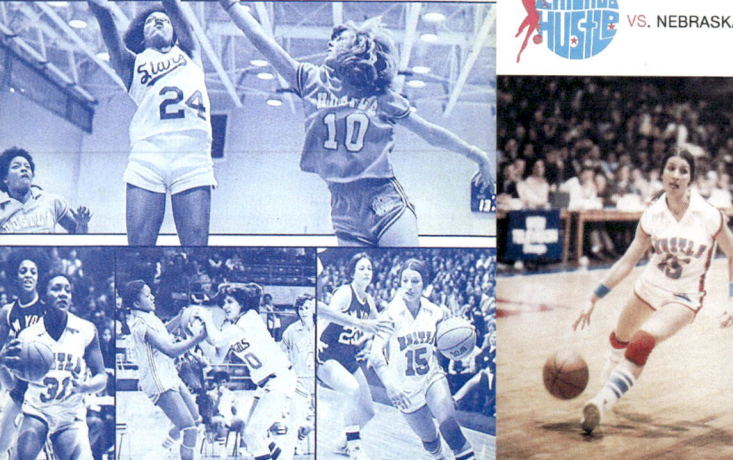

CHICAGO HUSTLE VS. NEBRASKA WRANGLERS

1980/81 OPENING GAME COLLECTORS PROGRAM

WBL

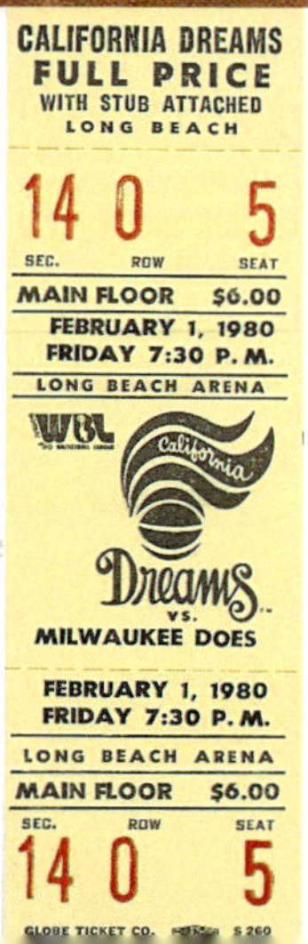

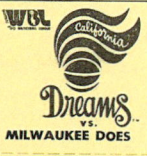

CALIFORNIA DREAMS
FULL PRICE
WITH STUB ATTACHED
LONG BEACH

SEC. 14 ROW 0 SEAT 5

MAIN FLOOR $6.00
FEBRUARY 1, 1980
FRIDAY 7:30 P.M.
LONG BEACH ARENA

WBL California

Dreams
VS.
MILWAUKEE DOES

FEBRUARY 1, 1980
FRIDAY 7:30 P.M.
LONG BEACH ARENA
MAIN FLOOR $6.00

SEC. 14 ROW 0 SEAT 5

GLOBE TICKET CO. S 260

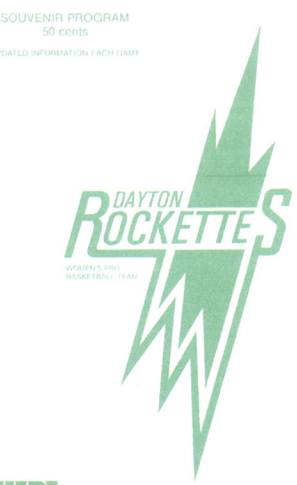

SOUVENIR PROGRAM
50 cents
UPDATED INFORMATION EACH NAME

DAYTON ROCKETTES
WOMEN'S PRO
BASKETBALL TEAM

WBL

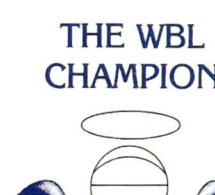

THE WBL CHAMPION

HOUSTON ANGELS

THE CHAMPS ARE BACK !!!

1979-80 Season Ticket Program

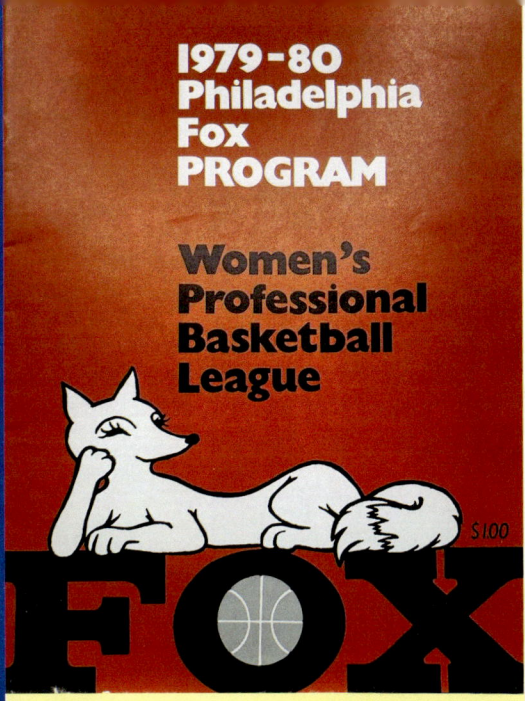

1979-80 Philadelphia Fox PROGRAM

Women's Professional Basketball League

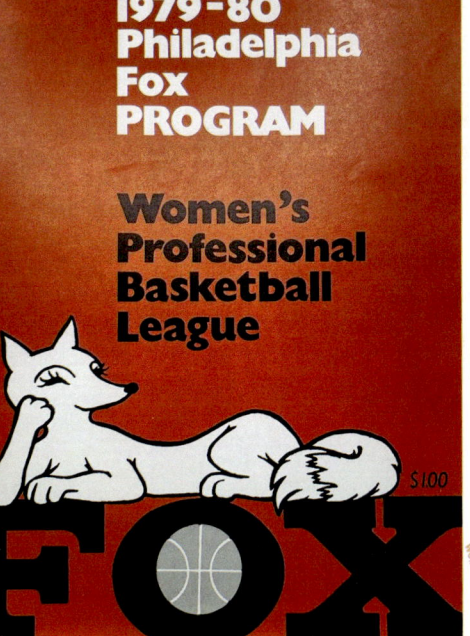

FOX

$1.00

St. Louis

1980-81 Official Program

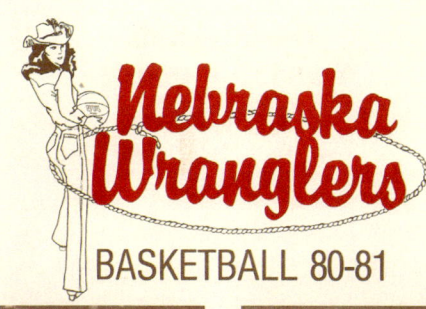

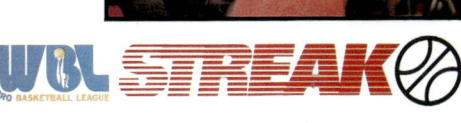

WBL STREAK

Minnesota Fillies

WBL Women's Pro Basketball
Premier Season/Met Center

$1.00

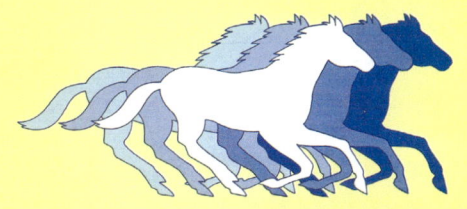

Nebraska Wranglers

BASKETBALL 80-81

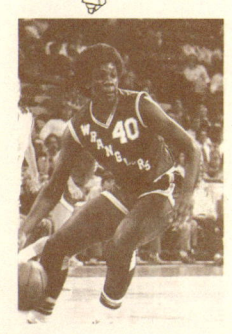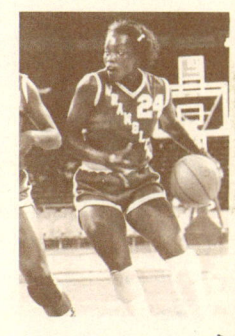

Follow Your...

California

Dreams
T.M.

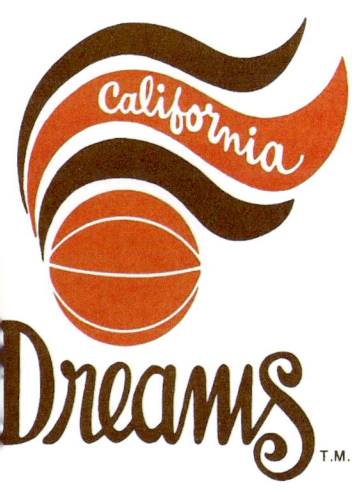

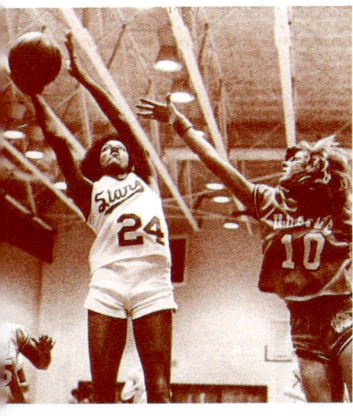

50 CENTS · FEBRUARY 9, 1981

WBL Presents the

ALL STAR GAME

EAST vs. WEST

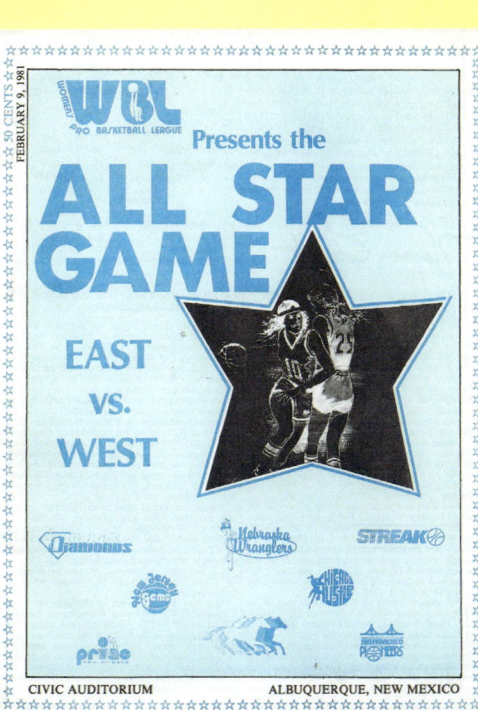

Diamonds · Nebraska Wranglers · STREAK

New Jersey Gems · Chicago Hustle

pride · Minnesota Pioneers

CIVIC AUDITORIUM   ALBUQUERQUE, NEW MEXICO

The Appraisal

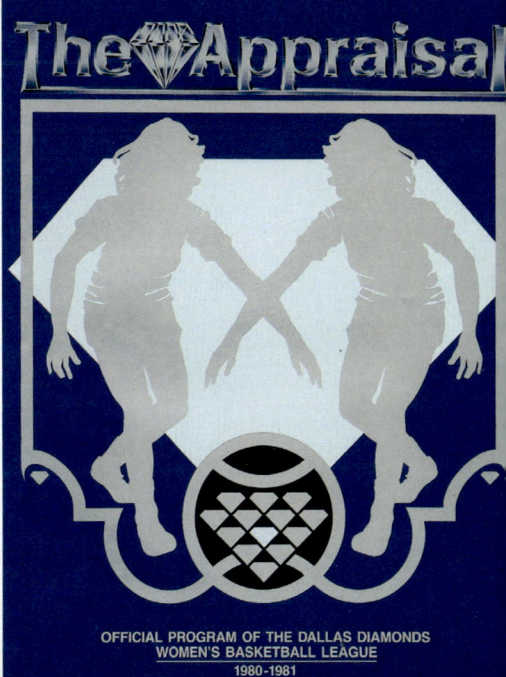

OFFICIAL PROGRAM OF THE DALLAS DIAMONDS
WOMEN'S BASKETBALL LEAGUE
1980-1981

though I had an eighteen-month-old baby and a family, there was nothing that was going to stop me from signing that contract," Bolin said. At merely twenty years old, her life changed in an instant. The WBL wanted to capitalize on her appearance and make her and her fluffy blond Farrah Fawcett–like hair the sexy symbol of their newly developed league. She was in commercials with NBA star Larry Bird. She posed for glamourized photoshoots for magazines like *Sports Illustrated* (yes, there's even one where she's in her Iowa uniform posing with a machine gun). But don't let this fool you, "Machine Gun" Molly could hoop, too. She scored 50-plus points in a single game four times in her WBL career, light work compared to the 63 points she scored on her sixteenth birthday. She snagged co-league MVP honors with sharpshooter Ann Meyers in the 1979–80 season after averaging 32.6 points per game for 1,174 total points.

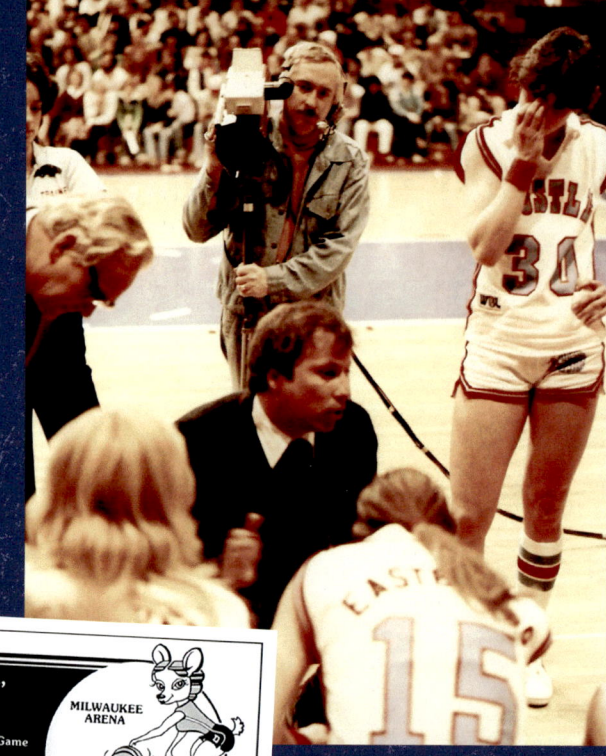

"We were playing against the best players of our time," Galloway added. "You had eight Olympians from that '76 Olympic team in the WBL. You had college All-Americans." Legendary names include Carol "the Blaze" Blazejowski, Lusia Harris, Nancy Lieberman, Pearl Moore, Muffet McGraw, and many more.

Charlene McWhorter wanted in on the WBL action, too, but coming into the league in year two served a rocky start. Originally from Georgia, McWhorter grew up playing basketball outside to get out of doing chores. She worked on her post-up game enough to earn a scholarship to Albany State College, an HBCU. When her senior season was wrapped, she was set to join the military as an officer, but her coach encouraged her to join a new WBL team in Washington, DC. She was drafted to the Washington Metros in 1979, but the team didn't have enough investors and their season only lasted thirty-three days. From there, McWhorter was picked up for a short stint with the Milwaukee Does. After a few missed paychecks, in February 1980, Chicago Hustle coach Doug Bruno drove to Milwaukee to pick up McWhorter so she could join the fiery frontcourt alongside Galloway. She didn't even tell the Does she'd be leaving. "Doug had that old red van backed up to my apartment, and he came up and said, 'Get your stuff, let's go. You're going to Chicago,'" McWhorter told *Chicago Tribune Magazine.*

This was a perfect fit. She made the All-Star team, won the game's MVP award after scoring 31 points, and felt like a celebrity. "We had public appearances. We did little outdoor clinics and things like that. They really did treat us like professionals," she said.

However, it was known that this wasn't the case for every team within the WBL. The Minnesota

TOP: Chicago Hustle head coach Doug Bruno talks to the huddle while a WGN cameraman looks on. The national cable station televised many Hustle home games.

ABOVE: An advertisement for the Milwaukee Does promoting the WBL's inaugural season.

PEARL MOORE

Guard, New York Stars and St. Louis Streak

She was first with the NY Stars, who she led to win the first WBL championship in 1979. While attending Francis Marion University (1975–79), Moore totaled a staggering 4,061 career points, which set an AIAW small-school record. Still, no player in the NCAA has passed this feat. She averaged 30.6 points per game and finished with three 50-point games, including a 60-point performance.

RIGHT: The Streak's five-foot-seven point guard Moore shoots a jumper over her defender in 1980.

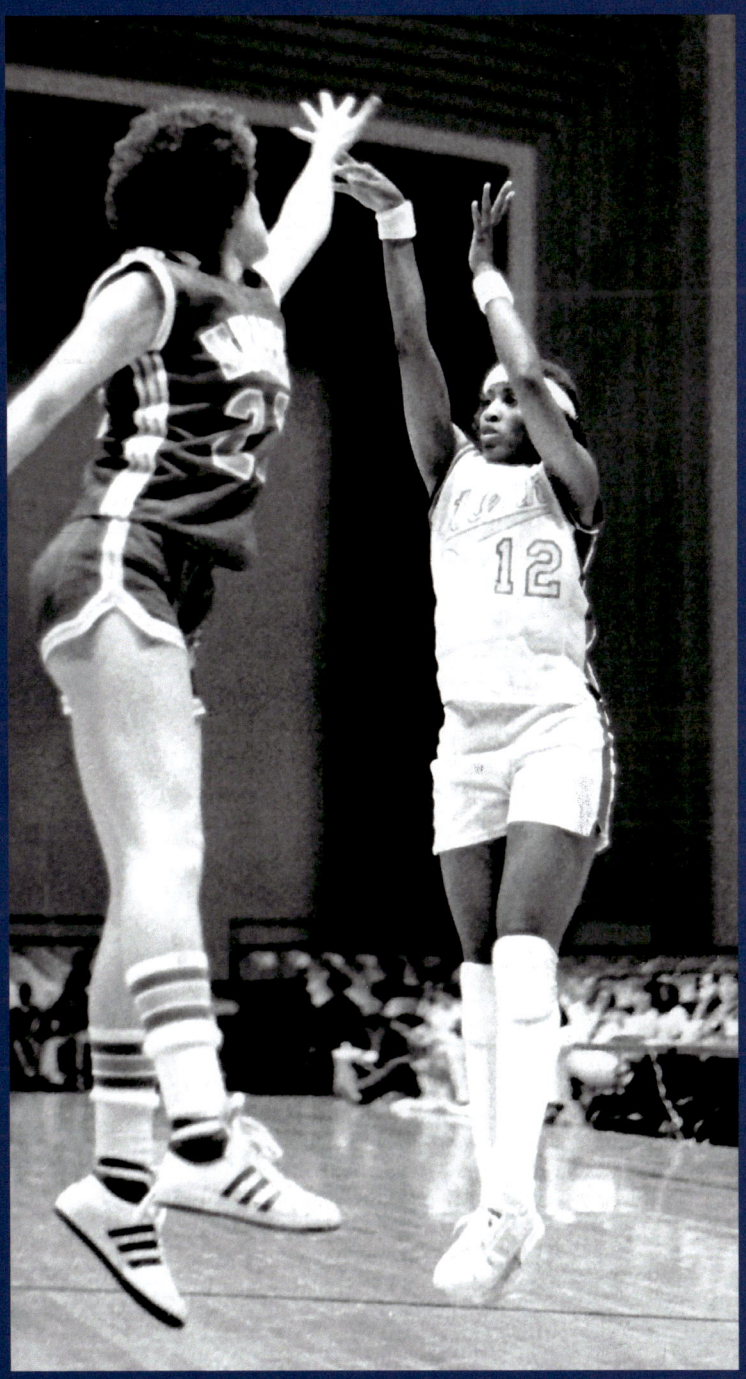

Fillies collectively scheduled a walk-out minutes before tip-off because of delayed paychecks. The league repossessed the Dayton Rockettes after their owner stopped paying the bills. The WBL officially closed its doors after the 1981 season, only its third.

"My heart was ripped out because I finally found my place in the world, I thought," Bolin said after she heard the news. "It was everything that I wanted to do. I loved every minute of it. I loved doing the promotions. I loved inspiring kids. I loved being on TV. I loved doing interviews. I loved playing basketball, and then *boom*. There was no closure. It was gone."

The WBL didn't have the necessity that Title IX brought to college athletics; people had to pay to see these women play. Sponsorships and advertisements became critical to building this league, and after totaling $14 million in losses so far, they had no other option but to shutter.

Seventeen teams came and went in three seasons—coast to coast, from New York to San Francisco—but the dream of a professional women's sports league wasn't enough to pay the players and profit. The Hustle attempted to crowdsource for investors to buy a minimum of ten shares (at $10 per share) into the team with a goal of 75,000 shares before the next season, stating the thirteen-player team roster and staff's salary totaled $200,000, but they didn't reach their goal.

"The people investing in the teams were not millionaires or billionaires," Galloway said. The California Dreams out of Long Beach was owned by four lawyers, a CPA, and a dentist. A thirty-two-year-old stock broker founded the New Orleans Pride.

Bolin adds that ESPN was in its infancy, and the WBL didn't get the chance to capitalize on the growth of national sports coverage. "The only way that someone across the country would hear about a player was the Associated Press and certain newspapers had to pick up stories that were happening in another city," she said. "But other than that, we were very localized."

The WBL forged a path for professional women's sports in only three seasons. It became a place for future Hall of Famers to compete and

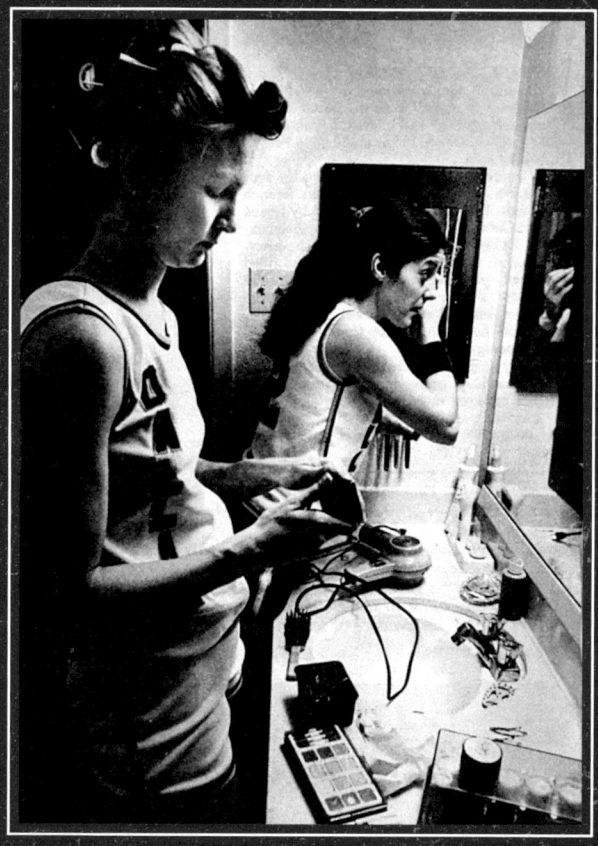

emphatically claim that women's basketball belongs at the pro level. Bolin, Galloway, and McWhorter are board members of Legends of the Ball Inc., a nonprofit dedicated to preserving the WBL's rightful place in hoops history.

"We are more than the three years we played," Galloway said in her TEDxBoston speech in 2022. "Yes, we folded, but we are not a league that failed, we are a league that propelled the game forward."

They became Title IX's wildest dreams. Born at the right place, at the right time. She added, hammering the importance of her generation's ballers: "We were unassuming trailblazers. We were just doing what we loved and then becoming trailblazers in the process."

ABOVE: Dallas Diamonds Sharon McClannahan (left) and Janice Baker (right) set their rollers and apply makeup pregame.

THE WBL PLAYERS' POV

The first wave of women's hoops pros want the record to reflect they could ball

MOLLY BOLIN
Guard, Iowa Cornets

The best game you ever played in?

The game I set the women's pro basketball scoring record, on March 2, 1980. We were playing our top rival in our division (Minnesota Fillies) for playoff seeding, so it was a really big game [and] we had one of our largest crowds ever. . . . I went on to have the best game of my pro career with 55 points.

CHARLENE MCWHORTER
Center, Washington Metros, Milwaukee Does, and Chicago Hustle

The best game you ever played in?

The 1980 WBL All-Star game, where I scored a game-high 31 points and won MVP. I only played twenty-four minutes.

Favorite shoes to play in?

Adidas Top Tens.

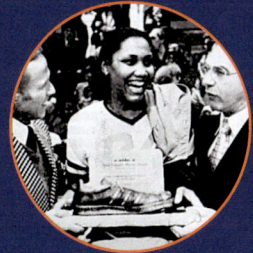

PEGGIE GILLOM
Forward, Dallas Diamonds

Your best game?

The best game I ever played in was at Tennessee while I was attending Ole Miss. I scored 45 points and that record is still the most points ever scored by a Tennessee opponent.

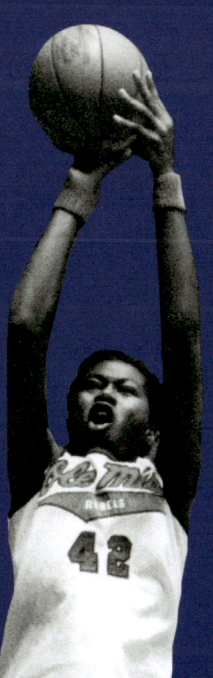

ADRIAN MITCHELL
Forward, Chicago Hustle and St. Louis Streak

The coach who made the biggest impact?

I often give thanks to Coach Marian Washington for changing my life. I was playing in a park district basketball tournament. . . . She asked me if I would be interested in playing basketball at the University of Kansas. . . . Through Title IX, she was able to give three scholarships that year (1975–76). My scholarship was only around $650.

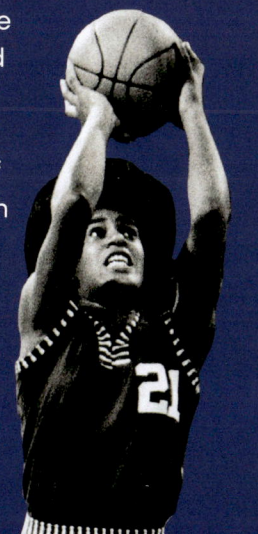

MATTER OF FACT
1970s

Numbers, People, and Moments That Defined the Era

NUMBERS

1% Percentage of college athletic budgets that went to women's sports programs before Title IX. At the high school level, male athletes outnumbered their female counterparts 12.5 to 1.

7,924 Fans attended the first WBL game in 1978, Milwaukee Does at Chicago Hustle.

21.5/ 10.1 Rita Easterling's point/assist averages for the WBL's Chicago Hustle during the 1979 season, earning her the league's first MVP award.

8 Total appearances in AIAW tournament by Southern Connecticut, the most of any school between 1972 and 1982.

PEOPLE

CAROL "THE BLAZE" BLAZEJOWSKI of Montclair State in New Jersey blitzed her competition with her sweet jumper. In 1977 she scored a career-high 52 points at Madison Square Garden (sans three-point line), a record that held until Kobe Bryant broke it in 2009. She was the first recipient of the Wade Trophy in 1978, named in honor of Delta State head coach Lily Margaret Wade. It is the oldest and most prestigious award for the best women's college player of the season.

GAIL MARQUIS, a two-time All-American at **QUEENS COLLEGE**, led the Knights to a national ranking for four straight years. On February 22, 1975, Coach **LUCILLE KYVALLOS** and her team faced perennial favorite Immaculata in front of 11,969 fans at Madison Square Garden, the venue's first-ever women's basketball game.

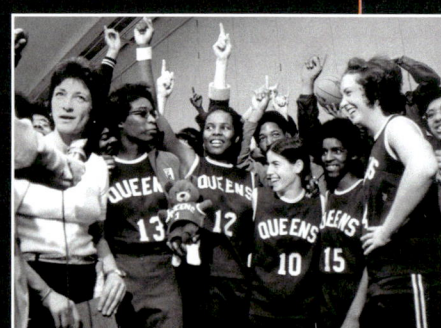

1976

Challenge of the Sexes: "A hotshot lady plays H-O-R-S-E with one of basketball's all-time greats," read the marketing copy from CBS. On the sports television show in 1976, former All-American Red Head **KAREN LOGAN** went up against Hall of Famer Jerry West, and her years of doing trick shots paid off—she won.

SEPT. 7, 1979

ESPN officially launches its anchor program, *SportsCenter*.

1977

KAREN LOGAN signs a contract with Nike worth $3,500 a year.

1978

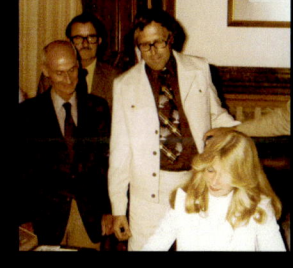

MOLLY BOLIN is the first player to sign with the WBL. Her salary was $6,000. She also earned $3,000 for being featured in the 1979 film *Scoring*, alongside "Pistol" Pete Maravich.

1979

KAYE AND FAYE YOUNG were twin sisters who played at NC State and then for the New York Stars and starred in national commercials— including one for Dannon yogurt, filmed in their Stars uniforms.

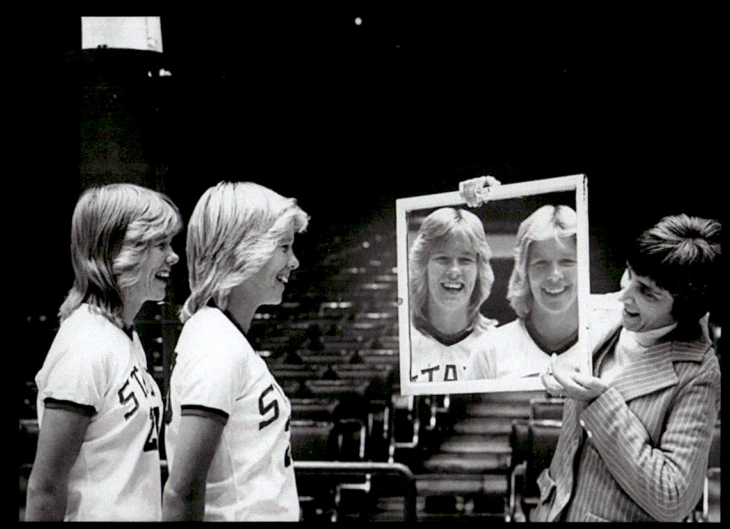

CHAPTER 3

1980s

THE TREND-SETTERS

IN COLLEGE, AT THE OLYMPICS, AND EVEN FOR THE HARLEM GLOBETROTTERS, WOMEN TOOK OFF AND STARTED PLAYING WITH STYLE.

RIGHT: Cheryl Miller with a slam dunk, 1983.

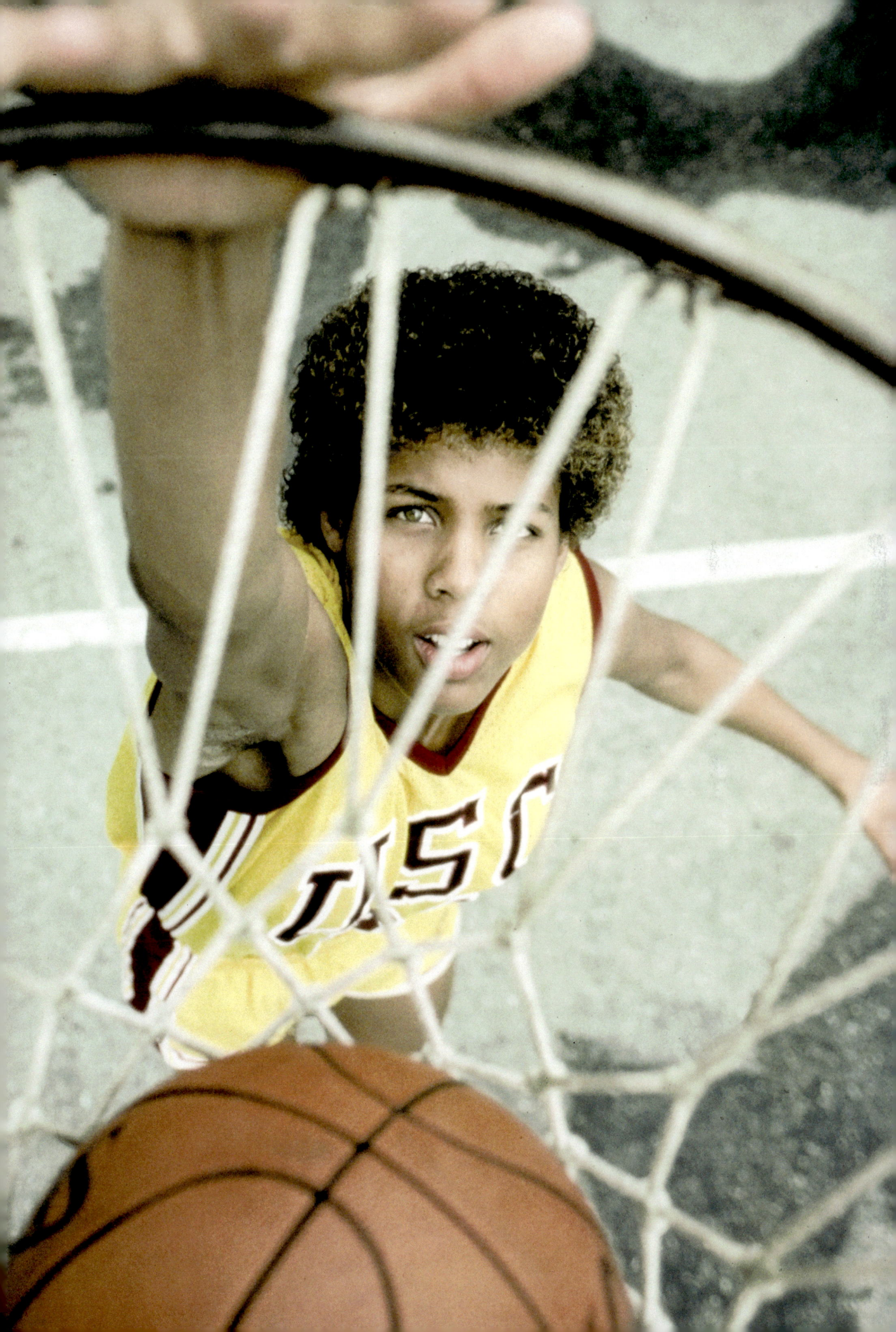

AIAW VS. NCAA

THE YEAR WITH TWO NATIONAL CHAMPIONSHIPS

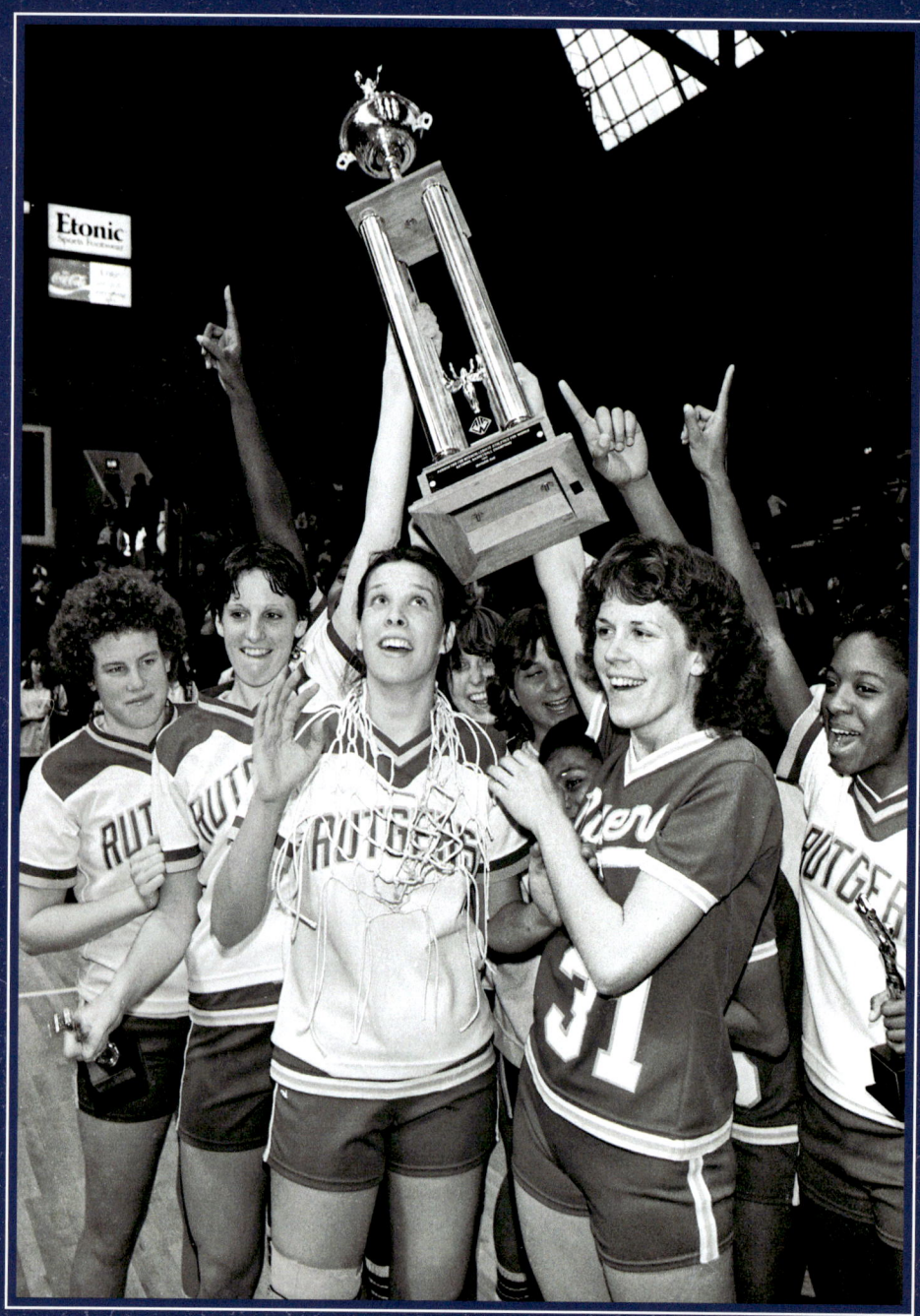

ABOVE: The NCAA record books would ultimately show Louisiana Tech as the 1982 champion. But Rutgers's AIAW victory, seen here, gave them a claim to the championship, too—complete with a trophy.

he 1982 women's college basketball season was like no other. Start with the fact that eight teams made the Final Four.

That year saw an intense, messy power struggle over the future of the game, and it ended with not one but two national tournaments. One was hosted by the AIAW—which had been founded more than a decade earlier to oversee college sports for women and had run the national championship ever since. One was hosted by the NCAA—which had long overseen college sports for men and was now angling to do the same for women. Their championship games were both scheduled for March 28, 1982, with Rutgers taking down Texas in the AIAW, while Louisiana Tech beat Cheyney State in the NCAA. But the most consequential battle of the day was the one between the respective governing bodies.

This was a fight about the logistics of college athletics. It was also a larger debate about what it would mean to chart a successful path for women in sports. That championship would be the last ever hosted in basketball by the AIAW. It would be the first of many for the NCAA. And under all of that discussion, past the questions of profit, control, and philosophy, there were two historic games.

The dueling 1982 championships were set when college athletics powerbrokers descended on the Fontainebleau Hotel in Miami in January 1981. It was the NCAA's annual convention, and this one was dedicated to a complicated, highly combustible question that might have seemed unthinkable to most of its members just a decade earlier: Should they sponsor national championships for women?

It was a concept in which the NCAA had not originally shown any interest. In fact, it had originally pushed *against* Title IX, first lobbying for a congressional amendment and then filing a lawsuit challenging the idea that it should apply to college sports at all. But the ground had begun to shift in the last few years. It was clear that Title IX would not easily be shaken or amended. There was no point in fighting it anymore. It was similarly clear that women's college sports were growing into a force under the AIAW.

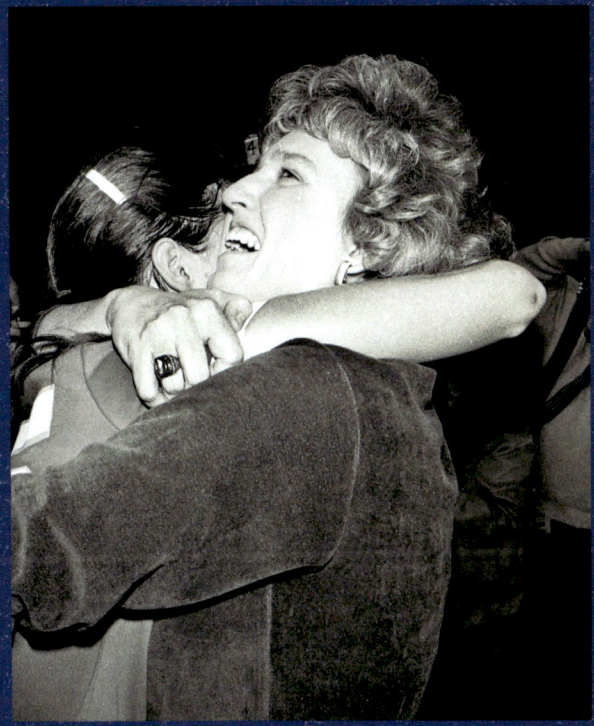

The organization had more than 950 schools playing seventeen sports with plans in motion to add two more. Money was limited and resources were modest, but they had used the last decade to build their own athletic departments, their own championships, and even their own television contracts. The 1980 women's basketball national championship between Old Dominion and Tennessee aired live on NBC and outdrew some NBA playoff coverage that year.

This opportunity was not lost on the NCAA. There did not seem to be hope for any kind of merger with or formal takeover of the AIAW. There was another option here, though. The NCAA could begin competing with the AIAW by holding its *own* national championships for women and simply let schools choose which one they wanted to join. That was the question put to a vote

ABOVE: Theresa Shank Grentz had been the star player at the first AIAW championship in 1972. She was the coach at the last AIAW championship in 1982. Here, she hugs player June Olkowski.

of NCAA delegates in January 1981.

The ensuing debate was fierce, but its divisions were not straightforward. There were NCAA men's coaches and directors strongly opposed to sponsoring anything for women. (Why should they give up any bit of their budgets?) There were AIAW women's coaches and directors with no interest in seeing another organization involved with their sports. (Why should they believe these men actually cared?) But there were also NCAA delegates who believed that women's sports could be a potentially good investment. (Wasn't it the wise thing?) And there were AIAW members who believed they would never be taken seriously if they were not part of the same governing body as the men. (Wasn't it the practical thing?) The NCAA's annual budget was about $22 million. The AIAW's was just under $1 million. Getting even a tiny fraction of that enormous pie could be transformational. There were strong arguments not just between the organizations but inside them.

It made for some unusual alliances. (Such as when the Arkansas football coach gave a rousing speech on the importance of women being allowed to control their own athletic departments . . . because he did not want to give up any of his budget. "He wasn't doing it for the right reasons, but that was all right," Iowa director of women's athletics and former AIAW president Christine Grant later told *Sports Illustrated*. "We adopted him at that convention.") It also made for some personal and deeply painful discussions. There were women who owed their careers to the existence of the AIAW—and now felt their best future might be under the NCAA. It was a group that included Tennessee coach Pat Summitt, already then gaining notice among the most accomplished, respected voices in the sport.

"The AIAW had been there from the beginning and allowed women an opportunity to compete,"

> **"The AIAW had been there from the beginning. . . . Yet, I knew realistically that the only way the sport could grow to the level we enjoy today was under the umbrella of the NCAA."**
>
> **—PAT SUMMITT, TENNESSEE COACH, 1993**

Summitt would reflect in 1993. "I almost felt like we were stabbing people in the back that had made our dreams possible at a very young age in women's sports. That bothered me because of the loyalty and dedication of AIAW. Yet, I knew realistically that the only way the sport could grow to the level we enjoy today was under the umbrella of the NCAA. That brought instant credibility to women's athletics. It gave us that name attachment; it gave us championships in a first-class arena, and we needed that. I thought that without that we may never have the opportunities to make the strides that are necessary for women to have what they have today."

When the NCAA brought the question to a vote of Division I schools at the convention, it was at first a tie, 124–124. But a recount showed the motion had been defeated by just one vote. It meant the NCAA would *not* sponsor women's championships: Much of the AIAW leadership was ecstatic. And then supporters of the motion called for another vote. They began working delegates they knew had been conflicted and ultimately managed to sway roughly a dozen of them. A final vote was held later that day, and now, the motion prevailed. The NCAA would begin holding championships for women in twelve sports in 1981–82.

There was no going back. It would be all but impossible for the AIAW to compete with the championship infrastructure from the NCAA. Much of the organization's budget came from school membership fees, and even a few jumping ship would be damning, especially if the group included the biggest names in premium sports like basketball. But it did not kill the AIAW—at least not yet. Instead, for one year, the landscape of the sport would fracture, and it would all end with twin national championships.

"I knew somebody would bring this up," Rutgers senior forward June Olkowski sighed at

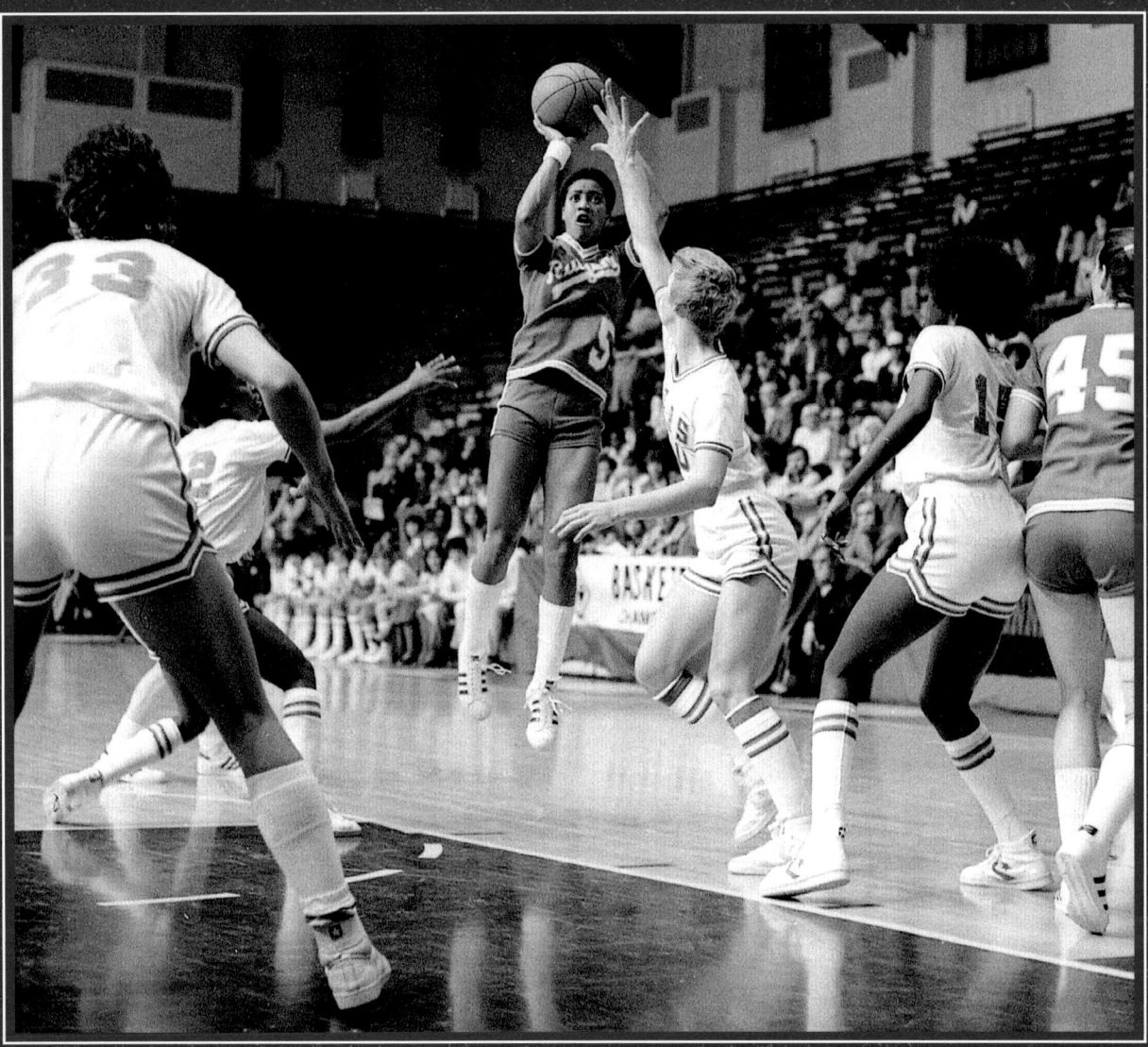

the 1982 AIAW National Division I Basketball Championship. "It really frustrates me that some people want to take that away from us."

She had just been asked if the championship her team was about to play in would mean anything. Rutgers was ranked No. 8 in the country. They had beaten top competition all year. Olkowski would be named an All-American. But come March, their athletic department had chosen to stick with the AIAW, instead of entering the new tournament hosted by the NCAA. It was already clear which championship would be considered more prestigious.

Many top programs had opted for the NCAA. For most athletic departments, choosing which

championship to play had been a financial question, not a strategic or philosophical one. The NCAA offered to pay travel costs. The AIAW could not afford that. (A decade had passed since the days of Immaculata scrambling to fly standby to the tournament in 1972, but for many programs, funding championship travel was still a yearly struggle.) Ultimately, seventeen of the schools ranked in the top twenty would choose the NCAA, including reigning AIAW champion Louisiana Tech.

ABOVE: Rutgers point guard Jennie Hall was named to the final AIAW All-Tournament Team.

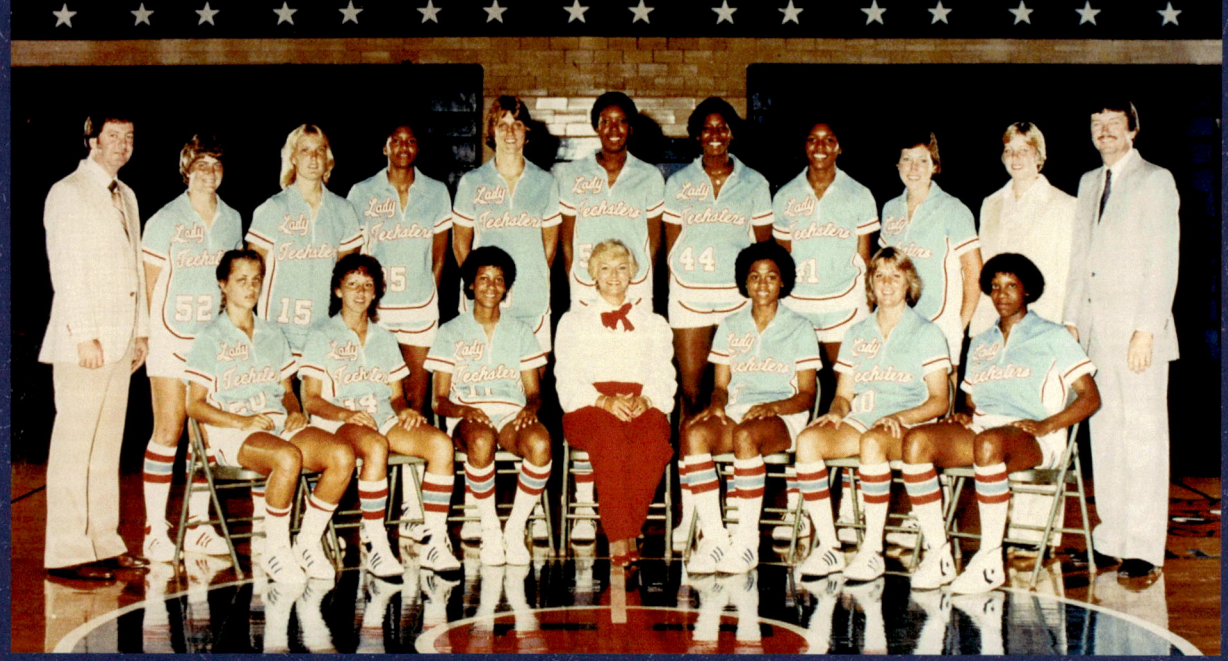

No one in the country had built a program quite like the Lady Techsters. With a coaching staff that had not one, not two, but *three* future Women's Basketball Hall of Famers, they helped introduce a style of play that shook off any lingering vestiges of six-on-six. Head coach Sonja Hogg was a masterful recruiter who focused on the image of the program and insisted that her players be ladylike. (She even designed the uniforms.) Players were instructed to call her "Miss Hogg" rather than "Coach." The on-court strategy came from her associate coach, Leon Barmore, who encouraged the group to move away from set shots and play with more creativity. The roster was led by dynamic six-foot-three center Janice Lawrence. At point guard, they had a petite, intense Louisiana native by the name of Kim Mulkey, who eventually would be much better known for her success as a coach. Crashing the boards was Debra Rodman, who grew up battling for rebounds with her brother, future NBA star Dennis. And their best player that season was someone else altogether. The Wade Trophy, given annually to the best female player in the country, went to three-time All-American Pam Kelly.

But they had a serious challenge in their path to another title. The championship game

> "If this is the last one,
> this is the best."
>
> **—THERESA SHANK GRENTZ,
> RUTGERS COACH**

would pit them against No. 2 ranked Cheyney State—a remarkably talented underdog. The small Pennsylvania school is still the only historically Black college or university ever to make an NCAA Final Four. They were coached by C. Vivian Stringer, who had accepted the job years earlier despite the fact it originally did not come with a salary, and she had steadily built up the program. (She would eventually become the first coach in

ABOVE: Louisiana Tech had three Hall of Famers as coaches and two future Olympians as players. Their success earned them a serious local fan base: Their home gym held 5,200 fans, but head coach Sonja Hogg learned that if she dangled free tickets for the fire marshal, he would let them pack in even more.

major college basketball, men's or women's, to lead three different programs to a Final Four.) Cheyney State could not match the depth of Louisiana Tech but they would counter it with pace, strategy, and incredible guard play.

"They might be better than we are," Barmore told reporters before the championship. "They're one of the best-coached teams I've ever seen."

The final between Louisiana Tech and Cheyney State was originally not meant to be on television. CBS had a deal with the AIAW to air its championship instead of the NCAA's. Yet the network backed out and brokered a new deal when it became clear that more top programs would be in the latter bracket. It meant a national audience would see Cheyney State jump out to a surprising early lead, only to ultimately be ground down by the overwhelming force of Louisiana Tech, with a final score of 76–62.

The Lady Techsters were the first NCAA women's basketball champions. A picture of Mulkey cutting down the nets in her signature French braids ran in newspapers across the country.

But there was another championship played a few hundred miles north on that same day. The battle for the AIAW crown ended up overshadowed by the NCAA. The players and coaches involved did not have a say in which tournament had been selected by their schools, and they would spend years reminding people they had played a compelling, tight championship matchup, too.

It offered a fascinating collection of historic figures. Rutgers was coached by Theresa Grentz, the star player on those Immaculata championship teams from the 1970s, now the first women's college basketball coach ever hired full-time. The Rutgers

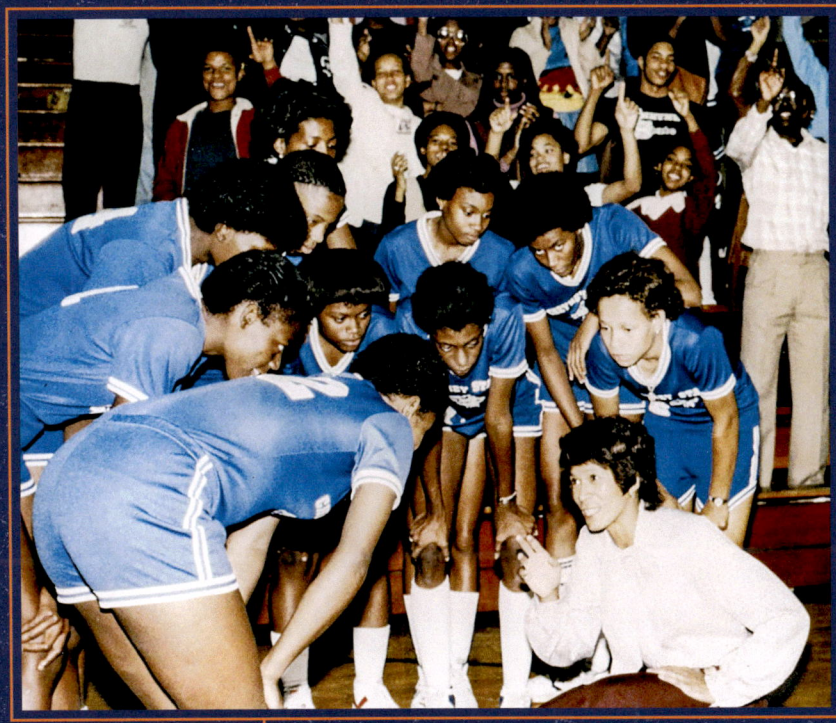

ABOVE: Cheyney State did not technically hire C. Vivian Stringer to be a coach. Instead, when she came to campus at the age of twenty-three in 1971, she was hired as a professor of physical education—and coaching was something she volunteered to do for free. The school had limited resources: Players had to wash their own uniforms. But under Stringer's dedicated, passionate eye, they became the first and only historically Black college to make a Division I Final Four.

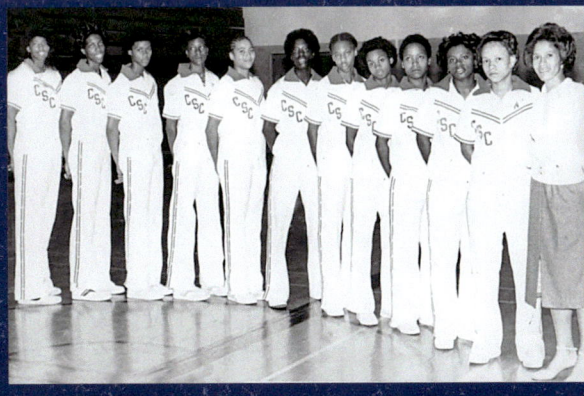

ABOVE: Cheyney State's ranking peaked at No. 2 in the country in 1982. The Lady Wolves' season included a twenty-three-game win streak.

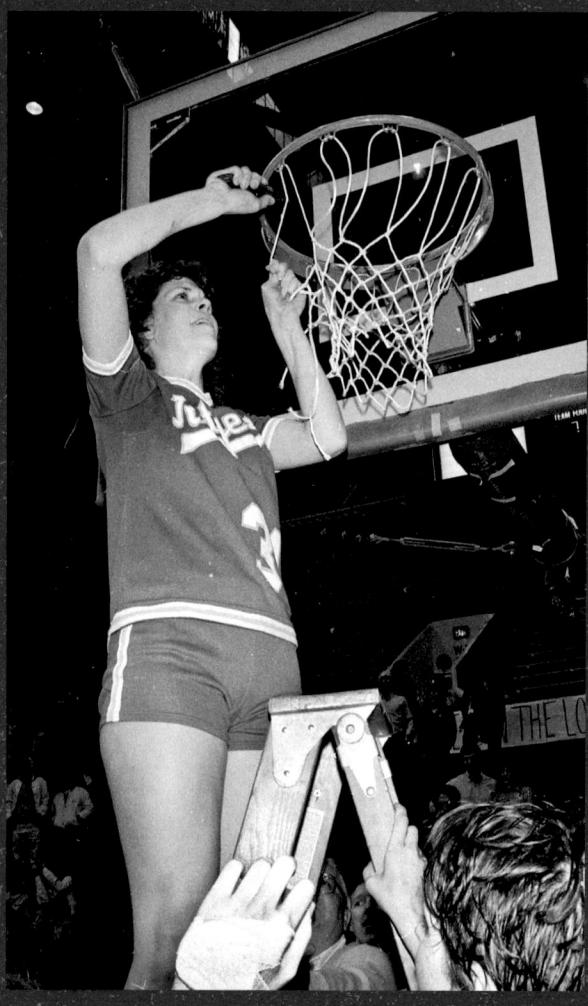
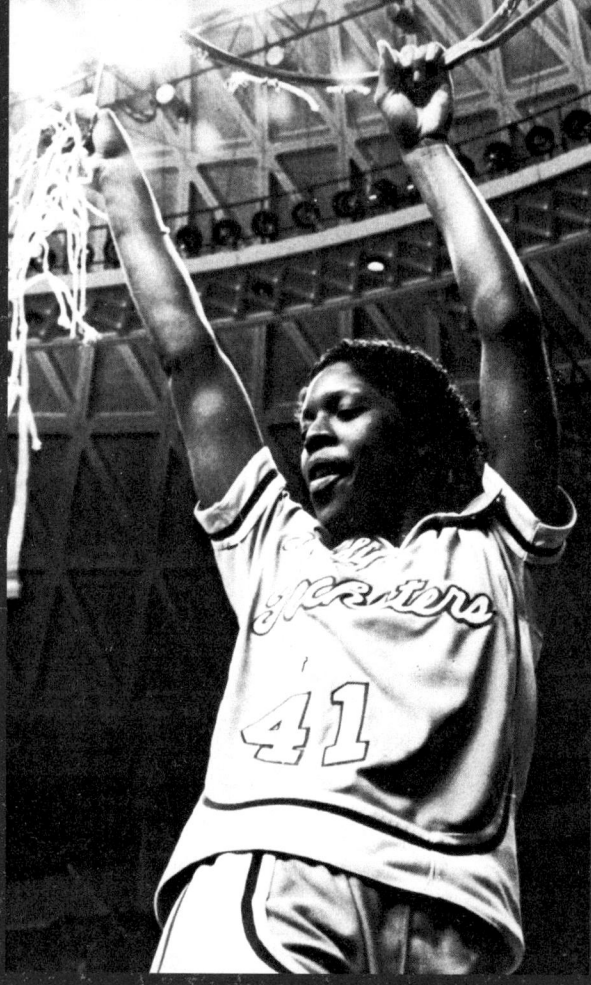

captain was a no-nonsense guard named Chris Dailey—who'd eventually be the most respected associate coach in the country with decades spent alongside Geno Auriemma at the University of Connecticut. Across the bracket from them in the Final Four had been the Wayland Baptist Queens, the little program that pioneered the college game back in the 1950s, long before the existence of the AIAW or the interest from the NCAA. In the championship, No. 8 Rutgers would face No. 5 Texas, who entered the game with the longest win streak in the country for either men or women. The Longhorns were coached by future Hall of Famer Jody Conradt—who'd originally been inspired to leave her tiny hometown when a local girl made the barnstorming All-American Red Heads. A tangle of connective threads from the last few decades of the game all led here.

The game was close down to the final minutes. Rutgers ultimately prevailed, 83–77, and the most dominant player of either title matchup was senior guard Patty Coyle, who scored 30. Yet the legacy of that championship seemed to fade as soon as the buzzer rang. The AIAW would be functionally dead within a few months. The organization's last attempt for survival was an unsuccessful antitrust lawsuit.

As the NCAA took over women's college sports, it wrote and maintained the record books, and so it shaped the history of the game. Its list of women's basketball champions begins in 1982 with Louisiana

ABOVE: Two national championships meant two sets of celebrations to cut down the nets. Rutgers senior Chris Dailey cuts down the net, left, and Louisiana Tech senior Pam Kelly does the same, right.

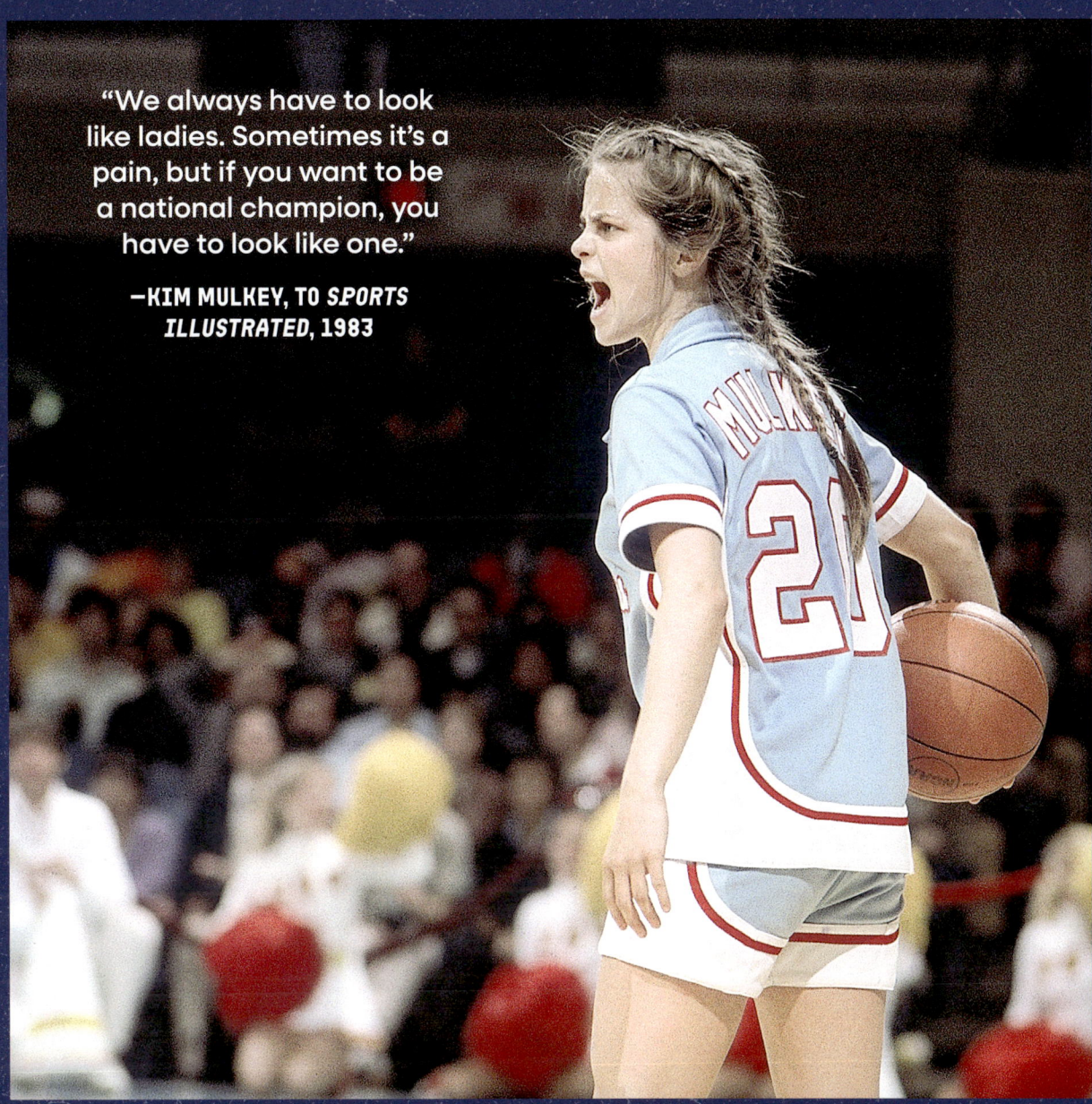

"We always have to look like ladies. Sometimes it's a pain, but if you want to be a national champion, you have to look like one."

—KIM MULKEY, TO *SPORTS ILLUSTRATED*, 1983

Tech. However, there was a record book that lived behind that one, allowing for its creation in the first place, with its own list of women's basketball champions ending in 1982 with Rutgers.

"From a coaching standpoint, I wanted to be there with the big schools and the bright lights and the potential for growth," Texas coach Conradt told *The Washington Post* decades later. "As I look back on it now, I have totally different feelings. I am so proud . . . that we stayed with AIAW that last year. Because it became a statement. It was a statement that, 'Yes, women can control their own destiny. We

are not dependent on the NCAA, male-dominated organization to create this opportunity for women's basketball.'"

ABOVE: Kim Mulkey scored just 6 points in the national championship win over Cheyney State. But the point guard was so effective in directing the offense that she was still named Most Valuable Player by the TV broadcast on CBS. (Her teammate Janice Lawrence was voted Most Outstanding Player by the print media.) Mulkey was often the smallest player on the floor at just five foot four, but she never lacked nerve.

CHERYL MILLER

A GENERATIONAL TALENT WHO MADE HISTORY

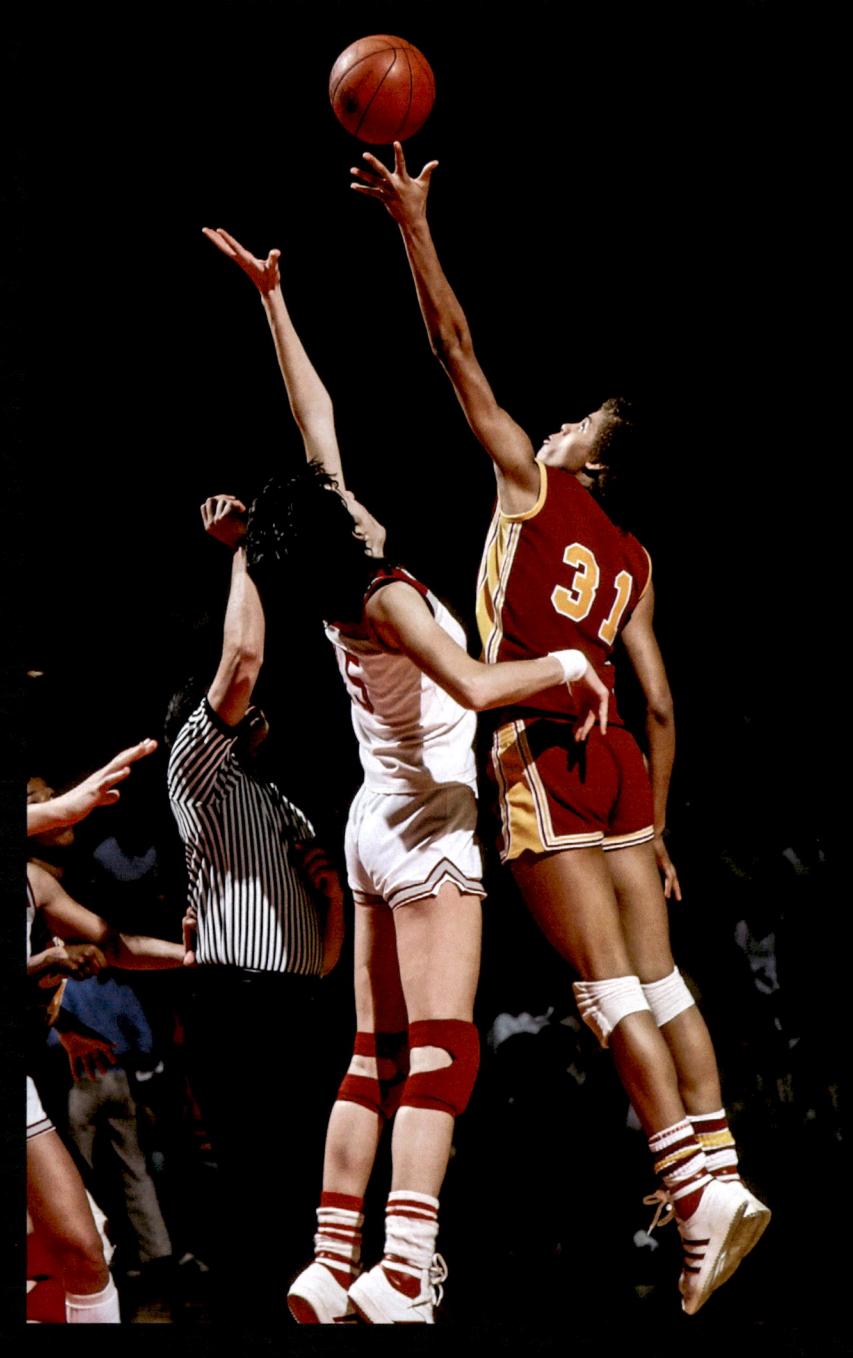

ABOVE: Miller leaps for the tip-off against Stanford in 1983 at Maples Pavilion.

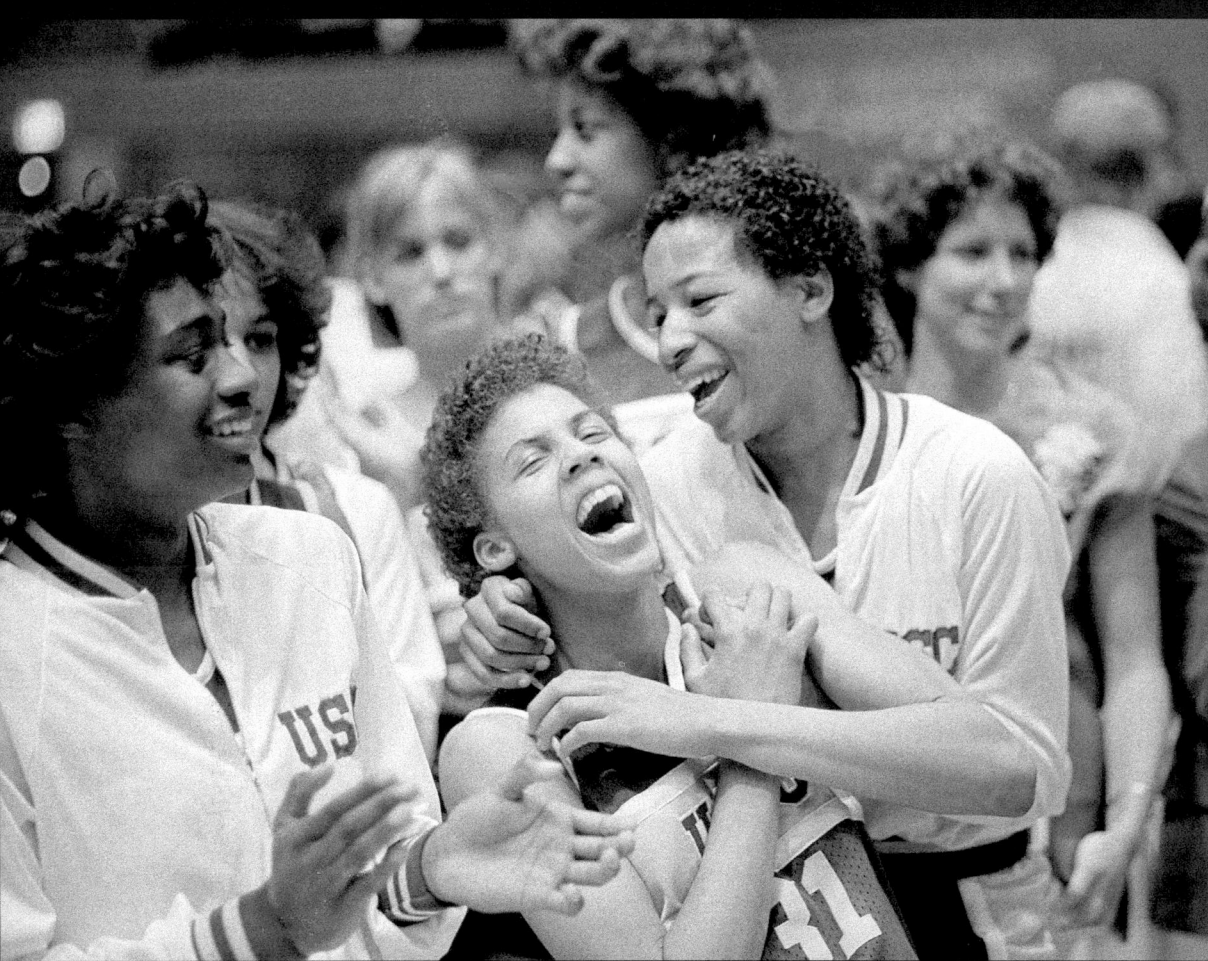

n the 1980s, the shiny shorts were extra short, and the tube socks were extra long. It was rare to see a ponytail bounce up and down the court; cropped, wafted haircuts were the rage. For superstar Cheryl Deann Miller, her long, lanky six-foot-two frame and juicy Wave Nouveau–drenched curls bounced as she soared at the rim. Her classic Adidas squeaked on the gym floor as she revved to intercept passes. Miller *was* eighties women's basketball personified.

At Riverside Polytechnic High School in Riverside, California, Miller became must-watch live entertainment. She'd dunk, throw no-look dimes, and drill it from deep. The neighboring kids already knew it. She'd been beating them one-on-one since grade school. Her six-foot-seven little brother, Reggie, knew it, too. Despite him being a local hotshot, she'd block his shot more times than she could count. She once scored 105 points (46–50

from the field) her senior year as her Poly crushed Norte Vista 179–15. Reggie excitedly scored 40 points the same night in his high school basketball game. Cheryl had 65 points *at halftime*.

Cheryl Miller finished high school ball in 1982, being a four-time state champion with a 132–4 record. She set a state high of 3,405 career points.

There were 250 colleges vying for Miller to wear their jersey and rep their school colors. At the time, schools couldn't fly prospects out. So, the handwritten letter from Tennessee's Pat Summitt was nice, but the Miller family didn't have the funds to fly cross-country for a campus tour. Local schools like the University of California, Los Angeles, and

---

ABOVE: Miller with teammate Cynthia Cooper (right) rejoicing after winning the 1984 national championship.

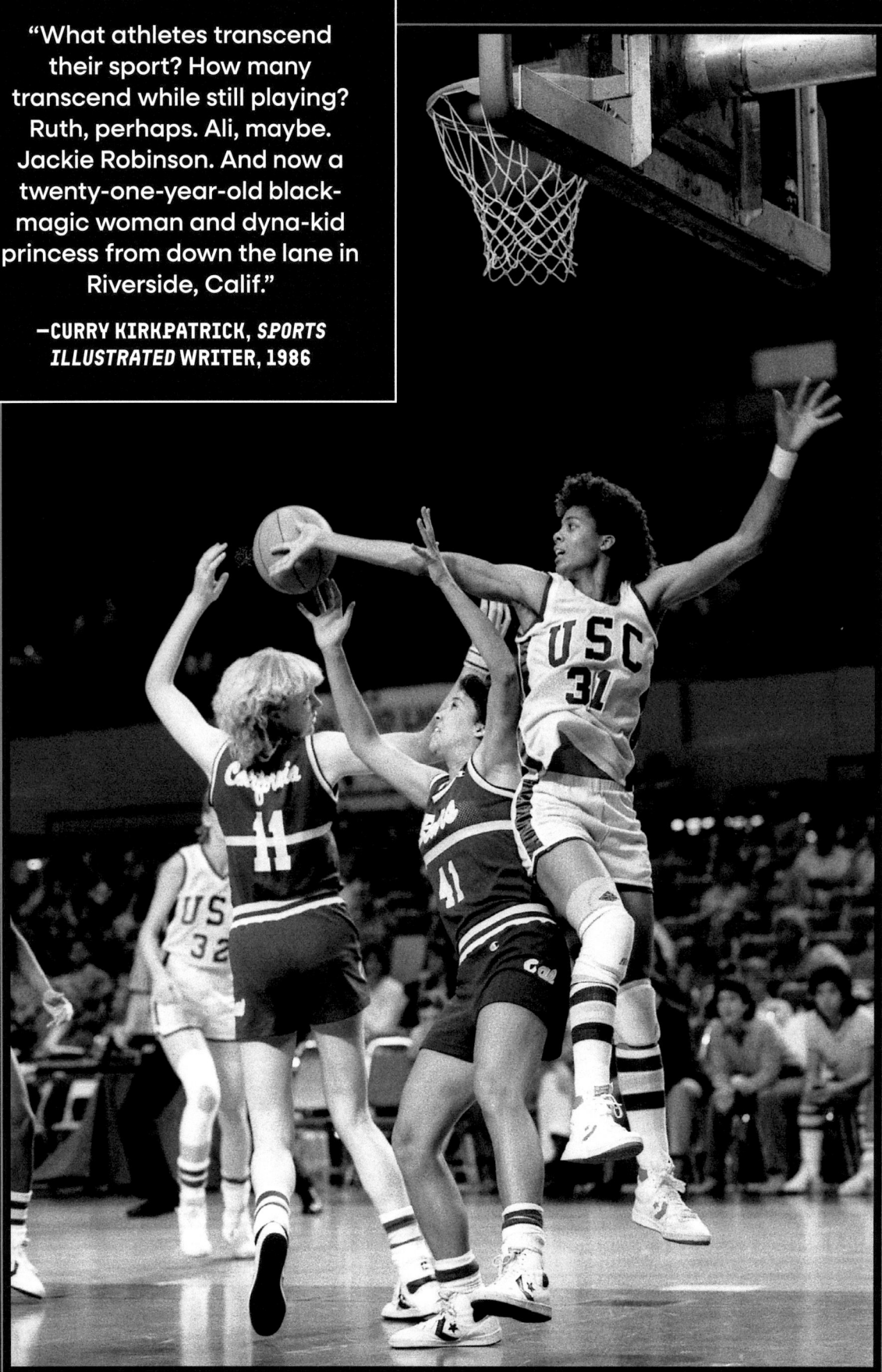

the University of Southern California had a leg up.

USC's head coach, Linda Sharp, brought sophomore All-American twins Pamela and Paula McGee with her on her recruiting visit to Miller's family home. The six-foot-three McGee sisters sandwiched Miller on the couch, and then Pam said, "You can either play two years with us or two years against us." She nearly guaranteed the three of them would win at least a few championships if Miller teamed up with their squad. "What's it gone be?" Paula prodded. And that was it. The USC Trojans (also known as the Women of Troy) was her choice. Another top freshman prospect, Rhonda Windham (Bronx, New York), would join Miller's recruiting class. With the McGee twins as veterans and a tough-as-nails point guard in Cynthia Cooper, a new women's basketball powerhouse was formed.

Miller said moving west from rural Riverside to South Central Los Angeles in the early eighties was a culture shock. Alumna Esther Williams once described USC's campus as "the world's most expensive ghetto." Despite the rapid rise of drugs and gang violence, Magic Johnson and the Showtime Lakers had the city buzzing with new basketball fans.

Coach Sharp wasted little time thrusting her new-look Women of Troy into the spotlight. Preseason matchups between Tennessee, reigning national champions Louisiana Tech, and Georgia were first up. Boisterous crowds of over 15,000 fans packed the gyms to see the highly touted team from the West Coast come to town. There were many boos and *Ghostbusters*-like signs with Miller's face, a bright red circle, and a slash through it, but USC swept the Southern tour.

For home games at Southern Cal, the men would play before the women's team most nights. "That was the wrong thing to do with a bunch of arrogant women," Miller said, smirking at the memory decades later. "After the game was over,

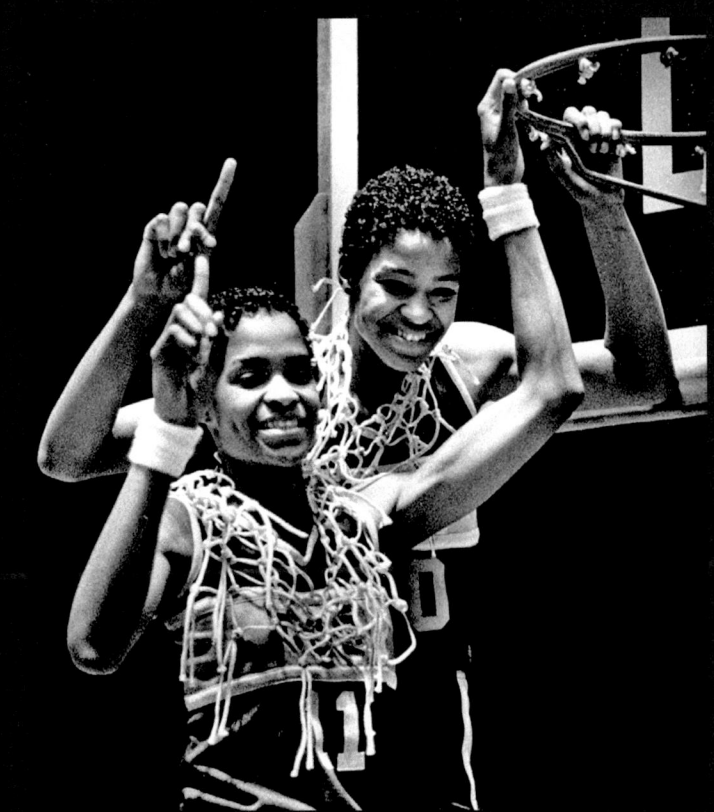

we'd slap them on the rear and say, 'Thanks for warming up the court!' We'd clown them. And then the crowd would come to watch us play." In Miller's freshman year, the Women of Troy broke eleven attendance records on the road and sold out four home games.

On April 3, 1983, in Norfolk, Virginia, USC would get a rematch with Louisiana Tech in the NCAA national championship game. It was nationally broadcast on CBS, peaking at 11.84 million viewers, up over 35 percent from last year's inaugural women's title. They'd win again, 69–67, earning the Trojans' first title in school history. And they did it in *style*. Anchored by high-flying All-American Miller—who finished with 28 points

---

OPPOSITE: Miller blocking a Cal player's shot backward. What can't she do?

ABOVE: USC made Black history on April 3, 1983, becoming the first all-Black starting five in women's basketball to win a title. They won again the next year. Here Paula and Pam McGee celebrate by cutting down the 1984 championship net.

with flair and panache. It was something women's basketball fans weren't used to yet. Tech's slow-but-steady style was tethered to yesteryear. With a pigtailed point guard in Kim Mulkey, they were pegged as "ladylike" and more withdrawn. Their early hoops reign came to an end—they hadn't faced Cheryl Miller yet.

"Cheryl enlarged her aura by creating an identity at the defensive end," USC men's coach Stan Morrison told *Sports Illustrated* in 1985. "She seems to search for those opportunities to hit the deck for a tie-up, dive into the crowd for a save, leap back over a press table for the loose ball. Everything and anything to turn the game her way."

After returning with the national championship trophy to Southern Cal, Miller admits her ego swelled. She was the queen of college basketball, in her prime, and very Hollywood. Miller shared the stage with Donna Summer at the Grammys during her performance of "She Works Hard for the Money," schmoozed with Michael Jackson, and filmed commercials with Dr. J in Philadelphia. She'd blow kisses to the crowd after made buckets, hold her follow-through as she backpedaled to defense, do back-arching cheerleader leaps in celebration, and perform cartwheels during gameplay. Her antics and sly comments to the media became a part of her persona. She had charisma, and the women's basketball world had to buckle up because she was just getting started.

The young, flashy USC team returned next season looking to pick up right where they left off. They finished the regular season 24–4, with sophomore Miller leading the way with 22 points and nearly eleven rebounds per game. The Women of Troy returned to the NCAA title game ranked fifth, going up against fifteenth-ranked Tennessee and Coach Pat Summitt's five senior starters.

It was April 1, 1984, at UCLA's Pauley Pavilion, so Southern California had the hometown advantage. Over 8 million people tuned in to CBS to see if Miller and the McGee twins could do it again. USC trailed by 2 points at the half but rallied late to win 72–61. They *did* do it again; they were back-to-back national champs. Pam and Paula

McGee had 17 points each, and Miller pitched in 16. Once again, Miller earned the crown of Player of the Tournament.

"I think they have a great front line. They've got experience, and they've got a Cheryl Miller to complement things," said Tennessee coach Pat Summitt after the loss. "No one else has a Cheryl Miller."

That summer, Coach Summitt *would* have Cheryl Miller on her team—the 1984 Los Angeles Olympic team, to be exact. Joining Team USA was a no-brainer for junior-to-be Miller, with the Games in her backyard at the Forum in Inglewood. Plus, she'd get the opportunity to play with the country's brightest women's basketball stars: Cathy Boswell, Denise Curry, Anne Donovan, Teresa Edwards, Lea Henry, Janice Lawrence, Carol Menken-Schaudt, Kim Mulkey, Cindy Noble, Lynette Woodard, and her USC teammate Pam McGee.

"While much of the Olympic world fussed over the considerable feats of Carl Lewis and Mary Lou Retton, Cheryl Miller demonstrated again tonight that she dominates her sport as much as any athlete at these Games," journalist Michael Wilbon wrote in the *Washington Post* in August 1984. "Miller, with undeniable brilliance, had 16 points, eleven rebounds, and five assists to lead the United States to an 85–55 gold-medal victory over South Korea before 11,280 in the Forum. It was the first gold medal a US women's basketball team had won in Olympic history."

With a gold medal around her neck, Miller said it was "ten times better than winning a national championship." At twenty years old, she'd unlocked a new level, and now the world knew her name.

Her final two years at USC didn't bear the same team success, but Miller still shined individually. Fresh off the gold medal, Miller led the country by averaging almost 27 points, sixteen rebounds, and three blocks per game during the 1984–85 season. She'd be crowned the Wade Trophy winner,

---

OPPOSITE: Miller's in-game antics were what made her special. Georgia's Teresa Edwards (background) wasn't amused.

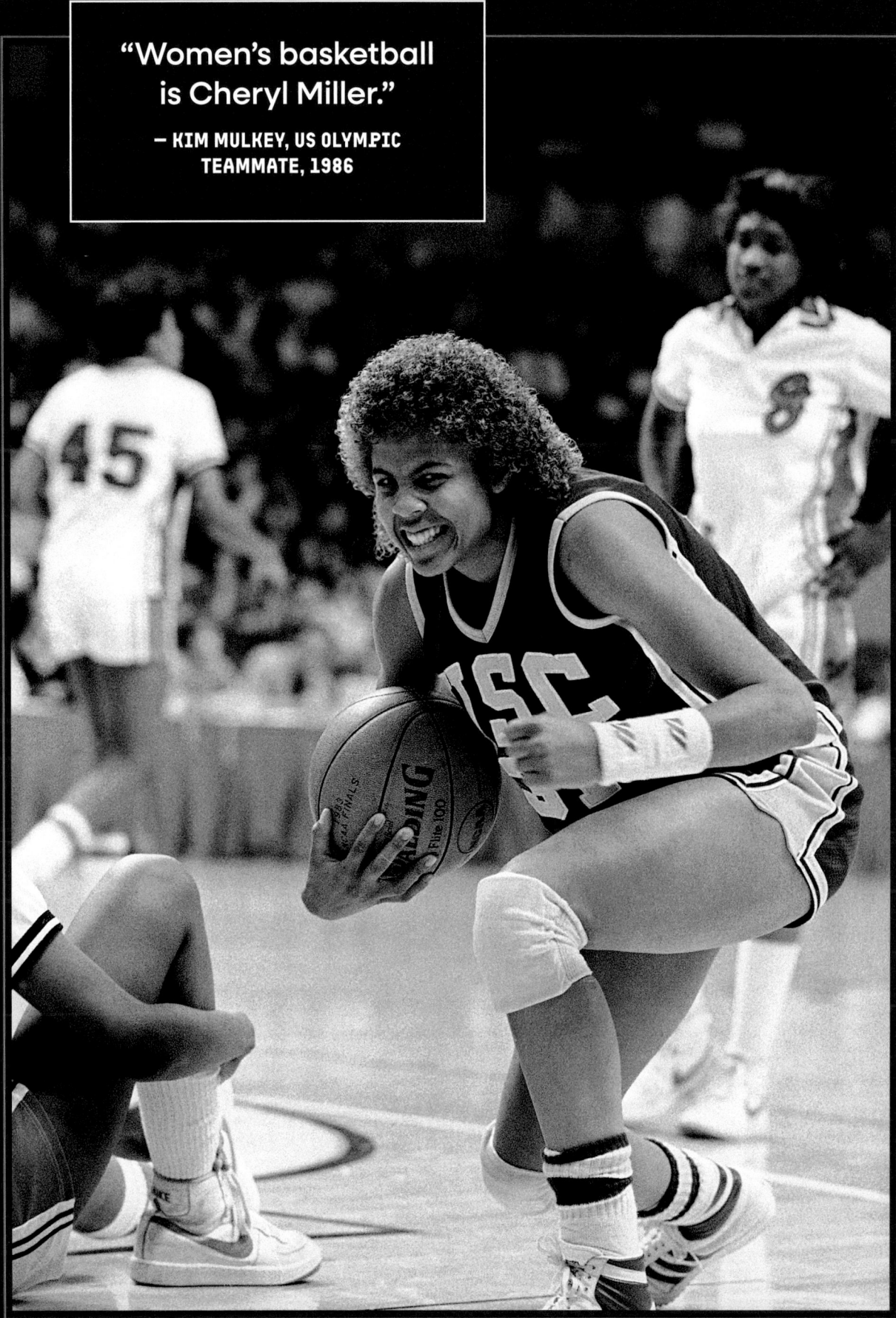

"Women's basketball is Cheryl Miller."

— KIM MULKEY, US OLYMPIC TEAMMATE, 1986

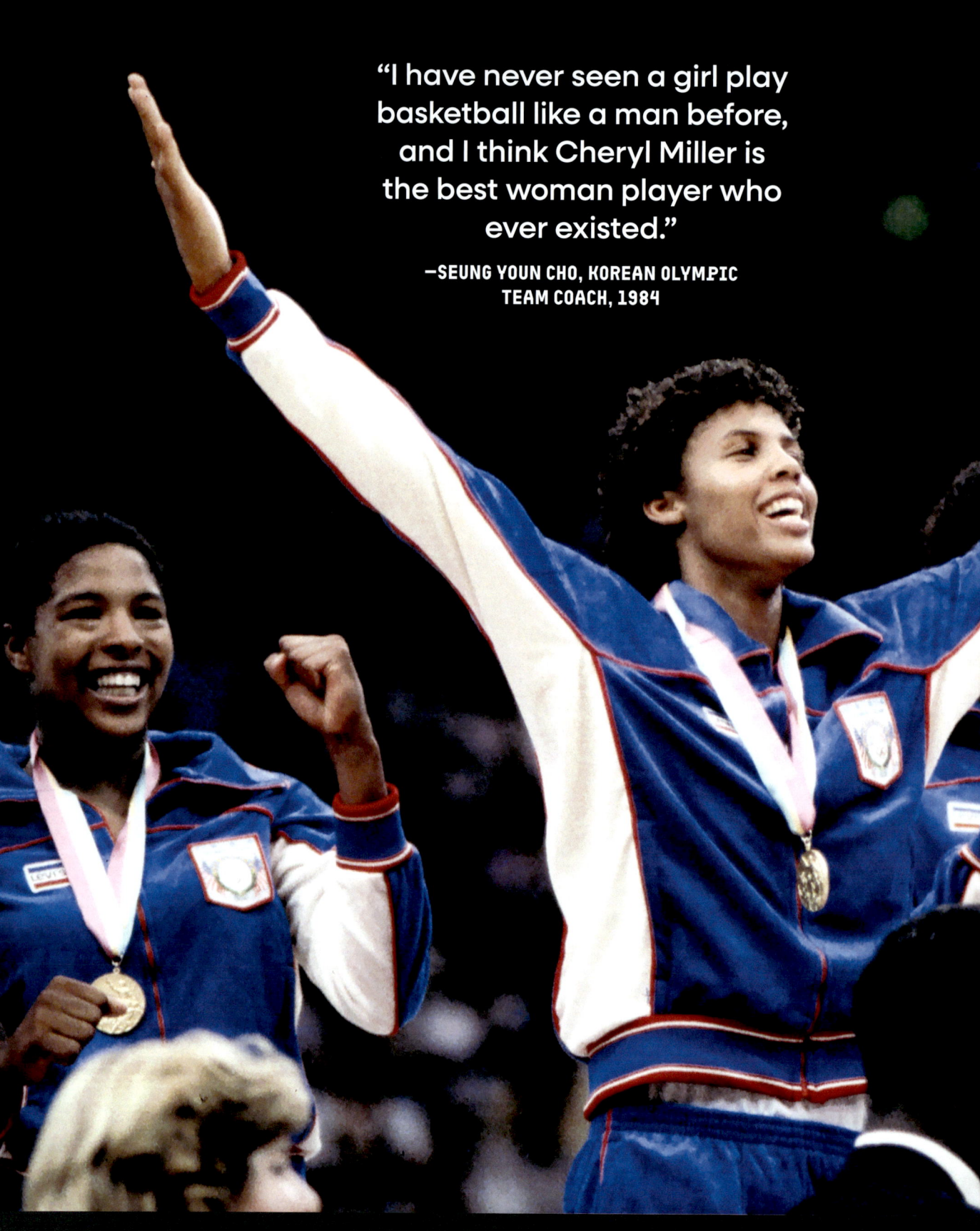

"I have never seen a girl play basketball like a man before, and I think Cheryl Miller is the best woman player who ever existed."

—SEUNG YOUN CHO, KOREAN OLYMPIC TEAM COACH, 1984

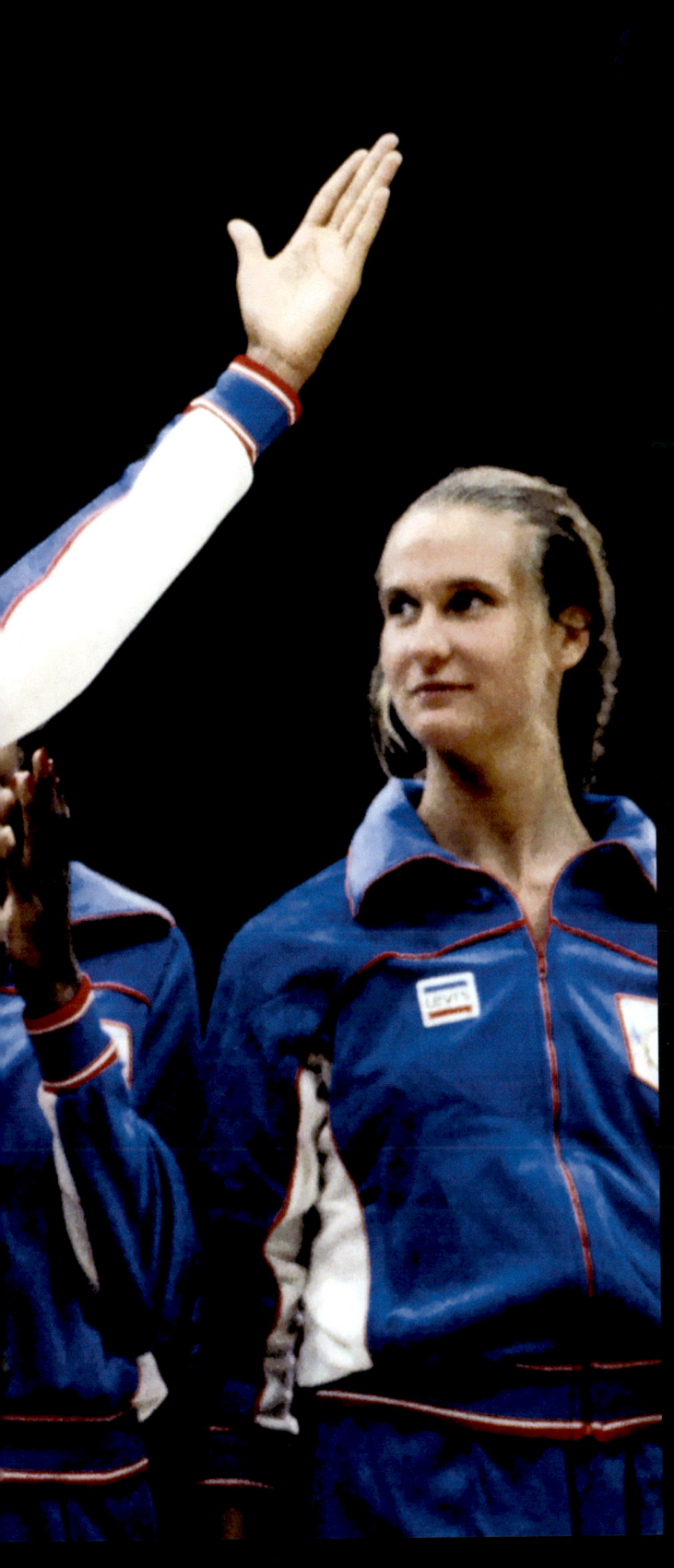

but third-ranked Long Beach State bounced the Women of Troy in the Sweet 16. Miller's '86 senior season wrapped with a 31–5 record, her third consecutive Naismith Player of the Year honor, and her fourth straight All-American badge, and *Sports Illustrated* named her the best male or female player in college basketball. Southern California would retire her number 31 jersey *before* her final game as a Trojan; she'd be their first basketball player (men or women) to have a jersey in their rafters.

After graduation, Miller planned to play overseas and in the 1988 Olympics. Her fallback plan was to become a sports broadcaster. But a random pick-up game on campus against football players would end her playing career. A guy fell before her, she tried to jump over him, and then *pop*. Miller devastatingly injured her ACL and a partial tear of her lateral meniscus in her knee. The diagnosis felt like a death sentence.

She remembers the doctor coming in and telling her, "Well, you had a great run. I guess now it's time for you to have kids." It was a reality check; all her accolades flashed before her eyes—hoisting trophies, cutting down nets, and shattering scoring records. It was a wrap. She tried rehabbing and returning to the Olympic team in '88, but she was waived after reaggravating her knee injury in a training scrimmage. Miller would retire at the age of twenty-four before ever playing professional ball.

She paid the game forward. USC's success and rise to one of the West Coast's premiere women's basketball programs led to another local six-foot-two superstar's desire to be a part of the Women of Troy—Lisa Leslie. Southern Cal would go on to dominate for decades, but it all started with the girl with a Jheri curl from Riverside. Cheryl Miller was, is, and will always be the standard.

LEFT: Cheryl Miller taking in the crowd at the Forum in Los Angeles after winning gold in the 1984 Olympics.

USA'S OLYMPIC DOMINANCE BEGINS

The 1984 Gold Medal Was Just the Beginning of a Historic Reign

Fresh off a runner-up finish in the first Olympic Games for women's basketball in 1976, Team USA entered the eighties on the vicious hunt for gold. They knew to get it, they must go through the Soviet Union. But in December 1979, the Soviet Union invaded Afghanistan, which led President Jimmy Carter to give Russia an ultimatum: Remove their troops, or the United States will boycott the Moscow-hosted 1980 Summer Olympics.

While awaiting the impending verdict, Team USA still competed in the qualifying tournament and went 6-1 in Bulgaria, where five players averaged double figures: Denise Curry, Cindy Noble, Holly Walker, LaTauyna Pollard, and Carol "the Blaze" Blazejowski. The USSR didn't budge, and so the US and sixty-four other nations didn't participate in the Games. The Soviets took gold once again in women's basketball. Some players, like Blazejowski, had one shot at medaling snatched from them.

"We couldn't even believe it," Blazejowski told the *Chicago Tribune* in 2020. She was an alternate in 1976 and a starter in 1980. "It was the whole range of emotions, from anger to sadness to resentment to 'Okay, what's next?' The unknown."

The 1984 Los Angeles Olympic team had pent-up energy and excitement to finally face their foe, but then it was the Soviets' turn to bow out of participation. Cheryl Miller and Lynette Woodard led Team USA to gold on a perfect 6–0 route, defeating teams by an average of 32.7 points per game. It was the first gold medal for women's hoops.

For the Seoul Games 1988, the message for the Olympic squad was clear: "Sole Goal—Seoul Gold." The triple threat of Katrina McClain, Teresa Edwards, and Cynthia Cooper met the Soviet Union in the semifinals; Team USA had yet to beat them

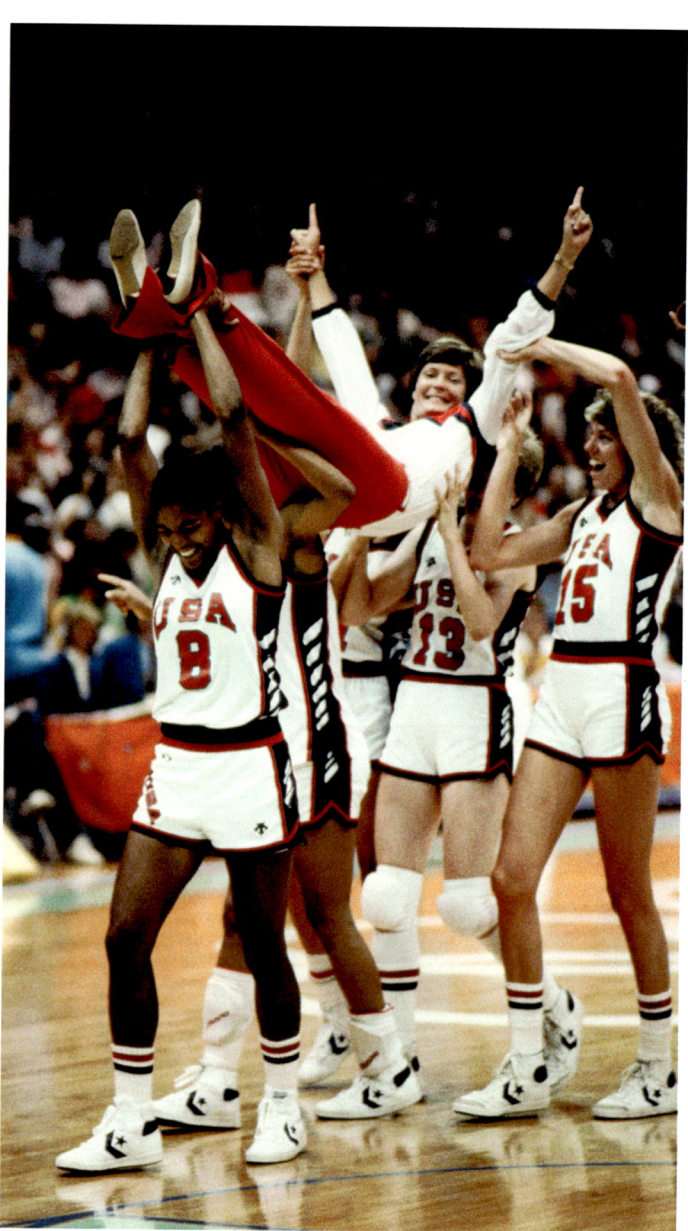

ABOVE: Coach Pat Summitt, victorious, is carried off by her team after defeating South Korea in the group stage in the 1984 LA Summer Olympics.

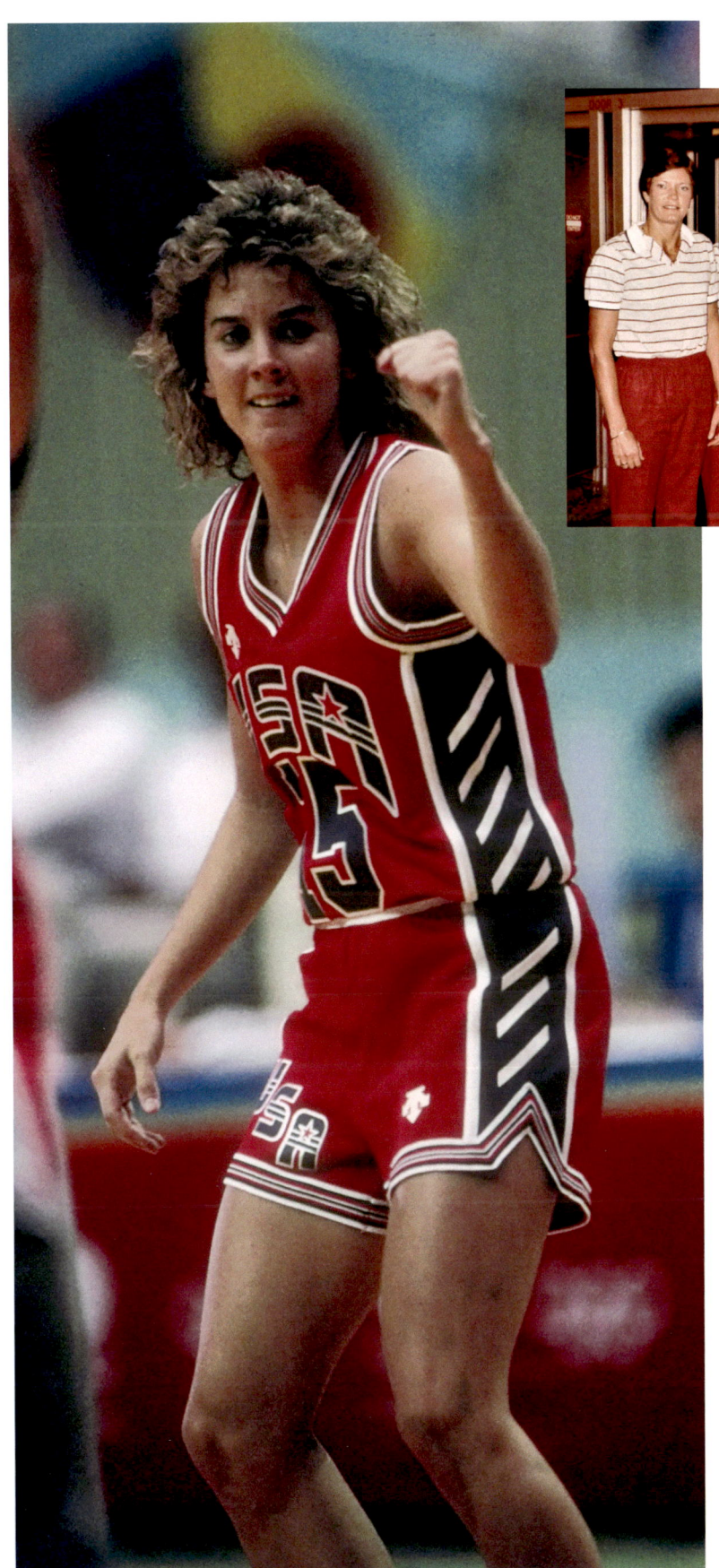

in the Olympic competition. But with head coach Kay Yow's sweltering pressure defense and fast-break offense, USA finally bested USSR 102–88. Cooper had 27 points, and McClain added 26 points and fifteen boards in the win.

Edwards became otherworldly in the gold-medal match versus Yugoslavia, scoring 14 of her 18 points in the second half. Team USA would win their second straight Olympic gold medal, 77–70, setting a new standard for women's hoops on the world stage.

ABOVE: Legendary women's basketball coaches led Team USA throughout the decade, shown here at the airport in 1984. From left to right: Pat Summitt, Kay Yow, Jody Conradt, Billie Moore, and Sue Gunter.

LEFT: Point guard Suzanne McConnell hailed from Penn State (1984–88), where she set the NCAA DI records for career total assists (1,307) and career per game average (10.2)—a record that still stands today. She won Olympic gold in Seoul in '88 and bronze in Barcelona in '92.

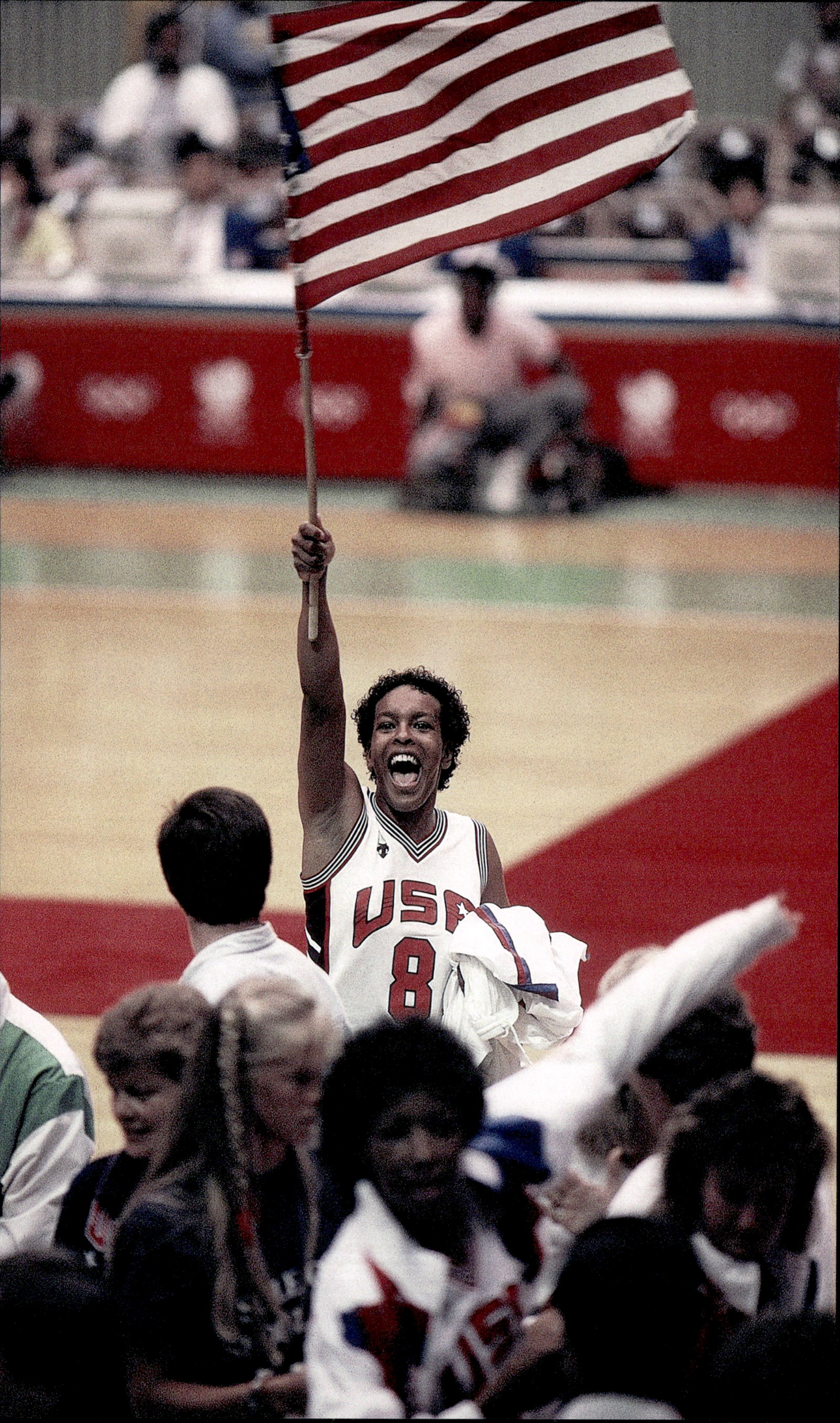

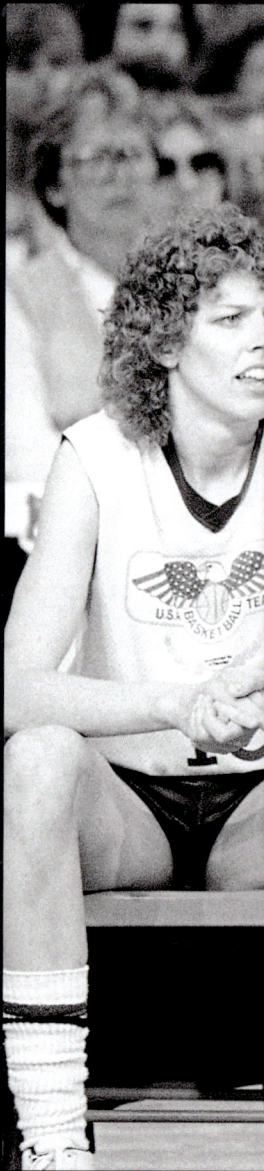

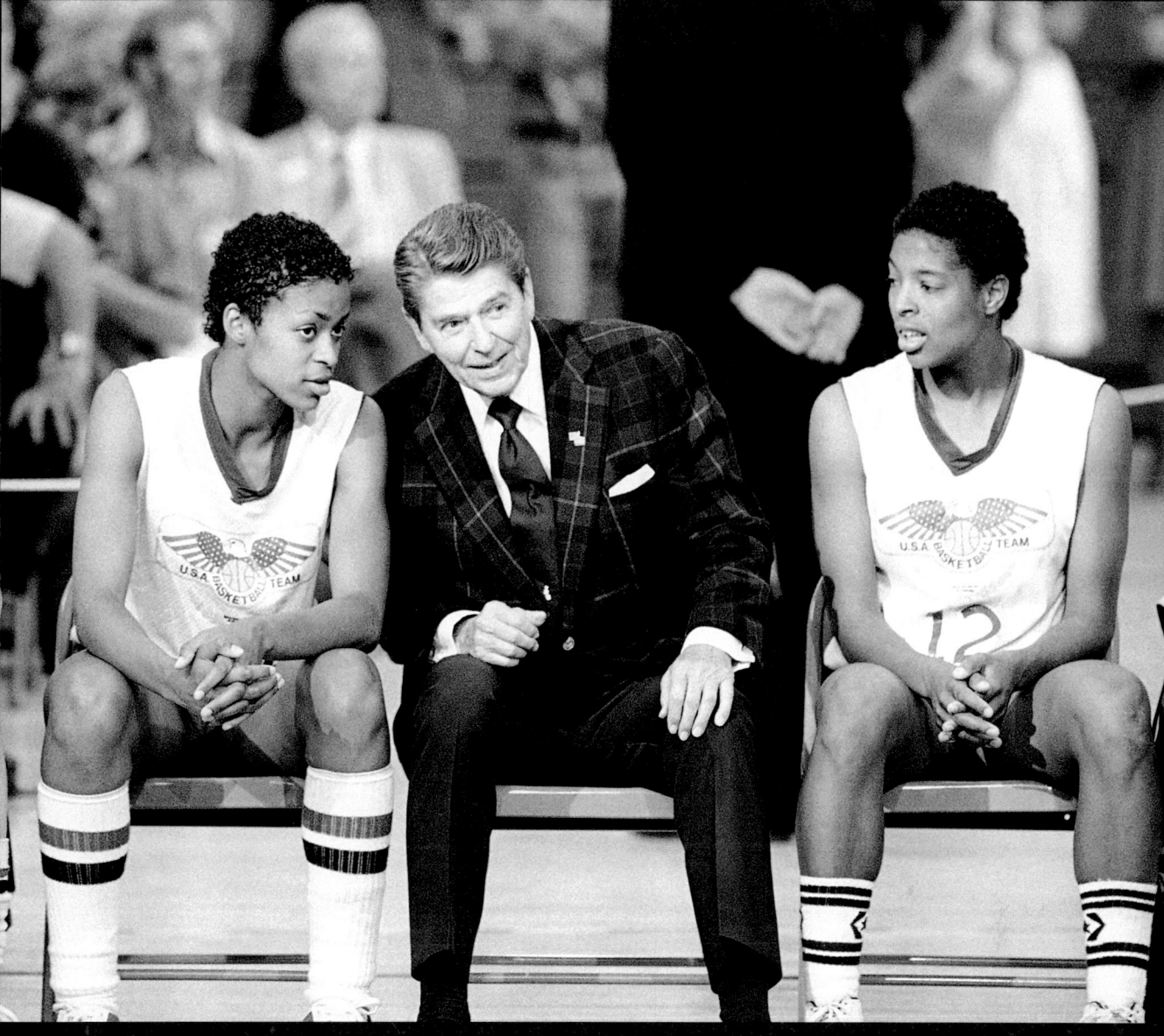

OPPOSITE: Teresa Weatherspoon had an incredible stretch in the spring/summer of 1988: She won the NCAA title with Louisiana Tech, won the Wade Trophy as the national POY, and finished the summer by winning an Olympic gold medal in Seoul. "The moment that you receive a gold medal, that's precious. And that's something you'll never forget," she said decades later. "You'll never forget the look and the smile on your teammates' faces when you accomplish a dream."

ABOVE: Pam McGee chats with President Ronald Reagan during his visit to the US Olympic Training Center in Colorado Springs ahead of the 1984 Los Angeles Olympics. Carol Menken-Shaudt (left) and Cathy Boswell (right) look on.

TERESA EDWARDS

The Gold Standard

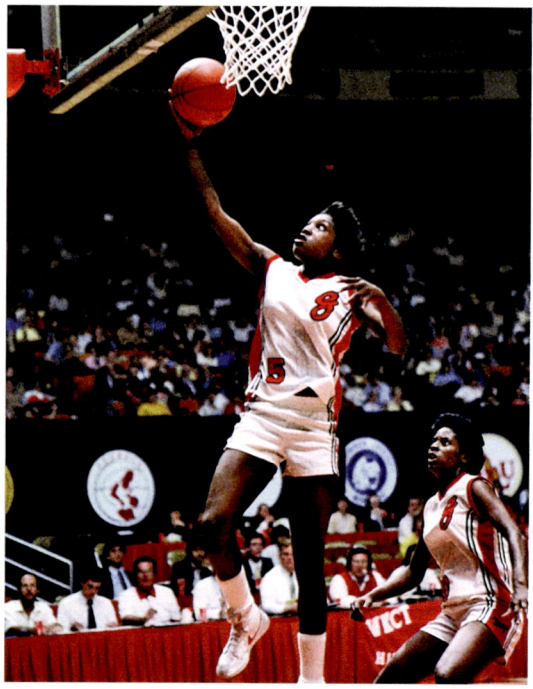

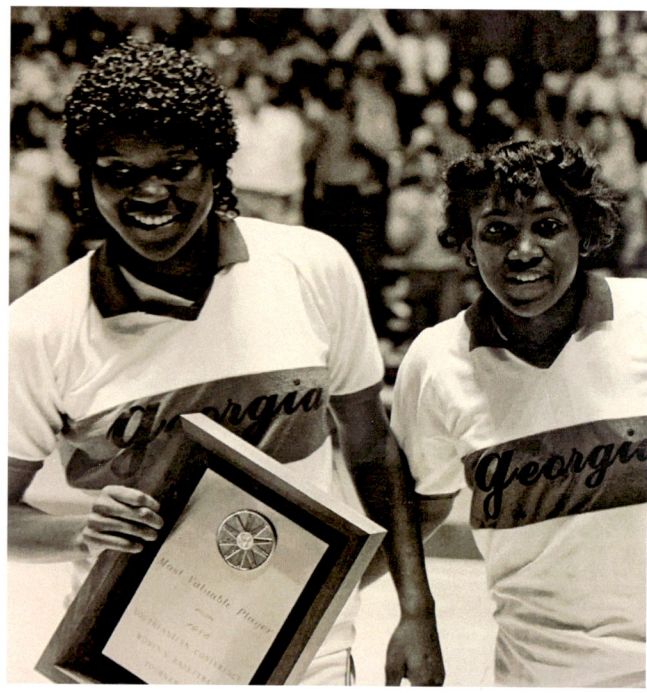

"She came downcourt going lickety-sizzle and bounced a pass behind her back left-handed to a teammate who laid it in. You could tell then that she was going places."

This was Tom Lehman, the president of the Chamber of Commerce in Cairo, Georgia, reflecting on watching local kid Teresa Edwards. He was describing a game that had taken place when she was just fifteen. She would be generating those kinds of highlights for the next two decades. Edwards was selected as the youngest member of the 1984 Olympic team. (She turned twenty the week before the Opening Ceremonies.) Every other player had been on the roster for a previous international competition, such as the Pan-Am Games. Not Edwards. The guard made a strong impression at trials shortly after leading the University of Georgia to its first Final Four. Her passing was wonderful, yes, but it was her defensive effort that especially stood out to coach Pat Summitt.

It was just the start of an Olympic career that would last decades. Edwards would go on to shine in Seoul in 1988, experience the frustration of bronze in Barcelona in 1992, find redemption in Atlanta in 1996, and do a victory lap in Sydney in 2000. She was the first woman to play basketball in five Olympics.

ABOVE LEFT: Teresa Edwards led the Lady Bulldogs to two Final Fours.

ABOVE RIGHT: Edwards was a two-time All-American alongside close friend and teammate Katrina McClain (left).

LYNETTE WOODARD

The First Lady

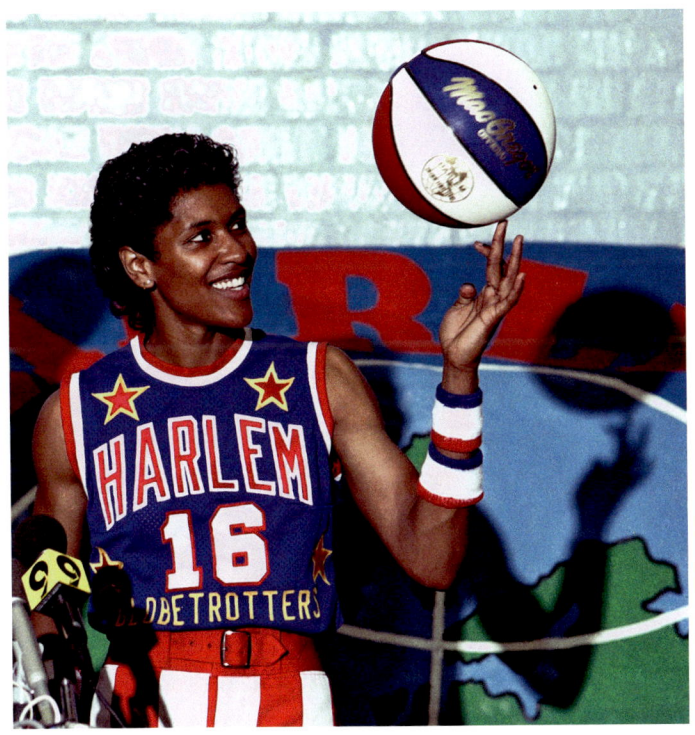

> "I want people to see me play with the Globetrotters and say a woman could also have the ability to play in the NBA."
>
> —LYNETTE WOODARD TO *THE NEW YORK TIMES*, 1985

By the fall of 1984, Lynette Woodard had done it all: four-time Kodak All-America guard at the University of Kansas, AIAW all-time leading scorer with 3,649 points, and team captain of her Olympic gold-medal team. But she felt in her spirit that she wasn't done. She kept training, awaiting another opportunity to showcase her skill at the highest level. Then she saw an announcement in the *USA Today*'s "Tip-Off" sports section that said the Harlem Globetrotters planned to go coed for the 1985–86 season. "My vision blurred," Woodard recounted on *The Doc Holliday Show* in 2022. "I looked again, and my heart just started palpitating."

Woodard grew up in Wichita, Kansas, with Globetrotter posters dotting her walls. She was a fan of the fancy handles and razzling routines but a bigger fan of what they stood for. The New York Harlem Globetrotters originated in the late 1920s to combat segregation by showcasing an all-Black, all-male roster's skills and outgoing personalities. By the fifties, they were goodwill ambassadors, even performing in front of 75,000 fans in Berlin in August 1951. Woodard's cousin, Hubert "Geese" Ausbie, thrilled Globetrotter audiences for twenty-four years. She wore the red, white, and blue Globetrotter wristbands he gifted her in every game while playing at Kansas—the opportunity to wear the stars and stripes as a pro was her lifelong dream.

Woodard and twenty-five other women traveled to Charlotte, North Carolina, the summer of 1985 to try out for the lone female roster spot. Woodard checked all the boxes; she had the fundamentals, the tricks, and the megawatt smile. That October, she became the first woman on a men's professional basketball team, and got to travel the world doing what she loved. Woodard told *The New York Times*: "I'm in basketball heaven."

ABOVE: Lynette Woodard at her introductory press conference as the first female Harlem Globetrotter, October 7, 1985, in Burbank, California.

NANCY LIEBERMAN

Lady Magic

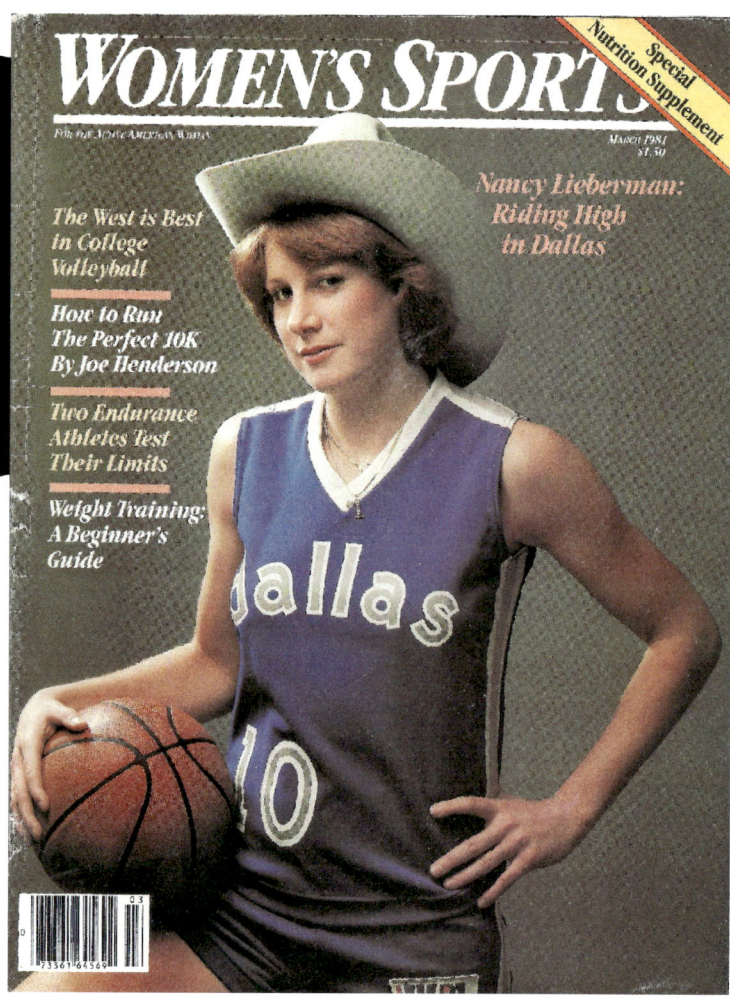

Nancy Lieberman grew up in Queens, New York, playing local boys in pickup and making regular trips to famous Rucker Park in Harlem. She eventually earned the nickname Lady Magic—she was such a slick passer that she reminded folks of Magic Johnson. Lieberman was just eighteen when she became the youngest basketball player to get a medal at the 1976 Olympics. She then breezed through college ball, winning two AIAW national championships at Old Dominion, and she was a no-brainer as the No. 1 pick for the Dallas Diamonds in the 1980 WBL Draft. But as she waited for her season to start with the Diamonds, she wanted to keep her game sharp, and Lieberman decided to go back to her roots: She wanted to toughen herself up by playing with the boys. And so Lieberman entered the New York Pro Summer League, suiting up alongside a group of former college players, fringe NBAers, and even a few big names. "She's not a woman out there," Nate Archibald told *Sports Illustrated*. "She's a player."

ABOVE: While Lieberman's biggest headlines came from playing alongside men in summer leagues, she got legitimate publicity for her regular gig with the Dallas Diamonds, too. She averaged 26.3 points a game and was named Rookie of the Year in 1981. After the original version of the Diamonds folded that year with the collapse of the WBL, she came back, ultimately joining its reincarnation in WABA in 1984.

ANOTHER SHOT AT PRO BALL

The Women's American Basketball Association (1984)

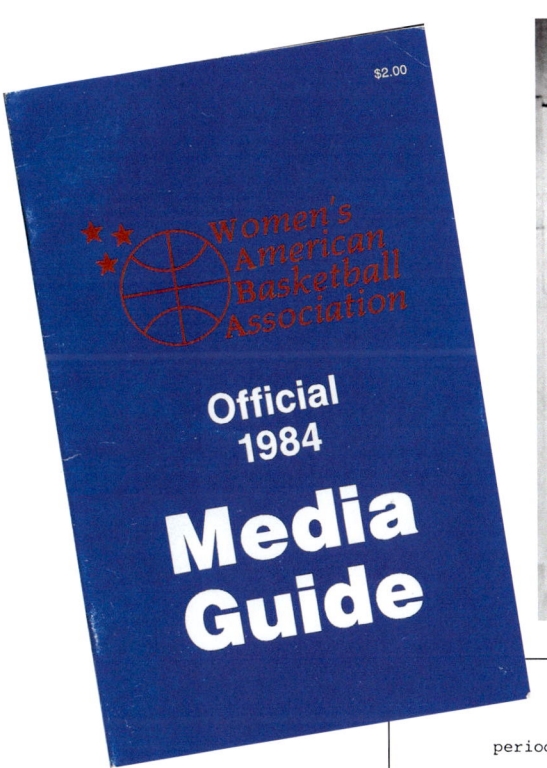

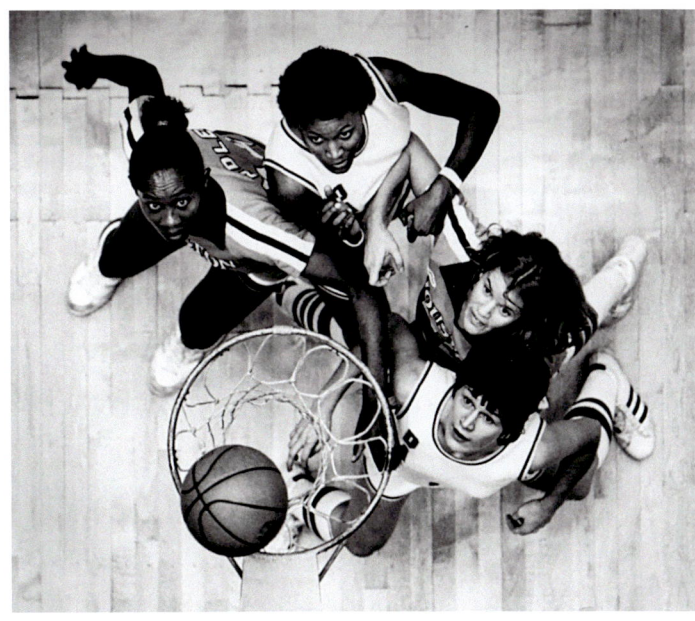

2.8 Contract Year.

The Contract Year is the ~~twelve (12)~~ *Three* 3 consecutive-month period from *October 7, 1984* to ~~October~~ *January 1, 1985* each year during the term of this Contract.

The WBL's founder, Bill Byrne, was undeterred after his first women's pro basketball league folded in 1981. He set out to start another one. The Women's American Basketball Association would have the same feel as his first endeavor, with even some of the same mega names, such as "Machine Gun" Molly Bolin and Nancy "Lady Magic" Lieberman. Tipping off on October 7, 1984, the league spanned five cities—Atlanta Comets, Chicago Spirit, Columbus Minks, Houston Shamrocks, Virginia Wave, and the resurrected Dallas Diamonds.

Financial troubles brewed early, however. By Thanksgiving, half the clubs had disbanded. Soon after, Byrne and the other league owners decided that the December All-Star game would be the final championship. The Dallas Diamonds were the runaway favorite. League MVP Lieberman, alongside '84 Olympic gold medalist Pam McGee, sprinted to a 19–2 record. For the Finals, they pitted the Diamonds against a hodgepodge of WABA All-Stars. The Diamonds won 101–94 in front of an estimated 1,500 fans at Southern Methodist University's Moody Coliseum. The league would fold after a single season.

TOP LEFT: In 1984, the WABA aimed to be another opportunity for women's pro hoops, but it was short-lived.

TOP RIGHT: Just as these WABA players waited for a rebound in 1984, they waited to see if this would be the professional league to stick.

ABOVE: A standard WABA player contract shows a revised three-month promise.

MATTER OF FACT
1980s

Numbers, People, and Moments That Defined the Era

NUMBERS

4

Triple doubles Ann Meyers had in the 1980 WBL season with the New Jersey Gems.

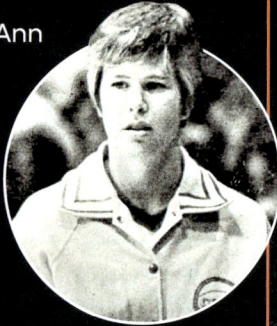

898

Points Tina Hutchinson scored as a freshman for San Diego State in 1984, a freshman record that would stand until 2024.

11.84 MILLION

CBS viewers for the 1983 Final USC vs. Louisiana Tech. Up 35 percent from the first NCAA championship game.

37–0

Record for University of Texas en route to the 1986 national title. Led by head coach Jody Conradt, the Longhorns became the first women's NCAA DI program to complete a flawless, undefeated season.

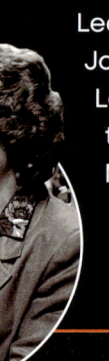

PEOPLE

West Virginia center **GEORGEANN WELLS** became the first woman to dunk in a college game, on December 21, 1984. While it was photographed and widely covered in the news, it was thought for decades that no video footage existed, until a tape was discovered in 2009.

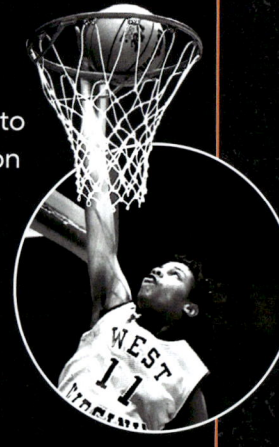

Georgia's **JANET HARRIS** was the first NCAA player to score 2,500 points and collect 1,250 rebounds.

Bethune-Cookman's **GWEN DAVIS** made 111 three-point field goals in 1988, which led the nation. It was the first season where the NCAA recognized three-pointers.

Pam and Paula McGee, Joyce Walker, Linda Page, and **SANDRA HODGE** were among the women who tried out for the Harlem Globetrotters with Lynette Howard in 1985. Hodge would make the team in 1987 and play in South America.

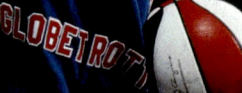

MARCH 31, 1982

Drake's **LORRI BAUMAN** sets the record for most points in an NCAA tournament game by dropping 50 in a loss to Maryland.

1982

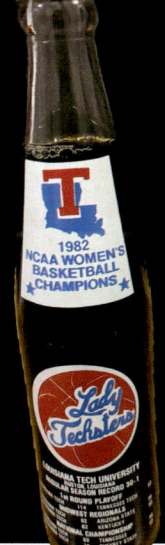

Coca-Cola made a commemorative soda label to celebrate Louisiana Tech's championship. One thing the **LADY TECHSTERS** did *not* get? Championship rings. The first NCAA women's basketball title did not include any of the classic hardware. They eventually, in 2017, received their rings, for the thirty-fifth anniversary of their championship.

FEB. 28, 1984

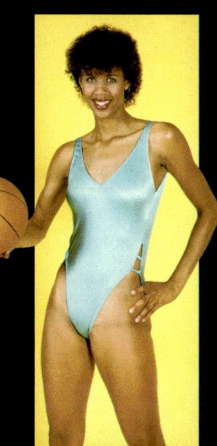

CHERYL MILLER appeared onstage during Donna Summer's "She Works Hard for the Money" live performance at the Grammy Awards. Miller was Hollywood and eighties personified.

SEPT. 27, 1988

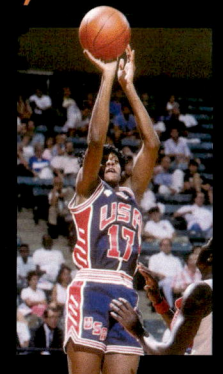

The US beats the Soviet Union in women's basketball at the Olympics for the first time, 102–88, during the semifinals of the '88 Games in Seoul.

1987

Total attendance for the women's **NCAA TOURNAMENT** surpasses 100,000 for the first time.

CHAPTER 4

1990s

THE DREAMERS

PRIME TV SLOTS, SOLD-OUT ARENAS, LUCRATIVE ENDORSEMENT DEALS—IT WAS NO LONGER JUST A DREAM. WOMEN'S BASKETBALL HAD ARRIVED.

RIGHT: Jennifer Azzi and the 1996 Olympic team celebrate after defeating Brazil 111–87 in the gold-medal game in Atlanta, Georgia.

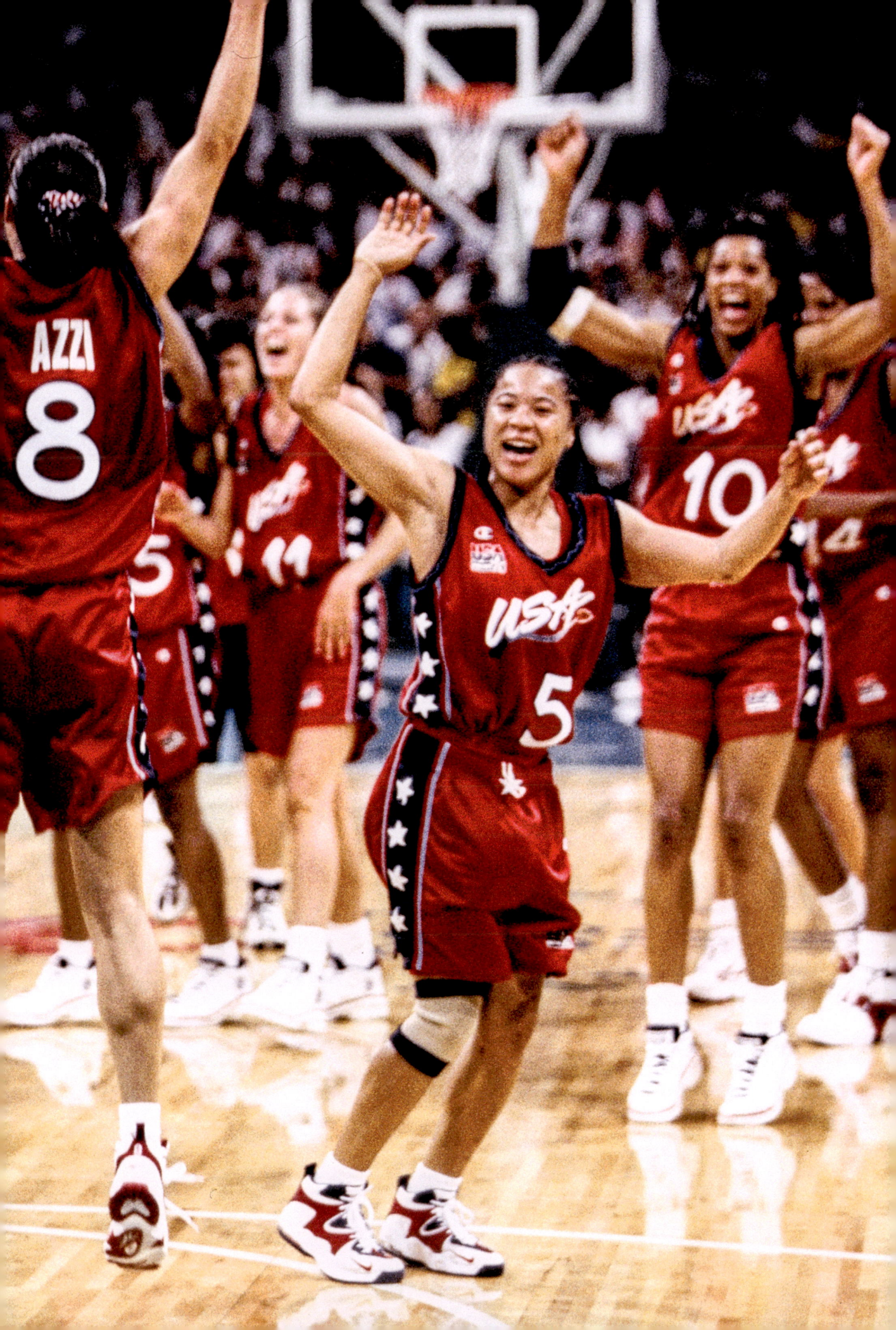

MARCH MADNESS

Unforgettable '90s Final Fours

They don't call it March Madness for nothing. These nineties Final Four hoopers danced their way to iconic title games for a shot at one shining moment.

Stanford 88, Auburn 81
April 1, 1990

Future Olympic players Jennifer Azzi and Katy Steding put together a balanced attack to help get Stanford head coach Tara VanDerveer her first championship.

Tennessee 70, Virginia 67, in overtime
March 31, 1991

Virginia was up by 5 points with 1:25 to play, but a series of frustrating late fouls and unfortunate missed shots ended up sending the game to overtime, and they ended up handing it to Tennessee. It marked the end of the road for a deep, talented Virginia team featuring Dawn Staley and identical twins Heather and Heidi Burge.

Texas Tech 84, Ohio State 82
April 5, 1993

Sheryl Swoopes scored a Final Four record of 47 points in the upset, being named the tournament's outstanding player. Her 144 total tournament points (35.4 ppg) in a five-game stretch still holds today, thirty years later.

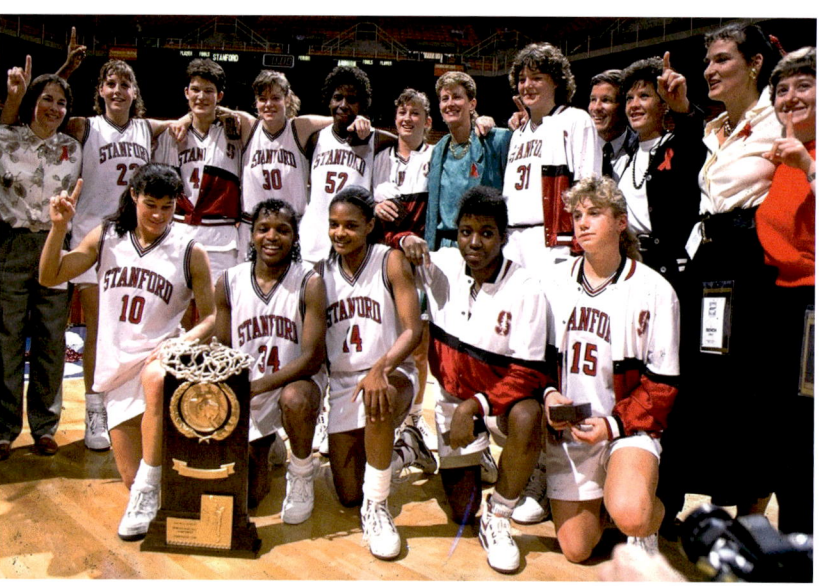

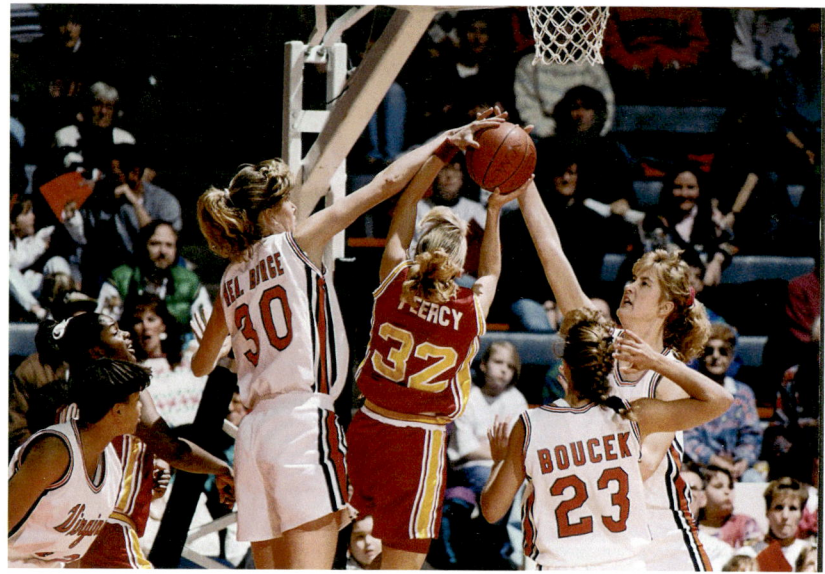

TOP: Stanford's first national championship came in Coach VanDerveer's fifth season as head coach.

ABOVE: At six-five, the Burge twins of Virginia gave a new definition of being double-teamed.

OPPOSITE: Sheryl Swoopes jumps for joy after leading the Red Raiders to their lone national title.

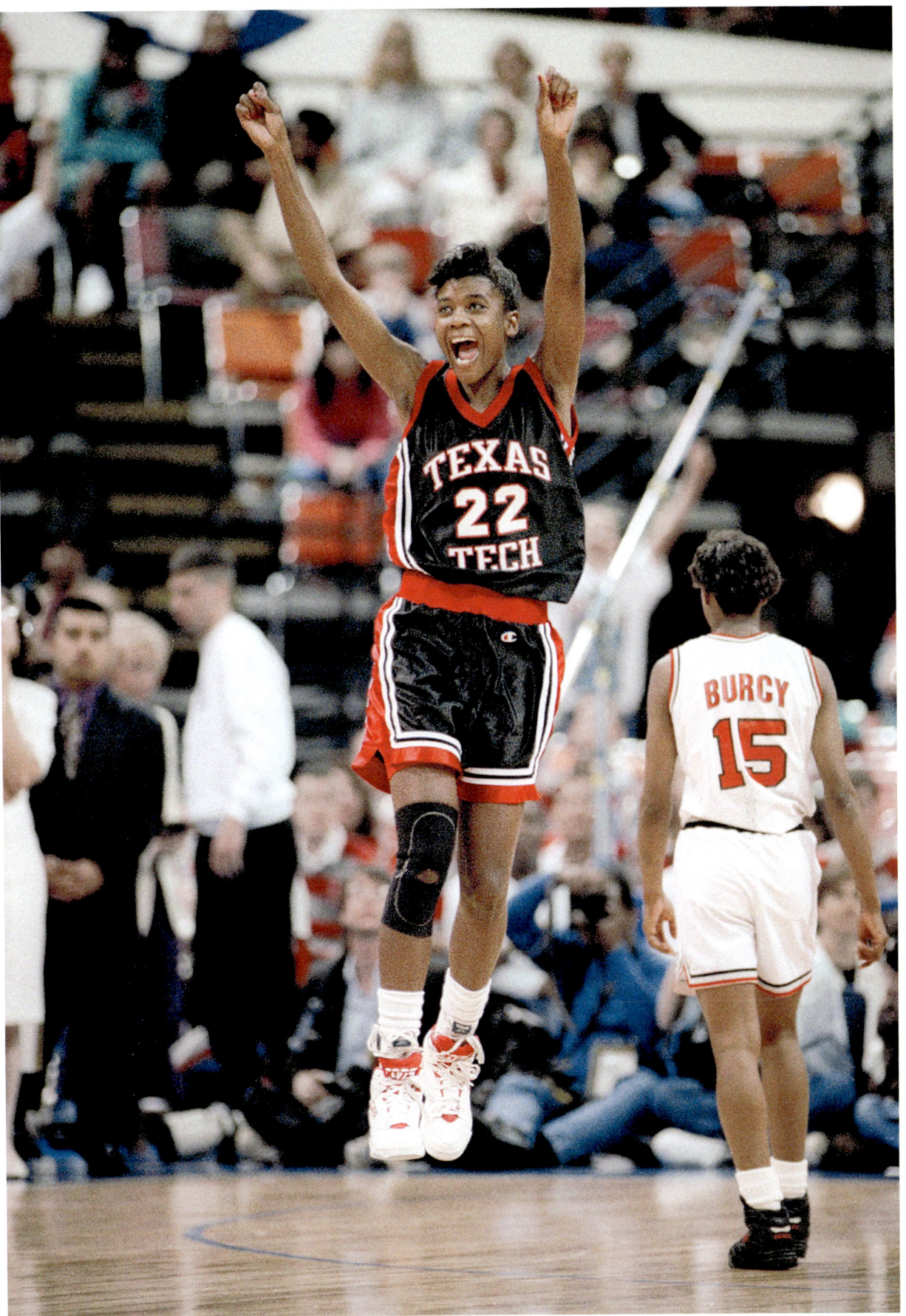

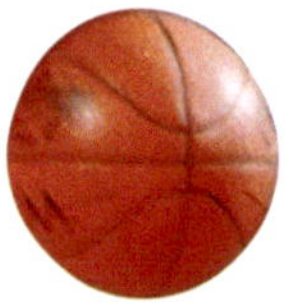

North Carolina 60, Louisiana Tech 59

April 3, 1994

North Carolina was trailing by 2 points with 0.7 seconds left, and Coach Sylvia Hatchell burned back-to-back time-outs. The first huddle's play was drawn for a six-foot-five center, Sylvia Crawley, to catch a lob and finish at the rim, but Louisiana Tech quickly caught on and clogged the paint. The next whistle, a new one was drawn up—a baseline out-of-bounds play that would go for the win. Charlotte Smith started on the ball-side block in a box set. On the whistle, she screened diagonal. Tech's miscommunication left Smith wide open for a weak-side three. The hometown kid sinks it. UNC's lone title is stamped as one of the most thrilling title finishes ever.

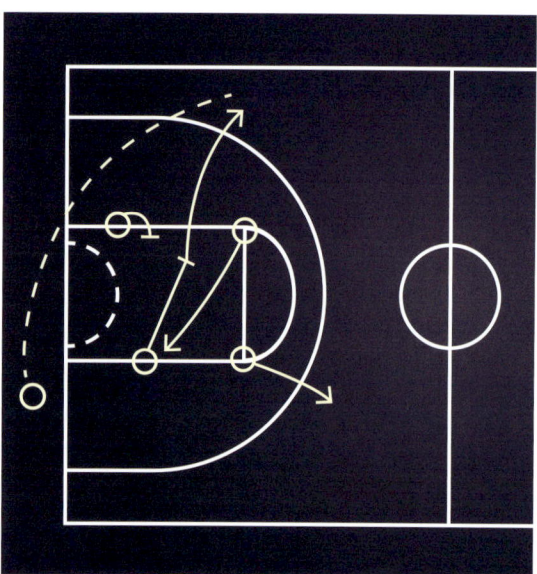

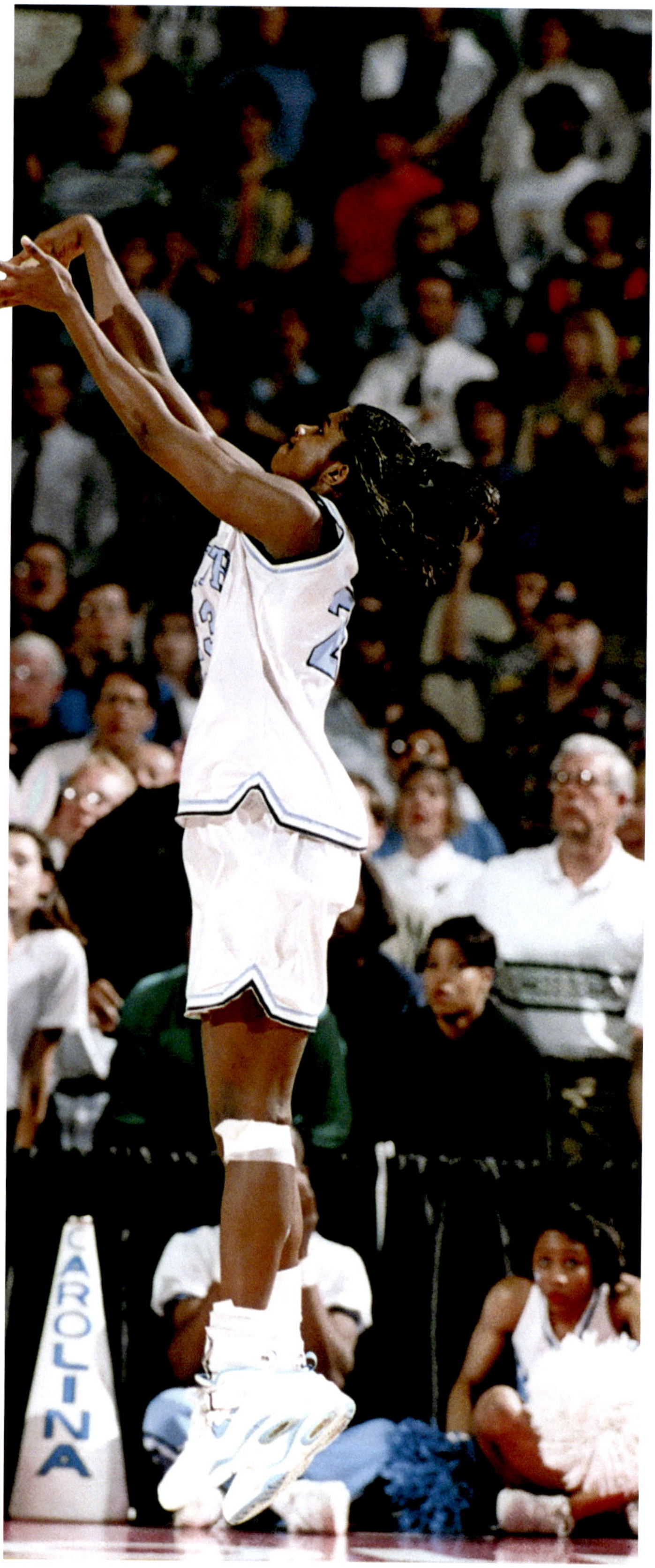

ABOVE: The championship-winning play that North Carolina's coach Sylvia Hatchell drew up.

RIGHT: Charlotte Smith became a household name after sinking this three-pointer at the buzzer. She finished the game with 20 points and twenty-three rebounds—the latter, a record that still holds today.

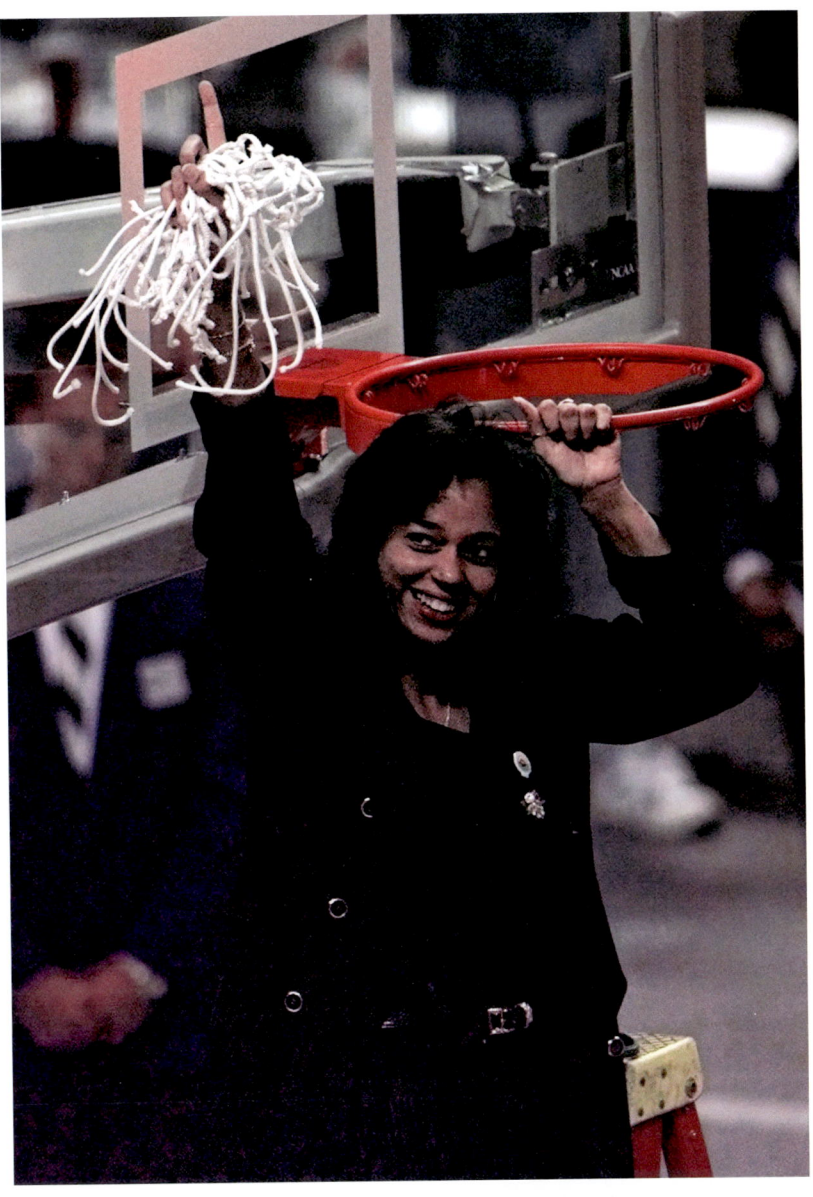

Purdue 62, Duke 45
March 28, 1999

When the game clock struck zeros on March 28, 1999, in San Jose, California, Purdue and their head coach Carolyn Peck were national champions. The top-ranked Boilermakers handily beat Duke, 62–45. It was Peck's last game before heading to the WNBA to be coach and GM to the Orlando Miracle. The 17,753 fans in the San Jose Arena went wild. Pom-poms waved toward the court. The Purdue band sounded off. Coach Peck, thirty-three, had just become the NCAA's first Black woman to win a national championship. She'd eagerly waited for this day; she'd been tying an old piece of gifted championship net into her game-day shoes for years as motivation. And when it was her turn to climb up the ladder to cut down her title net—with fans chanting, "Please don't go!" in the background—she snipped it with a smile, her index finger signaling "number 1."

ABOVE LEFT: Carolyn Peck became the first Black woman head coach to win an NCAA Division I national championship in 1999 with Purdue. There wouldn't be another championship-winning Black female coach for eighteen years.

LEFT: Wade Trophy winner Stephanie White cuts down her piece of the net. The two-time All-American is the Boilermakers' third all-time leading scorer.

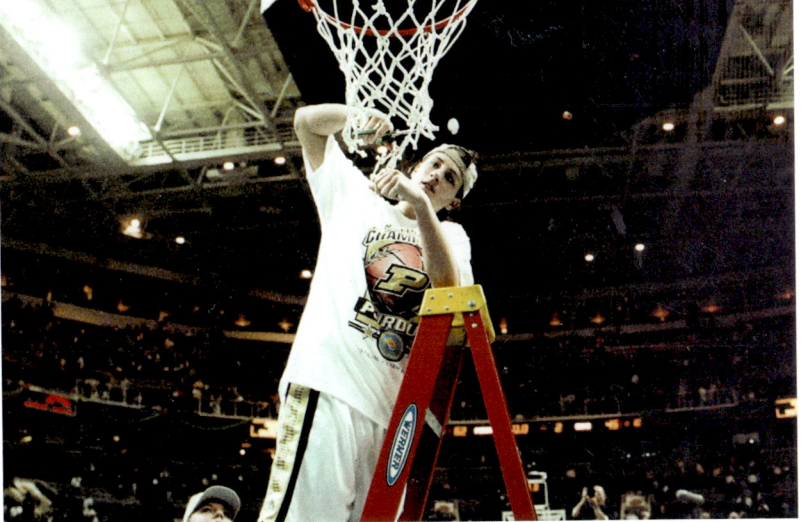

THE RIVALRY

The Beginnings of UConn vs. Tennessee

The first-ever basketball game between UConn and Tennessee was only a backup plan. It nonetheless sparked a rivalry that defined a decade and beyond.

In the summer of 1994, ESPN executive Carol Stiff began to schedule what she hoped might be an elite college hoops matchup. She had a prime slot for 1 p.m. Eastern on Martin Luther King Jr. Day in January 1995. It was unusual to have that kind of platform any day other than Sunday, typically a losing battle against the NFL, but here was a rare chance for the spotlight. Children would be home from school. Adults would be off work. Stiff hoped they might all turn on ESPN and see a plucky, talented squad in search of its first title facing off against the reigning champions. It could be a rematch of the Elite Eight from March of 1994: She wanted the University of Connecticut versus the University of North Carolina.

There was just one catch. Network contractual obligations with the Big East would require the game be hosted by UConn. This got a firm *no* from UNC head coach Sylvia Hatchell. She'd love to play the game at home, she told Stiff, but she didn't want to play a tough opponent on the road in the middle of their conference schedule. Stiff laid out her idea: ESPN, holiday afternoon broadcast, Robin Roberts

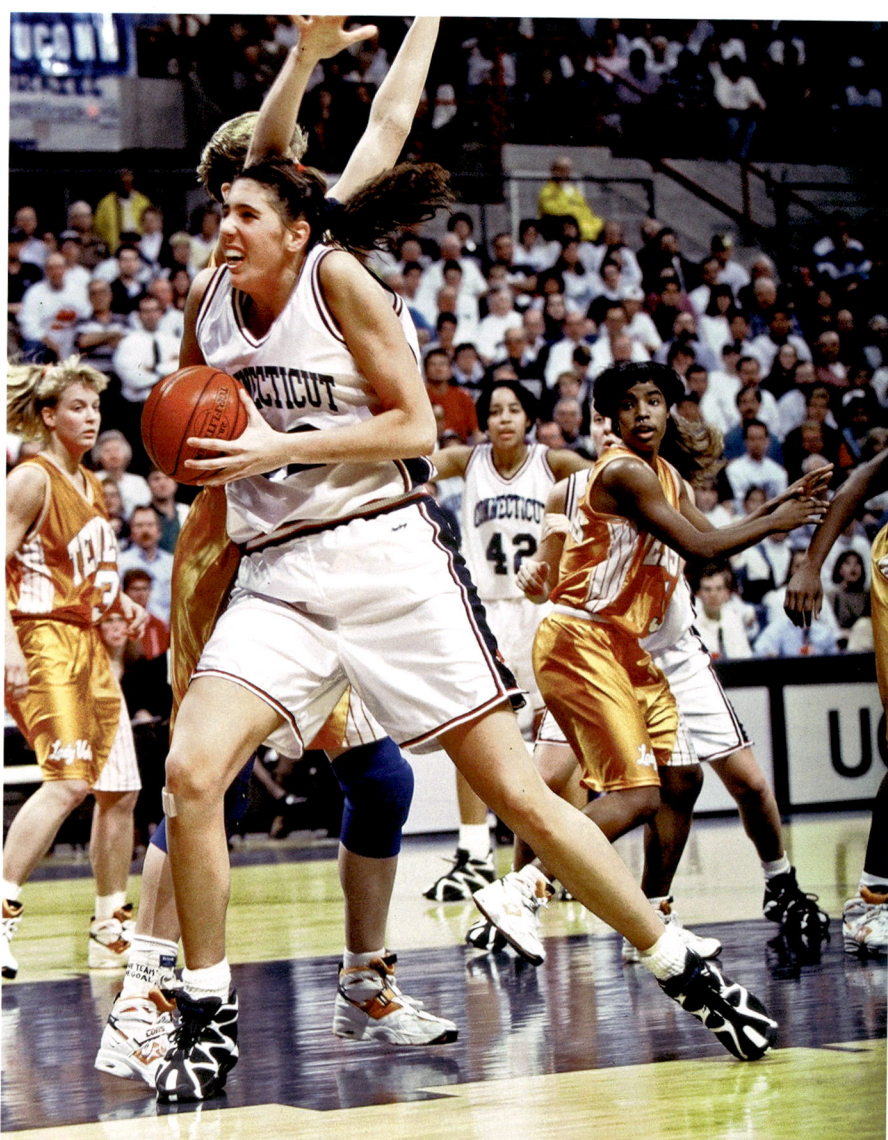

ABOVE: In 1995 and 1996, UConn and Tennessee played four times—twice in the regular season, once in the Final Four, once for a national championship. All four games were decided by single digits. Six-foot-seven UConn star Kara Wolters (*above, with ball*) led all scorers in the first of those matchups with 18 points.

OPPOSITE: UConn's victory over Tennessee in January 1995 gave the program its first-ever No. 1 ranking.

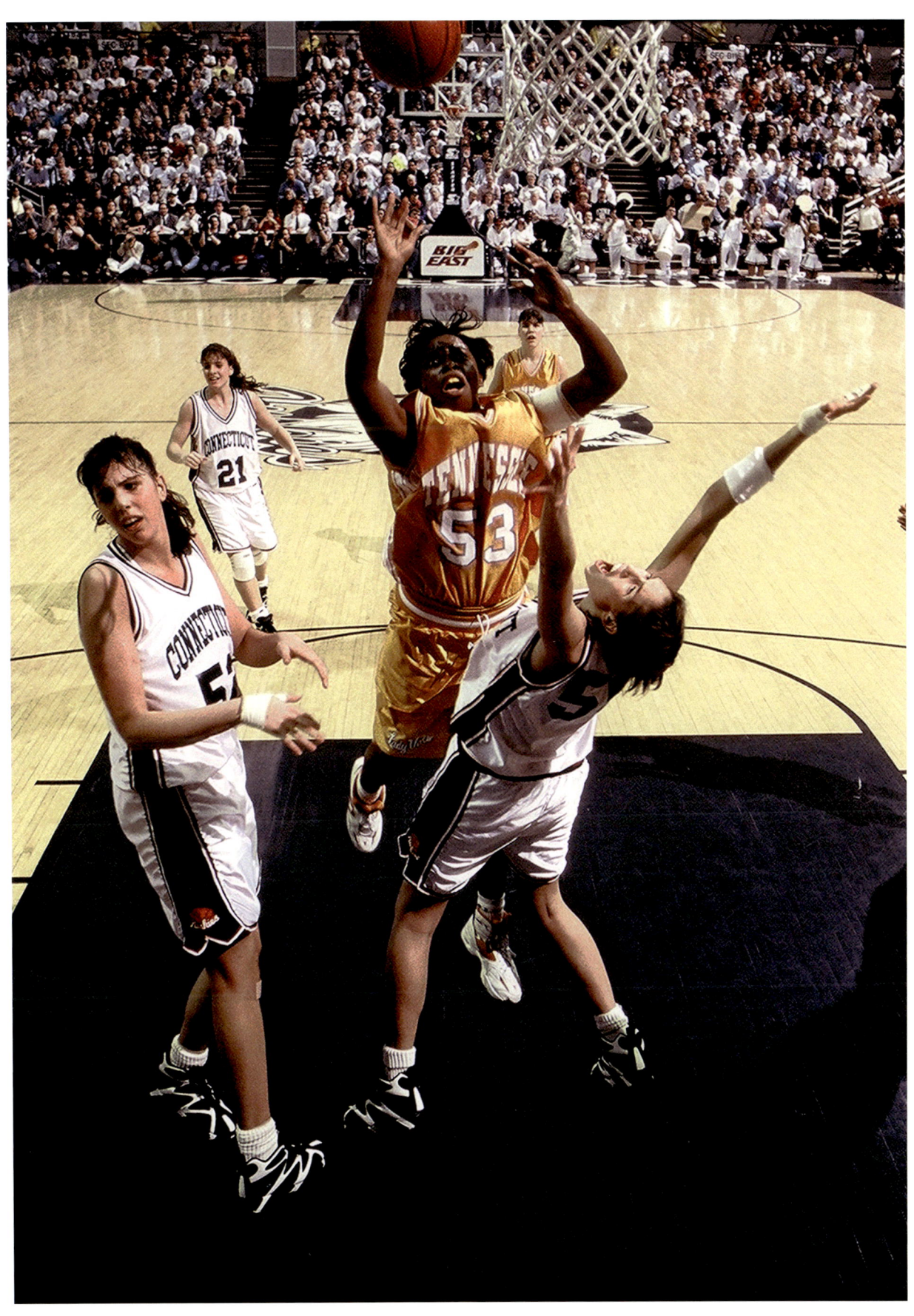

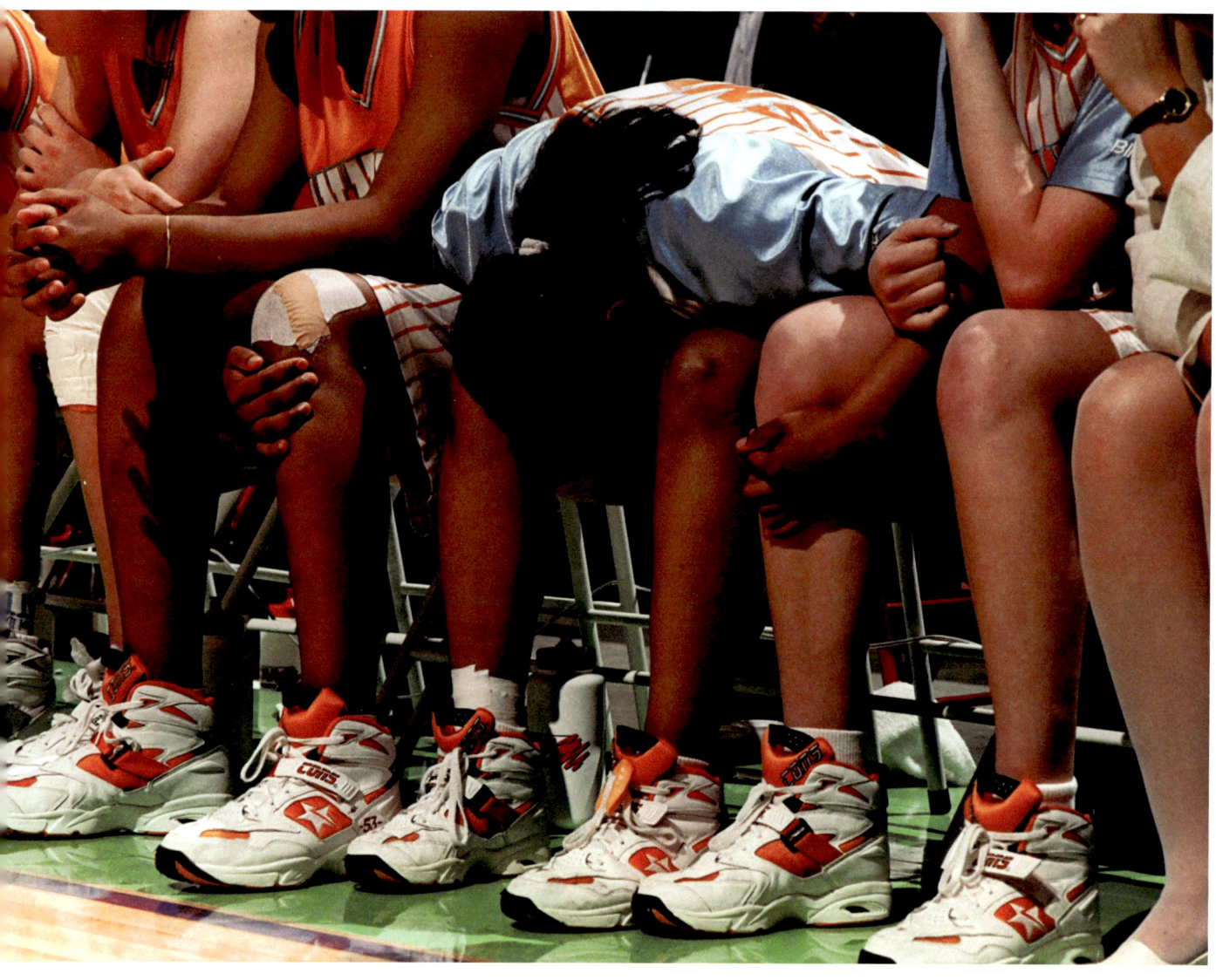

in the booth? *No, thanks*, said Hatchell. And so the broadcast executive moved on.

Stiff's next call was to Pat Summitt at the University of Tennessee. The three-time champion coach was not much happier about scheduling a road game against tough competition amid their conference schedule. But she could see the vision: It could be tremendous for women's basketball. She agreed to do it, "for the good of the game," Stiff would later recall.

There would be more good in that game than anyone could have imagined. As mid-January approached, Tennessee was No. 1 in the country, and UConn was No. 2. Both were undefeated. It was not just an exciting matchup but a potential

championship preview. The premium broadcast window selected months earlier would be home to what now seemed like the game of the year.

"Win or lose, this will be a great game for women's basketball, great for this opportunity on national live television," UConn coach Geno Auriemma told *The New York Times*.

The game sold out weeks in advance. The Connecticut crowd wore T-shirts reading BATTLE OF THE BEST, and they were treated to a remarkable,

---

ABOVE: Tennessee lost each of the first three games it played against UConn. Each loss was agonizing. But the program got revenge by winning four of the next five.

dominating win: No. 2 UConn, 77; No. 1 Tennessee, 66. "History is made, and Number One UConn now takes over!" Roberts declared on the broadcast. The upstart program had knocked off the heavyweight. As it turned out, the game *had* been a championship preview, and with a title on the line for the rematch in April, it would be No. 1 UConn, 70; No. 2 Tennessee, 64. It helped establish a rivalry that became the fiercest in the game.

It was defined by its coaches. Auriemma and Summitt had little in common besides their basketball acumen and their strong personalities. They would become two of the winningest leaders in women's basketball. (Of the sixteen national championships between 1995 and 2010, twelve featured either UConn or Tennessee, and four of those featured *both*.) Many of their most iconic matchups would be the ones played at the NCAA tournament. But for a decade and a half, they kept playing each other in season, too. What started as a happy accident of television scheduling had become a fierce tradition. And the way it ended was just more evidence of how personal the rivalry had become.

Summitt declined to schedule the game, beginning in 2008, after she accused Auriemma of recruiting violations.

"I think she should just come out and say she's not playing us because she hates my guts," Auriemma told the *Hartford Courant*. "She should just say that [Geno is] a dope, a smart-ass and then everyone could say that they agree with her."

The annual game was eventually revived in 2020. It continued a story in which each chapter might be described just as UConn senior forward Rebecca Lobo had described the first one in 1995.

"The electricity was bouncing off the walls," Lobo told reporters. "This is an example of what women's basketball can be."

THREE ICONIC GAMES FROM THE RIVALRY

1. **March 29, 1996: No. 4 Tennessee, 88; No. 2 UConn, 83; in overtime**
The Final Four. Overtime. This one had it all—and it was Tennessee's first win over UConn after losing its first three games in the rivalry. Lady Vols guard Michelle Marcinak hit a pair of clutch free throws to seal it.

2. **February 2, 2000: No. 4 Tennessee, 72; No. 1 UConn, 71**
The only loss UConn experienced all season. Tennessee came back from a first-half deficit and got a game winner from Semeka Randall.

3. **January 4, 2003: No. 3 UConn, 63; No. 5 Tennessee, 62; in overtime**
A Diana Taurasi performance for the ages. She hit a sixty-foot heave as the buzzer expired to tie this one going into halftime . . . and then hit a dagger of a three as regulation expired to send it to overtime . . . and then landed a floater to win it all. She finished with 25 points, eight rebounds, four blocks, and three steals.

PAT SUMMITT

A 1,098–208 RECORD OVER THIRTY-EIGHT YEARS, EIGHT-TIME NATIONAL CHAMPION, EIGHTEEN FINAL FOURS, ZERO LOSING SEASONS

Written by: Jordan Robinson, *Ren.* magazine, published by Kamp A.B.C., 2023

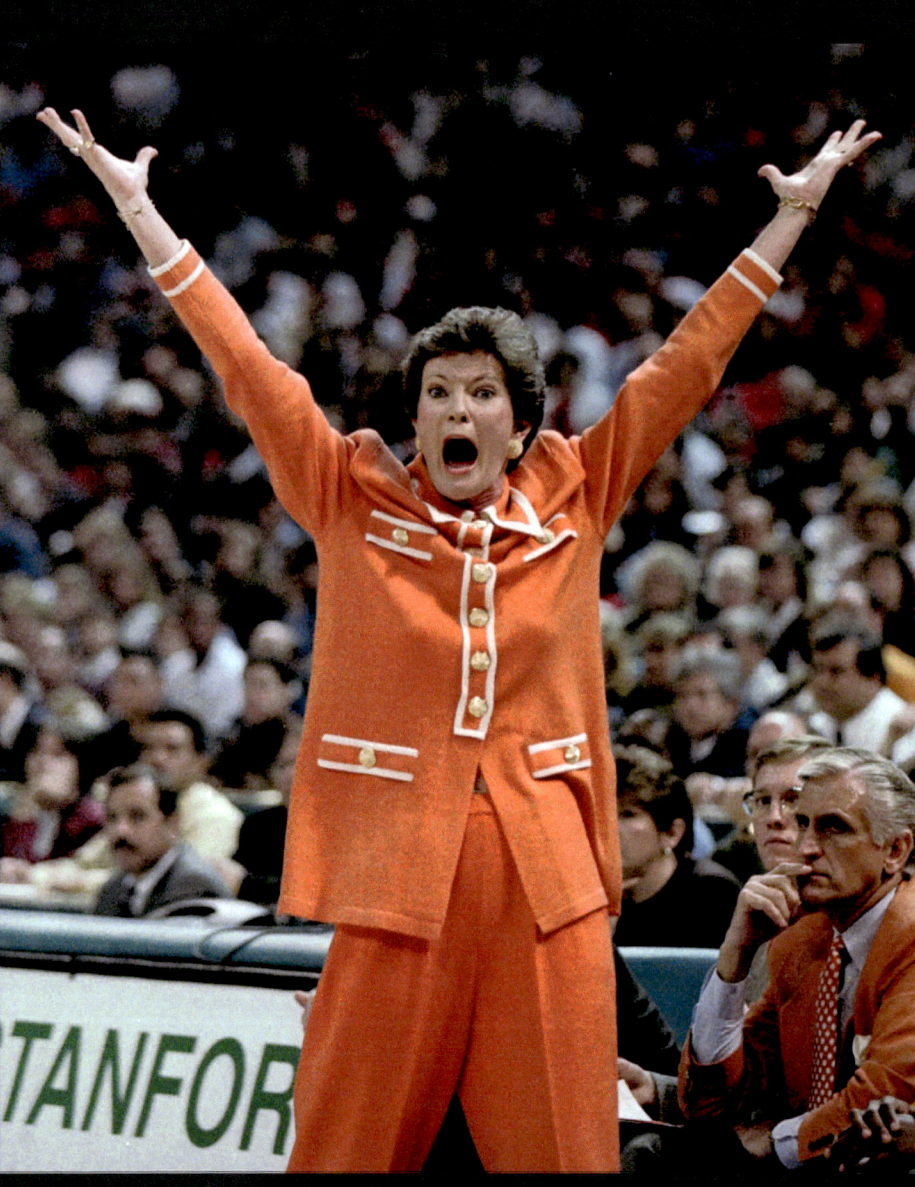

ABOVE: Coach Pat Summitt was always a spectacle on the sideline, from her gestures to her bold outfits. On March 31, 1996, she's animated during Tennessee's 83–65 win over Georgia in the championship game.

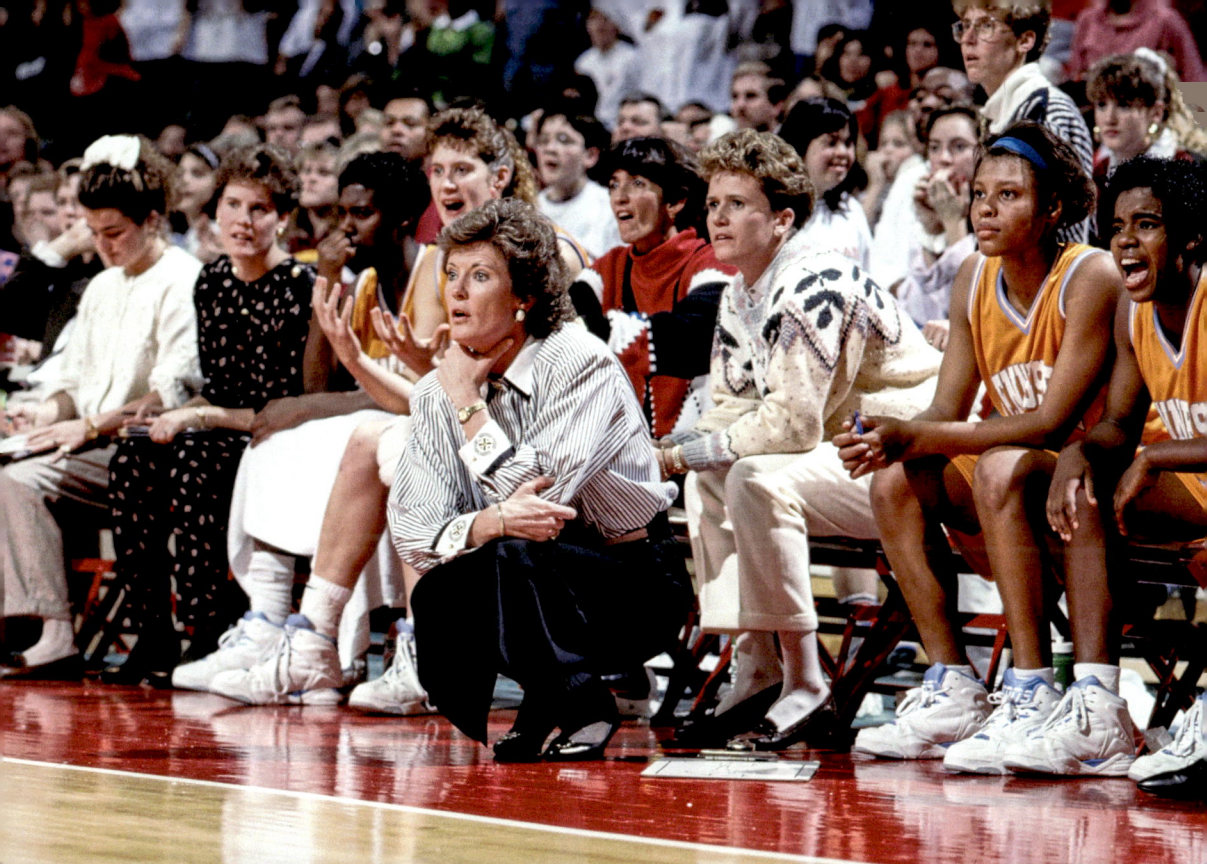

f you *did not* want to transfer from the University of Tennessee, something was wrong," Nikki Fargas, Tennessee guard (1990–94), said. "So many of us picked up the phone and said, 'Mom, I can't do this.'"

That was thanks to Pat Summitt. At only thirty-eight years old, the 1990–91 season was already Summitt's seventeenth year coaching. She had coached a national team to gold, tallied 400-plus wins, and made seven Final Four appearances by this point. Building a championship-level culture was what she knew how to do.

Despite how Summitt's résumé made it look, it wasn't easy. It was 4:30-a.m. wake-ups for wind sprints on the Tennessee track. It was accepting nothing less than perfection when doing drills. It was hard work.

She had kicked the 1989–90 team out of their palacelike locker room and squeezed them into the visitors' for five weeks; she said they didn't deserve such comfort. Coach also demanded players sit in

the front three rows in their classrooms. If you miss a class, you miss a game.

One time, when she heard the team had gone partying the night before, Summitt plopped trash cans at all four corners of the court at an early morning practice. She told them to run until they puked.

"If you don't like discipline, if you don't want to be in a structured environment, Tennessee's not right for you," Summitt said to the *Tampa Bay Times* in 1999. "I tell kids, 'If you want to be the showboat, you go somewhere else. If you want to be on the showboat, then you come here. If you're lazy, stay as far away from me and our program as

---

ABOVE: Summitt accepted the grad assistant coaching job at Tennessee in 1974 at twenty-two. Two weeks later, she'd be offered the head coach position because the previous one quit. Here in 1992, Pat (age forty) had already notched over 150 wins. Nikki Fargas is second from right.

you can because you'll be miserable.' We work hard. We're not ashamed of it. We're proud of it."

Recruits heard the horror stories, but they still jumped at the opportunity to suit up for Summitt. They didn't want to just *play* college basketball; they wanted to win with the best.

Playing high-level hoops during March Madness became routine. Hoisting trophies and cutting down nets became muscle memory. Everyone knew that when Summitt's Lady Vols stepped on the court, they meant business.

"When we walked on the floor, I think teams were already spotting us ten," Fargas said. "We just knew that you weren't going to outhustle us. You weren't going to outwork us."

The 1991 championship game in New Orleans was special. It marked the ten-year anniversary of the NCAA Women's Final Four. The riveting ballgame went down to final free throws as Tennessee topped Dawn Staley's University of Virginia Cavaliers in overtime, 70–67. The Lady Vols were led by standout Dena Head's tournament record of 28 points. A clutch charge taken by freshman Fargas sealed the deal.

The nearly sold-out crowd of 7,865 fans in the Big Easy was electric. (Summitt's first win at Tennessee, in contrast, came in 1975 in front of a crowd of only fifty-three people.) The camera crew panned over the student section. Someone held a sign that read CAN'T BEAT SUMMITT. The letters CBS were bolded, a nod to the network airing the national championship. The youngest fan in the crowd? Summitt's seven-month-old son, Tyler, wearing a onesie with the UVA mascot circled and struck out.

Coach Summitt, in her classic white-blazer, pencil-skirt combo, fiercely paced the sideline as she always did. A smile appeared only after the final buzzer sounded. Atop a ladder, she held a freshly cut piece of the championship net and looked out to the roaring crowd. Her players beamed back at her.

"I won a thousand and ninety-eight games and eight national championships," Summit, who died in 2016 due to Alzheimer's, once said during her retirement. "But what I see are not the numbers, I see their faces."

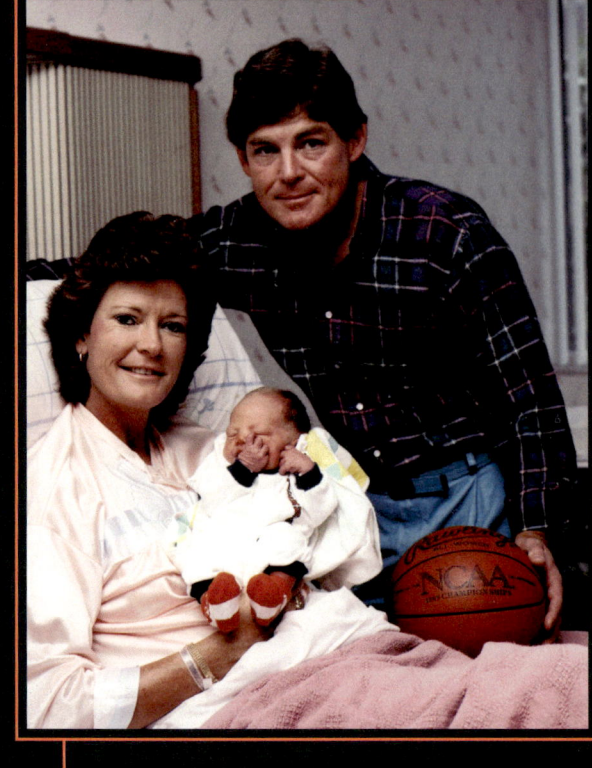

ABOVE: "Oh, I think my water broke," Summitt casually tells her long-time assistant coach, Mickie DeMoss. They'd just landed in Allentown, PA, for a recruiting visit. Despite her due date, Summitt was too stubborn to cancel the visit. She calls her doctor and gets the green light to continue to shmooze. Then contractions hit. Back on the plane, the flight crew was ready to make an emergency landing. DeMoss passed along a message to the cockpit from a heavy-breathing Summitt: "She's gonna have the baby on the plane or in Tennessee. It's sure as hell not going to be in Virginia." Ross Tyler Summitt was born on September 21, 1990, in Knoxville, just as Summitt desired.

Yeah, she pushed them during those three-hour practices. She yelled and screamed until her voice went hoarse. But she cared about all her players as young women.

"She did a great job of teaching you the real game. Not the one that's played ninety-four by fifty," Fargas says, "but the real game of life."

Summitt's famous "Definite Dozen" lists the twelve principles that encapsulate a championship program. Fargas tells me these same fundamentals, which led them to win the national championship in 1991, can lead anyone in business, personal life, or through academics. It was bigger than basketball for Pat.

Coach didn't subscribe to any particular *isms* or *movements* when it came to empowering women and shutting down societal gender norms. Her actions—and her trophy case—did all the talking. She constantly matched UT with the toughest programs in the country—like Geno Auriemma's University of Connecticut—to get more eyes on women's hoops. She had an all-female coaching staff and led the charge to ensure Tennessee had a separate athletic department dedicated to women's athletics. No hand-me-downs.

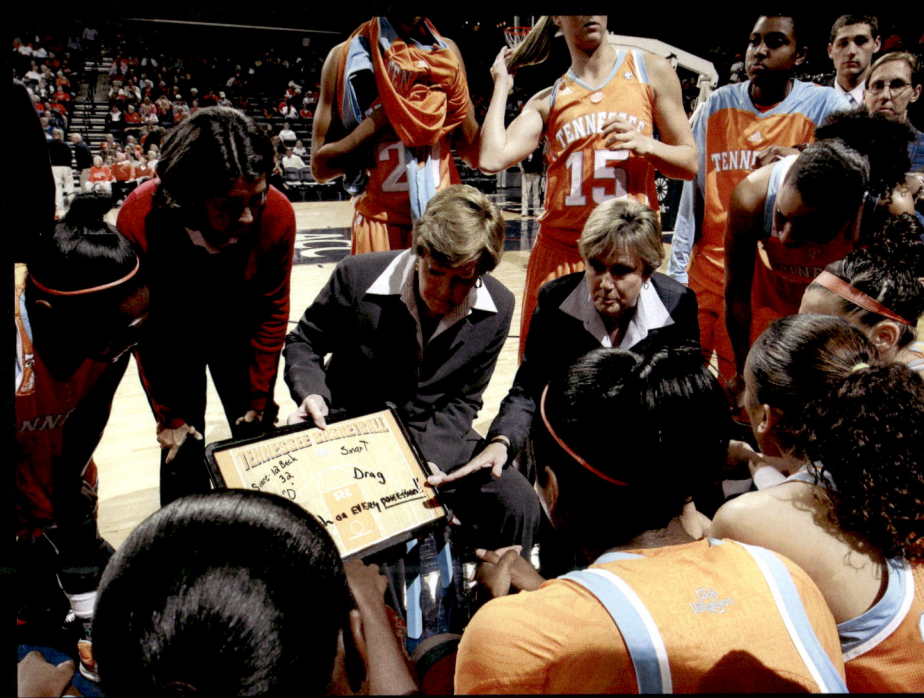

ABOVE: Summitt never had a losing season in her thirty-eight years as head coach. She is currently ranked the fourth-winningest coach (men's or women's), with those 1,098 wins.

PAT SUMMITT'S DEFINITE DOZEN

1. Respect Yourself and Others

2. Take Full Responsibility

3. Develop and Demonstrate Loyalty

4. Learn to Be a Great Communicator

5. Discipline Yourself So No One Else Has To

6. Make Hard Work Your Passion

7. Don't Just Work Hard, Work Smart

8. Put the Team Before Yourself

9. Make Winning an Attitude

10. Be a Competitor

11. Change Is a Must

12. Handle Success Like You Handle Failure

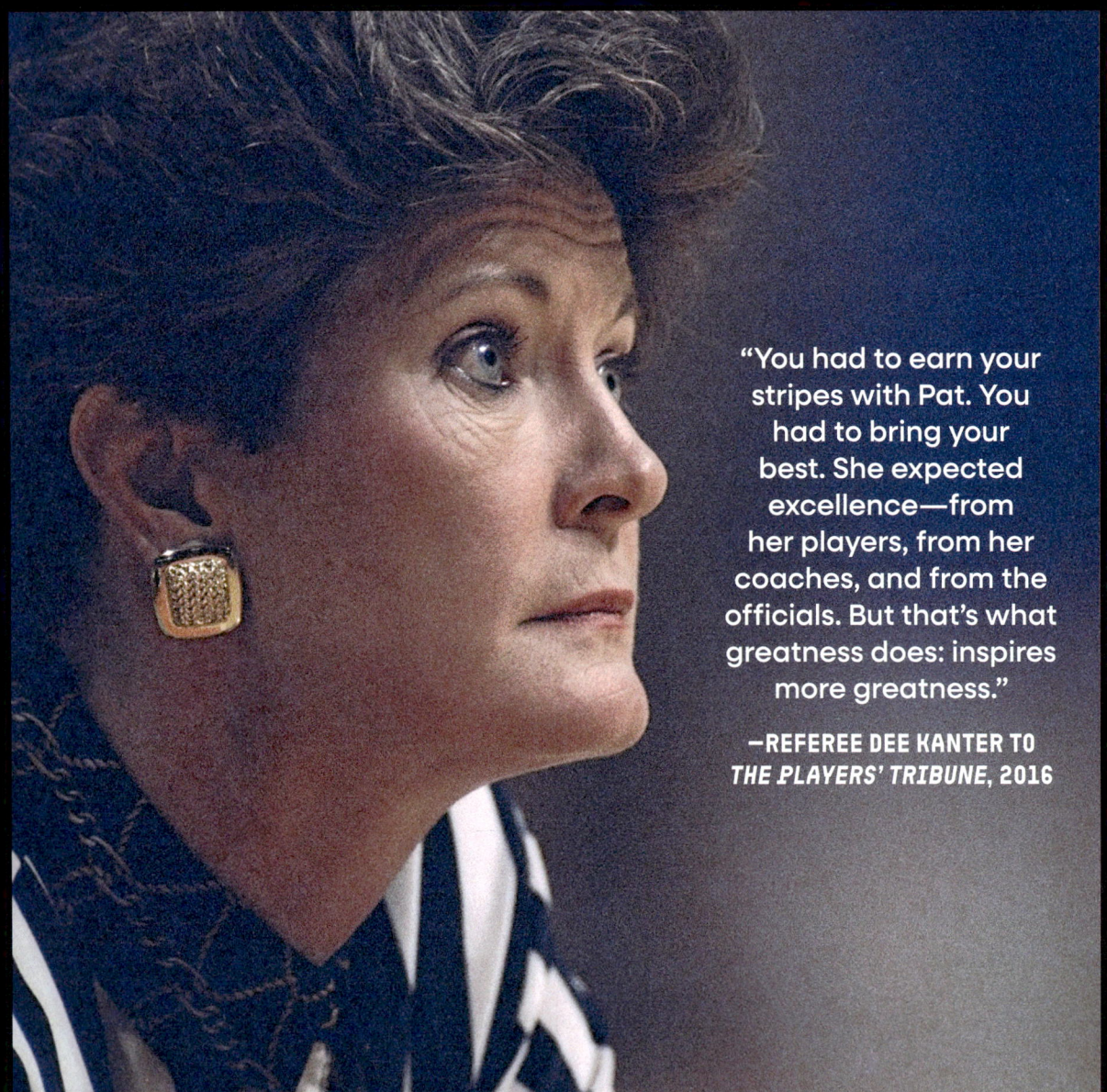

"You had to earn your stripes with Pat. You had to bring your best. She expected excellence—from her players, from her coaches, and from the officials. But that's what greatness does: inspires more greatness."

—REFEREE DEE KANTER TO *THE PLAYERS' TRIBUNE*, 2016

Both Summitt and UT women's athletic director, Joan Cronan, fought for equality. And it worked. In 1998 Tennessee set the NCAA single-game attendance record with 24,597. Later that year, Summitt became the first women's college basketball coach to appear on the cover of *Sports Illustrated*. She was a rock star. Her $1.125 million salary in 2006 was the most ever for a female coach. The mission was to elevate the women's game, and she did it.

The nineties catapulted women's basketball onto everyone's radar. Not only did Tennessee win four national titles in the decade, but the 1996 USA Olympic women's basketball team went 52–0 before winning gold. Two Tennessee players were on that roster. The next year, the WNBA tipped off at Madison Square Garden for the first time. At least four Lady Vols took the court as representations of Summitt in the league.

This isn't by accident. Summitt and her program in Knoxville became the blueprint. And that 1991 national championship was the start of a dynasty.

ABOVE: Coach Summitt in 1996.

THE THREE MEEKS

This Tennessee Trio Defined the '90s

The Three Amikas: Mik, Mique, and Meek. Not only did their names phonetically share the same middle syllable, they shared the same winning desire at Tennessee. "We wanted to go out there and dominate and embarrass people," Chamique Holdsclaw would say decades later. During the 1998 season, they did. A perfect 39–0 with a fairy-tale national championship ending. They each knew their role: Semeka Randall was the floor general, orchestrating Pat Summitt's offense to a T. Catchings was the defensive wizard, picking pockets and taking names. Holdsclaw was a precisionist, slicing through the defense like she was a contestant on *Iron Chef*; she still holds the spot of all-time scorer and rebounder in Lady Vols history. Together, they molded into a three-headed Meekmonster, virtually impossible to contain.

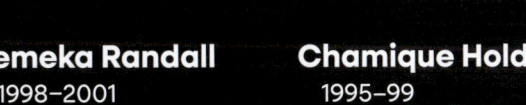

Semeka Randall
1998–2001
2-time All-American
National Champion

Chamique Holdsclaw
1995–99
All-time UT leading scorer
   and rebounder
4-time All-American
2-time Naismith Player of
   the Year
3-time National Champion

Tamika Catchings
1998–2001
4-time All-American
2000 Naismith Player
   of the Year
National Champion

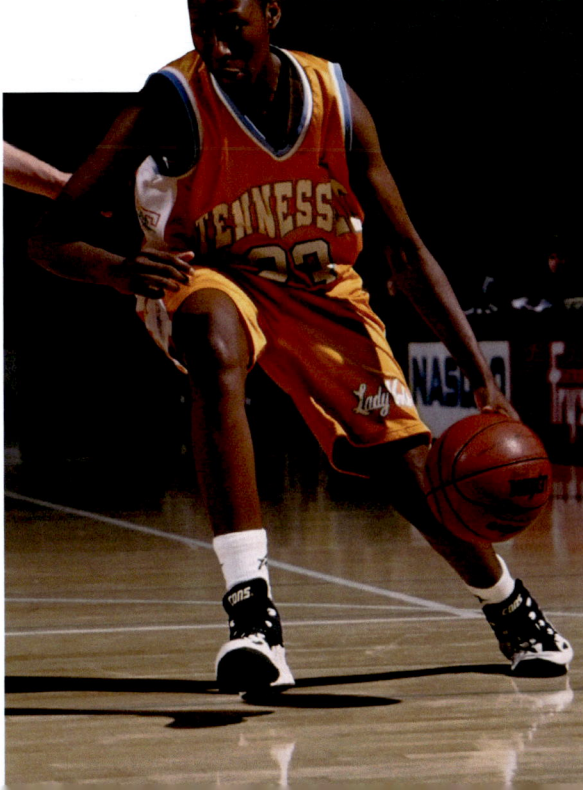

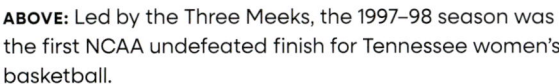

ABOVE: Led by the Three Meeks, the 1997–98 season was the first NCAA undefeated finish for Tennessee women's basketball.

LEFT: Chamique Holdsclaw drives against Stanford in 1995. Then in 1998 Holdsclaw—a Queens, NY, native—was the first woman to grace the cover of *SLAM* magazine. "It was a statement piece: Women's basketball had arrived," she declared. There wouldn't be another cover woman for twenty years.

GENO AURIEMMA

The Winningest Coach in Division I College Basketball History

"Geno's natural walk is a strut," UConn star Rebecca Lobo once told *Sports Illustrated*. No one would ever accuse the man of lacking in confidence. But the winningest coach in college basketball history could make that work for him just fine. In four decades on the sideline, Geno Auriemma racked up championships and records, coached some of the best players in the sport, and built a dynasty like no other at the University of Connecticut.

Auriemma agreed to come to UConn during a 1985 meeting with the school's athletic director at a Dunkin' Donuts. (Over the years, as the story took on the cadence of folklore, Auriemma was always sure to note their donuts were plain: There was no frosting, no sprinkles, no cream.) The Italian-born Auriemma was an assistant at the University of Virginia at the time. His only head coaching experience had come with a junior varsity high school team. But there was no real pressure for success at UConn.

In its eleven years of existence, the program had posted a winning record just once, and there was certainly never any talk of championships. The women had never so much as qualified for a postseason tournament. All of which changed, of course, under Auriemma and his longtime associate Chris Dailey.

It did not happen instantly. The Huskies went 12–15 in his first season at Connecticut—still the only losing season on his record. But he began shifting the culture right away. "He got us to play hard and to think about winning," UConn center Jennifer Weideman told her hometown newspaper after that first season under Auriemma. The young coach was relentless, with an unsparing attention to detail, and he did not particularly care if he occasionally rubbed people the wrong way.

That intensity could be difficult to handle, but it delivered results. The Huskies made their

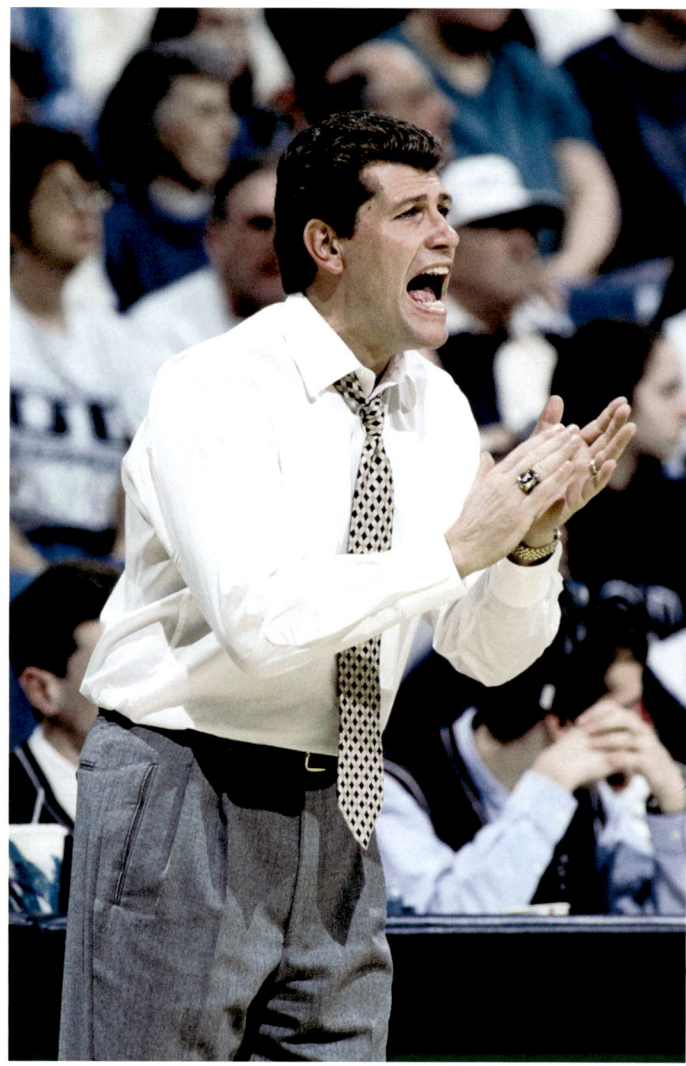

first Final Four in 1991, their sixth season under Auriemma, and won their first championship in 1995. That original championship season would go down as being among the most impressive displays of dominance in the history of the college

ABOVE: Auriemma has been an expressive force on the sideline for more than forty years.

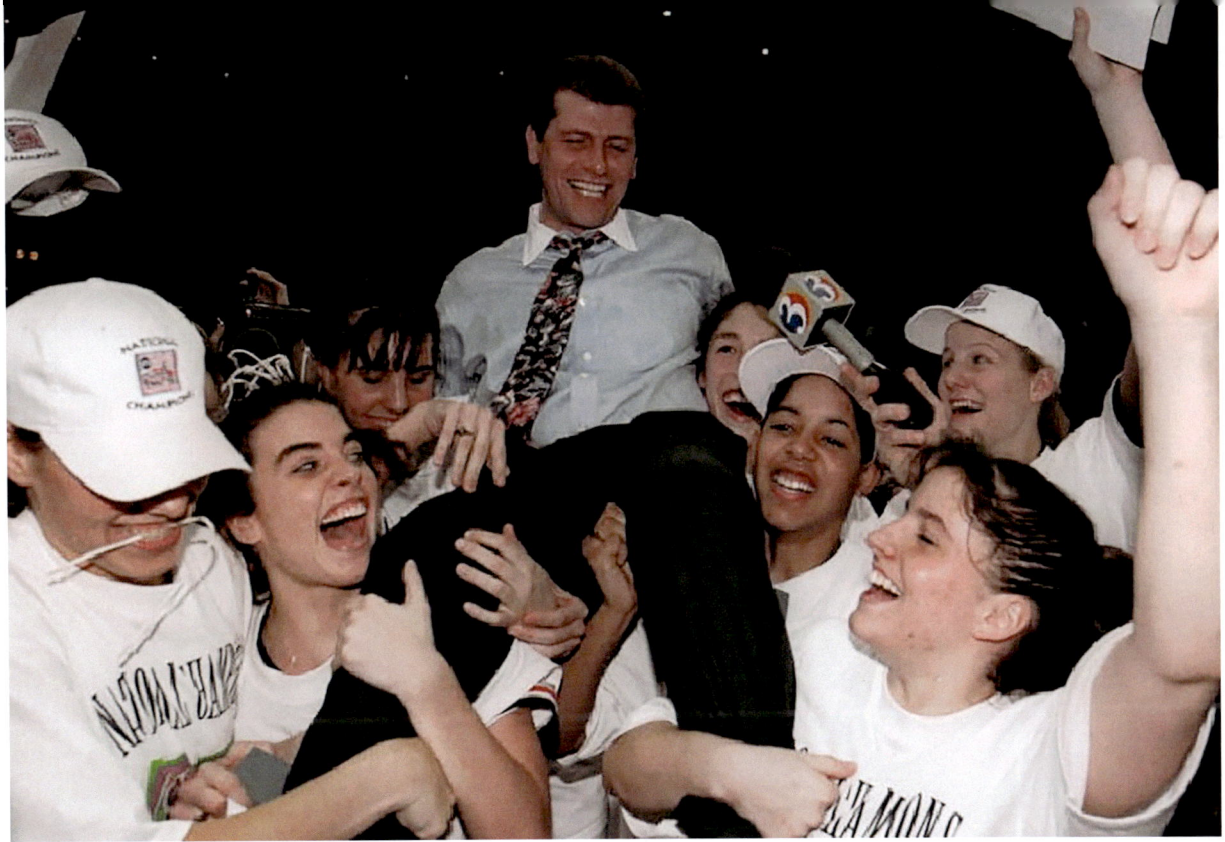

game. UConn went a perfect 35–0. They won every regular season game by double digits and set the record for highest average scoring margin, at 33.2. (That record would stand for twenty years before being broken by . . . Auriemma and UConn.) Their pursuit of perfection captured unprecedented national attention for women's basketball.

"Someone said the best thing that could happen to us was to lose one before the tournament to take the pressure off," Auriemma told *The Boston Globe*. "Oh, really? If we had lost one, then we would have been like everyone else. Tell me: What lessons can you learn by losing that you can't learn by winning?"

And he could find those lessons in any kind of win. When someone put on a tape of the championship game at their victory party, Auriemma seamlessly transitioned from celebrating to coaching, pointing out defensive lapses as if they were having a film session. His players were hardly surprised.

That approach did not change as the years passed and the championships piled up.

"Geno was different from all the other coaches," UConn phenom Diana Taurasi told *Sports Illustrated* in 2003. "He'd tell me things that were real."

Taurasi went 139–8 in her four years at UConn. She won three national championships on four trips to the Final Four. Auriemma never eased up on her.

"He'll pound away at you," Taurasi went on. "There were times I hated to come to practice because it was so mentally demanding. He'd put you in situations where you couldn't win. But it's like he says: 'You're going to prove me right. Or prove me wrong.' And I'm always determined to prove him wrong. You see, you hate him in a way you need to."

Over the decades, the game changed, and the players did, too. Auriemma came to UConn at a time when the program did not even have its own locker room. He stayed as the sport exploded in popularity and the structure of college athletics shifted completely, winning titles in the 1990s, 2000s, 2010s, and 2020s. And the success of his teams helped shape the potential of the sport. Maybe his natural walk *is* a strut. But it's hard to argue that he hasn't earned it.

ABOVE: When Auriemma led UConn to its first championship in 1995, his players chanted his name as they carried him out.

THE '96ERS
GOLD OR BUST

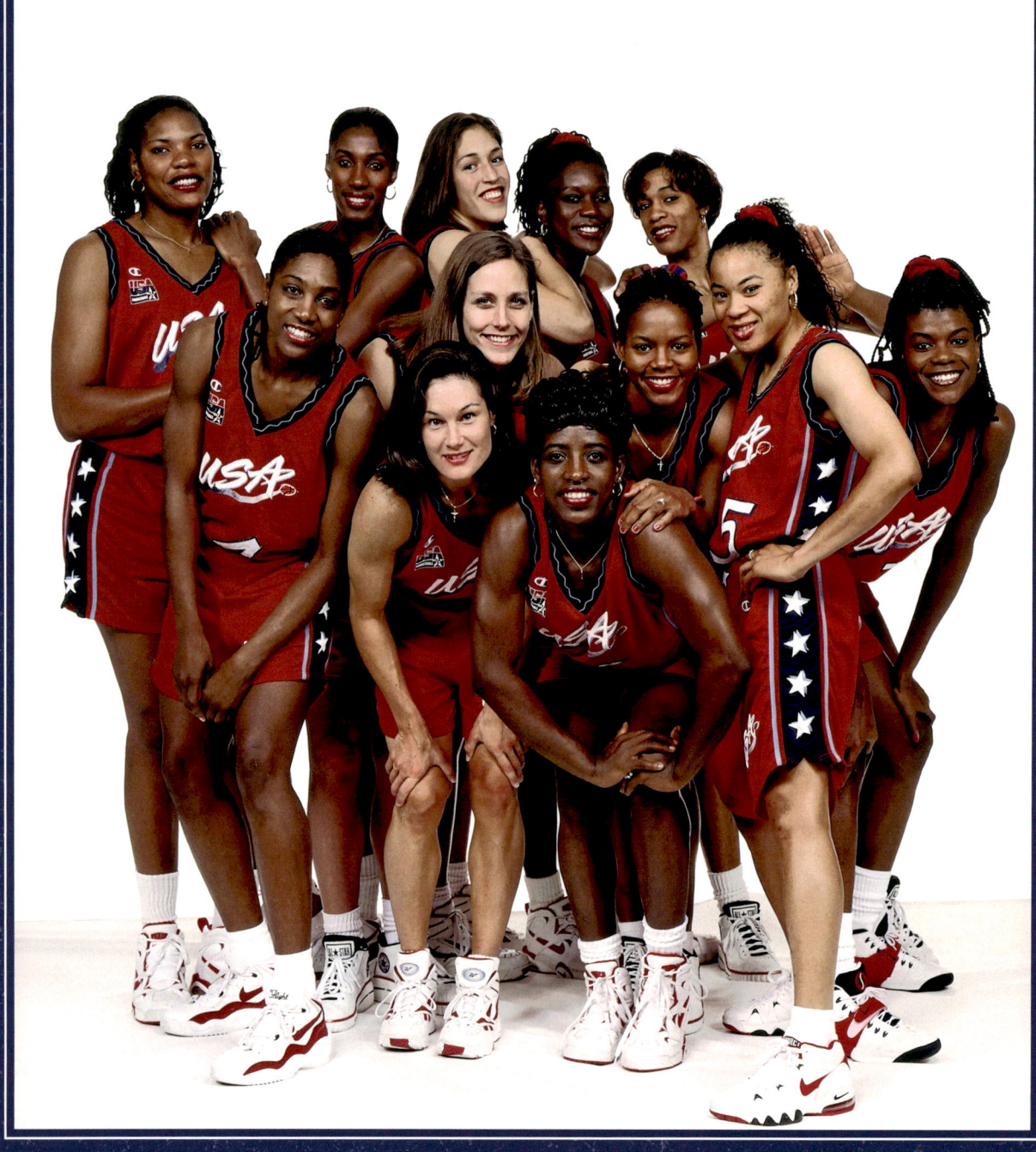

ABOVE: The 1996 US Olympic team.

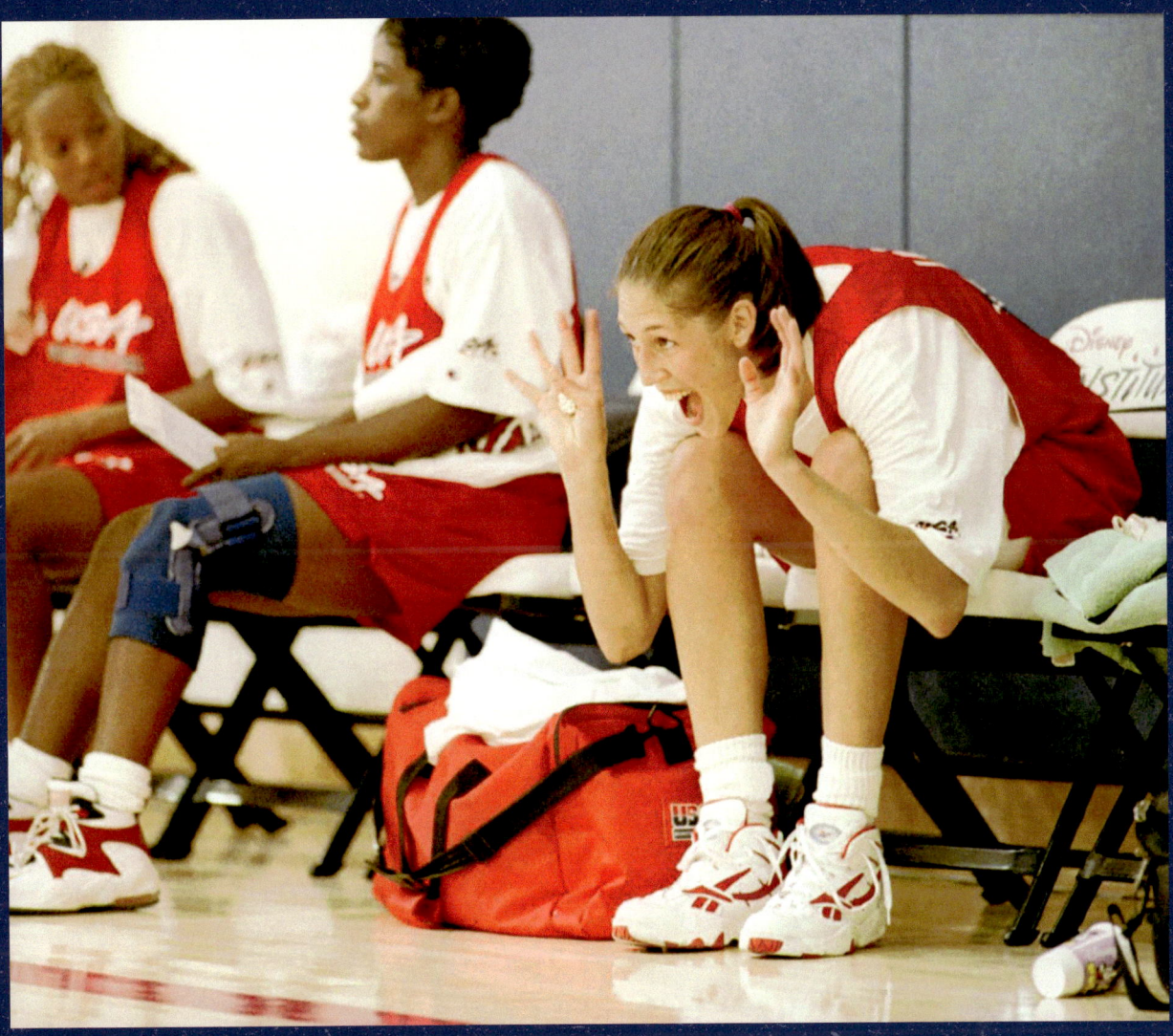

ome two dozen women gathered at the US Olympic Training Center in May 1995. They all wanted to make a roster unlike any that had come before. It was supposed to be the strongest national team ever, and if all went according to plan, it was also supposed to rewrite the future of the sport. This would eventually be the Olympic women's basketball squad for 1996. But it would first embark on a global barnstorming tour—playing exhibition games, courting media, and making public appearances in hopes of proving the market potential for their game to eventually support a league. They would ultimately spend ten months on the road and cover more than 100,000 miles.

And *then* would come their battle for a gold medal.

USA Basketball had decided their system needed a major shakeup. The women's national basketball team was traditionally selected just a few months before the Olympics: They'd practice together for a few weeks and then jump into competition. But that model had begun to crack as global competition grew tougher. Team USA had only barely secured bronze after being upset in the semifinals of the 1992 Olympics, and their next major international competition was similarly a bust, finishing third

ABOVE: The team logged hundreds of hours of practice in gyms all over the country (and the globe) on their barnstorming tour. They logged over 100,000 miles on the road, everywhere from Hawaii to Siberia.

at the 1994 Fédération Internationale de Basketball World Championships. USA Basketball decided it could not possibly see a repeat in 1996—especially on their own turf.

However, there was another organization involved in the early roster selection and subsequent barnstorming tour. That was the NBA—which had recently begun making gradual movements into women's basketball. It would now serve as the marketing agent of the national team and gauge the viability of something even bigger. Like, say, launching its own league for women. And it was not the only group to have noticed the potential there. An independent set of investors was already laying the groundwork for a separate domestic league. It was clear there was real interest (and money) in a new landscape for the women's game. It all hinged, at least in part, on the success of this barnstorming tour and subsequent quest for gold.

The yearlong program would be the most significant investment ever made in the women on the national team. It would also be the most that had ever been asked of the players. Anything less than gold would be considered a failure.

When the players arrived for tryouts at the Olympic Training Center in Colorado Springs, they were greeted by a countdown registering the 425 days until the 1996 Games would begin in Atlanta. It was a reminder of how seriously the selection committee was considering this—assembling the roster so far in advance—and of how much would be required of them. This would take up more than a year of their lives. Each player would be paid $50,000 for the barnstorming tour: Many of these women made far more playing overseas, generally six figures, some as much as $400,000. But they considered the financial hit worth it to potentially represent Team USA in the Olympics.

The group who had been called in that day provided a snapshot of the era. A few players were fresh out of college basketball, including Tennessee guard Nikki McCray and UConn center Rebecca

1996 OLYMPIC ROSTER

JENNIFER AZZI, guard, Stanford
RUTHIE BOLTON, guard, Auburn
TERESA EDWARDS, guard, Georgia
VENUS LACY, center, Louisiana Tech
LISA LESLIE, center, Southern Cal
REBECCA LOBO, center, Connecticut
KATRINA MCCLAIN, forward, Georgia
NIKKI MCCRAY, guard, Tennessee
CARLA MCGHEE, forward, Tennessee
DAWN STALEY, guard, Virginia
KATY STEDING, forward, Stanford
SHERYL SWOOPES, guard/forward, Texas Tech

Lobo, who had just played each other for the national title. (Lobo skipped her college graduation to come to the tryouts.) They had been under one of the brightest spotlights ever seen for women in the college game: The championship got more than seven million viewers on CBS. But nothing existed for players after the NCAA. The other women at tryouts had likewise starred in college, but with no basketball infrastructure to keep them in the public consciousness, their names began to fade as they went overseas for their only chances at playing.

"They develop almost a love-hate relationship with the game," Olympic coach Tara VanDerveer told *Sports Illustrated*. "They love basketball, but hate that they have to go away to play it."

With no domestic league available, American women instead played in countries like Italy, Japan, Spain, and Turkey. It was always considered an honor to represent their country on the world stage. There was also a special meaning in the 1996 Olympics. To have the Games in Atlanta would be a rare chance for these women to play meaningful games at home again in the United States.

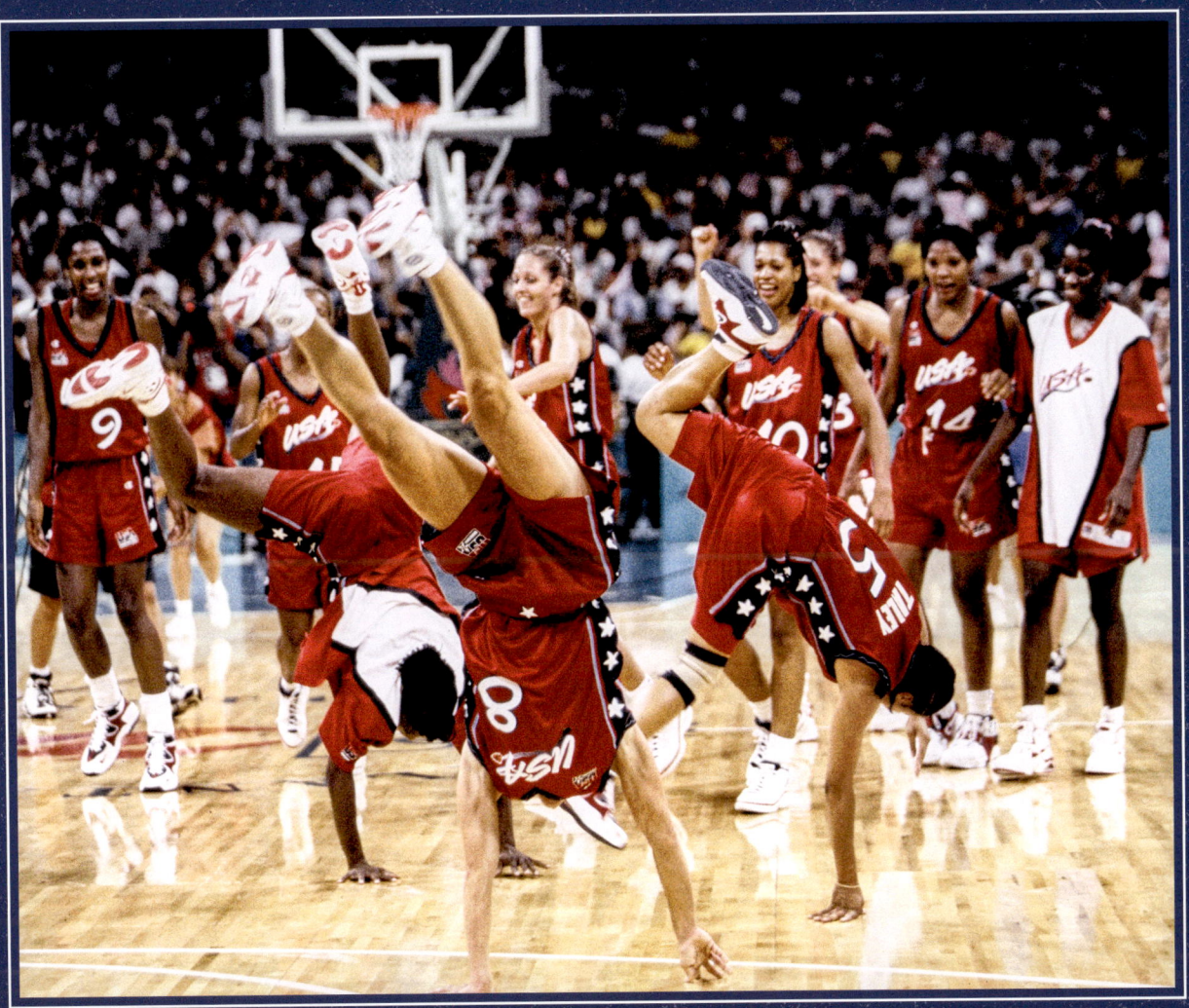

It produced especially tough competition at tryouts and it led to a roster that was almost entirely new. USA Basketball ultimately chose to keep only two players who had been to the last Olympics: Katrina McClain and Teresa Edwards, teammates and best friends at the University of Georgia in the 1980s, would now be cocaptains of Team USA for 1996. They were joined by a collection of first-timers, from five-foot-six point guard Dawn Staley to six-foot-five center Lisa Leslie, with plenty of talent in between. Some had played together before. Most had not. And now the group would spend the next year crisscrossing the globe together.

They would do it under the watchful eye of Tara VanDerveer. The head coach of Stanford, she was taking a sabbatical for a year to focus entirely on the Olympics, just like the players. She was known for being exacting, with ruthless attention to detail and a heavy emphasis on conditioning. The players learned that almost immediately. They'd had a bit of time at home after tryouts and before the start of training, and she gave them all detailed, intense workout plans to follow while they were away. When they reported back for training in Colorado Springs, VanDerveer felt that more than half the players had not met her standards. They would all make it up with grueling, early-morning cardio sessions, in a group that she nicknamed the Breakfast Club.

ABOVE: The gold medal had players jumping (and cartwheeling) for joy.

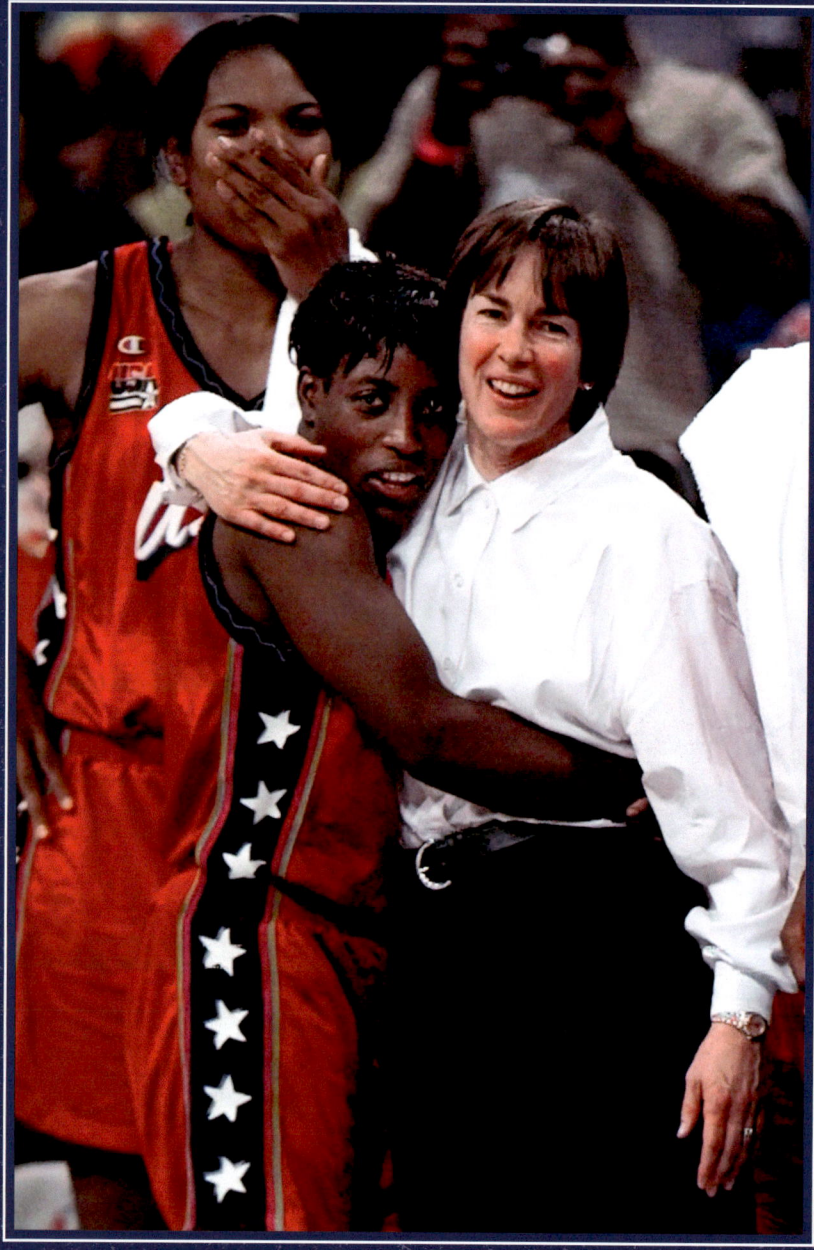

Indeed they did. Team USA would play all of the top college teams followed by all of the top international teams. They would make public appearances, participate in charity work, and greet the media as they went from city to city. A journalist was embedded with them to write a book. (This produced *Venus to the Hoop: A Gold Medal Year in Women's Basketball*, a fascinating, in-depth chronicle by Sara Corbett.) The travel would not be glamorous: Domestically, they would fly coach, rent minivans, and stay in modest hotels. And they would be expected to be ideal representatives of both womanhood and basketball at every turn.

This hit the tricky dual purposes of the barnstorming tour. It had been organized both to prepare them for the Olympics—to provide intense competition on the court—and to determine the success of what ultimately became the WNBA. Their journey was supposed to be about proving marketing potential as much as it was about basketball. They shot television commercials and held regular autograph signings. The NBA had secured major corporate sponsors for the women like State Farm and Kraft Foods. They were always supposed to be performing—in every sense of the word. In their regular open practices, VanDerveer was asked to wear a microphone so the crowd heard every word from her mouth. The result could feel more like a show than a practice. (VanDerveer eventually won a battle to ditch the

"The conditioning wasn't just for the basketball," VanDerveer later wrote in her memoir of that year, *Shooting from the Outside*. "We had a long year ahead of us."

ABOVE: No player on the team formed a closer bond with Tara VanDerveer than Ruthie Bolton. After the Olympics, she wrote the coach a thank-you note: "You are truly my Number One coach. You'll never know the impact that you've made on my life. You were the first coach to truly believe in me, and for that I owe you so much."

mic.) The players could never forget just how much was expected of them.

It was not just about winning. (Though, of course, it was about that, too: If they *didn't* win, all of this might be deemed moot.) It was about proving that people wanted to watch them.

"Winning the gold was the top priority, but riding on that success, just below the surface, was the future of women's basketball itself," VanDerveer wrote in her book. "Maybe that sounds like hyperbole, but it's not."

They hit the road under an enormous amount of pressure. They started by playing college teams across twenty states and Washington, DC. In the latter, they were invited on a jog with President Bill Clinton, wearing their red, white, and blue sweatsuits as they ran around the National Mall. They also visited Supreme Court Justices Sandra Day O'Connor and Ruth Bader Ginsburg:

As USA Basketball wrestled over how best to market women's hoops, it debated various nicknames for the team, including the question of whether it should represent its own concept or match the men's "Dream Team" moniker from 1992. Here are some of the options they considered, though none of them stuck:

- The Dreamettes
- Liberty Belles
- The Fab Femmes
- Dream Team Too
- The Hoop Troupe
- Golden Girls
- The '96ers
- Chicks Who Set Picks

"I wanted to meet you because what you're doing is important," O'Connor told Team USA. The justices then took them up to the Supreme Court gym. (O'Connor banked in a shot. Ginsburg . . . tried her best.) The task of playing for their country felt newly significant.

ABOVE: Lisa Leslie was among the biggest stars on the team, starring in television commercials, signing a modeling contract with Wilhelmina International, and of course, cleaning up on both ends of the court.

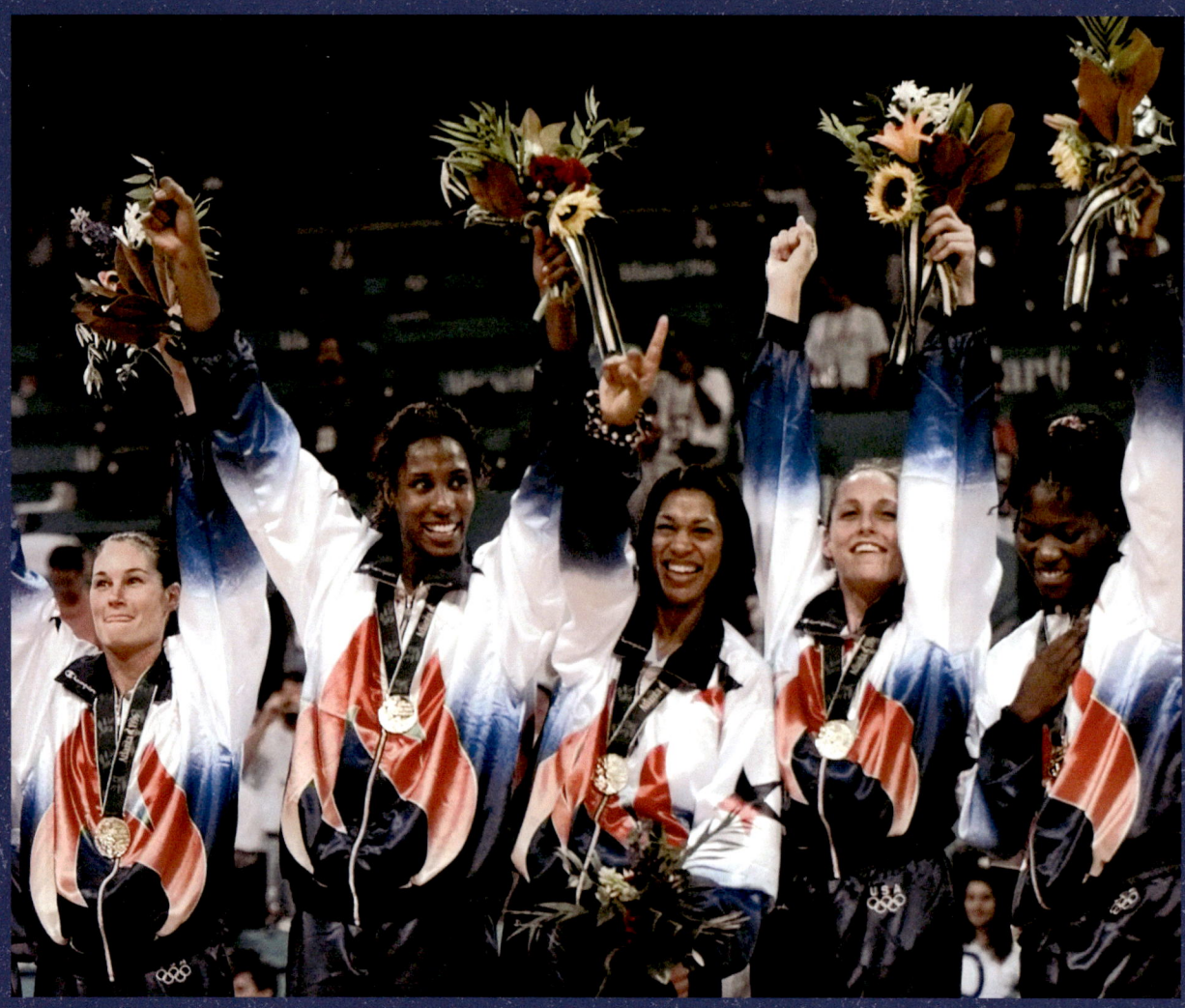

They covered more ground than any campaigning politician, California to Missouri to Tennessee to Washington to Kansas to Arkansas to Ohio, greeting fans everywhere. The real test would be what came after those college exhibitions. (Team USA won them all handily as expected: The average margin of victory was more than 40 points.) After their months on the road in the US, they next went overseas, playing in Russia, China, and Australia. They would now face some of the best teams in the world. Most of the players were banged up from their workload and growing steadily exhausted from their schedule. But they were beginning to come together as a group. This was a far more complete, seasoned, unified Team USA.

They won every single game they played abroad. It meant the US entered the Olympics riding a 52–0

record. They had not lost a game since the roster had been chosen a year ago, which only amplified the pressure for Atlanta.

After so much travel, all those months of grueling workouts, Team USA would now finally play the games they had been assembled to win. It had been one of the most draining experiences of their lives—and it was only the warm-up. In their first game against Cuba, a country they had played and beaten multiple times over the last year, they suddenly looked uncharacteristically shaky. They spent most of the first quarter looking flat

ABOVE: Their gold medal represented the end of a journey both literal (all over the globe) and emotional (their entire lives) for Team USA.

and getting beaten inside—but then came a change. *Here* was Team USA.

Leslie dominated in the paint and finished with 24 points. They got another 12 from Sheryl Swoopes, who had demonstrated over the past year that she could do just about everything on the court, and 11 from Katy Steding, a three-point specialist who always came through when needed. And the most dazzling highlights from that opening win came from none of the above. That honor went to a series of jaw-dropping, no-look passes from Staley.

Reporters noted Magic Johnson, sitting in the stands, jumping to his feet in awe. The postgame media session was full of questions about whether she did this kind of thing regularly. Staley answered honestly.

We've all been *like this. You've just never been able to watch.*

"I've been doing these same things for the last few years overseas," Staley told reporters. "It's a shame you guys didn't get a chance to see that."

They rolled from there. A different player led the roster in scoring for each game of group stage play: After getting those 24 points from Leslie against Cuba, there were big performances from speedy Ruthie Bolton, from point guard Jennifer Azzi, from the veteran McClain, and from youngster McCray. When they played their first game in the Georgia Dome, they set a record for the largest audience ever for a stand-alone women's basketball game. Team USA dominated in the quarterfinals and then in the semifinals. Their victories had begun to feel automatic.

This led them to the Olympic gold-medal game against Brazil.

> ## "What happened with the Olympic Dream Team was we showed what can happen when you market women's basketball. They found out how jerseys will sell and posters will sell."
>
> —REBECCA LOBO

"If we don't win," McClain said before the game, "to me, the whole year has been a waste."

They made sure their year had not been wasted. It was Brazil who had embarrassed the US in the semifinals of the 1994 FIBA World Championship, but now, two years later, the matchup was all USA. They were up by double digits at the half. Every member of the roster scored at least one bucket. As it turned out, there would be no suspense here, either, with a final score of United States 111, Brazil 87.

Some of the players turned cartwheels on the court. They hugged and cried and dumped a water cooler on VanDerveer. Now, finally, they knew where they were going: It had already been announced that not one but *two* new domestic basketball leagues would start play within the next year. But they mostly thought of where they had been. The country had just seen them win. Almost no one had seen what it required to get there.

"This is what we've been shooting for," Azzi told reporters, gold medal around her neck, amid the celebration they had waited so long for. "You can't imagine the workouts we've been through. The things no one saw, eating dinner in China, traveling in Russia . . . The relief and joy are indescribable."

FOLLOWING: In the homestretch of their global tour, Team USA played Cuba in Providence, Rhode Island, on May 26, 1996. They cruised to an easy victory: 106–58. But that stop on their tour was better remembered for something that happened off the court. NBA vice president Val Ackerman met with the team in a hotel that week in Providence and laid out the plans for the WNBA. "You have exceeded everyone's expectations," she told them. With most of the players already signed to the American Basketball League, however, the reaction was muted.

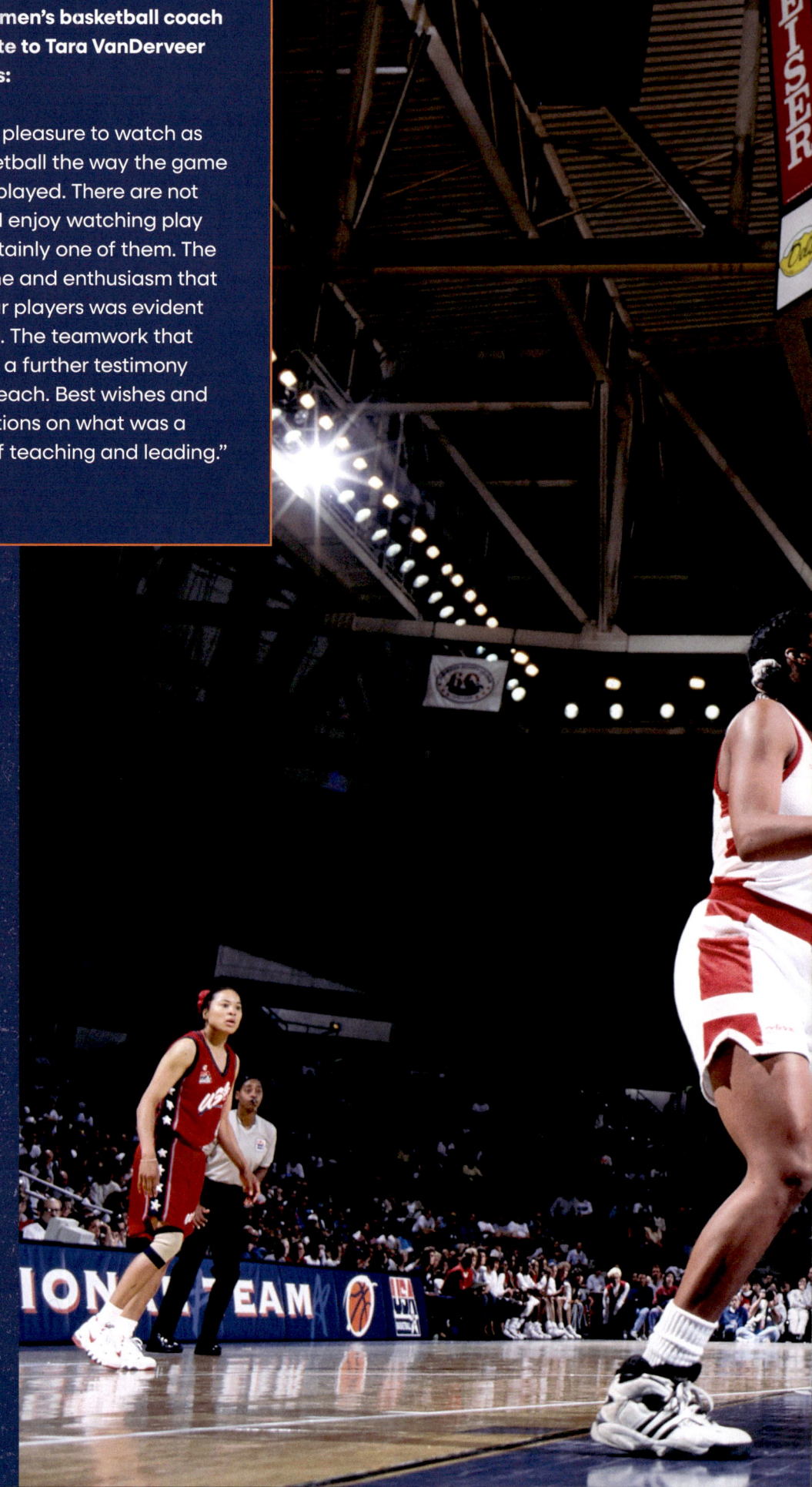

Longtime Indiana men's basketball coach Bobby Knight's note to Tara VanDerveer after the Olympics:

"Your team was a pleasure to watch as they played basketball the way the game was meant to be played. There are not many teams that I enjoy watching play but yours was certainly one of them. The teaching, discipline and enthusiasm that you instilled in your players was evident in all that they did. The teamwork that your kids had was a further testimony to your ability to teach. Best wishes and again congratulations on what was a magnificent job of teaching and leading."

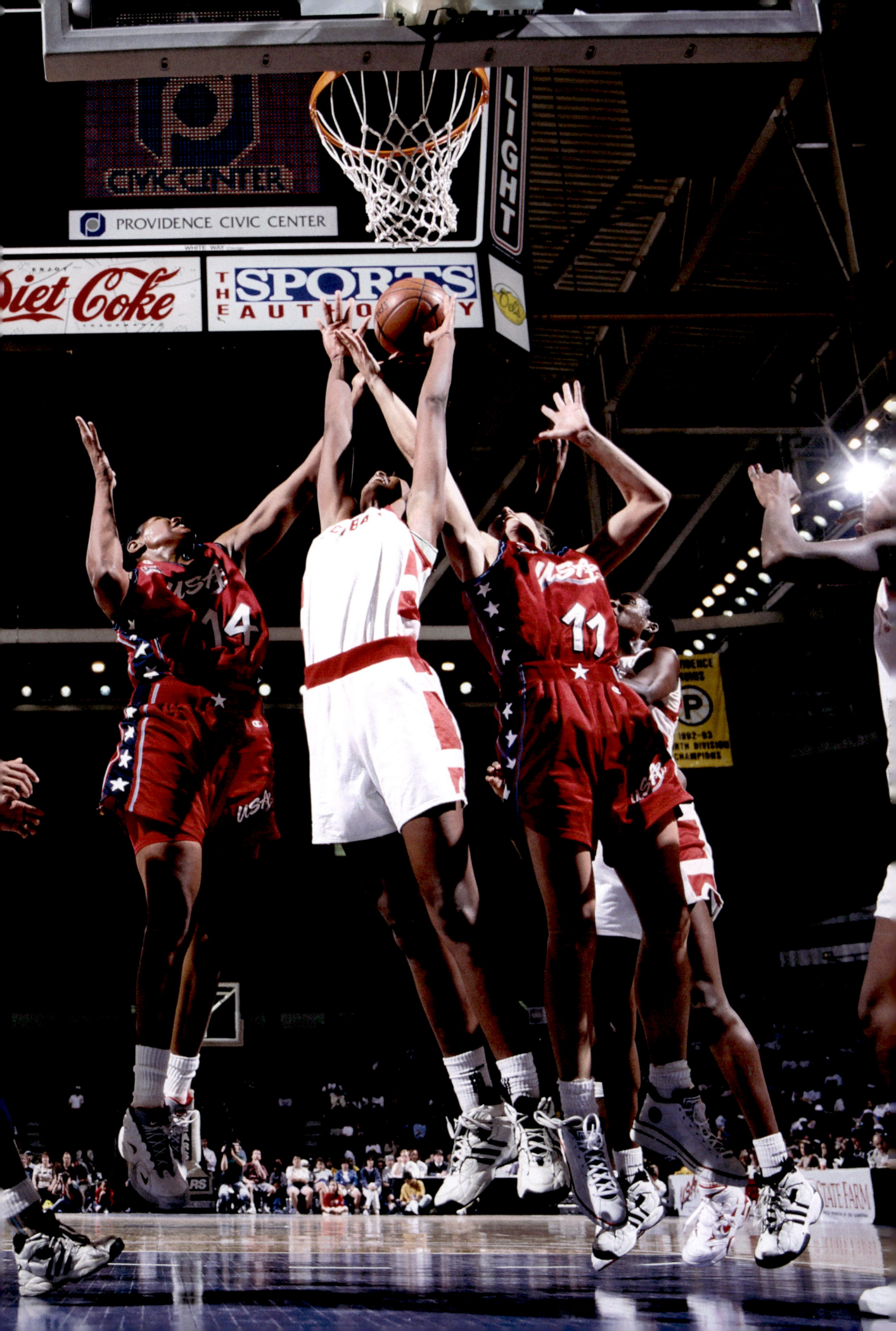

WE GOT NEXT

The Professional Game Gets Off the Ground

The desire for a women's professional basketball league was heightened around the 1996 national team, which went on a yearlong global undefeated romp, taking home gold during a humid summer in Atlanta. The itch to see these women continue to compete piqued the interest of fat wallets. Two leagues would spring up at the same time in the late nineties. Women hoopers suddenly found themselves not automatically needing to slug heaps of luggage overseas. Pro players now had something they'd never had in America: options. But which league would players choose to participate in?

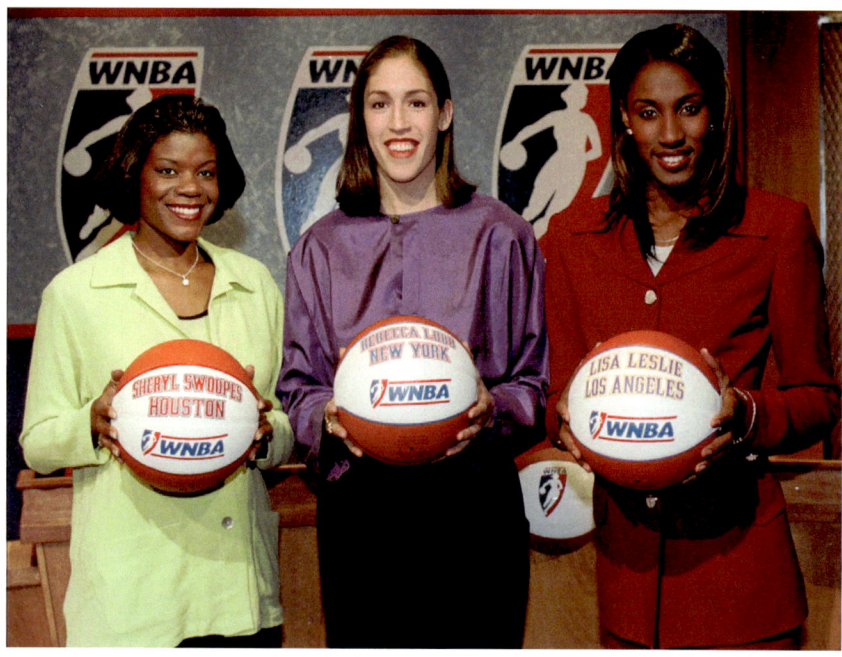

September 1995

Silicon Valley executives Steve Hams, Anne Cribbs, and Gary Cavalli spent '94 and '95 dreaming up the next women's pro basketball outlet, the American Basketball League (ABL). It was intentional for the word *woman* to be left out of the league's moniker. Olympic stars like Jennifer Azzi and Teresa Edwards would begin signing contracts with the promising player-first ABL. More than 600 women tried out (some in their forties) as they'd launch with eight teams strategically placed in towns with major college programs, such as the Richmond Rage, with Virginia's Dawn Staley, and the New England Blizzard, with UConn's Jennifer Rizzotti. They planned for a six-month, forty-game season and offered lucrative contracts ($40,000 to $100,000), year-round medical insurance, and stock options.

April 1996

The commissioner of the National Basketball Association (NBA), David Stern, officially declared at a press conference that a women's league would start the following summer, with each team competing in their NBA counterpart's first-class arena. Val Ackerman, then vice president of business affairs at the NBA and soon-to-be president of the WNBA, had her eyes set on signing Sheryl Swoopes, Lisa Leslie, and Rebecca Lobo—all of the past three national college players of the year and Olympians in their own right—to jump-start the league. Average contracts would range from $15,000 to $50,000 to start.

ABOVE: Sheryl Swoopes, Rebecca Lobo, and Lisa Leslie became the first to sign with the Women's National Basketball Association (WNBA) in 1996.

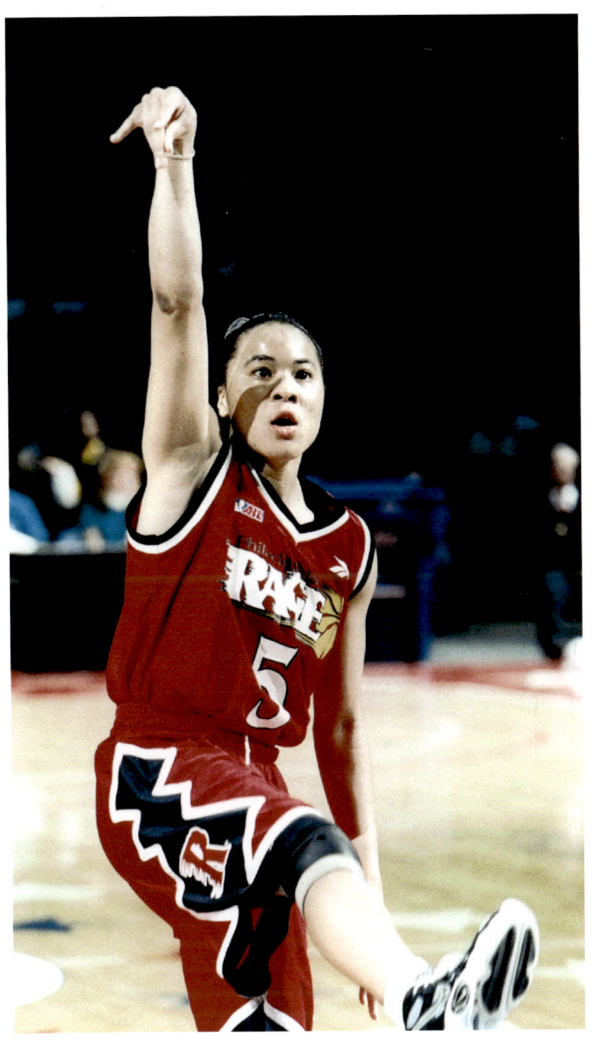

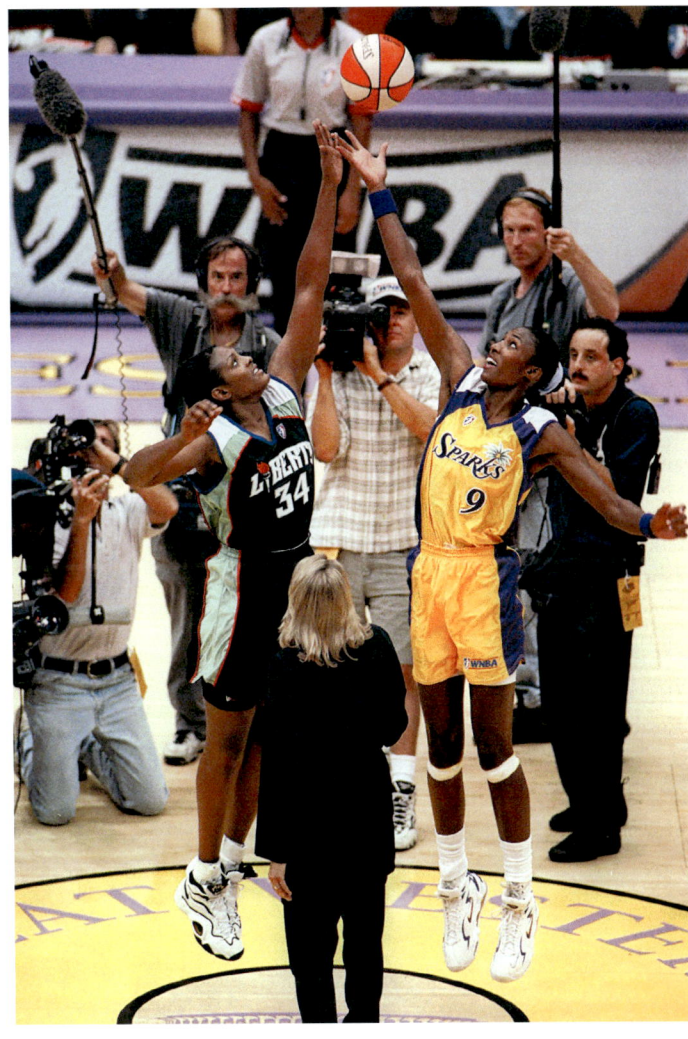

August 1996

Team USA wins an Olympic gold medal in Atlanta, the third for women's basketball.

October 1996

The first ABL game was in front of a sellout of 4,600 fans to see Azzi's San Jose Lasers go toe to toe with Edwards's Atlanta Glory. Reebok had signed on as an official sponsor, and Fox SportsNet was their national TV deal with reairs on BET. "What you saw tonight was just the beginning," Azzi said, postgame. The ABL averaged 3,500 fans in the first season, and the Columbus Quest won the championship with a dominant 31–9 record. Their star, Nikki McCray, averaged 19.9 ppg and became the league's first MVP.

June 1997

The WNBA first tips off in Los Angeles' Great Western Forum with Leslie's Sparks and Lobo's Liberty, with 14,000 fans in attendance. The Sparks' Penny Toler scored the first basket in league history—a baseline jumper assisted by Jamila Wideman. Thanks to the league's incredible marketing push—Ackerman and Rick Welts won

---

ABOVE LEFT: Dawn Staley, Philadelphia Rage guard, ABL 1997.

ABOVE RIGHT: NY Liberty's Kym Hampton and LA Sparks' Lisa Leslie perform the first jump ball in league history, which WNBA president Val Ackerman ceremoniously tossed.

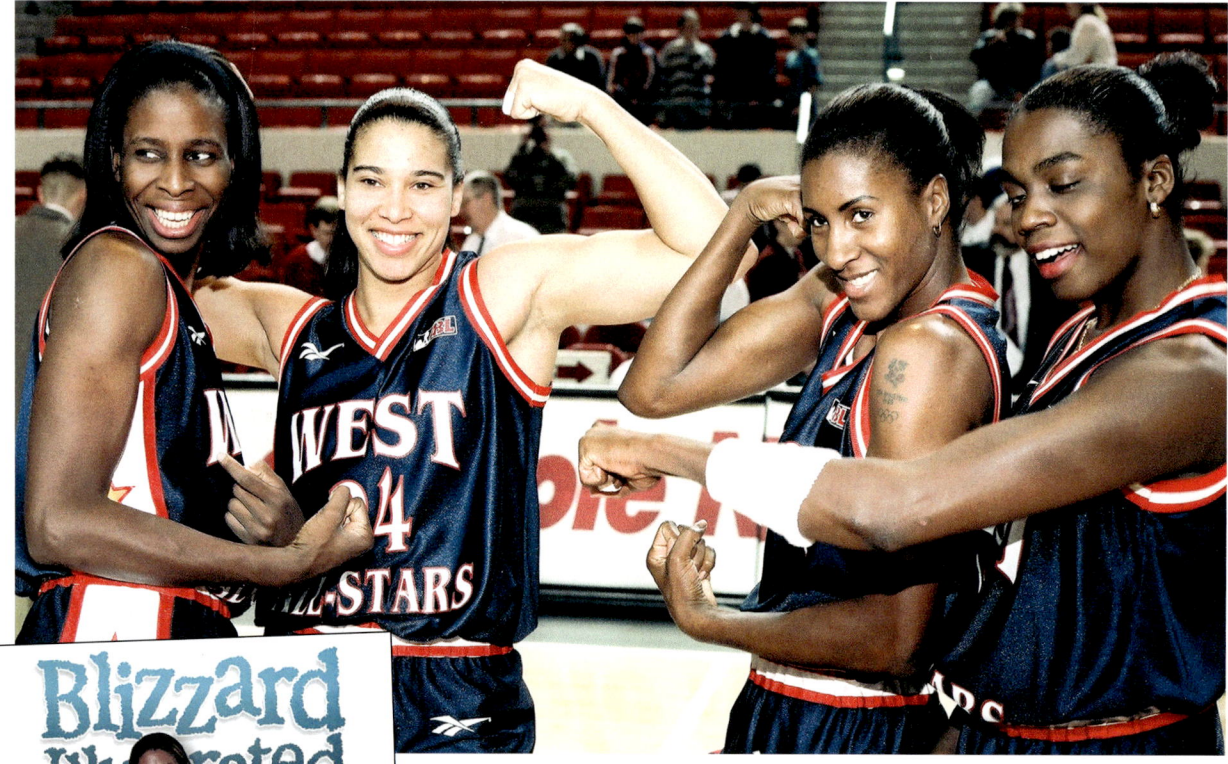

Brandweek's Marketers of the Year award—the "We Got Next" commercials sparked excitement for a new summer league nestled between the end of the NBA season and the start of NFL. Eight teams would launch (New York, LA, Sacramento, Phoenix, Cleveland, Utah, Houston, Charlotte), and lucrative TV deals were inked with NBC, ESPN, and Lifetime. Big brands like Nike, Coca-Cola, and McDonald's signed on as corporate sponsors as the league averaged nearly 10,000 fans in 112 regular season games in the first season.

October 1997

The ABL's second season tips off cautiously optimistic. Columbus Quest went back-to-back as champs, with the newest team addition, Long Beach Stingrays, as runner-ups. "The ABL wasn't an afterthought. It was the forerunner to the WNBA—we were the main event," said Quests' Valerie Still, who was named MVP of both championship series. There were some frustrations with their rival pro league because they felt the competition was stronger in the ABL. Yet, the league still lost its top talent to the WNBA— McCray left with a new Fila shoe deal in hand, and Staley dipped for the better, less-exhausting schedule.

ABOVE LEFT: The New England Blizzard's 1997–98 All-Stars: Stacey Lovelace, Carolyn Young, and Jennifer Rizzotti.

TOP: The ABL Western Conference All-Stars flex before the game in Hartford, Connecticut, on December 15, 1996. Pictured here, from left, Val Whiting, Natalie Williams, Cindy Brown, and Tari Phillips.

OPPOSITE: Sylvia Crawley takes flight during the ABL's All-Star Game dunk contest in January 1998. The Colorado Xplosion forward won the league's first slam dunk contest and a $5,000 prize

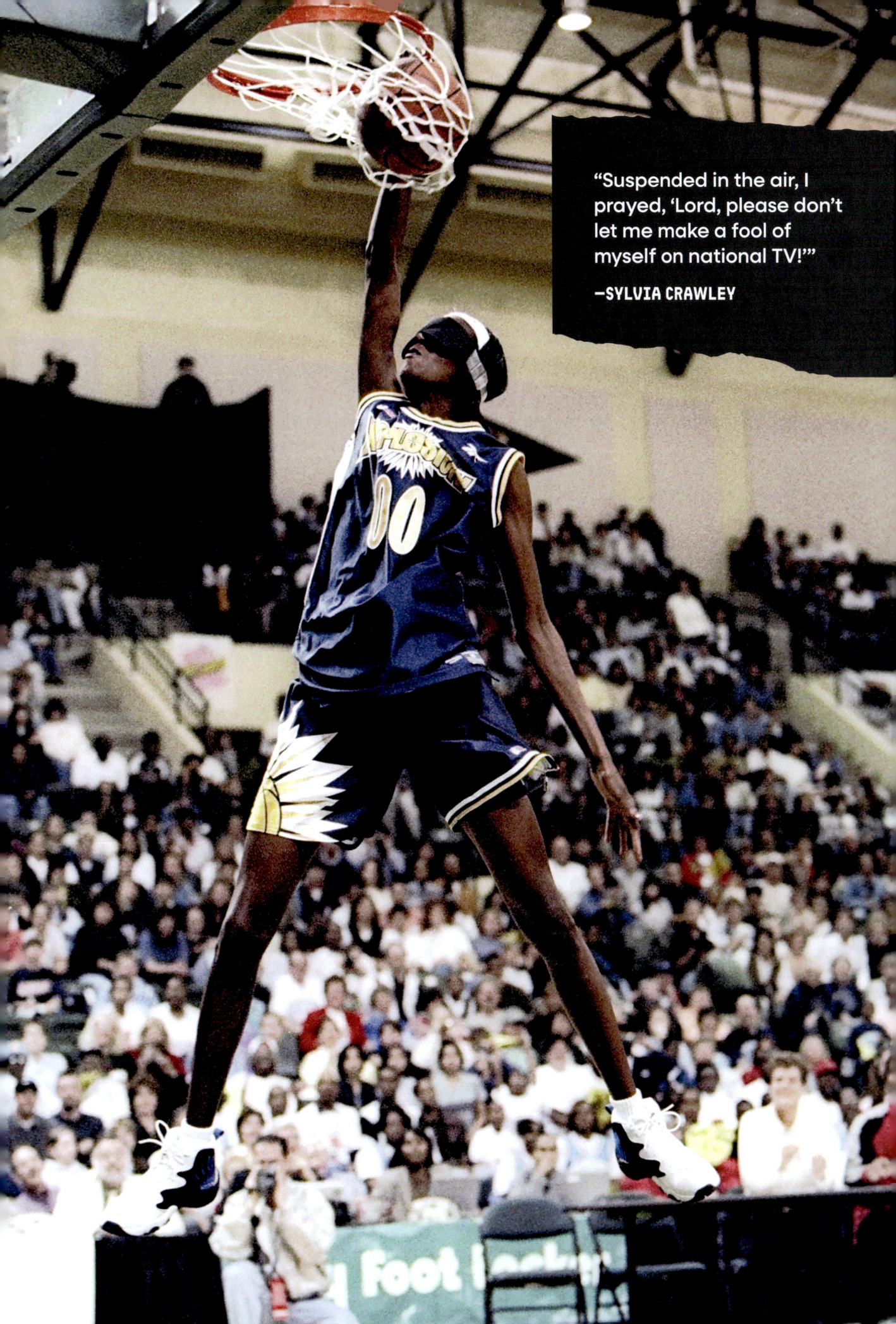

"Suspended in the air, I prayed, 'Lord, please don't let me make a fool of myself on national TV!'"

—SYLVIA CRAWLEY

December 1997

The ABL did not have the financial muscle to go toe to toe with the WNBA but it *did* have a deeper pool of talent. That was on full display at its annual All-Star Game, featuring players like two-time All-American Val Whiting and 2000 Olympian Natalie Williams. "I wanted to play in the ABL from the very beginning," said fellow All-Star Jennifer Azzi. "It changed the course of women's professional basketball in this country. . . . The ABL forced the WNBA to compete for players."

January 1998

Sylvia Crawley set the basketball world on fire when she completed a "blindfolded" dunk in the 1998 ABL's dunk contest, the first for women's pro basketball. She was the favorite but didn't tell the buzzing media her plans. She'd messed up too many times while practicing her steps and didn't want to jinx it. But then, she decided to go for it in the final round. She put on the blindfold (not too tight so she could still look down to the ground to see where she marked the floor earlier) and saluted the boisterous Walt Disney Sports Complex crowd. Crawley took off near mid-court—two dribbles, two long strides—and slammed it home with one hand. The NBA nixed the dunk contest in the '98 season, so Crawley was the sole dunk champ across pro hoops. She put on a show fans will never forget.

June 1998

After one season, the WNBA expanded cities, Detroit and Washington, DC, and their schedule from thirty-eight to forty games. TV ratings were solid, and merch was flying off the shelves. "It's safe to say that we were successful beyond our wildest dreams," Ackerman said. The growth was evident: Nearly 11,000 fans rallied per game across the league. And when league MVP Cynthia Cooper and reigning champions Houston Comets took on the Phoenix Mercury in the Finals, Game 2 set a playoff-viewership record with an average of 1.4 million viewers on ESPN. The Comets would win their second championship in as many years.

> "We are proud of what we accomplished as a pioneer in women's professional athletics. We put a great product on the floor. We gave America's best women athletes an opportunity to play professionally in this country during basketball season. We gave it our best shot; we fought the good fight, and we had a good run. But we were unable to obtain the television exposure and sponsorship support needed to make the league viable long-term."
>
> —ABL PRESS RELEASE, DEC. 23, 1998

December 1998

The '98 NBA lockout allowed the ABL to fill the void for hoop fans in the fall. The Lasers and Seattle Reign had a double-overtime thriller in the Supersonics' arena before a boisterous crowd of 7,400, setting a record for the Reign. But it was too little, too late. The ABL abruptly folded one-third through their third season, leaving ninety players out of work. "Nice Try, No Reward," a *New York Times* article was titled. Cavalli attempted to merge with the WNBA but to no avail. The league filed for bankruptcy, noting debts of over $10 million.

May 1999

The WNBA and its players union had recently signed the first Collective Bargaining Agreement (CBA) in women's team sports history. The players landed better wages (i.e., the rookie minimum was now $25,000); paid maternity leave, year-round medical and dental coverage; and limited ex-ABL players to two per team (and five each for the new

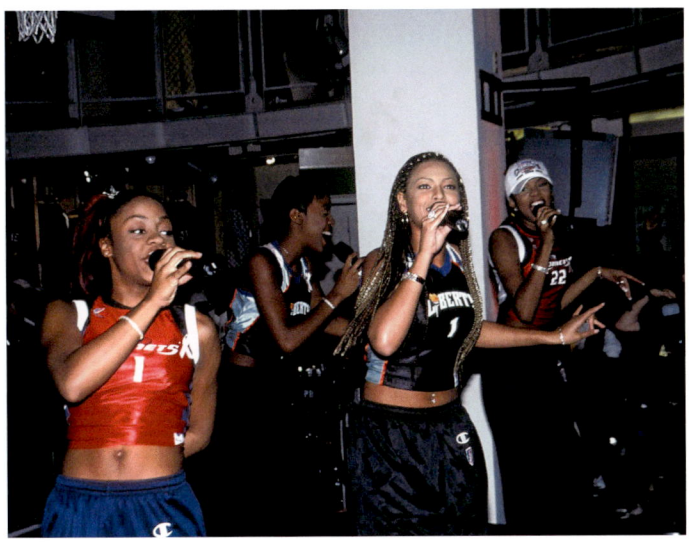

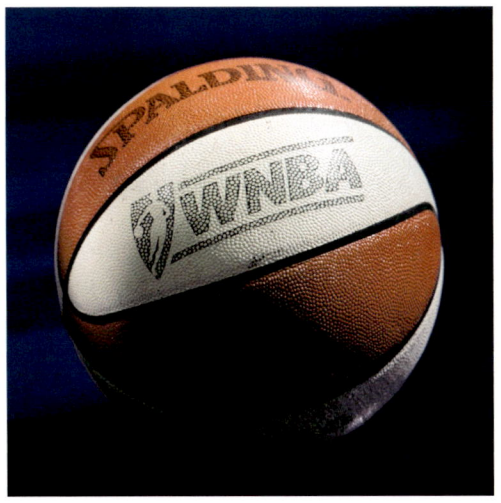

expansion teams in Minnesota and Orlando). Outside Tennessee's Chamique Holdsclaw being the number one pick in the 1999 draft, ten of the remaining eleven first-round selections were ex-ABL players. Yolanda Griffith, Natalie Williams, DeLisha Milton-Jones, and Azzi would headline, with Katie Smith and Shannon Johnson allocated to expansion teams the day prior.

June 1999

The WNBA's third season begins with now forty ex-ABL players in tow. The swirl of top rookies, seasoned veterans, and world-class international athletes boosted the league's overall talent pool. New York Liberty's Teresa Weatherspoon drained a half-court buzzer-beater in Game 2 of the Finals over the Houston Comets. The next game set a viewership record that stood for over twenty-five years: 3.25 million tuned in to ESPN to see the WNBA wrap. Former ABL standout Yolanda Griffith swept awards, winning MVP, Defensive Player of the Year (DPOY), and Newcomer of the Year. Just ahead of the millennium, the league had expanded again, with teams in Indiana, Miami, Portland, and Seattle.

ABOVE: The WNBA surged in 1999 after winning its battle against the ABL—expanding, hitting new ratings highs, and welcoming celebrity promoters like Destiny's Child.

THE WNBA BALL IS BORN

There were only eight months between Sheryl Swoopes signing the first WNBA contract and the inaugural season's tip-off. Val Ackerman was racing against the clock. All ideas were on the table regarding jersey designs: unitards, jumpers, skirts, and even dresses. The design team landed on shiny, two-toned shorts and jerseys—all eight teams having a similar template, just swapping out the colors.

For the Spalding ball, Ackerman wanted it to pop on viewers' TV screens. The colors of green, teal, and sky blue were mentioned. However, after paint-testing different options under the bright lights of Madison Square Garden, the alternating panels of orange and oatmeal caught everyone's eye. "You knew that was the right ball. Everybody felt it," Donna Goldsmith, former vice president of non-apparel licensing at the NBA, stated. "It was just perfect."

1999 WNBA ALL-STAR GAME

Twenty-three of the brightest stars of women's basketball came together for the 1999 inaugural WNBA All-Star Game at Madison Square Garden in New York City. Nearly 19,000 fans, a sold-out crowd, cheered on the East versus West matchup. Lisa Leslie of the Los Angeles Sparks earned the first All-Star Most Valuable Player honors with 13 points as the Western Conference rolled to a 79–61 victory over the East.

TOP ROW (L-R): Ticha Penicheiro, Chamique Holdsclaw, Kym Hampton, Taj McWilliams, Vicky Bullett, Vickie Johnson, Teresa Weatherspoon, Rebecca Lobo, Jennifer Gillom. **MIDDLE ROW (L-R):** Michele Timms, Nikki McCray, Cynthia Cooper, Natalie Williams, Yolanda Griffith, Tonya Edwards, Sheryl Swoopes, Lisa Leslie, Merlakia Jones. **BOTTOM ROW (L-R):** Ruthie Bolton-Holifield, Sandy Brondello, Nykesha Sales, Tina Thompson, and Shannon Johnson

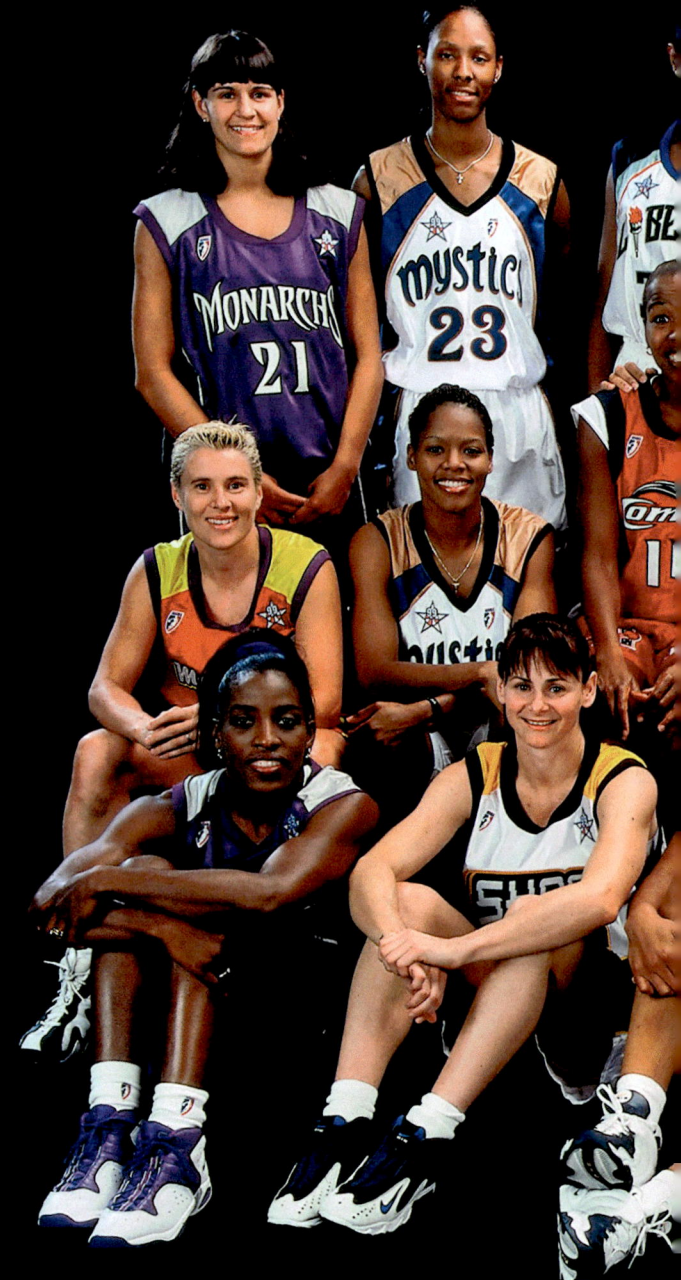

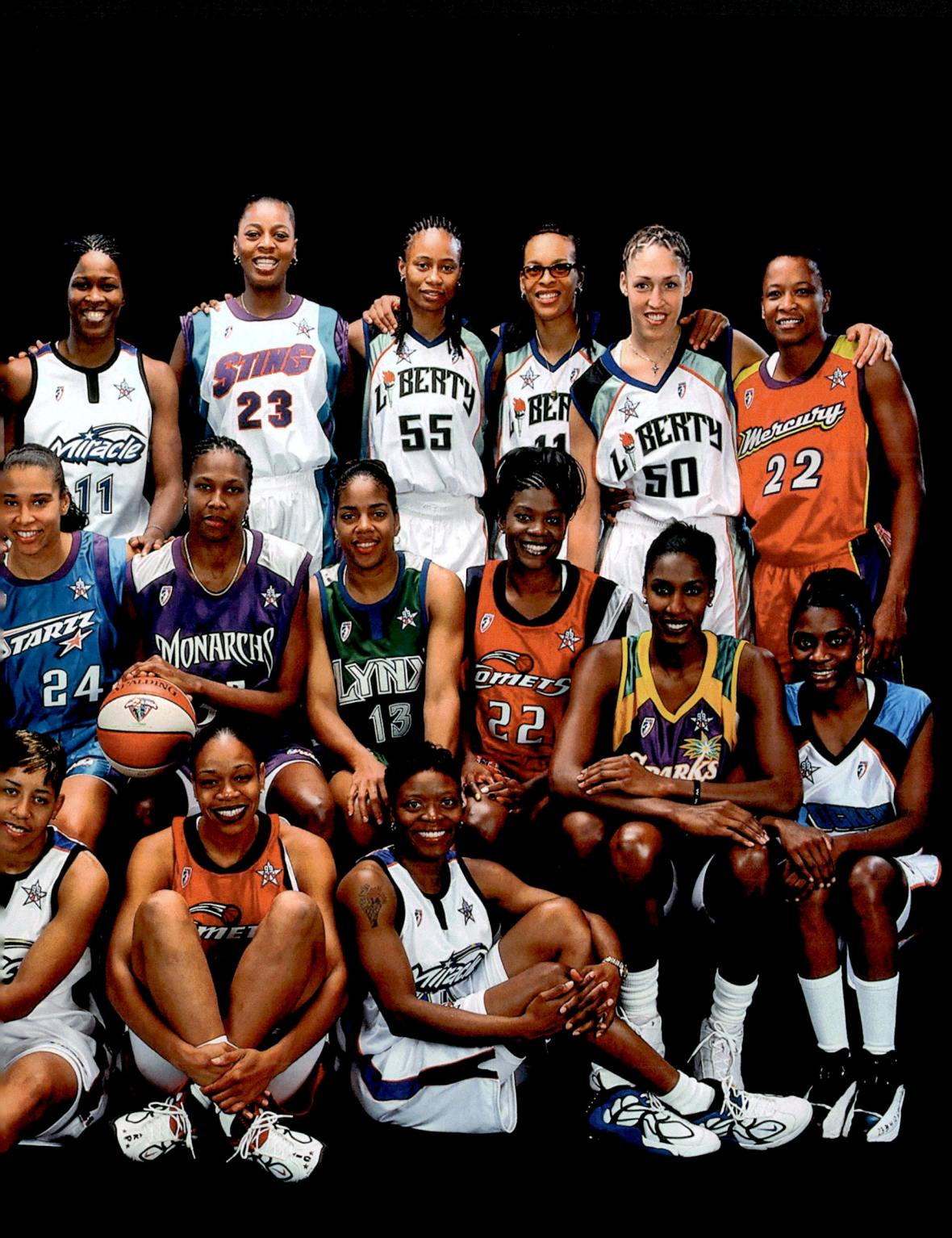

ALL HAIL THE HOUSTON COMETS

The WNBA's First Dynasty

There will never be another winning run like the Houston Comets had from 1997 to 2000. Four championships in four years. Four straight MVPs hailed from the Comets roster—three in a row for Cynthia Cooper and one for Sheryl Swoopes. Three straight Coach of the Year awards for their Van Chancellor. *Dominate* might not do it justice. *Dynamite?* Maybe.

Four days after the Comets first cut down the nets after bouncing the New York Liberty in a single championship game 65–51, Cooper grabbed the mic at the championship parade in front of Houston's City Hall. She rapped:

> We got next, as we flex, on the hardwood
> decks.
> It's not the size of checks, or even gender or
> sex.
> It doesn't matter.
> I'll serve you like a dish on a platter, male,
> female, tall, or even fatter.
> Hanging on the rim like a Shaquille shattah,
> rat-a-tat-tattah
> The WNBA is coming to your town,
> from the East to the West Coast we all get
> down.
> The WNBA is coming to your town.
> Bow down.

"Bow down" is right. The newly anointed basketball royalty wore COMETS across their chests. The roster was stacked. Sheryl Swoopes was the first woman to sign to the WNBA but missed part of the inaugural season because she had a baby. She

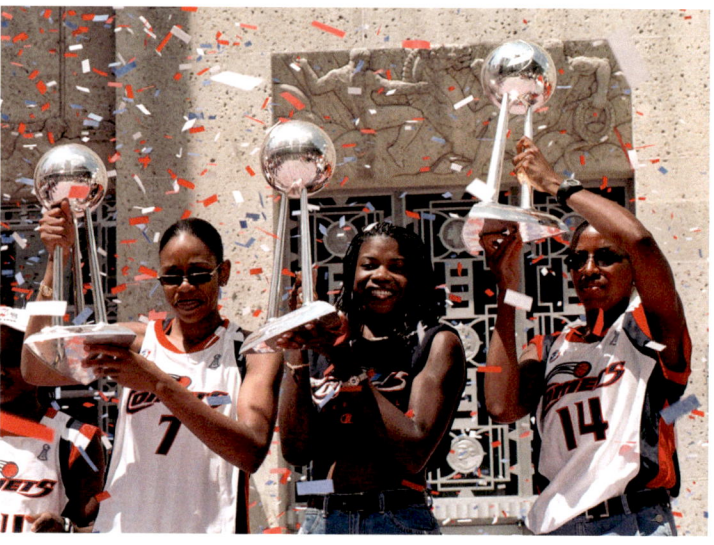

returned just forty-three days after giving birth, like only a mother could. Swoopes's defensive tenacity will be studied for generations to come (ahem, a three-time Defensive Player of the Year). She earned the nickname the Female Michael Jordan and became the first female player ever to have a signature shoe: the Nike Air Swoopes. During her three full seasons in this stretch, Swoopes averaged 18.3 points, 2.6 steals, and 1.0 blocks per game.

Tina Thompson was the youngest on the team by a long shot. She was bright-eyed and fresh from USC, but her age didn't make a difference as she soared for rebounds. Ball high, elbows higher. With

---

ABOVE: The first three WNBA championships were earned by the original "Big 3." Tina Thompson, Sheryl Swoopes, and Cynthia Cooper pose with their hardware in 1999.

OPPOSITE: Swoopes soars in for the rebound while teammates Janeth Arcain (left) and Tiffani Johnson (right) look on.

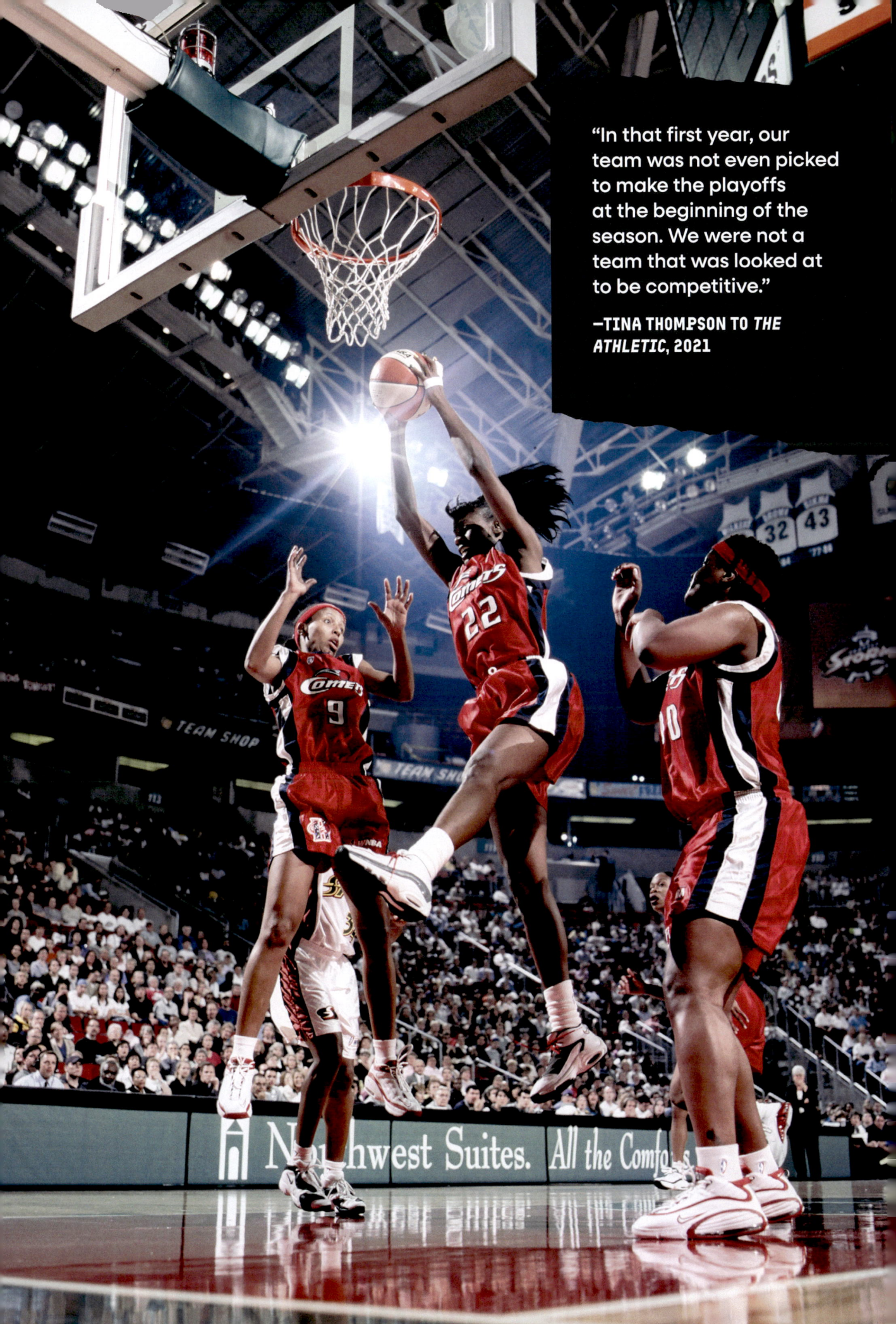

"In that first year, our team was not even picked to make the playoffs at the beginning of the season. We were not a team that was looked at to be competitive."

—TINA THOMPSON TO *THE ATHLETIC*, 2021

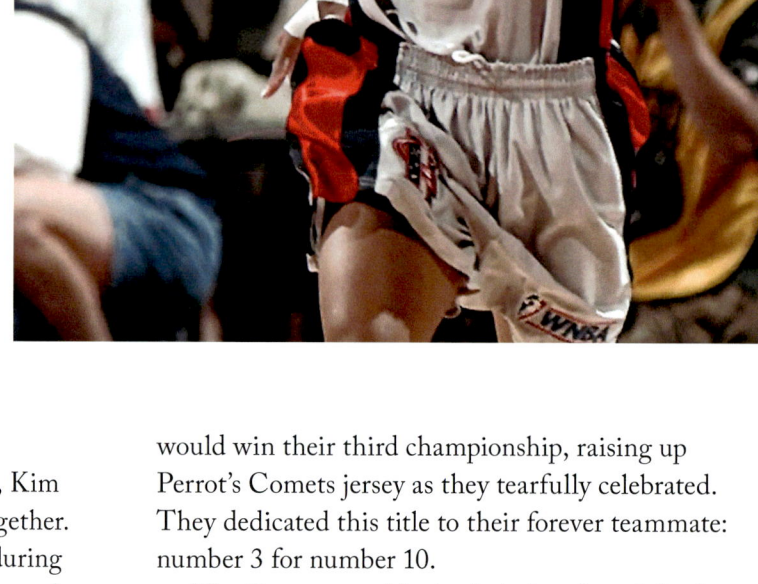

her striking red lipstick and slicked-back bun, she swished baseline jumpers like it was nothing. Her twelve years with the Comets were integral to her Hall of Fame career, which finished with her atop the WNBA's scoring leaderboard with 7,488 points.

With Cooper as the third member of this Big 3, she took pride in the right wing. When she got the ball there, it was like she was a chef ready to take your order. *Would you like me to rip through, blow by you, and finish with a left floater? Or how about you try today's special: a jab-step, pull-up jumper?* "Coop, play your game," Coach Chancellor would tell her with his classic Mississippi drawl.

A walk-on turned starting point guard, Kim Perrot, was the glue that held the Big 3 together. She nearly averaged five assists per game during the '98 season. "If I shoot, we don't have enough basketballs for Sheryl, Coop, and Tina," she'd say. At a feisty five foot five, Perrot was selfless and a flat-out winner. But in February 1999, Perrot was diagnosed with lung and brain cancer at thirty-two. She was still present during practices and games while undergoing chemotherapy—a true fighter. After a six-month battle, Perrot died in August. Almost two weeks later, the Comets

would win their third championship, raising up Perrot's Comets jersey as they tearfully celebrated. They dedicated this title to their forever teammate: number 3 for number 10.

The Comets would win their fourth and final championship in 2000. According to ESPN, they are one of only five domestic professional franchises to win four straight titles.

ABOVE: Comets guard Kim Perrot celebrates winning the 1997 title. In 2000, Perrot's number, 10, was the first jersey to be retired in the WNBA.

DIVAS OF THE COURT

The WNBA released its "soundtrack" through Sony Music in 1999. The track listing on *Divas of the Court—Songs from the WNBA: Volume I* tried to capture the full spread of women's basketball fandom, from Aretha Franklin to the Indigo Girls. Instead of song lyrics, the liner notes showed WNBA statistical leaders. Proceeds went to the National Alliance of Breast Cancer Organizations.

1. Opening Interlude: Welcome to the WNBA—Divas of the Court—Songs from the WNBA: Volume 1
2. Happiness—Vanessa Williams
3. Friends—Luscious Jackson
4. Don't Take It Personal (Just One of Dem Days)—Monica
5. Jumpin', Jumpin'—Destiny's Child
6. Interlude: WNBA Firsts—Divas of the Court—Songs from the WNBA: Volume 1
7. Round of Blues—Shawn Colvin
8. Legend of a Cowgirl—Imani Coppola
9. Everytime—Tatyana Ali
10. Heart and Shoulder—Heather Nova
11. Interlude: Offense—Divas of the Court—Songs from the WNBA: Volume 1
12. Jump to It—Aretha Franklin
13. We Got the Beat—The Go-Go's
14. Interlude: The Buzzer Beaters—Divas of the Court -Songs from the WNBA: Volume 1
15. Ladies First—Queen Latifah
16. Galileo—Indigo Girls
17. Ready to Go—Republica
18. Interlude: Dynasty—Divas of the Court—Songs from the WNBA: Volume 1
19. We Are Family—Sister Sledge

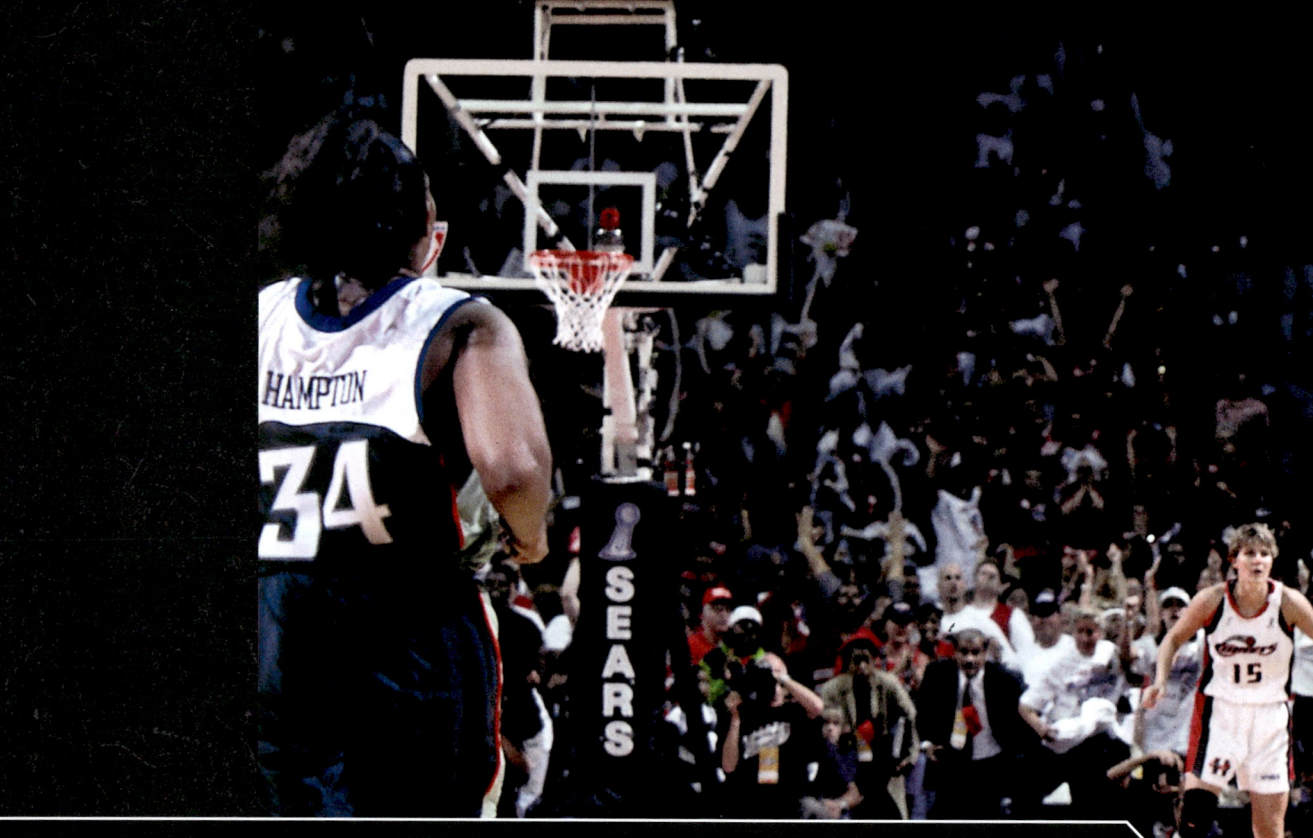

THE SHOT

SEPTEMBER 4, 1999. When the Comets went up over the Liberty with 2.4 seconds remaining in Game 2 of the '99 Finals, confetti started to fall: Arena staff had started dropping it early. They had not been counting on a miraculous, instant-classic, buzzer-beating forty-seven-foot heave from Teresa Weatherspoon. "She put it in!" Mike Breen delivered on the call. "She put it in!" The Comets ultimately won the series. But Weatherspoon delivered the moment that defined it.

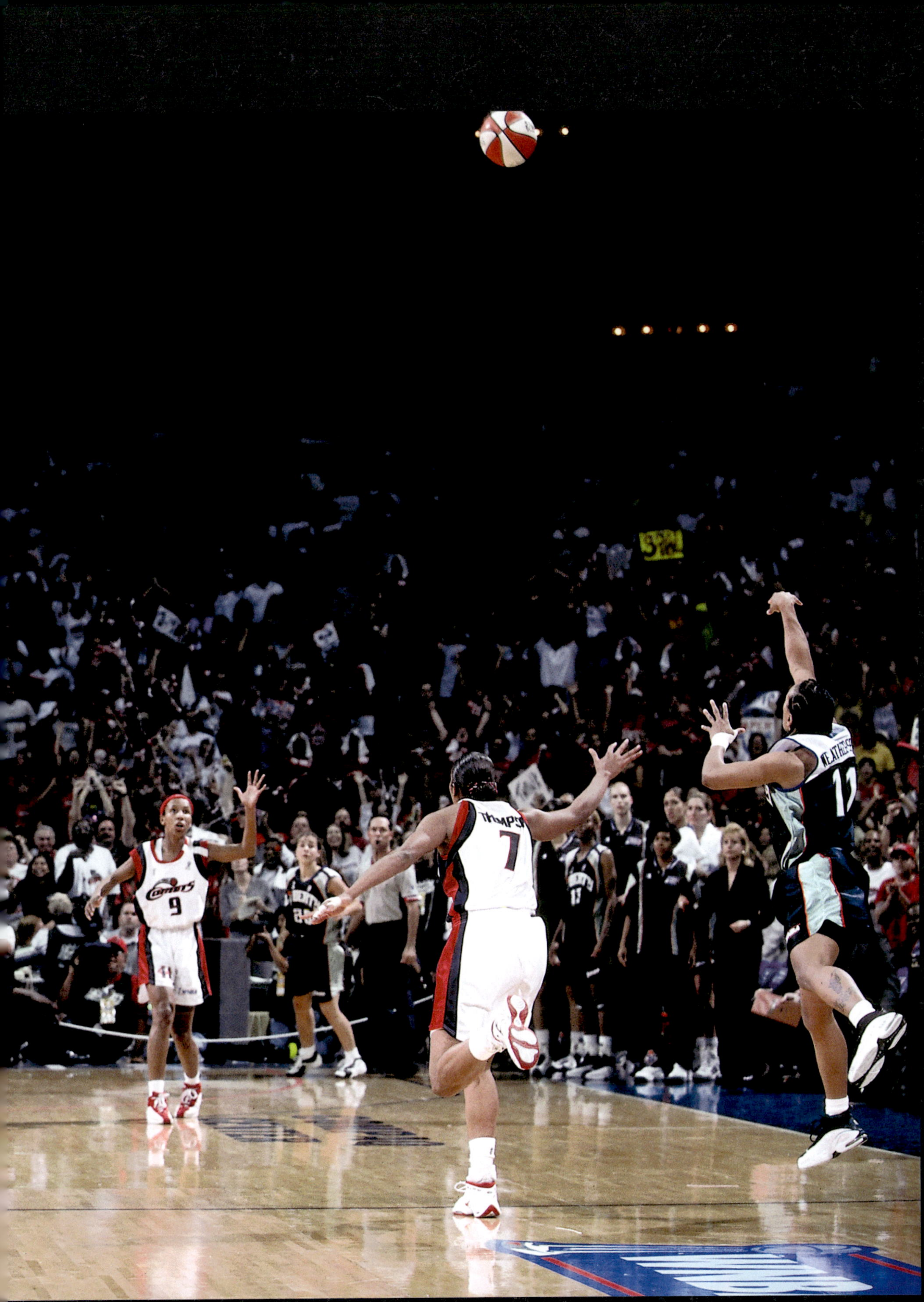

MATTER OF FACT
1990s

Numbers, People, and Moments That Defined the Era

NUMBERS

0-60 Record for 16 seeds in the NCAA tournament until Allison Feaster's Harvard beat No. 1 Stanford in 1998. Since then, no 14, 15, or 16 seed has won a single NCAA tournament game.

7 Tracy Reid was the seventh pick in 1998 and won the first Rookie of the Year award, the lowest pick to do so until Crystal Dangerfield in 2020 (sixteenth pick).

102.4 Average point total of the 1996 Olympic team.

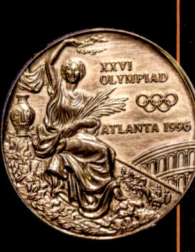

2,178 Career point total for UConn's Nykesha Sales, passing Kerry Bascom for the program record in 1998. She achieved the feat by making an uncontested layup in a cast after a season-ending Achilles injury.

PEOPLE

The tradition of **TINA THOMPSON** wearing her signature red lipstick during games started as an accident. While at USC, she attended an event in full glam and immediately jetted to the arena for her game, forgetting to wipe it off. She played stellar. "It must be the lipstick!" her teammates chanted after the final buzzer. From then on, MAC Diva lipstick became a part of her uniform.

In 1998, the Utah Starzz drafted **MARGO DYDEK**, the first international draftee in the WNBA. The seven-foot-two Polish center had an eighty-five-inch wingspan. By 2001, she set the record for single-game blocked shots with ten, and she still holds the record for career blocks, with 877, after a decade-long stint in the WNBA. The gentle giant's nickname back home was Ptyś—the Polish word for a sweet, whipped-cream-covered cake.

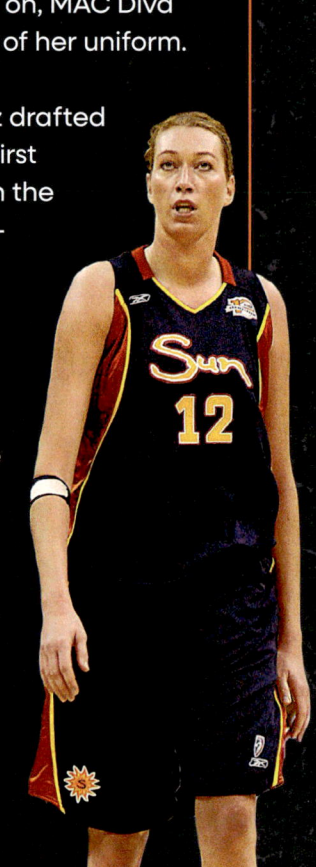

NOV. 7, 1996

Olympians **DAWN STALEY**, **SHERYL SWOOPES**, **REBECCA LOBO**, and **TERESA EDWARDS** appeared on the hit sitcom *Martin*.

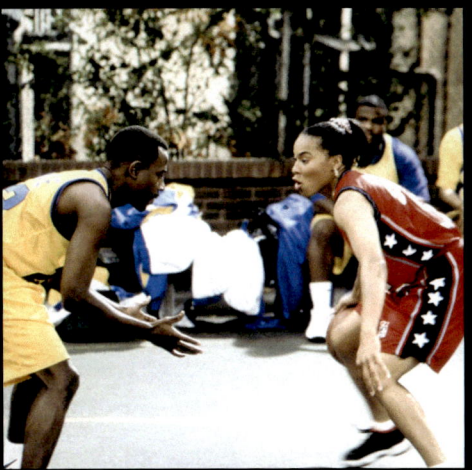

1996

LISA LESLIE signs a contract with Wilhelmina Models.

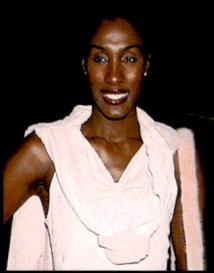

FEB. 10, 1998

WNBA BARBIE debuted at the American International Toy Fair, fitted with a jersey, shorts, and knee pads. "I can really shoot and pass!" the box states.

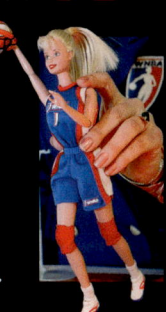

JULY 14, 1999

Grammy Award–winning artist **WHITNEY HOUSTON** sings the National Anthem in front of an electrified, sellout crowd at Madison Square Garden for the inaugural WNBA All-Star Game. This came eight years after her iconic rendition of "The Star-Spangled Banner" at Super Bowl XXV, arguably the best performance in history.

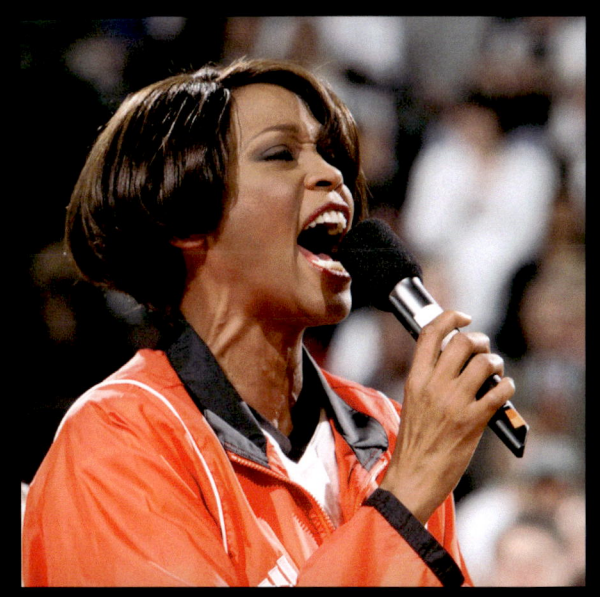

THE YOUNG GUNS

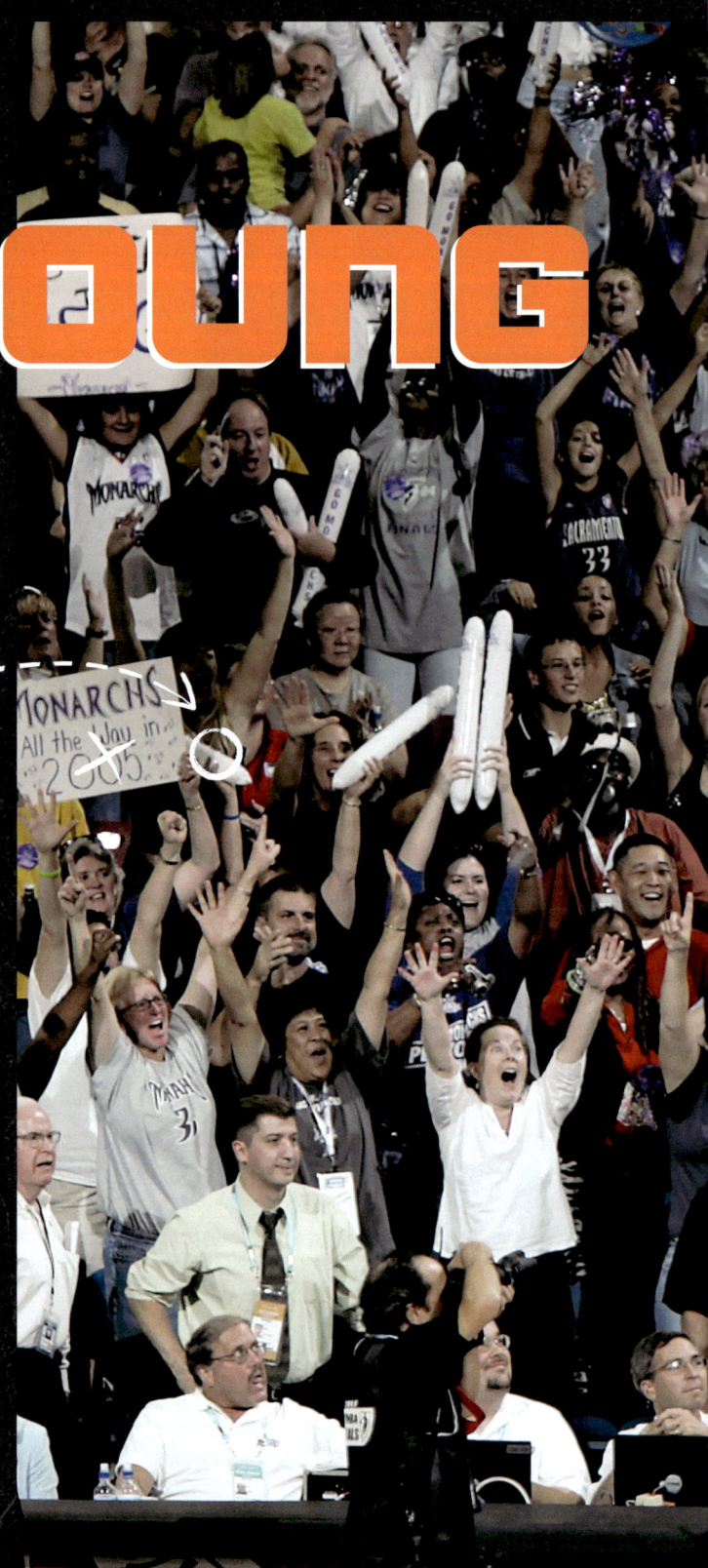

WHEN ONE DYNASTY ENDS, ANOTHER STARTS ANEW: A YOUNG LEAGUE BEGINS TO BUILD ITS OWN LORE.

RIGHT: Kara Lawson revels in the Sacramento Monarchs Finals crowd, 2005.

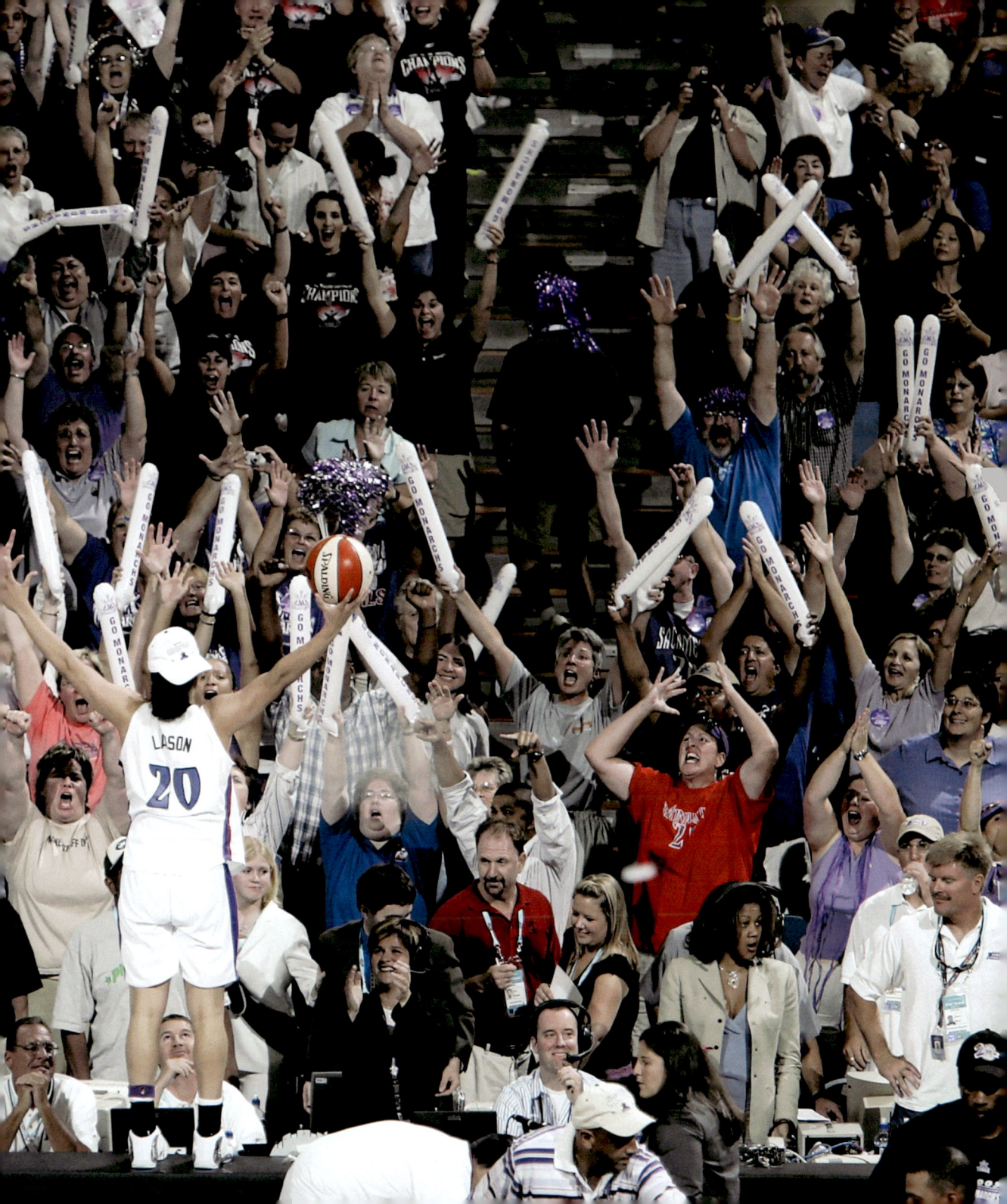

CHANGING OF THE GUARD

The Comets' Reign Comes to an End: There's New Talent in Town

At the turn of the century, the WNBA added four more franchises into the mix: the Indiana Fever, Miami Sol, Portland Fire, and Seattle Storm. Still, the Houston Comets held up four fingers as they hoisted the championship trophy so that even the fans in the Compaq Center's nosebleed seats could see it shine again. It was their fourth WNBA championship in as many years.

"I'm just glad I don't have to go to church tomorrow tied one–one and convince the Lord that I'm one of his boys," coach Van Chancellor said, after his Comets bested the New York Liberty (again) 79–73 in overtime, sweeping the series 2–0. "Was that a basketball game? This one was the sweetest of the four."

It *was* sweet and felt like an era closing and a new one beginning. Three-time league scoring champ Cynthia Cooper, thirty-seven, would retire after this season and accept the head coaching position of the Phoenix Mercury. Around the league, many trailblazers from the '97 allocation draft, like Mercury's Michele Timms and Liberty's Teresa Weatherspoon, were pushing forty. The recent additions of ex-ABL players who joined the WNBA in their career's twilight years were

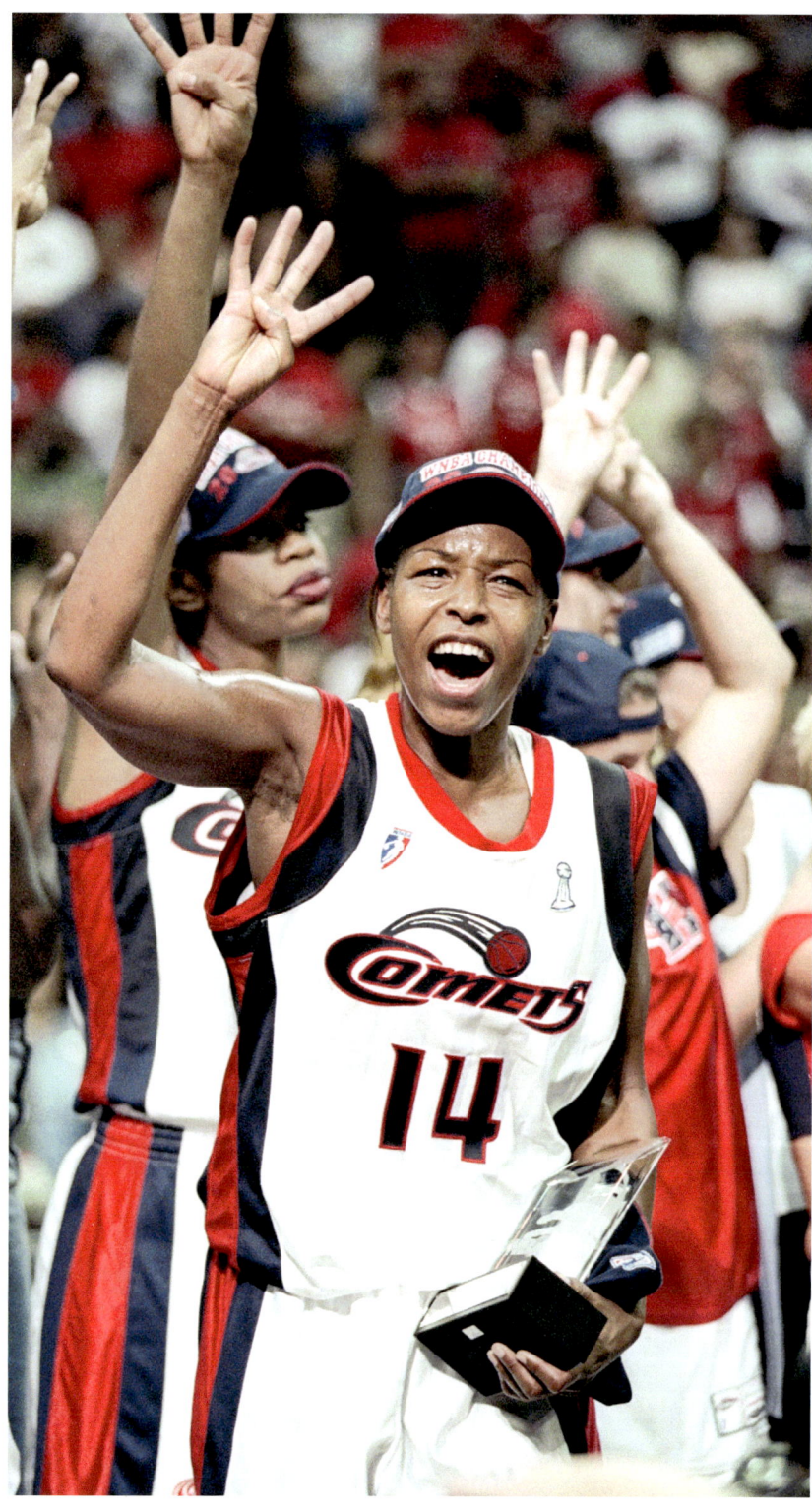

RIGHT: Cynthia Cooper celebrates in 2000, letting everyone know how many rings (and Finals MVPs) she owns.

phasing out, and young, spry college talent was sprinkling in.

The 2000 season comprised a full slate of thirty-two games (plus an All-Star break) and playoffs in just ninety days; this feverish pace was a young woman's game. This feeling of transition bubbled over to the 2000 Sydney Olympic squad as well. It was one last ride for stars like five-time Olympic legend Teresa Edwards (thirty-six) and fierce competitor Ruthie Bolton (thirty-three). Team USA still went undefeated to capture their second-straight Olympic gold. But the eighteen-year-old, six-foot-five Aussie who scored 20 points on a thirty-year-old Yolanda Griffith in the post during the gold-medal Final was a glimpse that the future was coming and ready to wreak havoc.

In 2001 Seattle Storm head coach and general manager Lin Dunn drafted that Australian Olympian, Lauren Jackson, number one overall. "Everyone was trying to get that pick. Other teams were offering almost their whole starting five," Dunn said at the time. "After seeing her perform in Sydney with her toughness, competitiveness, and long-term potential, there was no doubt. She was too good."

The opportunity was there; this would be the first draft class to complete four years of college ball since the WNBA's inception. The Storm's next draft pick in 2002 was a gritty point guard from New York with a slicked-back ponytail, Sue Bird. Dunn was building for the future—not just her team's, but the league's.

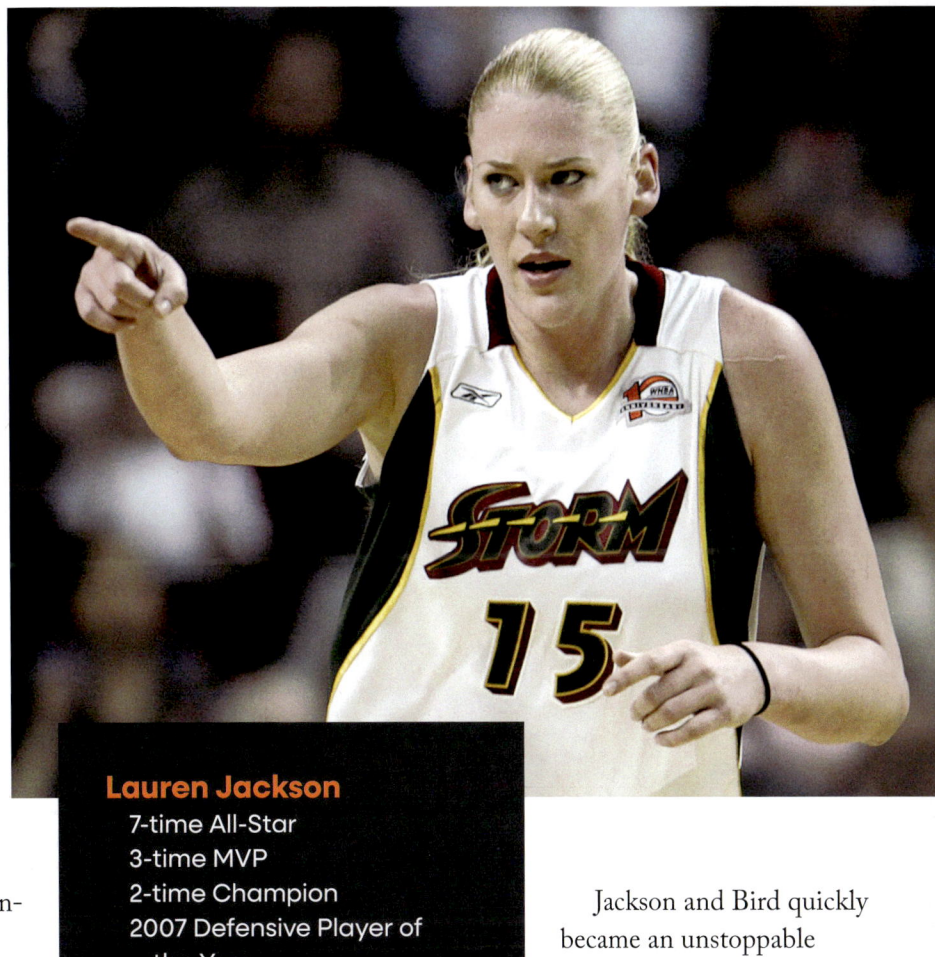

Lauren Jackson
7-time All-Star
3-time MVP
2-time Champion
2007 Defensive Player of the Year

Jackson and Bird quickly became an unstoppable pick-and-roll duo. Their youthful stamina was too much for their opponents. They'd win the franchise's first of four championships in 2004. Jackson was already a league MVP (the first of her three MVP awards and the only international player to receive the honor). Bird averaged almost six assists per game and dished out a single-game record fourteen times in the playoffs. And twenty-eight-year-old Betty "Big Buckets" Lennox took home the Finals MVP award by averaging 22.3 ppg in the series win over an All-Star Connecticut Sun squad led by Nykesha Sales, Katie Douglas, Taj McWilliams-Franklin, and rookie Lindsay Whalen. Seattle had arrived.

ABOVE: Lauren Jackson took Seattle by storm when she entered the league as a teenager in 2001. The Aussie is the first and only international player to earn the MVP award, and she did it three times.

SUE BIRD

13-TIME ALL-STAR, 5-TIME OLYMPIC GOLD MEDALIST,
4-TIME WNBA CHAMPION, 2-TIME NCAA CHAMPION,
ALL-TIME WNBA ASSIST LEADER

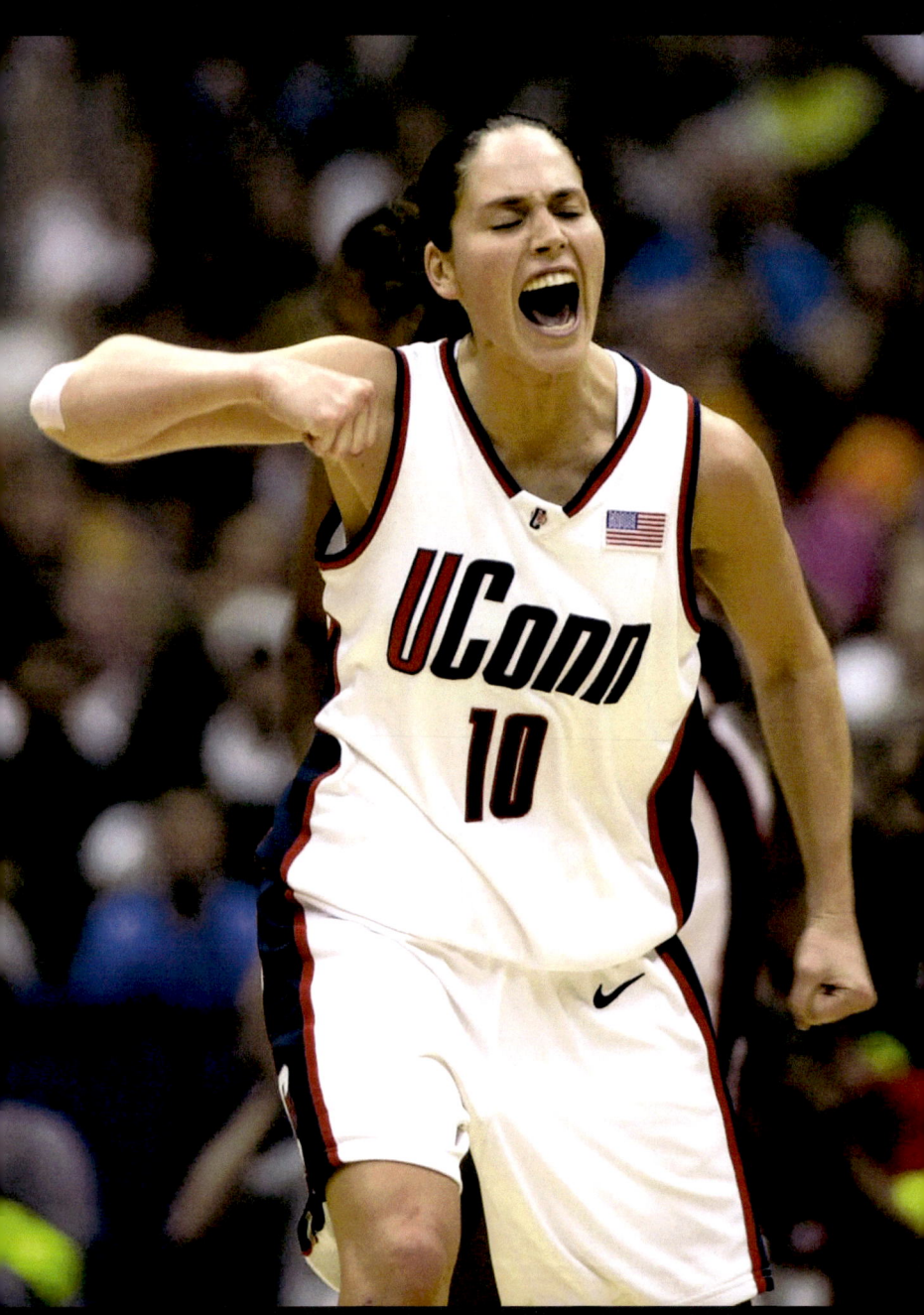

ABOVE: Bird screams against Tennessee on March 29, 2002,
during the NCAA Women's Final Four in San Antonio.

Seattle's Climate Pledge Arena is the house Sue Bird built. The portion of Second Avenue North where it sits is called Sue Bird Court for a reason. She was drafted to the Storm in 2002, only year three of the franchise. All eighteen playoff appearances and all four championship banners had her fingerprints.

Bird loved playing point guard because of the control: At the point, she could control the tempo, the play calling, and when to call her own number. It's cerebral. It's surgeonlike. Women's basketball fans sat in awe of Bird's decision-making, big-time shot-making, and no-look passing spanning four decades. When she hung up her sneakers in 2022, she'd be the WNBA's all-time assist leader and one of the most decorated Olympic athletes ever. Above all, though, she was a winner.

"Scrabble, Crazy 8, card games, Candy Land—you name it, Sue Bird had to win," Nancy Bird said about her daughter in the documentary *Sue Bird: In the Clutch*. "When she lost, she did not like it."

Bird started playing soccer while growing up in Syosset, New York, on Long Island. She'd score goals like it was going out of style. But by thirteen years old, hoops had fully consumed her life. Bird had transferred to the highly touted Christ the King Regional High School in Queens, whose team, after a perfect 27–0 season, won a New York state championship in 1998. When colleges came calling, they wanted a point guard to help their program win, and they knew she'd be the one to do it.

Bird doesn't like when people sugarcoat the truth. She knew University of Connecticut head coach Geno Auriemma would give it to her straight, and she respected that. She also respected the pedigree of what wearing "UConn" across her chest meant. When she was incoming in 1998, the Huskies had already won a championship in 1995 with Rebecca Lobo. Auriemma already had over 300 victories. She also knew it wouldn't be easy, especially at the point guard position.

"'You know, everything that happens out there is your fault, right?'" Bird recalled what Auriemma told her early in her career. "'If so-and-so turns it over, that's your fault. You need to take ownership of everything that's happening out there.'"

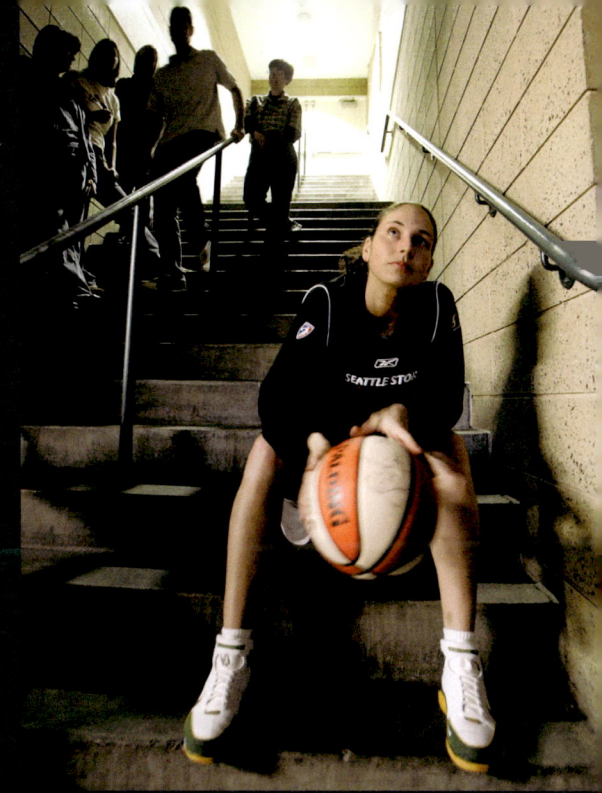

She'd earned the starting spot as a freshman but tore her ACL eight games in. During that rehab season, she could digest the pace of the college game, observe the right on-ball screen reads, and learn how her teammates could be best set up for success. In 1999, she came back stronger and more focused. Flanked by All-Americans Swin Cash and Asjha Jones—two future Olympians—Bird led the UConn Huskies to a national championship, averaging 11 points, four assists per game, and almost 50 percent from the three-point line. She did a belly slide onto the court as the final horn sounded.

"She's going to throw the ball to the right person at the right time to the right place every time," Auriemma said. "And if the game's on the line? She's going to shoot it, and it's going in."

A new freshman arrived on campus in the 2000–01 season. Diana Taurasi was confident

---

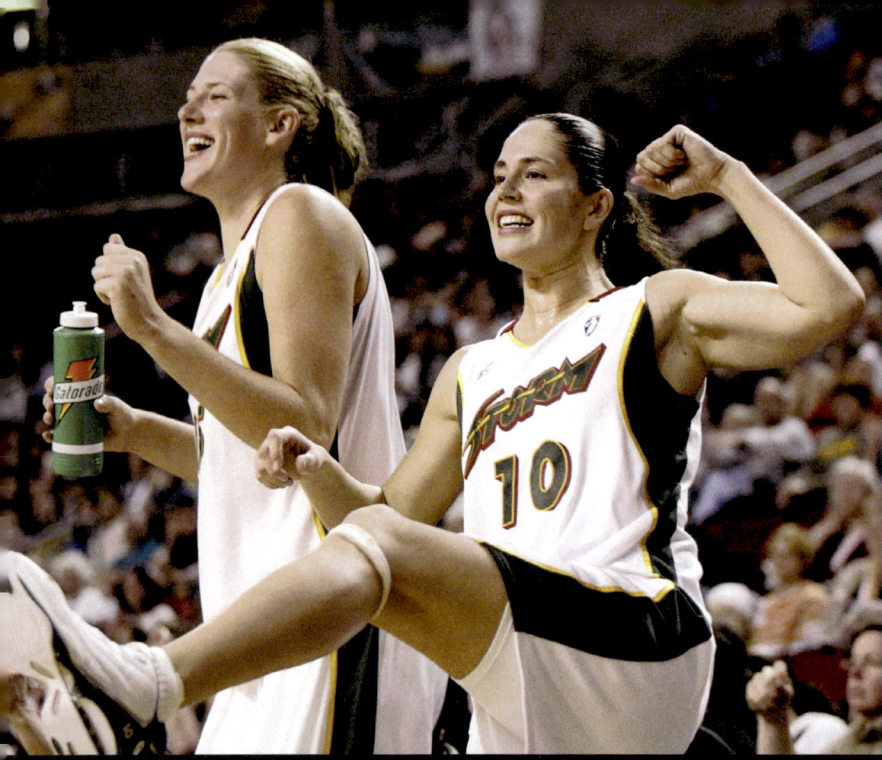

points) led them back to the Final Four, but this time a different result. Over 5.5 million viewers watched as another UConn undefeated season stamped history. "Thirty-nine and zero, and Connecticut is perfect!" said ESPN's Mike Patrick as the celebration ensued. Sue Bird had only lost four times in her entire college career.

"If we had won that semifinal against Notre Dame, maybe we don't go undefeated that next year. Maybe we don't win a national championship. Maybe that 2002 team doesn't go down as one of the best ever," Bird wrote in *The Players' Tribune* in 2018. "And we were one of the best. Ever."

and a little hotheaded. Bird's shyness balanced her out, and the best friendship materialized. The two shared a willingness to do anything to win. They went 15–1 in the Big East Conference and landed back in the Final Four, taking on Notre Dame for a chance to go to the championship again. The teams had been battling all season long. Notre Dame handily won the first meeting 92–76 in South Bend—the first win over UConn in school history. Then, for the Big East Championship, Bird hit the game-winning, buzzer-beater three-pointer, which sportswriter Jeff Goldberg described in his book *Bird at the Buzzer* as "the best women's college game ever played." The 2001 national semifinals rematch was must-watch TV, but Notre Dame's Niele Ivy and Ruth Riley combined for 39 points in the comeback win. Bird scored a team-high 18, but it wasn't enough. The team shot a dismal 6-for-30 from the three-point line. Heartbreak.

That Final Four loss made for an even sweeter senior season for Bird. She was confident that UConn was the best team in the country. They were untouchable. An unblemished 34–0 regular season (with an average winning margin of 37

A few weeks later, as the high had subsided, Bird got ready for the WNBA Draft. She was the first pick—the first UConn player to go number one—and packed her bags for Seattle, Washington, a city she knew little about. Bird was the Storm's second top draft pick in two years. Lauren Jackson had already begun her dominance, but they needed a floor general to push them to the next level.

"Playing with someone like that gives you so much confidence because she's so smart," Jackson said of her teammate of twelve seasons.

Jackson and Bird became a decade-defining duo. Bird's court awareness was extraordinary. She could stop on a dime and throw them. Her head was level, her emotions guarded; she made it all look effortless. In 2004 she and Jackson won the franchise's first title and their first championship together. "It was my first 'first,'" Bird said. She's

ABOVE: Bird, with teammate Lauren Jackson, celebrates from the bench during a regular-season win over the Silver Stars in 2003.

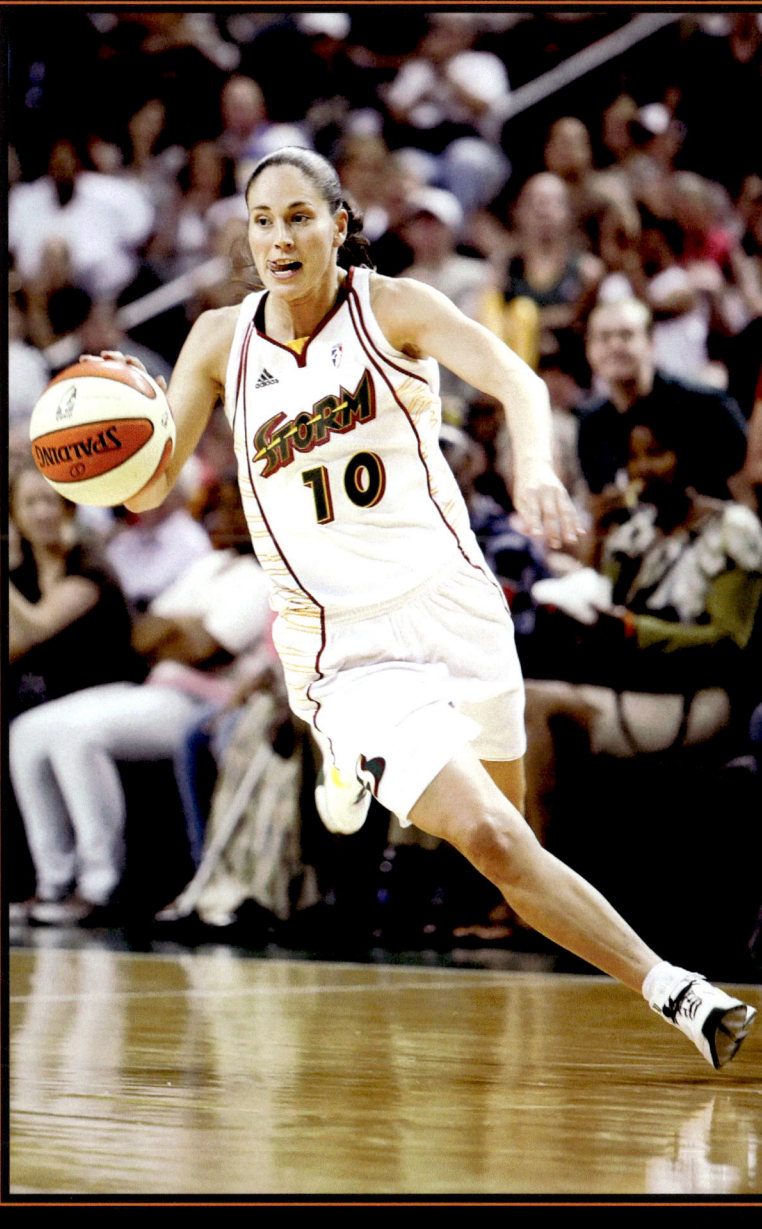

Sheryl Swoopes, Lisa Leslie, and Dawn Staley.

"The same way Dawn got to help me, I'd want to pass that on to somebody else," Bird said to ESPN in 2018. "I think that's what USA Basketball is about—it's about the older players showing the younger players the ropes a little bit, what it means to be a USA Basketball player, represent your country, represent the team, yourself, all that stuff. It's about showing younger players and then also going out and winning gold medals, that's all that matters."

The 2000s were full of Bird's "firsts." Her first undefeated regular season. Her being the first pick in the 2001 WNBA Draft. Her first professional championship. Her first gold medal. With Bird's unique skill set and tenacity, fans knew none of it would be her last. Throughout the next two decades of her career, she'd win three more 'ships for Seattle (2010, 2018, 2020), set a record of thirteen WNBA All-Star appearances, and finish atop a half dozen all-time lists.

never been a part of building something from the ground up. Christ the King had already had a legacy of greatness, and so had UConn. The Storm, still in its infancy, had an opportunity to create a new expectation of winning. And that was what Bird was all about.

Earlier in 2004, Bird sported the red, white, and blue for the first time with Team USA. The Athens Olympic team had a balance of youth and vets. Bird, Taurasi, Cash, Riley, and Tamika Catchings were all first-timers. They learned from the best as they chased gold again: three-time Olympians

"I feel like I've helped create a path for players in the WNBA that didn't exist before," Bird says in her documentary, *Sue Bird: In the Clutch.* "Not a lot of people can sit here and say the things that I'm saying. And then, on top of that, I won a lot. So it's not just feeling satisfied with how I carried myself. I also f— won, and you can never take that away."

ABOVE: By the time Bird retired in 2022, she'd be the WNBA's all-time assist leader.

DETROIT SHOCK THE WORLD

A Dynasty Emerges from Motor City

The youth movement also went through the Detroit Shock in 2003, a team with an average age of only 24.2 years old. After starting 0–13 the previous season and finishing last in the standings, the young, hungry squad led by six-foot-one forward Swin Cash wanted to rewrite their history. Flint, Michigan, native Deanna "Tweety" Nolan was a speedy midrange sniper who also shot over 42 percent from the three-point line. Rookie power forward Cheryl Ford, daughter of NBA player Karl "Mail Man" Malone, averaged a double-double in points and rebounds on her way to Rookie of the Year honors. And Ruth Riley, at six foot five, covered the paint ferociously. The Shock's insanely quick pace made it difficult for teams to keep up with their point production (a league-best 75.1 ppg) while keeping opponents to a league-low field-goal percentage.

"The 2003 Detroit Shock changed the way women's basketball was played forever," said head coach and general manager Bill Laimbeer, who orchestrated this iconic worst-to-first season by being aggressive in free agency and the draft. He was a key

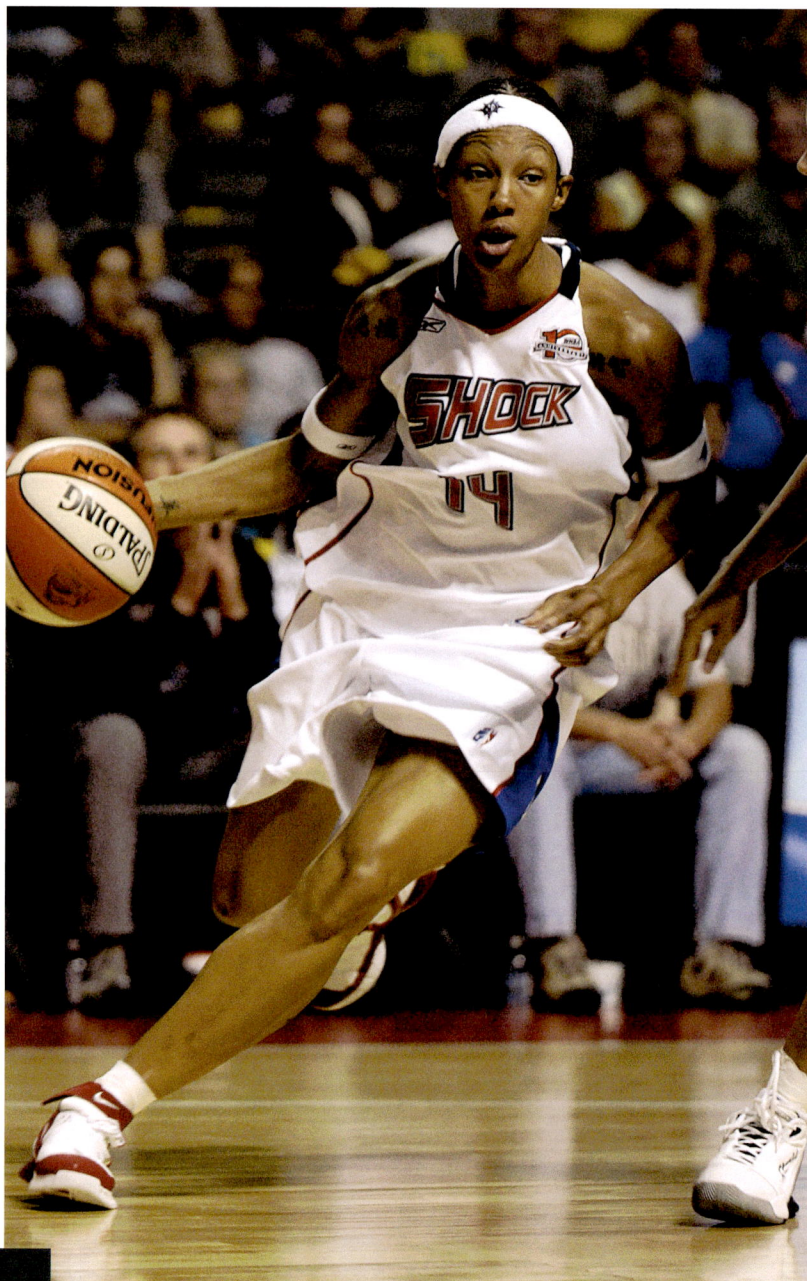

Deanna "Tweety" Nolan
5-time All-Star
3-time Champion
2006 Finals MVP

ABOVE: Deanna Nolan was crazy quick and had a fierce midrange game. Here, she's moving past her defender in the 2006 WNBA Finals en route to earning the Finals MVP award.

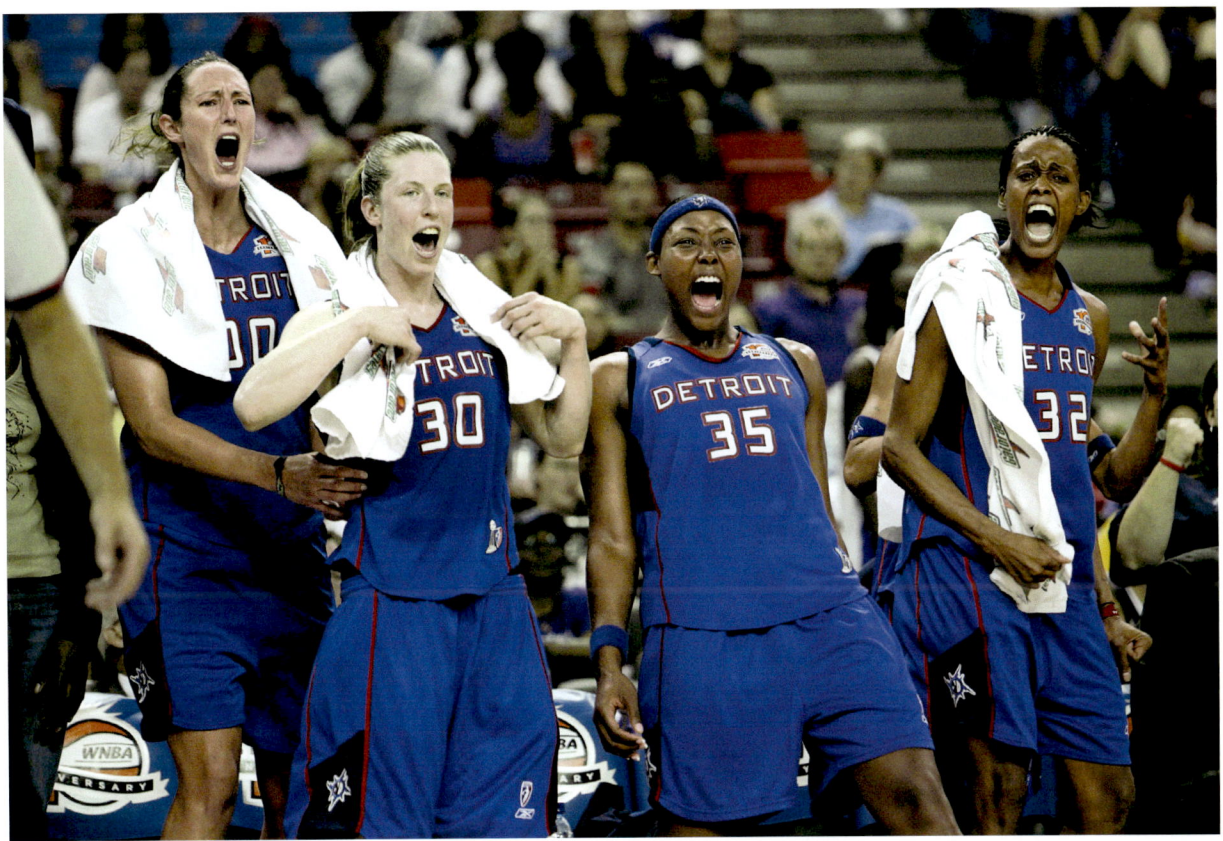

figure of the brash NBA Detroit Pistons' "Bad Boy" era of the late eighties, and it was rubbing off. "We go play physical basketball, and we go to play every game to win. We'd rip your heart out."

In a win-or-go-home Game 3 of the Finals, against the LA Sparks, a record 22,076 fans in Detroit watched their Shock become the youngest title-winning team in league history. "As it gets going, you see them start to mold themselves into the 'Bad Girls,'" Kristin Bernert, Shock VP of Operations, added. "Every good story has a villain." This kick-started a dynasty; Laimbeer led Detroit to win two more titles in the decade, 2006 and 2008.

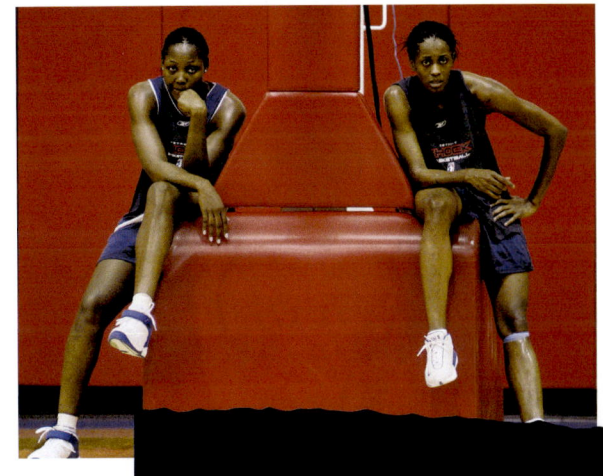

TOP: The Detroit "Bad Girls" always brought the energy. From left to right: Ruth Riley, Katie Smith, Cheryl Ford, and Swin Cash.

RIGHT: Cheryl Ford (left) and Swin Cash (right) take a breather during practice ahead of the 2003 WNBA Finals.

"Detroit is a big, tough, power team that'll knock your head off inside."

—JOHN WHISENANT, MONARCHS COACH, 2006

TAKING CENTER STAGE

When Radio City Music Hall Became an Unlikely Hoops Venue

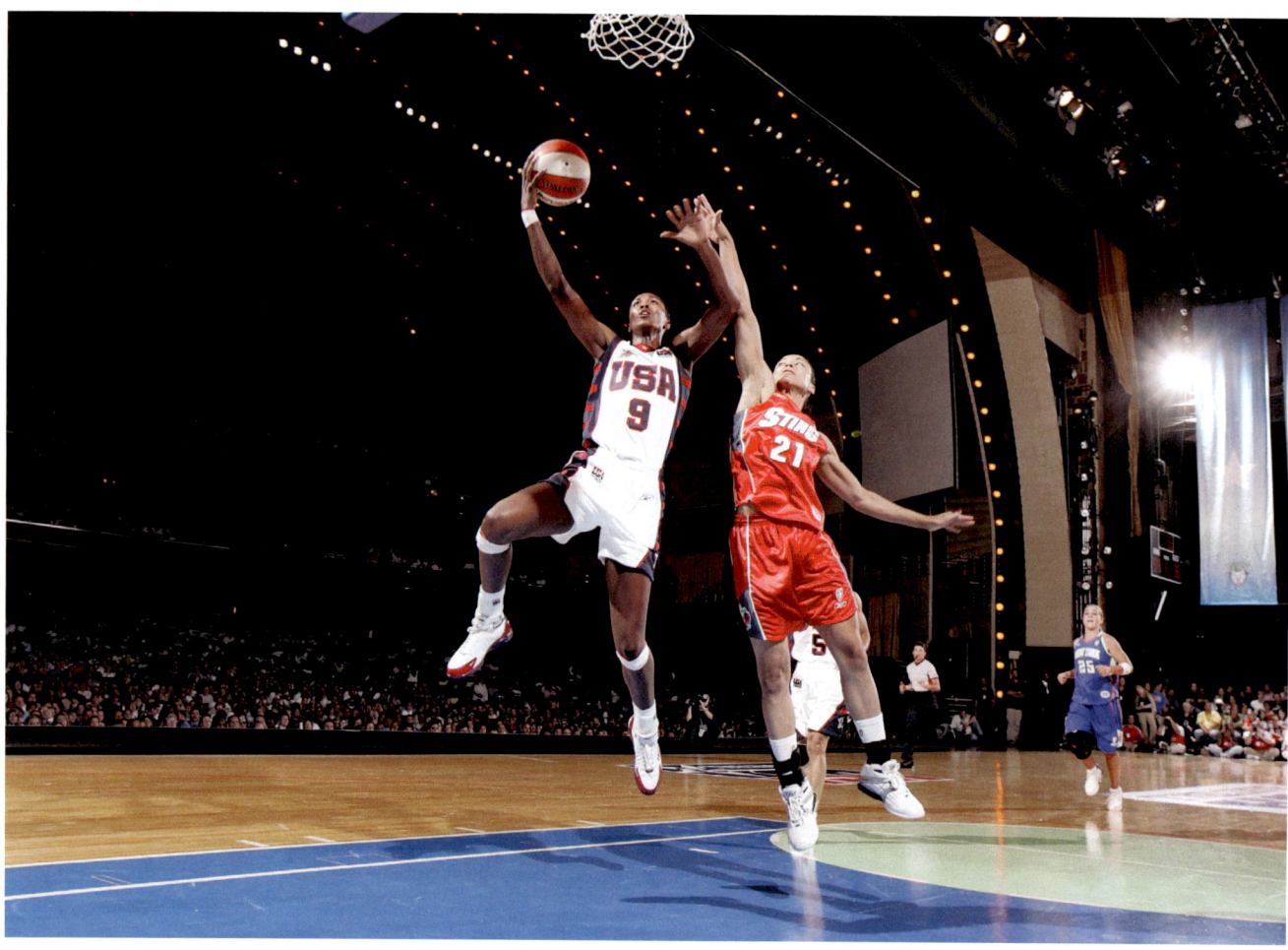

Right from the jump, WNBA teams got very familiar with getting bumped from their home gyms, forced to relocate games to accommodate everything from concerts to other sporting events to Disney on Ice. No team ever handled it quite how the Liberty did in the summer of 2004.

Their usual home of Madison Square Garden would begin hosting the Republican National Convention that August. But they would have to evacuate for more than just the convention itself: The event required so much preparation and security that the team would have to leave for a month. It would cover six home games. Rather than moving

to another arena, Liberty owner James Dolan threw out a different, decidedly more complicated plan. His corporate portfolio also included Radio City Music Hall. Why not just play there?

For one, the famed concert venue had never hosted any kind of team sporting event, for two, its capacity was half their average attendance, and for three, it was unclear a basketball court would even

ABOVE: Radio City Music Hall was also home to the All-Star Game, with a group of stars playing an exhibition against Team USA before it left for the 2004 Olympics.

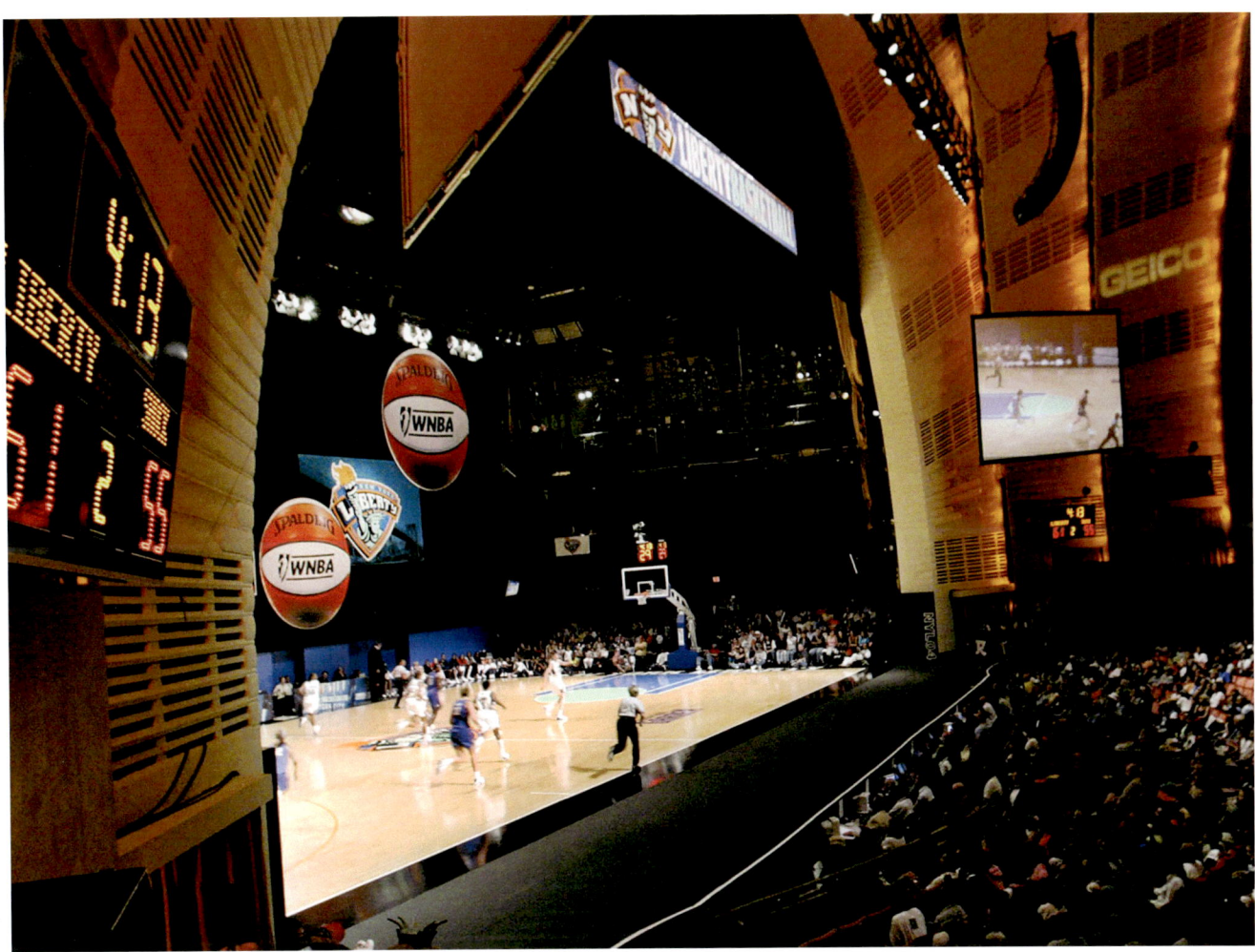

fit on the stage, New York Liberty general manager Carol Blazejowski later recalled. Dolan insisted they go for it anyway. So they did, and it created some of the most interesting, visually striking games ever seen in the league.

They pulled up their hardwood and moved it a few blocks north to set up onstage. (They had to bring *everything* with them: Liberty personnel would not be allowed in MSG for any reason while security preparations were ongoing, so they brought uniforms, basketballs, even laundry detergent.) They decided the players would jog down the aisles for pregame introductions. For halftime entertainment, they'd have, naturally, the Rockettes.

Radio City was not without a few mishaps. A league press release had tried to get ahead of one of them: "The court will be set back far enough so that players don't fall off the stage diving for loose balls." They did not count on the tenacity of Shock forward Swin Cash, who did, in fact, dive into the orchestra seats doing just that. (She popped right back up.) And the phenomenal acoustics onstage meant players and coaches had to be careful about what they said. *Everything* carried. But it left them with an experience that was one of a kind. That stage had been home to Frank Sinatra and Stevie Wonder, Ella Fitzgerald and Mariah Carey, the NFL Draft and the MTV Video Music Awards.

And how many of them could say they used it to show off their jump shot?

ABOVE: Fans still got a scoreboard and a video screen next to the action. It just looked a little different than usual.

THE BATTLE OF CALIFORNIA

Sacramento and Los Angeles Spark a Rivalry

What makes a rivalry? History, hate, and hostility are all key ingredients. The Comets and Liberty carried the crown through the previous decade, but in the early 2000s, new feuds brewed, forcing casual viewers to choose a side.

By 2005 Lisa Leslie had almost every award you could win—three All-Star Game MVPs, two league MVPs, two Finals MVPs, and Defensive Player of the Year. Her Sparks had recently won back-to-back titles in 2001 and 2002. (In the former, LA won eighteen games in a row, a WNBA record that still stands today.) No one liked battling the Sparks, but the Sacramento Monarchs, particularly, weren't keen on their California foe. This beef even crossed gender lines; the NBA's Los Angeles Lakers and Sacramento Kings *hated* each other.

The WNBA's LA-Sacramento battles raged with "Beat LA!" chants in ARCO Arena, wall-shaking boos when Sparks' Nikki Teasley graced the jumbotron, and rattling cowbells when any purple-and-gold player stepped up to the free-throw line. But in 2005—after the Sparks had ended their playoff hopes in 1999, 2001, and 2003—the Monarchs swept them in the playoffs on their way to the franchise's first and only title. They were a team full of hustlers: Point guard Ticha Penicheiro added the flair to the fast break, Kara Lawson was the muscle, Nicole Powell was pure from long range, and Rebekkah Brunson started to show her dominance inside. Finals MVP Yolanda Griffith shouted "2005" into the mic as they celebrated with purple and silver confetti flickering around them. The crowd echoed her. "All the way live!"

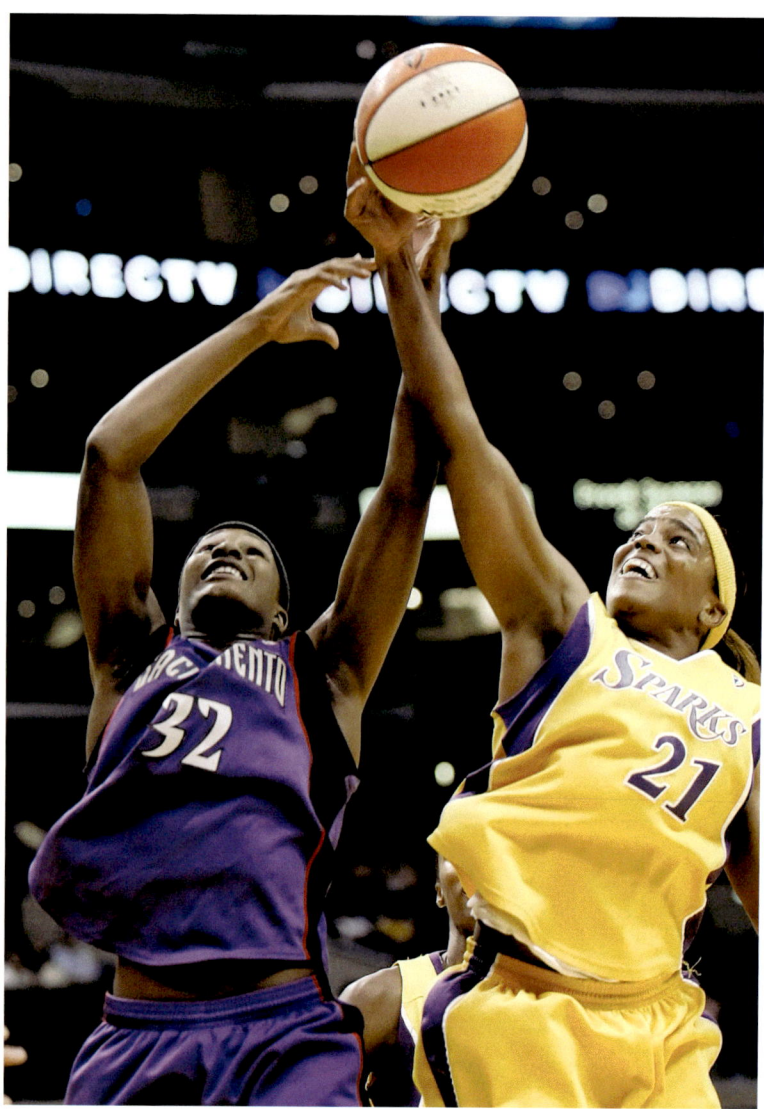

ABOVE: Every matchup between the Monarchs and Sparks was for bragging rights to be the state's premier team. Rebekkah Brunson (left) and Tamecka Dixon (right) battle on the boards in August 2005.

OPPOSITE: Griffith adds "Champion" and "Finals MVP" to her already-packed résumé of WNBA All-Star, DPOY, and Newcomer of the Year.

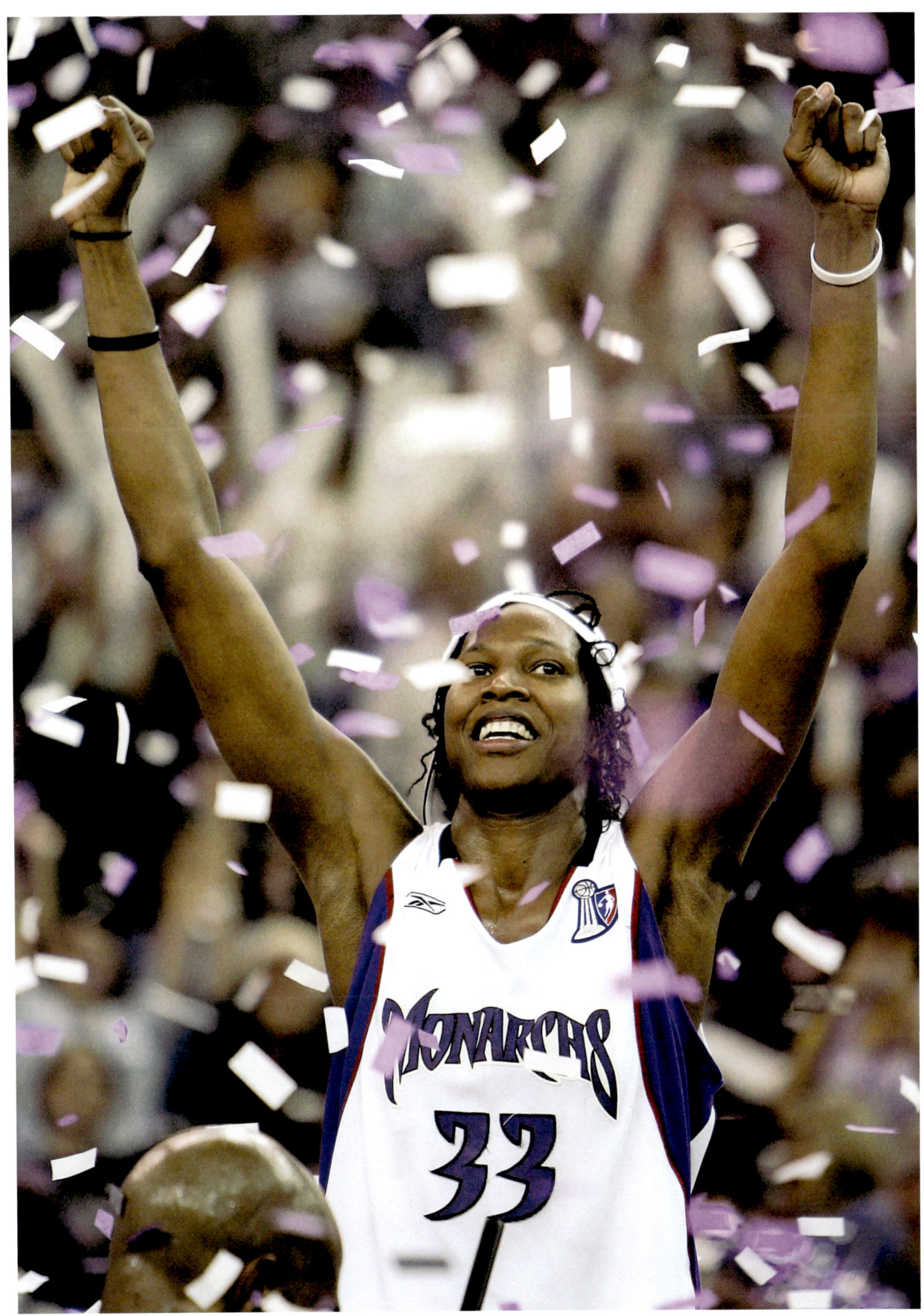

THE DUNKING QUEEN

Lisa Leslie Throws It Down

"Byears gets it up to Leslie. What's she gonna do? She dunked it! For the first time in WNBA history, someone has dunked in a game! It's Lisa Leslie with the dunk!"

—THE PLAY-BY-PLAY CALL

When the 1996 Olympic team embarked on its barnstorming tour before the Games, playing exhibitions and holding open practices across the country, Lisa Leslie pulled out a signature move.

She dunked.

Leslie was under strict instructions from US head coach Tara VanDerveer not to do so during national team games. (VanDerveer did not want any injury risks while preparing for the Olympics.) But outside game situations, during open practices and warm-ups, Leslie knew exactly how she wanted to treat the crowds full of excited little girls.

She dunked because it was fun, of course, but she also dunked

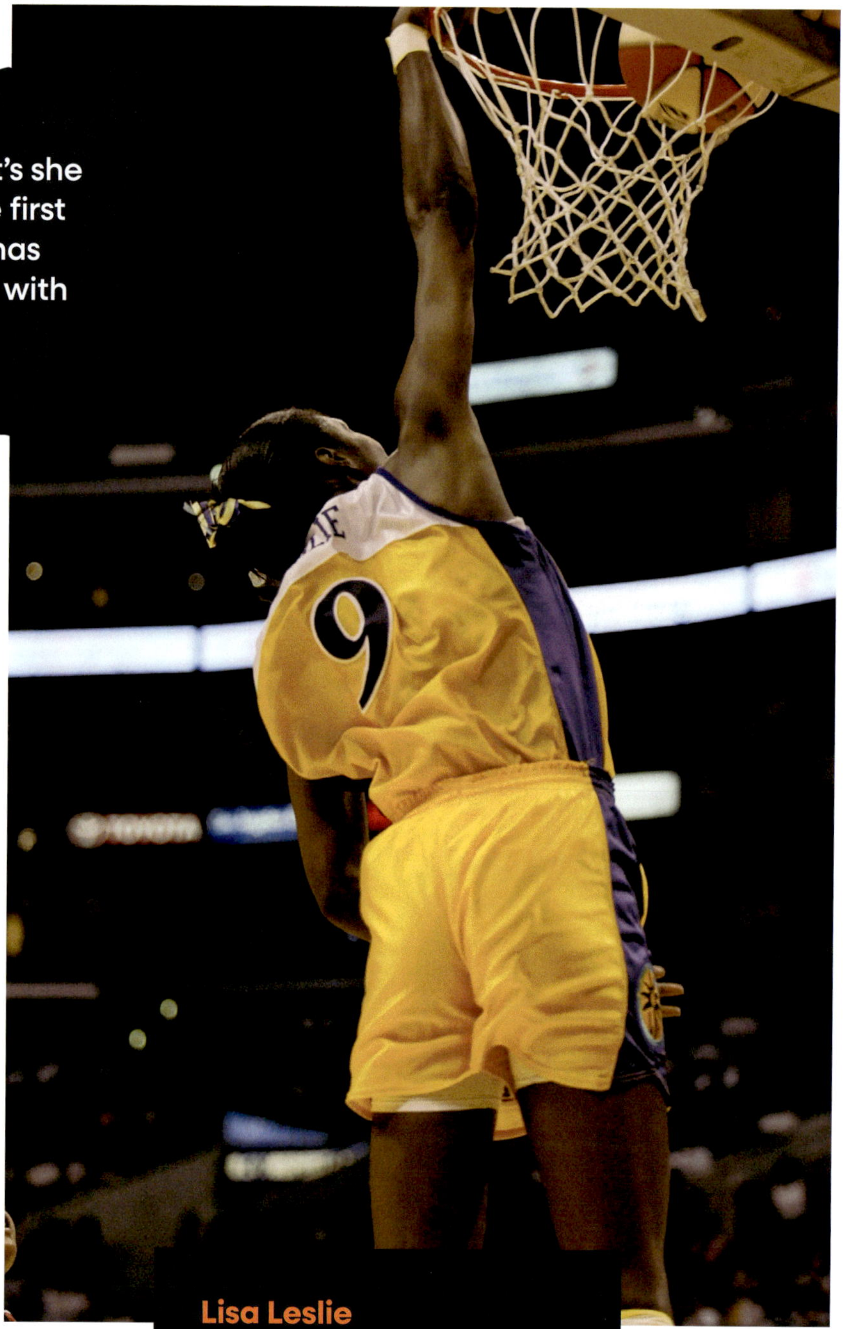

Lisa Leslie
8-Time All-Star
3-Time MVP
2-Time WNBA Champion

RIGHT: "They're saying now I've got to reverse it, and the Tomahawk is next," Leslie told reporters the day after her dunk.

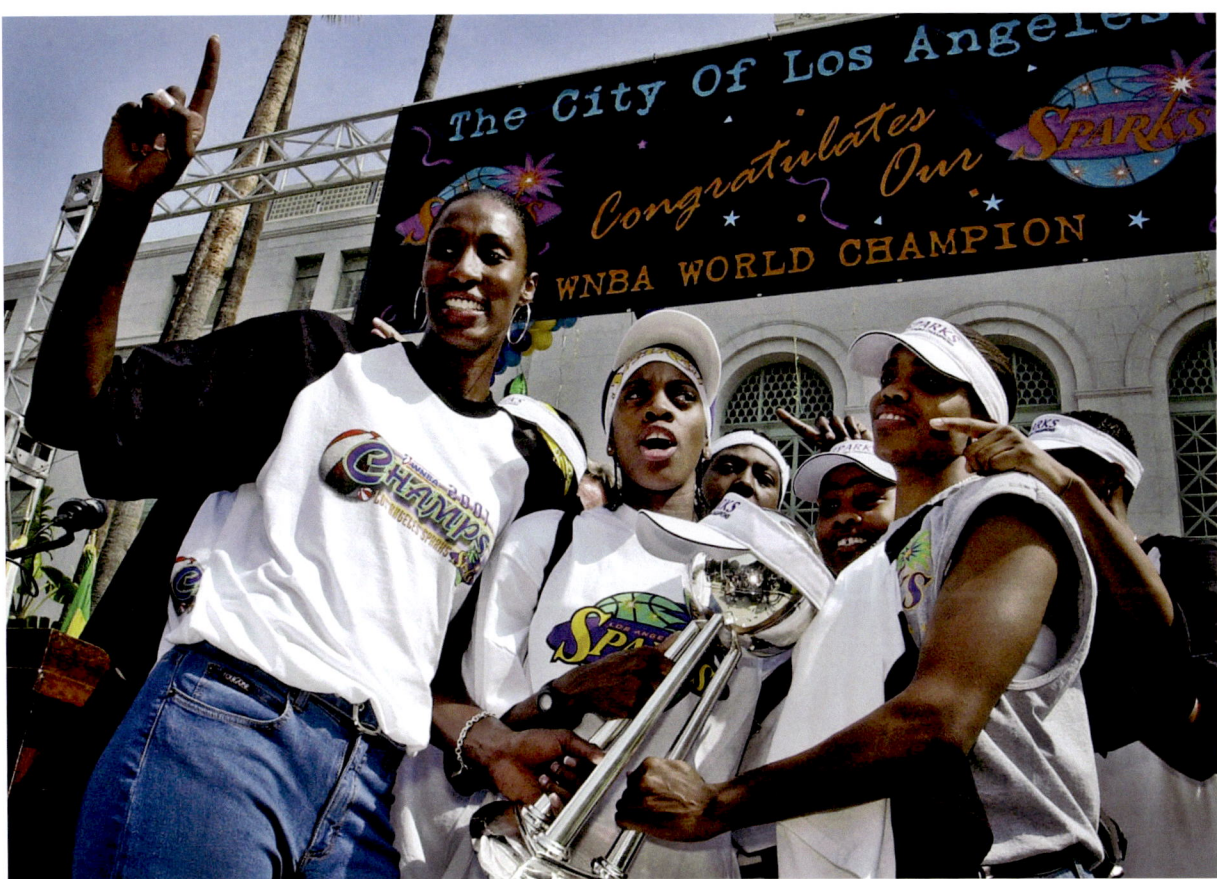

because she wanted people to see her doing it.

"If those girls see me doing something that people think women can't do, well, then, maybe they won't listen the next time somebody tells them women can't do something," she explained at the time.

She had wanted to deliver that same kind of signature moment for the first game ever in the WNBA. "I was thinking it'd be big for women's basketball, so as I'm dribbling, I'm contemplating, Do I do it? Do I not do it?" Leslie told reporters. "And then I ran right into the rim." She had been so anxious that she had barely slept the night before that inaugural game: She tried going to bed at 6 p.m., woke up at 11 p.m., fell back to sleep at 1 a.m., and woke up again at 3 a.m. and 5 a.m. The missed dunk made for a frustrating lowlight. She would not try again in a game for years.

But when she *did* go for that next dunk attempt, five years later, Leslie made it count. Midway through the second quarter on July 30, 2002, she found herself with an open lane and threw it down

with one hand. This one had been a no-doubter. Her Los Angeles Sparks ultimately lost that game to the Miami Sol. But her dunk won the day. Leslie's highlight was everywhere—an electric rejoinder to arguments that dunking would never happen in the W. It was part of an incredible stretch for Leslie and the Sparks.

The willowy center had won her first MVP in 2001, after being a finalist for years, and she then delivered the first title to the Sparks. They repeated as champs in 2002. She would keep piling up accolades until 2007—when she sat out a year on maternity leave, a lost season of sorts for the team, which gave them a poor record but a high draft pick. They would use that to draft a next-generation star, another dunker, a player to carry the next era. Leslie would pass the torch to Candace Parker.

ABOVE: The Sparks won consecutive titles in 2001 and 2002. It would be two decades before another team went back-to-back.

THE POSITIONLESS POWERHOUSE

CANDACE PARKER HAD AN ILLUSTRIOUS CAREER: TWO-TIME MVP, FINALS MVP, ROOKIE OF THE YEAR, DEFENSIVE PLAYER OF THE YEAR, AND SEVEN-TIME ALL-WNBA FIRST TEAM

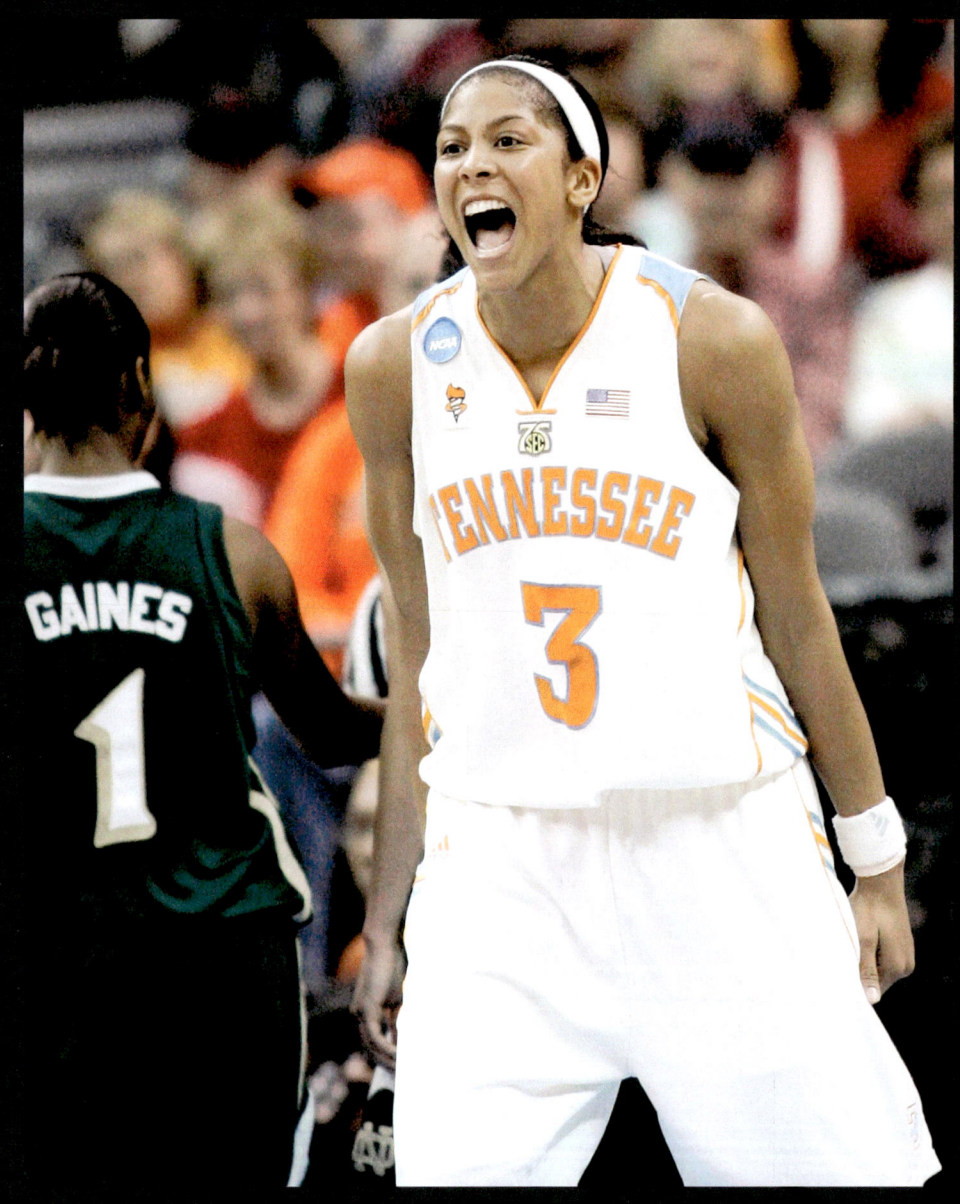

ABOVE: Parker's do-it-all skill set and passion lit up the college game.

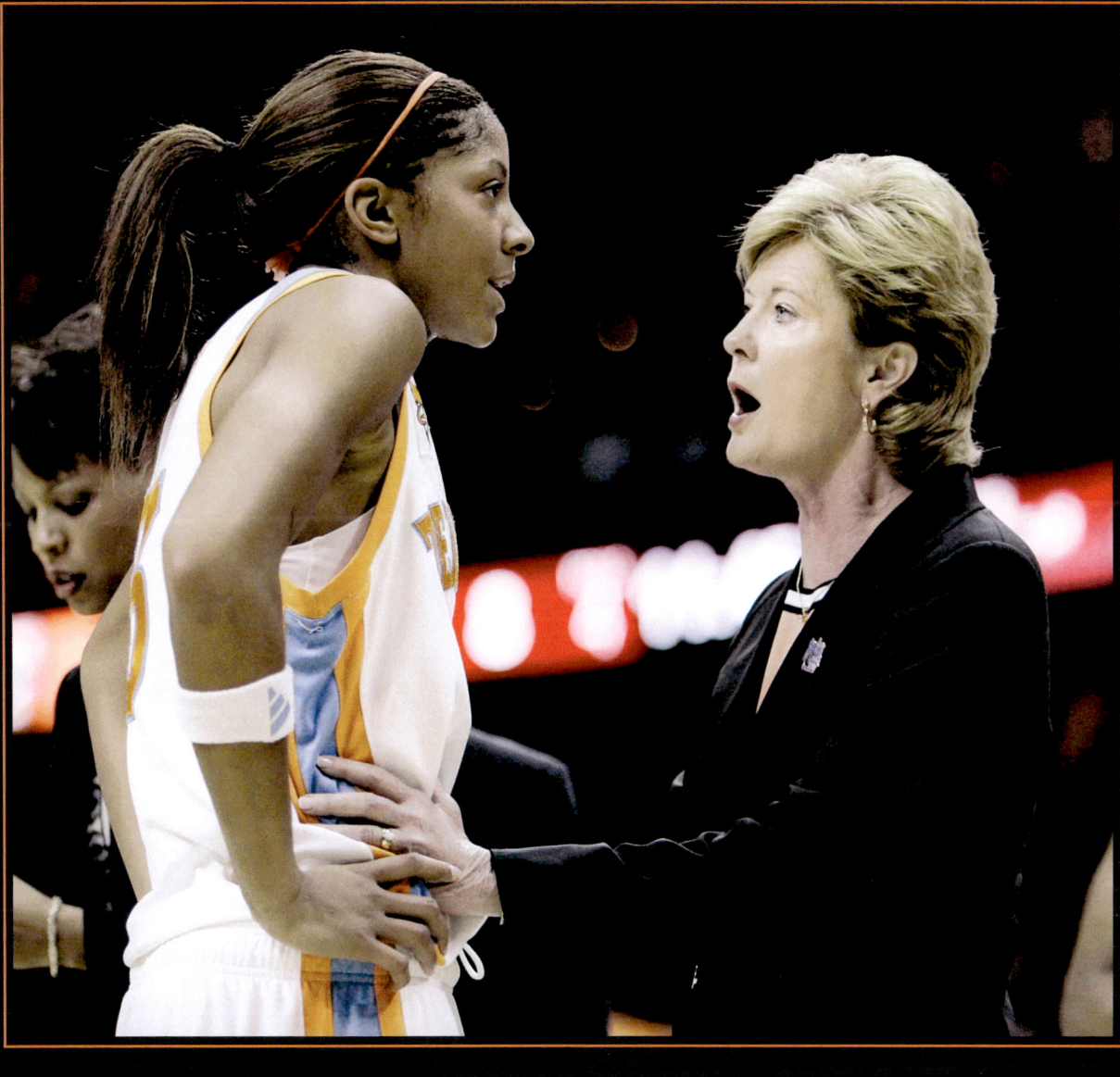

"H ype Machine Is Rolling" read the headline on a *Chicago Sun-Times* article on Candace Parker in July 2000. She was just fourteen years old—still a month away from starting high school. But it was hard to argue with the headline. The hype machine *was* rolling, and it would continue going right on ahead for years, making her the center of remarkable national attention. Yet she consistently managed to play up to expectations. Parker never let that rolling hype machine run her over.

The first national headlines came a year later, when fifteen-year-old Parker dunked in a high school game in her hometown of Naperville,

Illinois. There would be more of those headlines when she won the Naismith Prep Player of the Year Award, more when she won it *again* the following year, the first player to receive the honor twice, and more when she became the first girl to win the McDonald's All-American High School Dunk Contest. (For her grand finale, she went no-look, covering her eyes with her left hand before dunking

ABOVE: Parker's relationship with Summitt would be one of the guiding forces in her career. She eventually gave her third child the middle name "Summitt."

with her right.) When she decided to play for Pat
Summitt at Tennessee in November 2003, she made
the announcement in a special on ESPNEWS, the
first time a college decision by a woman had been
carried live on national television.

But what made her special was not the dunks,
not the raw physical gifts, not the constant
accompanying media circus. It was how she rewrote
the possibilities of the game. Parker was not quite
like anyone who had come before her. She was six
foot four, a record-breaking dunker, and . . . nothing
like a traditional big. Parker had the handles of a
point guard. She had the quickness and light touch
of someone much smaller. She could score from
anywhere, create her own shot, and bring the ball
up. And, of course, Parker
still had the post moves and
defensive acumen that you
would expect from someone
with her size and skill. There
were no compromises in her
game, and she helped usher
in a modern, positionless style
of basketball that would pave
the way for the next decade.

It was not that she was
ahead of her time so much as
it was that she forced the whole sport ahead in order
for it to catch up with her.

She began honing that versatility early. It
was partially a product of her father, Larry, who
coached her Amateur Athletic Union team. "If
some other coach had told her, 'You're tall, you're
going to be my center,' Candace would basically
be a center," Larry told *USA Today* in 2003. "She
wouldn't have developed those other skills." And
develop them she did.

It made her all but impossible to classify. When
Parker got to Tennessee, the school listed her as a
"forward/center/guard." There was no use in putting
one (or two) position(s) on her. She was everything.

Parker had chosen Tennessee largely because
of Summitt. She entered the program during a
relative dip. The Lady Vols had not won a title in
six years—not very long in the scheme of things,
perhaps, but a veritable drought for a program like

this one. Worse, it had lost eight of its last nine
matchups with dreaded rival UConn, including
three in the national championship and one in
the Final Four. (Diana Taurasi's years as a Husky
were not kind to the Lady Vols.) Parker wanted to
change that, and most of all, she wanted to play
under Summitt.

She wanted to be challenged.

Parker learned quickly just how that could
manifest. Early in her freshman year, rehabbing a
knee injury, she waited to sneak into an empty gym.
She was under strict instructions not to run or jump
while still recovering. It was unclear how much she
would be able to play in the upcoming season and
in those early, shifting months of college, Parker
wanted a private reminder
of what she could do. She
needed to dunk. Just once.
And so alone, in the quiet
gym, she worked herself up to
it, and she threw one down.
Parker left satisfied.

She got the message the
next day: *Coach needs to see you
in her office.*

Parker had no idea how
Summitt could have possibly
found out that she had been in the gym. ("I think
Pat is omniscient," Parker wrote in a reflection for
Sports Illustrated.) The coach was predictably furious
but she pushed the conversation beyond simple
anger. This demonstrated to Summitt that Parker
should not be playing *at all* that year: The decision
lay with Parker, but rather than rushing herself back
and potentially compromising her career, the most
hyped player in the country should really delay her
start in college and take a redshirt, Summitt said.

The freshman was heartbroken. But she listened.
"It was the best decision I ever made," Parker wrote
a few years later. It demonstrated something to her:
Summitt would push her, and she would sometimes
frustrate her, but it would always come from a place
of deep care. "Everything she did was to make me a
better individual," Parker wrote. Over the next few
years, player and coach would push the program
back to the highest level of the sport.

> "I know she was in a lot
> of pain. But we were in
> a lot of pain trying to
> guard her, too."
>
> —GARY BLAIR,
> TEXAS A&M COACH, 2008

The forward/center/guard lived up to the billing at Tennessee. In her first NCAA tournament game, Parker became the first woman to dunk in the tourney, and then, about twenty minutes later, she became the first woman to do it *twice*. Yet the season did not end the way they hoped: Tennessee lost in the Elite Eight. Parker was adamant that would not happen again. They won the national championship the next year, and she promised that another would be coming after that, too.

"You can mess around and do stuff one time, and people can doubt it. But if you do something twice, it's not by accident," Parker later told *Time*. "In order for my name to be mentioned with the greatest players at Tennessee, I have to win twice."

And, of course, she did. It resulted in one of the most impressive statlines of her career. Against Texas A&M in the Elite Eight, Parker put up 26 points, five rebounds, two blocks, two steals, and two shoulder dislocations. Twice she left the floor in pain. Twice she came back, compromised but determined, and battled to push her team over the edge.

Summitt had assumed that Parker was out after the second dislocation. The first one had looked playable—not for everyone, certainly, but for someone as fierce and determined as her star player, sure. But when Parker's left shoulder popped out of its socket again, this time at a freakish angle, it seemed like that

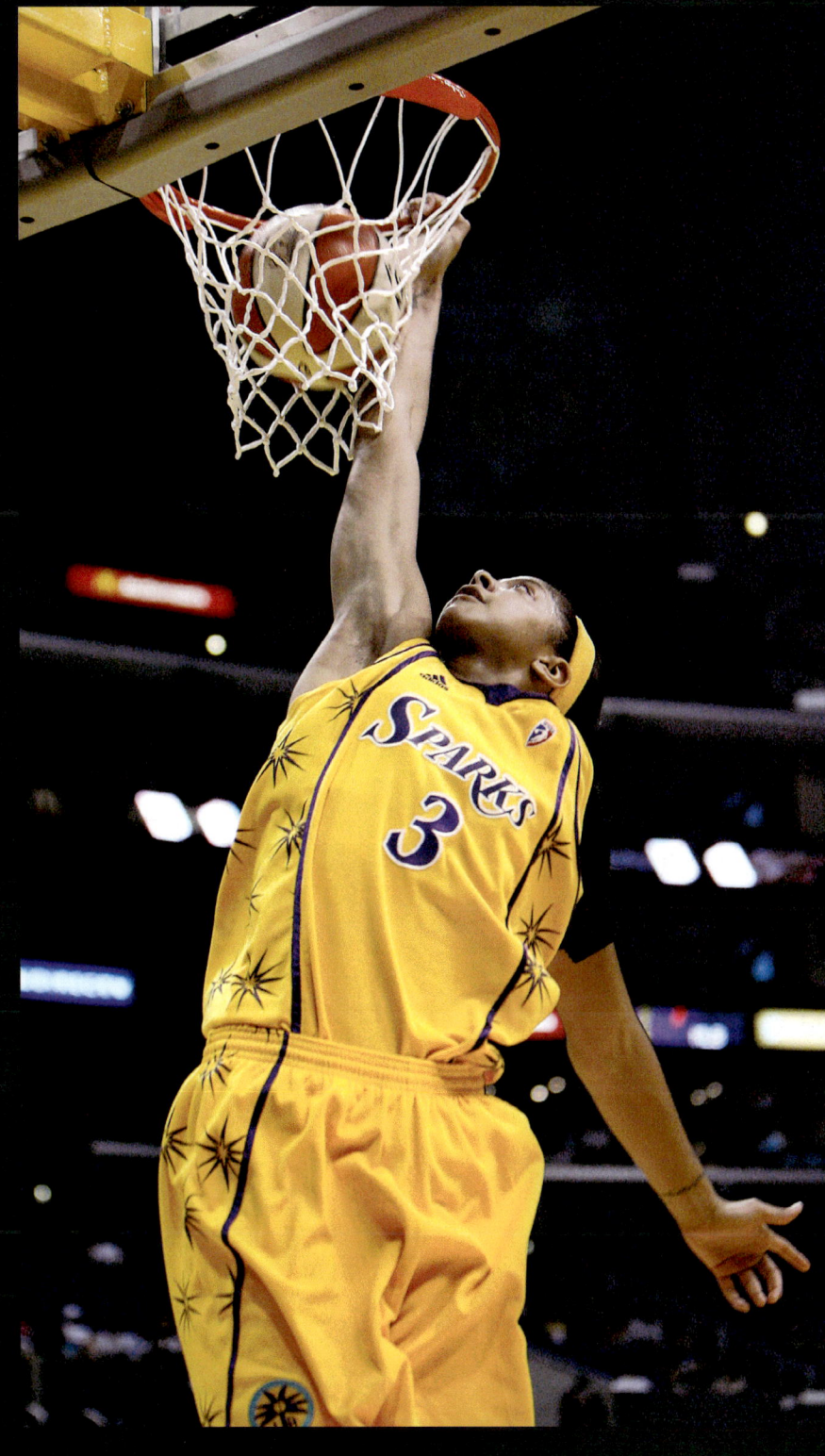

ABOVE: On June 22, 2008, Candace Parker became the second WNBA player ever to dunk, scarcely a month into her rookie season. For good measure, she dunked again in her very next game.

would be it. She initially did not return to the court after halftime. Tennessee came out flat and slipped behind Texas A&M: The end of the season looked imminent. Then an athletic trainer was sent to root under dirty laundry on the team bus to find a heavier brace. Parker was going back in.

It was obvious that she was compromised. (She could not quite hold her form; Parker missed her first two shots.) Yet just her presence shifted everything for Tennessee. With three minutes to play, she sank a pair of free throws to tie the game and then to take the lead, and a few moments later, she assisted on the basket that brought them some distance.

"I know she was in a lot of pain," Texas A&M coach Gary Blair told reporters. "But we were in a lot of pain trying to guard her, too."

One person knew just how much the injury hurt. That was Summitt: The coach had dislocated her own shoulder while shooing a raccoon off her porch earlier that season. (The team nicknamed her Davey Crockett.) It felt like just one more way the pair was linked in their intensity.

"Let me tell you, it is very, very painful," Summitt said. "Sometimes when you see a finesse player, you don't realize just how mentally tough they are until you see them fight through the adversity that she fought through."

She would keep fighting, through the Final Four and through an ugly, grinding slog of a national championship win. Parker was, of course, Most Outstanding Player. (She is one of just four players to receive the honor twice.) She had entered college as the most hyped player of her generation. And she had somehow made it all seem completely reasonable.

Oh, and one more thing: Tennessee beat UConn in every game they played while Parker was on campus.

Parker's schedule in April of 2008 went something like this: Win the national championship on Tuesday. Get selected as the No. 1 overall pick in the WNBA Draft on Wednesday. Turn around, pack everything up, move across the country, go through training camp, and prepare to start playing scarcely a month later. Make history with the best debut ever seen in the league. And then just keep going.

In her rookie debut with the Sparks, Parker dropped 34 points, twelve rebounds, and eight assists. She couldn't be too bummed about missing out on the triple-double: Parker didn't have much of an opportunity to pick up any more assists because at the end of the close game, in her very first moments in the WNBA, she was already the one taking the big shots.

"She's a shot maker," Sparks coach Michael Cooper told reporters that night. "She's the money player. She's anything but a rookie."

This was something that she would prove all season long. Less than two weeks later, she became the first WNBA player ever to post a 5x5 statline: 16 points, sixteen rebounds, six blocks, five assists, five steals. A month later, she became the first player to dunk since Lisa Leslie in 2002, and then she became the first player to dunk *twice*. Parker did not play like any rookie the WNBA had seen before. And she finished with an honor that no rookie had received before or since: In addition to being the obvious, no-doubt Rookie of the Year, Parker was also named MVP.

THE MIGHTY MERCURY

Diana Taurasi Leads Phoenix to Its First Ring

The Phoenix Mercury drafted a knock-down, long-range shooter from UConn in 2004, Diana Taurasi. Since stepping foot on a WNBA court, Taurasi made an enemy out of anyone standing across from her; it was Taurasi vs. Everybody. She was ruthless, exciting, and cold-blooded. It earned her the nickname White Mamba, a moniker mirroring NBA great Kobe Bryant's.

"My job is to be the best basketball player I can be and show up every single year better physically, mentally, skill-wise," Taurasi told *Rolling Stone* in 2024. "I'm here to ball out and try to kill whoever's in front of me."

In 2007 the Mercury had an all-star trio in Taurasi, Cappie Pondexter, and Penny Taylor, as they finished the regular season with a franchise-best twenty-three wins. Coach Paul Westhead—the Guru of Go—had the desert team blazing through competition at a frenetic pace. Taurasi's game matched well with his run-and-gun style. Taylor, the six-foot-one Aussie forward, was efficient and multifaceted. Pondexter, only a league sophomore, was fearless with a silky-smooth handle. The Mercury's first taste of the postseason came in 2007, which ended the longest drought by any franchise. After Taurasi bounced her former college teammate and BFF, Sue Bird, from the Western Conference semifinals and swept the San Antonio Silver Stars, Phoenix beat the defending champs Detroit Shock in a winner-take-all championship Game 5. Taurasi, Pondexter, and Taylor would win again in 2009.

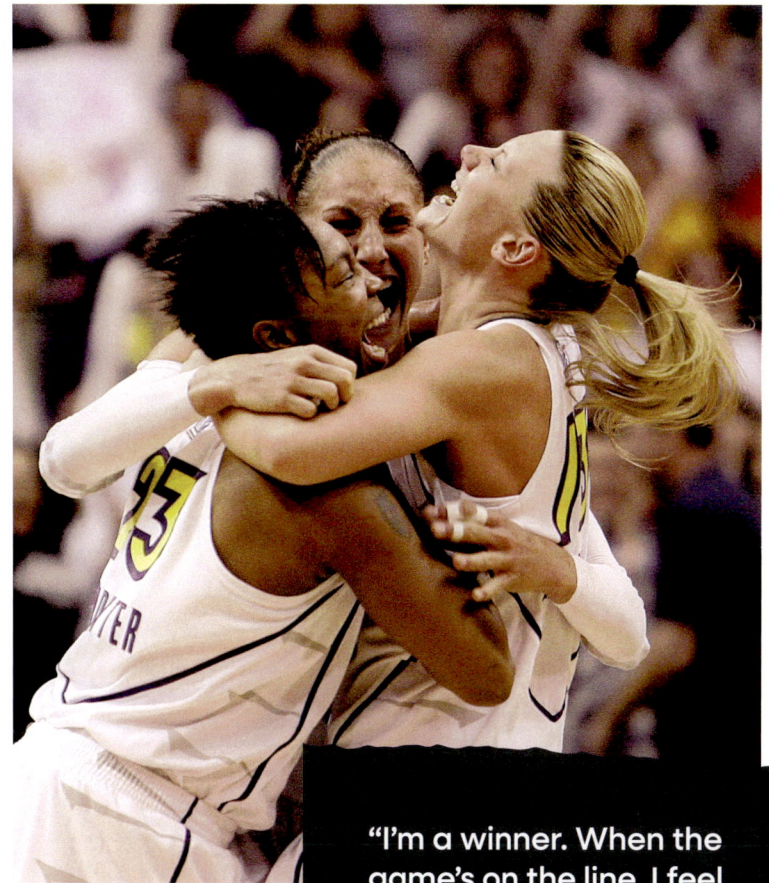

"I'm a winner. When the game's on the line, I feel like I can win every time. I just love having the ball and making things happen."

—CAPPIE PONDEXTER, 2007

ABOVE: The trio of Cappie Pondexter (left), Diana Taurasi (center), and Penny Taylor (right) won two WNBA titles in the decade. Here, they're celebrating their Game 5 win over the Indiana Fever in 2009.

MONEY, MONEY, MONEY?

Some W Franchises Fight to Survive

Financial turmoil hit the WNBA in the 2000s, just as it did the country as a whole. A wave of pluses and minuses burrowed through an adolescent league. In 2002 the NBA board of governors voted to change its single-entity ownership model, which opened the door for ownership beyond NBA teams. Franchise changes quickly ensued. The Orlando Miracle, after only four seasons in Florida, was sold to the Connecticut-based Mohegan Tribe and renamed the Sun. The Utah Starzz were forced to move to San Antonio (and again, to Las Vegas, in 2018). And after the 2002 season, two franchises shuttered after only three seasons, the Miami Sol and Portland Fire—the shortest-tenured franchises in league history. The Cleveland Rockers went up for sale but found no buyers.

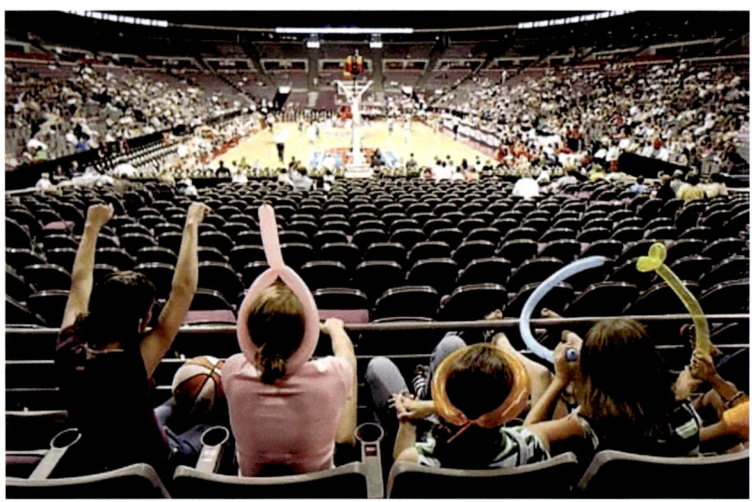

In 2003 the league's first Collective Bargaining Agreement (CBA) was up, and the Women's National Basketball Players Association (WNBPA) began discussions with the league to increase salaries and add free agency. However, NBA commissioner David Stern set an ultimatum in April after months without an agreement: Settle the contract dispute in ten days, or no WNBA season will be played.

"Many of these players are the most accomplished in their game," Stern said then. He claimed the NBA was losing $12 million per year because of the WNBA. "They see the men making so many times more than they make. But that's the nature of the world we live in."

A new CBA was signed on April 25, 2003, which increased the amount teams could spend on salaries, returned player group licensing rights to players, and inked the first free agency rights in women's professional team sports.

Then the 2008 economic crisis hit, making an already frugal league even more concerned about the bottom line. Despite recent ownership group expansions to Chicago and Atlanta, championship franchises like the Sacramento Monarchs and Houston Comets disbanded. The Detroit Shock was sold and moved to Tulsa (and again to Dallas in 2016). Some teams began seeking alternative revenue streams. Phoenix and Los Angeles secured jersey-front sponsorship deals: LifeLock, identity-theft prevention, for the Mercury, and Farmers Insurance for the Sparks. Then-WNBA president Donna Orender called the signings "consistent with the league's innovative mindset."

Like its professional league predecessors, the WNBA was doing anything to survive.

ABOVE: Though scattered, fans still came to cheer on their Detroit Shock in Auburn Hills in 2002. But seven years and three titles later, they'd get the boot to Tulsa.

THE LEAGUE'S LOST LEGACY

Every franchise that went defunct in the first decade of the league meant a lost opportunity to build history and legacy. Here's a look at which jerseys might have been hanging in the rafters through the 2000s and 2010s—had they been given the chance.

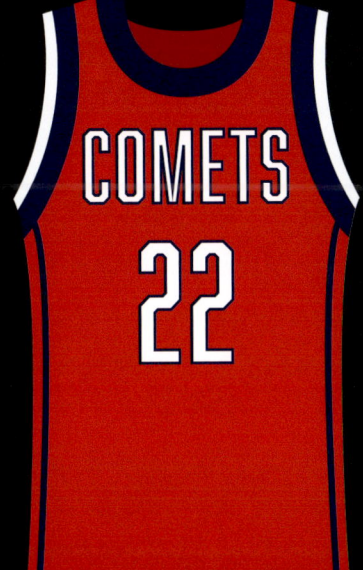

Sheryl Swoopes, Houston Comets, 3x WNBA MVP

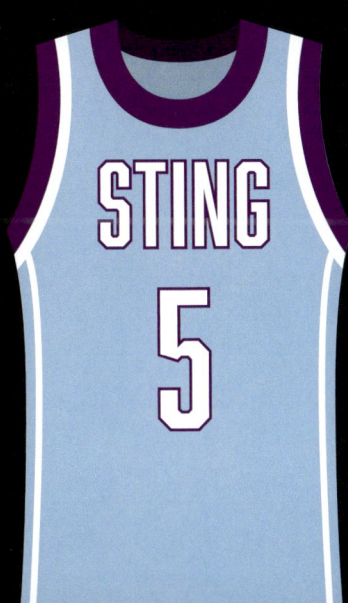

Dawn Staley, Charlotte Sting, 5x All-Star

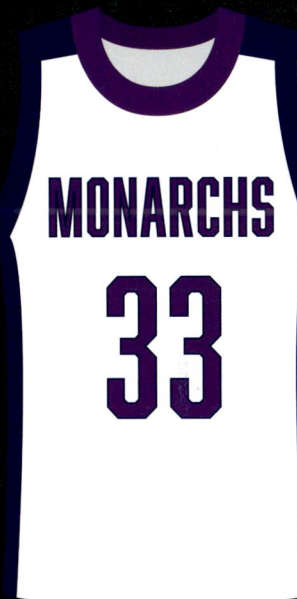

Yolanda Griffith, Sacramento Monarchs, MVP, DPOY

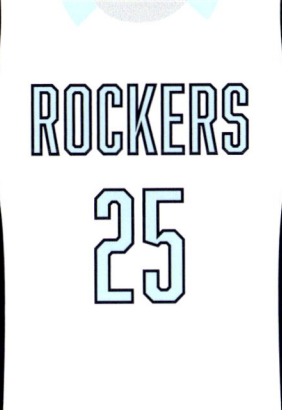

Merlakia Jones, Cleveland Rockers, 3x All-Star

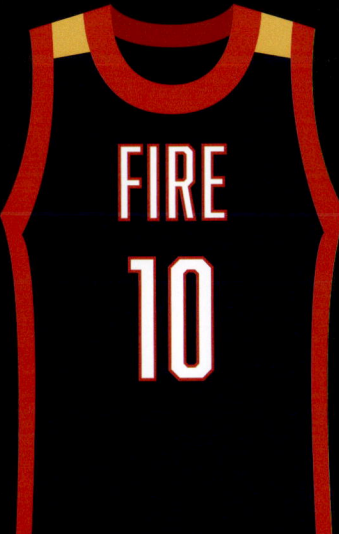

Jackie Stiles, Portland Fire, Rookie of the Year

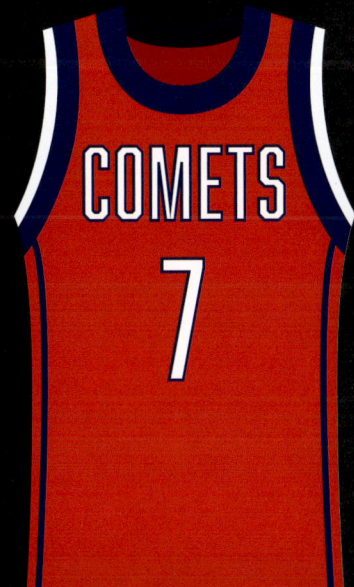

Tina Thompson, Houston Comets, 3x First-Team All-WNBA

THE POINT GAWDS

The Best PGs of the Decade

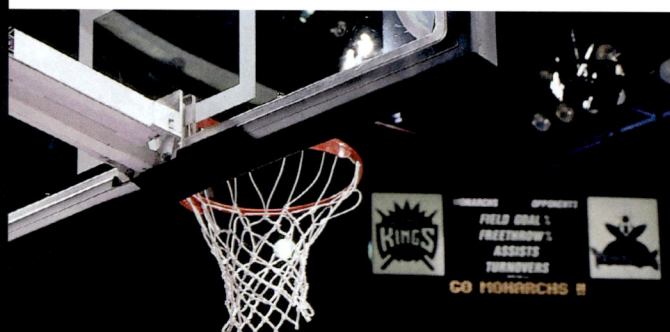

The floor generals. The playmakers. The dime dishers. The 2000s brought a hot spotlight to the point guard position and its importance. They were the players who wanted the rock in their hands when the game was close and the clock was winding. Salute to these legendary PGs.

Ticha Penicheiro
Sacramento Monarchs
Los Angeles Sparks
1998–2012

The Portuguese player burst onto the scene with her flashy passes and set a rookie assist record (225) that held for twenty-five years. Her single-game assist record (16), set twice in 1998 and 2002, wasn't broken until 2020.

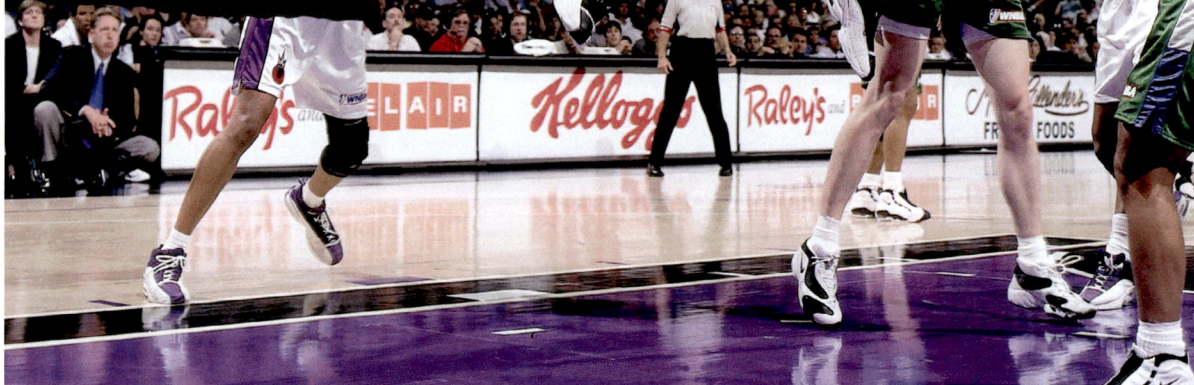

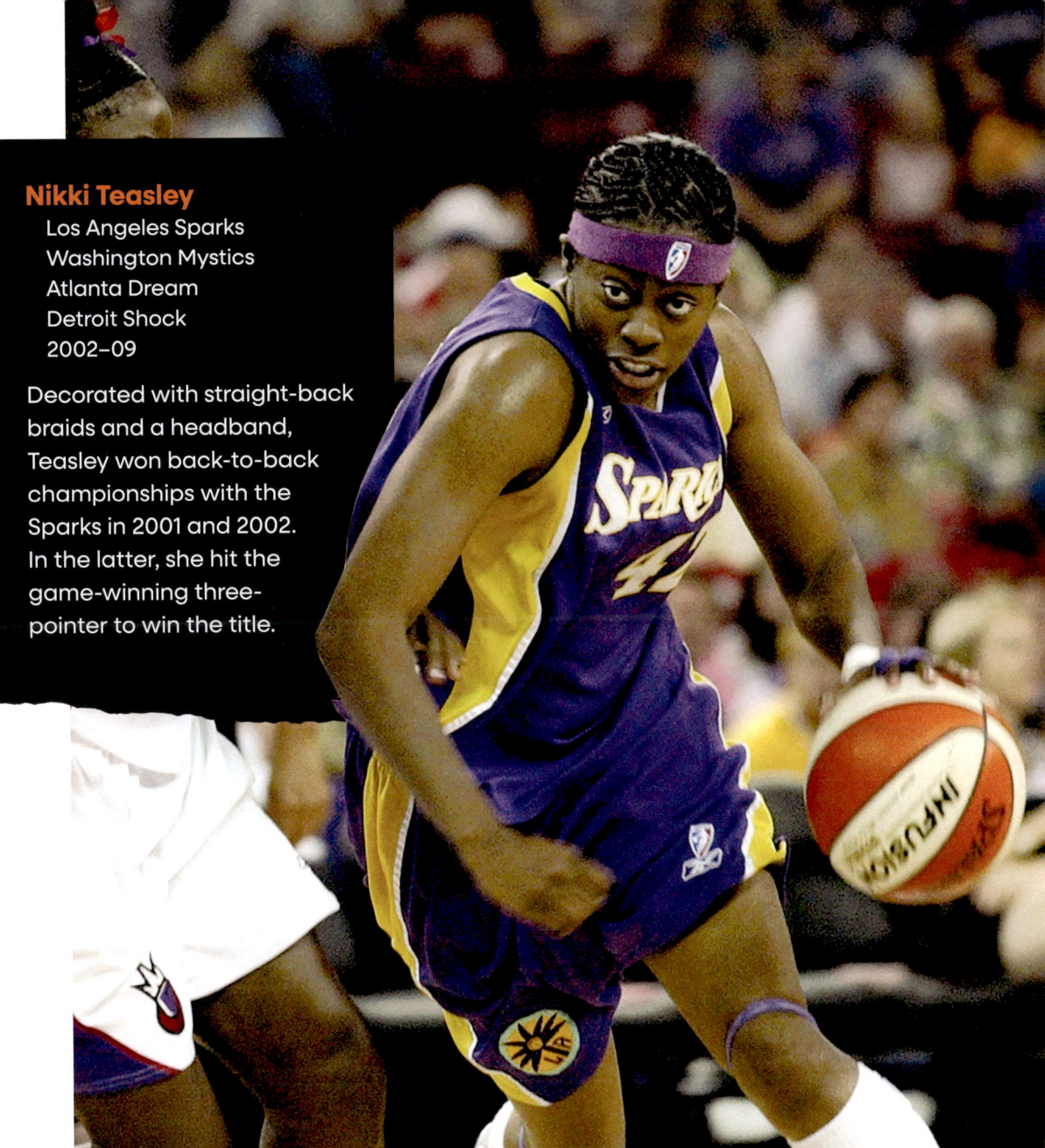

Nikki Teasley

Los Angeles Sparks
Washington Mystics
Atlanta Dream
Detroit Shock
2002–09

Decorated with straight-back braids and a headband, Teasley won back-to-back championships with the Sparks in 2001 and 2002. In the latter, she hit the game-winning three-pointer to win the title.

Dawn Staley

Charlotte Sting
Houston Comets
1999–2006

Staley was North Philly tough, an unrelenting competitor, and the quintessential leader. She led the Sting to their sole Finals appearance in 2001 and tallied over 2,200 points, 1,300 assists, and 300 steals in eight seasons.

Sue Bird

Seattle Storm
2002–2022

For twenty-one years, Bird dazzled fans with shifty passes, leaving the game as the all-time assist leader. The four-time champion is the only WNBA player to win a title in three different decades.

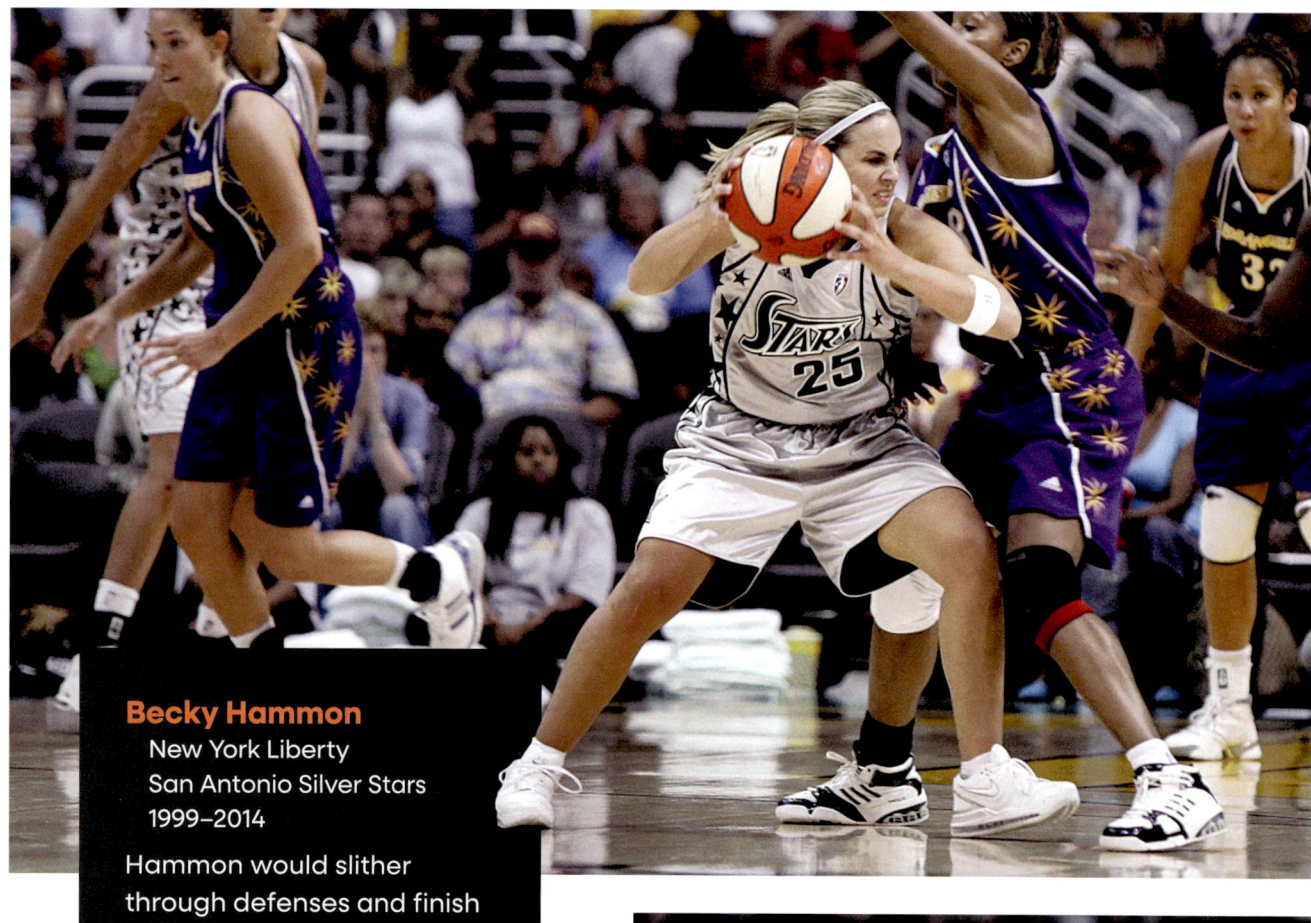

Becky Hammon

New York Liberty
San Antonio Silver Stars
1999–2014

Hammon would slither through defenses and finish at the rim with her elite layup package at five foot six. She led the Stars to a playoff berth each of her seven full seasons.

Cappie Pondexter

Phoenix Mercury	Chicago Sky
New York Liberty	LA Sparks
Minnesota Lynx	2007–2017

At seventeen years old, Pondexter got a tattoo of the WNBA logo with "The Future" inked above it. Her confidence paid off. The two-time champion is one of the best one-on-one guards in history and currently sits top-10 in career assists.

Lindsay Whalen

Connecticut Sun
Minnesota Lynx
2004–2018

Whalen hung four WNBA championship banners in her home state of Minnesota. She had eight seasons averaging over five assists per game and is the second-most winningest player in history, with 323 total wins.

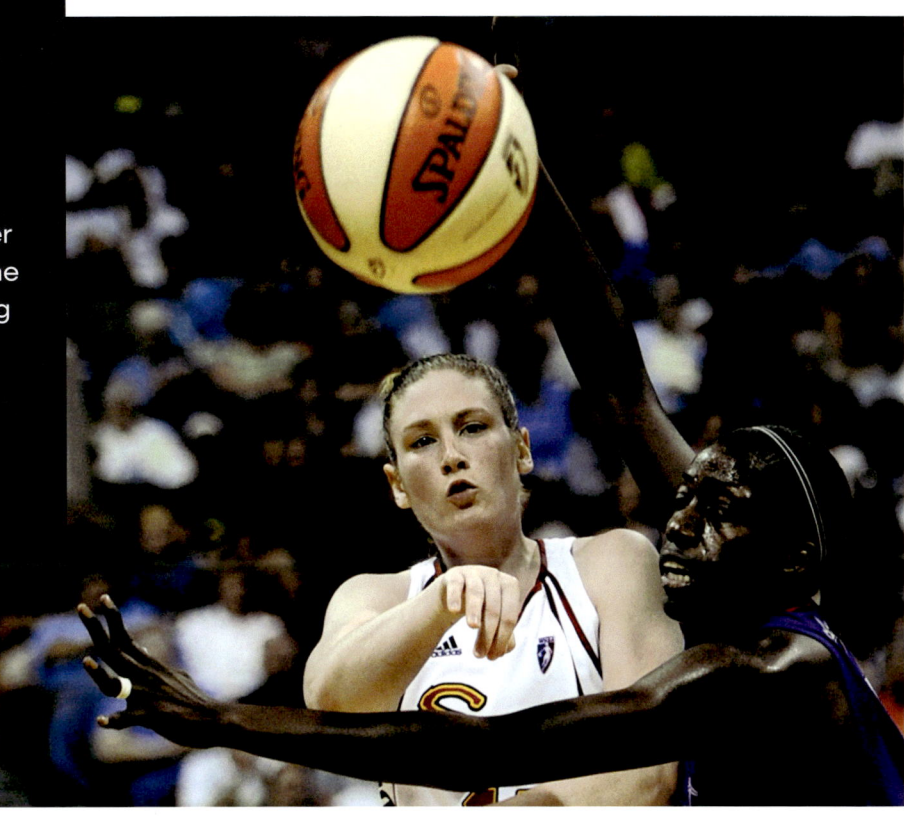

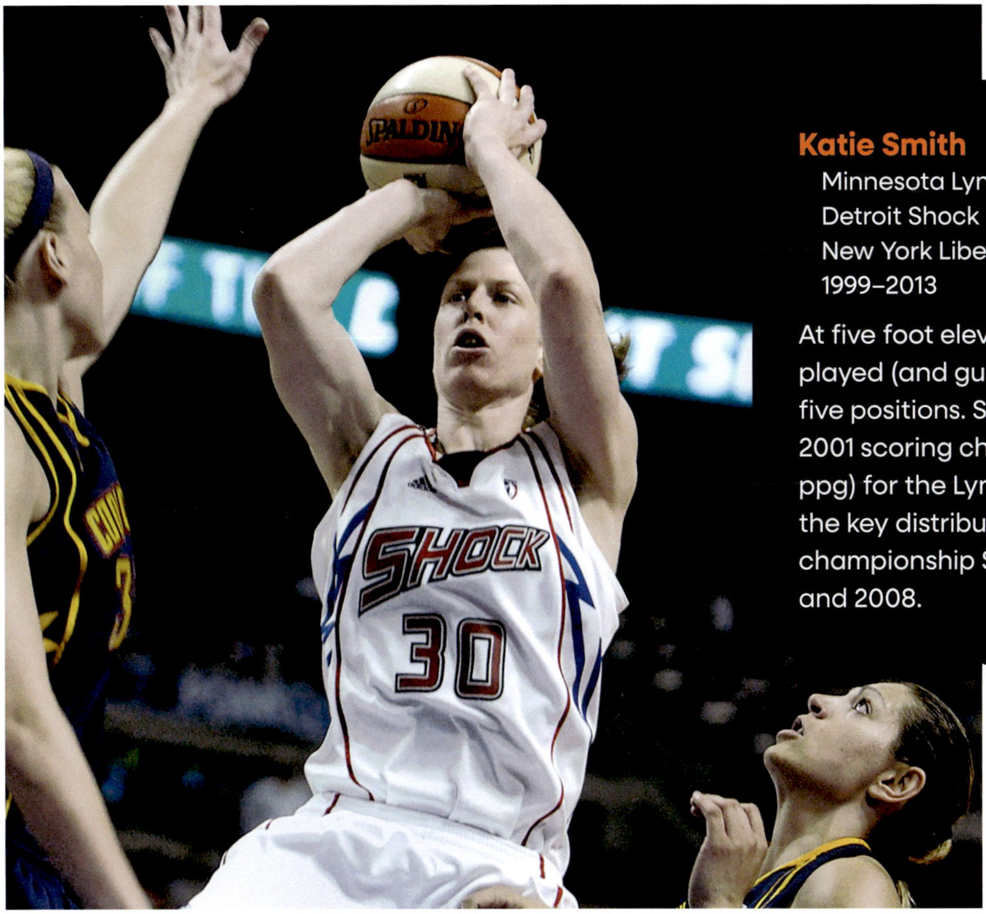

Katie Smith

Minnesota Lynx
Detroit Shock
New York Liberty
1999–2013

At five foot eleven, Smith played (and guarded) all five positions. She was the 2001 scoring champ (23.1 ppg) for the Lynx and then the key distributor for the championship Shock in 2006 and 2008.

MATTER OF FACT
2000s

Numbers, People, and Moments That Defined the Era

NUMBERS

5 Highest number of WNBA All-Stars hailing from a single team in a single year (Shock in 2005 and Sun in 2006).

6 The only number retired by the Sacramento Monarchs franchise for Ruthie Bolton.

10 Number of times Tamika Catchings finished top-5 in MVP voting.

24 Most rebounds by a player in a WNBA game: Chamique Holdsclaw, 2003.

112 Courtney Paris of Oklahoma recorded 112 consecutive double-doubles from 2006 to 2009, and became the first four-time first-team All-American in women's basketball history.

PEOPLE

During the 2004 Athens Summer Olympics opening ceremonies, **DAWN STALEY** was voted by her peers to carry the American flag, becoming the first to receive the honor for USA Basketball. Staley led Team USA to clinch their third straight gold medal with a 74–63 win over Australia. "I took one last look around . . . and thought: Unbelievable, the best athletes in the world are following a girl from the projects in North Philly," she'd recall in her 2013 Hall of Fame speech.

In 2002 Liberty forward **SUE WICKS** was asked in an interview with *Time Out New York* if she was a lesbian. "I am," she responded simply. "I think it's important that if you are gay, you not be afraid to say who you are." That made her the first athlete in American team sports to come out as gay. And it started what ultimately would become a proud legacy of LGBTQ+ acceptance and activism in the W.

FEB. 14, 2000

CYNTHIA COOPER wins her third consecutive ESPY Award for Best WNBA Player. The award debuted in 1998.

JAN. 18, 2002

Disney Channel original movie *Double Teamed* premiered on cable. It told the story of twin ballers **HEATHER AND HEIDI BURGE**.

APRIL 16, 2000

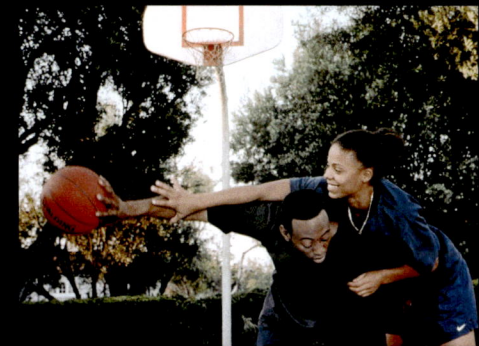

LOVE & BASKETBALL, a film where the protagonist is a women's basketball player at USC, hits theaters.

JULY 10, 2002

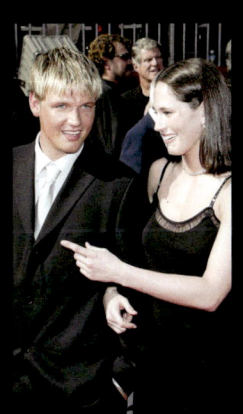

SUE BIRD and Backstreet Boy Nick Carter attended the tenth ESPY Awards as friends at the Kodak Theatre in Hollywood. The pair had the same manager.

FEB. 1, 2006

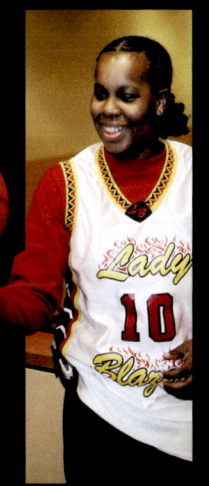

Seventeen-year-old Brooklynite **EPIPHANNY PRINCE** scored 113 points. Her 54/60 field goals shattered the previous girls' prep records of Cheryl Miller (105) and Lisa Leslie (101). She received quite a bit of backlash for the feat.

CHAPTER 6

2010s

THE BIG SHOT MAKERS

BUZZER-BEATER FADEAWAYS, SILKY-SMOOTH TURNAROUNDS, CLUTCH STEP-BACKS— ELECTRIC PERFORMANCES MARKED THE NEXT DECADE OF SCORERS.

RIGHT: Maya Moore shoots a jumper over the outstretched arm of defensive specialist Alana Beard during the 2017 WNBA Finals.

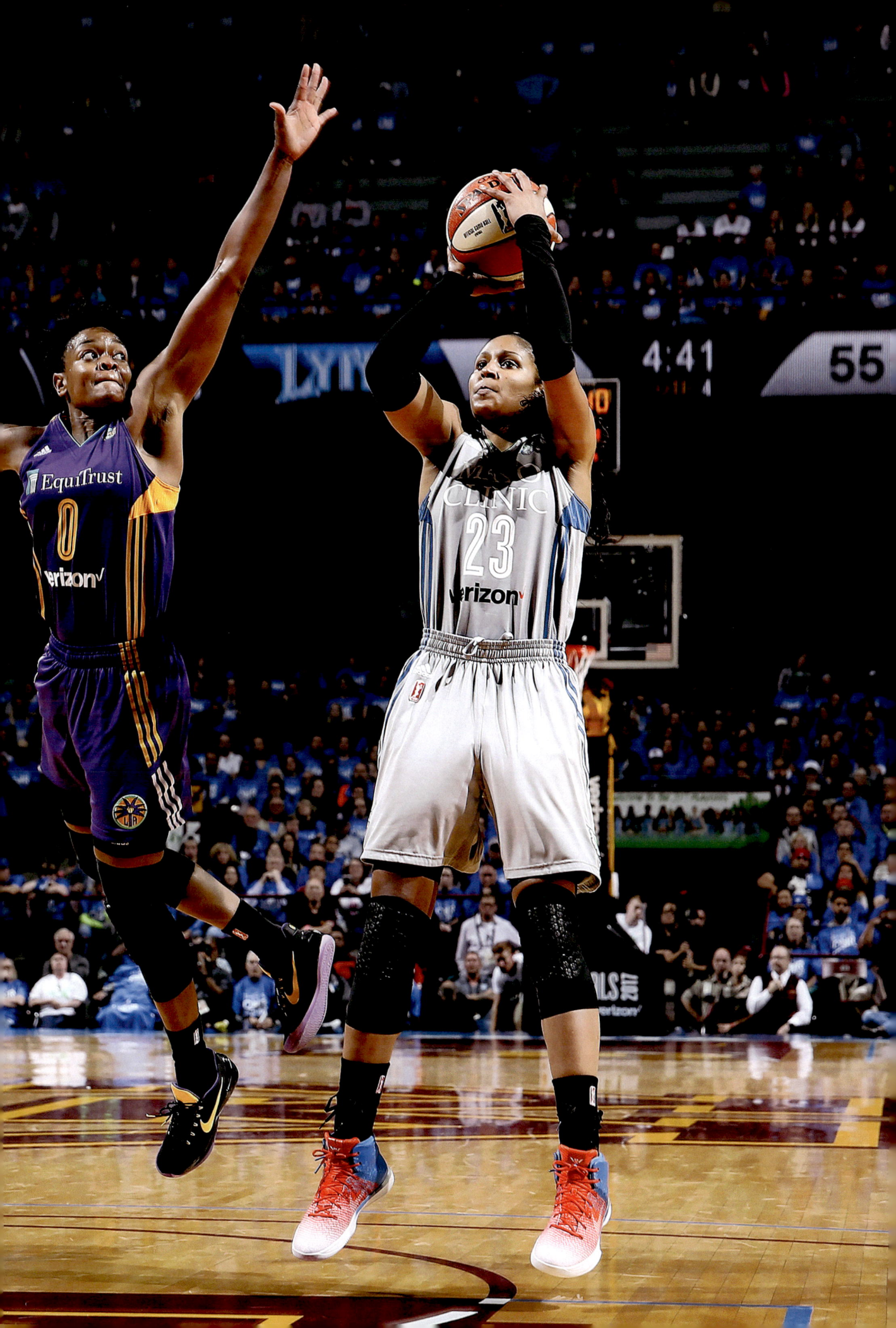

ONE FOR THE AGES

THE MINNESOTA LYNX VS. LA SPARKS
RIVALRY DEFINED THE DECADE

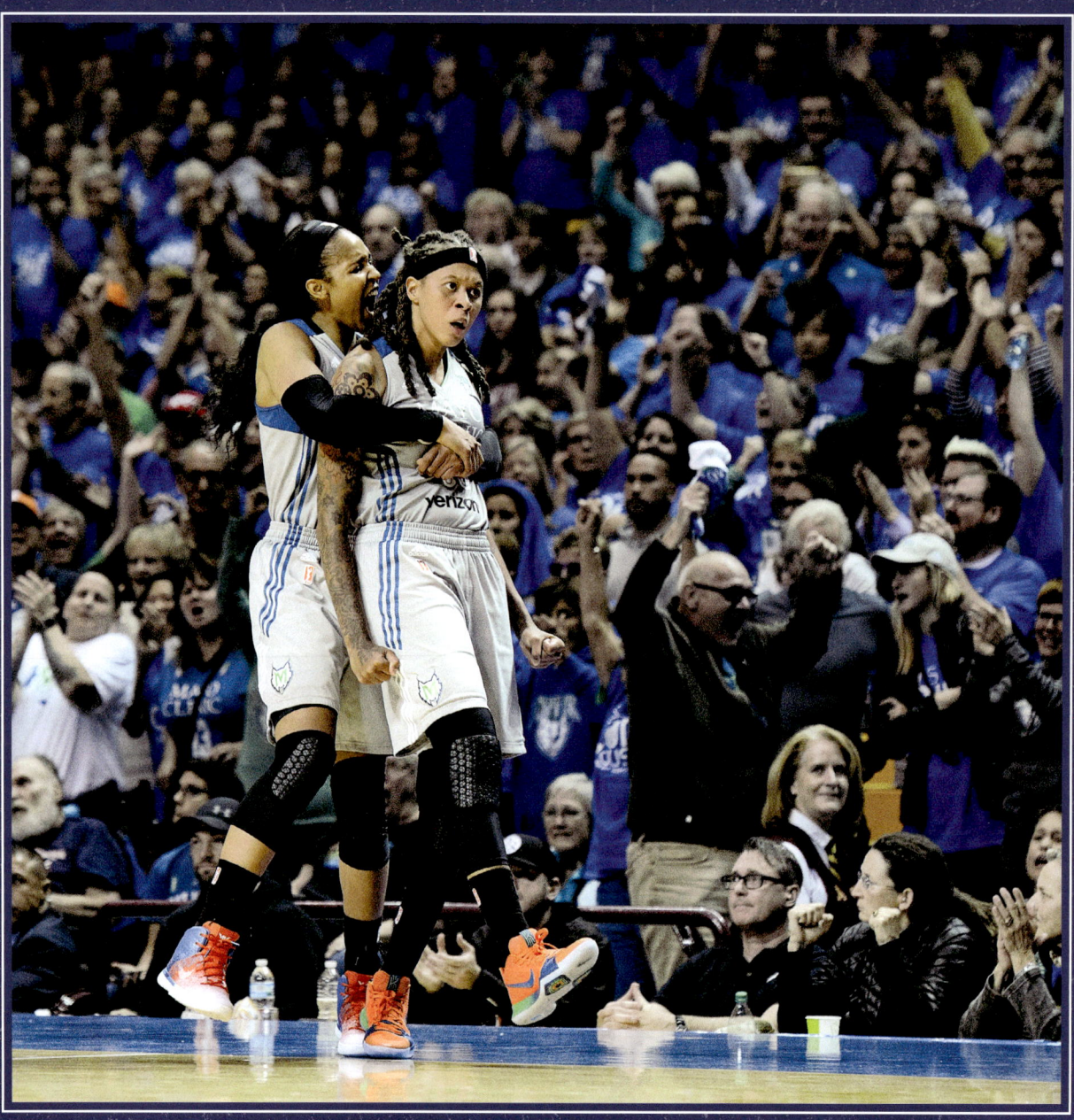

ABOVE: "The Lynx are marked by their leadership, their steadiness, their attention to detail on both ends of the floor. There's nothing gimmicky about the Lynx, just high-level and hard-nosed basketball." —Michelle Smith, ESPN, 2013

t was October 2017 when journalist Ramona Shelburne caught Minnesota Lynx forward Maya Moore in the locker room after her team won Game 4 of the WNBA Finals in Los Angeles. Her 15 points forced a winner-take-all Game 5 back in Minneapolis. Shelburne asked Moore a simple question: "Have you ever been in a rivalry like this?" Moore responded with an even simpler answer, "Never." Her teammate Renee Montgomery was close by, and she agreed. Shelburne followed up. "Well, what's it like?"

"It's fun," Moore replied, spent, "but it's really hard." Then she let out a laugh. She knew the contradiction in her answer.

The Minnesota Lynx defined the decade by reaching dynasty status in the 2010s. The greatest roster ever constructed? You be the judge. Regardless, they were built to win. And that's what they did. Out of the ten Finals that made up the decade, the Lynx appeared in six and won four. It was a complete takeover, and it started with hiring a new coach, in December 2009.

"I'm looking forward to this exciting opportunity to lead the Minnesota Lynx," said first-time head coach Cheryl Reeve. "I believe that with the rising young talent on this team, the return of Seimone Augustus, and the additions we'll make to the roster this offseason, the time is now for the Lynx to be the best in the West."

The Lynx had missed the playoffs for five seasons straight, but Reeve and general manager Roger Griffith rolled up their sleeves and immediately got to work. Augustus, who had the coldest crossover in women's basketball, was already their anchor, so they built around her. They got Rebekkah Brunson, traded for Lindsay Whalen in 2010, and added free agent Taj McWilliams-Franklin before the 2011 season. Oh, and they drafted Maya Moore with the number one pick in the 2011 draft.

"Every year, the goal is a championship," Moore told ESPN before her rookie season. "That's what I expect. I go on to every team expecting to win a championship, especially with the amount of talent we have. I don't want to limit to the playoffs, I want to win a championship."

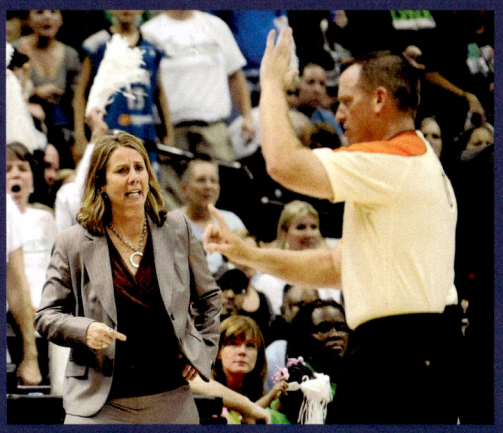

"Look, I can get a little passionate when it comes to game time. Remember the Great Jacket Toss of 2012?

The whole dang thing made national news. For forty-eight hours, there it was . . . replay after replay. I can't help but think a large part of why was because I'm a woman, and yet I was showing passionate anger in a way we usually associate with masculinity. If Bob Knight throws a chair it also makes national news— but we laugh at it. It's ridiculous, sure, but it doesn't make us uncomfortable.

I think I made a lot of people uncomfortable."

—Cheryl Reeve, *The Players' Tribune*, 2018

And she started in year one. Moore hailed from UConn (2007–2011) and only lost four games in four years. Winning was customary. In her first season with Minnesota, in 2011, she'd nab Rookie of the Year and her first championship in the same season. She had to go through a crafty scorer in Atlanta Dream's Angel McCoughtry to cut down the net. And then again in 2013. She fought through pesky defender Tamika Catchings in the

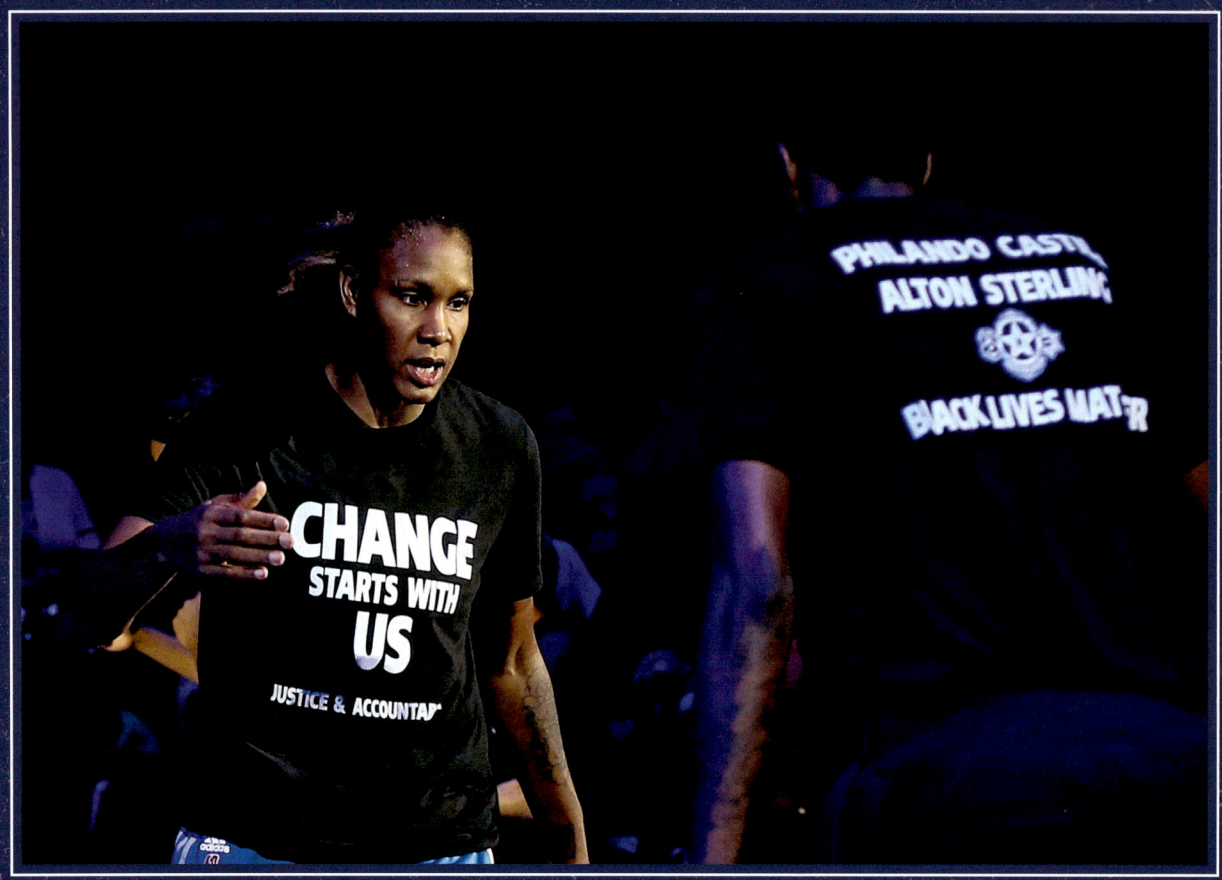

Finals twice, besting her the second time in 2015 thanks to her game-winning free-throw-line jumper.

But the rivalry with Candace Parker's LA Sparks was just different for Moore's Minnesota Lynx. They matched up well with each other; at its peak, there were four MVPs and twelve gold medals across the two rosters. The animosity is rooted in a down-to-the-wire Western Conference semifinal in 2015. The Lynx won 2–1 on their way to their third championship.

For the 2016 season, the league changed the postseason format, which ensured the best two teams—regardless of conferences—would meet in the Finals. And those two teams were the Lynx and Sparks. *Finally, this is what the people wanted to see.*

LA added Chelsea Gray, a flashy, pass-first point guard whose chemistry with Parker instantly clicked. This was center Sylvia "Sweet Syl" Fowles's first full season with Minnesota; she'd already earned Finals MVP in 2015. Heading into a win-or-go-home Game 5, Moore, Augustus, Fowles, and Lindsay

Whalen knew Parker and Nneka Ogwumike—the 2016 league MVP—were hungry for their first 'ship. It would be the Lynx's fourth in five years. It was a heavyweight boxing match at the Target Center in Minnesota, with each team going blow for blow— there were twenty-four lead changes. Parker and Moore were both flirting with thirty-piece double-doubles. The rivalry was thriving.

ABOVE: In 2016, the Lynx starting five wore these shirts as a call to action after the murder of Minnesota resident Philando Castile and Louisiana native Alton Sterling.

OPPOSITE: Tamika Catchings had a lot of accolades already: five DOYs, an MVP, and seven WNBA First-Team nods. But she didn't have a ring. In 2012 that changed, after her Indiana Fever shocked the top-seeded Lynx in the Finals, 87–78. Catchings led the way with 25 points. "When you come into this league, your goal and dream is to win a WNBA championship," Catchings said. "Twelve years later . . . It's so sweet right now."

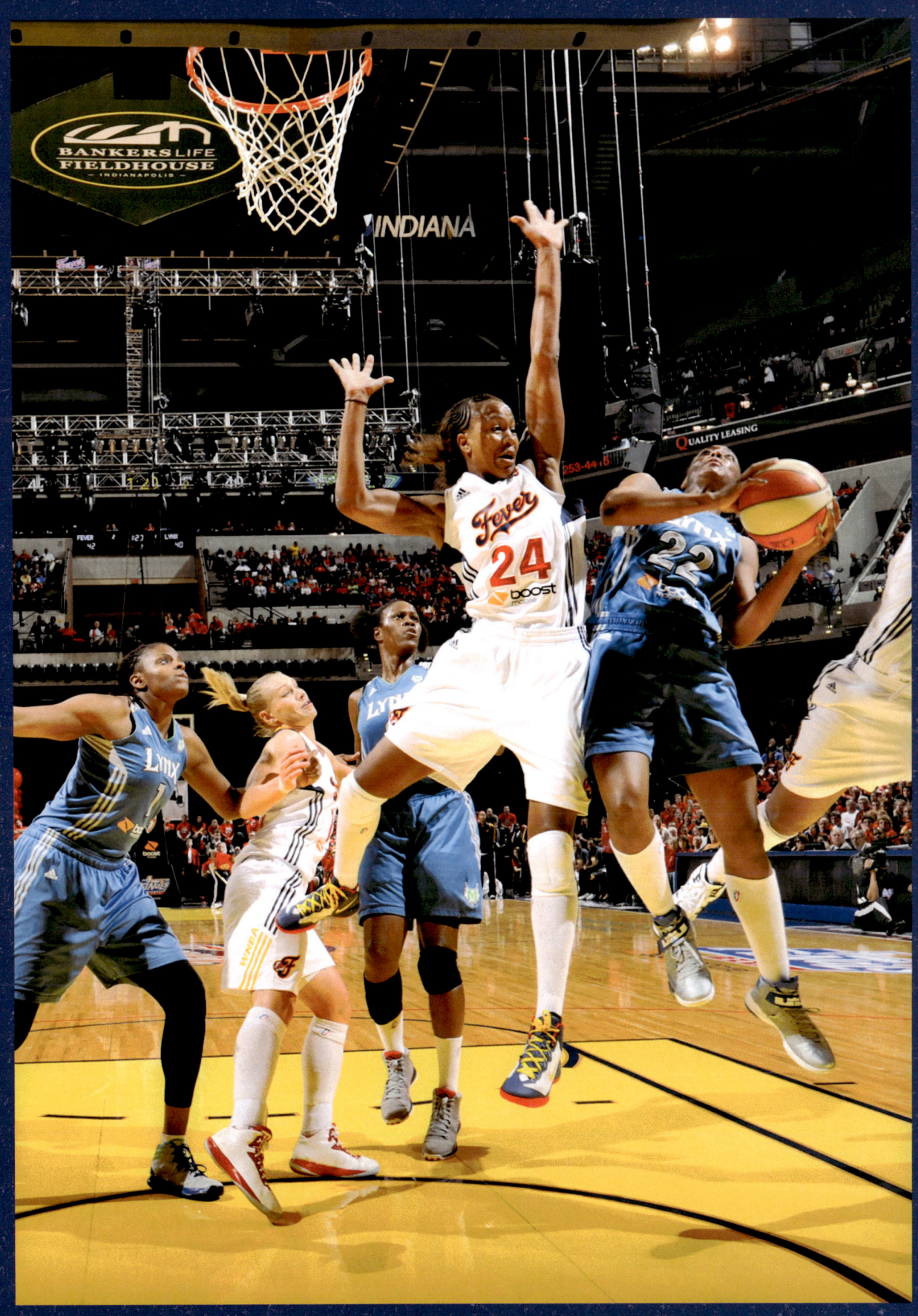

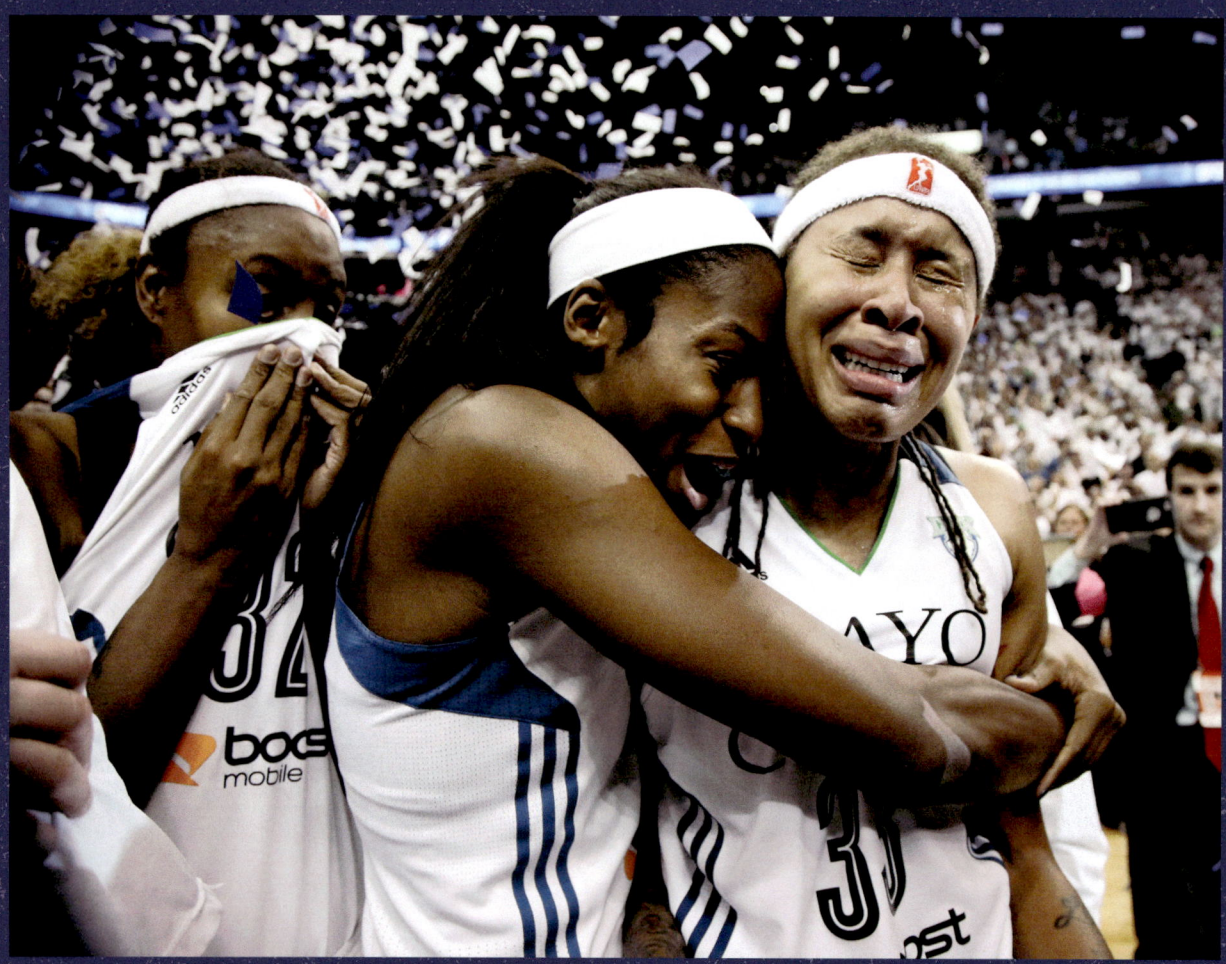

An award-winning playwright couldn't have written a better fourth quarter. Candace Parker's layup with 19.7 seconds left puts LA up by one. Moore drains a turnaround baseline jumper over a fallen Alana Beard after the Lynx time-out. Minnesota retakes the lead, 75–76, with 15.6 seconds remaining. Both teams are out of time-outs—the drama.

The Sparks' Gray shoots a fadeaway jump shot that misses long. Ogwumike gets the rebound, shoots it, gets blocked, and the ball ricochets back to her. Fading backward off one leg, she catches and launches it back at the rim. It drains with 3.7 seconds left. Whalen is forced to heave a last-second near half-court shot, to no avail. The backboard lights up red. Ball game. The Sparks were WNBA champions for the first time in fourteen years, and the Lynx were left in disbelief in front of their 19,400 fans.

Moore writes in her memoir years later: "It was the hardest loss of my career because we really played well enough to win."

The Lynx and Sparks would return to the Finals almost one calendar year later. Since Ogwumike's buzzer-beater, Moore, Augustus, Whalen, and Fowles had won a gold medal together in Rio. Famously, Parker and Ogwumike did not make this Team USA roster. The Lynx started the 2017 season 20–2 in their first twenty-two games on

ABOVE: Devereaux Peters (left) and an emotional Seimone Augustus (right) revel in winning the 2015 WNBA championship over the Indiana Fever.

OPPOSITE: Nneka Ogwumike's go-ahead fadeaway stunned the Minneapolis crowd and WNBA fans nationwide.

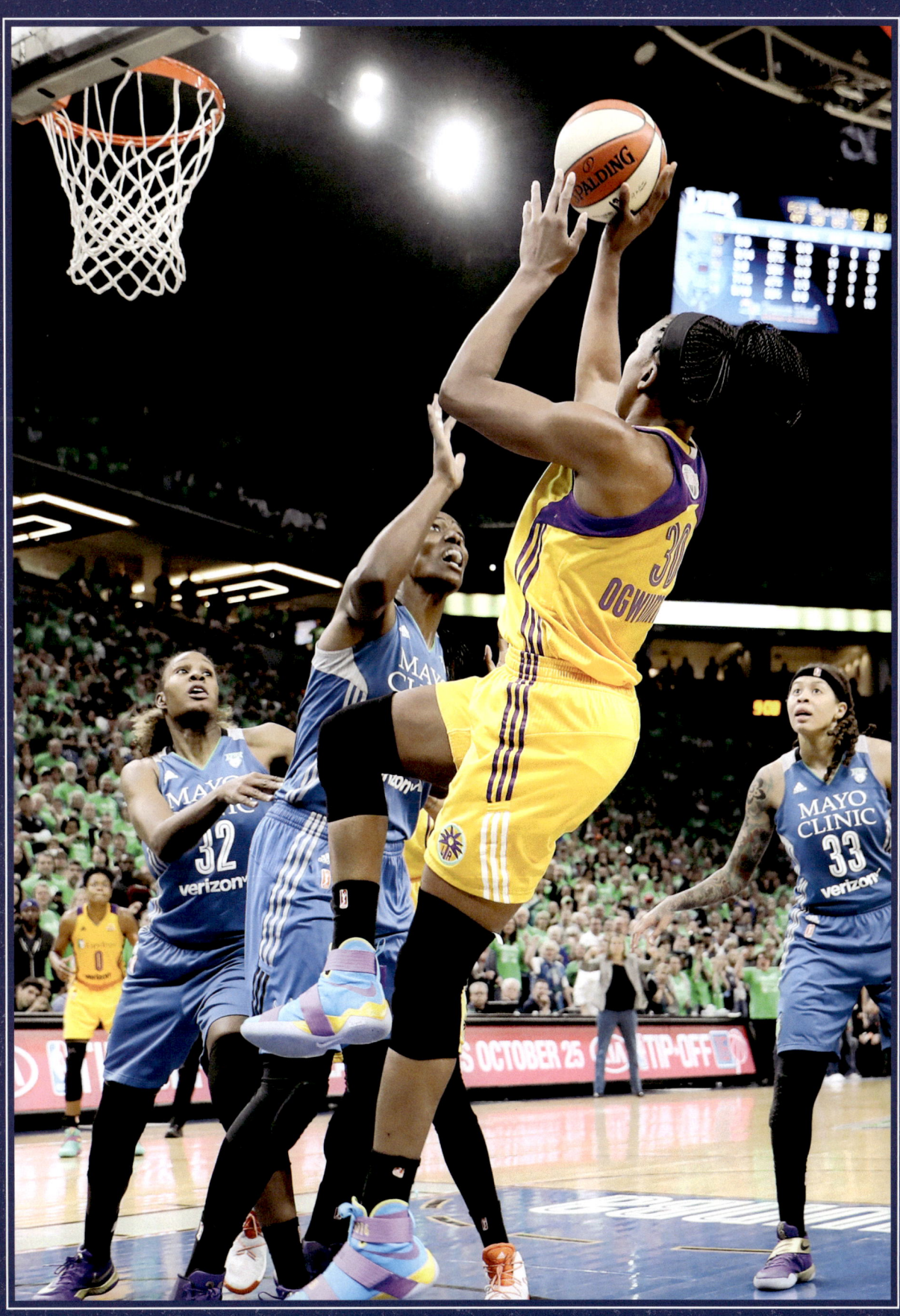

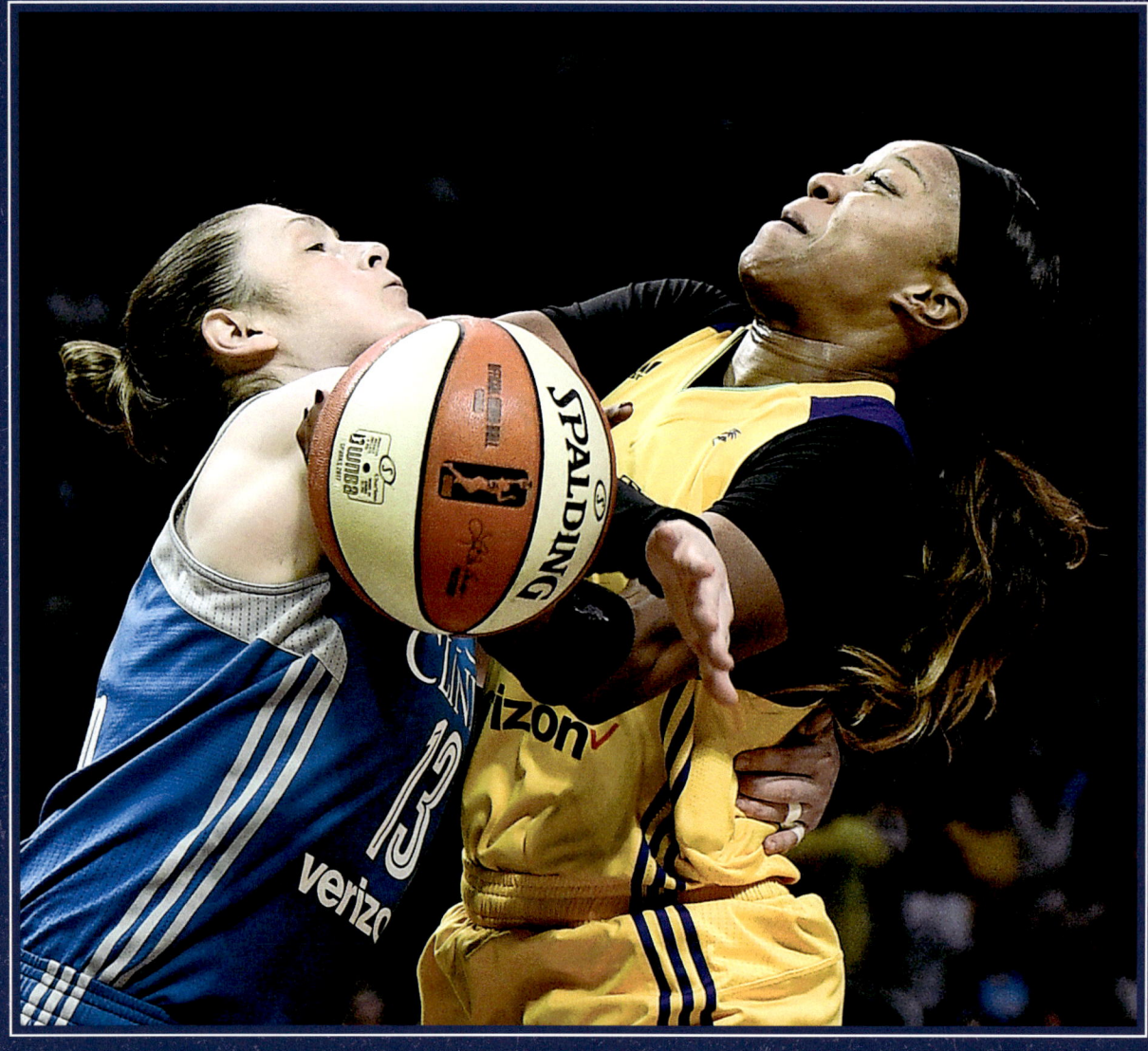

their way to a league-best 27–7 record. They'd inch out the Sparks for the best record in the Western Conference by a single point. It felt like one last ride for this group. Whalen and Brunson, both thirty-five years old, were wrapping up Hall of Fame careers.

This Finals rematch between LA and Minneapolis felt bloated with backstory. They'd split the series' first four games, with each team winning a road game. It would lead to a Game 5 (again) in Minneapolis (again). Let's skip to the good part: The Sparks trailed 79–67 with less than two minutes remaining in the fourth. Then a 9–0 burst, led by Odyssey Sims, closed the gap. Regular season MVP Fowles went otherworldly to

finish the game (she had a record twenty-rebound double-double en route to her second Finals MVP), but Moore's hang-in-the-air midrange floater with under thirty seconds left was the dagger. The crowd went nuts. They could feel it. Their fourth championship in seven years.

"Every time you do this, it gets a little more special," said Whalen afterward. The Lynx's Target Center was under construction for Game 5, so they played at the University of Minnesota, Whalen's

---

ABOVE: Sparks' Odyssey Sims (right) is fouled hard by Lynx's Lindsay Whalen minutes into Game 4 of the 2017 Finals.

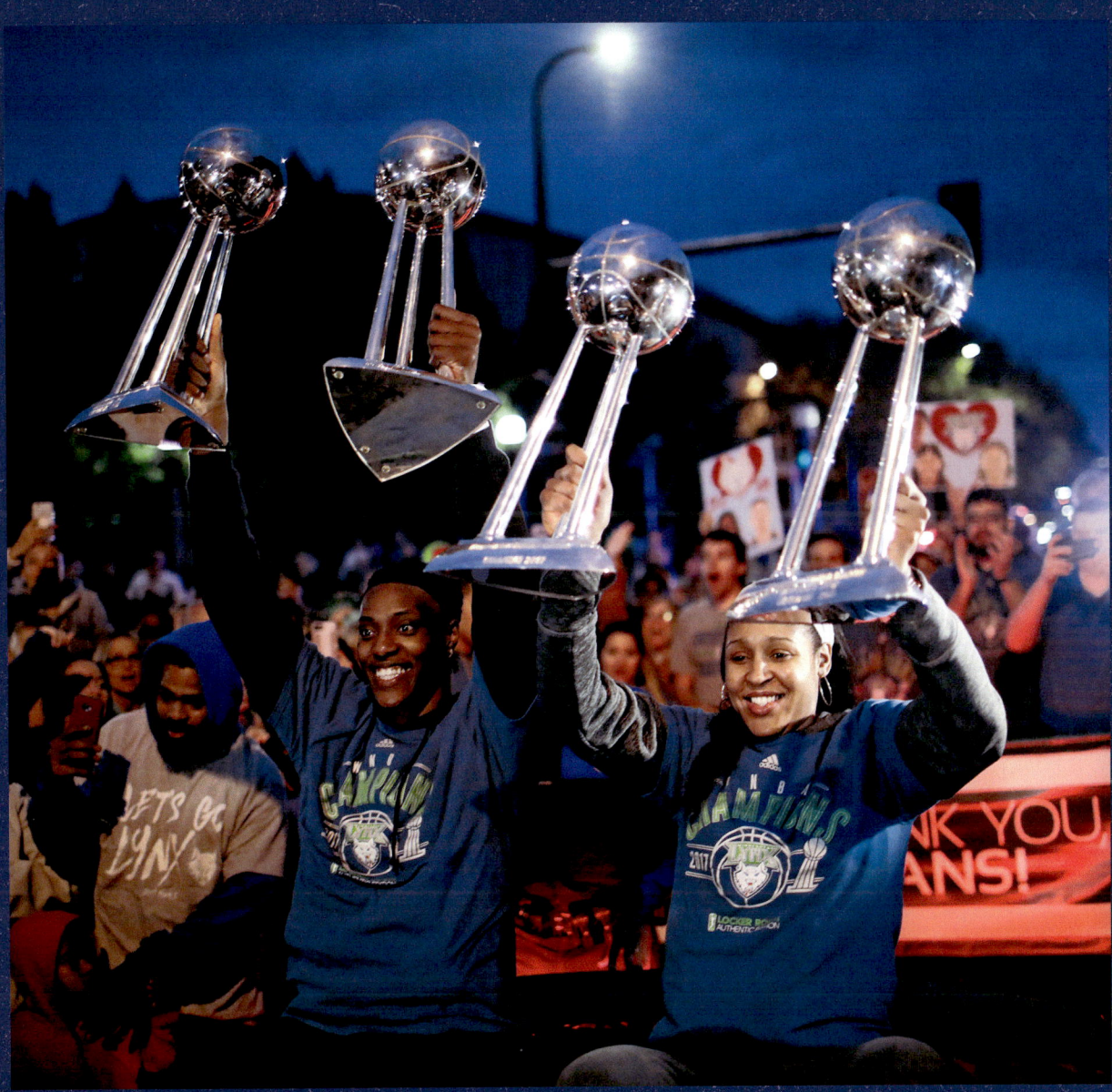

alma mater. "I felt good about our chances, being in this building. . . . It doesn't get any sweeter than to bring another trophy home, another ring, but to do it here is pretty cool."

The Lynx's 2018 home-opener opponent? The LA Sparks. It was ring night. Minnesota got to flash their bling in their rivals' faces.

"It definitely adds salt to the wound a little bit," Parker said at the time.

During the last two years of the decade, the Lynx had uncharacteristic early postseason exits. Whalen and Brunson retired after the 2018 season. Moore announced in February 2019 that she was taking a

sabbatical from hoops to focus on her faith, family, and social justice, extending her legacy beyond basketball. (She'd officially retire in 2024 without ever stepping foot on a WNBA court again.)

The Minnesota Lynx defined an era by compiling one of the best rosters in WNBA history. Moore went to six Finals in her eight-year career,

---

ABOVE: Fowles (left) and Moore (right) hold up all four championship trophies as they arrive at Williams Arena on October 5, 2017 in Minneapolis.

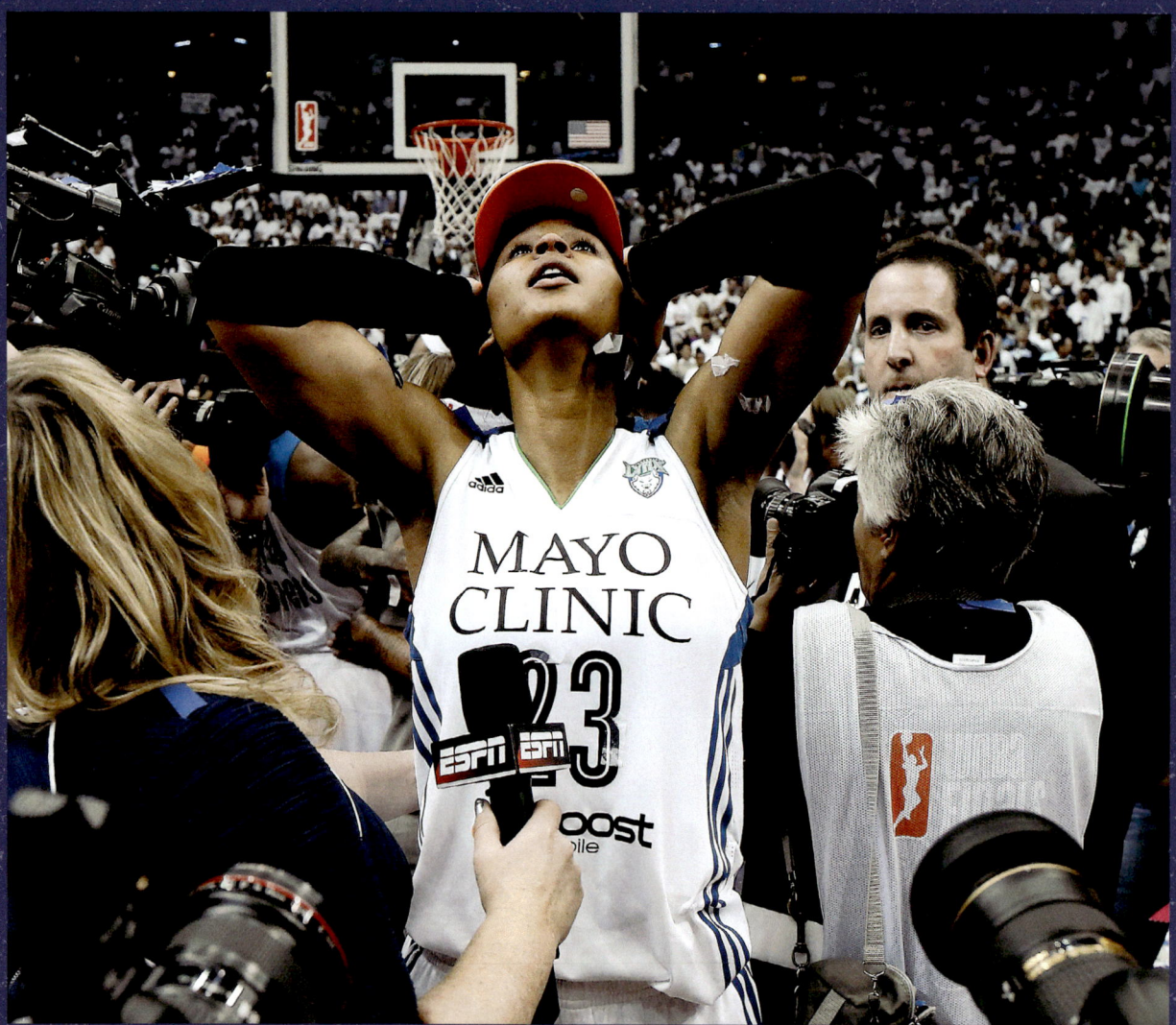

winning over half of them; she is one of women's basketball's best winners ever. Augustus retired after playing one season with the LA Sparks (oh, the irony) in 2020, leaving the game top-10 in scoring. Brunson holds the record for most WNBA championships, with five. When Fowles retired in 2022, she was the WNBA's all-time rebounder. It remains to be seen if another generational run like this will happen again. But until then, let's marvel at what was.

ABOVE: "I like to make history. I like to do things that have never been done before. We did a lot of that at UConn. I might as well keep it up." —Maya Moore, after the 2011 draft, to *The Minnesota Star Tribune*

"There are times that you're in the midst of something great and can't quite quantify it. But that's not the case when it comes to the Lynx and Sparks. When these teams are on the floor, you can't look anywhere without seeing a future Hall of Famer. We've had talent-filled rivalries before in the WNBA, but this one is special."

—MICHAEL VOEPEL, ESPN WRITER, 2017

THE THREE TO SEE

The Game-Changing 2013 Draft

There was a lot of hype around the 2013 WNBA season, and it started with the loaded draft on April 15 in Bristol, Connecticut. College superstars Brittney Griner, Elena Delle Donne, and Skylar Diggins were selected during the first-ever prime-time telecast of the draft, on ESPN. The league had recently struck a lucrative television extension with the network, and the caliber of talent justified the change.

Phoenix received the No. 1 pick via the draft lottery after finishing the 2012 season 7–27. The lottery was jokingly named "the Brittney Griner sweepstakes" because the six-foot-nine center was the obvious first choice. Griner led Baylor to a national championship and had a 49–0 conference record in her junior and senior seasons. Her seven-foot-four wingspan led her to graduate as the all-time Division I (men and women) blocks leader. She finished with a record eighteen dunks and was second-best ever in NCAA scoring.

Chicago picked Delle Donne, a six-foot-five forward with guard skills—she was a unicorn. Delle Donne took Delaware to new heights, including its first Sweet 16 appearance in school history. She graduated in the top five on the NCAA DI all-time scoring list after averaging 26.7 points, 8.5 rebounds, and 40 percent from the three-point line for her career. The Sky knew she'd make the perfect high-low partner to Sylvia Fowles.

For the third pick, Tulsa Shock selected Skylar Diggins from Notre Dame. The five-foot-nine

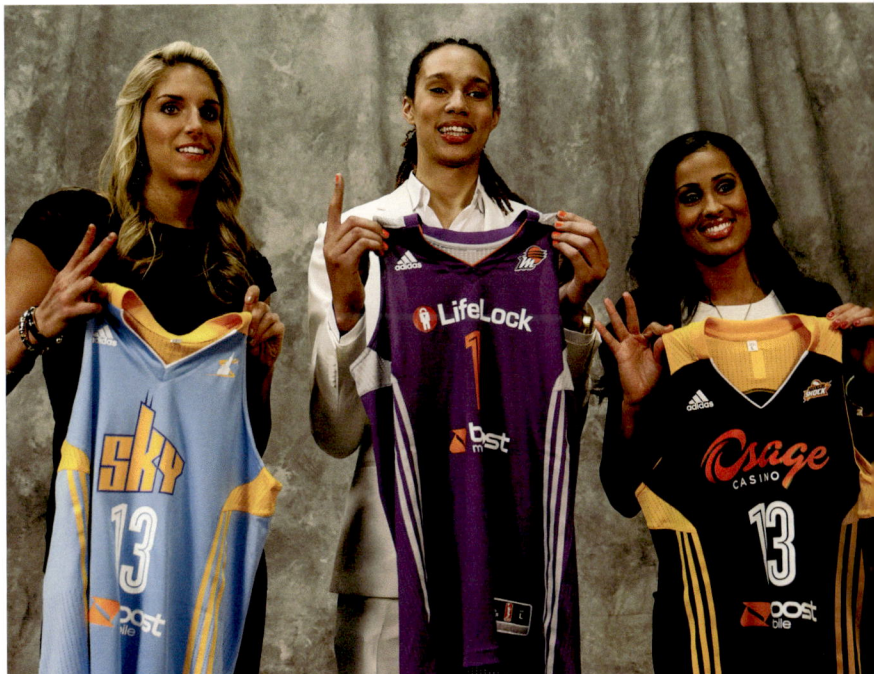

point guard led the Irish to two back-to-back national title appearances as a sophomore and junior. Diggins was a talented distributor but could also stretch defenses with her perimeter shooting. She was only the fourth player with 600 points, 200 assists, and 100 steals in a single season. Her then 300,000-plus Twitter followers were the most by any college athlete; rapper Lil Wayne repped her jersey while performing onstage; she made the polyester tie headbands cool.

These three surefire prospects had high expectations to drive the WNBA into the mainstream. The tide was shifting. The "Three to See" provided hope and promise.

ABOVE: The three fresh faces brought style and pedigree from college, ushering in a new era of the WNBA.

THE WHITE MAMBA

DIANA TAURASI RETIRED AS AN ELEVEN-TIME ALL-STAR, SIX-TIME OLYMPIC GOLD MEDALIST, THREE-TIME WNBA CHAMPION, THREE-TIME NCAA CHAMPION, AND THE ALL-TIME WNBA POINTS LEADER

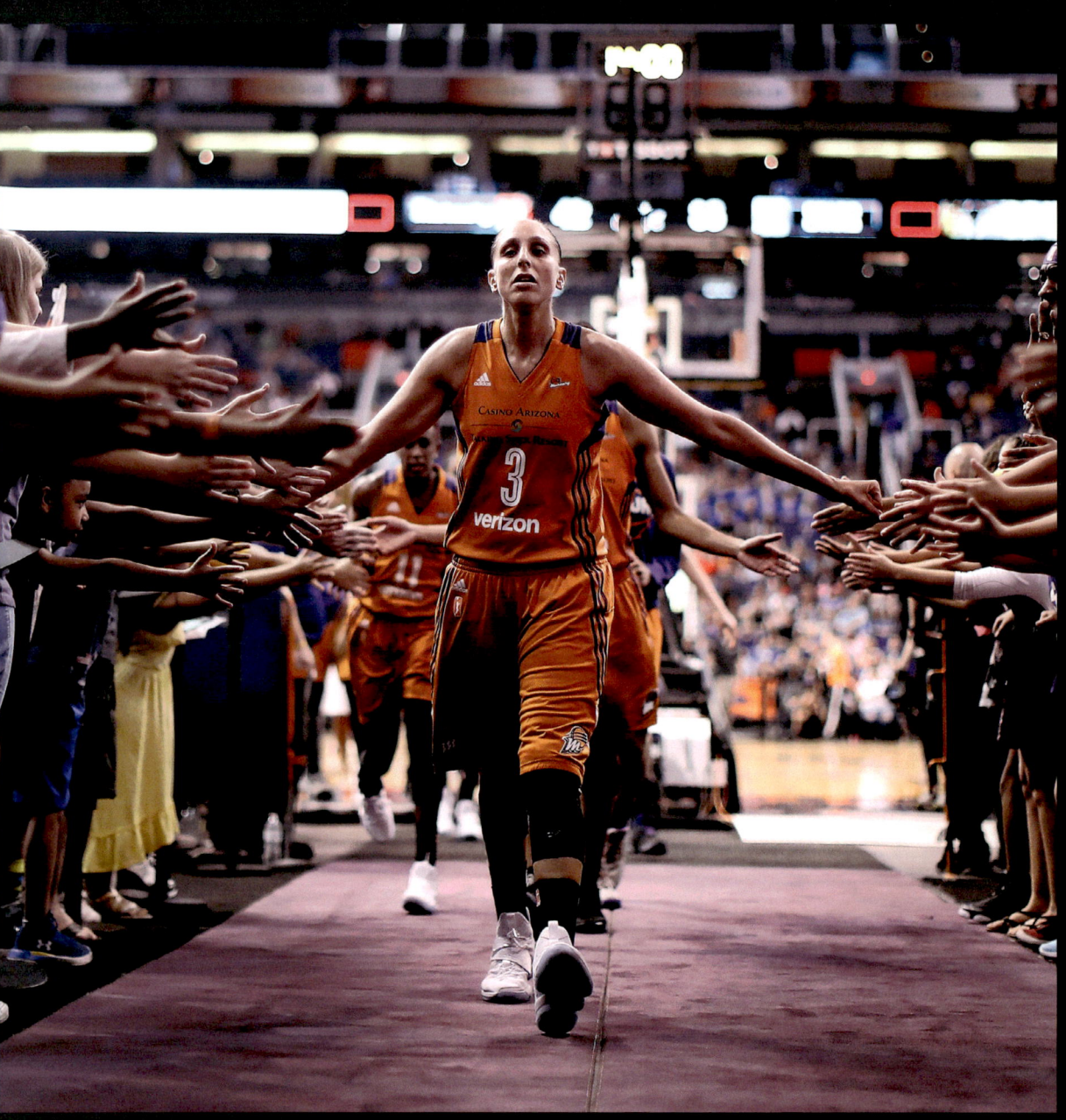

ABOVE: Taurasi spent her entire WNBA career in Phoenix and led the franchise to a pair of championships.

After an eighteen-year-old Diana Taurasi left her native California in 2000, prepared for the spotlight of major college basketball, UConn coach Geno Auriemma sat her down. He believed that she could be the best player in the world. The coach wanted to know if she was ready.

"You want that?" he asked her, according to *Sports Illustrated*.

"Yeah," Taurasi said. "I do."

She would spend the next two decades chasing it. After winning championships, breaking records, and unlocking a rare brand of star power in college, Taurasi built a singular career in the WNBA. She bridged generations of the game: Taurasi was a constant across more than twenty years of tumult and growth in the sport. No one scored like her, and no one talked trash like her, either. That she became the WNBA's all-time leader in scoring was as unsurprising as the fact that she became the all-time leader in technical fouls. Both were quintessential Taurasi.

In her freshman year, UConn collapsed against Notre Dame in the Final Four, and Taurasi vowed they would never lose a tournament game again while she was on campus. She was right. The next three years would bring three championships, and in each of the last two, Taurasi was named Most Outstanding Player.

All of that winning garnered a remarkable level of national attention. "Taurasi didn't just give her college three straight championships; she gave her game a fresh face," Frank Deford wrote in *Sports Illustrated*. The guard was tough and self-possessed, with a knack for coming through in the clutch, and the country took notice. Her senior year championship win over Tennessee became the most-viewed basketball game on ESPN at the time, men's or women's, college or professional. A week later, when Taurasi was selected by the Phoenix Mercury with the No. 1 pick in the WNBA Draft, the night set a draft viewership record that would hold for two decades. Thus began a professional career like no other.

Taurasi's scoring touch registered immediately. She won Rookie of the Year while averaging 17 points a game. With her intensity, court vision

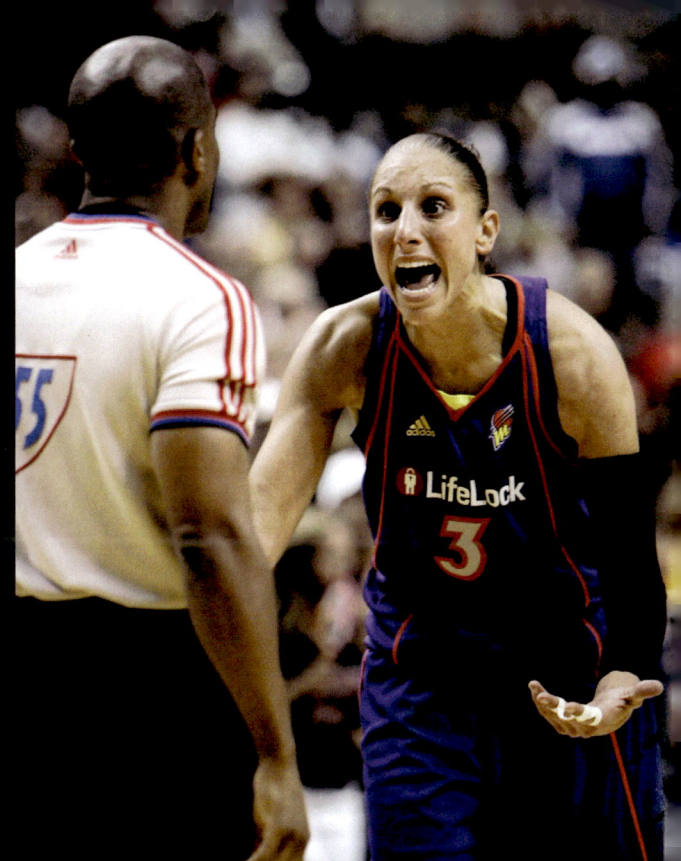

and three-point shooting, she quickly found a place among the greatest talents in the league. Taurasi would become the first WNBA player to average more than 25 points in a season. (Her record there would stand for nearly two decades.) She won three championships—two of them as Finals MVP. And she dominated overseas, too, with six titles in the EuroLeague.

She had an incredible sense of the moment in front of her. No situation was ever too big for Taurasi. To watch her work at the end of a close game was to see a master at home in her medium of choice. It was not just the numbers but also how she went about putting them up. Taurasi played with swagger—a confidence that might have been verging on cockiness were she not so prepared to

ABOVE: The heated conversation with a referee is a key ingredient in any classic Taurasi game.

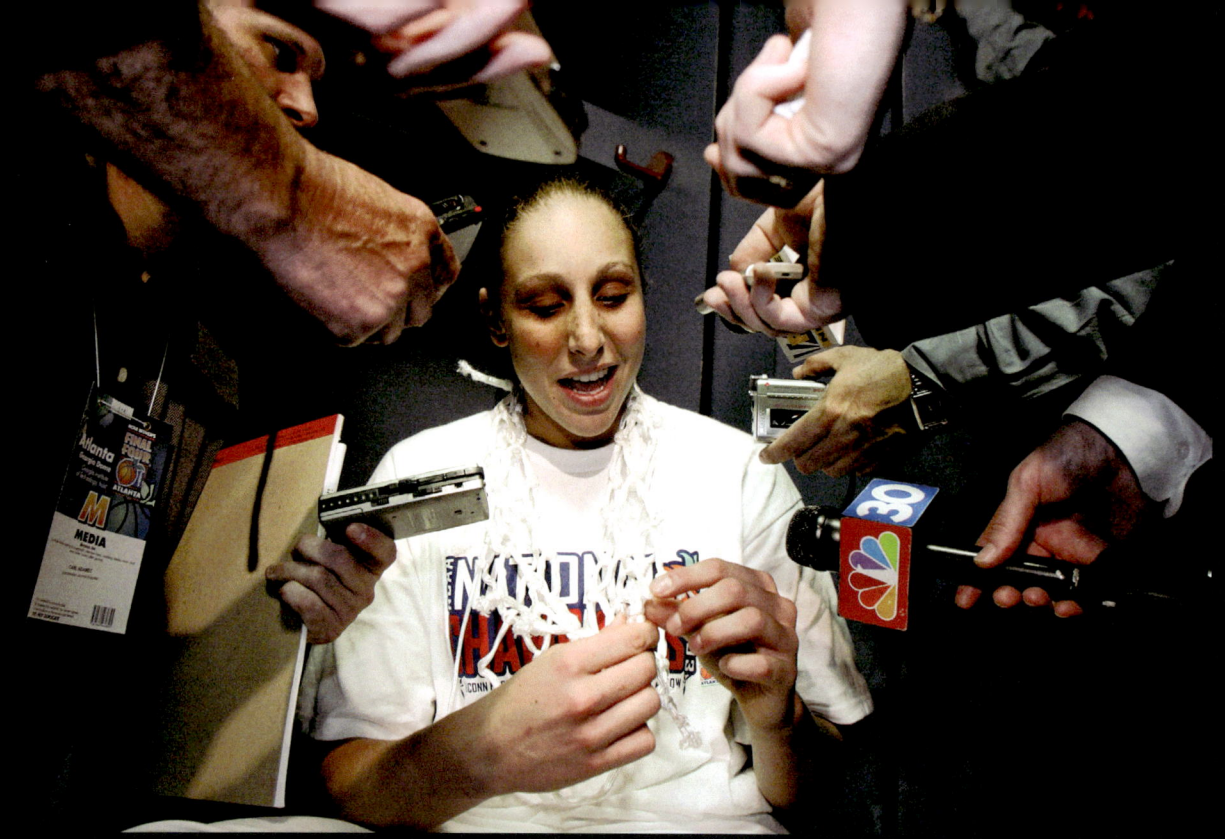

back it up. (This meant that some of her most iconic highlights occurred away from the basket: Think planting a playful kiss on Seimone Augustus's cheek during the 2013 playoffs.) Taurasi knew exactly how good she was. And she would be happy to remind anyone who might be at risk of forgetting it.

Yet her most remarkable feature of all may have been her longevity. Taurasi entered the league in its first decade of existence. She played as the W pushed through financial struggles and fought to secure its place in the broader sports landscape. (That was perhaps best demonstrated in her own career by her Russian team paying her to sit out the entire WNBA season in 2015: Taurasi's salary in Russia was more than ten times what she made playing in the US.) And she kept playing through to the boom of the early 2020s. She remained a focal point through a generation of change.

The league grew up around her. The culture evolved, the money increased, and the style of play changed. By the time she announced her retirement in February 2025, the WNBA bore little

resemblance to the fledgling league that she had entered in 2004. Taurasi stayed consistent. In the same baggy shorts, the same high, signature bun, she kept scoring in double figures the whole time.

"She's always thinking ten possessions ahead, which is crazy, but that's the way she sees the game," Olympic teammate A'ja Wilson said of Taurasi before the 2024 Games. "That's greatness."

That would be Taurasi's sixth trip to the Olympics with Team USA. It earned her a sixth gold medal, which, fittingly enough for her, was something that no basketball player had ever done and something that it would be hard to imagine anyone else doing.

ABOVE: In addition to winning three championships at UConn, Taurasi generated a remarkable level of media interest.

OPPOSITE: Taurasi driving strong to the hoop against Connecticut's Alyssa Thomas in 2017.

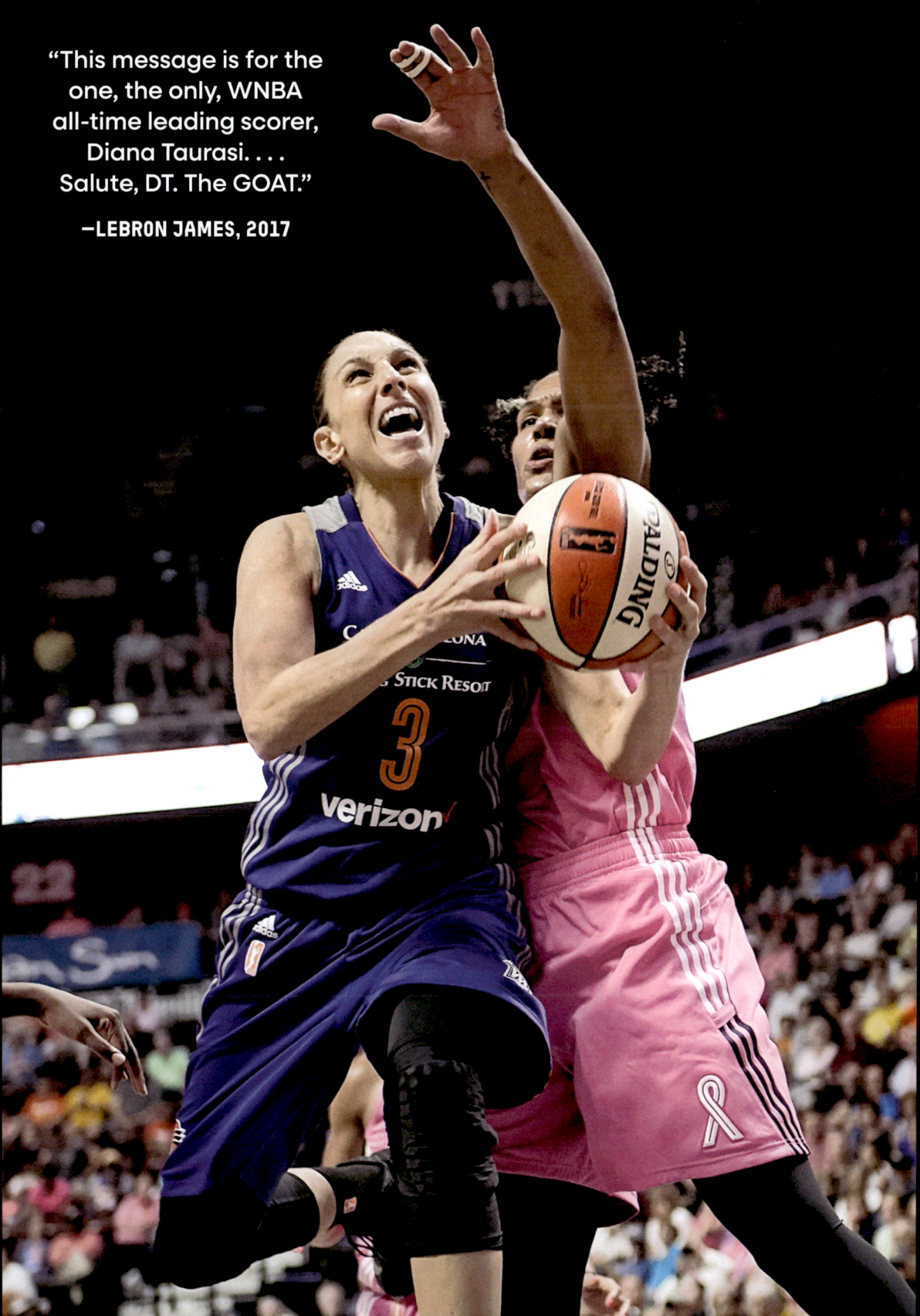

"This message is for the one, the only, WNBA all-time leading scorer, Diana Taurasi. . . . Salute, DT. The GOAT."

—LEBRON JAMES, 2017

FOUR FOR FOUR

A One-of-a-Kind College Career for Breanna Stewart

Breanna Stewart signed her letter of intent for UConn on the hood of her car.

The gangly forward was the best recruit in the country, but there was no media availability, no televised announcement, no big fuss around her college decision. Instead, she looked at what she needed to do, and she found the most straightforward way to make it happen. The letter had to be faxed, and her father had a fax machine at his office, so she might as well sign it right there in his office parking lot.

This began a college basketball career like no other. Stewart chose UConn in large part because she wanted to win. She would do so there in a way that no one ever had before and that no one ever may again. Start with the obvious. Four years. Four national championships. Four nods as the NCAA tournament's Most Outstanding Player. (Add in three Naismith College Player of the Years, two Wade Trophies, and a Sullivan Award, among various and sundry other honors.) Yet *how* she won ultimately felt more striking than *what* she won.

Every victory came to feel automatic. That was not a new concept at UConn: Almost every player in the program got to leave campus with a title, and many of those came in clear, overwhelming fashion. (To wit: Eighteen of the twenty recruiting classes before Stewart's won at least one championship.)

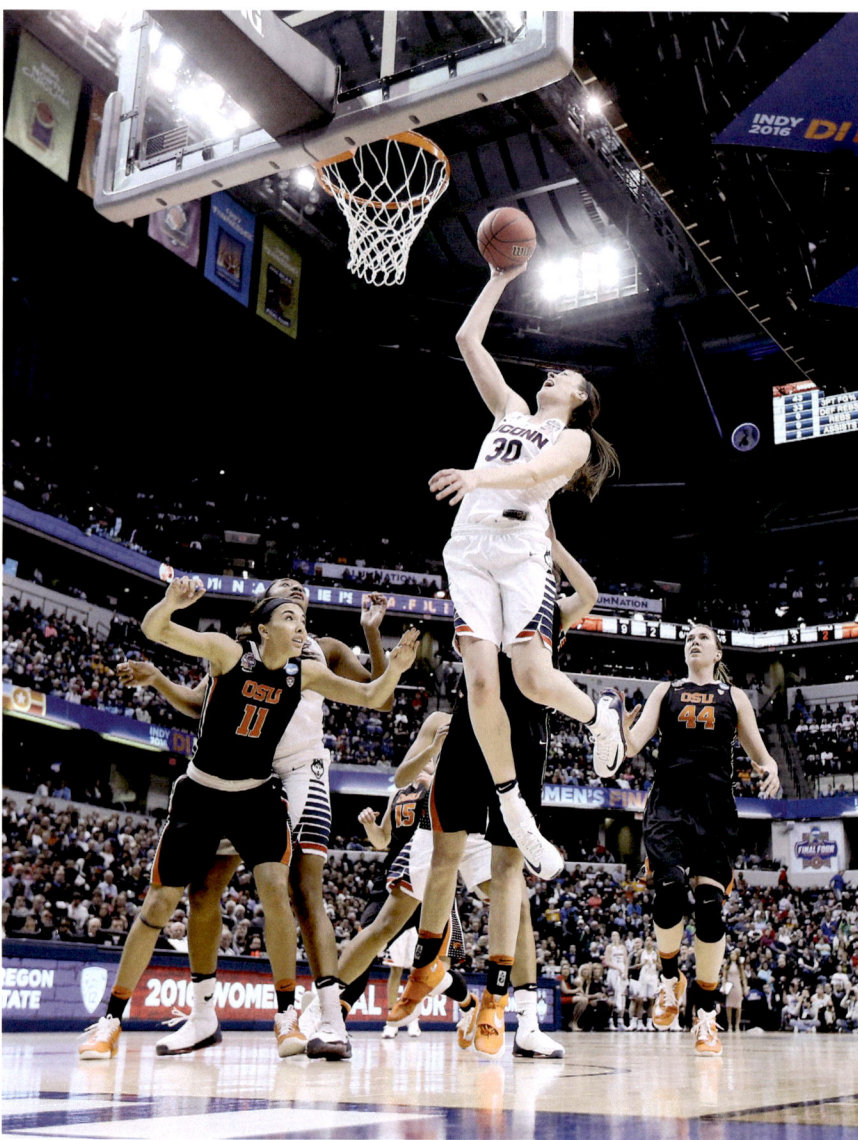

But no one had ever made it happen quite like *this*. The Division I record for average winning margin already belonged to UConn. When the 2002 team helmed by Sue Bird and Diana Taurasi became

ABOVE: No one won in college like Breanna Stewart.

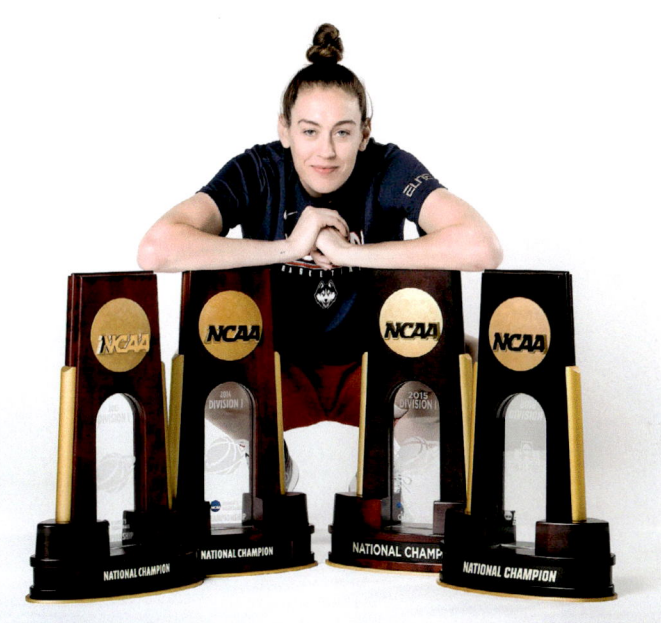

the first ever to win by an average of 35 points or more across an entire season, it seemed like the sort of total, consistent dominance that might never be matched. Yet the rosters led by Stewart broke that record, then broke it again, becoming the first to win by an average of 40 points or more. Their average margin of victory in just their four national championship games was 24. It could make the biggest stage in the game feel totally routine.

This was a kind of winning that had never quite been seen—even in the winningest place in modern college basketball.

Of course, those are team records, and Stewart was on a team surrounded by great players. The other two members of her recruiting class—the only players other than her ever to win four national championships—were Morgan Tuck and Moriah Jefferson. Both were notable talents in their own right. The clear No. 1 pick in the 2016 WNBA Draft was Stewart . . . and No. 2 was Jefferson . . . and No. 3 was Tuck. (If it goes without saying that one program had never gone one-two-three in the WNBA Draft, know that none had ever done that in any other major professional sport, either.) Their collective record in college was 151-5—and four of those five losses came in their freshman season. (Their lone defeat from their last three years of

college still went to overtime.) Yet what Stewart did individually was equally unprecedented. Even on a team full of stars and future pros, even with every other person on the floor a quality option, the best choice in big games was always, always Stewart.

Consider the handful of players who had two wins as Most Outstanding Player at the NCAA tournament. Taurasi did it at UConn. Cheryl Miller at USC. Chamique Holdsclaw and Candace Parker at Tennessee. No one had ever won more. Holdsclaw and Taurasi both got three national championships, and they went down as some of the greatest talents ever to play the college game, but they did not have three MOPs, which only makes sense. On any squad talented enough to pull off a rare three-peat, it stands to reason that *someone* else will shift into a starring role, if only for one major tournament game. Yet not with Stewart.

On these historically talented UConn teams, stacked with five-star recruits, every single one of the four championships ended with Stewart being named Most Outstanding Player.

It was easy to feel as if she could do everything. Stewart is six foot four, a master shot blocker, and a capable, rangy defender with a seven-foot wingspan. But her college years also showed her skill as a ball handler. She could work the perimeter. She could dish like a guard. She could rip apart mismatches. And she did it all in a way that looked so natural and unflashy that it almost felt casual. (The story about her signing her letter of intent on the hood of her car would be repeated so often in part because it fit her game so well.) Stewart won like no one else. And she did it with a range of skills that were all her own.

"Breanna is the one player we have who is able to change the game," UConn head coach Geno Auriemma told reporters after her very first game in college. "No one has an answer for her or what she can do."

She spent four years proving that.

ABOVE: Stewart came away from college with so much hardware that she told reporters she ended up stashing most of it at her parents' house.

THE STREAK-BREAKER

Morgan William Shoots Her Way into the History Books

n the midst of all that UConn winning in the 2010s, all of those records and championships, they handed the worst loss in the history of the Sweet 16 to Mississippi State.

The game was brutal. Mississippi State was a No. 5 seed in the 2016 NCAA tournament, a capable team, if still an obvious underdog against a power like No. 1 UConn. They were certainly not expected to win. But they were not expected to get completely *humiliated*. They lost by a score of 98–38. "Stewie looked like an NBA player playing against high school kids," Coach Auriemma would later say of the performance from Breanna Stewart. Even months later, Mississippi State coach Vic Schaefer would describe the game as "humbling" and "embarrassing." It was the worst feeling that most of his group had experienced on a basketball court.

Schaefer included. He'd been scheduled to give a talk about defensive principles for a coaching convention at that year's Final Four. He had to call up the organizer after the loss: *You really still want me to get up in front of all of my peers and give a presentation about defense?* It was overwhelming. But he did not want his group to forget how it felt. They watched the game back throughout the next season.

"We saw that film a lot," Mississippi State player Victoria Vivians said the next year. "It didn't leave our heads at all."

And it was more than film sessions. Mississippi State's strength coach wrote a giant 60 on the window of their weight room. This was the number of points they had lost by. Now they would look at it every day for the next year.

"It's annoying, honestly," Mississippi State guard Morgan William told reporters. "It's annoying to see that sixty. Like, dang, we got beat by sixty. It's a pride thing, too. Getting beat by sixty, that's personal."

But their group improved in 2017. They clawed their way through fierce competition in the tourney as a No. 2 seed: They pushed out No. 3

Washington, led by top WNBA Draft pick Kelsey Plum, and then emerged from their region having survived an overtime battle with No. 1 Baylor. That led them to a place that was both dream and nightmare.

Mississippi State was in the Final Four, a spot the program had never been before, and their opponent would be . . . UConn.

This would not be the same roster they had faced a year before. Stewart had graduated, and WNBA lottery picks Morgan Tuck and Moriah Jefferson had, too. But the UConn talent pipeline was as stocked as ever. "Let me tell you, this team is no different," Schaefer told reporters before the rematch. "I know the names have changed with some of them. The team is no different." It was hard to argue with him. UConn may have lost three stars, but they now had a *quartet* of future WNBA first-round draft picks in Gabby Williams, Napheesa Collier, Kia Nurse, and Katie Lou Samuelson, with a fifth waiting in the wings in Azurá Stevens. And they were riding a record win streak.

UConn had won 111 consecutive games. The streak had begun in the age of Stewart, but it continued right along under Collier, Williams & Co., who had made it the longest streak ever in modern college basketball. Once again, UConn was a heavy title favorite, and once again, they looked completely, intractably unbeatable, especially against a squad they had beaten a year ago by sixty.

This made an ideal setup for perhaps the most improbable shot in the modern college game.

Schaefer approached this game differently than their last tournament dance with UConn. For this one, they were not going to watch the

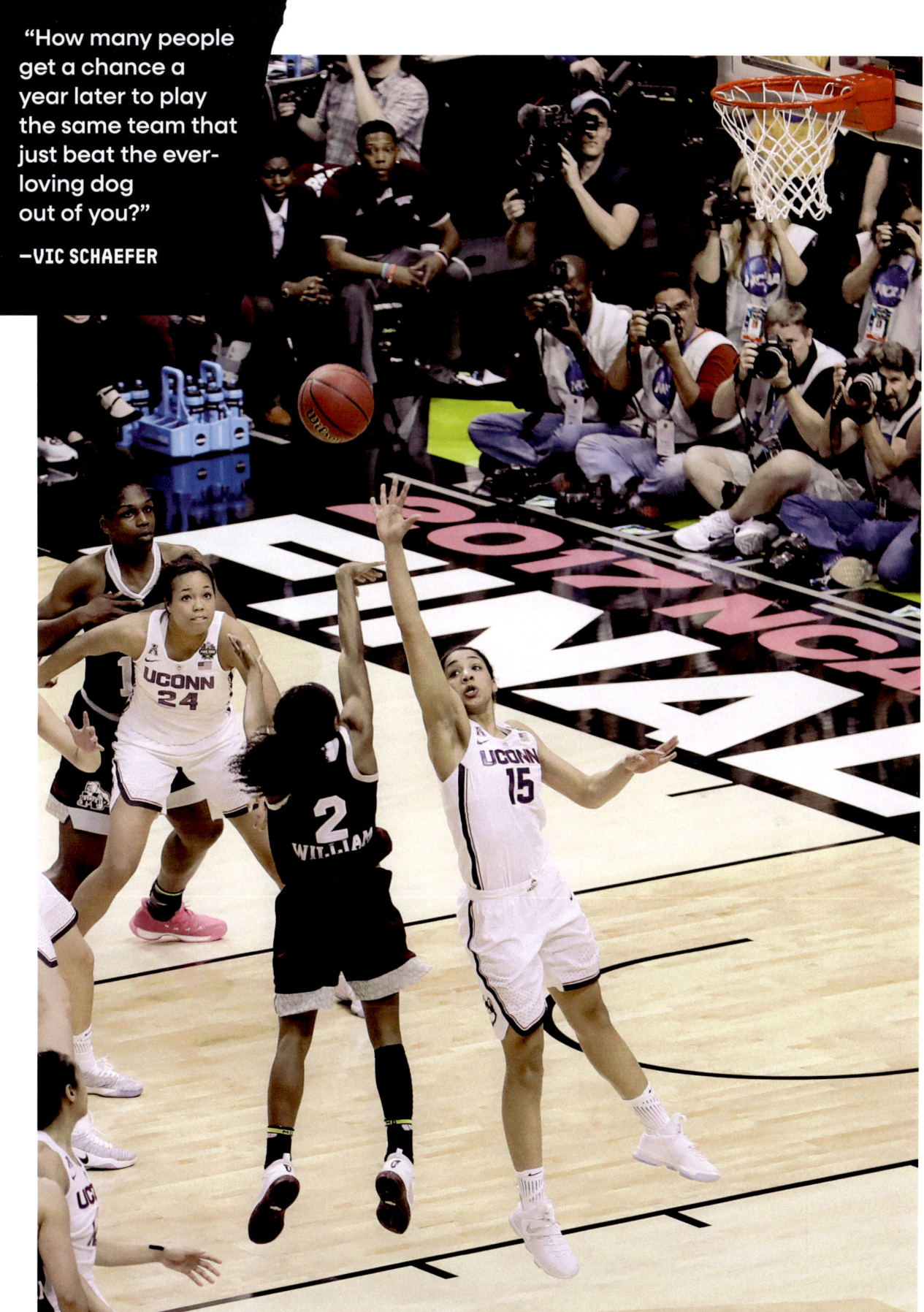

"How many people get a chance a year later to play the same team that just beat the ever-loving dog out of you?"

—VIC SCHAEFER

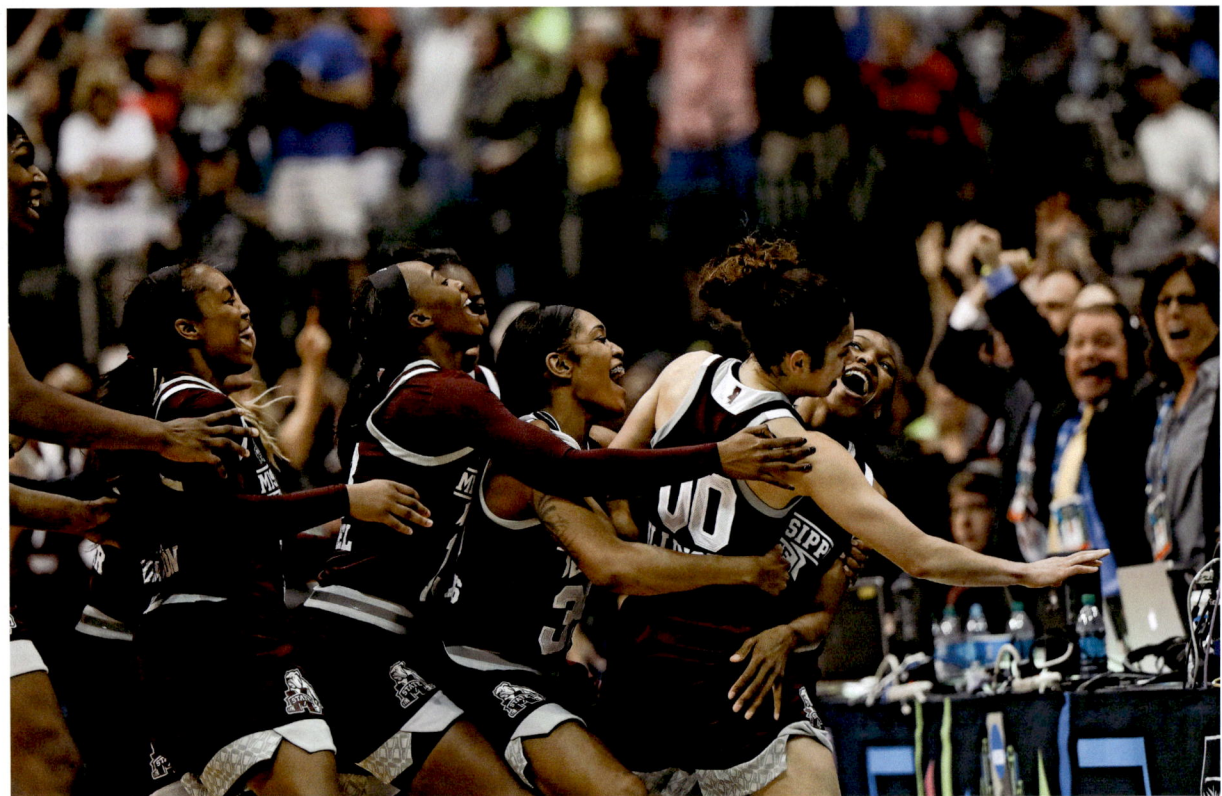

1980 US Olympic hockey team defeat the Soviets in the movie *Miracle*, and they were not going to hear a speech about David slaying Goliath. They knew they were the underdog. They didn't need a reminder. Instead, Schaefer thought about how much stronger this roster had grown over the last year, and he thought about how much confidence they had gained, and he told his players: Why *not* you? This group was talented enough, fierce enough, and defensively strong enough to make something magical happen once. And it only had to be once.

"We didn't have to play them the best out of seven, didn't have to play the best out of five," Schaefer said. "We just had to beat them one time."

And through forty tough, grinding minutes, they managed to get closer than anyone had all season. The game was tied. UConn had not been pushed to overtime in more than two years. But now, with a trip to the championship on the line, here they were, courtesy of Mississippi State.

Yet it seemed as if this might be as far as they went. Mississippi State's leading scorer was Vivians, who'd made an enormous three for their last shot of regulation, and she had fouled out in the first minute of overtime. The offense did not quite click without her, and it was only their methodical, intense defense that had kept them in the game. (After all: Schaeffer had been invited to give that speech on defensive principles the year before for a reason.) With 26.6 seconds left to play in overtime, the game was tied, and UConn had possession. The final shot would be theirs.

Only it wasn't. The Huskies made their drive bafflingly early, an uncharacteristic lapse for such a talented group, and the ball suddenly belonged to the Bulldogs. Schaefer used his last time-out. They would have 12.3 seconds for a potential game-winning shot. And he knew who he wanted to take it.

Itty-bitty guard Morgan William, the smallest player on the floor, very generously listed at five foot five. (She would later confirm: It's actually more like five foot three.) The junior was capable of incredible offensive performances: She'd dropped 41 points

ABOVE: Mississippi State teammates rushed Wiliam after her iconic shot.

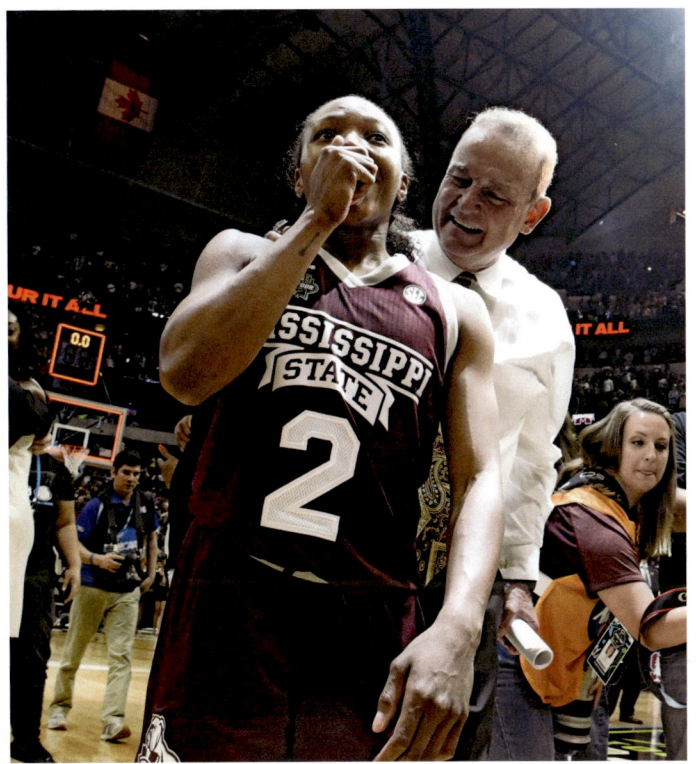

the week before to beat Baylor. Yet this was not that. William had 11 points on 5-of-16 shooting. She'd taken the final shot of regulation and watched her layup get blocked by Gabby Williams. But her coach wanted to return to her now.

Mo, he said in the huddle, *you're about to win the game.*

With the final seconds ticking off the clock, William drove from the top of the key only to be confronted by a defending Gabby Williams, who had blocked her shot to end regulation, who now had a hand up, who had a good seven inches on her.

None of it mattered.

The tiny guard pulled up, twisting slightly, all kinetic energy and spirit, and released a jumper from the elbow. Here was the David versus Goliath metaphor that Schaefer had not wanted to use: a small player shooting over a bigger one, a program that had never been here before versus a program that essentially lived here, a ball floating over an outstretched arm with the resolution of the story uncertain. The buzzer rang out. And the shot fell.

As the weight of the moment settled, Mississippi State players running and jumping and hugging and crying, the broadcast lingered for a fraction of

a second on someone else. There was UConn head coach Geno Auriemma, 111–0 in the last two and a half calendar years, 0–1 today, and he was smiling.

It was the final question of his press conference: *Why?*

"Look," he said. "We haven't lost in a while. But I understand it. I know how to appreciate when other people win."

ABOVE: "What an unbelievable, gutsy performance that no one in the country, including all of y'all, probably thought could happen, and that's okay," Schaefer declared in his press conference. "But we knew it could happen."

DAWN OF A NEW DAY

Dawn Staley Finally Cuts Down a Championship Net

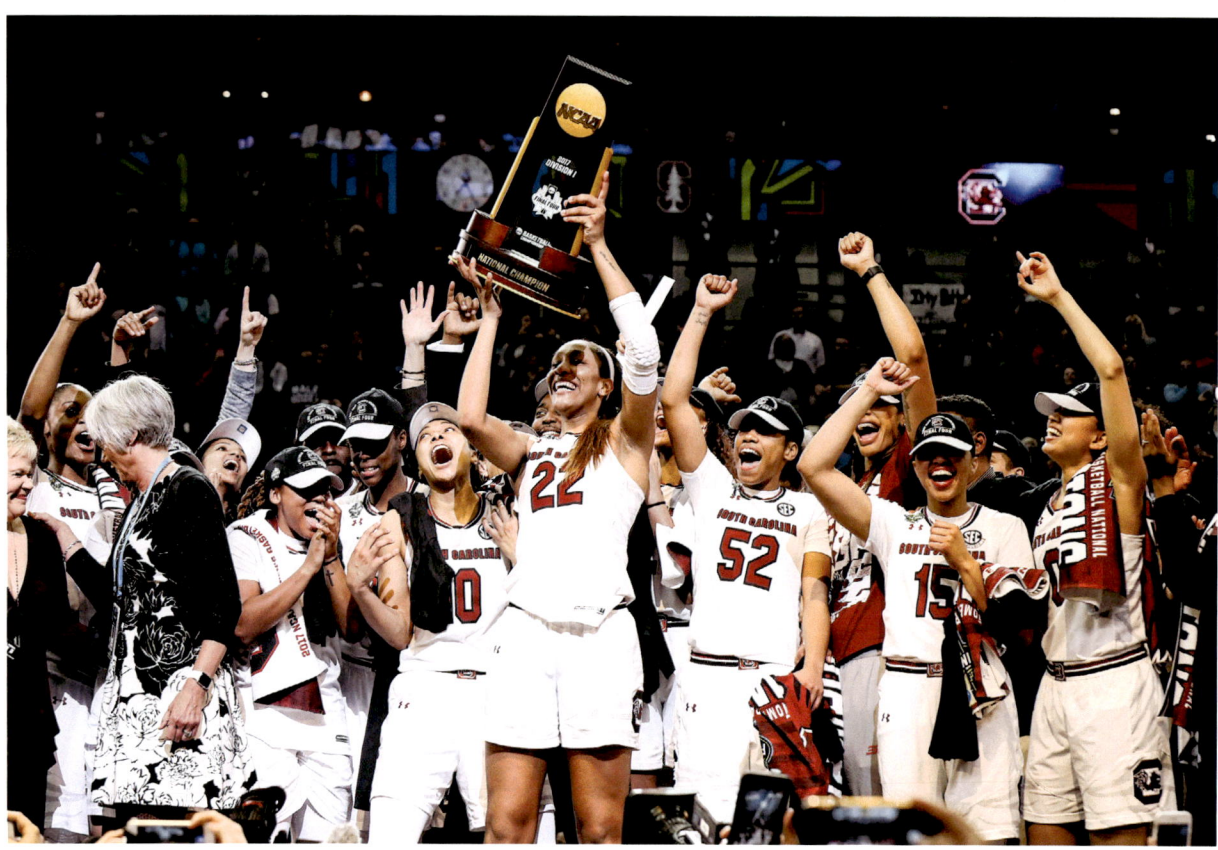

When Dawn Staley was growing up in North Philadelphia, playing neighborhood boys in pickup, her only two chances to see women play basketball on television were the NCAA national championship and the Olympics. The crafty guard decided those were her goals. She would cut down the nets wherever she went to college, and she would get a gold medal, too.

"Those are the things that I wanted," Staley reflected years later at a press conference. "That's what I saw. That's what I was shooting for."

She got the gold. (She got three, actually, with a turn in the Olympic spotlight as the United States' flagbearer, too.) But she never got the college championship. At the University of Virginia, Staley went to three Final Fours, yet she never finished her season with a win. (Though she did become the first and only player to lose the championship game and still win Most Outstanding Player: UVA fell in overtime to Tennessee in 1991, but Staley had 28 points, eleven rebounds, six assists and three steals.) She went on to have the pro career she could not have dreamed of as a child, playing overseas, in the ABL and finally in the WNBA, ultimately becoming a Hall of Famer. But she did not achieve that original goal, that college title she had wanted so badly as a little girl, and she believed that she never would.

ABOVE: A'ja Wilson scored 23 points with ten rebounds to lead South Carolina to its first national championship.

"When I couldn't get it done in college," Staley said, "I thought that was it."

She had not planned on ever becoming a coach. Her first gig was at Temple University in her native Philly, and though she'd had to be talked into even considering the job, she realized soon enough that she loved the work. When she left in 2008 to take over a struggling program at South Carolina, she headed on a path back to a dream that she thought she had long given up.

There was initially no talk of championships at South Carolina. They had not so much as qualified for the tournament in the five years before Staley arrived in Columbia. But she fixed herself on the slow journey of building the program back up—establishing a team identity, connecting with the community, eventually winning games and scoring tournament berths. Staley needed just four years to get back to the Sweet 16. Yet her biggest win of the season was not a tournament victory but a recruit: That early success laid the groundwork for Staley to land the biggest recruit in program history. Top prospect A'ja Wilson had decided to stay in her hometown of Columbia and play for the Gamecocks. The power forward had been recruited by essentially every elite program in the country, but she had felt the strongest connection with Staley.

Wilson changed the program immediately. As a freshman in 2015, she helped lead South Carolina to its first Final Four, ending up just a bucket shy of a trip to the national championship. There was widespread praise for Staley: She'd been known as a player for her ability to facilitate an offense, but she gained notice as a coach for cultivating a tough, fundamentally sound defensive identity. The groundwork was being laid for the program to become a regular contender. And two years later, Wilson and transfer guard Allisha Gray would have them in their first national championship game, their first chance to deliver that lifelong dream for Staley.

They made it look easy. South Carolina was facing Mississippi State, fresh off their miraculous Final Four buzzer-beater to knock off UConn, but against the Gamecocks, it looked as if the magic had worn off for the Bulldogs. They had no answer for Wilson. South Carolina was up by 10

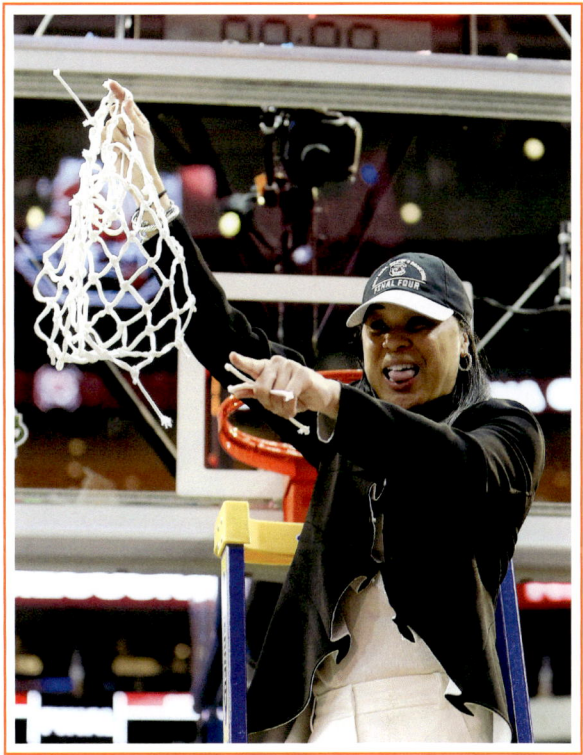

ABOVE: When she didn't win a national championship in college, Dawn Staley thought she would never cut down a net. Her players at South Carolina proved her wrong. Years ago, she had received a piece of a net from the former Purdue coach Carolyn Peck, the first Black woman to win a Division I basketball championship. Staley then cut up her own first net and sent pieces to other Black female coaches around the country.

at halftime. The rest of the game continued apace. Staley finally cut down that net.

There would be more championships to come at South Carolina. In the years that followed, Staley would bring in more top recruits and solidify a position for the school as having one of the best programs of a new era in the game. (There would even be a perfect season in 2023-24, the first since 1990 by any program other than UConn, Tennessee, or Baylor.) Yet there was nothing quite like that first one for Staley.

"Just because something takes a long time, I mean, you have to have patience, you have to persevere, stay with it," she would say afterward. "If something is a goal of yours to accomplish, you don't give up on it."

ICE IN HER VEINS

Arike Ogunbowale Is Cold-Blooded.
Relive Her Game-Winning Buckets from 2018.

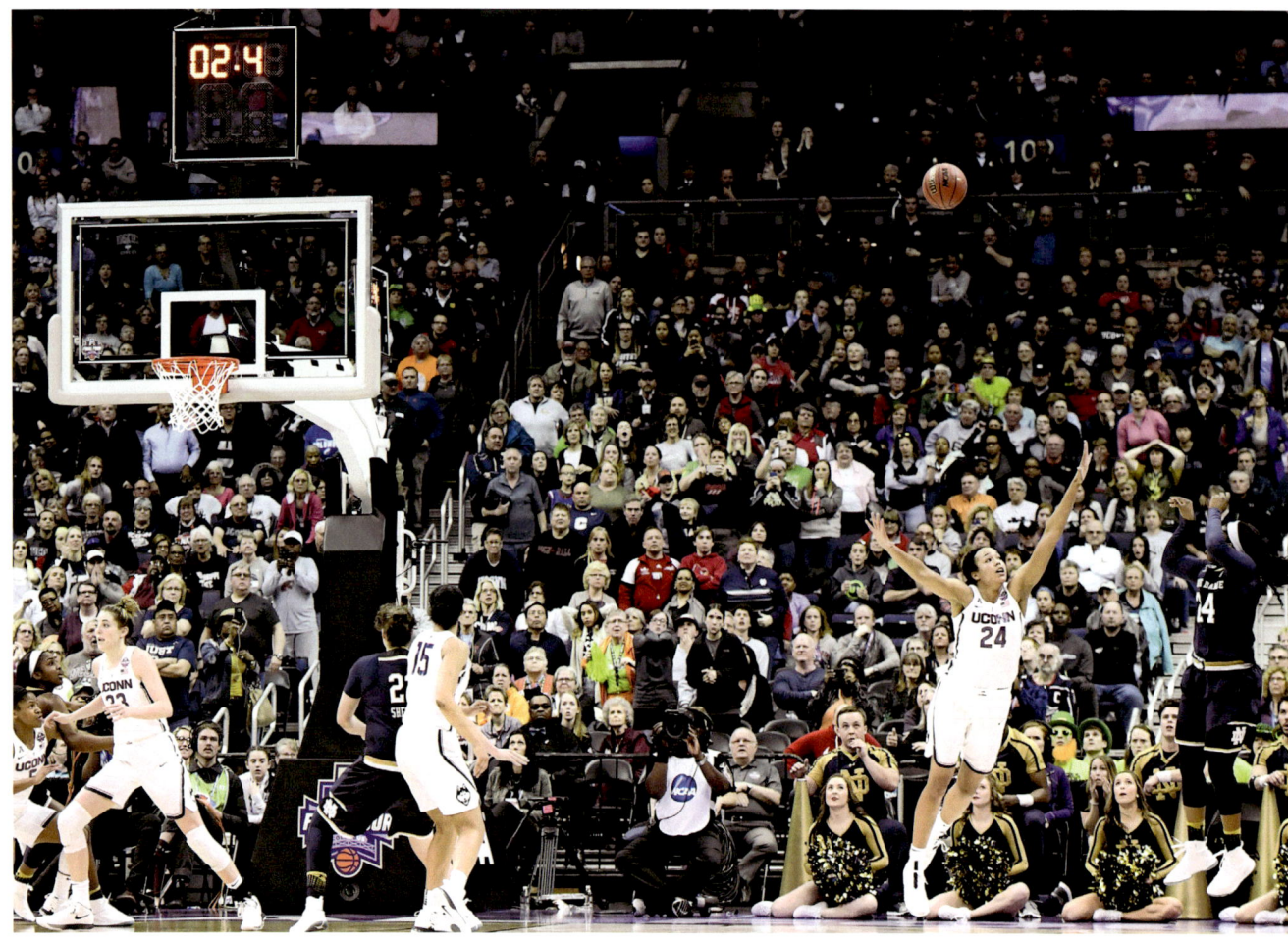

O n March 30, in the 2018 Women's Final Four, a star was born. Some basketball fans knew about a shooting guard at Notre Dame filling up the stat sheet, easily scoring on Atlantic Coast Conference teams like they were stagnant orange cones. Arike Ogunbowale, a junior, had averaged almost 20 points per game in conference play, and the Fighting Irish were in the Natty contender conversations as a No. 1 seed. When NCAA tournament time came, Arike ensured you wouldn't only know her name but you'd never forget it.

The UConn Huskies were expected to speed past the Final Four and win the whole thing. They had a ridiculous, star-studded lineup anchored by names like Napheesa Collier and Katie Lou Samuelson.

They were good. But Notre Dame had some serious hoopers of their own, too: Ogunbowale,

---

ABOVE: 3 . . . 2 . . . 1 . . . The shot you always practice as a kid. After this three-pointer in 2018, kids say, "Arike!" when tossing anything into a basket.

Marina Mabrey, Jackie Young, and Brianna Turner. The Irish weren't expected to dance much further because of UConn's high expectations and a very disciplined Mississippi State team (with rim protector Teaira McCowan) awaiting the winner. But Arike said to her team, "Get on my back." And they did—not once, but twice.

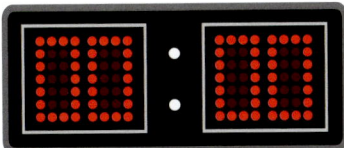

The buzzer sounds, and it's the end of regulation for Notre Dame vs. UConn. The score was deadlocked at 79. Players are exhausted. Fans are in anguish.

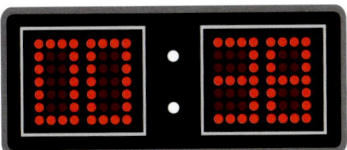

In overtime, with under a minute to go, Arike had a chance at the free-throw line to put her Irish up by 4 points, but it clanks the back of the rim. It was just enough time to allow Huskies' Crystal Dangerfield to drill a three on the other end to tie the game. Time-out Notre Dame.

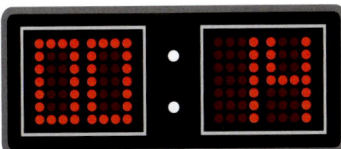

The Irish run a quick out-of-bounds play to get the ball to their center, Jessica Shepard, so she can drive to the basket. But she doesn't have anything. She dribbles it out, and Arike demands the ball as the play is broken. Gabby Williams—a lockdown defender—is guarding Arike at first, but a screen comes and Napheesa Collier takes the switch. Arike dribbles as the clock continues to tick. She shoots a long two, a foot-on-the-line jumper, and drills it with one second remaining.

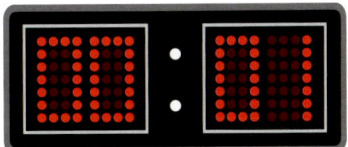

UConn had no more time-outs, but they had a decent look to tie—to no avail. The Notre Dame band strikes up a victory tune, the crowd is going absolutely wild. Arike finished with 27 points, and the last two sent Notre Dame to the 2018 national championship game.

Two days later, still on a buzzer-beater high, Arike and the Irish tip off against Mississippi State, a team who also inched out an overtime win, in their Final Four game over South Carolina. It was the first time that both semifinals went into overtime. The championship game continued the drama.

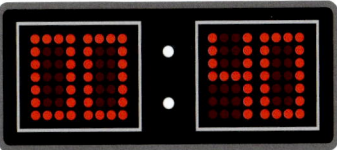

It's all tied up at 58. Notre Dame was down by as many as 15 points in this one but clawed their way back into it. Forty seconds remain in the fourth quarter, and Mississippi State has the ball out of bounds. They get it in, and the Irish are sagging in a matchup 2–3 zone to clog the paint. Teaira McCowan, their star center, has 18 points and seventeen rebounds. Everyone knew where the ball was going.

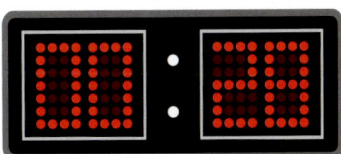

McCowan posts up Jessica Shepard, drop-steps, and misses the point-blank layup. Notre Dame secures the rebound. The shot clock is off.

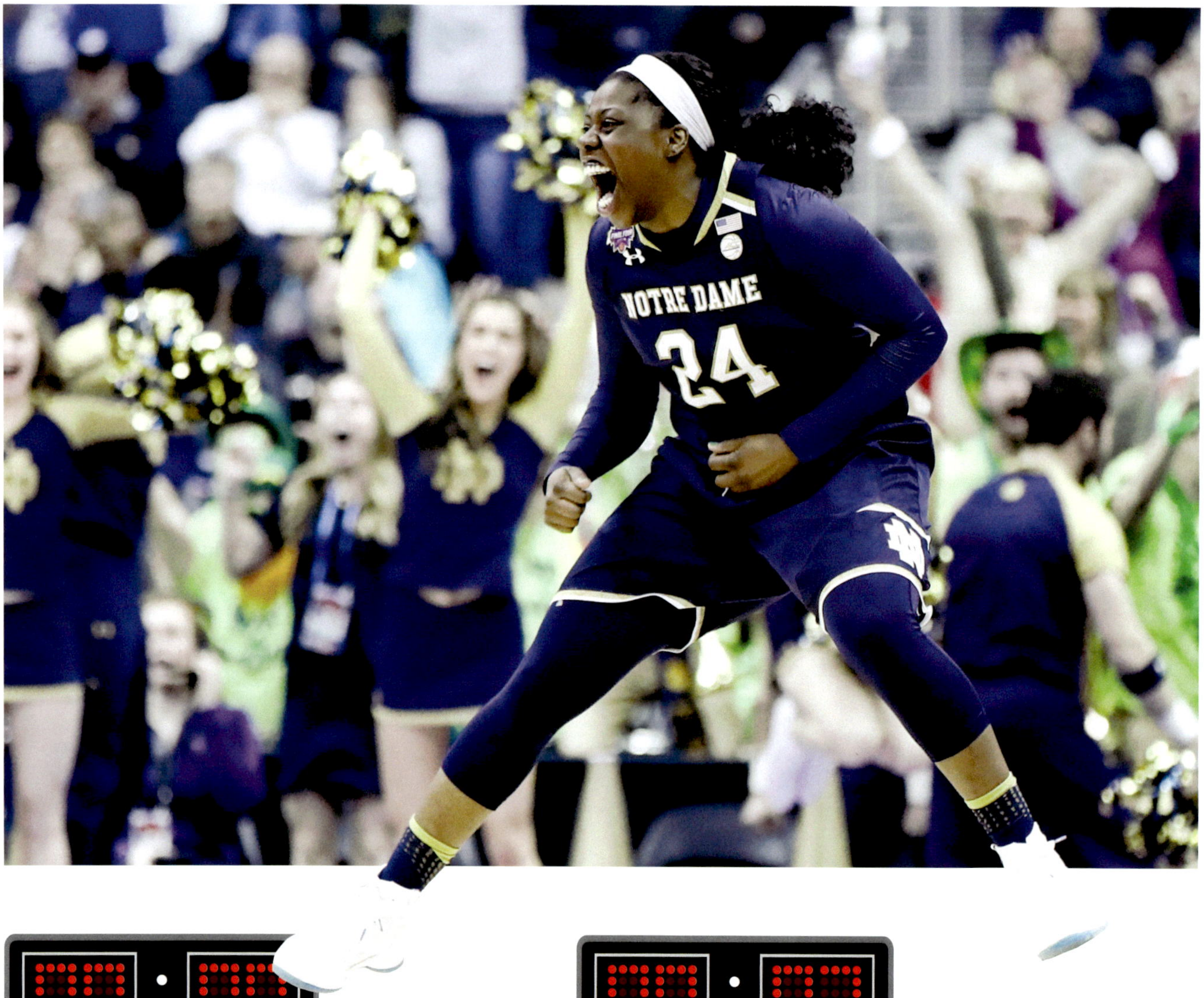

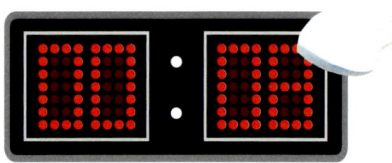

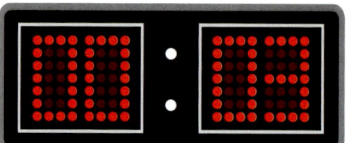

Notre Dame turns the ball over. Mississippi State starts a fast break, but Marina Mabrey picks the point guard from behind. The ball is loose at mid-court. The Irish's Jackie Young comes away with it and is fouled by McCown, her fifth and final foul. But the Bulldogs had a foul to give. Time-out on the floor.

ABOVE: She did the unbelievable. Then two days later, she did it again.

Young inbounds the ball to Arike near the sideline. It's congested, but it doesn't seem to matter. She takes two dribbles toward the baseline, shakes the defender, then pulls up from behind the arc, and shoots the three as she fades away.

"Ogunbowale, for the win," play-by-play announcer Ryan Ruocco says. Time seemed to stand still.

Nothing but the bottom of the net. The buzzer sounds.

"GOOOOOD!" Ruocco yells. "Arike Ogunbowale wins the national championship for Notre Dame!"

It was their first title in seventeen years. And it was all thanks to Arike's clutchness.

THE ORANGE HOODIE

The WNBA Breaks Out and Becomes Its Own Iconic Brand

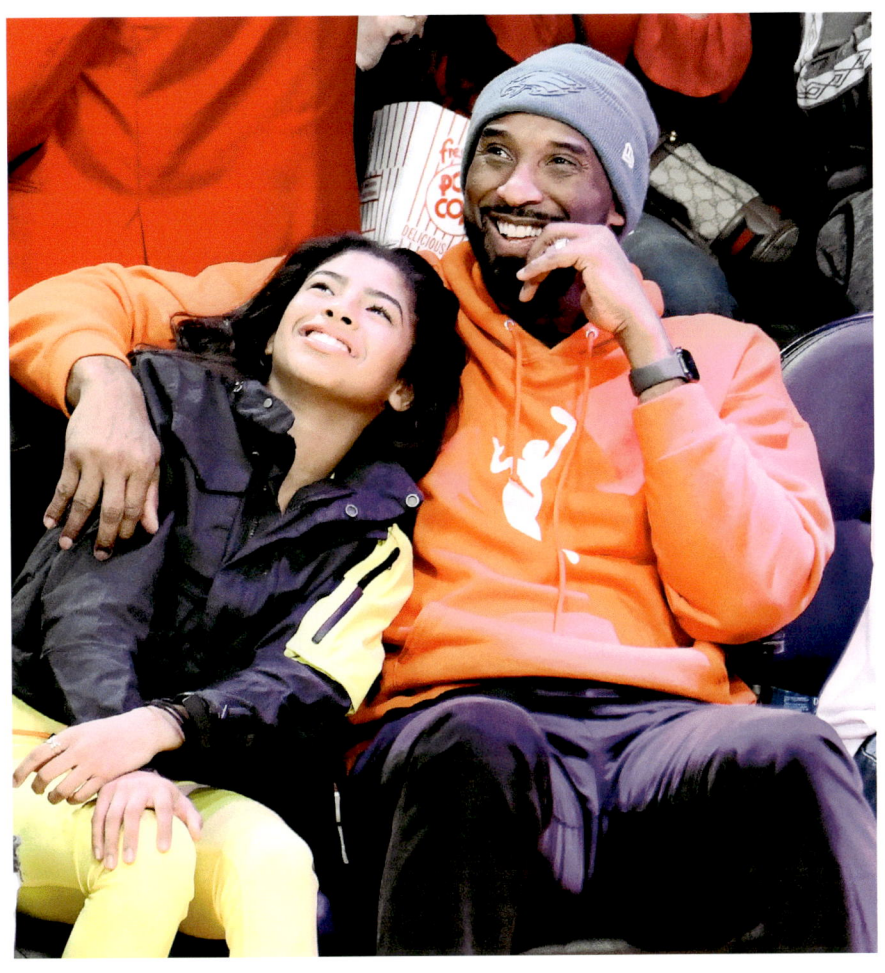

The third iteration of the WNBA logo, created in 2019, is more of a sleek symbol. The designers insisted the brand refresh wasn't based on a player, but fans argued the bun epitomized the WNBA's all-time points leader, Diana Taurasi, who's been rocking the hairstyle for over twenty-five years. The color switched to a deeper orange, and the box around the player was removed to show power, freedom, and expansion.

Then a white silhouette logo centered on an orange hoodie started a trend. In December 2019, Kobe Bryant wore the hoodie while sitting NBA courtside with his daughter, Gianna. It went viral on social media, and the clothing item became a phenomenon.

"It came at a time when people wanted, and needed, merch and wanted something better for the league," Eb Jones, then the WNBA's head of content and influencer strategy, said to *Sports Illustrated*. "If you're wearing the WNBA orange hoodie, it's because you believe in what the league stands for."

The *Sports Business Journal* named the hoodie 2020's "Best Fashion Statement of the Year," and it's the bestselling WNBA item ever.

ABOVE: Kobe Bryant (right) showed off his WNBA fandom with his daughter Gianna (left, while sitting NBA courtside in 2019.

There were more than fifty variations of the WNBA logo during its original design phase in 1996. "Move the shoe over, make her shoulders wider, make her hips smaller," said Tom O'Grady, then-NBA vice president and creative director. "It was created off a pose of three different people. She is definitely the Bride of Frankenstein." The red, white, and blue background mirrored the NBA's and was simple yet striking.

In 2013 the WNBA went orange. The bold, more athletic logo raised the question: Was it a layup or a dunk? The ponytailed player shuffled in a fresh era of women's basketball, leaving behind the NBA's color scheme and embarking on its own path.

MATTER OF FACT
2010s

Numbers, People, and Moments That Defined the Era

NUMBERS

22 Tina Charles's double-doubles as a rookie in 2010, setting a rookie record that held for 14 years (Angel Reese 2024).

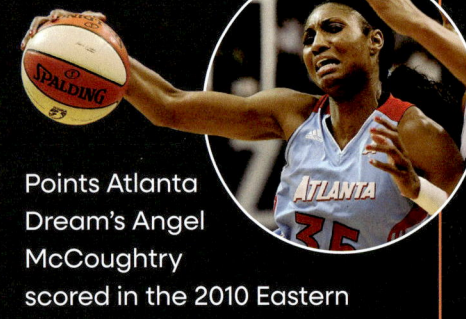

42 Points Atlanta Dream's Angel McCoughtry scored in the 2010 Eastern Conference Finals, setting a playoff record.

50-40-90

Elena Delle Donne becomes the first statistically qualifying player in WNBA history to end the season, making at least 50 percent from the field, 40 percent from the three-point line, and 90 percent from the free-throw line. Her statline was 51.5/43.0/97.4 in 2019, leading to her second MVP award.

PEOPLE

Maryland's **ALYSSA THOMAS** (2011-14) had 135 career starts, every game of her college career. She's the Terrapins all-time leader in six categories, including points (2,356), rebounds (1,235), and field goals made (890).

BRITTNEY GRINER made 206 blocks in the 2012 season, more than all but two DI teams (South Dakota and her own team, Baylor).

During her senior season at the University of Washington, **KELSEY PLUM** tallied seventeen 30-plus games, five 40-plus games, and one 50-plus, while also leading the team in assists per game (4.8). The five-foot-eight guard would graduate in 2017 as the NCAA scoring leader with 3,527 points, a crown she'd hold for seven years.

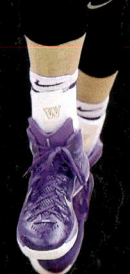

AUG. 11, 2012

TEAM USA takes gold at the Olympics with one of its most dominant rosters ever. Their average margin of victory was an incredible 32 points.

JUNE 2014

The WNBA announced that June would be the league's "Pride Month." To embrace LGBTQ+ fans, each team would host a "Pride Night" every season.

APRIL 5, 2017

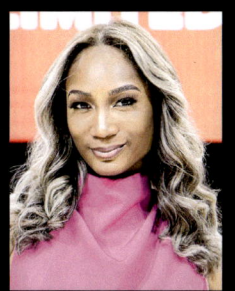

Women's sports creator **ARI CHAMBERS** tweeted "The WNBA is so important." It is liked 4,600 times.

APRIL 30, 2018

ARIKE OGUNBOWALE competed on the twenty-sixth season of *Dancing with the Stars* with her partner Gleb Savchenko, becoming the first college athlete to participate.

DECEMBER 2018

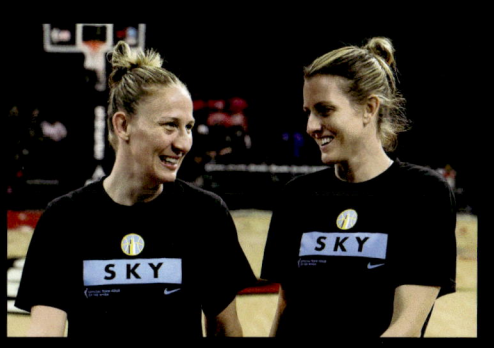

WNBA players **COURTNEY VANDERSLOOT** and **ALLIE QUIGLEY** tie the knot in Seattle. Then, in 2021, they became the first married teammates to win a professional championship together.

THE GAME CHANGERS

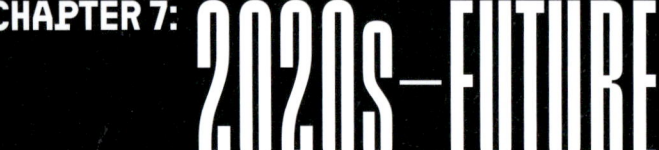

"SUPER" TEAMS, RECORD-BREAKERS, AND OFF-THE-COURT CHANGE-MAKERS RAISE THE GAME TO NEW HEIGHTS.

RIGHT: A'ja Wilson hyped after scoring a layup and getting fouled, May 2024.

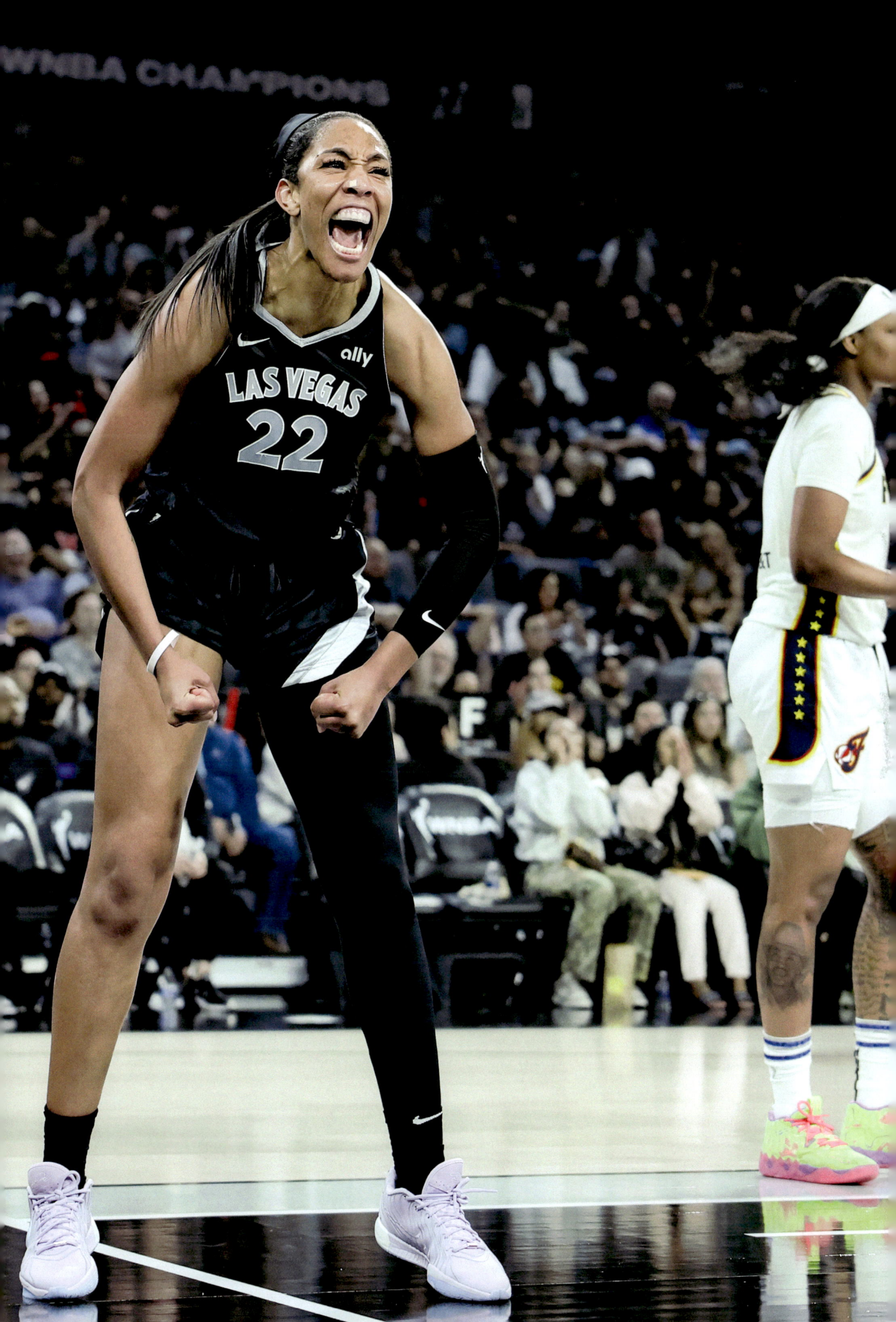

UNFINISHED BUSINESS

Sabrina Ionescu and the NCAA Tournament That Never Was

Sabrina Ionescu, by the Numbers:
- **2,562 points, 1,040 rebounds, and 1,091 assists,** the first DI NCAA player—male or female—to reach this feat.
- **26 career triple-doubles,** more than double the previous record.
- **8 NCAA single-season triple-doubles** in her junior and senior seasons.

"No question [this was one of my best teams]. This team was so extremely close. I liken them to the 2006 national championship team. . . . We kind of felt like this group probably was going to have another opportunity to hang another banner in Xfinity that we won't ever know."

—BRENDA FRESE, MARYLAND COACH, 2020

ESPN's bracketologist Charlie Creme created the championship probabilities heading into a simulated tourney based on his Basketball Power Index (BPI).

Oregon: 29.4%
Baylor: 19.3%
South Carolina: 19.1%
Maryland: 7.9%

UConn: 7.7%
Louisville: 6.0%
Stanford: 2.6%
Mississippi State: 2.1%
NC State: 1.9%

"There's a lot of 'What if?' conjecture happening in college basketball after the NCAA canceled the men's and women's tournaments because of the COVID-19 pandemic. The 2019–20 season will forever remain frozen in time, with no conclusive champion and no memories made during March Madness. It's a harsh reality for the players, especially those at the end of their careers, who didn't have the national platform to showcase their talents and add a final chapter to their legacies. The 'what if' scenarios are particularly painful when considering Oregon star Sabrina Ionescu's career. What if she hadn't returned to Oregon for her senior season? She may have been the No. 1 pick in last year's WNBA Draft, and in the running for Rookie of the Year as a member of the Las Vegas Aces. When Ionescu decided to return to college for her senior season, she did so to add to her record-breaking career and lead the Ducks to a national championship. She accomplished the former; we'll never know if she would have achieved the latter."

—JORDAN ROBINSON,
***THE RINGER*, 2020**

OPPOSITE: The Sabrina Effect: During Ionescu's freshman year, the Ducks' women's team accounted for only 19 percent of attendance for basketball games at Matthew Knight Arena. By her senior season, the Oregon women were responsible for 58 percent.

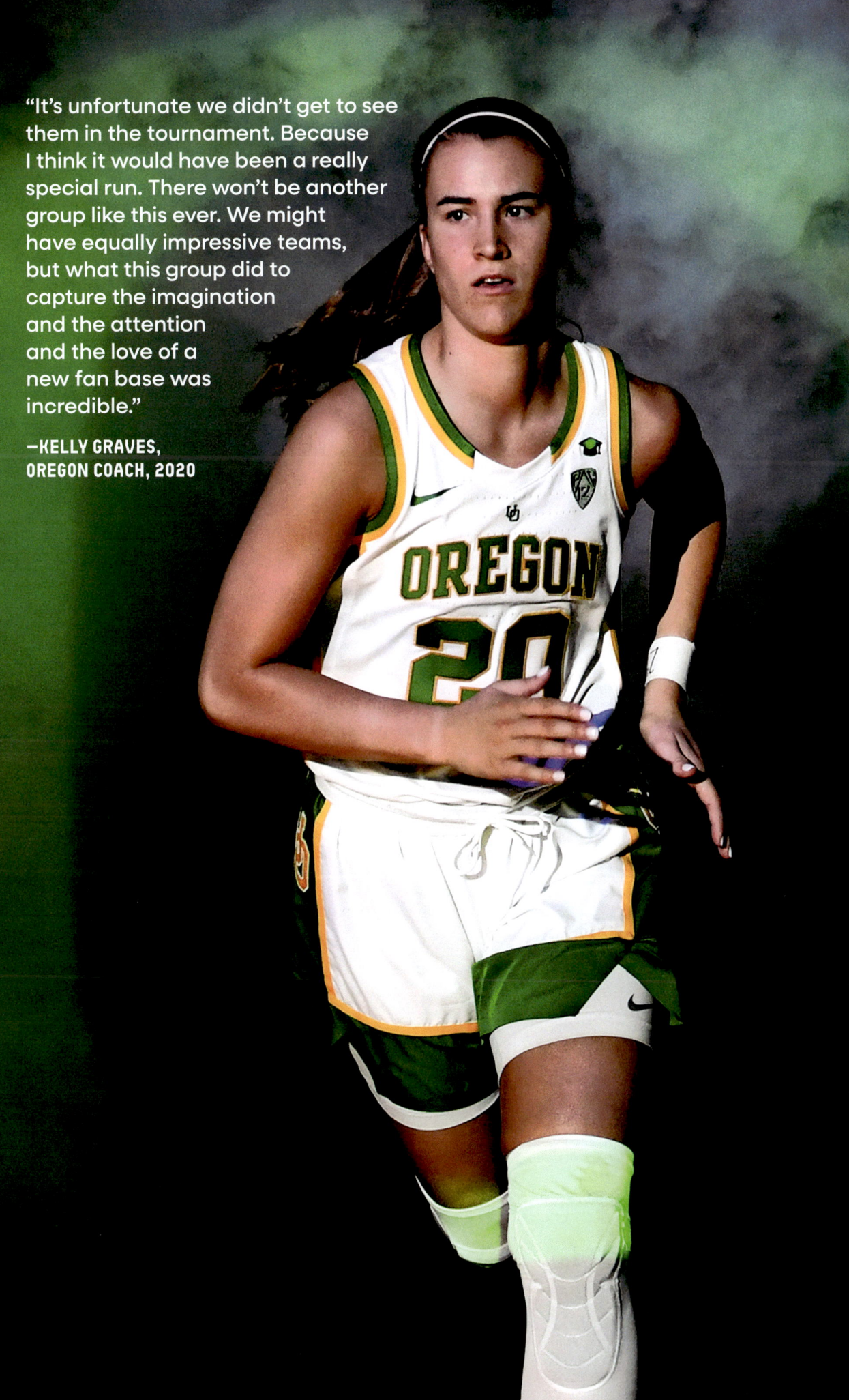

"It's unfortunate we didn't get to see them in the tournament. Because I think it would have been a really special run. There won't be another group like this ever. We might have equally impressive teams, but what this group did to capture the imagination and the attention and the love of a new fan base was incredible."

—KELLY GRAVES,
OREGON COACH, 2020

"SAY HER NAME"

A WNBA SEASON LIKE NO OTHER

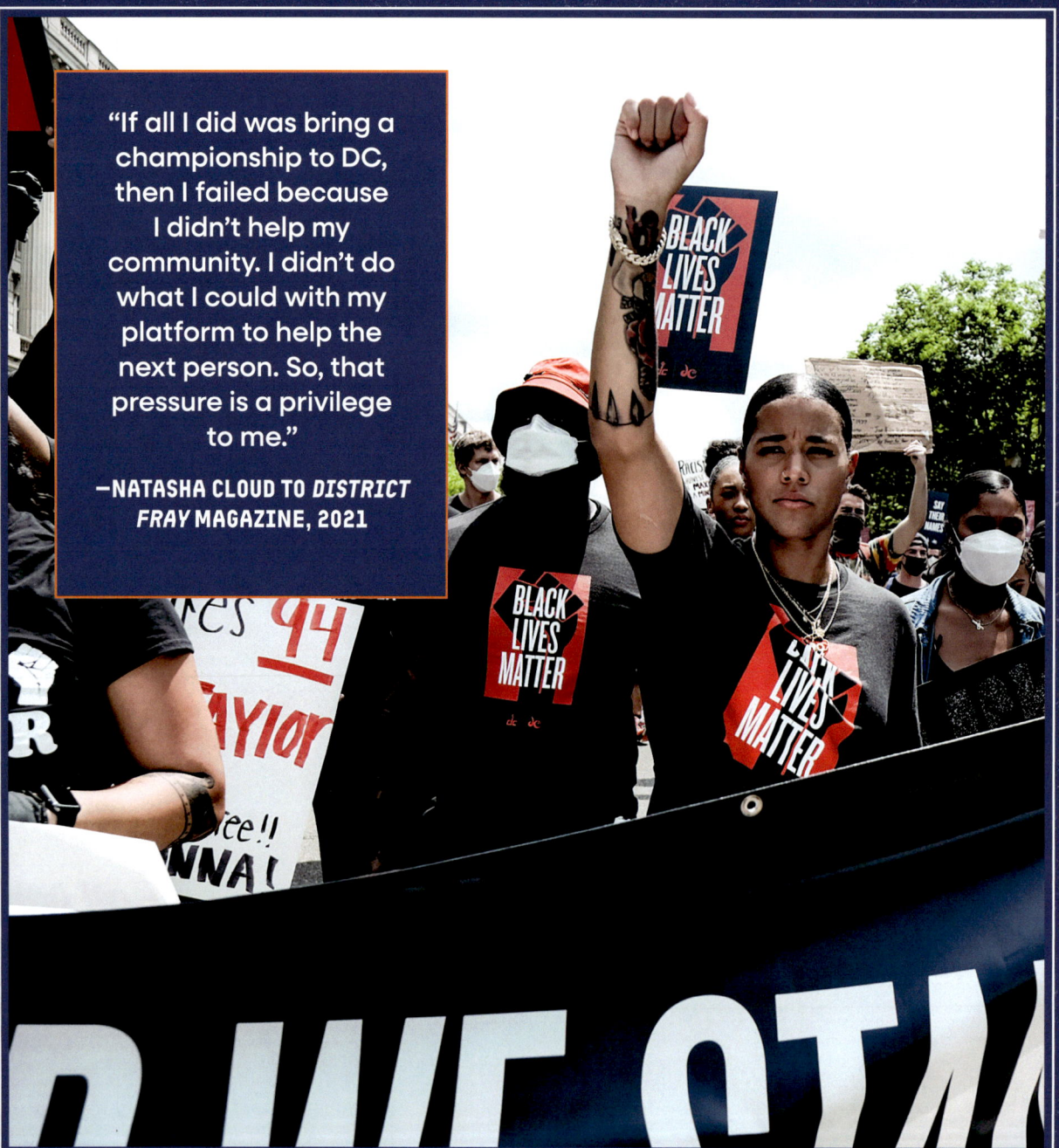

> "If all I did was bring a championship to DC, then I failed because I didn't help my community. I didn't do what I could with my platform to help the next person. So, that pressure is a privilege to me."
>
> **—NATASHA CLOUD TO** *DISTRICT FRAY* **MAGAZINE, 2021**

ABOVE: Natasha Cloud marching during a DC Juneteenth celebration in 2020.

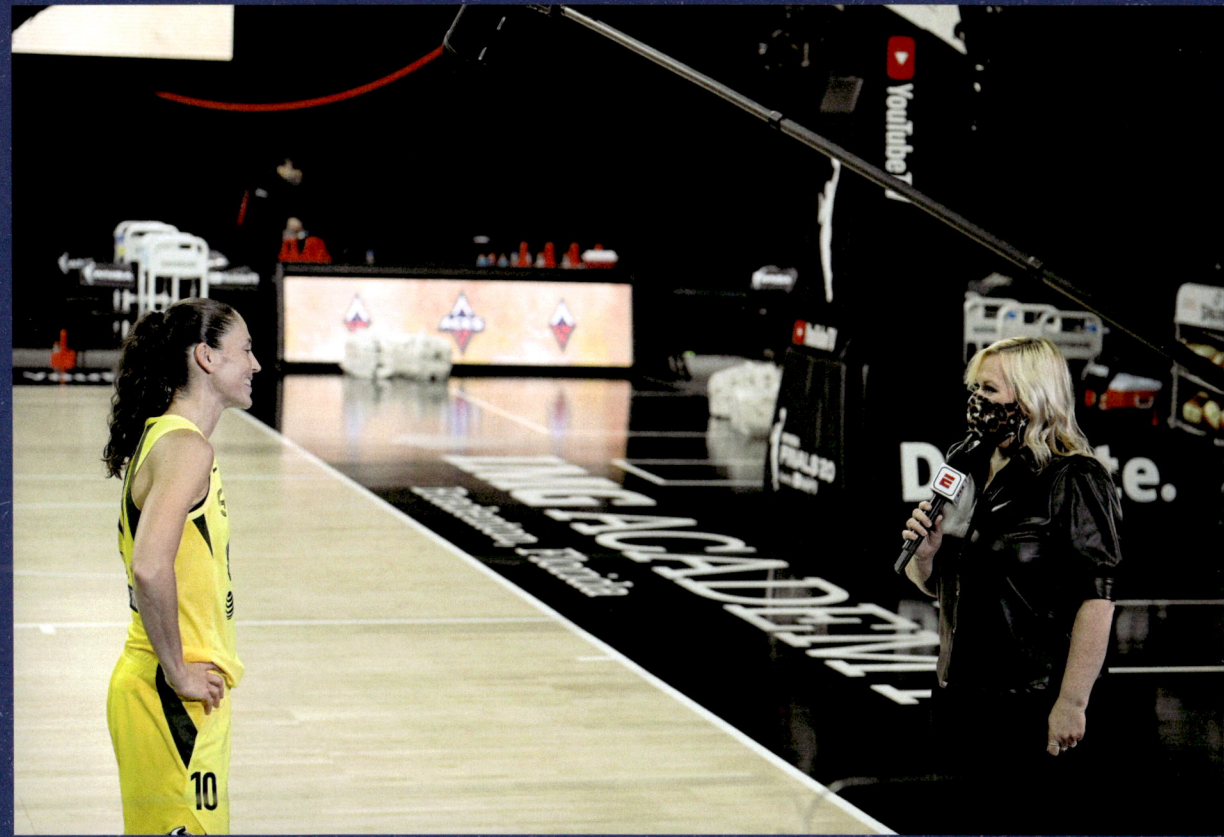

The year 2020 was unprecedented. So much so that *unprecedented* was Dictionary.com's word of the year. The time forced America to have tough conversations about politics, race, and sport, and how they intertwine. Outsiders called the players' advocacy a distraction, and some felt it should be separated. But the players? They knew it was necessary.

"We're onto something much greater. More recently than ever, athletes realize that we can have such impact with our platforms," forward Gabby Williams told me then. "It's almost a crime not to use them."

The WNBA was one of the first professional sports league to resume regular-season play amid a global COVID-19 pandemic and nationwide protests against police brutality and systemic racism. Play started on July 25, 2020—three months after their typical May tip-off—and the shortened season was only twenty-two games. Teams stayed in a quarantined bubble (nicknamed the Wubble) at IMG Academy campus in Bradenton, Florida, for ninety-seven days, with daily coronavirus testing and mask mandates. Select players could bring family members, and those with children could have caregivers. During games, there were no outside fans to cheer them on. Football, baseball, hockey, soccer, tennis—they had been paused for over a hundred days by the time the WNBA started. America was starving for live sports. It was an opportunity to put women's basketball front and center.

"Somebody's got to be the martyrs in getting sports back," Dawn Staley said.

The WNBA players were prepared for the spotlight. Advocacy and activism have been part of the WNBA's DNA since the league's first season in 1997 through its ongoing fight for equal pay and its stances on LGBTQ+ inclusion, reproductive rights,

---

ABOVE: Life inside the WNBA quarantine bubble looked different. Like media interviews being conducted with six-foot social-distancing protocols.

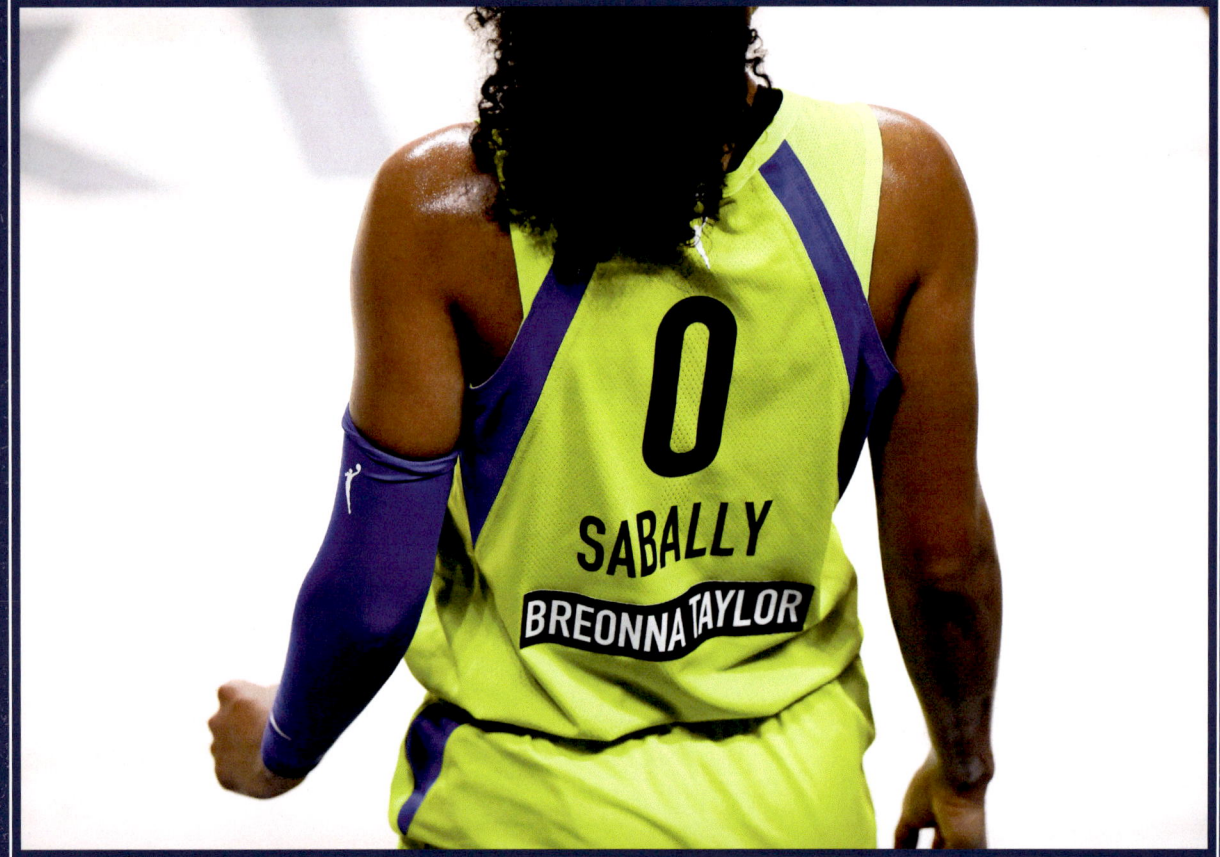

and racial injustice. In July 2016, Minnesota Lynx players wore "Change Starts With Us: Justice & Accountability" warm-up T-shirts after the killings of Philando Castile and Alton Sterling, two Black men shot by police officers. Later that season, the entire Indiana Fever team linked arms and kneeled during the national anthem; before Game 1 of the 2017 WNBA Finals, the Sparks stayed in the locker room during the anthem. Maya Moore, a four-time league champion, left the sport to advocate for criminal justice reform; her efforts helped overturn a fifty-year wrongful prison sentence for Jonathan Irons, a forty-year-old Georgia man who had served twenty-three years of his sentence after a conviction for burglary and assault with a gun.

"The WNBA and its players never shy away from speaking out on social injustices," Staley continued. "They're utilizing the same stamina, persistence, and perseverance that they've used to allow the WNBA to be in existence for twenty-four years."

Still, over twenty-five players decided to opt out of the season. Sun center Jonquel Jones said she didn't feel comfortable competing in an environment with "the resurgence and unknown aspects of COVID-19"; international players like Australian Liz Cambage didn't want to make the trip from overseas; and second-year Liberty standout AD Durr decided to opt out because of a "complicated and arduous" recovery process after testing positive for coronavirus a month prior. The reigning MVP, Elena Delle Donne, said she would not play for the Washington Mystics, citing her ongoing battle with Lyme disease; she felt that going to play in the bubble would put her compromised immune system at risk.

Other players opted against playing because they felt their time and focus were better spent addressing issues related to systemic racism and

ABOVE: Satou Sabally with Breonna Taylor's name honored on her jersey during the 2020 "Wubble" season.

police brutality. Atlanta Dream point guard Renee Montgomery was one of the first to opt out of the 2020 season for this reason, posting on social media, "There's work to be done off the court in so many areas in our community. Social justice reform isn't going to happen overnight but I do feel that now is the time and Moments equal Momentum."

Angel McCoughtry, though, wanted to have both: a chance to play and a chance to make a difference. "It was a no-brainer for me," she told me in 2020 when asked why she decided to go to the Wubble. The eleven-year vet hadn't played since 2016 because of flip-flop years of injuries and rehab. "I'm getting older in my career, and I know I don't have that much longer left, so I don't want to take anything for granted. I want to be out there as much as I can," she said. She also wanted to actively participate in the conversations surrounding the Black Lives Matter movement, so she came up with an idea for WNBA players to continue to "say her name" throughout the season by placing the names of women killed by police on their jerseys. McCoughtry, who played at the University of Louisville and is the program's all-time leading scorer, wanted to advocate for Breonna Taylor, a twenty-six-year-old who was gunned down by police in her Louisville home in March 2020. When McCoughtry posted her idea on social media, along with a petition asking for support, the mock jersey went viral.

The WNBA approved the idea as part of its larger initiative to center the opening weekend around the Black Lives Matter movement. A bold decal of the phrase "Black Lives Matter" was also placed on the basketball court. Each game thereafter, players had the option to continue to have Breonna Taylor's name under their own. "People say, 'Well, what does putting a name on a jersey going to do?' It does a lot," McCoughtry said. "We're planting the seed. We're representing that person. We're keeping their legacy alive."

Some players' motives to play the Wubble season were rooted in finances. For most players, their WNBA salary isn't their highest source of income. After a tough five-month season, many players hop on a plane to tend to their more lucrative overseas contracts. (For reference, Breanna Stewart made $900,000 in Russia, compared to the $56,000 she made in her entire 2018 championship and MVP season in the United States.) With the world shutting down, the international pay valve was closed; they were low on options. If they're lucky, players can also rely on endorsement deals. Natasha Cloud, who decided to forgo the season in favor of her activism, became the first women's basketball player to ink a shoe deal with Converse, and the brand covered her entire season's salary in addition to making a $25,000 donation to a grassroots Philadelphia organization of her choice. She told *USA Today* in 2021: "To have a company see your worth and your value and how much you can bring to them, that's a surreal feeling."

Roughly thirteen games into the season, Jacob Blake, a twenty-nine-year-old Black man, was shot in the back seven times and seriously injured by a police officer on August 23 in Kenosha, Wisconsin. After meeting for hours before the three-game slate on ESPN2, the players ultimately decided they would not play and instead use that national TV air time to talk about the issues that matter. "This is the reason for the 2020 season," Elizabeth Williams read on camera. "We will continue to use our platform to speak of these injustices and demand action for change." The Mystics players linked arms and wore white T-shirts with seven holes on their backs, mimicking gunshots.

> "What kind of first impression are we going to make? What kind of message are we going to send? Are people going to look at us and know that Black Lives Matter is a part of our identity as a league? We hold a lot of power this summer."
>
> —GABBY WILLIAMS TO *THE RINGER*, 2020

VOTE WARNOCK

On July 7, 2020, Georgia senator Kelly Loeffler, co-owner of the Atlanta Dream, said in a statement that she was "incredibly disappointed to read about efforts to insert a political platform into the league." The WNBA distanced itself from Loeffler's comments. A month later, the players responded with immense support for Democrat Raphael Warnock's candidacy for Loeffler's Georgia senate seat. They boldly wore black VOTE WARNOCK shirts, recruited poll workers, and helped with voter registration. By January 2021, Warnock had defeated Loeffler in the runoff election. He became Georgia's first Black senator, and flipped the seat so Democrats would control the Senate. One former Dream player added: "I need to have a shirt that says, 'We Did That.'"

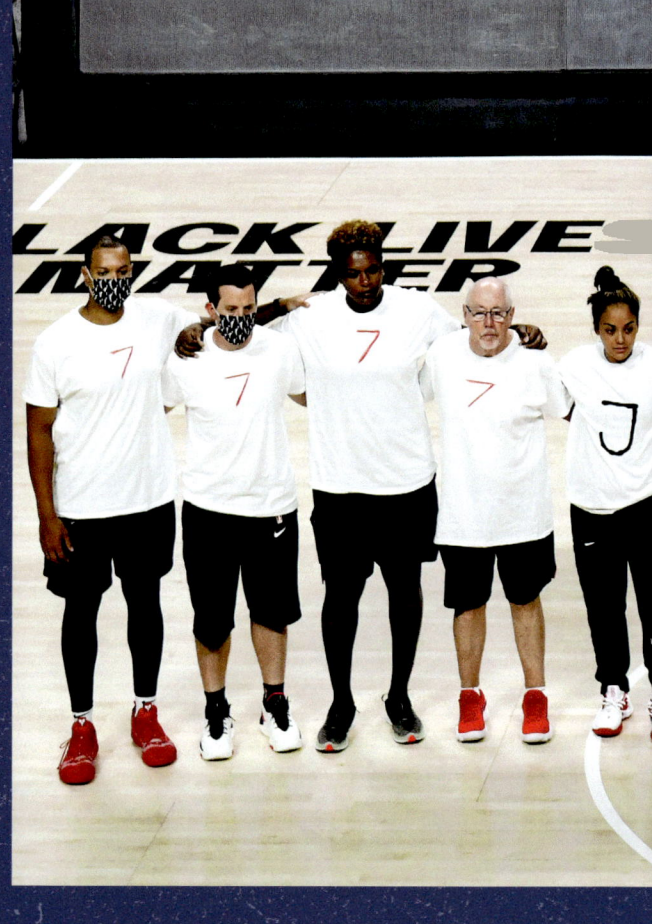

But when all 144 players met again to decide if they would forfeit the remaining competition in protest, Courtney Williams spoke up: "Let's be honest, I came here so I can get paid. I didn't want to come here, but I came here because I got people to feed. People eat off me. . . . I'm not willing to give up my check because that's the only reason why I'm here." It was a reality check; players didn't leave behind their families for months to *not* add to their bank accounts.

The league itself couldn't afford to skip the season, either. "For a women's league where we're trying to expand the fan base, if we would have been out of the sport's landscape for twenty months, the base would contract," Commissioner Cathy Engelbert told ESPN then. "I'm not sure it would have been recoverable."

Under the fresh Collective Bargaining Agreement—signed in January with a raise of the salary cap, among other benefits—the league began paying its players starting June 1. Because of this, the WNBA's twelve teams had to get their rosters down to a max of twelve players by May 26 to abide by the $1.3 million salary cap per team. There was one problem: The original training camp date was canceled due to health concerns. The majority of the women who got the boot were rookies. After the league's unconventional yet successful remote draft in April, rookies didn't have an opportunity to show what they could bring to the team without in-person play. Because of players opting out, however, there was a newfound chance for first-years; roughly twenty-two rookies started the season, which is high for a typically vet-driven league.

Seattle Storm rookie Ezi Magbegor had an experience of a lifetime. At twenty-one years old, she became the second-youngest player in history to win a WNBA championship. "I've taken a lot away," she said of her time in the Wubble. "More on-court stuff, reading the game and how much

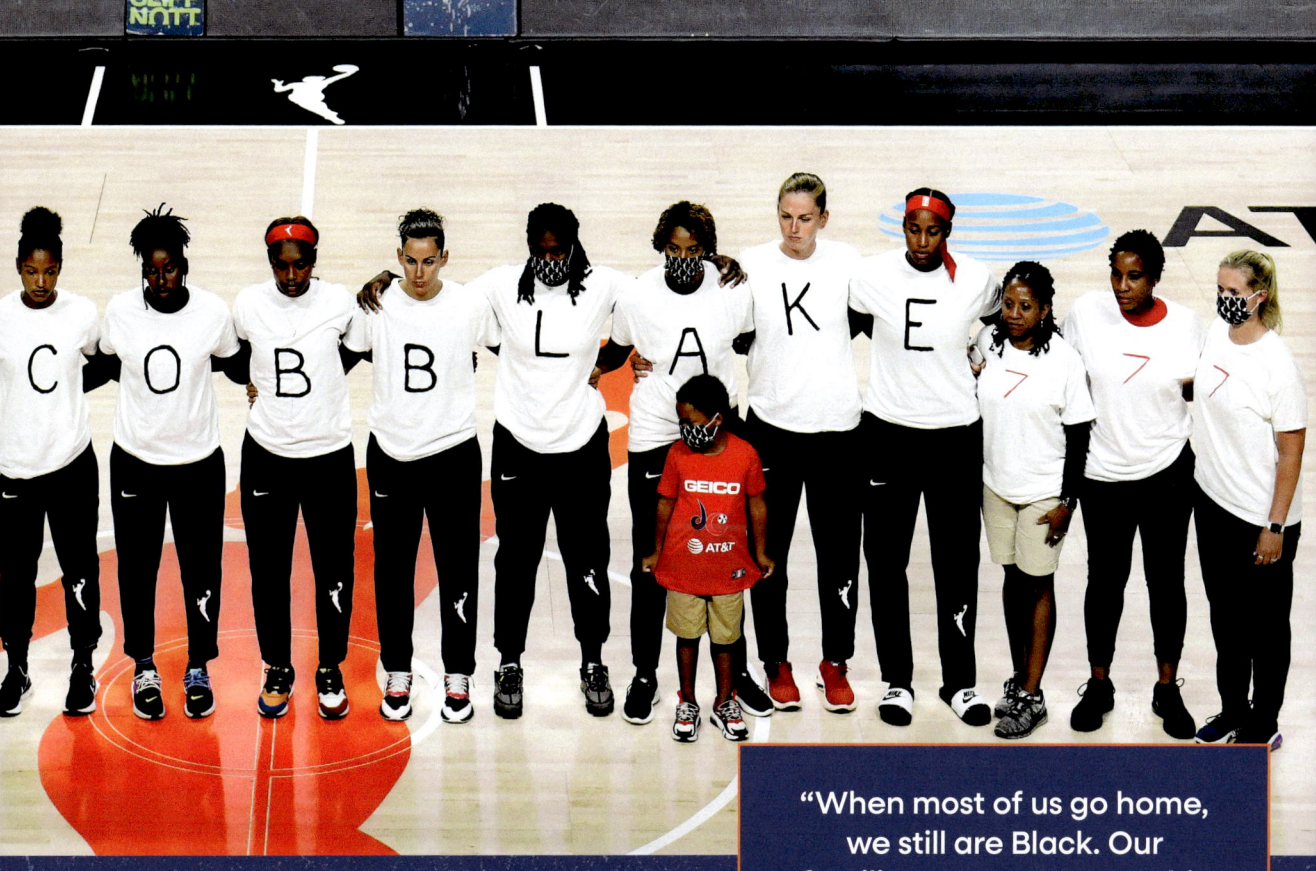

the little details matter and I think I've learned that from Sue [Bird]." The Storm trio of Bird, Jewell Loyd, and Breanna Stewart swept the Las Vegas Aces and earned their second title together while their fans virtually celebrated.

"The smiles, you can see them through the masks," announcer Ryan Ruocco said as the final buzzer sounded. "In a year we will never forget, the Seattle Storm is the team we will always remember."

When the bright lights of IMG Academy switched on for the first game of the 2020 WNBA season, it looked a little different. It felt different, too. Beyond the countless roster switches and no fans in attendance, the league had a different tone. But what wasn't different was a league dripping in advocacy, whose players put their careers on the line to give a voice to the voiceless. The phrases "Black Lives Matter" and "Say Her Name" framed the court's baselines as a reminder that even though the players couldn't be actively involved in the summer of protests in the streets of their home cities, they

found a new way to take part. "As a Black woman, as a queer woman playing in sports . . . my existence is political," Layshia Clarendon told ABC News in July 2020. "We are the movement."

> "When most of us go home, we still are Black. Our families matter. We got this little guy here that we see every day. His life matters. . . . That's what people need to understand. We're not just basketball players. If you think we are, then don't watch us."
>
> —ARIEL ATKINS, MYSTICS GUARD, ON ESPN2

ABOVE: On August. 26, 2020, the players decided to cancel their game, and the Washington Mystics used their national time slot to speak out.

TARA VANDERVEER

A 1,216–271 Record Over Forty-Five Seasons.
Three National Championships. Thirteen Final Fours.

Coach Tara VanDerveer's third championship at Stanford looked nothing like her first two. The celebratory press conference was held virtually, for one, and the arena had made only a fraction of its tickets available for sale. This was the COVID bubble tournament, in March and April of 2021, and if that ended a season that had been taxing for every team, it had been especially so for Stanford. The program had needed to spend nearly the entire season living and playing on the road due to local health regulations.

And they finished with VanDerveer's first championship in nearly thirty years. It had been a once-in-a-lifetime situation, and it had required an especially tricky coaching job, but it had taken them to a place the program had not been in decades. Yet for everything that made this group different from their predecessors at Stanford, there was much that made them similar, too.

"I know that these women are kind of on the shoulders of those women," VanDerveer said. "Former players would be so proud to be part of this team, because of the resilience they've shown, because of the sisterhood that they represent."

There was something very real in that concept of a sisterhood that spanned generations. Playing for VanDerveer had always been a unifying experience, beginning with her first college head coaching gig at Idaho in the AIAW era of the late 1970s. She worked her players hard, with a ruthless, uncompromising emphasis on conditioning and a remarkable eye for strategy. Yet their bonds were built on more than grueling workout sessions. They came from the passion that motivated VanDerveer, too. It was as true for her first teams at Idaho as it was for her championship squads at Stanford and for the 1996 Olympic team. Yes, she worked her players hard. But it came from a deep sense of joy and care for the sport.

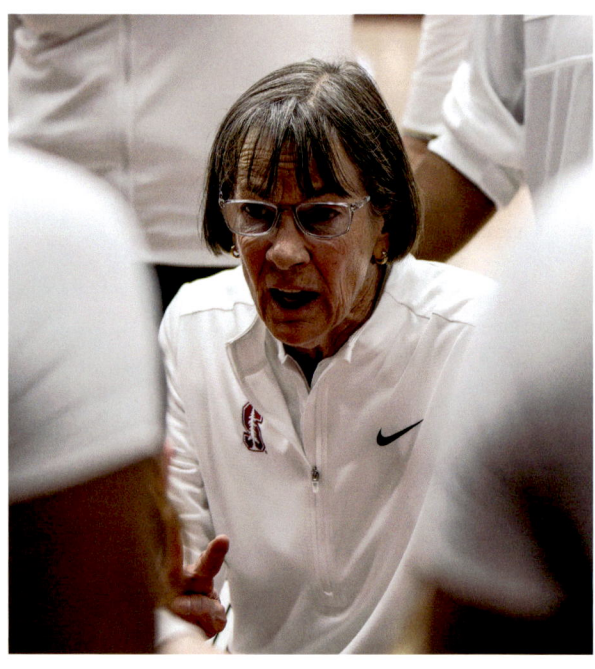

VanDerveer loved the game even when it did not love her back. There were no girls' teams at the schools she attended in Schenectady, New York, in the 1960s. Desperate to be part of the action in any way she could, VanDerveer asked to be the mascot for the boys' teams, watching the games through the eyes of a ratty bear suit. ("I was the worst mascot in the history of mascots," she wrote in her memoir: She was encouraged not to return the next season after taking off the head of her costume to see the game better one too many times.) Later, when she played in college at Indiana and led her team to the 1973 AIAW Final Four, she would sit in at practices for the men, taking notes on the strategies of coach Bobby Knight.

ABOVE: VanDerveer coached fifteen first-team All-Americans at Stanford, from Jennifer Azzi (1989) to Cameron Brink (2024).

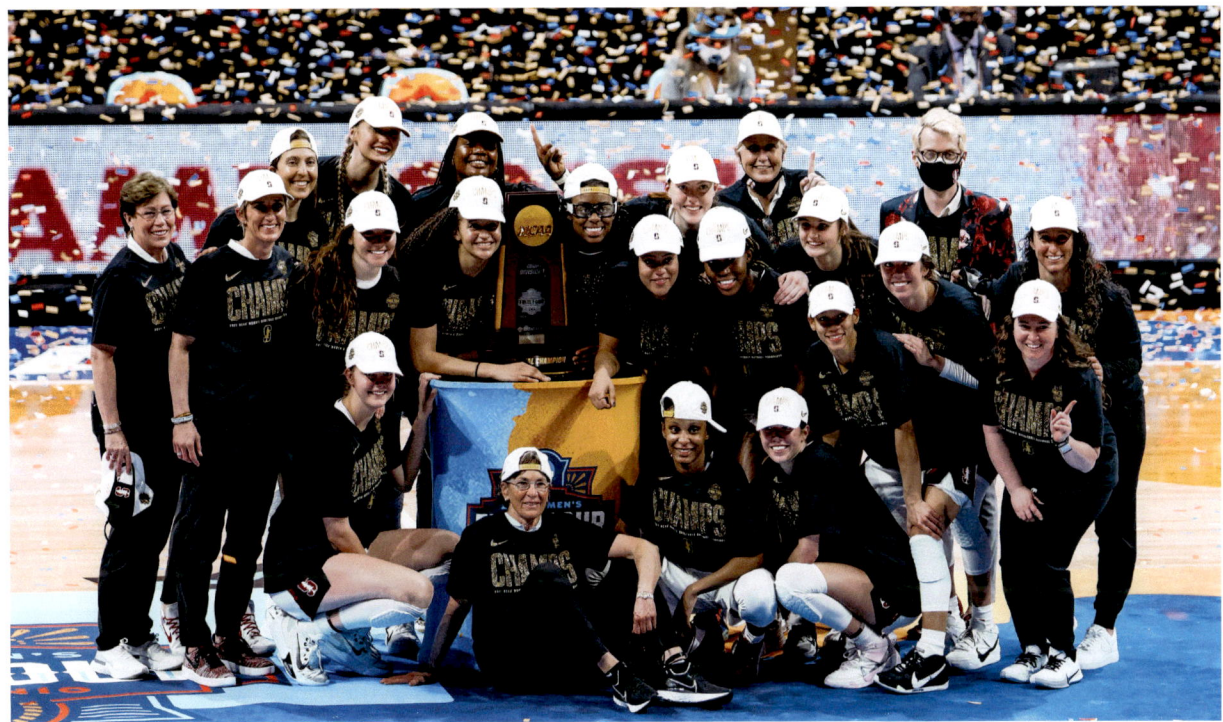

Like any coach of her era, she was made to spend the early years of her career battling for respect. When she was at Idaho, the women's team was once told that they could not play overtime because the men were scheduled to play immediately after the conclusion of their game. They would have a sudden death basket instead. "If anyone comes on the court, there will be sudden death," VanDerveer later recalled saying in response. "But I will be killing them." The young coach was always fighting to give her players more. She wanted the best for her teams, and she wanted the best for the sport, too.

That energy carried through all the many teams she coached over the years.

When she retired, VanDerveer was the winningest coach in college basketball, men's or women's, after passing Duke men's coach Mike Krzyzewski in early 2024. The record was later broken. But the spirit that built it never could be.

ABOVE: VanDerveer has always had incredibly high standards for conditioning with her players. That was true even with her first teams, at Idaho in the 1970s, in a time when most female athletes were not encouraged to hit the weight room. But VanDerveer was ahead of her time— and she always made sure to stay in great shape herself, as seen here, when she had to do push-ups for her players after they cracked her defense in a drill in 2008.

TOP: Stanford beat Arizona, 54–53, to win the national championship in the COVID bubble in 2021.

> "Stanford is not an average school. I'm not an average coach, and I don't want this to be an average program."
>
> **—TARA VANDERVEER, 1990**

A'JA WILSON

A STAR FINDS A WAY TO SHINE BRIGHTER

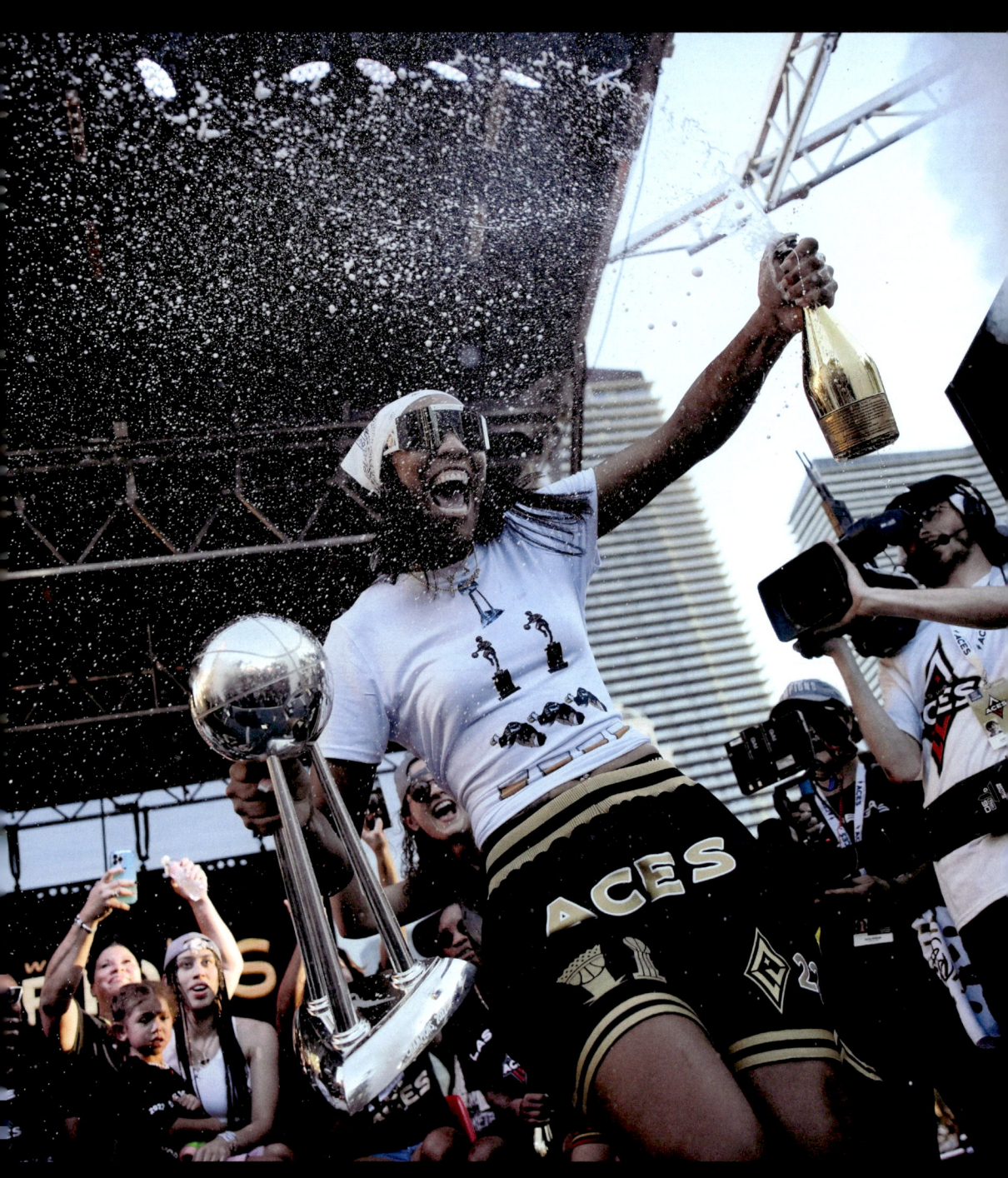

ABOVE: There's no party like an Aces' championship party. Wilson onstage in Las Vegas after winning back-to-back titles

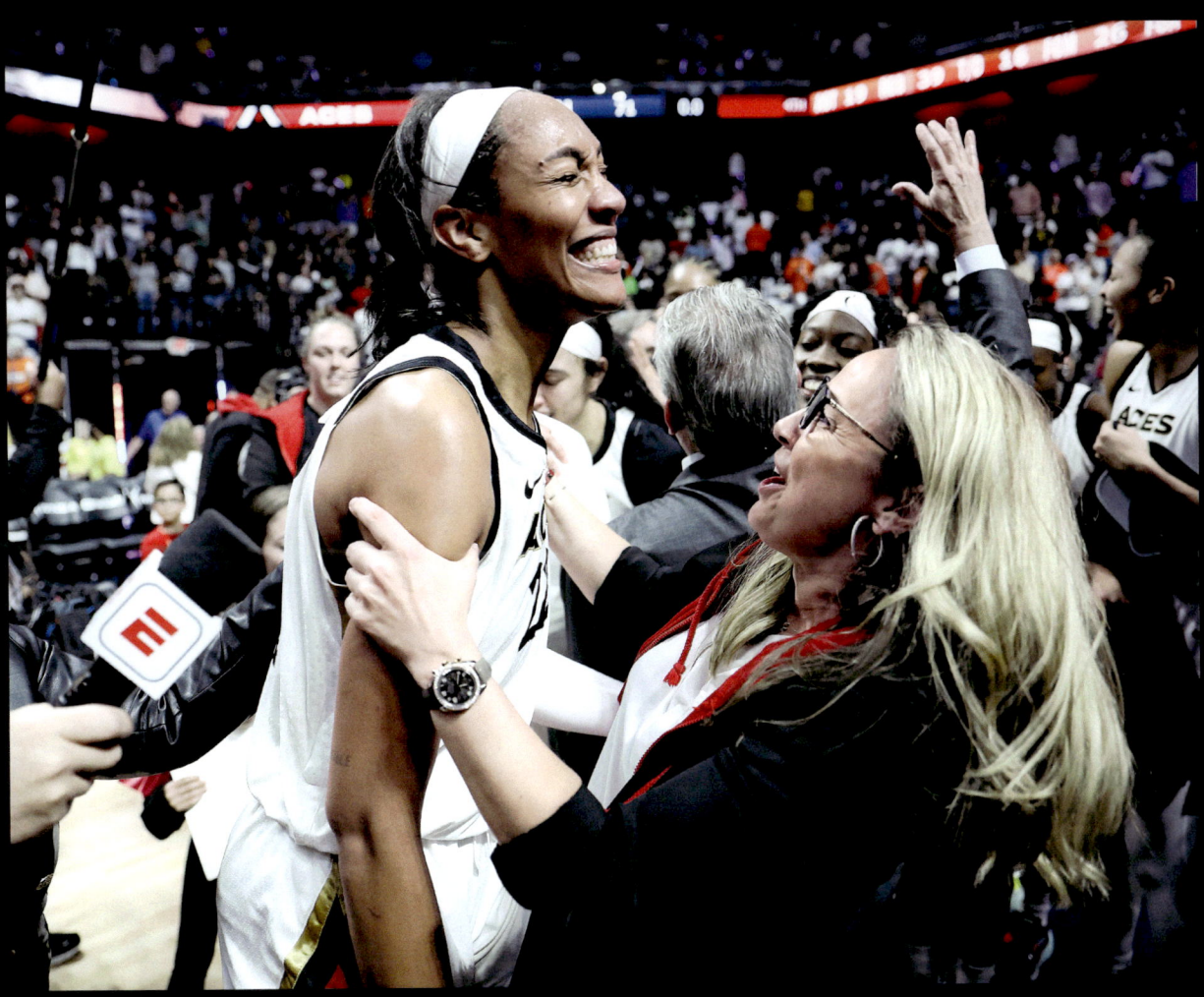

’ja Wilson was out shopping one day and saw a purse she liked. "Oh, that bag is top tier," the sales associate told Wilson. It wasn't top shelf; it was something beyond that. It was special. Since then, Wilson has made it her mission to be just that—incomparable and in rare air.

"When you think of 'top-tier,' 'top-shelf,' it's things that are up there for a reason," she told *Boardroom*. "And that is my standard."

Wilson's 2024 season could possibly be the best in WNBA history. The Las Vegas Aces forward was the first player to reach 1,000 points in a single season. She crushed the single-season scoring (1,021) and rebounding (451) records. Her 26.7 points per game led to being unanimously crowned league MVP, her third in five years—she's now in the legendary company of Lauren Jackson, Sheryl Swoopes, and Lisa Leslie. Plus, the two-time

Defensive Player of the Year had blocked a shot in eighteen consecutive games, the longest active streak in the league.

Wilson considers herself a "GOAT-in-Training," but with eye-popping numbers like these, she'll be in the GOAT conversations sooner than she thinks.

"It just takes a lot of pride, understanding where I am and knowing the personnel," Wilson told ESPN in 2023 about her defense. "I like to take that challenge of 'Can I guard a five? Can I guard a one?' I try to go out there and prove it every time."

Defense is about disruption—disrupting shots, passes, cuts—and Wilson is a disruptor.

ABOVE: Wilson with Aces head coach Becky Hammon.

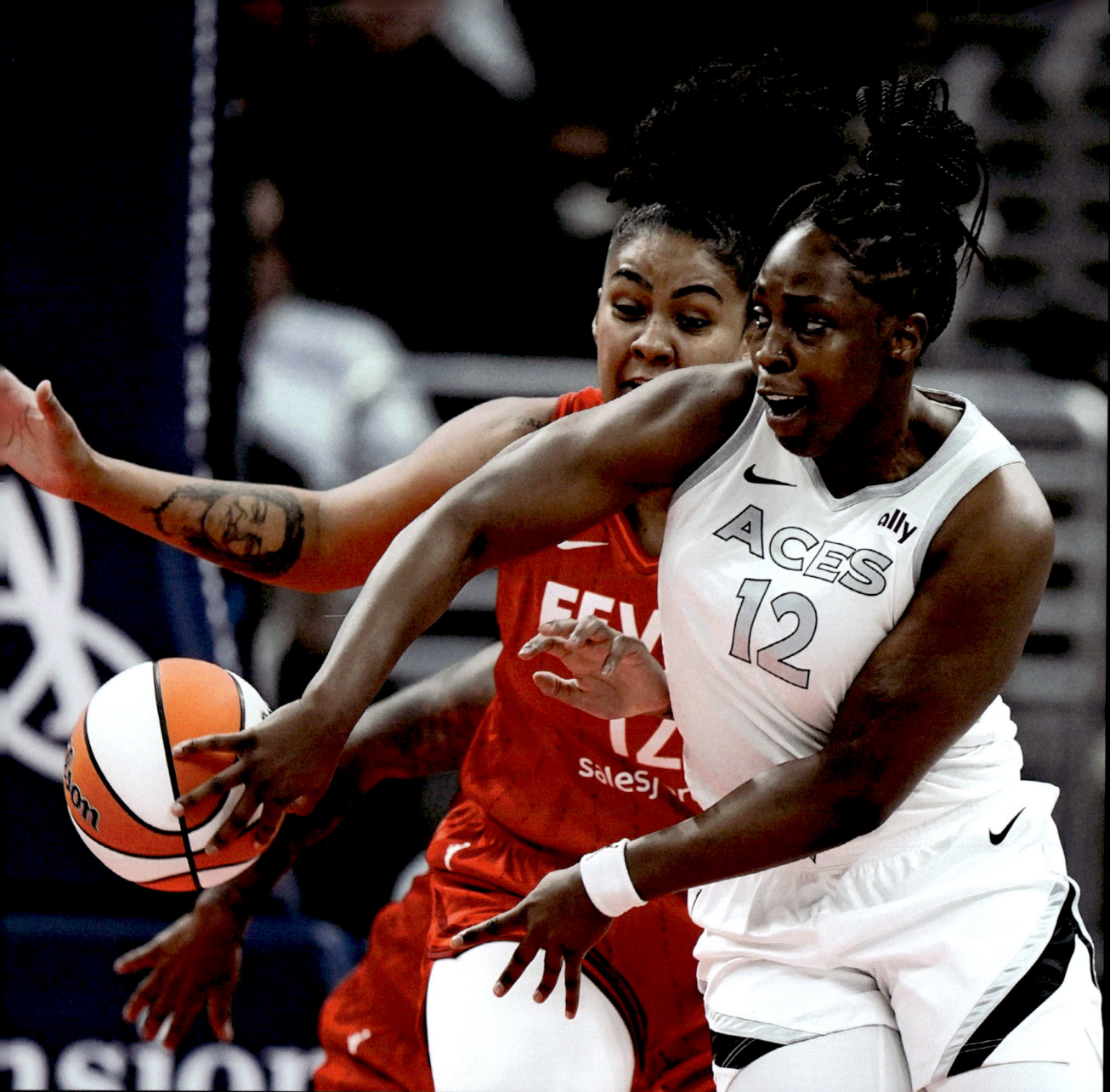

Wilson became the face of the franchise as soon as it moved to Las Vegas from San Antonio. She was the No. 1 pick in 2018 and won Rookie of the Year. The Aces got close to a championship in 2020. Then they added All-Star point guard Chelsea Gray to the roster, making them a so-called superteam. They'd win back-to-back championships in 2022 and 2023, the first time a team had since the Sparks in 2001 and 2002. Wilson took home the Finals MVP in 2023.

Wilson's leadership helped create a locker room in Vegas that was most desired. Between their laugh-out-loud pranks, pregame dance battles, or in-game antics, they've had some really good times. Winning contributes to that, but having a leader like

ABOVE: Las Vegas's "Point Gawd," Chelsea Gray, dishes a no-look pass. Casual.

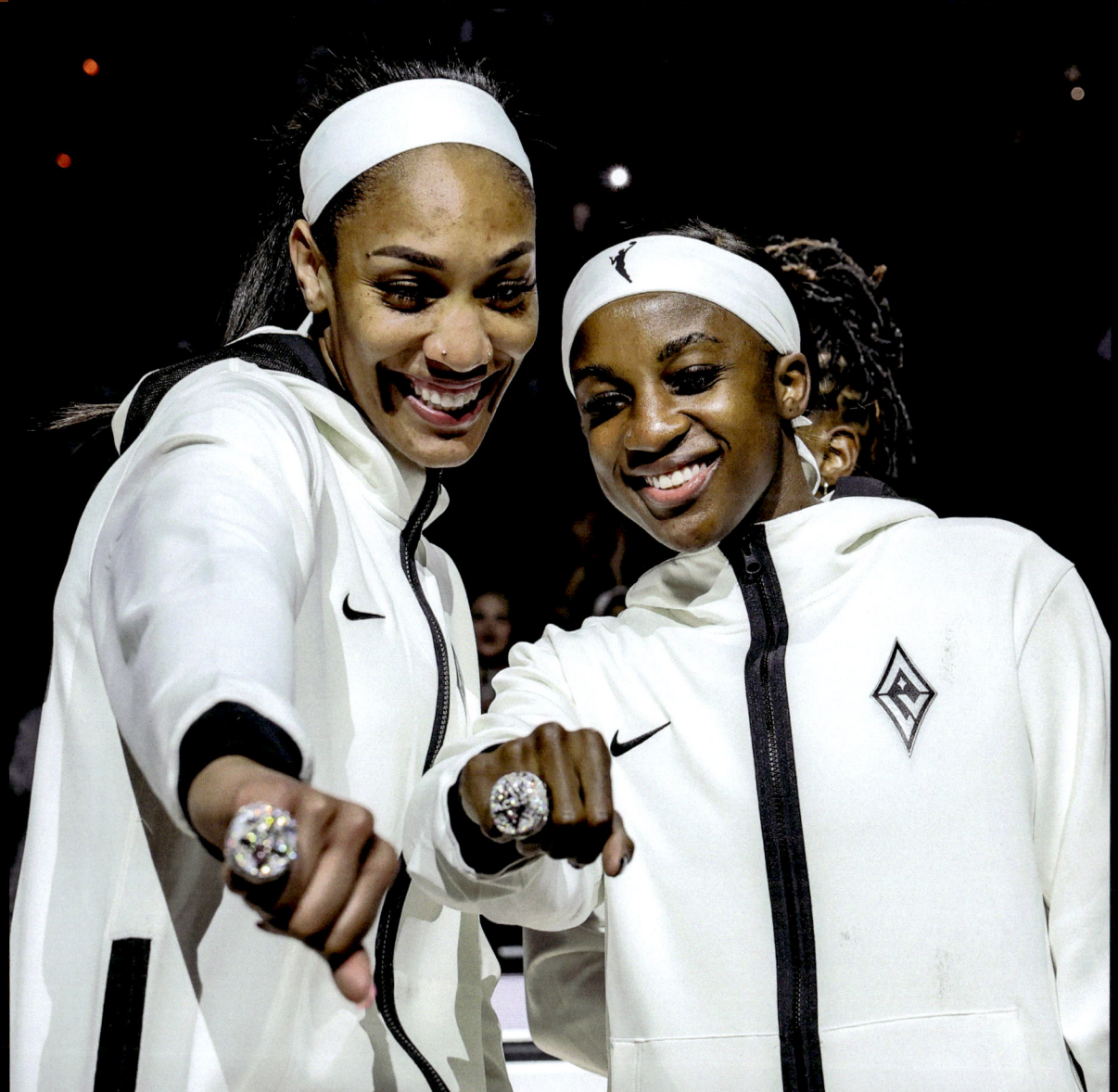

Wilson, who takes care of business on and off the court, makes for an easy follower. Yes, she dominates the box scores, but she's also dominating in the areas outsiders aren't always privy to. She's pouring into her teammates and instilling confidence in them. (Who can forget the incredible mic'd up moment to Jackie Young during a slump: "Shoot it. What's the worst that can happen? We get paid to shoot!") All things that build team morale. It's clear they want to win with her and for her.

"I'm sitting next to the best player in the world," Kate Martin said, motioning to Wilson. "And not only is she the best player in the world, she's the best leader I've ever been around. . . . Like, for the best player in the world to tell me to keep shooting it and stay aggressive, I feel on top of the world."

A'ja has an unwavering desire to be excellent. Her 2024 WNBA season was unprecedented greatness. Wilson is on the top tier all by herself.

ABOVE: A'ja Wilson (left) and Jackie Young (right) show off their second championship ring in 2024.

SUPER SUPERTEAMS

Star Players Join Forces

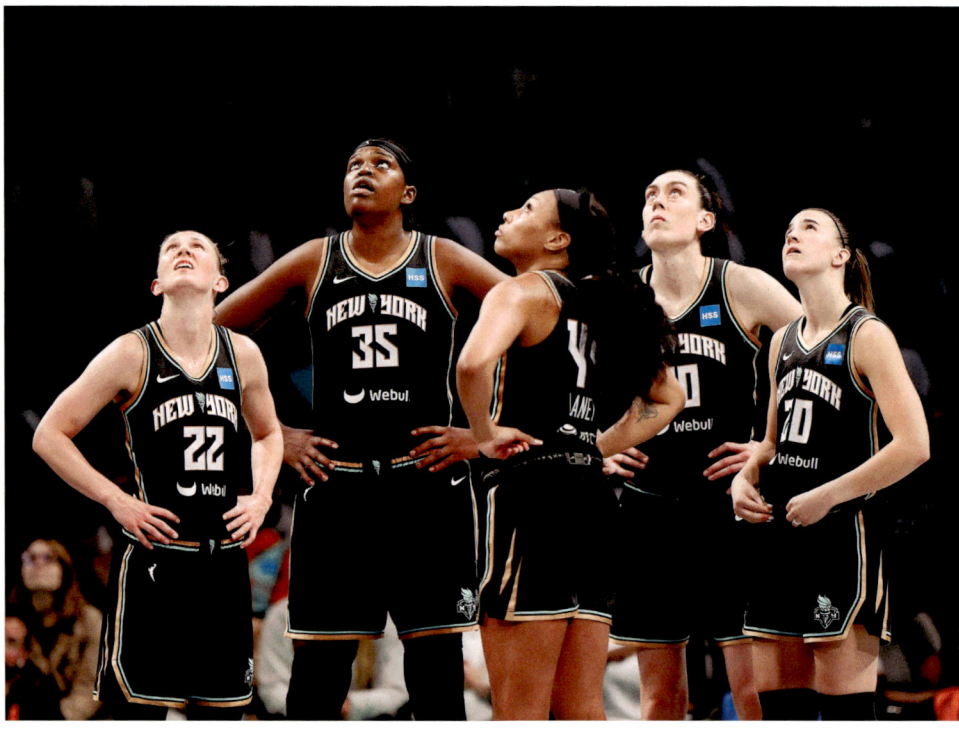

A new Collective Bargaining Agreement in 2020 reshaped much of the playing experience in the WNBA, with higher salaries, expanded maternity protections, and more. It changed the fan experience as well: The agreement reshaped free agency, making it a more dynamic process, and introducing a level of excitement and intrigue that had never been present in the offseason. It would no longer be so common for players to stay with one team for their whole careers. Teams had a new incentive to be competitive—not just in salary, but in terms of resources, practice facilities, and more. It meant the arms race was on.

The new model was exemplified by the free agency of Breanna Stewart in 2022. The former MVP was moving on from the Seattle Storm, and that meant she was being courted by the best teams in the league, a process she documented through regular posts of cryptic emojis. It was an offseason storyline that would have been impossible just a few years earlier. She ultimately chose to join the New York Liberty—a big splash made all the bigger by the fact that the team would also sign four-time All-Star point guard Courtney Vandersloot and trade for another former MVP in Jonquel Jones. The superteam era had officially begun.

It meant not just fresh storylines but also juice for fresh rivalries. The new-look Liberty immediately clashed with the Las Vegas Aces, a team similarly loaded with talent but assembled very differently. The Aces' roster had been created in the draft, with three No. 1 picks in A'ja Wilson, Kelsey Plum, and Jackie Wilson. The battles between the Aces and Liberty would mark a change for the WNBA. There was finally more than one way to build a contender. And while it took a season for the Liberty's loaded, new-look squad to gel, they made it worth the wait, bringing home the first championship in franchise history in 2024.

ABOVE: Jonquel Jones, Breanna Stewart, and Courtney Vandersloot all joined the Liberty ahead of the 2023 season. The group took the team to the Finals in their first year and won it all in their second.

OPPOSITE: New free agency rules meant new possibilities for rivalries—such as between the New York Liberty and the Las Vegas Aces.

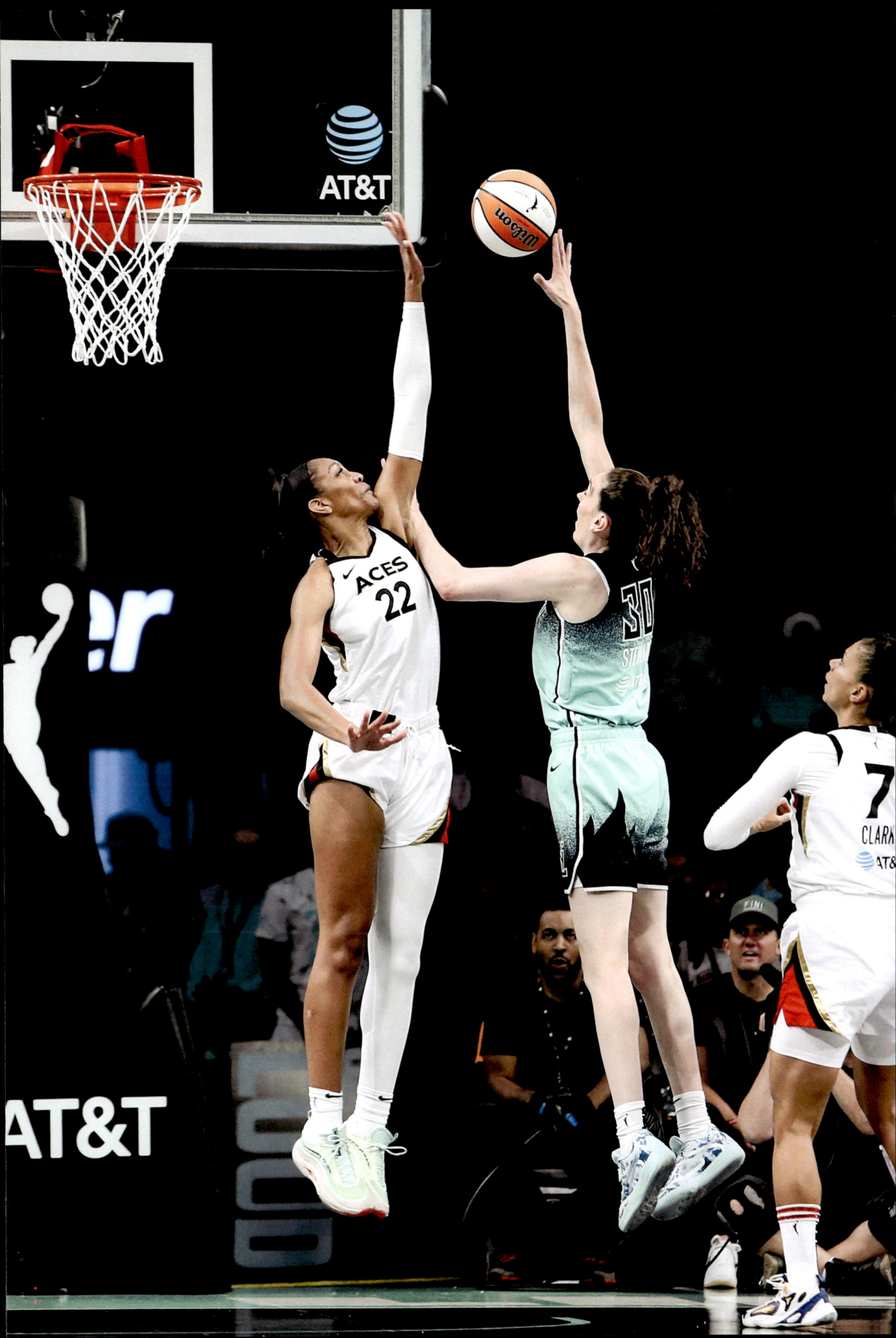

SIGNATURE SNEAKERS

Look good, play good. A brief history of the ladies who paved the way for today's sneakerheads.

SHERYL SWOOPES

The Air Swoopes (Nike, 1995)

Swoopes became the first female basketballer to earn a signature shoe. She'd release six iterations until 2002, but her Air Swoopes II's curved S-lace design was legendary.

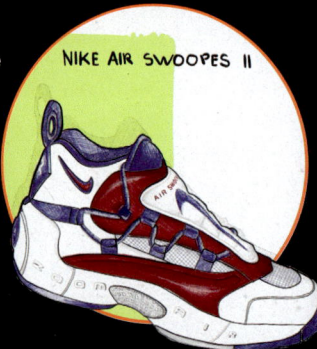

NIKKI MCCRAY

The Nikki Delta (Fila, 1999)

This shoe was perfectly personalized for McCray fans: flames for her quickness, number 15 on the sole, and colorways for both Team USA and the Washington Mystics.

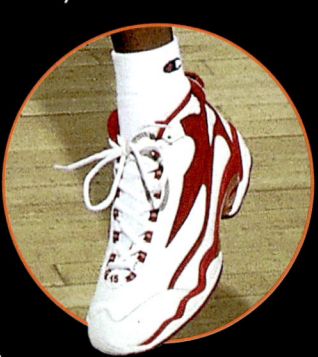

REBECCA LOBO

The Lobo (Reebok, 1997)

It was emblematic of the times: Fresh off an Olympic gold medal and starring in the bright lights of NYC, the shoe's clean white, blue, and red colors popped. A Knicks-centered blue-orange colorway was also pitched.

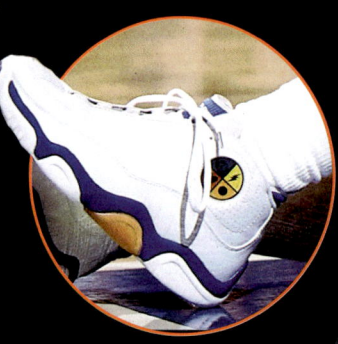

CANDACE PARKER

Ace Commander (Adidas, 2010)

The high-top design provided extra support and cushion, and there was a velcro strap across the top. Parker was the first female basketball player to release a design with Three Stripes. The Ace Versatility launched a year later.

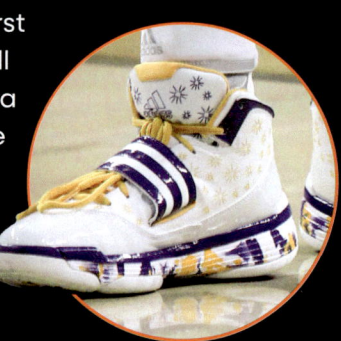

> "When Nike took a mold of my foot to make my shoe, and now they're selling it, I really do feel like everybody that buys and wears that shoe, they're walking in my footsteps."
>
> **—SHERYL SWOOPES TO *ANDSCAPE*, 2021**

ELENA DELLE DONNE
Air Deldon (Nike, 2022)

EDD used FlyEase technology in her sneaker design, inspired by her sister Lizzie. The collapsible heel allowed easy access for people with disabilities.

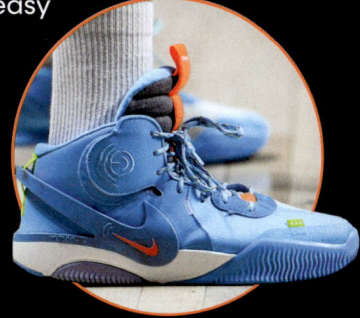

> "I recognized how Sheryl's shoe really impacted the lives of young girls and boys. It was amazing. To be able to say that I was one of a few women that had my own shoe, and it was a women's version, as well as a men's version."
>
> —NIKKI MCCRAY TO *ANDSCAPE*, 2021

BREANNA STEWART
PUMA x Stewie (Puma, 2022)

A low-top sneaker with electric colorways, Stewie's signature shoe is built for performance.

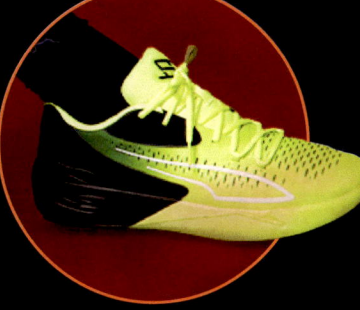

SABRINA IONESCU
Air Sabrina (Nike, 2023)

Its stylish design and grippy traction are tailored to help shooters like Sab stop on a dime. It's a crowd favorite; from 2023–24, the sneaker had a five-times year-over-year growth in revenue.

OTHER NOTABLE WNBA KICKS

- Dawn Staley, Zoom S5 (Nike, 1998)
- Lisa Leslie, Total 9 (Nike, 1998)
- Chamique Holdsclaw, Shox BB4 Mique (Nike, 2001)
- Diana Taurasi, Air Taurasi (Nike, 2005)

A'JA WILSON
A'Ones (Nike, 2025)

One of Nike's most anticipated shoe releases, the eye-catching "Pink Aura" A'One also launched with a clothing line, including an athleisure version of Wilson's signature one-leg sleeve.

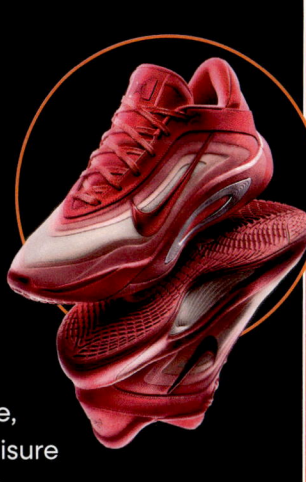

GAME, CHANGED

A RECORD AUDIENCE, A NEW MOVEMENT, AND THE 2023 NCAA NATIONAL CHAMPIONSHIP GAME

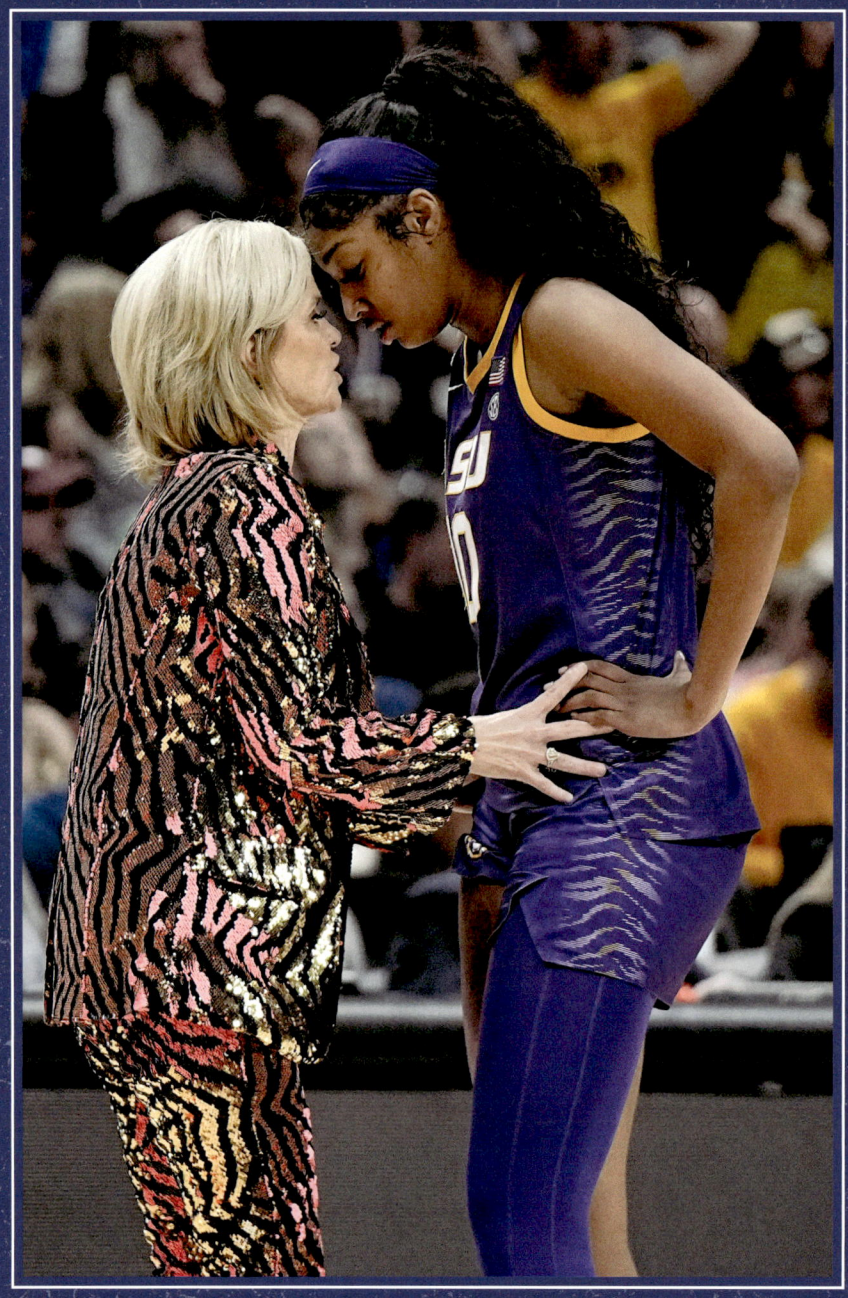

ABOVE: Reese entered the transfer portal in search of a fresh start. She found that with Mulkey and LSU.

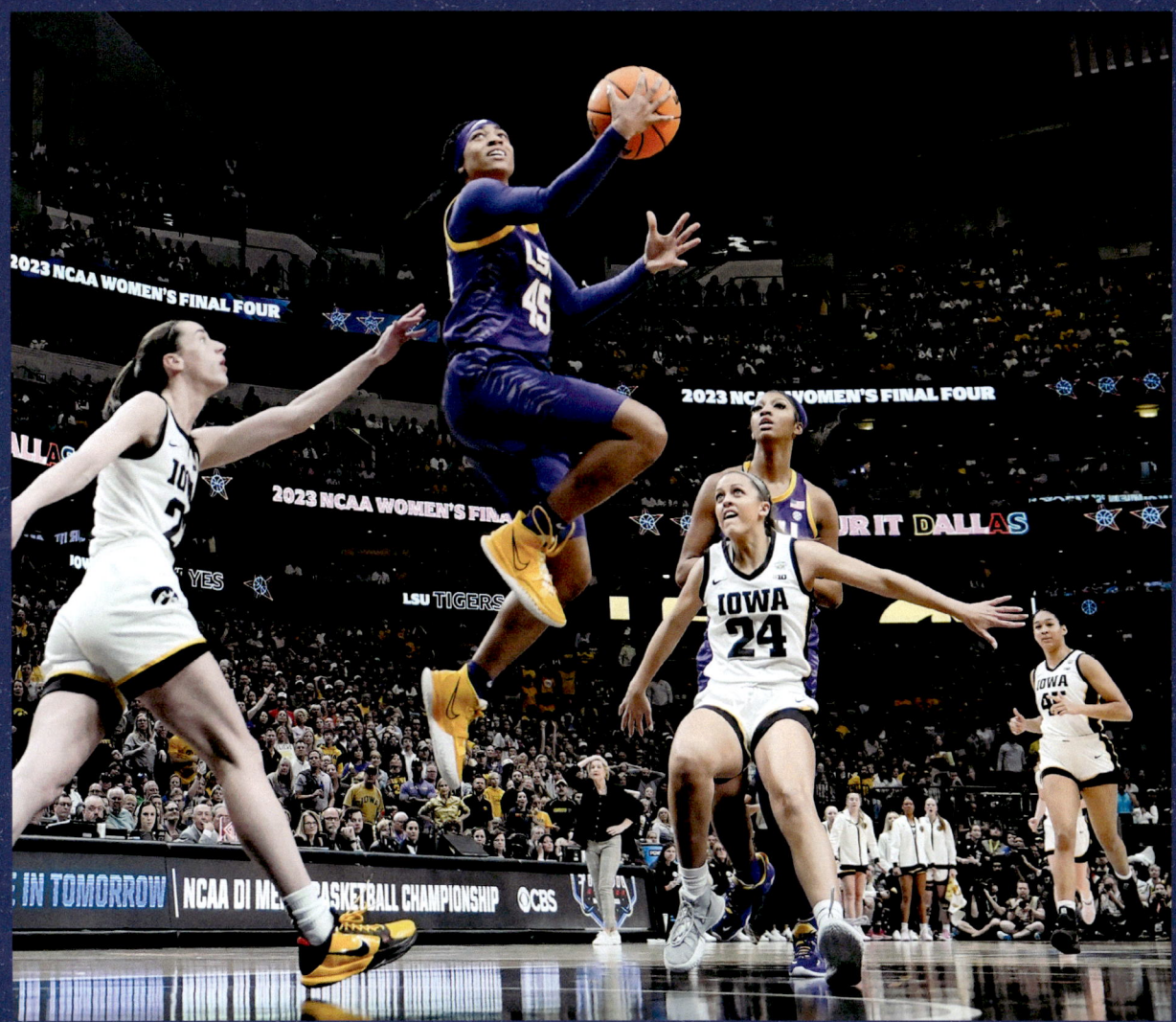

The 2023 national championship felt like a turning point even as it was happening. It did not capture the zeitgeist so much as it shaped an entirely new one. It reshaped the sense of possibility around the women's game. And underneath the ratings, the discourse, the cultural shift, almost easy to gloss over in retrospect, there was simply a great basketball game that was played that April day in Dallas.

It was the first national championship outing for Iowa junior Caitlin Clark. The point guard had been an electric offensive threat from the moment she entered college. A shooter with extraordinary range and a passer with impeccable vision, she had a habit of pulling off the unimaginable, and she had pulled her program right along with her. But Clark

had never done anything quite like what she did in March of 2023. Iowa had gotten bounced the year before without making the Sweet 16. Their star decided that she would not let that happen again. In the first three rounds of the tournament, Clark averaged 26 points and eleven assists, bending the bracket to her will. Next came a string of performances that felt almost literally unbelievable. She dropped a 40-point triple-double in the Elite Eight. (No one had ever done that, man or woman, in any round of the tournament.) She nearly did it

ABOVE: Alexis Morris was the only starter who had been on the team the year before. She showed out with 21 points and nine assists in the national championship game.

again in the Final Four, with 41 points, eight assists, and six rebounds en route to a remarkable upset over undefeated No. 1 South Carolina.

She had long established herself as a premier talent. But she was now establishing herself as something more like a legend. The story began to spread in the cadence of a fairy tale. Iowa had never been to the national championship before—and the program found itself there now because of a one-of-a-kind native Iowan. Their core had played together for years, something that felt almost charmingly retro in modern college hoops, and they were soon a national storyline. Viewership was spiking. Clark and the Hawkeyes had captured a rare level of mainstream attention. But one more game would be required to determine the ending of that fairy tale.

Clark and Iowa had to play LSU.

Here was another program that had never played for a national championship before. And it, too, was a compelling story, woven through with themes of homecoming and redemption. Head coach Kim Mulkey had won three national championships in two decades at Baylor. She was polarizing, often brash, and had never seemed to particularly care about cultivating admirers. The idea that she might ever leave the program she built had been almost inconceivable. But leave she did, returning to her native Louisiana in order to coach LSU, and she began remaking the program in just about every way. She raised over a million dollars in under two weeks on the job. She added someone to her staff to oversee branding opportunities for players. She began arranging for a new office, a new training space, a new weight room. The roster changed only modestly in her first year on the job. But in her second year? Here was a total shake-up.

Mulkey added nine players in one summer. They were the very picture of a modern team. The new-look LSU had been constructed almost entirely through the transfer portal—a feat that had traditionally been impossible. But that changed when the NCAA introduced new rules around transfers in 2021. A program could now remake itself in a few months. Yet this was bold even by those new standards. There was no blueprint for adding nine players at once, most of them looking

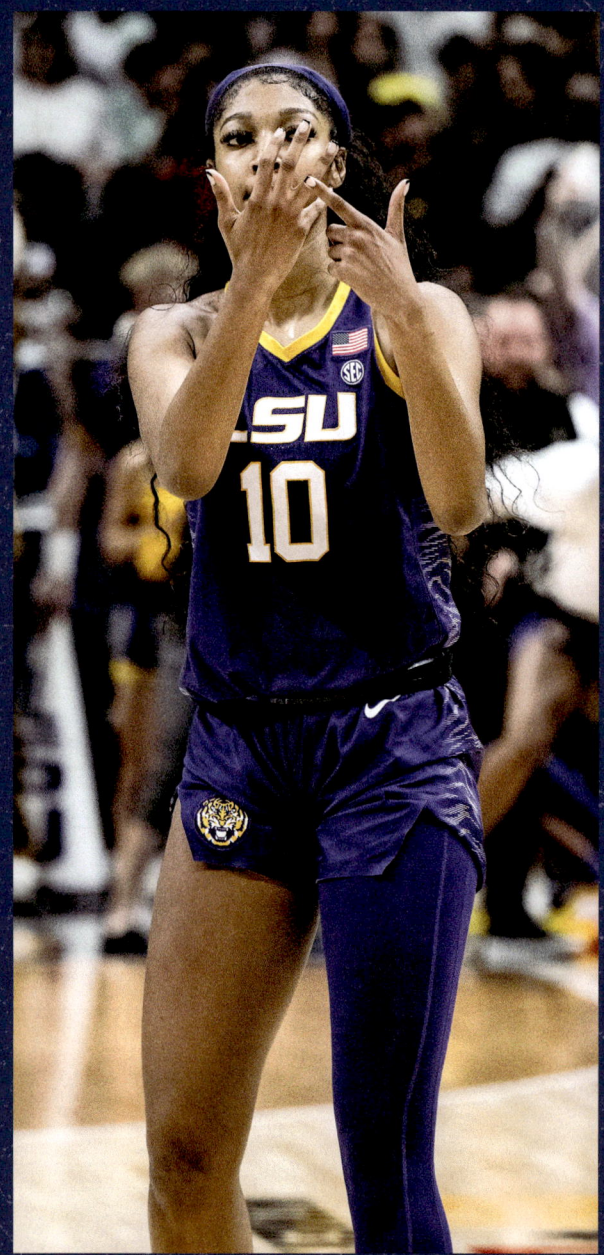

for second chances, hoping to prove themselves somewhere new.

And there was no prospect in that group of nine as intriguing as Angel Reese.

The Baltimore native had initially chosen to play at Maryland. She was ranked higher than any

ABOVE: Reese's ring-finger tap heard round the world ignited days of national discourse.

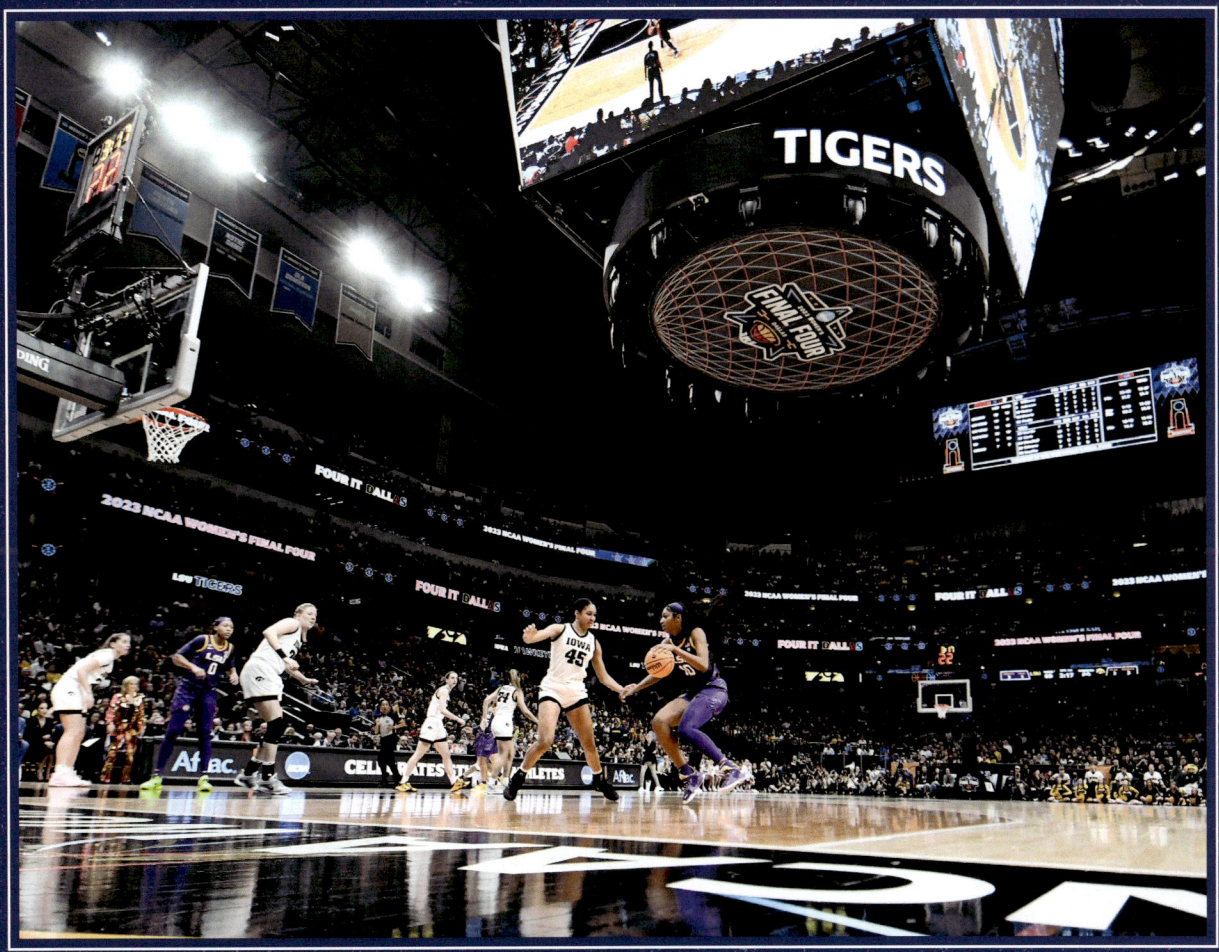

recruit in the history of the program, and she found success quickly despite a foot injury in her freshman year, still establishing herself as a masterful rebounder with a serious motor. As a sophomore, she averaged a double-double, 17.8 points, and 10.6 rebounds. Reese was named a third-team All-American. But she wanted something different. The forward decided that she needed a fresh start, and she needed to be pushed, and she needed to leave the state where she had grown up. She wanted someone who would demand more from her—in terms of grit, in terms of conditioning, in terms of leadership. She arranged for visits at marquee programs like South Carolina and Tennessee. But first, Reese went to see Mulkey at LSU, and she realized then she could just cancel those other visits. She had found what she wanted.

"I needed a coach to keep it real with me," Reese told reporters. "She's a coach that you could have those tough conversations with, and I don't feel like everybody can be coached by Kim Mulkey, but you need a Kim Mulkey. . . . You need somebody to humble you."

She was taking a risk. This was a program that was still very much in flux—building its future while sprinting toward it. But Reese decided that she trusted Mulkey. And it paid off. She had a career season in her first year at LSU, with 23 points and 15.4 rebounds per game, achieving nearly every goal on her list. She was a bigger presence later in games. She cut down on her fouls. She became a more

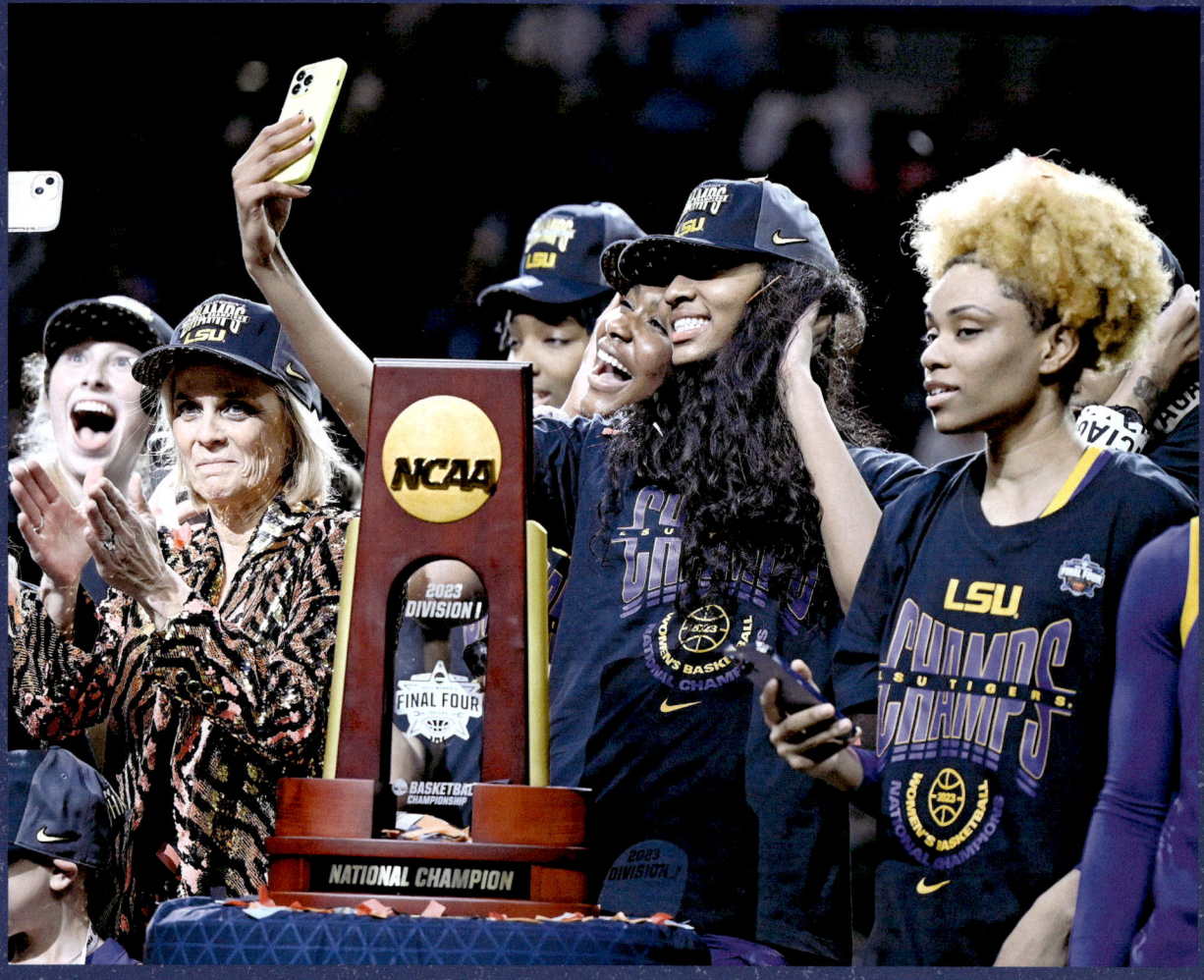

efficient shooter. Mulkey had not let any of it come easy, but that was just what she had wanted.

"Angel has grown up a lot," Mulkey said at the Final Four. "Angel can handle tough love."

That led her to the national championship, where two programs who had never been there before would battle in a matchup that was viewed, right from the jump, as one between its respective stars.

"I view matchups that people get really excited about as a really good thing for this game," Clark said after Iowa's win in the Final Four. "It's not going to be Caitlin versus Angel. That's not going to win a national championship. But that's what gets them excited about watching the game. I think more than anything, people are starting to understand women can play with excitement and a passion and a fire about themselves. That's what's fun."

She was right. Both players were first-team All-

Americans. Both were also prodigious trash-talkers. And they would bring that fire to a game under a remarkable spotlight.

These respective storylines would finally collide on track for a title. Their respective semifinals had made for the most-watched Final Four ever on ESPN. The audience would be even bigger for the championship. The game would ultimately draw a viewership of 9.9 million—a number that had not been recorded for women's basketball since USC was playing in the 1980s. This was a kind of audience that had not seemed possible for an entire generation. They would see a game that shifted everything.

ABOVE: Reese got the trophy—and a perfect selfie.

Those 9.9 million saw an LSU team who knew they could not stop Iowa's high-powered, lightning-fast offense, but maybe they could shoot past them. They saw Reese crash the boards. They saw Clark deliver as she always did, leading all scorers with a collection of head-turning, gasp-inducing threes. They saw LSU seal off the paint for Iowa. They saw an unfortunately miserable snap of refereeing. They saw LSU bench guard Jasmine Carson step up with the game of her life, 22 points, on seven-of-eight shooting. They saw LSU build what came to be an insurmountable lead, and they finally saw purple and gold confetti tumble down as the buzzer rang out, LSU 102, Iowa 85.

It had been electric. But the moment that would come to define the game was none of the above. Victory within reach, Reese had started tapping her ring finger, indicating where her new championship jewelry would go. She repurposed a gesture Clark had used in the Elite Eight, waving her hand in front of her face, and threw it back at her. Clark simply walked past to reach the handshake line. It started a national discourse on race, gender, and trash talk, a fire that would turn ugly as it burned for days. The moment had transcended sports. The reaction was unlike anything before in women's basketball.

The legacy of the game would be the audience it captured and the conversation it sparked. It had set up the personalities ready to define the coming years of the women's game. Those big-picture factors would ultimately come to overshadow what had actually happened on the floor. And that was something of a shame. If the game set the scene for the future in terms of drama, ratings, and discourse, it worked only because the action had delivered, too.

"I don't care about anybody else and what they have to say about me," Reese declared in the wake of her win, tiara perched atop her championship hat, confetti in her hair. "The biggest goal is to be a national champion. And that's what I did."

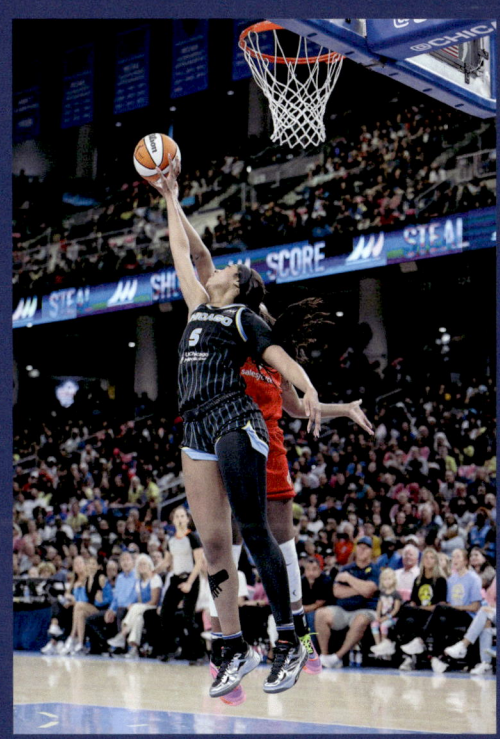

ANGEL REESE IN THE W

A year after that championship victory, Reese declared for the WNBA Draft with an announcement in *Vogue*, ultimately going seventh to the Chicago Sky. Her rebounding ability transferred seamlessly to the W. It set her up for a season that was not just special for a rookie, but special, period.

13.1: Reese's league record RPG
26: Double-doubles
3: Reese became the first player to record three consecutive games of twenty or more rebounds

ABOVE: Reese crashed the boards like no one else in her rookie season.

THE RECORD BREAKER

CAITLIN CLARK SHOT FROM THE LOGO—AND GREW THE GAME

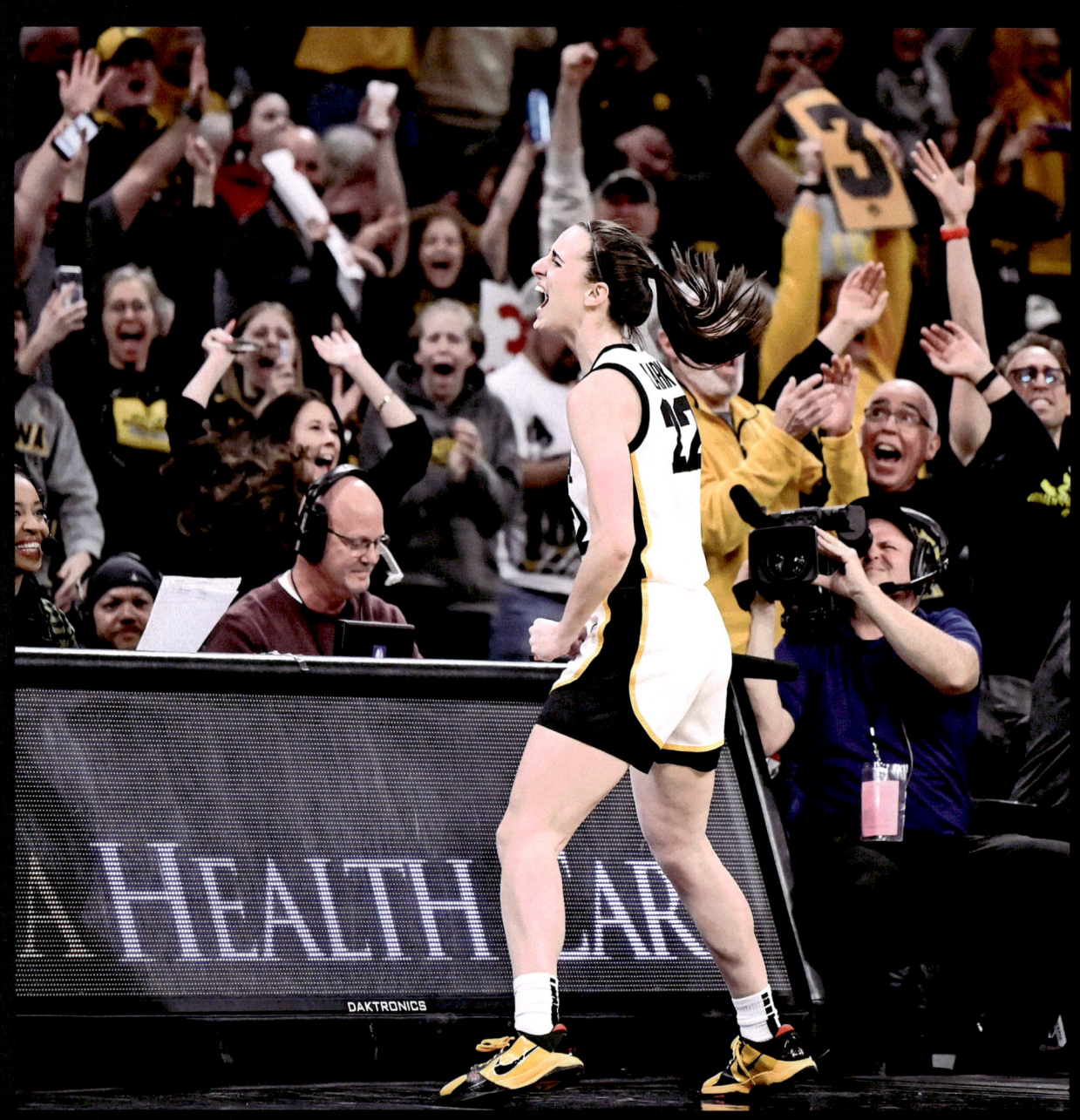

ABOVE: Clark broke the NCAA Division I women's scoring record in front of a raucous sellout crowd in Iowa City, which was nothing new: *Every* home game of her senior season was a sellout.

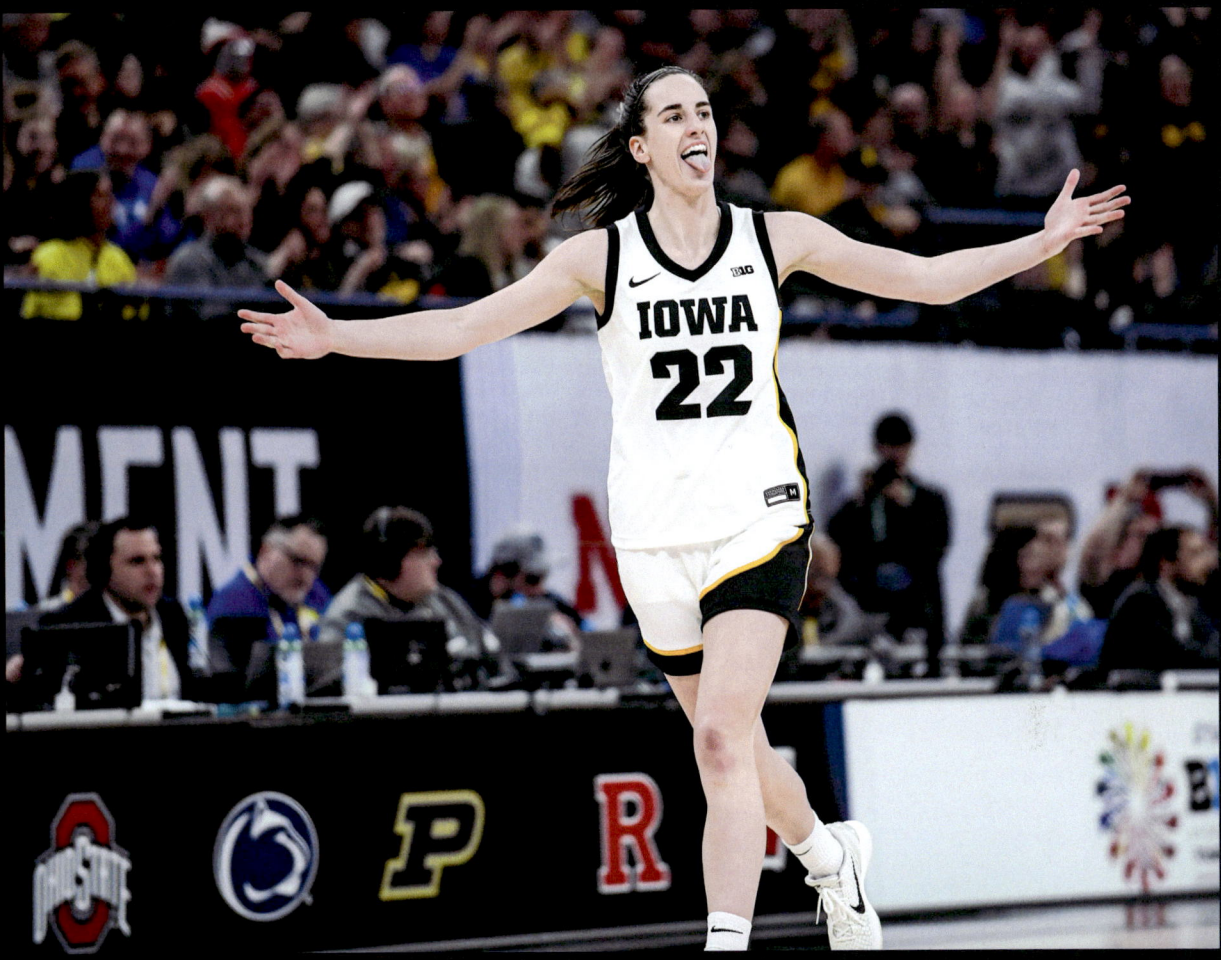

Caitlin Clark scored her first college points in largely empty gyms. Her freshman season began in the winter of 2020, when the game was still under pandemic restrictions, meaning that relatively few people saw those early games up close. Even when viewed from a distance, without the packed houses and roaring crowds and other dramatic cues that would soon become standard for her, it was clear that she could put on a show. There did not have to be anyone in the gym for it to feel obvious that Clark was something different.

The national attention and broken records and stuffed trophy case were yet to come. But what made her special was evident right from the jump. Some of those early games could feel almost literally unbelievable. Like, say, one in December of 2020, against Iowa State, a heated rivalry matchup, in which Iowa fought back after being down by 17. It gave them a chance to win the game: The

Hawkeyes were down by 1 with about thirty seconds to play. Clark brought the ball up, and with the shot clock ticking down, she had a choice: She could drive to the basket, or she could dish it to a teammate, or in the face of all prevailing wisdom, she could go for the low-percentage contested three in front of her. Iowa could afford to settle for two. Clark had a few seconds left to work. But settling was never her style.

What happened next felt stunning in the moment and totally obvious in retrospect. She called game (of course) and went for the wildly impractical three (of course) and made it (of course). It felt like theater as much as basketball.

Now *that* was her style.

ABOVE: Clark always knew how to put on a show.

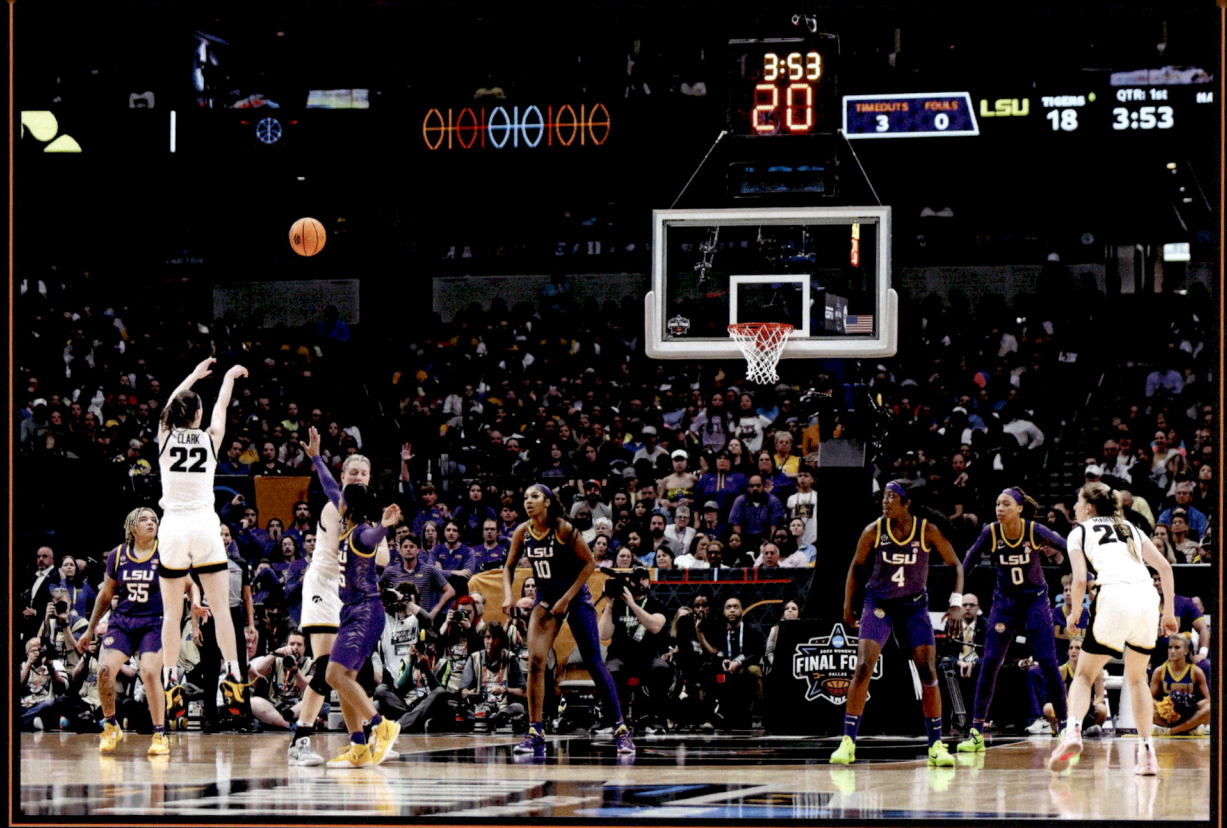

This was the fourth game of her freshman year. Clark had been playing college ball for about two weeks. The game-winning three was the last bucket of a 34-point effort, her best game yet, a personal record that lasted only a few days, until the next time she played, when she dropped 35. She made it all seem completely normal.

In the years to come, the "Caitlin Clark Effect" would come to describe the crowds she drew and the ratings she brought. But there was another kind of Caitlin Clark Effect, too, one that had manifested well before those external features did. It was not about how many people happened to be watching but about how she made them feel: She rewrote the sense of possibility around the game. The basic rules of the sport were seemingly thrown out the window. (Sometimes, the laws of physics were, too.) Clark made the impractical shot look practical. She made the daring pass feel reasonable. She made the crowd believe, however briefly, in something that bordered on fantastical. It was not that every shot landed or that every game finished in victory. (Many of them didn't.) But every one felt *possible*. Therein lay the Caitlin Clark Effect.

Her four years in college would see her mature as both person and player. Clark gained a better understanding of time and score. She worked to

ABOVE: Clark had range like no one else. She sank more threes individually than several entire programs did.

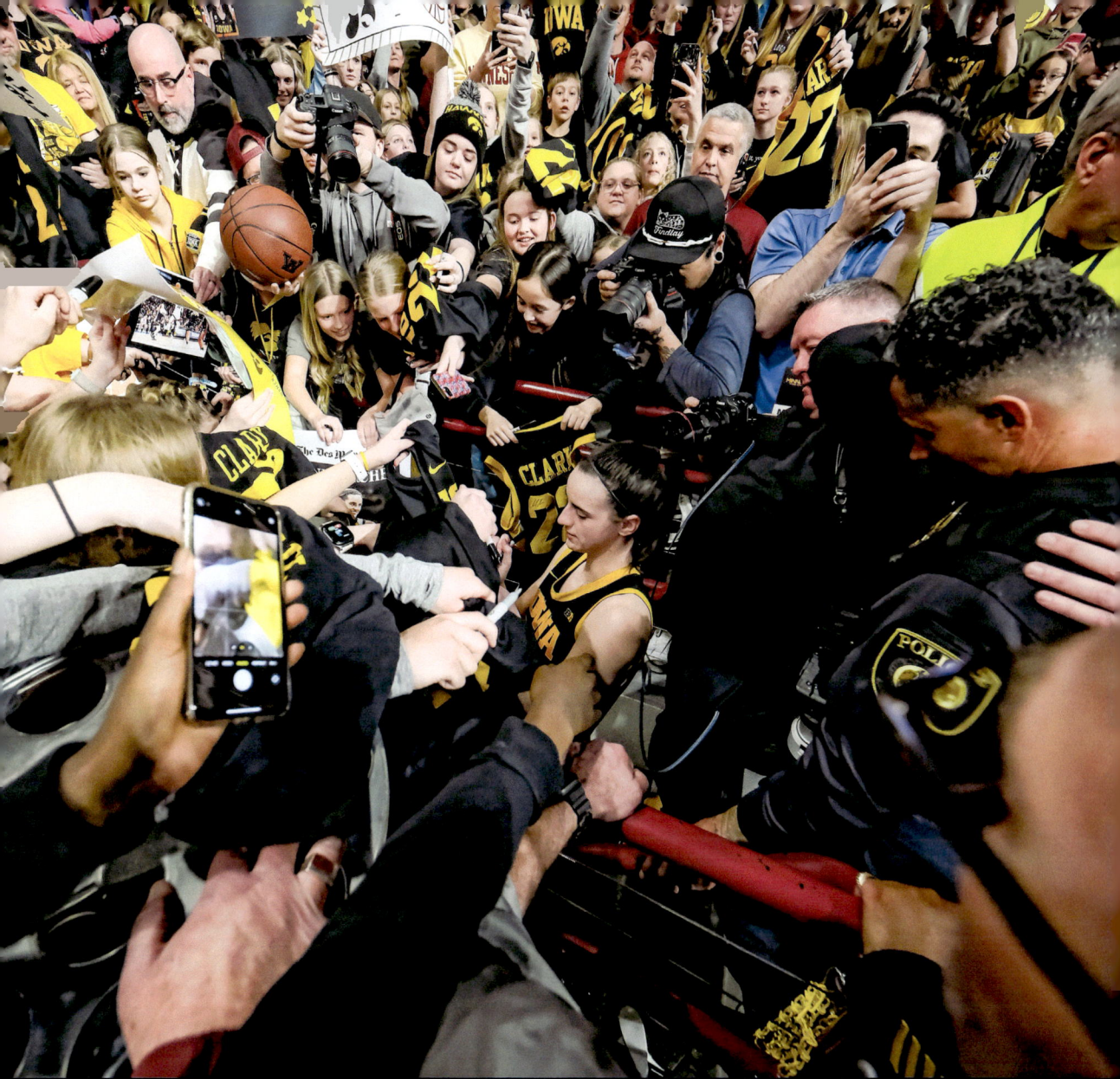

make sure her passion on the court fueled her rather than hold her back. She got physically stronger, less slight, better able to finish through contact. But the key pieces were all there from the beginning. She was the first player to lead the nation in scoring as a freshman. She became the first player to lead the nation in scoring *and* assisting as a sophomore. She scored more and assisted more as a junior. She then scored even more and assisted even more as a senior. Those per-game averages from her final season were almost literally unbelievable: 31.6 points and

8.9 assists.) All of which is to say that it had long seemed all but guaranteed that she would break major scoring records.

Clark ultimately sliced through multiple record books. She would finish college not only with more points than any other player ever in NCAA women's

ABOVE: Clark attracted unprecedented media and fan attention.

Division I, but also more than any player in NCAA men's Division I, and more than any player in the large-school division of the AIAW, too. (AIAW playing records are not recognized by the NCAA.) The first of those records would be the one to deliver the signature moment. This was the one with the fanfare, the coordinated television commercials, the pre-planned, postgame ceremony. (It was a safe bet: Clark had entered the February 15, 2024, game against Michigan just 8 points shy of former Washington guard Kelsey Plum's career 3,527.) And it was the one that showed the full range of her skill, not just as a scorer, but as a performer.

To score 8 points usually took her about a quarter. But this was a night that demanded some drama, a real sense of importance, and she delivered. Clark drove to the basket on the first possession of the game. *Two points in 15 seconds.* She nailed a three on the next possession. *Five points in 36 seconds.* And scarcely a minute later, fully aware this would be the record breaker, the one that would live on highlight reels, the moment that would

define a piece of her legacy, she delivered the only shot that made sense.

Clark pulled up from thirty-five feet. She was standing at the edge of the logo: If this was a spot that might suggest a desperation heave for other players, it was one that had come to seem like home for Clark, the place where she did her best and most audacious work. The shot was automatic.

"You all knew I was going to shoot a logo three for the record," Clark told reporters afterward, grinning, flush with hard-earned confidence. "Come on now."

She had scored the necessary 8 points in 132 seconds. Then she kept scoring, and scoring, and scoring. Clark finished with 49 points, not just a personal high but an Iowa program record, too, along with thirteen assists. She took a record and made it a show. What she had delivered was the same thing she had delivered in that nearly empty gym three and a half years prior. It was an incredible shot, of course, but it was something more. It was a sense of possibility.

THE REMATCH

Almost exactly a year after their championship showdown, LSU and Iowa met again in the 2024 Elite Eight. But the outcome would be different. With 41 points and twelve assists, Clark pushed the Hawkeyes to a win over the Lady Tigers, putting them back in the Final Four. (Reese had 17 points and twenty rebounds in defeat.) The game pulled an incredible 12.3 million viewers—at the time the largest audience ever for women's basketball. Kim Mulkey approached Clark in the handshake line. The coach had been around for decades. She had played for a college championship, played in the

Olympics, coached her way to multiple titles, watched many of the best in the game. And this was new to her.

"Girl, you're something else," Mulkey told Clark. "Never seen anything like it."

And the viewership mark would not stand very long. It was instead just one part of a remarkable, record-smashing run for Clark and the Hawkeyes. In the Final Four a week later, 14.2 million viewers tuned in to see Iowa take down UConn, and for the national championship game against undefeated South Carolina, the number was a historic 18.7 million. It was the first time ever the women had outdrawn the men.

CAITLIN CLARK IN THE W

The Phenom Goes Pro

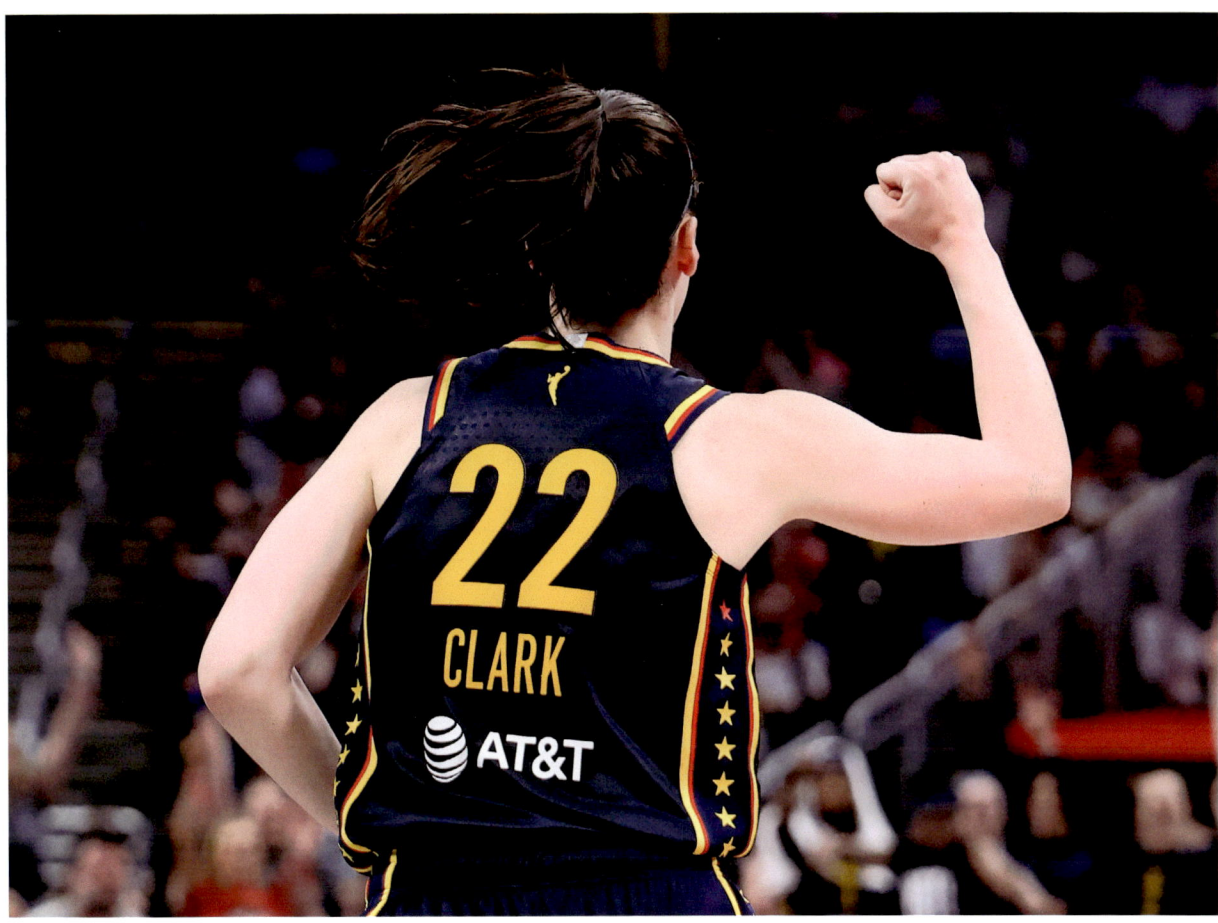

A record 2.45 million viewers tuned in to the 2024 WNBA Draft to see Caitlin Clark taken No. 1 by the Indiana Fever. And they saw a season of big performances to follow. Clark drew eyes to the league in a way that no one had previously: Indiana averaged more than one million viewers per game in her rookie season. She managed to live up to the hype.

Following a brief period of adjustment, Clark settled in with her trademark court vision and long-range shooting, and the point guard set about breaking records. She became the first rookie to be named First-Team All-WNBA since Candace Parker in 2008. She dished out a record nineteen assists in a single game. She also became the first rookie to record a triple-double—then recorded another for good measure. And she lifted her team up along with her. Her arrival helped revive a listless franchise. In her rookie year, Clark led the Fever back to the playoffs for the first time since the days of Tamika Catchings, and she set them up for more success to follow.

ABOVE: Clark broke records and captivated audiences like no one else.

A GAME ON THE RISE

Women's Pro Hoops Unlocked a New Level in the 2020s

As the game exploded in popularity, the professional landscape began to change significantly, with an influx of investment that allowed for new opportunities. The norm was no longer flying commercial, sharing practice courts with local rec leagues, and going overseas in the winter. It was a whole new ballgame.

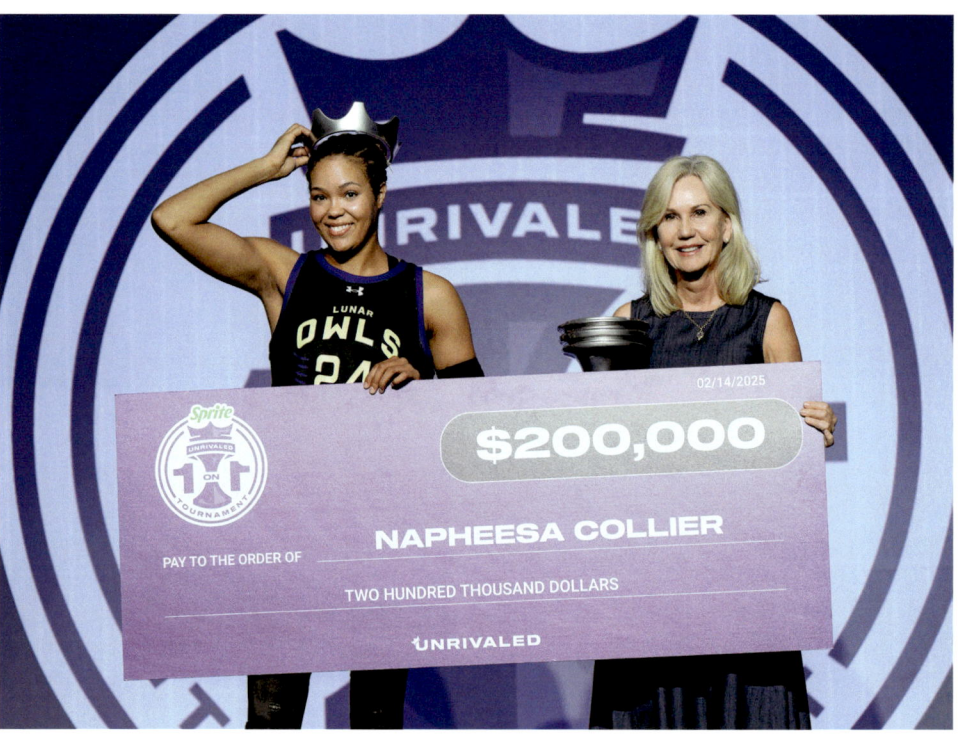

UNRIVALED

A Miami-based 3x3 league founded by WNBA stars Breanna Stewart and Napheesa Collier, Unrivaled started play in 2025 and gave players a chance to stay in the United States, earn higher salaries, and keep their names in the spotlight during the offseason. It had been standard for decades for WNBA talent to go overseas for playing opportunities in the winter. That came with drawbacks that were not always worth the money. Unrivaled offered players another path (not to mention equity in the league). It also introduced a one-on-one tournament—won first by Collier, who earned nearly as much in that one week as she would in an entire season in the WNBA, taking home a check for $200,000.

CHARTER FLIGHTS

Travel had long been one of the biggest frustrations for WNBA players. Flying commercial meant not just annoyingly cramped seats but also delays that occasionally jeopardized games. That finally came to an end in 2024, when the league introduced a full charter program, with private flights to every game.

PRACTICE FACILITIES

In the early years of the league, WNBA teams generally shared practice courts and locker rooms with other local squads, often without any space to call their own. That changed when the Aces built a $40-million, 64,000-square-foot practice facility in 2023. They were soon followed by other teams, including the Storm and Mercury, and as the league expanded and other franchises began to follow suit, it became clear that spaces like these were now the standard.

ABOVE: Collier helped found Unrivaled and then dominated its inaugural season.

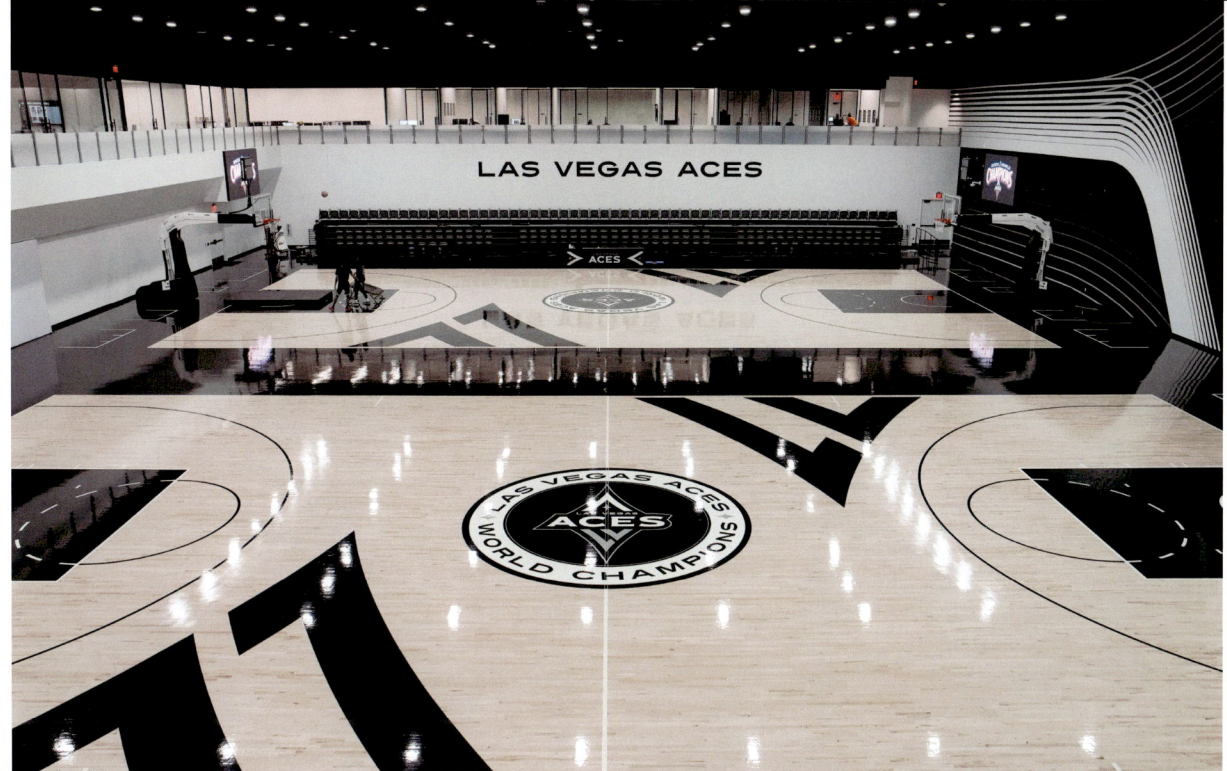

ALL-STAR STANDOUTS

The 2024 All-Star Game felt like a changing of the guard. Held in Phoenix, the weekend included plenty of celebrations of Diana Taurasi, who'd spent her entire iconic career in town with the Mercury. But the festivities were also a welcoming party for a new generation. Caitlin Clark and Angel Reese were the only rookies selected to the All-Star Team. They helped deliver a smash hit. The game attracted the largest television audience ever for a WNBA event on ESPN networks at the time: 3.4 million. Clark had ten assists with 4 points, Reese had eleven rebounds and 12 points, and they helped Team WNBA beat Team USA in an All-Star send-off to the Olympics.

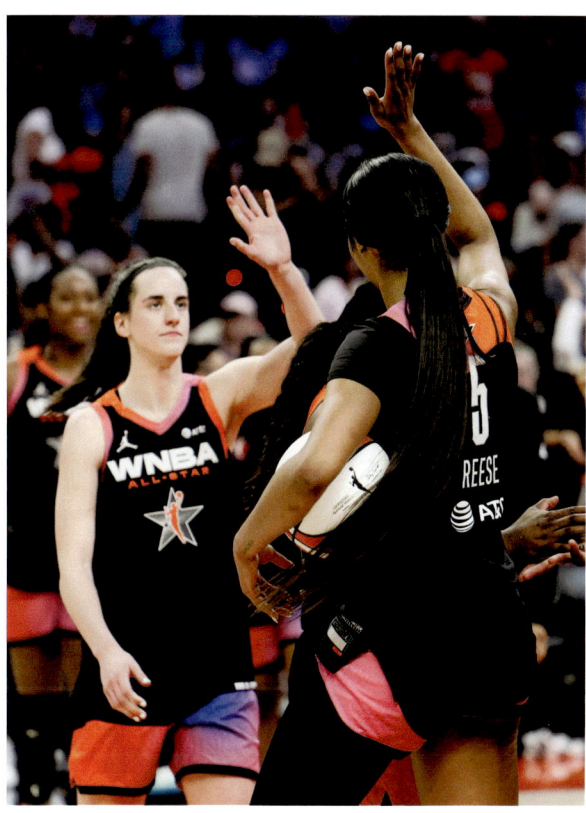

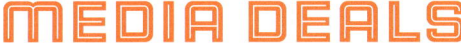

MEDIA DEALS

The WNBA signed a landmark media rights deal in summer 2024 amid rising viewership. The $2.2-billion, 11-year deal with Disney, Amazon Prime, and NBC represented a major increase in revenue for the league.

TOP: Specialized practice facilities became a factor in free agency and helped differentiate teams from one another.

ABOVE: The 2024 All-Star Game broke viewership records—and the players put on a show to match.

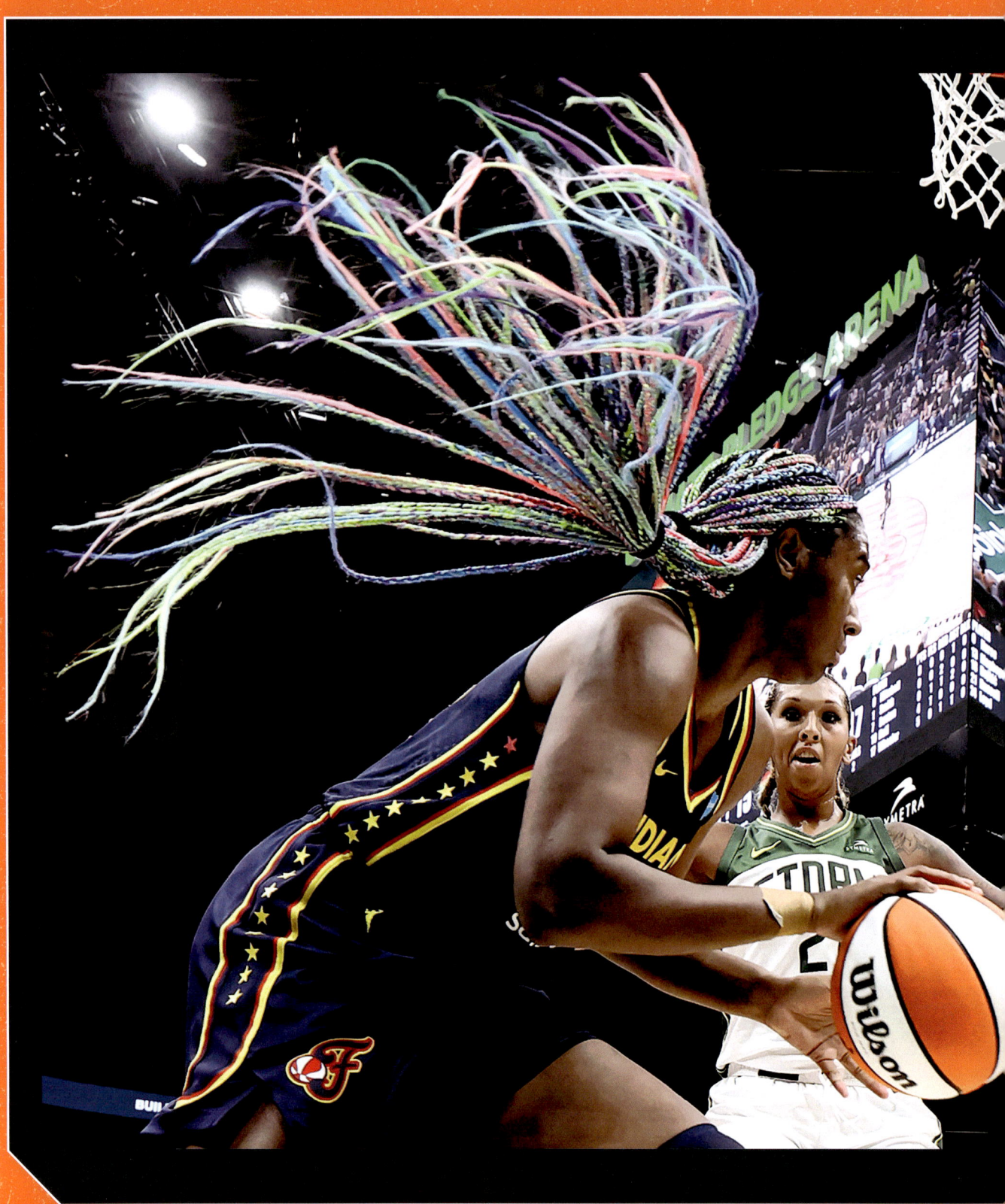

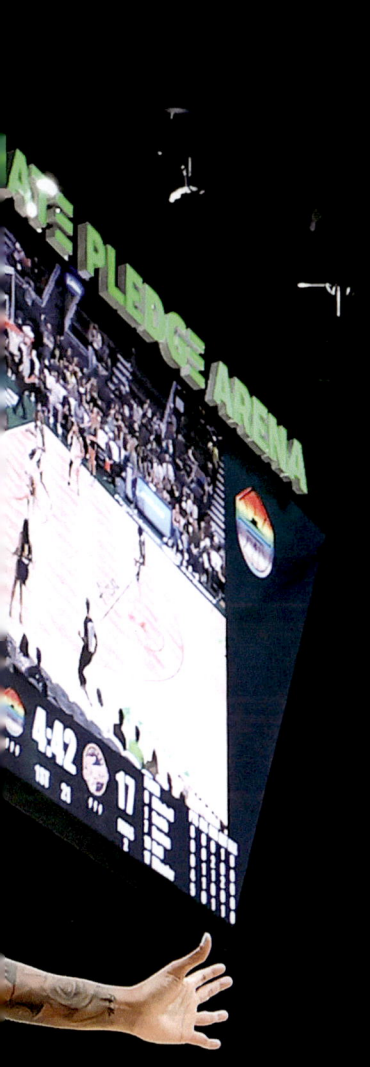

HAIR GAME STRONG

Hair has power. Rocking certain styles or hair colors is a way to stand out as an individual despite wearing a team uniform. This generation of women basketballers gets it; their game can speak for itself, but their bold hair also won't go unheard.

Indiana Fever's Aliyah Boston's brightly hued hair game is tough to beat. She pops off your TV screen with her Rolodex of ombré purple, turquoise, or a fiery yellow-green-orange combo. When you see her, you see the hair. Even some of her historic college career moments in South Carolina are hair-tied to the color she was donning at the moment. When she won the SEC Conference Finals MVP? Pink. When she broke the school's double-double streak record? Blue. When she won the 2022 national championship? Half pink, half purple.

"I hope that I'm able to inspire younger Black girls to have the confidence to play whatever sport they want," Boston said on Instagram. Hair is so much *more* than hair. Tresses can exude confidence, symbolize freedom, and weave in self-expression—on and off the court.

LEFT: Indiana Fever's Aliyah Boston guarded by Mercedes Russell of the Seattle Storm, 2024.

MATTER OF FACT
2020s

Numbers, People, and Moments That Defined the Era

NUMBERS

0
Number of confirmed COVID-19 cases among players during the WNBA's "Wubble" season.

$1 MIL.
Revenue in first eight months for the Sports Bra in Portland, Oregon. It's the first sports bar that's 100 percent dedicated to showing women's sports.

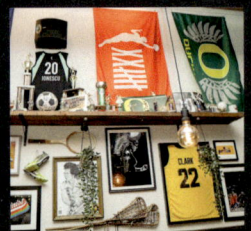

13
Number of 40-point games in the 2023 WNBA season (the previous record was four).

2,728
Playoff minutes DeWanna Bonner has played from 2009 to 2024.

54.4 PERCENT
Chelsea Gray's three-point percentage in the 2022 playoffs, the highest in postseason history, with at least thirty-two attempts.

PEOPLE

In Febuary 2022, Mercury center Brittney Griner was detained in Khimki, Russia, while playing overseas. She was accused of having vape cartridges containing cannabis oil, illegal under Russian law. Griner would remain imprisoned for ten months. Fans league-wide showed their support by writing her letters, contacting political officials to intervene, and using **#FREEBG**. Griner was released via prisoner swap in December 2022.

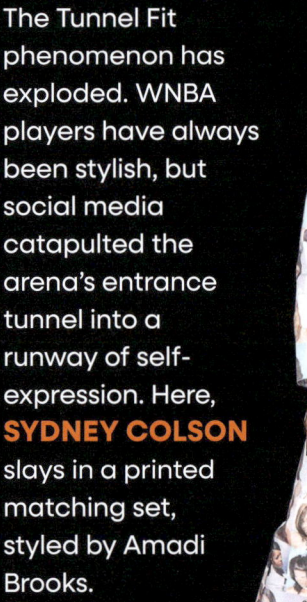

The Tunnel Fit phenomenon has exploded. WNBA players have always been stylish, but social media catapulted the arena's entrance tunnel into a runway of self-expression. Here, **SYDNEY COLSON** slays in a printed matching set, styled by Amadi Brooks.

MAY 6, 2021

ELLIE THE ELEPHANT makes her debut for the New York Liberty. The stylish mascot quickly established herself as far more than your average mascot, with major brand deals, elaborate halftime shows, and social media buzz all her own.

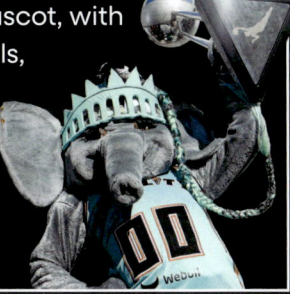

NOV. 23, 2022

Moolah Kicks, the first woman-owned basketball sneaker brand, signs guard **COURTNEY WILLAMS** to a contract. The brand boasts the first hoop shoe specifically designed for the female foot.

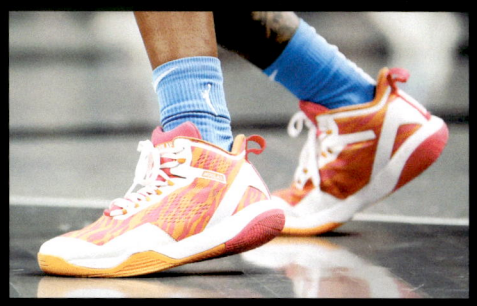

JAN. 23, 2022

AYOKA LEE scores 61 points, beating the NCAA single-game scoring records previously held by Long Beach State's Cindy Brown (60, in '87) and Minnesota's Rachel Banham (60, in '16).

MAY 6, 2024

Rookie **ANGEL REESE** fashionably walks the red carpet at the Met Gala in New York City. She's only the second WNBA player to receive the coveted invite (the first was Brittney Griner, in 2023).

APRIL 13, 2024

CAITLIN CLARK makes a surprise appearance on *Saturday Night Live*'s Weekend Update segment. "Way more nervous than I get for a basketball game," she told the AP.

ACKNOWLEDGMENTS

This book was a true labor of love for everyone who helped it come to life. Thank you to our indefatigable photography editor, Carolyn Davis, who brought an incredible eye and an even better sense of humor. Thank you to our data guru, Maddy Brown, for uncovering some incredible factoids to include throughout these pages. Thank you to our agent, Susan Canavan, who hand-selected us and believed in this project even before we did. Thank you to our editor, Lisa Tenaglia, and our designer, Katie Benezra, for making our ideas shine in such a beautiful format. And thank you to every last person who opened their photo archives, record books, and memories. Organizations like Legends of the Ball, Fun While It Lasted, and the Iowa Women's Archives were so gracious with their time and energy. We appreciate all the universities' sports information directors who opened the vaults for us, too. Most importantly? Thank you to every woman who helped to build this history and every girl who is carrying it forward.

FROM EMMA:

Thank you to my editors and coworkers at *Sports Illustrated*, who have encouraged and helped me over the years in covering women's basketball. To all the many friends, group chats, and fellow writers on press row, who make watching these games even more fun. To R. J. Anderson, for his belief and support. And to Paul, Nadine, and Olivia Baccellieri, for everything, always.

FROM JORDAN:

I would like to thank my parents, Jerold and La Shawn, for putting a basketball in my hand at the age of five and always encouraging me to shoot for the stars. To my siblings, La Shawnna and Shon Josef, thank you for your continuous love and support. And finally, to my husband, Fred, thank you for holding my hand throughout this entire process and being my number-one cheerleader. I love you all.

NOTES

Chapter 1

The Mother of the Game

3 She had been forced to leave . . . Conservatory of Music: Ralph Melnick, *Senda Berenson: The Unlikely Founder of Women's Basketball* (University of Massachusetts Press, 2007), p. 14.

3 She had turned down . . . opportunities he did: Melnick, *Senda Berenson*, pp. 13–14.

3 Berenson would visit . . . frailest of young women?: Melnick, *Senda Berenson*, pp. 14–16.

3 "How I hated . . . first few months!": Edith Naomi Hill, "Senda Berenson," *Research Quarterly of the American Association for Health, Physical Education and Recreation*, vol. 12, issue supplement 3, 1941, p. 659.

3 She could not . . . the standard exercises: Hill, "Senda Berenson," *Research Quarterly*, p. 659.

3 "It is impossible . . . whatever might come": Hill, "Senda Berenson," *Research Quarterly*, p. 659.

3 There was an opening . . . January of 1892: Hill, "Senda Berenson," *Research Quarterly*, p. 658.

3 Many of her . . . purpose of her work: Hill, "Senda Berenson," *Research Quarterly*, p. 660.

3 One day . . . few weeks later: "Where Basketball Was Invented: The History of Basketball," Springfield College, https://springfield.edu/about/birthplace-of-basketball.

4 "as a dubious . . . confessed": Senda Berenson, "Basket Ball for Women, Draft 1," Senda Berenson Papers, Smith College, series 6 speeches, ca. 1892–1920, p. 2.

5 "Above all . . . best to it": Berenson, "Basket Ball for Women, Draft 1," Senda Berenson Papers, p. 4.

5 A team of . . . all the same: Amy Nutt, "Hullabaloo Over Hoops," *Sports Illustrated*, 22 March 1993.

5 Berenson had fixed . . . for her girls: Melnick, *Senda Berenson*, p. 1.

5 "We took the girl . . . game went on": Hill, "Senda Berenson," *Research Quarterly*, p. 662.

5 "The scene . . . continual hum": "No Man In It," *Boston Globe*, 18 March 1894.

6 She felt basketball . . . in each section: Hill, "Senda Berenson," *Research Quarterly*, p. 662.

6 "It does away . . . to her territory": Luther Halsey Gulick, Theodore Hough, A. Bertha Foster, and Senda Berenson, *Line Basket Ball; or, Basket Ball for Women, as Adopted by the Conference on Physical Training, Held in June, at Springfield, Mass., Also Articles on the Game by Dr. Luther Gulick, Dr. Theordore Hough, Dr. A. Bertha Foster, and Miss Senda Berenson.* ed. by Senda Berenson, New York, American Sports Publishing Company, 1901, p. 25.

6 "She never lowered . . . know it, too": Hill, "Senda Berenson," *Research Quarterly*, p. 663.

6 "Certain elements . . . self-conscious": Gulick, Hough, Foster, and Berenson, *Line Basket Ball*, p. 22.

7 "It is impossible . . . with dignity": Gulick, Hough, Foster, and Berenson, *Line Basket Ball*, p. 22.

7 She left her job . . . United States Basket Ball Committee: Melnick, *Senda Berenson*, pp. 123–29.

8 "A bit temperamental . . . adored her": Hill, "Senda Berenson," *Research Quarterly*, p. 663.

College Ball Tips Off

5 All of the 700 . . . in the windows: "Stanford's Girls Win," *Sun*, New York, 19 April 1896.

5 Stanford won . . . when they returned: "Waterloo for Berkeley Girls," *San Francisco Examiner*, 5 April 1896.

5 In 1899 . . . for women: "Faculty at Stanford Abolishes Basket Ball," *San Francisco Call*, 16 December 1899.

Ora Washington

10 "Starting in 1925 . . . 1936": Renee Montgomery, "Ora Washington: The 'Queen of Two Courts' Whose Brilliance Was Ignored," *BBC Sport*, 12 October 2022, www.bbc.com/sport/63066765.

10 "She was probably . . . have now": Do Dang Phuc, "2018 Hall of Fame: Ora Washington." *YouTube*, 16 September 2018, www.youtube.com/watch?v=K-ozD5nNDEY.

10 "powerfully built . . . speed": Pamela Grundy and Susan Shackelford, *Shattering the Glass*, 1st ed. (The New Press, 2005), p. 63.

11 It was often referred . . . Ballard: Black Fives Foundation,. "All Hail the Philadelphia Tribune Girls! (Happy Birthday Ora Mae Washington) Black Fives," *Black Fives | Make History Now!*, 2 March 2018, www.blackfives.org/all-hail-the-philadelpha-tribune-girls-happy-birthday-ora-mae-washington/.

11 "She passes . . . envy": Randy Dixon, "Sports Ora Washington Capt., All-Philly Girls' Team Hornets' Ace Picked as Best Girl Player; Jersey Girl Gains Guard Berth First Team Consisting of Hill, Laws, Washington, Davis and Patterson, Is Best Ever Selected Hard Battle for Second Team Berths," *Philadelphia Tribune* (1912–2001), 17 March 1932, http://www.proquest.com.libproxy.temple.edu/.

11 "The game was . . . contest": BBC, *Untold Legends: Ora Washington*, podcast 4, BBC, 2022, www.bbc.com/audio/play/w3ct43ch.

11 "Queen Ora . . . Courts": Juliet Macur, "Overlooked No More: Ora Washington, Star of Tennis and Basketball," *New York Times*, 4 February 2022, www.nytimes.com/2022/02/04/obituaries/ora-washington-overlooked.html.

11 "the greatest girl . . . player": Dixon, "Sports: Ora Washington Capt.," *Philadelphia Tribune*, 17 March 1932.

11 "breaking down barriers . . . sports": Marilyn Morgan Westner, "Inez 'Pat' Patterson, The 'Mermaid of Philadelphia,'" *Pool A Social History of Segregation*, 2023, p.86, www.poolphl.com/pdfs/Pool_Magazine.pdf.

12 "She was one . . . around her": Rita Liberti, "We Were Ladies, We Just Played Basketball like Boys," African American Womanhood and Competitive Basketball at Bennett College, 1928–1942," *Journal of Sport History*, vol. 26, no. 3, 1999, https://www.academia.edu/30408972/_We_Were_

Ladies_We_Just_Played_Basketball_Like_Boys_African_American_Womanhood_and_Competitive_Basketball_at_Bennett_College_1928_1942.

13 "The players, winsome . . . attested": "Young Women Play Basketball," *New York Age*, 3 March 1910.

Six-on-Six

16 "Girls' basketball . . . the men's game": "Aberdeen Fans Follow Team," *News & Observer* (Raleigh, NC) 23 February 1950.

17 "Gentlemen, if you attempt . . . the train runs over you!": Iowa Girls High School Athletic Union, https://ighsau.org/history.

Denise Long

22 She took her . . . in Des Moines: Ron Maly, "Union-Whitten Wins It: 113–107," *Des Moines Sunday Register*, 17 March 1968.

22 In May 1969 . . . purple Jaguar: Alan Chazaro, "In 1969, Years Before the WNBA, the Warriors Drafted Denise Long," KQED (NPR), 6 October 2023, https://www.kqed.org/arts/13935961/denise-long-warriors-wnba.

23 "They included Lakers . . . didn't mean to": Daniel P. Finney, "That Time an Iowa Girls' Basketball Star Was Drafted Out of High School by the NBA's Warriors," *Des Moines Register*, 17 June 2019, https://www.desmoinesregister.com/story/news/2019/06/17/nba- draft-how-iowa-basketball-star-denise-long-rife-made-history-golden- state-warriors-girls-6-on-6/1409879001/.

The All-American Red Heads

24 "I called it Bozo . . . your face": "All-American Red Heads – Missouri Sports Hall of Fame," Mosportshalloffame.com, 2017, mosportshalloffame.com/inductees/all-american-red-heads/.

24 They won ninety-six . . . season: "The Naismith Memorial Basketball Hall of Fame: All American Red Heads," Hoophall.com, 2012, www.hoophall.com/hall-of-famers/all-american-red-heads/.

Wayland Baptist Flying Queens

28 A tiny religious . . . pants around campus: Skip Hollandsworth, "Hoop Queens," *Texas Monthly*, April 2013.

28 Not all . . . for every player?: Hollandsworth, "Hoop Queens," *Texas Monthly*.

28 Claude Hutcherson . . . Flying Queens: "The Flying Queens," *Sports Illustrated*, 2 April 1956.

29 They once found . . . a few tricks: Hollandsworth, "Hoop Queens," *Texas Monthly*.

Chapter 2

The Birth of the AIAW

34 "Must women follow . . . by men?": Virginia Hunt, *Governance of Women's Intercollegiate Athletics: An Historical Perspective* (University of North Carolina at Greensboro, 1976), p. 99.

The Mighty Macs

37 "I really didn't think . . . job": Phone interview with Cathy Rush, 11 December 2024.

37 "There was no anticipation . . . picture": Phone interview with Theresa Shank Grentz, 10 December 2024.

Lusia "Lucy" Harris

46 "It just came natural": *The Queen of Basketball*, directed by Ben Proudfoot, documentary short, *New York Times*, 2021.

47 "I had to be . . . big honor": Lusia Harris-Stewart, "Oral History with Ms. Lusia Harris-Stewart." Center for Oral History and Cultural Heritage of the University of Southern Mississippi, interview by Georgene Clark, 18 December 1999.

The WBL: "Unassuming Trailblazers"

52 Wilson was the first to . . . 1984: Payton Titus, "How Karen Logan and Her Legacy of the WNBA's Basketball Shows How Far Women's Pro Hoops Has Come," *Yahoo Sports*, 25 August 2022, sports.yahoo.com/how-karen-logan-and-her-legacy-of-the-wnba-basketball-shows-how-far-womens-pro-hoops-has-come-172938204.html.

56 She scored 50-plus . . . total points: Special thank-you to Tom Davis, a WBL assistant coach and statistician, who shared his personal archives.

56 After a few missed . . . going to Chicago: "When Chicago Hustled," *Chicago* magazine, October 2024, p. 55, https://www.chicagomag.com/chicago-magazine/october-2024/before-the-sky-there-was-the-hustle/.

58 The Hustle attempted . . . $200,000: Laurence M. Cooper, "1981 Chicago Hustle Public Stock Offering," Fun While It Lasted, *The Chicago Hustle*, WBL, 1981, funwhileitlasted.net/2017/01/30/1978-1981-chicago-hustle/.

58 The California Dreams out of . . . a dentist: Rich Roberts, "The Building of a Dream Team," *LA Times*, 28 August 1979, p. 32.

58 "We are more . . . forward": TEDx Talks. "A Women's Professional Basketball League Before the WNBA, Elizabeth Galloway McQuitter, TEDxBoston." YouTube, 7 June 2022, www.youtube.com/watch?v=0R5v0euYAFQ.

Chapter 3

AIAW vs. NCAA

65 "He wasn't doing it . . . at that convention": Mark Bechtel, "AIAW vs. NCAA: When Women's College Basketball Had to Choose, *Sports Illustrated*, June 2022, https://www.si.com/college/2022/06/14/aiaw-ncaa-womens-college-basketball-league-title-ix-daily-cover.

66 "The AIAW had . . . what they have today": 2002–2003 *Tennessee Lady Volunteers Basketball Media Guide*, p. 209.

66 "I knew somebody . . . that away from us": Will Pakutka, "Rutgers Up in 'Other' Tourney," *Daily Record* (Morristown, NJ), 22 March 1982.

68 "If this is the last . . . the best": "The Champion Lady Knights," *Home News* (East Brunswick, NJ), 30 March 1982.

69 "They might be . . . I've ever seen": Jim McLain, "Techsters in a New Role for Title Game," Gannett News Service, 28 March 1982.

71 "From a coaching . . . women's basketball": Liz Clarke, "How the NCAA Women's Final Four Was Born," *Washington*

Post, 31 March 2022, https://www.washingtonpost.com/sports/interactive/2022/first-womens-ncaa-tournament/.

Cheryl Miller

73 **She once scored 105 points . . . halftime**: *Winning Time: Reggie Miller vs. the New York Knicks*, directed by Dan Klores, ESPN Films, 2010.

75 **"You can either play . . . gone be?"**: Knuckleheads podcast, "Cheryl Miller Reflects on Her Championships with USC, the '84 Olympics in LA, the WNBA & More," YouTube, 5 October 2023, www.youtube.com/watch?v=luwJZcdSVEg.

75 **"That was the wrong . . . us play"**: Knuckleheads podcast, "Cheryl Miller."

76 **"Cheryl enlarged her aura . . . her way"**: Curry Kirkpatrick. "LIGHTS! CAMERA! CHERYL!" *Sports Illustrated Vault | SI.com*, 20 November 1985, vault.si.com/vault/1985/11/20/lights-camera-cheryl.

76 **"I think they have . . . Cheryl Miller"**: "USC Wins Women's Title Again," *Washington Post*, 2 April 1984, www.washingtonpost.com/archive/sports/1984/04/02/usc-wins-womens-title-again/8b566a5f-4a94-41d1-90d1-e31b41fff54b/.

76 **"While much of the Olympic . . . national championship"**: Michael Wilbon, "US Women Win Basketball Gold," *Washington Post*, 8 August 1984, www.washingtonpost.com/archive/sports/1984/08/08/us-women-win-basketball-gold/8410aacd-279d-42fc-ae28-350bb0041997/.

79 **She remembers . . . kids"**: Knuckleheads podcast, "Cheryl Miller."

USA's Olympic Dominance Begins

80 **"We couldn't even believe . . . unknown"**: Maggie Hendricks, "The 1980 US Basketball Teams Didn't Get to Play in the Summer Olympics That Year Either. But It Wasn't a Pandemic That Kept Them Away—It Was a Boycott," *Chicago Tribune*, 15 April 2020, www.chicagotribune.com/2020/04/15/the-1980-us-basketball-teams-didnt-get-to-play-in-the-summer-olympics-that-year-either-but-it-wasnt-a-pandemic-that-kept-them-away-it-was-a-boycott/.

83 **"The moment that you . . . a dream"**: Nina Mandell, "1988 Gold Medalist Teresa Weatherspoon on Why USA Basketball Will Win Another Gold," *For the Win*, 19 August 2016, ftw.usatoday.com/2016/08/1988-gold-medalist-teresa-weatherspoon-on-why-usa-basketball-will-win-another-gold.

Lynette Woodard

85 **"My vision blurred . . . palpitating"**: *The Doc Holliday Show*, "Episode 104 Lynette 'Legend' Woodard-Naismith Hall of Famer and 1st Female Harlem Globetrotter," YouTube, 28 July 2022, www.youtube.com/watch?v=QvQWHUj4IMs.

85 **"I'm in basketball heaven"**: Barry Jacobs, "Globetrotters Looking for Some New Wizards," *New York Times*, 17 July 1985.

Chapter 4

The Rivalry

96 **In the summer of 1994 . . . "for the good of the game"**: Lori Riley, "The UConn–Tennessee Rivalry Started with a Phone Call from an ESPN Employee. Here's How It Played Out," *Hartford Courant*, 22 January 2020, https://www.courant.com/2020/01/22/the-uconn-tennessee-rivalry-started-with-a-phone-call-from-an-espn-employee-heres-how-it-played-out/.

98 **"Win or lose . . . national live television"**: Frank Litsky, "At UConn, the Women Take On High Court," *New York Times,* 16 January 1995.

99 **"I think she . . . agree with her"**: John Altavilla and Lori Riley, "Geno Putting Press on Pat," *Hartford Courant*, 25 September 2007.

99 **"The electricity . . . basketball can be"**: Filip Bondy, "UConn Proves No Lady," *New York Daily News*, 17 January 1995.

Pat Summitt

101 **"If you don't like . . . proud of it"**: Antonya English, "Pressing for Success: The Real Pat Summitt," *Tampa Bay Times*, 9 March 1999, www.tampabay.com/archive/1999/03/09/pressing-for-success-the-real-pat-summitt/.

102 **"Oh, I think my water broke . . . Virgina"**: Martin Fennelly, "Fennelly: The Tale of Pat Summitt, a Recruiting Visit and the Dash to Have a Baby Born in Tennessee," *Tampa Bay Times*, 7 July 2016, www.tampabay.com/sports/basketball/college/fennelly-the-tale-of-pat-summitt-a-recruiting-visit-and-the-dash-to-have-a/2284374/.

102 **"I won one thousand ninety-eight . . . faces"**: Pat Summitt and Sally Jenkins, *Sum It Up: 1,098 Victories, a Couple of Irrelevant Losses, and a Life in Perspective* (Crown Publishing Group, 2014).

104 **"You had to earn . . . inspires more greatness"**: Dee Kantner, "Tennessee Titan," *Players' Tribune*, 14 June 2016, www.theplayerstribune.com/articles/dee-kantner-phillip-fulmer-pat-summitt.

The Three Meeks

105 **"We wanted to . . . embarrass people"**: *Players' Tribune*, "Chamique Holdsclaw Holdin' It Down with Q & D | Knuckleheads podcast S2E5 | The Players' Tribune." YouTube, 17 October 2019, www.youtube.com/watch?v=QbEPT8qYa-c.

105 **"It was a statement . . . arrived"**: Luke Kaiser, "Cover Woman," *SLAM*, 3 July 2014, accessed 3 March 2025, www.slamonline.com/wnba/chamique-holdsclaw-slam-magazine/.

Geno Auriemma

106 **"Geno's natural walk is a strut"**: Frank Deford, "Geno Auriemma + Diana Taurasi = Love, Italian Style," *Sports Illustrated*, 24 November 2003.

106 **"He got us . . . think about winning"**: Len Painter, "Jennifer Weideman's Future at Connecticut Now Clearer," *Grand Haven Tribune*, 15 March 1986.

107 **"Someone said . . . by winning?"**: Jackie MacMullan, "Striving Instructor," *Boston Globe*, 26 November 1995.

107 "Geno was different . . . that were real": Deford, "Geno Auriemma," *Sports Illustrated*.

107 "He'll pound . . . you need to": Deford, "Geno Auriemma," *Sports Illustrated*.

The '96ers: Gold or Bust

110 "They develop almost . . . away to play it": Alexander Wolff, "The Home Team," *Sports Illustrated*, 29 May 1995.

112 "The conditioning wasn't . . . ahead of us": Tara VanDerveer and Joan Ryan, *Shooting from the Outside: How a Coach and Her Olympic Team Transformed Women's Basketball* (Avon Books, 1997), p. 64.

112 "You are truly my Number One . . . so much": VanDerveer and Ryan, *Shooting from the Outside*, p. 251.

113 "Winning the gold . . . it's not": VanDerveer and Ryan, *Shooting from the Outside*, p. 146.

113 "I wanted to meet you . . . is important": VanDerveer and Ryan, *Shooting from the Outside*, p. 140.

115 "I've been doing . . . to see that": Sara Corbett, *Venus to the Hoop: A Gold Medal Year in Women's Basketball* (Anchor Books, 1998), p. 311.

115 "If we don't win . . . waste": VanDerveer and Ryan, *Shooting from the Outside*, p. 240.

115 "This is what . . . indescribable": Ann Killion, "VanDerveer & Co. Strike Gold," Knight-Ridder Newspapers, 5 August 1996.

115 "What happened . . . posters will sell": Adrian Wojnarowski, "WNBA Has the Hype, But Not the Hoops," *Fresno Bee*, 12 August 1997.

116 "Your team was . . . teaching and leading": VanDerveer and Ryan, *Shooting from the Outside*, pp. 251–52.

We Got Next

119 "What you saw . . . beginning": Maitreyi Anantharaman, "How the ABL Lost the Fight for the Soul of Women's Basketball," *Defector*, 5 November 2020, defector.com/how-the-abl-lost-the-fight-for-the-soul-of-womens-basketball?giftLink=91be3abfff82082c4bbd315a008f2ade.

120 "The ABL wasn't an afterthought . . . event": Dorothy J. Gentry, "The American Basketball League Helped Pave the Way for the WNBA," *Sports Illustrated*, 12 May 2021, www.si.com/wnba/2021/05/12/american-basketball-league.

121 "Suspended in the air . . . national TV!": UNC Athletic Communications, "Celebrate Carolina Crawley's Memorable Dunk—University of North Carolina Athletics," *University of North Carolina Athletics*, 2 July 2020, goheels.com/news/2020/7/2/womens-basketball-celebrate-carolina-crawleys-memorable-dunk.

122 "It's safe to say . . . dreams": Kelly Whiteside, *A Celebration: Commemorating the Birth of a League* (Harper Paperbacks, 1998), p. 95.

122 The league filed . . . $10 million: Selena Roberts, "PRO BASKETBALL; Nice Try, No Reward as A.B.L. Goes Dark," *New York Times*, 23 December 1998, www.nytimes.com/1998/12/23/sports/pro-basketball-nice-try-no-reward-as-abl-goes-dark.html.

123 "You knew that was . . . just perfect": Whiteside, *A Celebration*, p. 63.

All Hail the Houston Comets

126 "We got next . . . Bow down": Whiteside, *A Celebration*, p. 19.

128 "Coop, play your game": Whiteside, *A Celebration*, p. 31.

128 "If I shoot . . . Coop and Tina": Zachary Draves, "Kim Perrot Will Forever Be in the Hearts of the Houston Comets and Van Chancellor," *Swish Appeal*, 19 August 2024, www.swishappeal.com/wnba/2024/8/19/24223287/wnba-kim-perrot-houston-comets-passing-van-chancellor-memory-legacy-dynasty-cooper-swoopes-thompson.

Chapter 5

Changing of the Guard

136 "I'm just glad . . . of the four": ESPN, "Cooper's Career Ends with 4th Crown," espn.com, 2000, www.espn.com/wnba/2000/20000826/recap/nylhou.html.

137 "Everyone was trying . . . too good": Seattle Storm, "Key Moments in Lauren Jackson's Seattle Storm Career: An Oral History," wnba.com, 14 July 2016, storm.wnba.com/news/key-moments-lauren-jacksons-seattle-storm-career-oral-history.

Sue Bird

139 "Scrabble, Crazy 8 . . . like it": *Sue Bird: In the Clutch*, directed by Sarah Dowland, documentary, Netflix, 2024.

139 "You know, everything . . . out there": Adriana Morga, "Former UConn Basketball Player Sue Bird Interviewed on '60 Minutes,'" *CT Insider*, 21 March 2022, www.ctinsider.com/sports/uconn/article/sue-bird-uconn-megan-rapinoe-60-minutes-17018707.php.

139 "She's going to throw . . . going in": *Sue Bird*, Netflix, 2024.

140 "the best . . . ever played": Jeff Goldberg, *Bird at the Buzzer*. U of Nebraska Press, 2019.

140 "If we had won . . . Ever": Sue Bird, "We Had Control," *Players' Tribune*, 21 March 2015, www.theplayerstribune.com/articles/sue-bird-uconn-ncaa-tournament.

140 "Playing with . . . smart": *Sue Bird*, Netflix, 2024.

141 "The same way Dawn . . . that matters": Kevin Pelton, "USA Basketball Continues Search for Sue Bird's Successor," espn.com, ESPN, 25 April 2018, www.espn.com/wnba/story/_/id/23316354/usa-basketball-continues-search-sue-bird-successor.

141 "I feel like I've helped . . . that away": *Sue Bird*, Netflix, 2024.

Detroit Shock the World

142 "The 2003 Detroit Shock . . . heart out": Detroit Pistons, "Under the Hood | Episode 13: Shock & Awe," YouTube, 3 April 2023, www.youtube.com/watch?v=Lyti9AIoJGo.

143 "As it gets going . . . a villain": Detroit Pistons. "Under the Hood."

143 "Detroit is a big . . . inside": Vince Prygoski, *Worst to First: Or a 'Shock'ing Tale of Women's Basketball in Motown* (Outskirts Press, 2006).

The Battle of California

146 "2005 . . . All the way live!": WNBA, "WNBA at 20–2005," YouTube, 12 May 2016, www.youtube.com/watch?v=YZVCCcOwwEc.

The Dunking Queen

149 **"If those girls . . . do something"**: Corbett, *Venus to the Hoop*, p. 118

149 **"I was thinking . . . into the rim"**: Tom Friend, "A Rough Start as Women Take the Court," *New York Times*, 22 June 1997.

The Positionless Powerhouse

152 **"If some other . . . those other skills"**: Mike Dodd, "The Hardest Position: Sitting," *USA TODAY*, 12 November 2003.

152 **"I think Pat is omniscient"**: Candace Parker, "Ain't She Grand?" *Sports Illustrated*, 16 February 2009.

152 **"It was the best decision . . . better individual"**: Parker, "Ain't She Grand?" *Sports Illustrated*.

153 **"You can mess around . . . win twice"**: Sean Gregory, "Why Candace Parker Pretty Much Rules Basketball Right Now," *Time*, 21 October 2021, https://time.com/6108927/candace-parker-wnba-chicago-sky/.

154 **"I know she . . . guard her, too"**: Gary Blair, "Texas A&M Aggies Postgame Media Conference," NCAA Women's Regionals Semifinals & Finals: Oklahoma City, transcribed by ASAP Sports, 1 April 2008, https://www.asapsports.com/show_interview.php?id=48698.

154 **"Let me tell you . . . fought through"**: Pat Summitt, "Tennessee Lady Vols Postgame Media Conference," NCAA Women's Regionals Semifinals & Finals: Oklahoma City, transcribed by ASAP Sports, 1 April 2008, https://www.asapsports.com/show_interview.php?id=48699.

154 **"She's a shot maker . . . but a rookie"**: Christopher Ramirez, "Parker's 34 Points Set Scoring Mark for Debut," *Arizona Republic*, 18 May 2008.

The Mighty Mercury

155 **"My job is . . . front of me"**: Kate Storey, "For the Win," *Rolling Stone*, 8 June 2024, www.rollingstone.com/culture/culture-sports/wnba-womens-basketball-olympics-1235030924/.

155 **"I'm a winner . . . things happen"**: Phoenix Mercury, "2007 Phoenix Mercury: The Beginning of a Dynasty," wnba.com, 3 June 2020, mercury.wnba.com/news/2007-phoenix-mercury-the-beginning-of-a-dynasty.

Money, Money, Money?

156 **"Many of these players . . . live in"**: "Stern Tells WNBA to Settle in 10 Days," *Midland Daily News*, 8 April 2003, www.ourmidland.com/news/article/Stern-Tells-WNBA-to-Settle-in-10-Days-7154096.php.

156 **"consistent with . . . innovative mindset"**: "MERCURY: Mercury, LifeLock Break New Ground with Partnership," wnba.com, 2009, www.wnba.com/archive/wnba/mercury/news/lifelock_release_090601.html.

Matter of Fact: 2000s

162 **"I took one last look . . . in North Philly"**: Official Hoop Hall, "Dawn Staley's Basketball Hall of Fame Enshrinement Speech," YouTube, 9 September 2013, www.youtube.com/watch?v=1rIqn-Ii0dI.

Chapter 6

One for the Ages

167 **"Never . . . really hard"**: Ramona Shelburne, "Minnesota Lynx-Los Angeles Sparks Has Become One of Best Rivalries in WNBA History," espn.com, 2 October 2017, www.espn.com/wnba/story/_/id/20896940/minnesota-lynx-los-angeles-sparks-become-one-best-rivalries-wnba-history.

167 **"I'm looking forward . . . the West"**: "Lynx Cheryl Reeve Named Lynx Head Coach," wnba.com, 8 December 2009, www.wnba.com/archive/wnba/lynx/news/Cheryl_Reeve_Named_Lynx_Head_Coach_2009_12_08.html.

167 **"Look, I can get . . . people uncomfortable"**: Cheryl Reeve, "No Excuses," *Players' Tribune*, 11 April 2018, www.theplayerstribune.com/articles/cheryl-reeve-gender-equality.

167 **"Every year . . . to win a championship"**: "Maya Moore Selected First Overall by Minnesota Lynx," espn.com, 11 April 2011, www.espn.com/wnba/news/story?id=6330896.

168 **"When you come into . . . sweet right now"**: Indiana Fever, "Recapping the Fever's 2012 Championship Run: Championship Dreams Finally Come True," wnba.com, 21 October 2022, fever.wnba.com/news/recapping-the-fevers-2012-championship-run-championship-dreams-finally-come-true.

170 **"hardest loss . . . to win"**: Maya Moore Irons and Jonathan Irons, *Love and Justice*. (Andscape, 2023) ch. 19.

172 **"Every time you do this . . . pretty cool"**: Bob Sansevere, "Sansevere: Lindsay Whalen Shows Lynx Teammates That Ol' Barn Magic," *Twin Cities*, 5 October 2017, www.twincities.com/2017/10/04/lindsay-whalen-shows-lynx-teammates-that-ol-barn-magic/.

173 **"It definitely adds . . . bit"**: Sloane Martin, "The Lynx-Sparks Rivalry Will Waste No Time Getting Intense This Time Around," *New York Times*, 19 May 2018, www.nytimes.com/athletic/359795/2018/05/19/lynx-sparks-preview-candace-parker-seimone-augustus-maya-moore-lindsay-whalen/.

174 **"I like to make history . . . it up"**: Rachel Blount, "Moore Could Be Strong Voice for Women's Basketball," *Minnesota Star Tribune*, 2 June 2011, www.ctpost.com/default/article/Moore-could-be-strong-voice-for-women-s-basketball-1405894.php.

174 **"There are times . . . this one special"**: Michael Voepel, "Minnesota Lynx, Los Angeles Sparks Take WNBA Rivalry to New Level," espn.com, 14 August 2017, www.espn.com/wnba/story/_/id/20337340/minnesota-lynx-los-angeles-sparks-take-wnba-rivalry-new-level.

The White Mamba

177 **"You want that . . . I do"**: Deford, "Geno Auriemma," *Sports Illustrated*.

177 **"Taurasi didn't just . . . a fresh face"**: Frank Deford, "UConn's Flashy Finish," *Sports Illustrated*, 19 April 2004.

178 **"She's always thinking . . . greatness"**: A'ja Wilson, interview, 19 July 2024.

179 **"This message . . . The GOAT"**: "@KingJames salutes @DianaTaurasi for becoming the @WNBA's all-time leading scorer in history. #Respect," @uninterrupted, X (formerly Twitter), 18 June 2017, 7:14 p.m., https://x.com/uninterrupted/status/876578918836256768.

Four for Four

181 "Breanna is . . . can do": John Altavilla, "Impressive Debuts: Stewart, Huskies Couldn't Ask for Better First Game," *Hartford Courant*, 12 November 2012.

The Streak-Breaker

182 "Stewie looked . . . high school kids": Geno Auriemma, "UConn Huskies Pregame Media Conference," NCAA Women's Basketball Championship: Final Four, transcribed by ASAP Sports, 30 March 2017, https://www.asapsports.com/show_interview.php?id=128856.

182 "humbling . . . embarrassing": Vic Schaefer, "Mississippi State Bulldogs Pregame Media Conference," NCAA Women's Basketball Championship: Final Four, transcribed by ASAP Sports, 30 March 2017, https://www.asapsports.com/show_interview.php?id=128859.

182 "We saw . . . at all": Victoria Vivians, "Mississippi State Bulldogs Pregame Media Conference," NCAA Women's Basketball Championship: Final Four, transcribed by ASAP Sports, 30 March 2017, https://www.asapsports.com/show_interview.php?id=128859.

182 "It's annoying . . . that's personal": Doug Feinberg, "Mississippi St. Remembers 60 Point Loss to UConn," *Associated Press*, 31 March 2017.

182 "Let me tell . . . no different": Schaefer, "Mississippi State Bulldogs Pregame Media Conference," 30 March 2017.

183 "How many people . . . out of you?": Tara Sullivan, "Five Storylines to Love About Mississippi State's Win," *Record* (Bergen, NJ), 1 April 2017, https://www.northjersey.com/story/sports/columnists/tara-sullivan/2017/04/01/sullivan-five-storylines-love-mississippi-states- win/99905344/.

184 "We didn't have . . . one time": Schaefer, "Mississippi State Bulldogs Postgame Media Conference," NCAA Women's Basketball Championship: Final Four, transcribed by ASAP Sports, 31 March 2017, https://www.asapsports.com/show_interview.php?id=128938.

185 "Look . . . other people win": Geno Auriemma, "UConn Huskies Postgame Media Conference," NCAA Women's Basketball Championship: Final Four, transcribed by ASAP Sports, 31 March 2017, https://www.asapsports.com/show_interview.php?id=128937.

185 "What an unbelievable . . . it could happen": Schaefer, "Mississippi State Bulldogs Postgame Media Conference," 31 March 2017.

Parity Party

185 "I think it breathes . . . the past decade": Dawn Staley, "South Carolina Gamecocks Media Conference," NCAA Women's Basketball Championship, transcribed by ASAP Sports, 1 April 2017, https://www.asapsports.com/show_interview.php?id=128939.

Dawn of a New Day

186 "Those are the things . . . shooting for": Dawn Staley, "South Carolina Gamecocks Postgame Media Conference," NCAA Women's Basketball Championship, transcribed by ASAP Sports, 2 April 2017, https://www.asapsports.com/show_interview.php?id=128993.

187 "When I couldn't . . . that was it": Staley, "South Carolina Gamecocks Postgame Media Conference," 2 April 2017.

187 "Just because something . . . give up on it": Staley, "South Carolina Gamecocks Postgame Media Conference," 2 April 2017.

The Orange Hoodie

191 "Move the shoe over . . . simple yet striking": Whiteside, *A Celebration*, p. 61.

191 "It came at a time . . . league stands for": Ben Pickman, "How One Hoodie Became the WNBA's Defining Symbol," *Sports Illustrated*, 10 May 2021, www.si.com/wnba/2021/05/10/orange-hoodies-kobe-bryant-aja-wilson-eb-jones.

Chapter 7

Unfinished Business

196 "There's a lot of . . . achieved the latter": Jordan Robinson, "Oregon's Sabrina Ionescu Deserved a Better Send-Off," *Ringer*, 19 March 2020, www.theringer.com/2020/03/19/college-basketball/sabrina-ionescu-oregon-college-basketball-wnba.

196 "No question . . . we won't ever know": Gus Martin, "'Really Grateful': Despite Early End to Year, Brenda Frese Is Proud of Maryland Basketball," *Diamondback*, 14 March 2020, dbknews.com/2020/03/13/maryland-womens-basketball-brenda-frese-season-canceled-coronavirus/.

197 "It's unfortunate we . . . was incredible": James Crepea, "'There's Always Going to Be a Little Hole in My Heart': Oregon Women's Basketball Coping with Reality of Fore," *Oregon Live*, 14 March 2020, www.oregonlive.com/ducks/2020/03/theres-always-going-to-be-a-little-hole-in-my-heart-oregon-womens-basketball-coping-with-reality-of-forever-unfinished-business.html.

"Say Her Name"

199 "We're onto something . . . not use them": Jordan Robinson, "'Say Her Name': The WNBA Wants to Make a Statement When It Returns," *Ringer*, 21 July 2020, www.theringer.com/2020/07/21/wnba/say-her-name-wnba-wants-to-make-statement-when-it-returns.

200 "complicated and arduous": Graham Hays, "Liberty's Asia Durr Won't Play This Season after Bout with Coronavirus," espn.com, 7 July 2020, www.espn.com/wnba/story/_/id/29423503/liberty-asia-durr-play-season-bout-coronavirus.

201 "There's work to be . . . Momentum": Renee Montgomery, X (formerly Twitter), 18 June 2020, x.com/ReneeMontgomery/status/1273615398961844224?s=20.

201 "To have a company . . . feeling": Bryan Kalbrosky, "Converse Is Hoping to Re-Create Its Niche by Aligning with Outspoken Basketball Stars." *For the Win*, 2 April 2021, ftw.usatoday.com/2021/04/converse-basketball-draymond-green-natasha-cloud-shai-gilgeous-alexander-kelly-oubre.

201 "This is the reason . . . for change": Hoopfeed, "Elizabeth Williams Gives Statement on Why WNBA Players Refused to Play on August 26, 2020," YouTube, 26 August 2020, www.youtube.com/watch?v=h_TVBwiLwmQ.

202 **"Let's be honest . . . I'm here"**: *144*, directed by Jenna Contreras and Lauren Stowell, documentary, ESPN Films, 2021.

202 **"For a women's league . . . been recoverable"**: Michael Voepel, "How Commissioner Cathy Engelbert Saved the 2020 WNBA Season," espn.com, ESPN, 2 October 2020, www.espn.com/wnba/story/_/id/30018211/how-commissioner-cathy-engelbert-saved-2020-wnba-season.

202 **"I've taken a lot . . . Sue [Bird]"**: Roy Ward, "'I've Taken a Lot Away': Ezi's Joy as Storm Sweep Aces to Claim Fourth WNBA Title," *Sydney Morning Herald*, 7 October 2020, www.smh.com.au/sport/ezi-s-joy-as-storm-sweep-aces-to-claim-fourth-wnba-title-20201007-p562vh.html.

203 **"As a Black woman . . . the movement"**: ABC News, "WNBA Commissioner: Using Season as a 'Call to Action,'" YouTube, 7 July 2020, www.youtube.com/watch?v=fOS7FMru4GY.

Vote Warnock

202 **"I need . . . 'We Did That'"**: Sean Gregory, "'We Did That': Inside the WNBA's Strategy to Support Raphael Warnock," *Time*, 7 January 2021, time.com/5927075/atlanta-dream-warnock-loeffler/.

Tara VanDerveer

204 **"I know that these women . . . sisterhood that they represent"**: Tara VanDerveer, "Stanford Cardinal Finals Postgame Media Conference," NCAA Women's Basketball Championship, transcribed by ASAP Sports, 4 April 2021, https://www.asapsports.com/show_interview.php?id=164126.

204 **"I was the worst . . . history of mascots"**: VanDerveer and Ryan, *Shooting from the Outside*, p. 34.

205 **"If anyone comes . . . will be killing them"**: Tara VanDerveer, as told to Elizabeth Merrill, "Stanford Coach Tara VanDerveer on Her Decades-Long Love Affair with Basketball and Her Fight for Equality," espn.com, 28 March 2021, https://www.espn.com/womens-college-basketball/story/_/id/31141865/stanford-coach-tara-vanderveer-decades-long-love-affair-basketball-fight-equality.

A'ja Wilson

207 **"When you think . . . my standard"**: Vinciane Ngomsi, "Watch the Throne: A'ja Wilson Is Coming for Everything," *Boardroom*, 14 May 2024, boardroom.tv/aja-wilson-cover-story/.

207 **"It just takes a lot of pride . . . every time"**: Michael Voepel, "Aces Star A'ja Wilson Wins Second Straight DPOY Award" espn.com, ESPN, 22 September 2023, www.espn.com/wnba/story/_/id/38461630/aces-star-aja-wilson-wins-second-straight-dpoy-award.

209 **"Shoot it . . . paid to shoot!"**: Las Vegas Aces, "'Just Shoot It. What's the Worst That's Gonna Happen? Who Cares? Shoot It. We Get Paid to Shoot,'—A'ja Wilson to Jackie Young, EspnW | by Las Vegas Aces | Facebook," Facebook, 2022, www.facebook.com/watch/?v=374586894640541.

209 **"I'm sitting next to . . . of the world"**: Dustin Schutte, "Kate Martin Praises Aces Teammate A'ja Wilson as 'Best Player, Leader' in WNBA," *Fastbreak on SI*, Sports Illustrated, 10 June 2024, www.si.com/fannation/nba/fastbreak/news/las-vegas-aces-rookie-kate-martin-gushes-teammate-aja-wilson-best-leader-been-around-best-womens-basketball-player-world-2024-wnba.

Game, Changed

217 **"I needed a coach . . . to humble you"**: Angel Reese, "LSU Tigers Finals Pregame Media Conference," NCAA Women's Basketball Championship, transcribed by ASAP Sports, 1 April 2023, https://www.asapsports.com/show_interview.php?id=186069.

217 **"This was for . . . bigger than me tonight"**: Angel Reese, "LSU Tigers Final Postgame Media Conference," NCAA Women's Basketball Championship, transcribed by ASAP Sports, 2 April 2023, https://www.asapsports.com/show_interview.php?id=186123.

218 **"Angel has grown . . . tough love"**: Kim Mulkey, "LSU Tigers Finals Pregame Media Conference," NCAA Women's Basketball Championship, transcribed by ASAP Sports, 1 April 2023, https://www.asapsports.com/show_interview.php?id=186068.

218 **"I view matchups . . . what's fun"**: Caitlin Clark, "Iowa Hawkeyes Pregame Media Conference," NCAA Women's Basketball Championship," transcribed by ASAP Sports, 1 April 2023, https://www.asapsports.com/show_interview.php?id=186071.

219 **"I don't care . . . what I did"**: Angel Reese, "LSU Tigers Final Postgame Media Conference," NCAA Women's Basketball Championship, transcribed by ASAP Sports, 2 April 2023, https://www.asapsports.com/show_interview.php?id=186123.

The Record Breaker

222 **"Of course I love . . . shoot out there"**: Molly Bolin Kazmer, email interview, 6 December 2024.

224 **"You all knew . . . Come on now"**: Amna Nawaz, "Iowa Phenom Caitlin Clark Breaks NCAA Women's Basketball Record for Career Points," *PBS News Hour*, 16 February 2024, https://www.pbs.org/newshour/show/iowa-phenom-caitlin-clark-breaks-ncaa-womens-basketball-record-for-career-points.

224 **"Girl, you're something . . . like it"**: Kim Mulkey, "LSU Tigers Elite 8 Postgame Media Conference," NCAA Women's Basketball Championship Regional Final, transcribed by ASAP Sports, 1 April 2024, https://www.asapsports.com/show_interview.php?id=195958.

Hair Game Strong

229 **"I hope that . . . sport they want"**: "Instagram on Instagram: 'University of South Carolina Student Athlete Aliyah Boston (@Aliyah.boston), #SeeMe, Photo of @Aliyah.boston by @Kevindliles for @Sportsillustrated and @Sifullframe,'" Instagram, 21 March 2021, www.instagram.com/p/CMr7LFWMKSw/.

Matter of Fact: 2020s

231 **"Way more nervous . . . basketball game"**: Doug Feinberg, "Iowa Star Caitlin Clark Makes Surprise 'SNL' Appearance," *AP News*, 14 April 2024, apnews.com/article/snl-clark-weekend-update-3fcb51d9c43ba45627e65628ff9e1bee.

PHOTO CREDITS

Preface: Bob Thomas/Popperfoto via Getty Images/Getty Images vi · Courtesy of Iowa Girls' High School Athletic Union vii · **Chapter One:** FPG/Archive Photos/Getty Images viii · *Senda Berenson with rope in gym, circa 1890s*. Senda Berenson papers, Record ID 536, Smith College Special Collections, Northampton, Massachusetts 2 · *Ball about to be tossed up at centre, with Senda Berenson officiating at a Smith College basketball game*, 1903. Photograph by Katherine E. McClellan. Box 1346, Record ID 302. Athletics Subject Files, Smith College Archives, Smith College Special Collections, Northampton, Massachusetts 4 · *San Francisco Examiner*, Public Domain 5 · Gulick, L. H., Hough, T. & Foster, A. B., Berenson, S., ed. (1901) *Line basket ball; or, Basket ball for women, as adopted by the Conference on Physical Training, held in June, at Springfield, Mass., also articles on the game by Dr. Luther Gulick, Dr. Theodore Hough, Dr. A. Bertha Foster, and Miss Senda Berenson*. New York, American Sports Publishing Company. [PDF] Retrieved from the Library of Congress, https://www.loc.gov/item/03011986/6 · American Association for Health, *P. E. Basketball Guide, with Official Rules and Standards*. [Washington Division for Girls and Women's Sports, American Association for Health, Physical Education, and Recreation] · [Periodical] Retrieved from the Library of Congress, https://www.loc.gov/item/08033026/7 · *Rosedale Girls Basketball team, 1924*. National Photo Company Collection, Library of Congress, Prints & Photographs Division, [LC-DIG-npcc-12782] 8 · *P. M. Gen. New with girls basketball team of Dept., 3/1/26*. National Photo Company Collection, Library of Congress, Prints & Photographs Division, [LC-DIG-npcc-15577] 8 · Photograph by Leigh Richmond Miner/Hampton University Archives 8 · Johnston, F. B., photographer. (1899) *Female students playing basketball, Western High School, Washington, D.C.* Washington D.C., 1899. [Photograph] Retrieved from the Library of Congress, /9 · Johnston, F. B., photographer. (1899) *Five girls lying on mat in gymnasium in front of basketball scoreboard, Western High School, Washington, D.C.* Washington D.C., 1899. [Photograph] Retrieved from the Library of Congress, https://www.loc.gov/item/97505150/9 · John W. Mosley Photograph Collection, Charles L. Blockson AfroAmerican Collection, Temple University Libraries, Philadelphia, PA 10 · Courtesy of the Greensboro History Museum 12 · WorldPhotos/Alamy 13 · Heritage Art/Heritage Images via Getty Images 14–15 · Courtesy of Iowa Girls' High School Athletic Union 16–22 · Art Frisch/San Francisco Chronicle via AP 23 · Courtesy of Tammy Moore Harrison/All American Red Heads 24 · Gunther/Keystone/Hulton Archive/Getty Images 25, 26–27 · Courtesy Flying Queens Museum/Wayland Baptist University 28, 29 · Courtesy of Iowa Girls High School Athletic Union 30 · North Carolina Sports Hall of Fame 30 · *Fort Shaw Girls Basketball Team posing with Trophy*. [THM 2001.020.0002] Great Falls History Museum, MT 31 · Courtesy of the Women's Basketball Hall of Fame 31 · **Chapter Two:** Peter Read Miller/*Sports Illustrated* via Getty Images 32–33 · Special Collections and University Archives/University of Maryland 34 · Courtesy of Immaculata University 36–39 · Dan Farrell/NY Daily News via Getty Images 40 · Courtesy of Immaculata

University 41–43 · UCLA Athletics/UCLA Library Special Collections 44 · UCLA News Service 45 · Reed Saxon/AP Photo 45 · John G. Zimmerman /*Sports Illustrated* via Getty Images 46 · Courtesy of Margaret Wade Collection/Delta State University/Delta State University Charlie Capps Archives 47 · ABC Photo Archives/Disney General Entertainment Content via Getty Images 48 · AP Photo 49 · Fred Bunch/*Houston Chronicle* via Getty Images 50 · Courtesy of Molly Bolin Kazmer 51 · Courtesy of Fun While It Lasted (2) 51· Courtesy of Molly Bolin Kazmer 52 · *Iowa Cornets jacket*, IWA0669, Box 3, Rhonda Penquite papers, Iowa Women's Archives, Iowa City, Iowa (inset) 53 · Bettmann Archive/Getty Images 53 · Courtesy of Fun While It Lasted 54–55 · Courtesy of Molly Bolin Kazmer 56 · Courtesy of Fun While It Lasted (inset) 56 · Courtesy of Molly Bolin Kazmer 57 · Courtesy of OriAnn Miller Phillips/The Dallas Diamonds 58 · Courtesy of Molly Bolin Kazmer 59 (top two) · Ole Miss Athletics 59 (bottom left) · Kansas Athletics 59 (bottom right) · Bettmann Archive/Getty Images 60 (top) · Courtesy of Fun While It Lasted (left) 60 · Courtesy of Queens College Athletics (bottom) 60 · Courtesy of Molly Bolin Kazmer (top) 61 · University Archives Photograph Collection. Athletics Photographs, 1893 Queens College Athletics 2003 (UA023.004), Special Collections Research Center at NC State University Libraries (bottom) 61 · **Chapter Three:** Tony Duffy/Getty Images 62–63 · Thomas P. Costello for Rutgers University via "Forgotten Champions" 64–67 · Wikimedia Commons 68 · Courtesy of Rutgers University (2) 69 · Thomas P. Costello for Rutgers University via "Forgotten Champions" (left) 70 · Wikimedia Commons/Louisiana Tech Athletics (right) 70 · Jerry Wachter/*Sports Illustrated* via Getty Images 71 · David Madison/Getty Images 72 · Lennox McLendon/AP Photo 73 · *Los Angeles Times* Photographic Archive, UCLA Library Special Collections 74 · AP Photo 75 · Bob Bryant/AP Photo 77 · Disney General Entertainment Content via Getty Images 78–79 · Wally McNamee/CORBIS/Corbis via Getty Images 80 · Gray Mortimore/Allsport/Getty Images 81 · Courtesy of Molly Bolin Kazmer (inset) 81 · Richard Mackson/*Sports Illustrated* via Getty Images 82 · John Swart/AP Photo 83 · Courtesy of UGA Athletic Association (left) 84 · Athletic Association Records, UA0055, University of Georgia Archives, Hargrett Rare Book and Manuscript Library, The University of Georgia Libraries (right) 84 · Bob Riha, Jr./Getty Images 85 · Courtesy of Molly Bolin Kazmer 86 · Courtesy of Fun While It Lasted (left) 87 · Courtesy of OriAnn Miller Phillips/The Dallas Diamonds (top) 87 · Courtesy of Fun While It Lasted (bottom) 87 · Courtesy of Molly Bolin Kazmer (top left) 88 · Dale Sparks/WVU Athletics Communications Photo (top right) 88 · Wikimedia Commons (bottom left) 88 · Ken Levine/Allsport/Getty Images (bottom right) 88 · Tony Duffy/Getty Images (left) 89 · Joe Patronite/Getty Images (bottom right) 89 · **Chapter Four:** Alexander Hassenstein/Bongarts/Getty Images 90–91 · Stanford Athletics (top) 92 · University of Virginia Athletics (bottom) 92 · Elise Amendola/AP Photo 93 · Jim Gund/Getty Images (right) 94 · Paul Sakuma/AP Photo (top) 95 · Courtesy of Purdue Athletics (bottom) 95 · Bob Stowell/Getty Images 96–97 · Jonathan

INDEX